foundations of economics

david begg

stanley fischer   rudiger dornbusch

The McGraw-Hill Companies

London *Burr Ridge, Il* *New York* *St Louis* *San Francisco* *Auckland* *Bogotá*
Caracas *Lisbon* *Madrid* *Mexico* *Milan* *Montreal* *New Delhi* *Panama*
Paris *San Juan* *São Paulo* *Singapore* *Sydney* *Tokyo* *Toronto*

Published by
McGraw-Hill Publishing Company
Shoppenhangers Road, Maidenhead, Berkshire, SL6 2QL, England
Telephone +44 (0)1628 502500
Facsimile +44 (0)1628 770224
Website: www.mcgraw-hill.co.uk

British Library Cataloguing in Publication Data
A catalogue record for this book is available from the British Library

ISBN 0 07 709754 8

Publisher	Andy Goss
Senior Sponsoring Editor	Tony Johnston
Development Editor	Caroline Howell
Editorial Assistant	Catriona Watson
Senior Marketing Manager	Jackie Harbor
Production Manager	Penny Grose

Produced for McGraw-Hill by the independent production company
Steven Gardiner Ltd

McGraw-Hill
A Division of The McGraw-Hill Companies

Cover and text design by DesignDeluxe
Typeset by Ward Partnership, Saffron Walden, Essex
Printed and bound in Malta by Interprint Limited

We wish to thank the following organizations for permission to publish tables and figures in the text: in each case the source is given.
American Economic Association; Bank of England; Blackwell Publishers; Cambridge University Press; Centre for Economic Research; EBRD; Economic Journal; Financial Times; Harvard University Press; HM Treasury; HMSO; IMF; Institute of Economics Budapest; Institute of Economics and Statistics; International Trade Centre; OECD; Office for National Statistics; Oxford University Press; Times Newspapers Limited; The Economist; The United Nations; University of Munich.

1 2 3 4 5 IP 4 3 2 1 0

brief contents

contents

■■■ 8   money, interest rates, and output   246

12 trade and development 385

preface

Useful foundations need to be reliably up to the job, light enough to carry around for the rest of your life, and fun enough to make you want to bother.

Foundations of Economics is a short yet rigorous textbook for students taking an introductory economics course in higher education. It is suitable for all types of students whether they are studying economics or other subjects such as business studies. The book retains all of the features that make its parent text, *Economics 6/e* by Begg, Fischer and Dornbusch, the 'student's bible' for economics (BBC Radio 4, September 1999).

Foundations of Economics provides a concise coverage of core topics but continues to train readers in economic analysis rather than being merely descriptive. It encourages readers to think for themselves, using a wide range of examples and data to reinforce theoretical analysis, and offers authoritative commentary on topical issues. Through clear and imaginative presentation, it maintains the rigour of *Economics 6/e* but distils the central principles of economics to a course suitable for students who do not have the luxury of devoting all of their time to introductory economics.

▨▨▨ why study economics?

Economics is much too interesting to be left to professional economists. It affects almost everything we do, not merely at work or at the shops but also in the home and the voting booth. It influences how well we look after our planet, the future we leave for our children, the extent to which we can care for the poor and the disadvantaged, and the resources we have for enjoying ourselves.

These issues are discussed daily, in bars and on buses as well as in cabinet meetings and boardrooms. The formal study of economics is exciting because it introduces a toolkit that allows a better understanding of the problems we face. Everyone knows a smoking engine is a bad sign, but sometimes only a trained mechanic can give the right advice on how to fix it.

This book is designed to give you the toolkit and teach you how to use it. Nobody carries an enormous toolbox very far. Useful toolkits are small enough to be portable but contain enough proven tools to deal both with routine problems and unforeseen circumstances. With practice, you will be surprised at how much light this analysis can shed on daily living. This book is designed to make economics seem as useful as it really is.

If you are approaching the study of economics for the first time, this book is designed to help you develop an understanding of the key principles of this fascinating subject. Although you may not continue to study economics after reading this book, we hope that it will provide you with a working knowledge of the economic forces that shape our day-to-day lives.

■■■ how much do economists disagree?

There is an old complaint that economists never agree about anything. This is simply wrong. The media, taxi drivers, and politicians love to talk about topics on which there is disagreement; it would be boring TV if all participants in a panel discussion held identical views. But economics is not a subject in which there is always an argument for everything. There *are* answers to many questions. We aim to show where economists agree – on what and for what reason – and why they sometimes disagree.

■■■ economics for the new millennium

Our aim is to help students to understand today's economic environment. This requires mastering the theory and practising its application. Just as the theory of genetics or information technology is steadily progressing, so the theory of economics continues to make progress, sometimes in dramatic and exciting ways.

We believe in introducing students immediately to the latest ideas in economics. If these can be conveyed simply, why force students to use older approaches that work less well? Two recent developments in economics underlie much of what we do. One is the role of information; the other is globalisation.

How information is transmitted and manipulated is central to many issues in incentives and competition, including the recent boom in e-commerce. Easy access to information, coupled with lower transport costs, also explains trends towards globalisation, and associated reductions in national sovereignty, especially in smaller countries. Modern economics helps us make sense of our changing world, think about where it may go next, and evaluate choices that we currently face. We back up this claim with a section showing that the information economy in general, and the Internet in particular, are merely following standard economic principles.

■■■ learning by doing

Don't just read about economics, try to do it! Few people practise for a driving test just by reading a book. Even when you think you understand how to do a hill start, it takes a lot of practice to master the finer points. We give you lots of examples and real-world applications not just to emphasise the relevance of economics but also to help you master it for yourself. We start at square one and take you slowly through the tools of theoretical reasoning and how to apply them. We do not use algebra and there are very few equations in the book. The best ideas are simple and robust, and can usually be explained quite easily.

■■■ how to study

It is easy, but mistaken, to read on cruise control, highlighting the odd sentence and gliding through paragraphs we have worked hard to simplify. Active learning needs to be interactive. When the text says 'clearly', ask yourself 'why' is it clear? See if you can construct the diagram before you look at it. As soon as you don't follow something, go back and read it again. Try to think of *other* examples to which the theory could be applied. The only way to check you are really understanding things is to try problems and see if you got the right answer. The best way to do this is to explore the online resources centre we have developed for this textbook.

To assist you in working through this text, we have developed a number of distinctive study and design features. To familiarise yourself with these features, please turn to the Guided Tour on pages xviii–xix.

student CD-ROM

Free with your copy of *Foundations of Economics* is a Student CD-ROM. This CD contains a range of electronic resources to help you study economics, including case studies, chapter-by-chapter revision notes, weblinks, suggestions for further reading, and other useful extra material.

This has been designed to help you to better understand the concepts you read about in the text, so take time to explore the CD-ROM as you work through the chapters in the book. You will find all these resources and more on the textbook's Online Learning Centre at www.beggecon.com.

online resources

For this new abridged version of Begg, Fischer and Dornbusch *Economics 6/e*, we have worked hard to provide a range of online resources to support both students in their studying, and lecturers in their teaching of economics. Please visit our online resources centre at www.beggecon.com to gain access to an extensive and frequently up-dated range of materials.

■■■ acknowledgements

We would like to thank the following university experts who took the time and effort to take part in the market research for this book. They have added enormously to the development of this text.

Ian Jackson, Staffordshire University
David McCausland, University of Aberdeen
Norman Stang, University of North London
Dorron Otter, Leeds Metropolitan University
John Lipczynski, London Guildhall University
Paul Seaman, Dundee University
Kostas Mavromaras, Newcastle University
Steve Bradley, Lancaster University
Nat Levy, Middlesex University
Damien Ward, Bradford University
F. Forsythe, University of Ulster
Les Simpson, Heriot-Watt University
Sara Connolly, University of East Anglia
Alex Tackie, University of Kingston
Clive Lewis, Buckinghamshire Chilterns University College
Steve Millard, Buckinghamshire Chilterns University College

guided tour

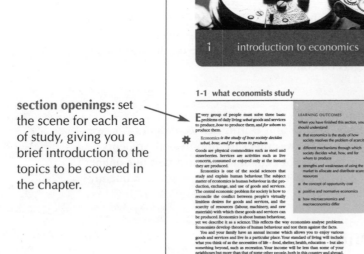

section openings: set the scene for each area of study, giving you a brief introduction to the topics to be covered in the chapter.

learning outcomes: identify the primary topics you should understand after studying each section.

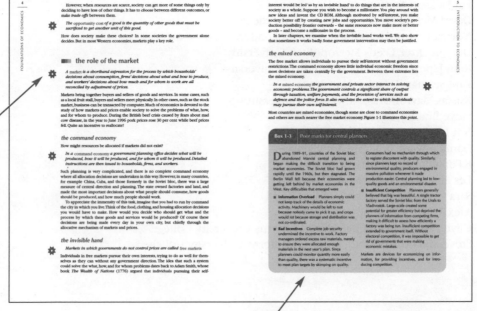

key terms: are in colour and are accompanied by an icon in the margin. The definition follows, giving you a handy reference for new concepts and techniques when they first appear in the text.

illustrative boxes: provide additional examples to highlight the practical application of concepts, and to encourage you to critically analyse and discuss real-world issues.

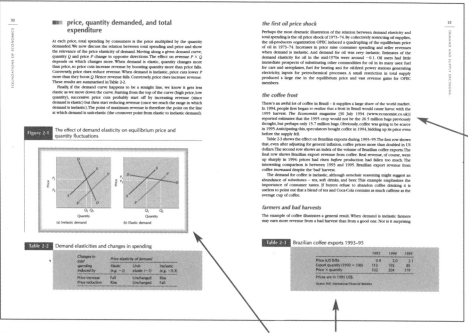

weblinks: are provided throughout the book, pointing you to websites that will help you to further explore and analyse the topics covered in the chapter.

graphs and tables: are presented in a simple and clear design; the use of colour will help you to understand and absorb key economic data and concepts.

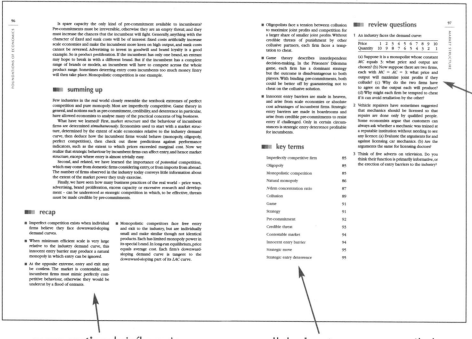

review questions: encourage you to review and apply the knowledge you have acquired from each chapter. These questions can be undertaken either individually or used as a focus for group discussion.

recap section: briefly reviews and reinforces the main topics you will have covered in each chapter.

all the **key terms** are compiled into an end-of-chapter glossary with a page reference to help you quickly locate and revise the key terms.

1 | introduction to economics

1-1 what economists study

Every group of people must solve three basic problems of daily living: *what* goods and services to produce, *how* to produce them, and *for whom* to produce them.

Economics *is the study of how society decides what, how, and for whom to produce.*

Goods are physical commodities such as steel and strawberries. Services are activities such as live concerts, consumed or enjoyed only at the instant they are produced.

Economics is one of the social sciences that study and explain human behaviour. The subject matter of economics is human behaviour in the production, exchange, and use of goods and services. The central economic problem for society is how to reconcile the conflict between people's virtually limitless desires for goods and services, and the scarcity of resources (labour, machinery, and raw materials) with which these goods and services can be produced. Economics is about human behaviour, yet we describe it as a science. This reflects the way economists analyse problems. Economists develop theories of human behaviour and test them against the facts.

You and your family have an annual income which allows you to enjoy various goods and services and live in a particular place. Your standard of living will include what you think of as the necessities of life – food, shelter, health, education – but also something beyond, such as recreation. Your income will be less than some of your neighbours but more than that of some other people, both in this country and abroad. Nations also have different levels of income. A nation's income, or national income, is

LEARNING OUTCOMES

When you have finished this section, you should understand

- that economics is the study of how society resolves the problem of scarcity

- different mechanisms through which society decides what, how, and for whom to produce

- strengths and weaknesses of using the market to allocate and distribute scarce resources

- the concept of opportunity cost

- positive and normative economics

- how microeconomics and macroeconomics differ

the sum of the incomes of all its citizens. World income is the sum of all countries' incomes or the sum of the incomes earned by all the people in the world.

 The income distribution *(in a country or in the world) tells us how income is divided between different groups or individuals.*

Income distribution is closely linked to the what, how, and for whom questions. Table 1-1 shows income per person for each group. In poor countries the average income per person is only £213 *per year*. In the rich industrial countries income is £15 690 *per person per year*, over *seventy* times larger. *For whom* does the world economy produce? Essentially, for the 16 per cent of its population living in the rich industrial countries. This answer about for whom the goods and services are produced also suggests the answer to *what* is produced. World production is directed chiefly to the goods and services consumed in the rich countries.

Why are there huge differences in incomes between groups? This relates to the question of *how* goods are produced. In poor countries there is little machinery, and few people have professional and technical training. Workers in poor countries are less productive because they work under less favourable conditions.

Income is unequally distributed within each country as well as between countries. In Brazil, the richest 20 per cent of families receive 64 per cent of Brazil's national income. In countries such as Denmark, the richest 20 per cent of families receive 35 per cent of national income. Denmark levies high taxes on high incomes to reduce the buying power of the rich, and levies high taxes on inheritances to reduce the concentration of wealth in the hands of a few families.

Table 1-1   World population and income

	Poor countries	Middle-income countries	Rich countries
Income per head (£)	213	1154	15 690
% of world population	35	49	16
% of world income	2	18	80

Source: World Bank, *World Development Report*, 1998–99.

Box 1-1   Service with a smile: the changing composition of what is produced

Production is divided into three sectors: agriculture, services, and industry. Agriculture is really quite a small part of national output. Even French farmers produce only 2 per cent of national output! Industrial output is usually around 30 per cent of national output. Services are over two-thirds of national output.

What are these services? The most important are financial services (banking and insurance), transport (road, sea and air), communications (mail, phone, satellite), tourism, and leisure and entertainment.

% of national output		Japan	France	UK
1965	Agriculture	10	8	3
	Industry	44	39	46
	Services	46	53	51
1997	Agriculture	2	2	2
	Industry	38	27	30
	Services	60	71	68

Source: World Bank, *World Development Report*, 1998/99.

The degree to which income is unequally distributed will also affect what goods are produced. In Brazil, where income is unequally distributed, many people work as domestic servants, chauffeurs, and maids. In Denmark few people can afford to hire servants.

scarcity and opportunity cost

A scarce resource *is one for which demand at a zero price would exceed available supply.*

Economics is the study of scarcity. When things are so abundantly supplied that everyone can have as much as they want, society need not waste time worrying about how and for whom these things should be produced. In the Sahara, there is no need to worry about the production of sand.

Box 1-2 | Developing a healthy scepticism

A TV presenter is interviewing two politicians about health services. The opposition politician is angry about cuts in government support for hospitals: fewer beds, fewer nurses, longer waiting lists. The government minister says the government is spending more than ever before on health.

UK opinion polls confirm widespread concern about cutbacks in services. The opposition politician was telling the truth. But so was the government minister. The table below shows that real (inflation-adjusted) government spending on health increased more than 27 per cent during 1990–98.

We are all living longer. The fraction of the UK population over 65 is projected to increase from 23 per cent in 1980 to 31 per cent by 2030. Older people need more health care than younger people. Moreover, advances in medical technology not merely keep us alive longer, they make available some very sophisticated and expensive treatments.

The real issue is *scarcity*. If we want to maintain past standards across a population now comprising many more older people, and if we want all medical breakthroughs to be widely available, we shall have to spend so much more on health that we shall have to spend *much less* on something else. This cutback could be in the public sector (defence cuts) or in the private sector (fewer consumer goods, allowing us to pay more income in taxes to finance health).

If we cannot cut back much on peacekeeping troops and consumer electronics, we had better face the consequences for health. Somehow, we shall have to ration people's access to health services in order to prevent total spending on health rising to such an extent that it crowds out everything else. This rationing can be done through markets (making people pay for some health services) or through rules (restricting entitlement to treatment). Politicians face huge temptations to leave difficult issues to their successors.

UK government spending on health, 1990–98

	1990	1995	1998
Real spending (£bn, 1998 prices)	36	44	46
Spending as % of national output	5.0	5.6	5.5

Source: ONS, *UK National Accounts*.

However, when resources are scarce, society can get more of some things only by deciding to have less of other things. It has to *choose* between different outcomes, or make *trade offs* between them.

The opportunity cost *of a good is the quantity of other goods that must be sacrificed to get another unit of this good.*

How does society make these choices? In some societies the government alone decides. But in most Western economies, markets play a key role.

the role of the market

A market *is a shorthand expression for the process by which households' decisions about consumption, firms' decisions about what and how to produce, and workers' decisions about how much and for whom to work are all reconciled by adjustment of prices.*

Markets bring together buyers and sellers of goods and services. In some cases, such as a local fruit stall, buyers and sellers meet physically. In other cases, such as the stock market, business can be transacted by computer. Much of economics is devoted to the study of how markets and prices enable society to solve the problems of what, how, and for whom to produce. During the British beef crisis caused by fears about mad cow disease, in the year to June 1996 pork prices rose 30 per cent while beef prices fell. Quite an incentive to reallocate!

the command economy

How might resources be allocated if markets did not exist?

In a command economy *a government planning office decides what will be produced, how it will be produced, and for whom it will be produced. Detailed instructions are then issued to households, firms, and workers.*

Such planning is very complicated, and there is no complete command economy where all allocation decisions are undertaken in this way. However, in many countries, for example China, Cuba, and those formerly in the Soviet bloc, there was a large measure of central direction and planning. The state owned factories and land, and made the most important decisions about what people should consume, how goods should be produced, and how much people should work.

To appreciate the immensity of this task, imagine that you had to run by command the city in which you live. Think of the food, clothing, and housing allocation decisions you would have to make. How would you decide who should get what and the process by which these goods and services would be produced? Of course these decisions are being made every day in your own city, but chiefly through the allocative mechanism of markets and prices.

the invisible hand

Markets in which governments do not control prices are called free markets

Individuals in free markets pursue their own interests, trying to do as well for themselves as they can without any government direction. The idea that such a system could solve the what, how, and for whom problems dates back to Adam Smith, whose book *The Wealth of Nations* (1776) argued that individuals pursuing their self-interest would be led 'as by an invisible hand' to do things that are in the interests of society as a whole. Suppose you wish to become a millionaire. You play around with new ideas and invent the CD ROM. Although motivated by self-interest, you make society better off by creating new jobs and opportunities. You move society's production possibility frontier outwards – the same resources now make more or better goods – and become a millionaire in the process.

In later chapters, we examine when the invisible hand works well. We also show that sometimes it works badly. Some government intervention may then be justified.

the mixed economy

The free market allows individuals to pursue their self-interest without government restrictions. The command economy allows little individual economic freedom since most decisions are taken centrally by the government. Between these extremes lies the mixed economy.

> *In a* mixed economy *the government and private sector interact in solving economic problems. The government controls a significant share of output through taxation, welfare payments, and the provision of services such as defence and the police force. It also regulates the extent to which individuals may pursue their own self-interest.*

Most countries are mixed economies, though some are close to command economies and others are much nearer the free market economy. Figure 1-1 illustrates this point.

Box 1-3	Poor marks for central planners

During 1989–91, countries of the Soviet bloc abandoned Marxist central planning and began making the difficult transition to being market economies. The Soviet bloc had grown rapidly until the 1960s, but then stagnated. The Berlin Wall fell because their economies were getting left behind by market economies in the West. Key difficulties that emerged were

- **Information Overload** Planners simply could not keep track of the details of economic activity. Machinery would be left to rust because nobody came to pick it up, and crops would rot because storage and distribution was not co-ordinated.

- **Bad Incentives** Complete job security undermined the incentive to work. Factory managers ordered excess raw materials, merely to ensure they were allocated enough materials in the next year's plan. Since planners could monitor quantity more easily than quality, there was a systematic incentive to meet plan targets by skimping on quality.

Consumers had no mechanism through which to register discontent with quality. Similarly, since planners kept no record of environmental quality, producers engaged in massive pollution whenever it made production easier. Central planning led to low-quality goods and an environmental disaster.

- **Insufficient Competition** Planners generally believed that big was beautiful. A single tractor factory served the Soviet bloc from the Urals to Vladivostok. Large-scale created some potential for greater efficiency but deprived the planners of information from competing firms, making it difficult to assess how efficiently a factory was being run. Insufficient competition extended to government itself. Without electoral competition, it was impossible to get rid of governments that were making economic mistakes.

Markets are devices for economizing on information, for providing incentives, and for introducing competition.

positive and normative

It is important to distinguish 'positive' and 'normative' economics.

> Positive economics *deals with objective or scientific explanations of the working of the economy.* Normative economics *offers recommendations based on personal value judgements.*

The aim of positive economics is to explain how society makes decisions about consumption, production, and exchange of goods. The purpose of this investigation is twofold: to satisfy our curiosity about why the economy works as it does, and to have some basis for predicting how the economy will respond to changes in circumstances. In positive economics, we hope to act as detached scientists. We are concerned with propositions of the form: if *this* is changed then *that* will happen. In this regard, positive economics is similar to the natural sciences such as physics, geology, or astronomy.

Economists of widely differing political persuasions would agree that, when the government imposes a tax on a good, the price of that good will rise. The normative question of whether this price rise is desirable is entirely distinct. Many propositions in positive economics command widespread agreement among professional economists. Of course, as in any other science, there are unresolved questions where disagreement remains. These disagreements are at the frontiers of economics. Research in progress will resolve some of these issues but new issues will arise and provide scope for further research.

Normative economics is based on subjective value judgements, not on the search for any objective truth. Is it more important to devote resources to health or to education? It is simply a subjective value judgement based on the feelings of the person making the statement. There is no way that economics can be used to show that one of these normative judgements is correct and the other is wrong. Positive economics can be used to clarify the menu of options from which society must eventually make its normative choice.

micro and macro

Many economists specialize in a particular branch of the subject. Labour economics deals with problems of the labour market. Urban economics deals with city problems: land use, transport, congestion, and housing. We can also classify branches of

| Figure 1-1 | Market orientation |

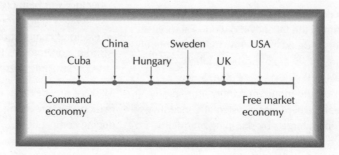

economics according to the approach that is used. The very broad division of approaches into microeconomic and macroeconomic cuts across subject groupings.

Microeconomic analysis *offers a detailed treatment of individual decisions about particular commodities.*

For example, we might study why individual households prefer cars to bicycles and how producers decide whether to produce cars or bicycles. We can then aggregate the behaviour of all households and all firms to discuss total car purchases and total car production. Within a market economy we can discuss the market for cars. Comparing this with the market for bicycles, we may be able to explain the relative price of cars and bicycles and the relative output of these two goods.

However, in studying the whole economy, the analysis becomes so complicated that we lose track of the phenomena in which we were interested. The interesting task for economics is to devise judicious simplifications which keep the analysis manageable without distorting reality too much. Microeconomists tend to offer a detailed treatment of one aspect of economic behaviour but ignore interactions with the rest of the economy in order to preserve the simplicity of the analysis. Sometimes, the indirect effects are too important to be swept under the carpet and an alternative simplification must be found.

Macroeconomics *emphasizes the interactions in the economy as a whole. It deliberately simplifies the individual building blocks of the analysis in order to retain a manageable analysis of the complete interaction of the economy.*

Macroeconomists typically do not worry about the breakdown of consumer goods into cars, bicycles, televisions, and calculators. They treat them all as a single bundle called 'consumer goods' because they are more interested in studying the interaction between households' purchases of consumer goods and firms' decisions about purchases of machinery and buildings.

Box 1-4	Green piece

Many people are worried that our planet is running out of natural resources such as rain forests, fish stocks, and clean air. Why do we manage the environment so badly? An economist's automatic response is to say 'because we do not price it like other commodities'. Why don't we simply price the environment, encouraging people to look after it and penalizing its degradation?

Historically, much of the answer has been technological. We have not had the means to exclude people who refuse to pay. Anyone can walk in a field, dump rubbish after dark, pump chemicals into a river, or drive down a public street. Turnstiles every 50 metres would not be feasible. Gradually, however, electronic monitoring of usage is becoming easier and cheaper. At some point, it may become possible to treat aspects of the environment as just another commodity to be

marketed. Of course this will immediately give rise to a vigorous debate about the what, how, and for whom questions.

It is already feasible to charge cars for using a particular street at a particular time. A smart card in the car would pick up signals as the car passed various charge points. The driver would get a monthly bill like a credit card bill. Rush-hour city traffic could be made to pay more than drivers in places or times where congestion was not a problem. The for whom question could be addressed. Residents could get a 'poll subsidy', a flat rate annual payment, in exchange for agreeing road pricing. Pricing the environment has one big advantage. It introduces a feedback mechanism, however crude, so that when society does stupid things an alarm bell rings *automatically*.

■■■ recap

- Economics analyses what, how, and for whom society produces. The central economic problem is to reconcile the conflict between people's virtually unlimited demands with society's limited ability to produce goods and services to fulfil these demands.

- Industrial countries rely extensively on markets to allocate resources. The market is the process by which production and consumption decisions are co-ordinated through adjustments in prices.

- In a command economy, decisions on what, how, and for whom are made in a central planning office.

- Modern economies are mixed, relying mainly on the market but with a large dose of government intervention. The optimal level of intervention remains a subject of controversy.

- Positive economics studies how the economy actually behaves. Normative economics makes prescriptions about what should be done.

- Microeconomics offers a detailed analysis of particular activities in the economy. For simplicity, it may neglect some interactions with the rest of the economy. Macro-economics emphasizes these interactions at the cost of simplifying the individual building blocks.

■■■ key terms

Economics	1
Income distribution	2
Scarce resource	3
Opportunity cost	4
Market	4
Command economy	4
Free markets	4
Mixed economy	5
Normative economics	6
Positive economics	6
Microeconomics analysis	7
Macroeconomics	7

■■■ review questions

1 How are the problems, what, how, and for whom settled within your own family?

2 Which of the following are scarce? (a) water in the desert, (b) water in a rainforest, (c) economics textbooks, (d) hours a day for work, rest, and play.

3 Which of the following statements are positive and which are normative? (a) The rate of inflation has fallen below 2 per cent per annum. (b) Because inflation has fallen the government should now expand its activity. (c) The level of income is higher in the UK than in Poland.

1-2 tools of economic analysis

It is more fun to play tennis if you know how to serve, and felling trees is much easier with a chain saw. Every activity or academic discipline involves a basic set of tools. The tools may be tangible, like the dentist's drill, or intangible, like the ability to serve in tennis. To analyse economic issues we use both *models* and *data*.

A model *or theory makes a series of simplifying assumptions from which it deduces how people will behave. It is a deliberate simplification of reality.*

Models are frameworks for organizing the way we think about a problem. They simplify by omitting some details of the real world to concentrate on the essentials.

An economist uses a model in the way a traveller uses a map. A map of London misses out many features of the real world – traffic lights, round-abouts, the exact width of streets – but if you study it carefully you can get a good picture of how the traffic is likely to flow and what will be the best route to take. This simplified picture is easy to follow, yet helps you understand real-world behaviour when you must drive through the city in the rush hour.

LEARNING OUTCOMES

When you have finished this section, you should understand

■ why theories are deliberate simplifications of reality

■ time-series and cross-section data

■ how to construct index numbers

■ nominal and real variables

■ how to build a simple theoretical model

■ how to interpret scatter diagrams

■ how 'other things equal' allows important influences to be ignored temporarily but not forgotten

Data *are pieces of evidence about economic behaviour.*

The data or facts interact with models in two ways. First, the data help us quantify the relationships to which our theoretical models draw attention. It may be insufficient to work out that all bridges across the Thames are likely to be congested. To choose the best route we need to know how long we would have to queue at each bridge. We need some facts. The model is useful because it tells us which facts are likely to be the most important. Bridges are more likely to be congested than six-lane motorways.

Second, the data help us to test our models. Like all careful scientists, economists must check that their theories square with the relevant facts. Here the crucial word is *relevant*. For example, the number of Scottish dysentery deaths was closely related to the actual inflation rate in the UK over many decades. Is this a factual coincidence or the key to a theory of inflation? The facts alert us to the need to ponder this question, but we can make a decision only by recourse to logical reasoning.

In this instance, since we can find no theoretical connection, we regard the close factual relationship between Scottish dysentery deaths and UK inflation as a coincidence that should be ignored. Without any logical underpinning, the empirical connection will break down sooner or later. Paying attention to a freak relationship in the data increases neither our understanding of the economy nor our confidence in predicting the future.

FOUNDATIONS OF ECONOMICS

 ## economic data

Initially we focus on the data or facts. How might we present them to help us think about an economic problem?

 Time series data *measure of a variable at different points in time.* Cross-section data *record at a point in time the way an economic variable differs across different individuals or groups of individuals.*

Table 1-2 shows a cross-section of unemployment rates in different countries in 1998.

To compare numbers without emphasizing the units to which they refer, we can present data as index numbers.

 An index number *expresses data relative to a given base value.*

Most countries keep track of the prices faced by consumers. In the UK this is called the *retail price index* (RPI). Announced monthly, and closely watched by the news media and economic commentators, the RPI is an index of the prices of consumer goods purchased by a typical household.

 The inflation rate *is the annual rate of change of the price index.*

The first row of Table 1-3 shows the average price of a new house, which increased from £2500 in 1960 to £96 700 in 1998. Are houses really 40 times as expensive as in 1960? Not when we allow for inflation, which has also raised incomes and the ability to buy houses.

Nominal values *are measured in the prices ruling at the time of measurement.* Real values *adjust nominal values for changes in the price level.*

Inflation led to substantial increases in the price level, and hence the RPI, during 1960–98. The third row calculates an index of real house prices, expressed in 1998 prices.

Table 1-2 Unemployment by country, 1998 (% of labour force)

USA	Japan	Germany	France	UK
4.5	4.1	11.2	11.8	6.2

Source: OECD, *Economic Outlook.*

Table 1-3 UK house prices (average price of a new house)

	1960	1980	1998
House price (£'000s)	2.5	27.2	96.7
RPI (1998 = 100)	7.7	41.1	100.0
Real price of houses (1998 £'000s)	32.5	66.2	96.7

Source: ONS, *Economic Trends.*

To calculate the real price of houses in 1960, by expressing them also at 1998 prices, we take the nominal price of £2500 and multiply by (100/7.7) to allow for subsequent inflation, yielding £32500. Real prices have roughly tripled since 1960. Most of the increase in nominal house prices in the top row of Table 1-3 was actually due to inflation.

When the price of goods rises, we say that the purchasing power of money falls because £1 buys fewer goods.

> *The* purchasing power of money *is an index of the quantity of goods that can be bought for £1.*

The distinction between real and nominal variables is sometimes expressed by saying that real variables measure nominal variables as if the purchasing power of money had been constant. Another way to express this idea is to say that we distinguish between measurements of nominal variables in *current* pounds and real variables in *constant* pounds.

Table 1-3 described the trend in real prices of houses by measuring house prices in 1998 pounds. We could of course have used 1960 pounds instead. Although the level of the real price index for houses would have been different, it would have grown at exactly the same rate as the final row of Table 1-3.

▬ measuring changes in economic variables

During the BSE crisis in 1996, UK beef production fell from 90000 tonnes in January to 50000 tonnes in April. The *absolute change* was −40000. The minus sign tells us output fell.

> *The* percentage change *is the absolute change divided by the original number, then multiplied by 100.*

Thus, the percentage change in UK beef output was $(100) \times (-40000)/(90000) = -44$ per cent. Whereas absolute changes specify units (e.g. tonnes) percentage changes are *unit-free*. It is often convenient to display data in this way.

When we study time series data over long periods such as a decade, we do not want to know just the percentage or absolute change between the initial date and the final date.

> *The* growth rate *is the percentage change per period (typically per year).*

Box 1-5	Millionaire: not the tag it once was

One in every 550 adults in Britain is now a millionaire. A million pounds in 1999 was worth only 1/43rd of a million pounds in 1938.

Being a millionaire is getting easier all the time, because of inflation.

£1 million in prices of year:	1988	1978	1968	1948	1938
Value in 1999 prices (£ million)	1.6	3.4	10.1	21.0	43

Sources: ONS, *Economic Trends*; United Nations, *Economic Surveys of Europe*.

■■ economic models

Now for an example of economics in action. The London Underground is losing money. Some people think it cannot survive without government subsidies. Others think that if it was run differently it could break even. You are called in to advise on the level of fares that would raise most revenue. How would you analyse the problem? To organize our thinking, or – as economists describe it – to build a model, we require a simplified picture of reality which picks out the most important elements of the problem: Revenue = fare × number of passengers. London Transport directly controls the fare, but can influence the number of passengers only through the fare that is set. (Cleaner stations and better service might also matter, but we neglect these for the moment.)

It is possible to travel by car, bus, taxi, or tube, and decisions about the mode of transport are likely to be sensitive to the relative costs of the competing alternatives. We must model the *demand* for tube journeys. First, the fare itself matters. Higher tube fares reduce the quantity of tube journeys demanded. Of course what matters is the price of the tube relative to the price of other means of transport – cars, buses, and taxis. If their prices remain constant, lower tube fares will encourage tube passengers. Rises in the price of these other means of transport will also encourage tube passengers even though tube fares remain unaltered. Finally, if passengers have larger incomes, they can afford more tube journeys. We now have a bare-bones model of the demand for tube journeys.

Writing down a model is a safe way of forcing ourselves to look for all the relevant effects, to worry about which effects must be taken into account and which are minor and can probably be ignored in answering the question we have set ourselves. Without writing down a model, we might have forgotten about the influence of incomes on tube journeys, an omission that might have led to serious errors in trying to understand and forecast revenue raised from tube fares.

■■ models and data

Theory alone cannot answer our question. Whether or not higher tube fares raise or lower total revenue depends entirely on the *empirical* or factual issue of how many passengers are discouraged by higher fares. Nevertheless, our model tells us that the key fact we have to discover is how many passengers are put off by higher fares alone, holding constant the price of all other means of transport. Knowing this, we can calculate whether higher or lower fares are better for revenue.

empirical evidence

We need some empirical research to establish the facts. *Experimental* sciences, including many branches of physics and chemistry, can conduct controlled experiments in a laboratory, varying one factor at a time while holding constant all the other relevant factors. Like astronomy, economics is primarily a *non-experimental* science. Astronomers cannot suspend planetary motion to examine the relation between the earth and the sun in isolation; economists can rarely suspend the laws of economic activity to conduct controlled experiments.

Thus most empirical research in economics must deal with data collected over periods in which many of the relevant factors were simultaneously changing. The problem is how to disentangle the separate influences on observed behaviour. We approach this in two stages. First, we proceed by examining the relationship of interest – the dependence of journeys on fares – neglecting the possibility that other relevant factors were changing. Then we indicate how economists deal with the harder problem in which variations in other factors are also included in the analysis.

A scatter diagram *plots pairs of values simultaneously observed for two different variables.*

In Figure 1-2 along the vertical axis we measure real tube fares in 1998 pence per passenger kilometre. Along the horizontal axis we measure the real tube revenue in billions of 1998 pounds. Real revenue is simply the real fare per passenger kilometre multiplied by the number of passenger kilometres travelled. The years of lowest real revenue coincides with the years in which the real tube fare was lowest.

If it is possible to draw a line or curve through all the points or crosses, this suggests, but does not prove, that there is an underlying relationship between the two variables. If, when the points are plotted, they lie all over the place, this suggests, but does not prove, that there is no strong underlying relationship between the two variables. Only if economics were an experimental science, in which we could conduct controlled experiments guaranteeing that all other relevant factors had been held constant, could we interpret scatter diagrams unambiguously. Nevertheless, they often provide helpful clues.

fitting lines through scatter diagrams

In Figure 1-2 we draw a line through the collection or scatter of points we had plotted. The line shows the average relation between fares and revenue during the period 1979–98. Given a particular scatter of points, how do we decide where to draw the line, given that it cannot fit all the points exactly?

Econometrics *is the branch of economics devoted to measuring relationships using economic data.*

Figure 1-2   Fares and revenues, 1979–98

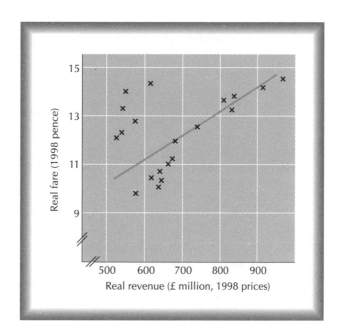

The details need not concern us here, but the idea is simple enough. Having plotted the points describing the data, a computer works out where to draw the line to minimize the dispersion of points around the line. After some practice, most people get used to working with two-dimensional diagrams such as Figure 1-2. A few gifted souls can even draw diagrams in three dimensions. Fortunately, computers can work in 10 or 20 dimensions at once, even though we cannot imagine what this looks like.

And therein lies the answer to the problem of trying to hold other things constant. The computer can measure the tube fare on one axis, the bus fare on another, petrol prices on a third, passenger incomes on a fourth, and tube revenue on a fifth, plot all these variables at the same time, and fit or work out the average relation between tube revenue and each of these influences when they are simultaneously considered. Although technically quite difficult, conceptually it is simply an extension of fitting lines through scatter diagrams. By disentangling separate influences from data where many different factors are all moving at once, econometricians can conduct empirical economic research even though economics is not an experimental science like physics.

■■■ 'other things equal'

Between 1979 and 1998 Britain's national income, in constant 1995 prices, increased from £516 billion to £773 billion. People had a lot more spending power by 1998. They

Box 1-6	Get a Becker view: use an economist's spectacles

Most people accept that the economic analysis of markets – thinking about how incentives affect resource allocation – helps us understand trends in things like inflation or unemployment. Can the same tools be applied to other social behaviour? To marriage? To drug use?

Since many of our tools embody the assumption that individual behaviour is driven by self-interest, rather than, say, by an altruistic concern for others, some economists are doubtful of the ability of economics to shed useful light on highly inter-active 'social' situations. Other economists have no such fears. In 1992 Chicago economist Gary Becker was awarded the Nobel Prize for Economics for his pioneering efforts to apply the logic of economic incentives to almost every facet of human behaviour. Some examples of Becker in action . . .

Drugs Prohibition of alcohol gave the US Al Capone but failed to stop drinking. The end of Prohibition 'was a confession that the US experiment in banning drinking had failed dismally. It was not an expression of support for

heavy drinking or alcoholism'. Becker's solution for drugs is the same – legalize, boost government tax revenue, protect minors, and cut out organized crime's monopoly on supply.

Marriage and divorce 'The courtroom is not a good place to make judgements about the unique circumstances of each marriage or relationship. We should replace judicial determination with marriage contracts that specify, among other things, the financial and child custodial terms of a divorce. Marriage contracts would become much more common if we set aside the legal tradition that they are not unenforceable.'

Do such views shed new light on old problems or merely reveal the limitations of traditional economic analysis? You must make up your own mind. But, even if you are unconvinced, it is helpful to ask what feature of a particular social situation you think renders it immune to economic analysis.

Source: G. S. Becker and G. N. Becker, *The Economics of Life*, McGraw-Hill, 1997.

could afford more tube journeys even if (real) prices remained unchanged. Unless we take account of this, we omit a key determinant of demand and misinterpret what was going on. Figure 1-3 replots Figure 1-2 but divides it into two periods: 1979–83, when national income averaged £510 billion a year, and 1984–98 during which national income averaged nearly £658 billion a year. Once we allow for the fact that higher incomes tend to increase demand for tube journeys, the underlying positive relationship between fares and revenue becomes much clearer.

Other things equal *is a device for looking at the relation between two variables, but remembering other variables also matter.*

some popular criticisms

You may have some nagging doubts about some of these techniques or about the whole approach. We conclude this chapter by discussing some of the popular criticisms of economics and economists.

No two economists ever agree   Even if all economists agreed on a positive economic analysis of how the world works, there would be enormous scope for disagreement on normative recommendations based on differing value judgements. A great deal of the disagreements between economists fall under this heading. Nor is it surprising that there are important and persistent disagreements in positive economics. Economics can only rarely be an experimental science. It would be prohibitively expensive to induce half of the population to become unemployed merely to find out how the economy then works.

Finally, it would be a mistake to suppose that there are not serious disagreements between physicists or doctors or engineers. These may be less apparent than disagreements between economists. Most ordinary citizens do not pretend to know

| **Figure 1-3** | Other things equal |

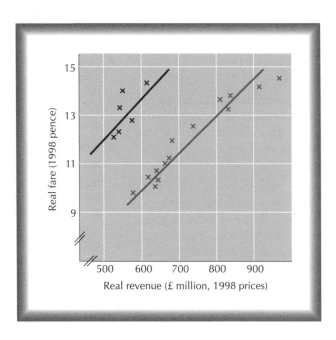

much about physics; everybody thinks he or she knows a bit about the problems that economists study.

Models in economics are hopelessly simple   A model is a deliberate simplification to help us think more clearly. A good model simplifies a lot but does not distort reality too much. It is successful in capturing the main features of the problem. The test of a good model is not how simple it is, but how much of observed behaviour it is capable of explaining.

People are not as mercenary as economists make out   We can certainly think of decisions where this is a fair comment. Marriage is typically though not exclusively determined by non-economic considerations. Economists believe that most of the phenomena they study, such as the decision about whether to travel by bus or tube, are determined primarily by economic incentives. This is very different from asserting that only economic incentives matter.

A knowledge of politics, sociology, and psychology would be necessary to provide a more complete description of human behaviour. These are all factors that economists subsume under the heading of 'other things equal'. Social attitudes change only slowly and for many purposes may be treated as being held constant. However, if an economist were told, or discovered, that there had been an important change in social attitudes, it would be straightforward to include this in the analysis.

People are human beings. You cannot reduce their actions to scientific laws
Physicists accept that molecules behave randomly but that it is possible to construct and test theories based on average or systematic behaviour. Economists take the same view about people.

If behaviour shows no systematic tendencies – tendencies to do the same thing when confronted by the same situation – there is really nothing to discuss. The past will be no guide to the future and every decision is a one-off decision. Not only is this view unconstructive, but it is not usually supported by the data. In the last resort the economic theories that survive are those that are consistently compatible with the data.

▩ recap

- A model is a simplified framework for organizing the way we think about a problem.

- Data or facts suggest relationships which we should aim to explain. Having formulated our theories, we can also use data to test our hypotheses and to quantify the effects that they imply.

- Index numbers express data relative to some given base value. The retail price index summarizes changes in the prices of all goods bought by households. The annual percentage change in the retail price index is the usual measure of inflation.

- Nominal or current price variables refer to values at the prices ruling when the variable was measured. Real or constant price variables adjust nominal variables for changes in the general level of prices.

- Scatter diagrams show the relationship between two variables plotted in the diagram. It is possible to fit a line through these points to summarize the average relationship. Econometricians use computers to fit average relationships between many variables simultaneously. In principle, this allows us to get round the other-things-equal problem which always applies in two dimensions.

◼◼ key terms

◼◼ review questions

1 The table below shows total consumption (spending by households) and total income received by households in the UK, both in £ billion at 1995 prices. (a) Plot the scatter diagram showing consumption on the vertical axis and income on the horizontal axis. (b) Sketch in a fitted line through these points. (c) Suggest a relation between consumption and income of households? Does this make sense?

	Income	Consumption
1992	462	421
1993	476	434
1994	482	447
1995	495	454
1996	505	471
1997	525	489
1998	525	505

2 You have been employed to study whether the level of crime is affected by the percentage of people unemployed. (a) How would you test this idea? What data would you want? (b) What other-things-equal problems would you bear in mind?

3 If economics cannot conduct controlled laboratory experiments, can it claim to be a science?

1-3 markets in operation

Some markets (shops and fruit stalls) physically bring together the buyer and seller. Other markets (the Stock Exchange) operate through intermediaries (stockbrokers) who transact business on behalf of clients. E-commerce is now conducted via the Internet.

Although superficially different, these markets perform the same economic function. They determine prices that ensure that the quantity people wish to buy equals the quantity people wish to sell. In fixing the price of a Rolls-Royce at 20 times the price of a small Ford, the market ensures that production and sales of small Fords will greatly exceed the production and sale of Rolls-Royces. These prices guide society in choosing what, how, and for whom to produce.

We require a model of a typical market. The essential features are demand, the behaviour of buyers, and supply, the behaviour of sellers. We can study the interaction of these forces to see how a market works in practice.

 Demand *is the quantity of a good buyer's wish to purchase at each conceivable price.*

Thus demand is not a particular quantity, such as six bars of chocolate, but rather a full description of the quantity of chocolate the buyer would purchase at each and every price which might be charged. The line *DD* in Figure 1-4 shows the demand for chocolate. Even when chocolate is free, only a finite amount is wanted. People get sick from eating too much chocolate. As the price of chocolate rises, the quantity demanded falls, other things equal.

 Supply *is the quantity of a good seller's wish to sell at each conceivable price.*

Supply is not a particular quantity but a complete description of the quantity that sellers would like to sell at each possible price. The line *SS* in Figure 1-4 shows how much sellers wish to sell at each price. Chocolate cannot be produced for nothing. Nobody would wish to supply if they receive a zero price. In our example, it takes a price of £0.10 before there is any incentive to supply chocolate. At higher prices it is increasingly lucrative to supply chocolate bars and there is a corresponding increase in the quantity supplied.

Notice the distinction between *demand* and the *quantity demanded*. Demand describes the behaviour of buyers at every price. At a particular price there is a particular quantity demanded. The term 'quantity demanded' makes sense only in relation to a particular price. The same applies to *supply* and *quantity supplied*.

In everyday language, we say that when the demand for football tickets exceeds their supply some people will not get into the ground. Economists must be more precise. At the price charged for tickets, the quantity demanded exceeded the quantity supplied. A higher ticket price would have reduced the quantity demanded, perhaps leaving empty space in the ground. Yet there has been no change in demand, the schedule describing how many people want admission at each possible ticket price. The quantity demanded has changed because the price has changed.

The demand schedule relating price and quantity demanded and the supply schedule relating price and quantity supplied are each constructed on the assumption of 'other things equal'. In the demand for football tickets, one of the 'other things' is whether or not the game is being shown on television. If it is, the quantity of tickets demanded at each and every price will be lower than if the game is not televised. To understand how a market works, we must first explain why demand and supply are what they are. (Is the game on television? Has the ground capacity been extended by building a new stand?) Then we examine how the price adjusts to balance the quantities supplied and demanded, given the underlying supply and demand schedules relating quantity to price.

> *The* equilibrium price *clears the market for chocolate. It is the price at which the quantity supplied equals the quantity demanded.*

Figure 1-4 shows that the equilibrium price is £0.30: 80 bars is the quantity buyers wish to buy and sellers wish to sell at this price. We call 80 bars the *equilibrium quantity*. At prices below £0.30, the quantity demanded exceeds the quantity supplied and some buyers will be frustrated. There is a shortage, what we call *excess demand*, a convenient shorthand for the more complicated expression: the quantity demanded exceeds the quantity supplied *at this price*.

Conversely, at any price above £0.30, the quantity supplied exceeds the quantity demanded. Sellers will be left with unsold stock. To describe this surplus, economists use the shorthand *excess supply*, it being understood that this means excess in the quantity supplied *at this price*. Only at £0.30, the equilibrium price, does the quantity demanded equal the quantity supplied. The market clears and people can buy or sell as much as they want at the equilibrium price.

Is the market automatically in equilibrium? If so, what brings this about? Suppose the price of chocolate is initially £0.40, higher than the equilibrium price. Producers

Figure 1-4 The market for chocolate

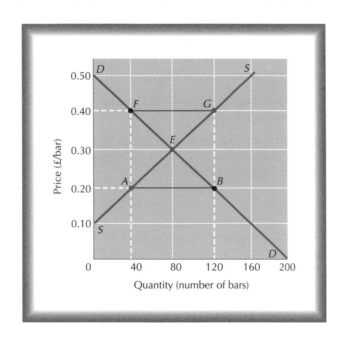

wish to sell 120 bars. Sellers have to cut the price to clear their stock. Cutting the price has two effects. It increases the quantity demanded and reduces the quantity producers wish to supply. Both effects reduce the excess supply. The process of price-cutting will continue until the equilibrium price of £0.30 is reached and excess supply has been eliminated. At this price the market clears.

When the price lies below the equilibrium price the process works in reverse. At a price of £0.20, the quantity demanded is 120 bars but the quantity supplied is only 40 bars. Sellers run out of stock and can charge higher prices. This incentive to raise prices continues until the equilibrium price is reached, excess demand *AB* is eliminated, and the market clears.

behind the demand curve

The demand curve depicts the relation between price and quantity demanded *holding other things constant*. The other things relevant to demand curves can be grouped under three headings: the price of related goods, the income of consumers (buyers), and consumer tastes or preferences.

the price of related goods

A rise in bus fares or petrol prices would increase the quantity of tube travel demanded at each possible price. In everyday language, buses and cars are ***substitutes*** for the tube. A journey may be made by bus or car instead of by tube. Similarly, petrol and cars are *complements* because you cannot use a car without also using fuel. A rise in the price of petrol tends to reduce the demand for cars.

A price increase for one good raises the demand for substitutes ***for this good, but reduces the demand for*** complements ***to the good.***

Most of the time goods are substitutes for each other. Complementarity is usually a more specific feature (CD players and CDs, coffee and milk, shoes and shoelaces).

consumer incomes

The second category of 'other things equal' when we draw a particular demand curve is consumer income. When incomes rise, the demand for most goods increases. Typically, consumers buy more of everything. However, there are exceptions.

For a normal good ***demand increases when incomes rise. For an*** inferior good ***demand falls when incomes rise.***

As their name suggests, most goods are normal goods. Inferior goods are typically cheap but low-quality goods which people would prefer not to buy if they could afford to spend a little more.

tastes

The third category of things held constant along a particular demand curve is consumer tastes or preferences. In part, these are shaped by convenience, custom, and social attitudes. The fashion for the mini-skirt reduced the demand for textile material. The emphasis on health and fitness has increased the demand for jogging equipment, health foods, and sports facilities while reducing the demand for cream cakes, butter, and cigarettes.

■■■ shifts in the demand curve

We are now in a position to distinguish between movements along a given demand curve and shifts in the demand curve itself. In Figure 1-4 we drew the demand curve for chocolate bars for a given level of the three underlying factors: the price of related goods, incomes, and tastes. Movements along the demand curve isolate the effects of chocolate prices on quantity demanded holding other things equal. Changes in any of these three factors will shift the demand for chocolate. Figure 1-5 shows a *shift* in the demand curve from *DD* to *D'D'*. The entire demand curve shifts to the right.

This changes the equilibrium price and quantity in the chocolate market. Equilibrium has changed from *E* to *E'*. The new equilibrium price is £0.40 and the new equilibrium quantity is 120 bars.

We can even sketch the transition from the old equilibrium at *E* to the new equilibrium at *E'*. Consider the instant when ice cream prices rise. The demand curve for chocolate shifts from *DD* to *D'D'*. Until the price changes from £0.30 there is an excess demand *EH* at this price: 160 bars are now demanded but only 80 bars are supplied. This excess demand puts upward pressure on prices until the new equilibrium price of £0.40, is reached.

We draw two general lessons from this example. First, the quantity of chocolate demanded depends on four things: its own price, prices of related goods, incomes, and tastes. We could choose to draw a two-dimensional diagram showing the relation between quantity of chocolate demanded and any one of these four factors. The other three factors would then become the 'other things equal' for this particular diagram. In drawing demand curves, we single out the price of the commodity itself (here the price of chocolate bars) to put in the diagram with quantity demanded. The other three factors become the 'other things equal' for drawing a particular demand curve, and changes in any of these other three factors will shift the position of demand curves.

Why do we single out the price of the commodity itself to plot against quantity demanded? By focusing on the price of chocolate, we have been able to show the self-correcting mechanism by which the chocolate market reacts to excess demand or excess supply through changes in *chocolate prices* to restore equilibrium.

Figure 1-5 | Ice cream prices and chocolate demand

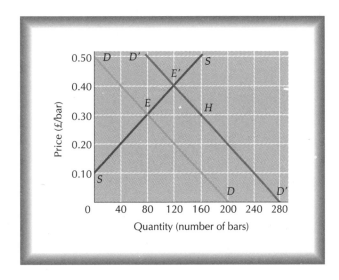

Second, our example shows the method of analysis by *comparative statics*.

In comparative static analysis *we change one of the 'other things equal' and examine the effect on equilibrium price and quantity.*

The analysis compares the old and new equilibrium positions, and it is static because it compares only the two equilibrium positions. In each equilibrium, prices and quantities are unchanging. Comparative static analysis is not interested in the dynamic path by which the economy moves from one equilibrium to the other.

■■■ behind the supply curve

We now examine three categories of 'other things equal' along a supply curve. These categories are: technology available to producers, the cost of inputs (labour, machines, fuel, and raw materials), and government regulation. Along any particular supply curve, all of these are held constant. A change in any of these categories will shift the supply curve by changing the amount producers wish to supply at each price.

technology

A supply curve is drawn for a given technology. Better technology will shift the supply curve to the right since producers will supply a larger quantity than previously at each price. An improvement in cocoa refining makes it possible to produce more chocolate for any given total cost. Faster shipping and better refrigeration lead to less wastage in spoiled cocoa beans. Technological advance enables firms to supply more at each price. As a determinant of supply, technology must be interpreted very broadly.

Box 1-7	One little piggy went to market

The 1996 BSE crisis led to a collapse of the demand for British beef. With a lower demand curve, the equilibrium price of beef fell. Consumers switched to chicken and pork, bidding up the price of pig meat by almost 40 per cent. Many farmers switched from rearing cows to pigs, but it took nearly two years before these new ventures could get pigs to market. Unfortunately there was a surge of pig supply and prices collapsed again!

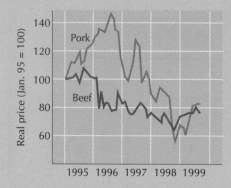

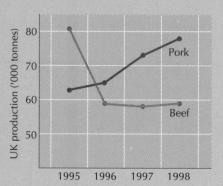

Sources: ONS, *Monthly Digest of Statistics*.

Improved weather forecasting might enable better timing of planting and harvesting. A technological advance is any idea that allows more output from the same inputs as before.

input costs

A particular supply curve is drawn for a given level of input prices. A reduction in input prices (lower wages, lower fuel costs) will induce firms to supply more output at each price, shifting the supply curve to the right. Higher input prices make production less attractive and shift the supply curve to the left.

government regulation

Government regulations can sometimes be viewed as imposing a technological change that is *adverse* for producers. If so, the effect of regulations will be to shift the supply curve to the left, reducing quantity supplied at each price. More stringent safety regulations prevent chocolate producers using the most productive process because it is quite dangerous to workers. Anti-pollution devices may raise the cost of making cars. Whenever regulations prevent producers from selecting the production methods they would otherwise have chosen, the effect of regulations is to shift the supply curve to the left.

■■■■ shifts in the supply curve

Along a given supply curve we hold constant technology, the prices of inputs, and the extent of government regulation. What happens when a change in one of these 'other

Figure 1-6   A reduction in supply

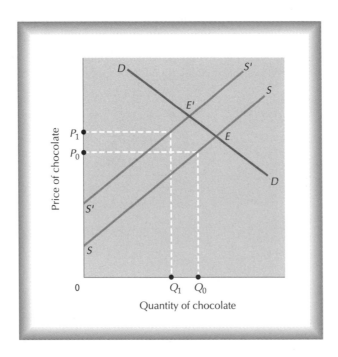

things equal' categories leads to a reduction in supply? Suppose, an increase in the stringency of safety legislation makes it more expensive to produce chocolate bars in mechanized factories. In Figure 1-6 we show a shift to the left in the supply curve from *SS* to *S'S'*. Equilibrium shifts from the point *E* to the point *E'*. Thus equilibrium price rises but equilibrium quantity falls. Conversely, a supply curve shift to the right can be analysed by supposing the supply curve is initially *S'S'* and the market is in equilibrium at the point *E'*. A change that increases supply will shift the supply curve to the right, say to the position shown by the supply curve *SS*. The new equilibrium will be at the point *E*. Thus an increase in supply leads to a higher equilibrium quantity and lower equilibrium price.

▰▰ free markets and price controls

 Free markets *allow prices to be determined purely by the forces of supply and demand.*

Box 1-8 | Who really pays the tax?

Suppose cigarettes cost £1 a packet. Then the government imposes a tax of 50p per packet. Do smokers end up paying the tax, or is it borne by manufacturers of cigarettes? How much of the tax producers pass on to the consumer depends on the slopes of the supply and demand curve.

We plot the (after-tax) price to the consumer on the vertical axis. *DD'* shows the demand curve, which depends on the price to smokers (consumers). Since the price received by the producer is the consumer price minus the 50p tax, the effect of the tax is to *shift* the supply curve from *SS* to *SS'* in both diagrams. Each possible quantity supplied

depends on the price received by the producer, which will be the same as before only if consumer prices are 50p higher; that is why we shift the supply curve up by 50p.

In part (a), with a flat supply curve and steep demand curve, the tax is borne mainly by cigarette consumers. Point B is nearly 50p higher than point A. Producers can pass on most of the tax in higher prices. Consumers pay £1.45 and producers get £0.95 a packet. In part (b), with a flat demand curve and a steep supply curve, most of the tax is borne by cigarette producers. Consumers pay £1.05 and producers get £0.55 a packet.

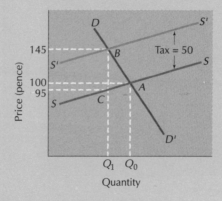

(a) Steep demand, flat supply

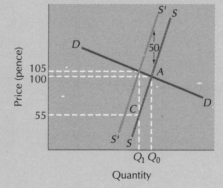

(b) Flat demand, steep supply

Government actions may shift demand and supply curves, as when changes in safety legislation shift the supply curve, but the government makes no attempt to regulate prices directly. Markets will not be free when effective price controls exist.

> Price controls *are government rules or laws that forbid the adjustment of prices to clear markets.*

Price controls may be *floor* prices (minimum prices) or *ceiling* prices (maximum prices).

Price ceilings make it illegal for sellers to charge more than a specific maximum price and are typically introduced when a shortage of a commodity threatens to raise its price by a substantial amount. High prices are the device by which a free market rations goods in scarce supply, but they may lead to a solution that society believes to be unfair, a normative value judgement. For example, high food prices mean considerable hardship for the poor. Faced with a national food shortage, a government might prefer to impose a price ceiling on food so that poor people can buy adequate quantities of food.

In Figure 1-7 we show the market for food. Perhaps war has disrupted imports of food. The supply curve lies far to the left and the free market equilibrium price P_0 is very high. Instead of allowing free market equilibrium at the point E, the government imposes a price ceiling at P_1. The quantity sold is then Q_1 and excess demand is given by the distance AB. The price ceiling creates a shortage of supply relative to demand by holding food prices below their equilibrium level.[1]

Figure 1-7	The effect of a price ceiling

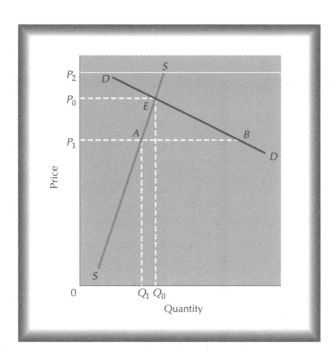

---

[1] Notice that a price ceiling imposed at P_2 above the equilibrium price would simply be irrelevant. The free market equilibrium at E could still be attained.

The ceiling price P_1 allows some of the poor to buy food they could not otherwise have afforded. However, it has reduced total food supplied from Q_0 to Q_1. Furthermore, since there is excess demand AB at the ceiling price, some form of rationing must be used to decide which potential buyers are actually supplied. This rationing system could be highly arbitrary. Food suppliers may reserve supplies for their friends, not necessarily the poor, or accept bribes from those who can afford to pay to jump the queue: a 'black market'. For this reason, the imposition of ceiling prices may be accompanied by government-organized rationing by quota, to ensure that available supply is shared out fairly, independently of ability to pay.

Whereas the aim of a ceiling price is to reduce the price for consumers, the aim of a floor price is to raise the price for suppliers. One example of a floor price is a national minimum wage. Figure 1-8 shows the demand curve and supply curve for labour. The free market equilibrium is at the point E, where the wage is W_0. A minimum wage below W_0 will be irrelevant since the free market equilibrium can still be attained. Suppose the government imposes a minimum wage at W_1. Firms will demand the quantity Q_1 and there will be excess supply AB. The lucky workers who manage to sell as much labour as they wish will be better off than before, but some workers may be worse off since total number of hours worked has fallen from Q_0 to Q_1.

Many countries set floor prices for agricultural products. In previous examples we have assumed that the quantity traded would be the smaller of quantity supplied and quantity demanded at the controlled price since private individuals cannot be forced to participate in a market. There is, however, another possibility: the government may intervene not only to set the control price but also to buy or sell quantities of the good to supplement private purchases and sales. However, the government may agree to purchase the excess supply so that neither private suppliers nor private demanders need be frustrated. Because European butter prices are set above the free market

| **Figure 1-8** | A minimum wage |

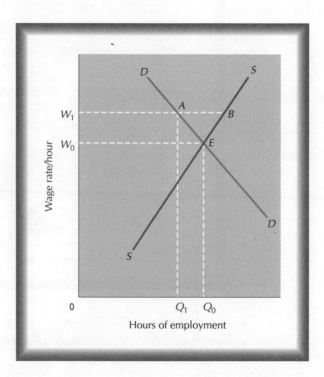

equilibrium price as part of the Common Agricultural Policy, European governments have been forced to purchase massive stocks of butter which would otherwise have been unsold at the controlled price. Hence the famous 'butter mountain'.

■■■ recap

- Demand is the quantity that buyers wish to buy at each price. Other things equal, the lower the price, the higher the quantity demanded. Demand curves slope downwards.

- Supply is the quantity of a good sellers wish to sell at each price. Other things equal, the higher the price, the higher the quantity. Supply curves slope upwards.

- The market clears, or is in equilibrium, when the price equates the quantity supplied and the quantity demanded. At this point supply and demand curves intersect. At prices below the equilibrium price there is excess demand (shortage), which itself tends to raise the price. At prices above the equilibrium price there is excess supply (surplus), which itself tends to reduce the price. In a free market, deviations from the equilibrium price tend to be self-correcting.

- Along a given demand curve, the other things assumed equal are the prices of related goods, consumer incomes, and tastes or habits. Changes in these shift demand curves.

- Along a given supply curve the other things assumed constant are technology, the price of inputs, and the degree of government regulation. An improvement in technology, or a reduction in input prices, will increase the quantity supplied at each price.

- Any factor inducing an increase in demand shifts the demand curve to the right, increasing equilibrium price and equilibrium quantity. Any factor increasing supply shifts the supply curve to the right, increasing equilibrium quantity but reducing equilibrium price.

- To be effective, a price ceiling must be imposed below the free market equilibrium price. It will then reduce the quantity supplied and lead to excess demand unless the government itself provides the extra quantity required. An effective price floor must be imposed above the free market equilibrium price. It will then reduce the quantity demanded unless the government adds its own demand to that of the private sector.

■■■ key terms

■■■ review questions

1 Supply and demand data for toasters are shown below. Plot the supply curve and demand curve and find the equilibrium price and quantity.

Supply and demand for toasters

Price (£)	Quantity demanded	Quantity supplied
10	10	3
12	9	4
14	8	5
16	7	6
18	6	7
20	5	8

2 What is the excess supply or demand when price is (a) £12? (b) £20?

3 What happens to the demand curve for toasters when the price of bread rises? Show in a supply–demand diagram how the equilibrium price and quantity of toasters change.

4 Suppose that cold weather makes it more difficult to catch fish. What happens to the supply curve for fish? What happens to price and quantity?

2 | demand and supply decisions

2-1 measuring demand responses

 the price responsiveness
of demand

The downward slope of the demand curve shows
that quantity demanded increases as the price of a
good falls. Frequently we need to know by how
much the quantity demanded will increase. It is
often best to examine the percentage change, which
is unit-free.

> *The* price elasticity of demand *is the percentage
> change in the quantity demanded divided by
> the corresponding percentage change in its
> price.*

LEARNING OUTCOMES

When you have finished this section, you
should understand

■ the price elasticity of demand

■ how (own) price elasticity relates to the
revenue effect of a price change

■ why bad harvests can help farmers

■ the fallacy of composition

■ the income elasticity of demand, and
and how it relates to inferior, normal,
and luxury goods

Whenever economists speak of *the demand
elasticity* they mean the price elasticity of demand.

If a 1 per cent price increase reduces the quantity demanded by 2 per cent,
the demand elasticity is −2. Because the quantity *falls* 2 per cent, this is a change of
−2 per cent. If a price fall of 4 per cent increases the quantity demanded by 2 per cent,
the demand elasticity is −½ since the quantity change of 2 per cent is divided by the
price change of −4 per cent. The price elasticity of demand tells us about movements
along a downward-sloping demand curve and the demand elasticity must be a
negative number.[1]

We say that the demand elasticity is *high* when it is a large negative number. The
quantity demanded is then very sensitive to the price. We say the demand elasticity

---

[1] For further brevity, economists sometimes omit the minus sign. It is easier to say the demand
elasticity is 2 than to say it is −2.

is *low* when it is a small negative number and the quantity demanded is relatively insensitive to the price. 'High' or 'low' thus refer to the magnitude of the elasticity ignoring the minus sign. The demand elasticity falls when it becomes a smaller negative number and quantity demanded becomes less sensitive to the price.

If the demand curve for football tickets is a straight line with constant slope the demand elasticity falls as we move down the demand curve from higher prices to lower prices.[2] Although a price cut of £1 always leads to the same absolute change in quantity since the demand curve has a constant slope, in *percentage terms* the quantity change is larger and price change smaller when we begin with low quantity and high price (near the top of the demand curve). For simplicity, we tend to talk about demand curves whether the relation is a straight line or a true curve.

It is possible to construct curved demand schedules (still, of course, sloping downwards all the time) along which the price elasticity of demand remains constant. Generally, however, the price elasticity changes as we move along demand curves, and we expect the elasticity to be high at high prices and low at low prices.

elastic and inelastic demand

Although elasticity typically falls as we move down the demand curve, an important dividing line occurs at the demand elasticity of −1.

Demand is elastic *if the price elasticity is more negative than* −1. *Demand is* inelastic *if the price elasticity lies between* −1 *and* 0. *If the demand elasticity is exactly* −1, *we say that demand is* unit-elastic.

Whether or not demand is elastic is the key piece of information required in setting tube fares in the example of Chapter 1.

the determinants of price elasticity

What determines whether the price elasticity of demand for a good is high (say, −5) or low (say, −0.5)? Ultimately the answer must be sought in consumer tastes. If it is socially essential to own a television, higher television prices may have little effect on quantity demanded. If televisions are considered a frivolous luxury, the demand elasticity will be much higher. Psychologists and sociologists may be able to explain more fully than economists why tastes are as they are. Nevertheless, as economists, we can identify some considerations likely to affect consumer responses to changes in the price of a good. *The most important consideration is the ease with which consumers can substitute another good that fulfils approximately the same function.*

Consider two extreme cases. Suppose first that the price of all cigarettes is raised 1 per cent. Do you expect the quantity of cigarettes demanded to fall by 5 per cent or by 0.5 per cent? Probably the latter. People who can easily quit smoking have already done so. In contrast, suppose the price of one particular brand of cigarettes is increased by 1 per cent, all other brand prices remaining unchanged. We should now expect a much larger quantity response from buyers. Consumers will switch away from the more expensive brand to other brands that basically fulfil the same function of nicotine provision. For a particular cigarette brand the demand elasticity could be quite high.

---

[2] There are two special cases of linear demand curves where this is not true. A horizontal or infinitely elastic demand curve has an elasticity of −∞ at all points since the price never changes. A vertical or completely inelastic demand curve has an elasticity of zero at all points since the *quantity* never changes.

Ease of substitution implies a high demand elasticity for a particular good. Our example suggests a general rule. The more narrowly we define a commodity (a particular brand of cigarette rather than cigarettes in general), the larger will be the price elasticity of demand.

measuring price elasticities

To illustrate these general principles we report estimates of price elasticities of demand in Table 2-1. The table confirms that the demand for general categories of basic commodities, such as fuel, food, or even household durable goods, is inelastic. As a category, only services such as haircuts, the theatre, and sauna baths, have an elastic demand. Households simply do not have much scope to alter the broad pattern of their purchases. In contrast, there is a much wider variation in the demand elasticities for narrower definitions of commodities. Even then, the demand for some commodities, such as dairy produce, is very inelastic. However, particular kinds of services such as entertainment and catering have a much more elastic demand.

using price elasticities

Price elasticities of demand are useful in calculating the price rise required to eliminate a shortage (excess demand) or the price fall required to eliminate a surplus (excess supply). One important source of surpluses and shortages is shifts in the supply curve. Harvest failures (and bumper crops) are a feature of agricultural markets. Because the demand elasticity for many agricultural products is very low, harvest failures produce large increases in the price of food. Conversely, bumper crops induce very large falls in food prices. When demand is very inelastic, shifts in the supply curve lead to large fluctuations in price but have little effect on equilibrium quantities.

Figure 2-1(a) illustrates this point. SS is the supply curve in an agricultural market when there is a harvest failure and $S'S'$ the supply curve when there is a bumper crop. The equilibrium price fluctuates between P_1 (harvest failure) and P_2 (bumper crop) but induces little fluctuation in the corresponding equilibrium quantities. Contrast this with Figure 2-1(b), which shows the effect of similar supply shifts in a market with very elastic demand. Price fluctuations are much smaller but quantity fluctuations are now much larger. Knowing the demand elasticity helps us understand why some markets exhibit volatile quantities but stable prices, while other markets exhibit volatile prices but stable quantities.

Table 2-1 Estimates of price elasticities of demand in the UK

Good (general category)	Demand elasticity	Good (narrower category)	Demand elasticity
Fuel and light	−0.47	Dairy produce	−0.05
Food	−0.52	Bread and cereals	−0.22
Alcohol	−0.83	Entertainment	−1.40
Durables	−0.89	Expenditure abroad	−1.63
Services	−1.02	Catering	−2.61

price, quantity demanded, and total expenditure

At each price, total spending by consumers is the price multiplied by the quantity demanded. We now discuss the relation between total spending and price and show the relevance of the price elasticity of demand. Moving along a given demand curve, quantity Q and price P change in opposite directions. The effect on revenue $P \times Q$ depends on which changes more. When demand is elastic, quantity changes more than price, so price cuts increase revenue by boosting quantity more than price falls. Conversely, price rises reduce revenue. When demand is inelastic, price cuts lower P more than they boost Q. Hence revenue falls. Conversely, price rises increase revenue. These results are summarised in Table 2-2.

Finally, if the demand curve happens to be a straight line, we know it gets less elastic as we move down the curve. Starting from the top of the curve (high price, low quantity), successive price cuts probably start off by increasing revenue (since demand is elastic) but then start reducing revenue (once we reach the range in which demand is inelastic). The point of maximum revenue is therefore the point on the line at which demand is unit-elastic (the crossover point from elastic to inelastic demand).

| Figure 2-1 | The effect of demand elasticity on equilibrium price and quantity fluctuations |

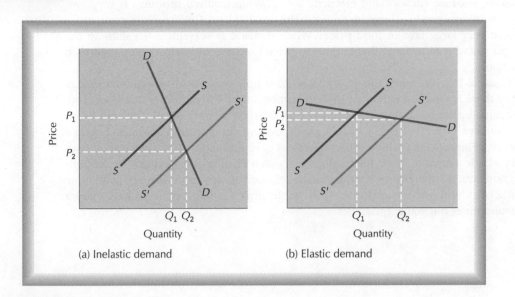

(a) Inelastic demand   (b) Elastic demand

| Table 2-2 | Demand elasticities and changes in spending |

Changes in total spending induced by	Price elasticity of demand		
	Elastic (e.g. −3)	Unit-elastic (−1)	Inelastic (e.g. −0.3)
Price increase	Fall	Unchanged	Rise
Price reduction	Rise	Unchanged	Fall

the first oil price shock

Perhaps the most dramatic illustration of the relation between demand elasticity and total spending is the oil price shock of 1973-74. By collectively restricting oil supplies, the oil-producers organization OPEC induced a quadrupling of the equilibrium price of oil in 1973-74. Increases in price raise consumer spending and seller revenues when demand is inelastic. And demand for oil was *very* inelastic. Estimates of the demand elasticity for oil in the mid-1970s were around −0.1. Oil users had little immediate prospects of substituting other commodities for oil in its many uses: fuel for cars and aeroplanes, fuel for heating and for oil-fired power stations generating electricity, inputs for petrochemical processes. A small restriction in total supply produced a large rise in the equilibrium price and vast revenue gains for OPEC members.

the coffee frost

There's an awful lot of coffee in Brazil – it supplies a large share of the world market. In 1994, people first began to realize that a frost in Brazil would cause havoc with the 1995 harvest. *The Economist* magazine [30 July 1994 (www.economist.co.uk)] reported estimates that the 1995 crop would not be the 26.5 million bags previously thought, but perhaps only 15.7 million bags. Obviously, coffee was going to be scarce in 1995. Anticipating this, speculators bought coffee in 1994, bidding up its price even before the supply fell.

Table 2-3 shows the effect on Brazilian exports during 1993-95. The first row shows that, even after adjusting for general inflation, coffee prices more than doubled in US dollars. The second row shows an index of the volume of Brazilian coffee exports. The final row shows Brazilian export revenue from coffee. Real revenue, of course, went up sharply in 1994: prices had risen *before* production had fallen too much. The interesting comparison is between 1993 and 1995. Brazilian export revenue from coffee *increased* despite the 'bad' harvest.

The demand for coffee is inelastic, although armchair reasoning might suggest an abundance of substitutes – tea, soft drinks, and beer. This example emphasizes the importance of consumer tastes. If buyers refuse to abandon coffee drinking it is useless to point out that a blend of tea and Coca-Cola contains as much caffeine as the average cup of coffee.

farmers and bad harvests

The example of coffee illustrates a general result. When demand is inelastic farmers may earn more revenue from a bad harvest than from a good one. Nor is it surprising

Table 2-3 Brazilian coffee exports 1993–95

	1993	1994	1995
Price (US $/lb)	0.9	2.0	2.1
Export quantity (1990 = 100)	113	102	85
Price × quantity	102	204	179

Prices are in 1995 US$.

Source: IMF, *International Financial Statistics*.

that the demand elasticity is low for many commodities such as coffee, milk, and wheat. These are part of the staple diet of most households and eating habits are slow to change, even when prices of these commodities change.

If bad harvests raise farmers' revenues and good harvests lead to a collapse in agricultural prices and hence farmers' revenue, you may now be wondering why farmers do not get together like OPEC to restrict their supply to increase revenues in the face of inelastic demand. If so, you are beginning to think like an economist. If it were easy to organize such collusion between farmers, it would occur more frequently. Later we discuss the difficulties that arise in trying to maintain a co-operative policy to restrict supply.

When demand is inelastic, suppliers *taken together* will be better off if supply can be reduced. However, if one farmer has a fire that destroys part of the crop but all other farmers' crops are unaffected, the unlucky farmer will definitely be worse off (unless fully insured). The reduction in a single farmer's output, unlike the reduction of all farmer's outputs simultaneously, will have only a negligible effect on supply. Market price will be unaffected and the unlucky farmer will simply be selling less output at the price that would have prevailed in any case. This illustrates an important lesson in economics.

The fallacy of composition *means that what is true for the individual is not necessarily true for everyone together, and what is true for everyone together does not necessarily hold for the individual.*

The individual producer faces a demand that is very elastic – consumers can easily switch to the output of similar farmers – even if the demand for the crop as a whole is very inelastic.

■■■ short run and long run

The price elasticity of demand varies with the length of time that consumers have to adjust their spending patterns when prices change. The dramatic oil price rise of 1973–74 caught many households owning a new but fuel-inefficient car. The immediate response to higher oil prices may have been to *plan* to buy a smaller car with greater fuel economy, but some households were unable to buy smaller cars immediately. In the *short-run*, they were stuck. Unless they could rearrange their lifestyles to make less use of a car, these households had to pay the higher petrol prices. That is why the demand for petrol was so inelastic.

Box 2-1 | Overegging the pudding

Egg, the direct-banking arm of the Prudential (www.egg.com) won 500 000 new customers during its first six months of operation but traded at a loss. An Egg savings account offered generous interest rates, sometimes a few tenths of a per cent above its rivals. To cut its costs, in April 1999 Egg closed its doors to telephone customers, accepting new savings only via the Internet. The example confirms that each lender faces a very elastic demand.

In June 2000, the Prudential sold 20 per cent of its Egg shares to the stock market, at a price of 160 pence a share, which put the total value of Egg at around £1.3 billion.

Over a longer period, consumers had time to sell their cars and buy cars with better fuel economy, or to move from the distant suburbs closer to their place of work. Over this longer period, they could reduce the quantity of petrol demanded much more than they could initially.

The price elasticity of demand is lower in the short run than in the long run when there is more scope for substitution of other goods. This result is very general. Even if addicted smokers cannot adjust to a rise in the price of cigarettes, fewer young people will start smoking if the price rises and gradually the number of smokers will fall.

how long is the long run?

The *short run* refers to the period immediately after prices change and before long-term adjustment can occur. The *long run* is the period necessary for complete adjustments to a price change. Its length depends on the type of adjustments consumers wish to make. Demand responses to a change in the price of chocolate should be completed within a few months, but full adjustment to changes in the price of oil or cigarettes may take several years.

▬▬ the cross price elasticity of demand

The price elasticity of demand tells us about movements along a given demand curve holding constant all determinants of demand except the price of the good itself. We now hold constant the own price of the good and examine the effect of variations in the prices of related goods. The cross price elasticity tells us the effect on the quantity demanded of the good i when the price of good j is changed. As before, we use percentage changes.

> *The* cross price elasticity of demand *for good* i *with respect to changes in the price of good* j *is the percentage change in the quantity of good* i *demanded, divided by the corresponding percentage change in the price of good* j.

The cross price elasticity may be positive or negative. It is positive if a rise in the price of good j increases the quantity demanded of good i. Suppose good i is tea and good j is coffee. An increase in the price of coffee raises the demand for tea. The cross price elasticity of tea with respect to coffee is positive. Cross price elasticities tend to be positive when two goods are substitutes and negative when two goods are complements. We expect a rise in the price of petrol to reduce the demand for cars because petrol and cars are complements.

▬▬ the effect of income on demand

Next, holding constant the own price of a good and the prices of related goods, we examine the response of the quantity demanded to changes in consumer incomes. For the moment we neglect the possibility of saving. Thus a rise in the income of consumers will typically be matched by an equivalent increase in total consumer spending.

Higher consumer incomes tend to increase the quantity demanded. However, demand quantities typically increase by different amounts as incomes rise. Thus the pattern of consumer spending on different goods depends on the level of consumer incomes. We define the budget share of a good as the fraction of total consumer spending for which it accounts.

The budget share *of a good is its price multiplied by the quantity demanded, divided by total consumer spending or income.*

Table 2-4 reports the share of consumer spending in the UK devoted to food and to services (personal and leisure activities such as eating out and going to the theatre) between 1990 and 1998. Real consumer spending (and incomes) rose over the period. The budget share of food fell, whereas the budget share of services rose. Since the real price of both food and services has remained fairly constant over the period, these changes in budget share mainly reflect changes in real consumer incomes.

The income elasticity of demand *for a good is the percentage change in quantity demanded divided by the corresponding percentage change in income.*

Since our strategy for analysing demand has been to consider varying one determinant at a time, the income elasticity of demand measures the effect on quantity demanded when incomes are changed but the own price of the good and the prices of related goods are held constant.

normal, inferior, and luxury goods

The income elasticity of demand measures how far the demand curve shifts horizontally when incomes change. The income elasticity is larger if the given rise in income shifts the demand curve a lot to the right. When an income rise shifts the demand curve to the left, the income elasticity of demand is a negative number. Higher incomes are associated with smaller quantities demanded at any given prices. Earlier, we distinguished *normal* goods, for which demand increases as income rises, and *inferior* goods, for which demand falls as income rises.

A normal good *has a positive income elasticity of demand. An* inferior good *has a negative income elasticity of demand.*

We also distinguish luxury goods and necessities.

A luxury good *has an income elasticity larger than one. A* necessity *has an income elasticity less than one.*

All inferior goods are necessities, since their income elasticities of demand are negative. However, necessities also include normal goods whose income elasticity of demand lies between zero and one.

These definitions also tell us what will happen to budget shares when incomes are changed but prices remain unaltered. The budget share of inferior goods must fall as incomes rise. Higher incomes (budgets) are associated with lower quantities

| **Table 2-4** | Budget shares 1990–98 |

	(1) Real consumer spending (1998 £ bn)	*(2)* % budget share:	*(3)*
		Food	Services
1990	430	12.4	43
1998	523	10.3	47

Source: ONS, *UK National Accounts.*

demanded at constant prices. Conversely, the budget share of luxuries must rise when income rises. Because the income elasticity of demand for luxuries exceeds one, a 1 per cent rise in income increases quantity demanded (and hence total spending on luxury goods) by more than 1 per cent. Rises in income *reduce* the budget share of normal goods that are necessities. A 1 per cent income rise leads to a rise in quantity demanded by less than 1 per cent, so the budget share must fall.

Inferior goods tend to be low-quality goods for which there exist higher-quality, but more expensive, substitutes. Poor people satisfy their needs for meat and clothing by buying low-quality cuts of meat and polyester shirts. As their incomes rise, they switch to better cuts of meat (steak) and more comfortable shirts (cotton). Rising incomes lead to an absolute decline in the demand for cheap cuts of meat and polyester shirts.

Luxury goods tend to be high-quality goods for which there exist lower-quality, but quite adequate, substitutes: Mercedes cars rather than small Fords, foreign rather than domestic holidays. Necessities that are normal goods lie between these two extremes. As incomes rise, the quantity of food demanded will rise but only a little. Most people still enjoy fairly simple home cooking even when their incomes rise. Looking back at Table 2-4, we see that services are luxuries whose budget share increased as UK incomes rose after 1990. Food cannot be a luxury, since its budget share fell as incomes rose, but it is not an inferior good either. At constant (1998) prices which adjust for the effects of inflation, real food spending *increased* from £53 billion in 1990 to £55 billion in 1998. Table 2-5 summarizes the demand responses to changes in incomes holding constant the prices of all goods. The table shows the effect of income increases. Reductions in income have the opposite effect.

Table 2-6 reports income elasticities of demand in the UK. Notice that tobacco (chiefly cigarettes) is not only a necessity but an inferior good. Although inessential for

Table 2-5 Demand responses to a 1 per cent increase in income

Type of good	Income elasticity	Change in quantity demanded	Change in budget share	Example
Normal	Positive	Increases		
Luxury	Larger than 1	Increases by more than 1%	Increases	Yachts
Necessity	Between 0 and 1	Increases by less than 1%	Falls	Food
Inferior	Negative	Falls	Falls	Bread

Table 2-6 Income elasticities of demand in the UK

Broad categories of goods	Income elasticity of demand
Tobacco	−0.50
Fuel and light	0.30
Food	0.45
Alcohol	1.14
Clothing	1.23
Durables	1.47
Services	1.75

physical survival, tobacco has the largest budget share among poor people. Richer people get their kicks in other (more expensive) ways.

using income elasticities of demand

Income elasticities are key pieces of information in forecasting the pattern of consumer demand as the economy grows and people become richer. Suppose we think that incomes will grow at 3 per cent per annum for the next five years. Given the estimates of Table 2-6, a 15 per cent change in incomes will reduce the demand for tobacco by 7.5 per cent but will increase the demand for services by 26 per cent. The growth prospects for these two industries are very different.

■■■ inflation and demand

In Chapter 1 we distinguished *nominal* variables, measured in prices at the time, and *real* variables, measured in constant prices to adjust for inflation. Suppose all nominal variables double. Every good costs twice as much, but all incomes are twice as high. Relative prices are unaltered and every bundle of goods previously affordable remains affordable. Nothing has really changed. Quantities demanded should be unaltered.

How do we reconcile this with price and income elasticities of demand? The former measured the effect of changing one price, holding constant other prices and nominal income. It is no longer relevant when all prices and incomes are inflated at the same rate. Similarly, income elasticities measure the effect of higher nominal income, holding all prices of goods constant. They measure the consequences of changes in real income. But real income does not change under pure inflation. The statement that pure inflation has no real effects on quantities demanded does not contradict our analysis of price and income elasticities of demand.

■■■ recap

■ The price elasticity of demand measures the sensitivity of quantity demanded to changes in the own price of a good, holding constant the prices of other goods and income. Demand elasticities are negative since demand curves slope down.

■ Demand is elastic if the price elasticity is more negative than −1. Price cuts then increase total spending on the good. Demand is inelastic if the demand elasticity lies between −1 and 0. Price cuts then reduce total spending on the good. When demand is unit-elastic the demand elasticity is −1 and price changes have no effect on total spending.

■ Demand elasticities will typically rise (become more negative) with the length of time allowed for adjustment.

■ The cross price elasticity of demand measures the sensitivity of quantity demanded of one good to changes in the price of a related good. Positive cross elasticities tend to imply that goods are substitutes. Negative cross elasticities tend to imply that goods are complements.

■ The income elasticity of demand measures the sensitivity of quantity demanded to changes in income, holding constant the prices of all goods.

■ Inferior goods have negative income elasticities of demand. Higher incomes reduce the quantity demanded and the budget share of such goods. Luxury goods have income elasticities larger than 1. Higher incomes raise the quantity demanded and the budget share of such goods.

■ Goods that are not inferior are called normal goods and have positive income elasticities of demand. Goods that are not luxuries are called necessities and have income elasticities less than 1. All inferior goods are necessities, but normal goods are necessities only if they are not luxuries.

■ Doubling all nominal variables should have no effect on demand since it alters neither the real value (purchasing power) of incomes nor the relative prices of goods.

■■ key terms

■■ review questions

1 Consider the following goods: (a) milk, dental services, beer; (b) chocolate, chickens, train journeys; (c) theatre trips, tennis clubs, films. For each of the three categories, state whether you expect demand to be elastic or inelastic. Then rank the elasticities within each category. Explain your answer.

2 Where along a straight line demand curve does consumer spending reach a maximum? Explain why.

3 The following table shows price and income elasticities for vegetables and catering services. For each good, explain whether it is a luxury or a necessity, and whether demand is elastic or inelastic.

	Price elasticity	Income elasticity
Vegetables	−0.17	0.87
Catering services	−2.61	1.64

4 In 1974 UK households spent £1.3 million on bread and cereals and in 1999 they spent over £5 million on bread and cereals, yet bread is supposed to be an inferior good. How do you account for this?

2-2 understanding demand decisions

adjustment to a price change: substitution and income effects

As the price of a good falls, people buy more of it. Demand curves slope down. Unfortunately, things are not this simple. Suppose the price of potatoes falls. For the rest of your life, you need to remember this has two quite different effects.

The substitution effect *says that, because the relative price of a good has fallen, people will demand more of it.*

Your intuition will always discover the substitution effect, the bit that is obvious. You have to train yourself to look for, and find, the second effect.

The income effect *says, for a given nominal income, a fall in the price of a good leads to a rise in real income, which will affect the demand for all goods.*

If potatoes are a normal good, the demand for them will increase when real income (spending power) increases. Both the income effect and the substitution effect lead to an increase in quantity demanded when the price of potatoes falls. For normal goods, the demand curve slopes down. Price cuts lead to a higher quantity demanded.

However, if potatoes are an inferior good, a rise in real income leads to a *fall* in the quantity demanded. Now the income effect of a price cut pulls in the opposite direction from the substitution effect. A fall in the price of potatoes makes them relatively cheaper, but also increases spending power and reduces the quantity of inferior goods demanded. Theoretical reasoning alone cannot deduce which of the two effects is larger. We need empirical evidence to resolve the issue.

In practice, demand curves for goods and services usually slope down. As their name suggests, inferior goods are less common than normal goods. When might we have any change of discovering an upward sloping demand curve? When the good is inferior and initially takes a large share of consumer spending, for then the price change has a big income effect. Sir Robert Giffen claimed to document an upward-sloping demand curve for potatoes during the Irish famine of the 1840s. As the price of potatoes rose, poor people got even poorer and had to give up other goods entirely. Consumption of potatoes rose. Goods whose demand curve slopes up are called Giffen goods.

These are a rarity in markets for goods and services. In analysing other markets, the sting in the tail from an income effect that outweighs the obvious substitution effect is much more common. Here is a quick taster of things to come. Higher interest rates increase incentives to save, don't they?

Saving *means giving up consumption today in order to get more consumption later.*

Think of the interest rate as the price of time, the bribe for waiting or the cost of consuming today instead of later. When the cost of consuming today rises, you choose less of it. Surely?

Your intuition has uncovered the substitution effect, the way you respond to a change in the relative price of today and tomorrow. Where is the income effect lurking? To afford that foreign holiday tomorrow, you do not have to save so much if interest rates are higher and your assets cumulate more quickly! This effect can make you save less.[3] Empirically, it is very hard to find much effect of interest rates on total saving. Politicians think higher interest rates boost saving, and are always devising schemes like PEPs and ISAs to provide tax breaks for savers in the hope that high after-tax interest rates will boost national saving. Economists are not optimistic this will work. Much of it is simply a subsidy to the rich.

■■■■ adjustment to income changes

Real income can increase either because nominal income increases while prices remain constant, or because the price of a commodity falls while nominal income remains unaltered. The former corresponds to a pure income effect, the latter needs to be decomposed into separate income and substitution effects.

Successive increases in real income lead to large increases in the quantity demanded when the good (or service) is a luxury with a large income elasticity of demand. Quantity demanded still increases for normal goods or services that have positive income elasticities. Thus, items we think of as luxuries are mainly purchased in the world economy by people whose incomes are already high. For example, Internet music sales are forecast to reach 8 per cent of worldwide recorded music by 2004 and 20 per cent by 2010. If people in poor countries have little Internet access, it is mainly consumers in advanced countries who will be downloading tracks from the Internet.

■■■■ tastes and demand

Prices and income tell us what goods people can afford and what the cost of one good is in relation to another. Which of the many affordable bundles of goods an individual actually chooses depends on her tastes. Different people may have different tastes, and therefore make different choices even when facing the same prices and enjoying the same income.

> Tastes *describe the utility a consumer gets from the goods that are consumed.* Utility *is happiness, pleasure or satisfaction.*

Utility is not directly observable in the way we observe prices or incomes. On what do tastes depend? On a host of influences: culture, history, familiarity, relationships with others, advertising, and so on. Explaining these influences is the role of other social sciences, like psychology and sociology. Economists treat them as an 'other things equal' assumption behind a particular demand curve. This does not mean that

---

[3] Provided you are a lender not a borrower, higher interest rates make you better off. Since consumption today and consumption tomorrow are both normal goods, you demand more of both. This income effect cuts saving today. If initially you were a borrower, higher interest rates make you worse off, and the income effect goes the other way. You are poorer and reduce consumption demand today and tomorrow.

tastes cannot change or that such changes may not be really important. For example, in the last three decades there has been a profound change in social attitudes to organic food, and the formality of dress. Economists represent these as a shift in the demand curve for organic vegetables or bowler hats. Constantly changing tastes is the very essence of the fashion industry.

■■■ marginal utility and demand

Fred goes clubbing and drinks lager. His utility depends only on the quantities he himself consumes. Initially, he goes to one club but has no lager. Fred is thirsty and can't enjoy himself. If he got a lager, he'd be a lot happier.

The marginal utility *of a good is the increase in total utility obtained from consumption of one more unit of the good, holding constant the quantity of other goods consumed.*

Fred's first lager gives him high marginal (or extra) utility. Suppose he gets another lager at the club. The second one gives him extra utility, but not as much extra utility as the first one did. A third and fourth lager add less and less extra utility.

Tastes display diminishing marginal utility *from a good if each extra unit adds successively less to total utility when consumption of other goods remains constant.*

Figure 2-2 shows Fred's marginal utility, which falls the more he drinks. It also shows the price of each lager. If a lager costs £4 (expensive club!), and Fred gets £6 of marginal utility from it, he should buy another one. If he only gets £2 of marginal utility from his last lager, he has already bought too many. He should buy lager up to the point the marginal cost (£4 for the last lager) equals the marginal benefit or marginal utility. Figure 2-2 shows Fred choosing point A when lagers cost £4 each.

Figure 2-2 suggests that if the price of lager falls, say from £4 to £3, Fred will definitely buy more lager because of diminishing marginal utility. But the figure is only

Figure 2-2 | Marginal utility and lager demand

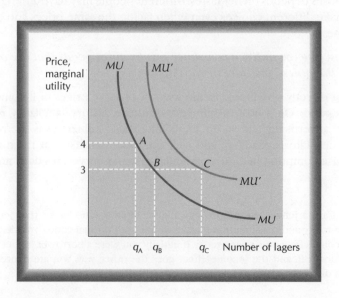

showing the substitution effect! The marginal utility curve assumes quantities of other goods remains constant. However, as the price of lager falls, Fred can afford more club nights too.

If lager is a normal good, the income effect shifts the marginal utility curve outwards to MU' in Figure 2-2. This also makes Fred consume more lager (point C). Income and substitution effects go in the same direction. The demand curve for lager, drawn through A and C slopes down. But if lager had been an inferior good, the MU curve might have shifted *inwards* enough to make Fred consume less lager when its price fell.

So far, marginal utility analysis has only reinforced our earlier and simpler discussion of income and substitution effects. However, it was worth learning. Here are two reasons why.

the water diamond paradox

Why is the price of water, essential for survival, so much lower than the price of decorative diamonds? One answer is that diamonds are scarcer than water. Yet consumers clearly get more total utility from water (without it they die). Marginal utility solves the problem.

The marginal benefit of the first unit of water is enormous. But we each consume lots of water. Since water is relatively abundant, the supply curve for water lies well to the right and the equilibrium price is low even when it is privately supplied. Hence consumers have moved a long way down their marginal utility of water curve.

In fact, where the state supplies water free, this analysis suggests consumers should use water up to the point its marginal utility is zero. May as well wash the car again. Even a small rise in price may lead to a large cutback in usage – demand is very elastic in this region of the demand curve.

risk aversion

Our second example concerns risk. We live in a world where we choose to take some risks (the lottery, the Grand National) but are forced by nature to take many other risks (heart attacks, traffic accidents, fires, earthquakes). Suppose Fred faces risk in the lager market. Suppose half the time nature gives him a *quantity* of 1 lager, and half the time a *quantity* of 3 lagers. Would he rather get 2 lagers for sure all the time? On average he would get just as many lagers but he would get more utility! Because of diminishing marginal utility, the downward slope of the MU curve in Figure 2-2, Fred gets less extra benefit from going from 2 to 3 lagers than he loses in going down 2 to 1 lager.

Even if in the long run he gets the same total quantity of lager, it does not yield him the same total utility. Risk hurts. Fair bets in money terms are not fair bets in utility terms. The boom years yield only a little extra pleasure. This does not compensate for the years of starvation. It would be better to even things out.

Risk aversion *means people dislike risk and would decline a fair bet.*

This explains why people are keen to insure their house and their possessions. They happily pay a small premium to have the risk taken away. If the bad situation arises, they get suitably compensated, and never face real starvation.

How then do we simultaneously explain insurance, the avoidance of risk, and gambling, a voluntary increase in risk? This puzzle has fascinated mathematicians and economists for centuries. Figure 2-2 again provides some of the answer. For large risks, there is a big difference in the marginal utility of winning and losing. For small stakes, the MU curve does not have much space in which to decline. Provided the odds are fair in money terms, losing sacrifices only a little more utility than is gained from winning.

Once we add in separately the thrill factor, this may be enough to 'pay for' the small loss implied by diminishing marginal utility. People playing the lottery are partly paying for a good night's entertainment – dreams and excitement – just as they would pay for other recreation activities like cinema and restaurants. And the value to them of this thrill must be quite large, because the National Lottery is nowhere near close to a fair bet even in money terms. Because of money deducted for operating expenses, good causes, and money for the Treasury, it only pays out about half the revenue it brings in from ticket sales.

from individual to market demand curve

Having examined the theory of individual demand decisions, our next task is to explain how individual behaviour is aggregated to give the total demand in a particular market.

The market demand curve *is the horizontal sum of individual demand curves in that market.*

Recall that we plot price on the vertical axis. All consumers in a market face the same price. Suppose at a price of £1 the first consumer demands a quantity of 2 and the second consumer a quantity of 3, the market demand is a quantity of 5 when the price is £1. Repeating this procedure at each and every possible price we trace out the market demand curve.

▥ recap

■ A price change has both a substitution (relative price) effect and an income (purchasing power) effect. Intuition usually locates the substitution effect. You must also find the income effect.

■ Demand curves slope down for normal goods. A sufficiently inferior good could have an upward sloping demand curve.

■ Because of the income effect, higher interest rates need not encourage more saving.

■ Higher incomes increase demand for normal goods and reduce demand for inferior goods.

■ Marginal utility is the extra benefit of consuming the last unit of a good, holding constant consumption of other goods. Tastes display diminishing marginal utility.

■ This explains both the water diamond paradox and risk aversion.

■ At each price, the market demand curve is the sum of the quantities demand by different people facing that price.

▥ key terms

1 Which of the following statements are true: A luxury good must have elastic demand; an inferior good has a negative income elasticity; spending on inferior goods falls when the price rises.

2 'A rise in the wage rate raises labour supply by making work more attractive than leisure.' 'A rise in the wage rate makes people better off, and will increase the quantity of leisure demanded.' Which is the income effect and which is the substitution effect? Will higher (after-tax) wages lead to more hours of work or more hours of leisure?

3 A person declines to insure their house even though a government ministry has confirmed that the insurance company was quoting a premium that reflected the true odds of house damage. What would you have to conclude about this person's marginal utility?

4 Give three examples where your own utility depends only on the quantity of the good that you consume, and three cases in which your utility depends on the quantities someone else consumed.

2-3 the supply decision

We now turn to the theory of supply. How much do firms decide to produce and offer for sale? For each possible output level, the firm need to answer two questions: how much will production cost and what revenue will be earned from sales? Profits are the excess of revenue over costs. The key to the theory of supply is the assumption that each firm chooses the output level that maximizes its profit.

types of firm

Businesses come in three forms: self-employed sole traders, partnerships, and companies. A sole trader owns the business, keeps any profit but is responsible for any loss no matter how large. A partnership is a business jointly owned by several people who share the profits or losses. Partnerships are one way for a business to attract extra financial backing. Like sole traders, partners face *unlimited liability*. If the firm loses enough they can be forced to sell personal assets, and may even go personally bankrupt. Really large firms have huge financial needs, and taking on more and more partners would get complicated. Instead the firm becomes a company.

A company *is an organization with a legal existence, allowed to produce and trade.*

Ownership is divided among a large number of shareholders. Since it is unreasonable to expect all of them to take a close interest in every business in which they hold shares, shareholders of a company have *limited liability*. If you buy £100 of shares and the company then loses £1 million, you shares become worthless but you cannot be forced to sell personal possessions to cover the company's debt. Although there are lots of sole traders in the UK, many are tiny. In value terms, most of the business is actually conducted by the large companies whose shares are traded every day on the stock market. Such companies are run by boards of directors, who must report annually to a shareholders' meeting, giving dissatisfied shareholders an opportunity to sack the board.

a firm's accounts

Firms report two sets of accounts, one for stocks and one for flows.

Stocks *are measurements at a point in time,* flows *are corresponding measurements during a period of time.*

The water flowing out of a tap is different per second and per minute. The measurement requires a time interval to make sense of it. The stock of water in the basin at any instant is a number of litres, and requires no time dimension to make sense of it. A firm reports profit-and-loss accounts per year (flow accounts) and a balance sheet showing assets and liabilities at a point in time (stock accounts). The two are of course related, as they are for the basin of water. The inflow from the tap is what changes the stock of water over time, even though the latter is only measured in litres at each point in time.

flow accounts (profit and loss)

A firm's revenue *is income from sales during the period, its* costs *are expenses incurred in production and sales during the period, and its* profits *are the excess of revenue over costs.*

This sounds very easy, but there are a few tricky complications. Economists and accountants adopt different definitions because they are interested in different things. Accountants have to certify that nobody is stealing cash from the business. They care about cash flow.

Cash flow *is the net amount of money received by a firm during a given period.*

Economists are interested in what, how and for whom goods are produced. Recall from Chapter 1 that a market economy using money is only one of the possible ways to organize things. Accountants keep track of actual cash spent. Economists focus on opportunity cost.

Opportunity cost *is the amount lost by not using resources in their best alternative use.*

Suppose you quit a job as a teacher of IT and start an internet business, paying out £5000 in the first year as you camp in an internet café, whose facilities are in effect your office. An accountant treats your costs as £5000. An economist stresses that your time was not free – you could have used it to earn £20 000 a year teaching IT. It only makes sense to switch your labour resources into the internet job if you can earn at least £25 000. For an economist, interested in incentives to reallocate resources, a revenue of £25 000 is merely break even; for an accountant it is £20 000 profit.

Normal profit *is the accounting profit to break even after all economic costs have been taken into account.* Economic (supernormal) profits *in excess of normal profit are a signal to switch resources into the industry. Earning less than normal profit is a signal that the resources could earn more elsewhere.*

Here is a second case in which economists and accounting definitions are different. The internet startup also requires the IT lecturer to plough in £2000 of her savings to cover everyday expenses. The accountant treats this personal financial injection by the owner as free, but an economist recognizes the opportunity cost. If the money could have earned £100 in interest during the year, that is another economic cost to be deducted in calculating economic profit.

What happens when stocks and flows get mixed up? Here both economists and accountants agree that the right procedure is to try to keep them separate. Suppose the internet startup company does so well that it moves out of the internet café and buys its own office.

Physical capital *is the input to production not used up within the production period. Examples include machinery, equipment, and buildings.* Investment *is additions to physical capital.*

This capital is a stock and not a flow, but we cannot exclude it entirely from the firm's flow accounts. How does it show up? First, the capital becomes less valuable during the period for which flow accounts are drawn up. This depreciation is a proper charge on the flow accounts.

Depreciation *is the cost of using capital during the period.*

It reflects both wear and tear, and the fact that it gradually becomes obsolete and less valuable. Notice too that in purchasing an office and computer equipment, the firm has tied up £100 000 of money. Whether it came out of the owner's pocket (and could otherwise have been earning interest) or whether it was borrowed from a bank (in which case the cost is evident to the accountant as well), either way the interest payments need to be entered into the flow accounts of the firm to get the right economic answer.

stock accounts (balance sheet)

The balance sheet shows at a point in time the assets and liabilities that the firm has built up as a result of its flow behaviour in all preceding periods.

Assets *are what the firm owns.* Liabilities *are what is owes.* Net worth *is assets minus liabilities.*

Assets include cash in the bank, money owed by customers, inventories, and physical capital such as plant and machinery. Liabilities are debts the firm still has to repay to suppliers and its bankers. Suppose your accountant tells you that a company has identifiable net worth of £300 000. If you wanted to buy the company, is that what the company is worth? You should probably bid more. Maybe much more. The company is not just its physical and financial assets and liabilities. It is also a *going concern* with a reputation, customer loyalty, and a host of intangibles that economists call *goodwill*. You have to add a guess about this value as well. Goodwill represents the ability of the firm to make money in the future, just as valuable an asset as what it has so far cumulated from past behaviour. The consultancy Interbrand tries to do these calculations by comparing the stock market value of companies with the identifiable physical and financial resources involved. Table 2-7 shows that US giants such as Coca Cola top the worldwide list. Microsoft, Nokia and Yahoo! are well up the list. So are Nike and Adidas. Interestingly, the big banks perform poorly in this rating.

Table 2-7	The value of a good name

Rank	Company	Brand value (£bn)
1	Coca Cola	50
2	Microsoft	36
3	IBM	25
4	Ford	20
5	Disney	19
11	Nokia	12
18	Sony	8
25	Citibank	8
28	Nike	5
52	Heineken	1

Source: Financial Times, 22 June 1999

Suppose you are considering switching resources between uses. Should you think about the flow accounts for the year or the stock accounts at the time of your decision? The former shows recent behaviour, the latter shows the long run position. If you can afford to take a long run view, you may be more interested in the stock accounts. However, if you have to worry about short-term considerations, the flow accounts may be more informative. In practice, you probably need to think about both.

Box 2-2 | Corporate finance and corporate control

Corporate finance refers to the ways companies raise money by ploughing back profits, issuing new shares, or borrowing. Borrowing can be from banks or by selling pieces of paper (corporate debt) whereby the firm promises to pay interest for a specified period and then to pay off the debt. Different countries have very different systems of corporate finance.

The United States and the UK have market-based or *outsider* systems, relying on active stock markets trading existing shares and debt, and available for launching new shares and debt. Japan and much of continental Europe, most notably Germany, have an *insider* system, in which financial markets play only a small role. German companies get long-term loans from banks, who then sit on company boards with access to inside information about how the firm is doing.

Distinguishing finance and control

Large firms finance most of their new investment from their own retained profits. Over 90 per cent of UK corporate investment is financed in this way; less then 7 per cent comes from sales of new shares on the stock market. The key difference in the two systems of corporate finance lies not in the ease with which they provide firms with finance, but in the way they award *control rights* to those providing that finance.

Under the bank-based insider system, representatives of the bank sit on the firm's board, and can use this inside position to press for changes in company policy or top management when mistakes are made. The market-based system entails a much smaller role for banks, and a more significant role for stock markets and debt markets. Failure to meet interest payments on debt usually gives debtholders the right to force the company into bankruptcy, a radical transfer of corporate control in which the existing management rarely survives. Similarly, the existence of publicly quoted shares raises the possibility of a stock market takeover in which a new management team effectively buys control on the open market. Outsider market-based systems of corporate finance thus become markets for corporate control itself.

Hostile takeovers: good or bad?

In Germany, hostile takeovers have been rare. In contrast, a large fraction of UK takeover activity reflects hostile bids uninvited by existing managers. Some economists see hostile bids as a vital force for efficiency. The threat of hostile takeovers may deter managers from departing too much from the profit-maximizing policies desired by shareholders.

However, hostile takeovers also undermine the existing managers. Suppose you want workforce co-operation in moving to new production methods. You promise to reward employees handsomely in the future once all the changes have been made and productivity has risen. The workers know you always keep your word. Even so, they may feel unable to trust you. While the changes are being made, profits will temporarily fall and you may become the victim of a takeover raid. The new owner may start firing workers to save money. So the workers reject your plan to bring changes to the company.

Hostile takeovers, by undermining the ability of managers to make commitments to their workers, may thus inhibit investment and encourage *short-termism*.

■■■ do firms really maximize profits?

Firms are in business to make money. Economists assume that firms make supply decisions to maximize profits. Some business executives, and even some economists, question the assumption that firms have the sole aim of maximizing profits. Sole traders are accountable only to themselves and may take into account other things about which they care (nice location, popularity with the local community, and so on). However, most business is done by large companies.

Companies are not run directly by their owners. The directors have day-to-day discretion and only account formally to shareholders at the annual shareholders meeting. In practice, shareholders rarely dismiss the directors. The directors have inside information about the true prospects of the firm, so it is hard for shareholders to be sure that new directors could do better. Economists call this a separation of ownership and control. The shareholders want maximum profits, but those in day-to-day control may pursue their own agenda. This may not simply be executive perks, such as nice cars and a company jet. If status depends partly on size, directors may pursue size rather than profits, for example by too much advertising or by holding prices lower than would be ideal for profits and shareholders' interests.

Even so, there are two good reasons why the assumption of profit maximization is a good place to start in developing a theory of supply. First, even if shareholders are kept partly in the dark, other firms in the industry may be better informed. Companies not pursuing profits will have low profits, and hence low share prices. A takeover raider can buy the company cheaply, change the management policy, make extra profits, and cash up as the share price soars. Fear of takeovers may force the directors to pursue profit maximization.

Second, shareholders are fully aware of the general problem and take action to minimize its adverse effect on themselves. They offer directors profit-related bonuses and share options. The total value of these is small relative to total profits but large relative to what directors earn in salary alone. It becomes worth while to do what the shareholders want.

■■■ an overview of the supply decision

Let's think first about (economic) costs of production. The total cost of production will vary with the level of output. Obviously, to make more costs extra. At each particular output level, there will generally be more than one available production technique. A field of wheat can be farmed with lots of workers and few implements or one worker with a lot of machinery.

The firm considers a particular output, examines the price of each input, the different production techniques available, and calculates the lowest cost way to make that output. Then it thinks about each other level of output it could possibly make, in each case working out the lowest cost method of making that output.

The total cost curve *shows the lowest cost method of producing each output level.*

Table 2-8 shows different outputs in the first column and the corresponding levels of total cost in the second column. Whatever it produces the firm has a cost of 10, perhaps the cost of paying interest on old debts. As output increases from 1 to 4, total costs increase from 18 to 54. Extra output incurs extra costs. The third column shows marginal cost.

Marginal cost *is the change in total cost as a result of producing the last unit.*

Thus, the marginal cost of the first unit of production is the increase in total cost from 10 to 18 in column 2. This marginal cost of the first unit produced is shown as 8 in column 3. Similarly, the marginal cost of producing the fourth unit of output is 14, the increase in total costs from 40 to 54. Try drawing a graph with total cost on the vertical axis and output level on the horizontal axis. Plotting columns 1 and 2 of Table 2-8 you will discover that marginal cost is simply the slope of the total cost curve at each output level, the rise in total cost when output increases by one unit.

Now we do the same for revenue. Column 4 shows total revenue from selling the output produced. With no output the firm gets no revenue. The first unit of output can be sold at a price of 20, giving a total revenue of 20. This is also the marginal revenue of going from zero to one unit of output sold.

Marginal revenue *is the change in total revenue as a result of producing and selling the last unit.*

As output and sales increase, column 4 shows that revenue rises for a bit but eventually gets smaller as sales increase. To sell more and more output, the firm has to reduce prices to induce purchasers to demand this output. Since all output is sold for the same price, cutting the price to sell new units reduces the revenue earned on previous units. This second effect eventually outweighs the first. Beyond 3 units, extra sales actually cut revenue. Column 5 does the sums for you, showing the marginal revenue from the last unit sold, which takes into account the effect on total revenue of bidding down the price that previous units have been sold for. By the bottom row of Table 2-8, marginal revenue is actually negative.

Armed with the first five columns of Table 2-8, you now advise the firm what output to produce and sell. One method is simply to subtract total cost from total revenue to obtain economic or supernormal profits. Column 6 shows that that profit maximizing output level is an output of 2, at which profits are 3. This is similar to the method used by a mountaineer who checks the top has been reached by making sure he can look down on all surrounding sides. But there is another way to check you are at the top. Work out the slope you are standing on. If it slopes in any direction, go on in an upwards direction. When you reach the very top, the slope at that particular point is zero. There is no direction you can move in order to get any higher. This is the marginal principle.

The marginal principle *says that if the slope is not zero there is always one direction to move to make things better, and another to make things worse. Only at a maximum (or a minimum) is the slope temporarily zero.*

Table 2-8 The supply decision: a first look

Output q	Total cost TC	Marginal cost MC	Total revenue TR	Marginal revenue MR	Supernormal profits	MR − MC
0	10	–	0	–	−10	
1	18	8	20	20	2	12
2	28	10	31	11	3	1
3	40	12	36	5	−4	−7
4	54	14	35	−1	−19	−15

Economists use the marginal principle a lot. Here we say that marginal profit must be zero. Otherwise, there would exist a direction to change output. But marginal profit is simply marginal revenue minus marginal cost. Column 7 shows how to use this decision rule. If marginal revenue exceeds marginal cost, you made a marginal profit by producing the last unit. Keep going. If marginal revenue is smaller than marginal cost, you made a marginal loss on the last unit, and already went too far. This rule says that, with a marginal profit of 1 it was a good idea to produce as much as 2 units; however, with a marginal loss of 7 from producing a third unit, it is best to stop at 2 units. This, of course, is the same answer we obtained by calculating total profit from total revenue and total cost. Sometimes, however, it is a much easier method to implement.

▪▪▪▪ plotting *MC* and *MR* curves

Table 2-8 is simply an artificial if useful example. Firms don't always have to produce in integer units such as 0, 1, 2, 3, 4. Dairies can produce 1284.8 litres of milk if this is the best output level. In Figure 2-3 we summarize much of the above discussion of the supply decision by plotting continuous curves for marginal cost and marginal revenue. We show an *MR* curve steadily declining as output increases and price cuts are necessary to get customers to buy. For most of its range we show a rising *MC* curve, as producing the last unit gets harder and harder. For example, a coal mine may have to go ever deeper to produce extra output.

The profit-maximizing firm chooses to supply the output q^*, at which marginal profit is zero because marginal revenue exactly equals marginal cost. At any lower output, marginal revenue exceeds marginal cost and the firm can add to profits by expanding. At any output above q^*, marginal cost exceeds marginal revenue and the firm can add to profits by contracting output.

| Figure 2-3 | A firm's supply decision |

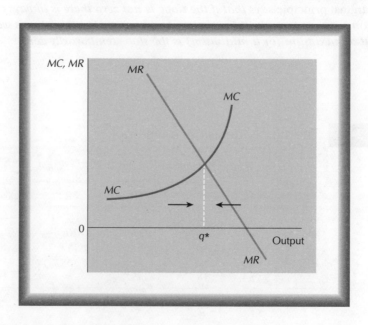

We can also use Figure 2-3 to do comparative static analysis. Anything that leads to an upward shift in a firm's marginal cost curve (such as wage increase or tougher pollution controls that it has to obey) will mean that *MC* crosses *MR* at a lower output. The firm will supply less. Conversely, a change in demand behaviour that shifts the *MR* curve upward will increase the output level that the firm wishes to supply.

do firms really know their MC and MR curves?

There are two ways in which profit maximization might be achieved. The first is by having a highly professional management with access to excellent management information. Marginal cost and marginal revenue are indeed what they should be trying to discover. But the firm may simply be run by an intuitive genius who happens to get things right without necessarily going through all the laborious steps above. If she were not a genius, she'd have been fired long ago. But if she does get things right, she is maximizing profit, and this guarantees that *MC* must equal *MR* whether anyone in the firm knows it or not. Using the marginal principle is how we mere mortals can keep track of what proven business leaders do instinctively. Later, it will allow us to deduce how they will react when economic circumstances change.

▪▪▪ so we've mastered the supply decision?

We have discovered the basic principle from which all else follows, but there is still some important detail to fill in. First, both revenue and costs may be different in the short run and in the longer run. In Chapter 1, for example, we noted that the overnight reaction of customers to OPEC's oil price rise was different from the eventual demand response. So the firm may have to react to a marginal revenue schedule that changes over time. Even more important, a firm's cost curves are likely to change over time. The rest of this chapter highlights key differences between short run and long run.

We also have to aggregate across individual suppliers to obtain the market supply curve. This aggregation depends on how many suppliers there are and how they react to one another. The next chapter explains the different forms of market structure and what this means for the supply decision.

▪▪▪ recap

■ Flows are measured over time, stocks at a point in time. Profit is the difference between the flow of revenue and cost.

■ Economic costs include all opportunity costs. Normal profit is the accounting profit that just covers all economic costs. Supernormal profits are any profits above this level.

■ Firms are assumed to maximize profits even when shareholders cannot directly observe the behaviour of their directors. Maximizing profits automatically entails marginal cost equal to marginal revenue.

■ An upward shift in marginal revenue leads to a higher level of chosen output. An upward shift in marginal costs reduces desired supply of output.

■■■ key terms

■■■ review questions

1 Why might firms, such as accountants and lawyers, where the trust of the customer is important, choose to be partnerships with unlimited liability?

2 You are drawing up a new set of 'Green accounts' for the UK. You decide that environmental depreciation should be deducted from a proper measure of the flow of UK net output each year. Give three examples you might deduct. Could they be measured?

3 Think about a region with lots of hills. At the very top of each hill, what is the slope? Does having a zero slope guarantee you have found the highest hill? What else might you check? How could a business use this insight?

4 Is there a difference between maximizing profits in the short run and in the long run? Could long run profit maximization justify any practices that look wasteful in the short run? Are any business practices hard to square even with long-run profit maximization?

2-4 production costs and supply

Firms don't always close down when they start losing money. Sometimes they expect demand to increase, or they may think that, given time, they can reduce their production costs enough to get back into profit. We distinguish between the *short-run* and the *long-run* output decisions of firms. No firm will stay in business if it expects to make losses for ever. We show how and why cost curves differ in the short run, when the firm cannot fully react to changes in conditions, and the long run in which the firm can fully adjust to changes in demand or cost conditions. In fact, we have to consider the short-run and long-run versions of three different cost curves: total cost; marginal cost; and average cost.

Figure 2-4 summarizes the material of this section.

inputs and output

> *An* input *(or* factor of production*) is any good or service used to produce output.*

Inputs include labour, machinery, buildings, raw materials, and energy. The term 'input' covers

LEARNING OUTCOMES

When you have finished this section, you should understand

- the production function and its relation to the avoidance of waste

- technology and a technique of production

- how a firm's choice of production technique is affected by input prices

- total, average and marginal cost, both in the long run and in the short run

- returns to scale and their relation to the shape of average cost curves

- fixed and variable factors in the short run, and the law of diminishing returns

- a firm's chosen output level, in the short run and long run, including temporary shutdown and permanent exit

---

Figure 2-4 | The complete theory of supply

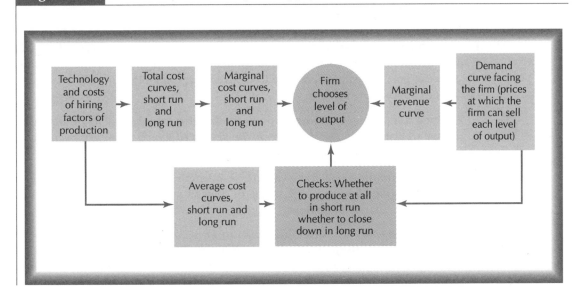

everything from senior management to bandages in the first-aid room. Suppose our firm uses inputs to make snarks. This is an engineering and management problem.

The production function *specifies the maximum output that can be produced from any given amount of inputs.*

The production function summarizes the *technically efficient* ways of combining inputs to produce output. A production method is technically *inefficient* if, to produce a given output, it uses more of some inputs and no less of other inputs than some other method that makes the same output. Since profit-maximizing firms will not be interested in wasteful production methods, we restrict our attention to those that are technically efficient.

A technique *is a particular method of combining inputs to make output.* Technology *is the list of all known techniques. The* production function *is the list of all techniques that are technically efficient.*

By *technical progress* economists mean an invention or improvement in organization that allows a given output to be produced with fewer inputs than before. A technique that used to be technically efficient has been rendered inefficient by the technical advance that has introduced a new, more productive production technique.

The production function relates volumes of inputs to volume of output. But costs are values. Suppose the firm wants an output level of 100 and has three different technically efficient ways to produce it. It examines input prices and chooses the lowest cost technique. This is the *economically efficient technique* for producing an output of 100 *given the input prices that the firm faces.* If wages rise, one of the less labour intensive techniques may then become the efficient way to produce an output of 100. But whenever input prices change, the firm can restrict its search to the few technically efficient techniques in the production function.

The firm has now discovered one point on its total cost curve, namely the lowest cost way to produce an output of 100, given existing input prices and technology. It now repeats the exercise for each and every possible output level to obtain the total cost curve, showing how costs vary with output. Notice that the firm may switch between techniques as output changes. We don't use mass production for very low output levels.

▦ long-run costs

Faced with an upward shift in its demand and marginal revenue curves, a firm will want to expand production. However, adjustment takes time. In the first few months, the firm can get its existing workforce to do overtime. Over a longer period it may be cheaper to build a new factory.

The long run *is the period long enough for the firm to adjust all its inputs to a change in conditions. The* short run *is the period in which the firm can make only* partial *adjustment of its inputs to a change in conditions.*

The firm may have the flexibility to vary the shift length almost immediately. Hiring or firing workers takes longer, and it might be several years before a new factory is designed, built, and fully operational.

Long-run total cost (*LTC*) *describes the minimum cost of producing each output level when the firm can adjust all inputs.* Long-run marginal cost (*LMC*) *is the increase in long-run total cost if output is permanently increased by one unit.*

LTC must rise with output. It must cost more to produce more output than less. How fast do total costs increase with output? Can large firms produce goods at a lower unit cost than small firms? Might it be a disadvantage to be large?

Long-run average cost (*LAC*) *is LTC total cost divided by the level of output.*

As output increases, average cost often starts out high, then falls, then rises again. This common pattern of average costs, called the U-shaped average cost curve, is shown in Figure 2-5.

returns to scale

There are economies of scale *(or* increasing returns to scale*) when long-run average costs decrease as output rises,* constant returns to scale *when long-run average costs are constant as output rises, and* diseconomies of scale *(or* decreasing returns to scale*) when long-run average costs increase as output rises.*

The three cases are illustrated in Figure 2-6. The U-shaped average cost curve has increasing returns to scale up to the point *A*, where average cost is lowest. At higher output levels there are decreasing returns to scale. Why should there be economies of scale at low output levels but diseconomies of scale at high output levels? This is a technological question about the most efficient production techniques. Figure 2-6 shows other posssible *LAC* curves.

economies of scale

There are three reasons for economies of scale. The first is *indivisibilities* in the production process, some minimum quantity of inputs required by the firm to be in business at all whether or not output is produced. These are sometimes called *fixed*

Figure 2-5 A typical *LAC* curve

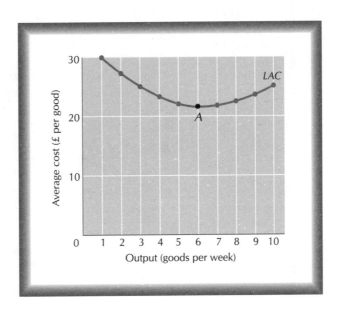

costs, because they do not vary with the output level. To be in business a firm requires a manager, a telephone, an accountant, a market research survey. The firm cannot have half a manager and half a telephone merely because it wishes to operate at low output levels. Beginning from small output levels, these costs do not initially increase with output. There are economies of scale because these fixed costs can be spread over more units of output. As the firm expands further, it has to hire more managers and telephones and these economies of scale die away. The average cost curve stops falling.

The second reason for economies of scale is *specialization*. As the firm expands and takes on more workers, each worker can concentrate on a single task and handle it more efficiently. The third reason for economies of scale is that large scale is often needed to take advantage of better machinery. Sophisticated but expensive machinery also has an element of indivisibility. No matter how productive a robot assembly line is, it is pointless to install one to make five cars a week. Average costs would be enormous.

Figure 2-6 Returns to scale and long-run average cost curves

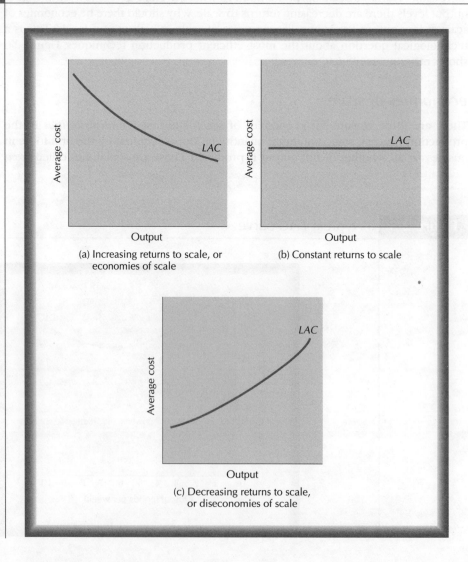

(a) Increasing returns to scale, or economies of scale

(b) Constant returns to scale

(c) Decreasing returns to scale, or diseconomies of scale

diseconomies of scale

The main reason for diseconomies of scale is that management becomes more difficult as the firm becomes larger: there are *managerial diseconomies of scale*. Large companies need many layers of management, which themselves have to be managed. The company becomes bureaucratic, co-ordination problems arise, and average costs may begin to rise. Geography may also explain diseconomies of scale. If the first factory is located in the best site, to minimize the cost of transporting goods to the market, the site of a second factory must be less advantageous. The shape of the average cost curve thus depends on two things: how long the economies of scale persist, and how quickly the diseconomies of scale occur as output is increased.

returns to scale in practice

At low output levels, average costs fall rapidly. As output rises, average costs fall but more slowly. Economists have tried to measure the output level at which further economies of scale become unimportant for the individual firm, the point at which the average cost curve first becomes horizontal. This output level is called the *minimum efficient scale (MES)*.

Table 2-9 contains some estimates of the MES for firms operating in different industries in the UK and the United States. The first column gives an idea of how steeply average costs fall before minimum efficient scale is reached. It shows how much higher average costs are when output is one-third of the output at minimum efficient scale. The second and third columns show the *MES* output level relative to the output of the industry as a whole. This provides a benchmark of the importance of economies of scale to firms in each industry. Since firms in the UK and the United States essentially have access to the same technical know-how, differences between the second and third columns primarily reflect differences in the size of the industry in the two countries rather than differences in the *MES* output level for an individual firm.

Table 2-9 Minimum efficient scale

Industry	% increase in average costs at ⅓ MES	MES as % of market in UK	USA
Cement	26.0	6.1	1.7
Steel	11.0	15.4	2.6
Glass bottles	11.0	9.0	1.5
Bearings	8.0	4.4	1.4
Fabrics	7.6	1.8	0.2
Refrigerators	6.5	83.3	14.1
Petroleum refining	4.8	11.6	1.9
Paints	4.4	10.2	1.4
Cigarettes	2.2	30.3	6.5
Shoes	1.5	0.6	0.2

Source: F. M. Scherer *et al.*, *The Economics of Multiplant Operation*, Harvard University Press, Tables 3.11 and 3.15.

Box 2-3 | Scale economies and the internet

Serious parents used to purchase for their children a bookshelf filled with *Encyclopaedia Britannica*. This prestige reference work was the market leader for two centuries, despite commanding a premium price, which peaked at about £1300.

Noting a fall in the price and availability of home PCs, Microsoft decided to produce PC software for an encyclopaedia called *Encarta*, at a fraction of the price of *Britannica*. *Encarta* was not only cheaper but the software was portable and often easier to use than a book, given the electronic hyperlinking and speed of access to information. To see how to order the current CD, visit the Microsoft *Encarta* website (http://www.encarta.msn.com). *Britannica* was not threatened by a new entrant to the 32-volume book business but by a new technology that changed the nature of the niche. A few months after the launch of *Encarta*, *Britannica* quickly responded to *Encarta*'s entry. It had been planning its own CD-ROM and released this on the market. Being originally aimed at libraries or other institutional users, this CD version was expensive at first but, recognising the potential of the home user market, *Britannica* now prices very competitively. To see material on the CD version of *Britannica*, visit *Encyclopaedia Britannica* (http://www.britannica.co.uk). In 1998 *Britannica* took the decision to disband its book sales force: those consumers using computers often pay little attention to traditional sales methods.

Some lessons of this case study? Once upon a time, *Encyclopaedia Britannica* enjoyed considerable market power. In part this was based on the one-off costs of amassing the huge volume of information for the encyclopaedia. Although new editions needed a little updating, information on the Roman empire or the geography of South America could be carried over from previous editions.

Britannica therefore enjoyed scale economies that made it difficult for new entrants to compete. They were then able to use their hard-won position of market leadership to enjoy an element of monopoly profit. Since the demand curve for £1300 encyclopaedias was probably fairly inelastic, setting marginal cost equal to marginal revenue then led to a large mark-up and a high price. Digital technology changed all this. Although the one-off costs of assembling the information remained large, the marginal cost of further production and sales fell almost to zero. No more encyclopaedia salesmen in the foyer of Foyles (an old-fashioned London bookstore) and production of expensive 32-volume sets of books. This sharp fall in marginal cost meant that marginal revenue could be driven down substantially, allowing many more copies to be sold and now CDs retail below £50.

Temporarily, *Encarta* got a technical edge and completely undercut *Britannica*'s old market. But *Britannica* did not have to collect new information, merely change the medium through which its existing information was presented and distributed. Once it had released its own CD, it was able to get back in the game.

Note too that *Encarta* also offers dictionary services. Similar forces are therefore at work in the traditional market for dictionaries. The unabridged *Oxford English Dictionary* has also become available in CD form, currently retailing at just under £300. This high price may indicate that *OED* has not lost its monopoly position to the same extent, but also reflects the fact that the demand for full-length dictionaries remains quite small. Even avid fans of the hardest Sunday crossword usually only require a (much shorter) one-volume dictionary to check their solutions. Interestingly, the 2000 disk edition of *Britannica* includes the *New Oxford Dictionary of English* free.

Questions for discussion

Since the marginal cost of making and distributing CDs is only a few dollars, why does competition not bid down the price of encyclopaedia CDs to this level? Should we be surprised that many products offered on the internet are free? Is this likely to continue?

These figures suggest that in heavy manufacturing industries economies of scale are substantial. At low outputs, average costs are much higher than at minimum efficient scale. We would expect similar effects in aircraft and motor car manufacture, which have very large fixed costs for research and development of new models and which can take advantage of highly automated assembly lines if output is sufficiently high. Yet in a large country such as the United States, minimum efficient scale for an individual firm occurs at an output that is small relative to the industry as a whole. Most firms will be producing on a relatively flat part of their averge cost curve with few economies of scale still to be exploited.

In smaller countries such as the UK, the point of minimum efficient scale may be large relative to the industry as a whole. However, there are many industries, even in the manufacturing sector, where minimum efficient scale for a firm is small relative to the market as a whole and average costs are only a little higher if output is below minimum efficient scale. These firms will be producing in an output range where the *LAC* curve is almost horizontal.

Finally, there are a large number of firms, especially those outside the manufacturing sector, whose cost conditions are well represented by a U-shaped average cost curve. With only limited opportunities for economies of scale, these firms run into rising average costs even at quite moderate levels of output.

We begin by discussing the output decision of a firm with a U-shaped average cost curve. Then we show how this analysis must be amended when firms face significant economies of scale.

■■■■ average cost and marginal cost

■ *LAC* is falling when *LMC* is less than *LAC*, and rising when *LMC* is greater than *LAC*.

■ *LAC* is at a minimum at the output level at which *LAC* and *LMC* cross.

Neither is an accident. The relation between average and marginal is a matter of arithmetic, as relevant for football as for production costs. A footballer with 3 goals in 3 games is averaging 1 goal per game. Two goals in the next game, implying 5 goals from 4 games, would raise the average to 1.25 goals per game. In the fourth game the marginal score is 2 goals, the increase in total goals from 3 to 5. Because the marginal score exceeds the average score in previous games, the extra game must drag up the average.

The same relation holds for production costs. When the marginal cost of the next unit exceeds the average cost of the existing units, making the next unit must drag up average cost. Conversely, when the marginal cost of the next unit lies below the average cost of existing units, an extra unit of production drags down average costs. When marginal and average cost are equal, adding a unit leaves average cost unchanged.

In Figure 2-7 average and marginal cost curves cross at the point of minimum average cost. Why? To the left, *LMC* lies below *LAC* so average cost is still falling. To the right, *LMC* lies above *LAC* so average cost is rising. *A* must be the output level at which average costs are at a minimum. As in the football example, this relation rests purely on arithmetic. With a U-shaped average cost curve, the marginal cost curve lies below the average cost curve to the left of minimum average costs but above the average cost curve to the right of minimum average cost. The marginal cost curve crosses the average cost curve from below at the point of minimum average cost.

■■■ the firm's long-run output decision

Figure 2-7 shows *LAC* and *LMC*. It also shows the marginal revenue (*MR*) curve. We know that the output level of maximum profit or minimum loss occurs at *B*, the output at which marginal revenue equals marginal cost. The firm then has to check whether it makes profits or losses at this output. It should not stay in business if it makes losses for ever.

Total profits are average profits per unit of output multiplied by the number of units of output. Hence total profits are positive only if average profits per unit of output exceed zero. Average profits are average revenue per unit minus average cost per unit. But average revenue per unit is simply the price for which each output unit is sold. Hence *if long-run average costs at B exceed the price for which the output* Q_1 *can be sold*, the firm is making losses even in the long run and should close down. If, at this output, price equals *LAC*, the firm just covers its costs and breaks even. And if price exceeds *LAC* at this output, the firm is making long-run profits and should happily remain in business.

Notice that this is a two-stage argument. First we use the *marginal condition* (*LMC = MR*) to find the profit maximizing or loss minimizing output provided the firm stays in business, *then* we use the *average condition* (the comparison of *LAC* at this output with the price or average revenue received) to determine whether the profit maximizing or loss minimizing output in fact yields profits and hence allows the firm to stay in business in the long run. If even the best output from the firm's viewpoint yields losses, then the firm should close down.

Figure 2-7	The firm's long-run output decision

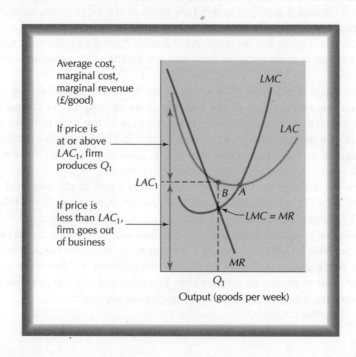

short-run cost curves and diminishing marginal returns

The short run is the period in which the firm cannot fully adjust to a change in conditions. In the short run the firm has some fixed factors of production.

A fixed factor of production *is a factor whose input level cannot be varied.*
A variable factor *can be adjusted, even in the short run.*

How long this short run lasts depends on the industry. It might take ten years to build a new power station but only a few months to open new restaurant premises. The existence of fixed factors in the short run has two implications. First, in the short run the firm has some fixed costs.

Fixed costs *do not vary with output levels.*

These fixed costs must be borne even if output is zero. Second, because in the short run the firm cannot make all the adjustments it would like, its short-run costs of production must be different from its long-run production costs, and must be higher. When adjustment eventually becomes possible, the firm has an incentive to make this adjustment only if it can get on to a lower cost curve by doing so.

short-run fixed and variable costs

Variable costs *are costs that change as output changes.*

Variable costs are the costs of hiring variable factors, typically labour and raw materials. Although firms may have long-term contracts with workers and material suppliers, which tend to reduce the speed at which adjustment of these factors can be accomplished, in practice most firms retain important elements of flexibility through overtime and short time, hiring or non-hiring of casual and part-time workers, and raw material purchases in the open market to supplement contracted supplies.

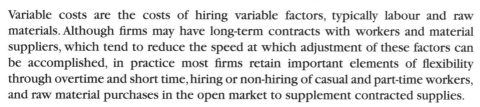

Short-run total cost = short-run fixed cost + short-run variable cost.
(STC)   (SFC)   (SVC)

Since fixed costs do not increase with output, short run marginal cost (*SMC*) is the increase both in short-run total costs and in short-run variable costs as output is increased by 1 unit.

The short-run marginal cost curve has the same general shape as the long-run marginal cost curve shown in Figure 2-7, but for a very different reason. The short-run marginal cost curve assumes that there is at least one fixed factor, probably capital. To increase output as we move along the short-run marginal cost curve, the firm must be adding ever-increasing amounts of labour to a given amount of plant and machinery.

the marginal product of labour and diminishing marginal productivity

The marginal product *of a variable factor (in this example, labour) is the increase in output obtained by adding 1 unit of the variable factor, holding constant the input of all other factors (in this example, capital).*

At low levels of output and labour input, the first worker has a whole factory to work with and has to do too many jobs to produce very much. A second worker helps, and a third helps even more. Suppose the factory has three machines and the three workers are each specializing in fully running one of the factory's machines. The marginal product of the fourth worker is lower. With only three machines, the fourth worker gets to use one only when another worker is having a rest. There is even less useful machine work for the fifth worker to do. By now there are diminishing returns to labour.

Holding all factors constant except one, the law of diminishing returns *says that, beyond some level of the variable input, further increases in the variable input lead to a steadily decreasing marginal product of that input. This is a law about technology.*[4]

short-run marginal costs

Figure 2-7 shows that, as output is increased, short-run marginal costs first fall then rise. Every worker costs the firm the same wage. While the marginal product of labour is increasing, each worker adds more to output than the previous workers. Hence the extra cost of making extra output is falling. *SMC* is falling so long as the marginal product of labour is rising.

Short-run marginal cost *is the extra cost of making one extra unit of output in the short-run while some inputs remain fixed.*

Once diminishing returns to labour set in, the marginal product of labour falls and *SMC* starts to rise again. It takes successively more workers to make each extra unit of output.

short-run average costs

Short-run average fixed cost *(SAFC) equals short-run fixed cost (SFC) divided by output.* Short-run average variable cost *(SAVC) equals SVC divided by output and* short-run average total cost *(SATC) equals STC divided by output. Thus*

$$
\begin{array}{ccc}
\text{Short-run} & \text{short-run} & \text{short-run} \\
\text{average total cost} = \text{average fixed cost} + \text{average variable cost} \\
(SATC) & (SAFC) & (SAVC)
\end{array}
$$

Look first at Figure 2-8. We already understand the shape of the *SMC* curve that follows from the behaviour of marginal labour productivity. The usual arithmetical relation between marginal and average explains why *SMC* passes through the lowest point on the short-run average total cost curve. To the left of this point, *SMC* lies below *SATC* and is dragging it down as output expands. To the right of *A* the converse holds.

Variable costs are the difference between total costs and fixed costs. Since fixed costs do not change with output, marginal costs also show how much total *variable* costs are changing. The same arithmetic relation between marginal costs and average *variable* costs must hold and the usual reasoning implies that *SMC* goes through the lowest point on *SAVC*. To the left of this point, *SMC* lies below *SAVC* and *SAVC* must be falling; to the right, *SAVC* must be rising. Finally, since average total costs exceed average variable costs by average fixed costs, *SAVC* must lie below *SATC*.

[4] Notice that economists use *diminishing* returns to describe the addition of one variable factor to other fixed factors in the short run, but *decreasing* returns to describe diseconomies of scale when *all* factors are freely varied in the long run.

■■■ the firm's output decision in the short run

Figure 2-8 illustrates the firm's choice of output in the short run. Since fixed factors cannot be varied in the short run, it is short-run marginal cost that must be set equal to marginal revenue to determine the output level Q_1 which maximizes profits or minimizes losses.

Next, the firm decides whether or not to stay in business in the short run. Profits are positive at the output Q_1 if the price p at which this output can be sold covers average total costs. It is the short-run measure $SATC_1$ at this output that is relevant. If p exceeds $SATC_1$, the firm is making profits in the short run and should certainly produce Q_1.

Suppose p is less than $SATC_1$. The firm is losing money because p does not cover costs. In the long run the firm closes down if it keeps losing money, but there the difference between the long run and the short run appears. Even at zero output the firm must pay the fixed costs in the short run. The firm needs to know whether losses are bigger if it produces at Q_1 or produces zero. If revenue exceeds variable cost the firm is earning something towards paying its overheads. Thus the firm will produce Q_1 provided revenues exceed variable costs even though Q_1 may involve losses. The firm produces Q_1 if p exceeds $SAVC_1$. If not, it produces zero.

The firm's short-run output decision *is to produce Q_1, the output at which* MR = SMC, *provided the price at least equals the short-run average variable cost (SAVC$_1$) at that output level. If the price is less than SAVC$_1$ the firm produces zero.*

Table 2-10 summarizes the short-run and long-run output decisions of a firm.

Figure 2-8   The firm's short-run output decision

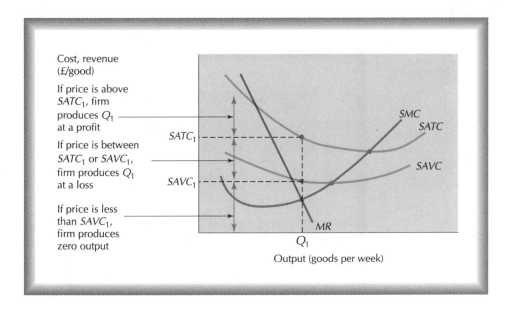

▬▬ short-run and long-run costs

Even if it is making losses in the short run, a firm will stay in business if it is covering its variable costs. Yet in the long run it must cover all its costs to remain in business. A firm may reduce its costs in the long run, converting a short-run loss into a long-term profit. Figure 2-9 shows a U-shaped *LAC* curve. At each point on the curve the firm is producing a given output at minimum cost. The *LAC* curve describes a time scale sufficiently long that the firm can vary *all* factors of production, even those that are fixed in the short run.

Suppose, that 'plant' is the fixed factor in the short run. Each point on the *LAC* curve involves a particular quantity of plant. Holding constant this quantity of plant, we can draw the short-run average total cost curve for this plant size. Thus, the $SATC_1$ curve corresponds to the plant size at point *A* on the *LAC* curve and the $SATC_2$ and $SATC_3$ curves correspond to the plant size at points *B* and *C* on the *LAC* curve. In fact, we could draw an *SATC* curve corresponding to the plant size at each point on the *LAC* curve.

By definition, the *LAC* curve describes the minimum-cost way to produce each output when all factors can be freely varied. Thus, point *B* describes the minimum

Table 2-10	The firm's output decisions	
	Marginal condition	*Check whether to produce*
Short-run decision	Choose the output level at which $MR = SMC$	Produce this output unless price lower than *SAVC*. If it is, produce zero.
Long-run decision	Choose the output level at which $MR = LMC$	Produce this output unless price is lower than *LAC*. If it is, produce zero.

Figure 2-9	*LAC* and *SATC*

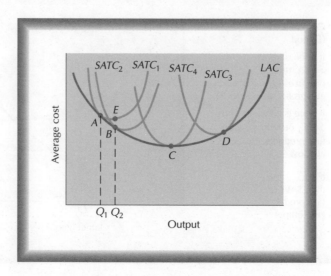

average-cost way to produce an output Q_2. Hence it *must* be more costly to produce Q_2 using the wrong quantity of plant, the quantity corresponding to point E. For the plant size at A, $SATC_1$ shows the cost of producing each output including Q_2. Hence $SATC_1$ must lie above LAC at every point except A, the output level for which this plant size happens to be best.

This argument can be repeated for any other plant size. Hence $SATC_3$ and $SATC_4$ corresponding respectively to the fixed plant size at C and at D, must lie above LAC except at points C and D themselves. In the long run the firm can vary all its factors and will generally be able to produce a particular output more cheaply than in the short run, when it is stuck with the quantities of fixed factors it was using previously. A firm currently suffering losses because demand has fallen can look forward to future profits after it has had time to build a plant more suitable to its new output.

| Box 2-4 | Sunk costs |

*S*unk costs are sunk. If certain costs have already been incurred and cannot be affected by your decision, ignore them. They should not influence your future decisions. In deciding how much to produce in the short run, the firm ignores its fixed costs which must be incurred anyway.

It may seem a pity to abandon a project on which a lot of money has already been invested. Poker players call this throwing good money after bad. If you do not think it will be worth reading the next ten chapters in their own right, you should not do it merely because you have put a lot of effort into the first two chapters.

---

recap

- In the long run the firm can fully adjust all its inputs. In the short run, some inputs are fixed.

- The production function specifies the maximum amount of output that can be produced using any given quantities of inputs.

- The total cost curve is derived from the production function, for given input prices. The long-run total cost curve is obtained by finding, for each level of output, the method of production that minimizes costs when all inputs are fully flexible.

- Average cost is total cost divided by output. The long-run average cost curve (LAC) is typically U-shaped. There are increasing returns to scale on the falling part of the U. The rising part of the U is a result of managerial diseconomies of scale.

- When marginal cost is below average cost, average cost is falling. When marginal cost is above average cost, average cost is rising.

Average and marginal cost are equal only at the lowest point on the average cost curve.

- In the long run the firm produces at the point where long-run marginal cost (LMC) equals MR provided price is not less than LAC at that output. If price is less than LAC, the firm goes out of business.

- The short-run marginal cost curve (SMC) reflects the marginal product of the variable factor holding other factors fixed. Beyond some output, diminishing returns to the variable factor make SMC rise.

- Short-run average total costs ($SATC$) are equal to short-run total costs (STC) divided by output. $SATC$ is equal to short-run average fixed costs ($SAFC$) plus short-run average variable costs ($SAVC$). The SMC curve cuts both the $SATC$ and $SAVC$ curves at their minimum points.

■ The firm sets output in the short run at the level at which *SMC* is equal to *MR*, provided price is not less than short-run average variable cost. In the short run the firm is willing to produce at a loss provided it is recovering at least part of its fixed costs.

■ The *LAC* curve is always below the *SATC* curve, except at the point where the two coincide. This implies that a firm is certain to have higher profits in the long run than in the short run if it is currently producing with a plant size that is not best from the viewpoint of the long run.

■■■ key terms

■■■ review questions

1 (a) What information does the production function provide? (b) Explain why the production function does not provide enough information for anyone actually to run a firm.

2 (a) What are economies of scale and why might they exist? (b) The following table shows how output changes as inputs change. Assume the wage rate is £5 and the rental rate of capital is £2. Calculate the lowest-cost method of producing, 4, 8, and 12 units of output. (c) Do you have increasing, constant, or decreasing returns to scale between those output levels? Which applies where?

Capital input	Labour input	Output
4	5	4
2	6	4
7	10	8
4	12	8
11	15	12
8	16	12

3 (a) Calculate the marginal and average costs for each level of output from the following total cost data. (b) Show how marginal and average costs are related. (c) Are these short-run or long-run cost curves? Explain how you can tell.

Output	Total cost (£)
0	12
1	27
2	40
3	51
4	60
5	70
6	80
7	91
8	104
9	120

3 | market structure

3-1 perfect competition

An industry is the set of all firms making the same product. The output of an industry is the sum of the outputs of its firms. Yet different industries have very different numbers of firms. Letters in the UK are delivered by the Post Office, which we call a nationalized industry because it is owned and run by the state. However, some sole suppliers are private firms. Eurostar is the only supplier of train journeys from London to Paris. In contrast, the UK has 200 000 farms and 30 000 grocers.

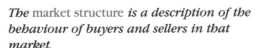

The market structure *is a description of the behaviour of buyers and sellers in that market.*

We assume that there are many buyers whose individual downward-sloping demand curves can be aggregated to yield the market demand curve. This chapter assumes different market structures reflect differences not in the number of buyers but in the number of sellers. We begin with perfect competition.

In a perfectly competitive industry *nobody believes that their own actions affect the market price.*

LEARNING OUTCOMES

When you have finished this section, you should understand

- the concepts of perfect competition and pure monopoly

- why a perfectly competitive firm chooses the output at which price equals marginal cost

- incentives for entry and exit

- how to derive the supply curve of a perfectly competitive industry

- the effect of shifts in demand or costs

Such an industry must have many buyers and many sellers. In London the New Covent Garden fruit market confronts many buyers with many sellers. Neither buyers nor sellers believe their own actions affect the market price.

Each firm in a perfectly competitive industry faces a horizontal demand curve. Whatever output the firm sells, it gets exactly the market price. This horizontal demand curve is the crucial feature of a perfectly competitive firm. To be a plausible description of the demand curve facing the firm, we need to have in mind an industry with four characteristics. First, there must be a large number of firms in the industry so that each is trivial relative to the industry as a whole. Second, the firms must be making a reasonably standard product, such as wheat or potatoes. Even if the car industry had a large number of firms it would not be sensible to view it as a competitive industry. A Ford Mondeo is not a perfect substitute for a Vauxhall Vectra. Each producer will cease to be trivial relative to the relevant market and will no longer be able to act as a price-taker.

This example alerts us to the problem of which goods can be grouped together within the same market or industry. In a perfectly competitive industry all firms must be making essentially the same product, *for which they all charge the same price*. Why don't all the firms in the industry do what OPEC did in 1973–74, collectively restricting supply, to increase the price of their output by moving the industry up its market demand curve? A crucial characteristic of a perfectly competitive industry is *free entry and exit*. Even if existing firms could organize themselves to restrict total supply and drive up the market price, the consequent increase in revenues and profits would simply attract new firms into the industry, thereby increasing total supply again and driving the price back down. Conversely, as we shall shortly see, when firms in a competitive industry are losing money, some firms will close down and, by reducing the number of firms remaining in the industry, reduce the total supply and drive the price up, thereby allowing the remaining firms to survive.

the firm's supply decision

In Chapter 2 we developed a general theory of the supply decision of the individual firm. First, the firm uses the marginal condition ($MC = MR$) to find the best positive level of output; then it uses the average condition to check whether the price for which this output is sold covers average cost. *The special feature of perfect competition is the relationship between marginal revenue and price.* The competitive firm faces a horizontal demand curve. Unlike the more general case, in which the firm faces a downward-sloping demand curve, the competitive firm does *not* bid down the price as it sells more units of output. Since there is no effect on the revenue from existing output, the marginal revenue from an additional unit of output *is* simply the price received: $MR = P$.

the firm's short-run supply curve

Provided it produces at all, any firm chooses the output at which $MC = MR$. For a perfectly competitive firm this means $MC = MR = P$. Then the firm checks whether zero output is better. Figure 3-1 shows the short-run cost curves we developed in Chapter 2.

P_1 *is the* shutdown price *below which the firm is failing to cover even variable costs in the short run. At all prices above* P_1, *the firm chooses output to make* $P = SMC$. *Hence the firm's* supply curve *is the part of its* SMC *curve above* P_1.

This shows how much the firm wants to make at each price it might be offered. For example, at a price P_4, the firm chooses to supply Q_4.

the firm's long-run supply curve

The same principles apply in deriving the long-run supply curve of the perfectly competitive firm. Figure 3-2 shows the firm's average and marginal costs in the long run. Facing a price P_4, the marginal condition leads the firm to choose the long-run output level Q_4 at the point D. Again we must check whether it is better to shut down than to produce this output. In the long run, shutting down means leaving the industry altogether. The firm exits from the industry only if price fails to cover long-run average cost LAC at the best positive output level. At the price P_2 the marginal

---

Figure 3-1   Short-run supply by perfectly competitive firm

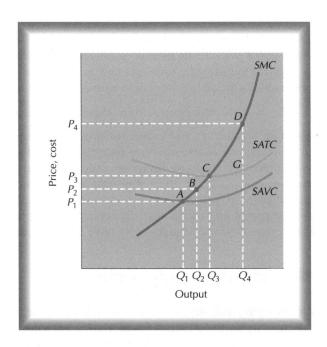

Figure 3-2   Long-run supply by perfectly competitive firm

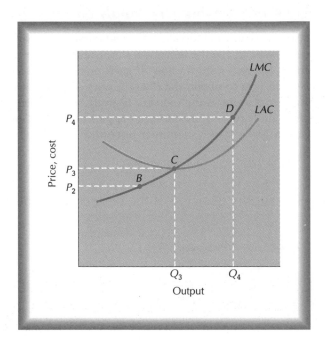

condition leads to the point B in Figure 3-2, but the firm is losing money and should leave the industry in the long run.

Thus the firm's *long-run supply curve*, the schedule relating output supplied to price in the long run, is the portion of the *LMC* curve to the right of point C corresponding to the price P_3. At any price below P_3 the firm can find no positive output at which price covers *LAC*. At the price P_3 the firm produces Q_3 and just breaks even after paying all its economic costs. It makes only normal profits.

entry and exit

The price P_3 corresponding to the minimum point on the *LAC* curve is called the *entry or exit price*. Firms are making only normal profits. There is no incentive to enter or leave the industry. The resources tied up in the firm are earning just as much as their opportunity costs, what they could earn elsewhere.

Entry *is when new firms join an industry.* Exit *is when existing firms leave.*

Any price less than P_3 will induce the firm to exit from the industry in the long run.

However, we can also interpret Figure 3-2 as the decision facing a potential entrant to the industry. The cost curves now describe the post-entry costs. P_3, the price that just covers the lowest average cost at which the entrant could produce, is the critical point at which entry becomes attractive. Any price above P_3 yields supernormal profits and means that the return on the owners' time and money will be higher than their opportunity costs. Table 3-1 summarises our discussion so far.

■■■ industry supply curves

A competitive industry comprises many firms. In the short run two things are fixed: the quantity of fixed factors employed by each firm, and the number of firms in the industry. In the long run, each firm can vary all its factors of production, but the number of firms can also change through entry and exit from the industry.

the short-run industry supply curve

Just as we can add individual demand curves by buyers to obtain the market demand curve, we can add the individual supply curves of firms to obtain the industry supply curve. Figure 3-3 shows how. At each price we add together the quantities supplied by each firm to obtain the total quantity supplied at that price. In the short run the number of firms in the industry is given. Suppose there are two firms, A and B. Each firm's short-run supply curve is the part of its *SMC* curve above its shutdown price. Firm A has a lower shutdown price than firm B. Firm A has a lower *SAVC* curve,

Table 3-1	The supply decision of the perfectly competitive firm

Marginal condition	Average condition	
	Short run	Long run
Produce output where $P = MC$	If $P < SAVC$ shut down temporarily	If $P < LAC$ leave industry

perhaps because of a more favourable geographical location. Each firm's supply curve is horizontal at the shutdown price. At a lower price, no output is supplied.

The industry supply curve is the horizontal sum of the separate supply curves. The industry supply curve is discontinuous at the price P_2. Between P_1 and P_2 only the lower-cost firm A is producing. At P_2 firm B starts to produce as well. When there are many firms, each with a different shutdown price, there are a large number of very small discontinuities as we move up the industry supply curve. In fact, since each firm in a competitive industry is trivial relative to the total, the industry supply curve is effectively smooth.

comparing short- and long-run industry supply curves

However, unlike the short run, the number of firms in the industry is no longer fixed in the long run. Not only can existing firms leave the industry, but also new firms can enter. As the market price rises, the total industry supply rises in the long run for two distinct reasons: each existing firm will move up its long-run supply curve, and new firms will find it profitable to enter the industry.

Conversely, at lower prices, higher-cost firms lose money and leave the industry. Entry and exit in the long run play a role analogous to shutdown in the short run. In the long run, entry and exit affect the number of producing firms whose output must be horizontally aggregated to obtain the industry supply. In the short run, although the number of firms in the industry is given, the fraction that is producing rather than being temporarily shut down is not. Again, the industry supply curve is the horizontal sum of the outputs of those actually producing at the given market price.

Hence, the long-run supply curve is flatter than the short-run supply curve for two reasons: each firm can vary its factors more appropriately in the long run; and higher prices attract *additional* firms into the industry, causing industry output to rise by more than the additional output supplied by the firms previously in the industry.

The marginal firm For each firm, the height of the minimum point on its *LAC* curve shows the critical price at which it can just survive in the industry making only normal profits. Suppose different firms have *LAC* curves of different heights, and hence face different exit prices. At any price there will be a marginal firm only just able

Figure 3-3   Deriving the industry supply curve

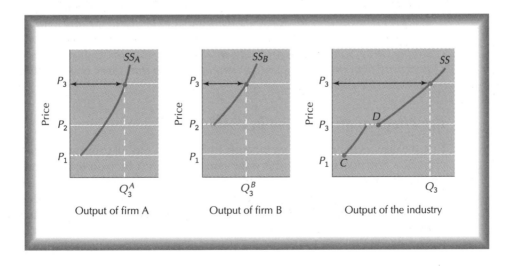

Output of firm A   Output of firm B   Output of the industry

to survive in the industry (and a marginal potential entrant just waiting to enter if only the price rises a little).

the horizontal long-run industry supply curve

Each firm has a rising *LMC* curve and hence a rising long-run supply curve. The industry supply curve is somewhat flatter. Higher prices not merely induce existing firms to produce more; they also induce new firms to enter the industry. In the extreme case the industry long-run supply curve is horizontal. This case occurs when all existing firms and potential entrants have *identical cost* curves. Suppose *P** is the entry and exit price for all existing firms and potential entrants. Below *P** no firm will wish to supply. Although it takes a price above *P** to persuade each individual firm to expand output beyond that at minimum *LAC*, no higher price than *P** is required to expand industry output. At any price above *P**, every firm makes supernormal profits. Since potential entrants face the same cost curves, there would be a flood of new firms entering the industry. Hence the industry supply curve is horizontal in the long run at the price *P**.

There are two reasons why the general case of a rising long-run industry supply curve is much more likely than the special case of a horizontal long-run supply curve for a competitive industry. First, it is unlikely that every firm and potential firm in the industry has identical cost curves. Second, even if all firms face the same cost curves, we draw a cost curve for given technology *and* given input prices. Although each small firm can affect neither output prices nor input prices, the collective expansion of output by all firms may bid up input prices. If so, it requires a higher output price to allow an increase in industry output that will bid up input prices and shift the cost curves for each individual firm upwards. Thus in general we expect the long-run supply curve of the industry to be rising. It requires a higher price to call forth a higher total output.

■■■ comparative statics for a competitive industry

Having discussed the industry supply curve, we can now examine how supply and demand interact to determine equilibrium price in the short run and the long run.

In short-run equilibrium *the market price equates the quantity demanded to the total quantity supplied by the given number of firms in the industry when each firm produces on its short-run supply curve. In* long-run equilibrium *the market price equates the quantity demanded to the total quantity supplied by the number of firms in the industry when each firm produces on its long-run supply curve. Since firms can freely enter or exit from the industry, the marginal firm must make only normal profits so that there is no further incentive for entry or exit.*

the effect of an increase in costs

First we discuss the effect of an increase in costs that hits all firms: an increase in the price of a raw material, or in the wage rate which must be paid in the industry. For simplicity, we discuss the case in which all firms face the same costs. Before costs increase, the industry is in long-run equilibrium. Every identical firm is producing the output at the bottom of its *LAC* curve and making only normal profits. Price equals this value of *LAC*. The market demand curve shows total industry output at this price. Previous entry and exit has made sure that the total number of firms is appropriate to produce the right industry output when each produces the output at its minimum *LAC*.

When all firms' *LAC* curves shift up, they all start losing money. Eventually some will leave the industry. This reduces industry output, and raises the equilibrium price as the industry moves up its demand curve. When enough firms have left, and industry output has become scarce enough to bid up prices in line with the rise in costs, the remaining firms are breaking even again. That is the new long-run equilibrium. Two points about the change in the long-run equilibrium. First, the rise in average costs is eventually passed on to the consumer in higher prices. Second, since higher prices reduce the total quantity demanded, industry output must fall.

a shift in the market demand curve

The previous example discussed only long-term effects. We can of course discuss short-run effects as well. Figure 3-4 illustrates the effect of a shift up in the market demand curve from *DD* to *D'D'*.

Figure 3-4 | A shift in demand in a competitive industry

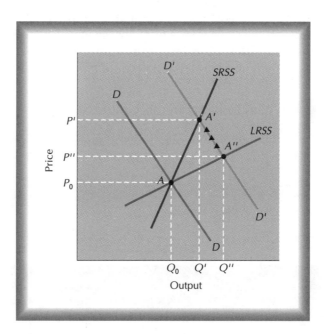

Box 3-1 | Truck off

After a bumper year in 1998, makers of trucks expected a bad year in 1999. Sharp rises in road tax and fuel duty raised costs for everyone in the industry in the UK. Producers were also nervous about looming restrictions on drivers' hours under the EU Working Time Directive. As the industry supply curve shifted left, equilibrium output was expected to fall. Industry forecasts ranged from a 10 per cent to an 18 per cent fall in 1999 alone.

The industry begins in long-run equilibrium at *A*. Overnight, each firm has fixed factors and the number of firms is fixed. Horizontally adding their short-run supply curves, we obtain the industry supply curve *SRSS*. The new short-run equilibrium occurs at the point *A'*. When demand first increases it requires a large price rise to persuade individual firms to move up their steep short-run supply curves with given fixed factors.

In the long run, firms can adjust all factors and move on to their flatter long-run supply curves. In addition, supernormal profits attract extra firms into the industry. Figure 3-4 assumes that the long-run industry supply curve is rising. Either it takes higher prices to attract higher-cost firms into the industry, or the collective expansion bids up some input prices, or both. The new long-run equilibrium occurs at *A"*. Relative to short-run equilibrium at *A'* there is a further expansion of total output but a more appropriate choice of factors of production and the entry of new firms combine to increase supply and reduce the market-clearing price.

The most spectacular example of a demand curve shift is probably provided by the oil price shock in 1973–74 when oil prices tripled. Since oil and coal are substitutes as energy sources, we should expect a large outward shift in the demand for coal. In many European countries the coal industry was regulated by the government. The best example of a competitive coal industry was the case of the United States. Table 3-2 presents some statistics for the 1970s which confirm the prediction of Figure 3-4. In 1974–77, immediately following the oil price shock, there was a 52 per cent rise in the real price of coal but only a modest 12 per cent rise in production of coal. This matches the move from *A* to *A'*. For the period 1978–80 output rises a lot but the real price falls back, as the move from *A'* to *A"* predicts.

Table 3-2   The coal industry in the United States

Years	Real price*	Output
1970–73	100	100
1974–77	152	112
1978–80	145	129

*Index for 1970–73 = 100.

Box 3-2   The elasticity of supply

The elasticity of supply measures the responsiveness of the quantity supplied to a change in the price.

$$\text{Supply elasticity} = \frac{(\% \text{ change in quantity supplied})}{(\% \text{ change in price})}.$$

Supply elasticity = (% change in quantity supplied) Because supply curves slope upwards, the elasticity is always *positive*. Higher prices induce higher quantities supplied. The more elastic is supply, the larger the percentage response.

■■■ recap

- In a competitive industry each buyer and seller acts as a price-taker, believing that individual actions have no effect on the market price. Competitive supply is most plausible when a large number of firms make a standard product under conditions of free entry and exit from the industry, and customers can easily verify that the products of different firms really are the same.

- For a competitive firm, marginal revenue and price coincide. Output is chosen to equate price to marginal cost. The firm's supply curve is its *SMC* curve above *SAVC*. At any lower price the firm temporarily shuts down. In the long run, the firm's supply curve is its *LMC* curve above its *LAC* curve. At any lower price the firm eventually leaves the industry.

- Adding at each price the quantities supplied by each firm, we obtain the industry supply curve. It is flatter in the long run both because each firm can fully adjust all factors and because the number of firms in the industry can vary.

- An increase in demand leads to a large price increase but only a small increase in quantity. The existing firms move up their steep *SMC* curves. Price exceeds average costs and the ensuing profits attract new entrants. In the long run output increases still further but the price falls back. In the long-run equilibrium the marginal firm makes only normal profits and there is no further change in the number of firms in the industry.

- An increase in costs for all firms reduces the industry's output and increases the price. In the long run the marginal firm must break even. A higher price is required to match the increase in its average costs.

■■■ key terms

■■■ review questions

1 The domestic economy has only one firm, but it faces a flood of international imports if it tries to charge more than the world price. Is it a dangerous monopoly or a perfectly competitive firm?

2 Suppose an industry of identical competitive firms enjoys a technical breakthrough that reduces everyone's costs. What will happen in the short run and the long run? Try to distinguish what is happening at the firm level and at the industry level.

3 If every firm is a price taker, who changes the price when a shift in demand causes initial disequilibrium?

4 Which industry has a more elastic long run supply curve: coal mining or hairdressing? Why?

3-2 pure monopoly

The perfectly competitive firm is too small to worry about the effect of its own decisions on industry output. In contrast, a pure monopoly is the entire industry.

> A monopolist *is the sole supplier or potential supplier of the industy's output.*

A sole national supplier need not be a monopoly for two reasons. If it raises prices, it may face competition from imports or from domestic entrants to the industry. A pure monopoly does not need to worry about potential competition. Some firms, such as the Post Office, have a monopoly conferred by the state and may have other concerns than profit. Other firms, such as privatised water companies, posed such a threat to competition that the government decided to regulate them. Think of the ensuing analysis as showing how each local monopolist would have behaved unregulated, and acting only in pursuit of private profit.

■■■ profit-maximizing output

To maximize profits, a firm chooses the output at which marginal revenue MR equals marginal cost MC (SMC in the short run and LMC in the long run) then checks that it is covering average costs ($SAVC$ in the short run and LAC in the long run). Figure 3-5 shows the average cost curve AC with its usual U-shape. Marginal revenue MR lies below the down-sloping demand curve DD. The monopolist recognizes that to sell extra units it has to lower the price, even for existing customers. Setting $MR = MC$, the monopolist chooses the output level Q_1. However, to find the price for which Q_1 units can be sold we must look at the demand curve DD. The monopolist sells Q_1 units of output at a price P_1 per unit. Profit per unit is given by $P_1 - AC_1$, price minus average cost when Q_1 is produced. Total profits are the area $(P_1 - AC_1) \times Q_1$.

Even though we are studying the long run, the monopolist continues to make these *supernormal* profits. They are sometimes called *monopoly* profits. Unlike the competitive industry, supernormal profits of a monopolist are not eliminated in the long run. By ruling out the possibility of entry, we remove the mechanism by which supernormal profits tend to disappear in the long run. Table 3-3 summarizes the monopolist's output decision.

Price-setting   Whereas the competitive firm is a *price-taker*, taking as given the equilibrium price determined by the interaction of market supply and market demand, the monopolist actually sets prices and is a price-setter. Having decided to produce Q_1, what the monopolist actually does is to quote a price P_1 knowing that customers will then demand exactly Q_1 units of output.

Elasticity and marginal revenue   When demand is elastic, lower prices and higher output increase revenue. The marginal revenue from the extra output is positive. When MR is negative, demand must be inelastic. The monopolist sets MC

equal to *MR*. Since *MC* must be positive, so must *MR*. The chosen output must lie to the left of Q_2. Hence, we say that *a monopolist will never produce on the inelastic part of the demand curve* where *MR* is negative.

Price, marginal cost, and monopoly power   At any output, price exceeds the monopolist's marginal revenue since the demand curve slopes down. Hence, in setting *MR* equal to *MC* the monopolist sets a price that exceeds marginal cost. In contrast, a competitive firm always equates price and marginal cost, since its price is also its marginal revenue. The competitive firm cannot raise price above marginal cost and has no monopoly power.

The excess of price over marginal cost is a measure of monopoly power

comparative statics for a monopolist

Figure 3-5 may also be used to analyse the effect of changes in costs or demand. Suppose there is a change in costs, for example an increase in input prices, which

| **Figure 3-5** | The monopolist's decision |

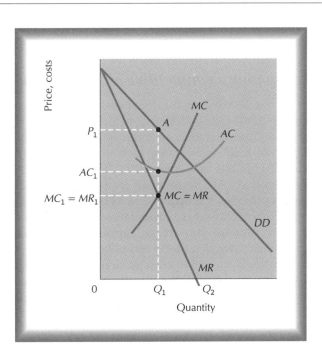

| **Table 3-3** | Monopolists' criteria for maximizing profits |

				Average condition			
	Marginal condition			Short-run		Long-run	
	MR > MC	MR = MC	MR < MC	P ≥ SAVC	P < SAVC	P ≥ LAC	P < LAC
Output decision	Raise	Optimal	Lower	Produce	Shut down	Stay	Exit

shifts the *MC* and *AC* curves upwards. The higher *MC* curve must cross the *MR* curve at a lower level of output. Provided the monopolist can sell this output at a price that covers average costs, the effect of the cost increase must be to reduce output. Since the demand curve slopes down, this reduction in output will be accompanied by an increase in the equilibrium price.

Now suppose for the original cost curves that there is an outward shift in demand and marginal revenue curves. *MR* must now cross *MC* at a higher level of output. Thus an increase in demand leads the monopolist to increase output.

▐▌▌ output and price under monopoly and competition

We now compare a perfectly competitive industry with a monopoly. For this comparison to be of interest the two industries must face the same demand and cost conditions. We are interested in how the *same* industry would behave if it were organized first as a competitive industry then as a monopoly. Clearly this is a tricky comparison. In the next section we develop a theory of market structure that aims to explain why some industries are competitive but others are monopolies. If this theory has any content, can it be legitimate to assume that the same industry could be competitive or monopolized? The answer turns out to be yes in some circumstances but no in other circumstances.

comparing a competitive industry and a multi-plant monopolist

In Section 3-3 we show that the reason some industries are competitive and others are monopolies lies in differences in the cost structure and demand curves. It is not generally the case that an industry could be either competitive or a monopoly. However, there is one case in which the comparison makes sense. Suppose an industry has lots of identical firms. From Section 3-1 we know its long-run supply curve is horizontal since it can always expand or contract output by changing the number of firms. If it operated as a competitive industry, long-run equilibrium would occur where this supply curve intersected the industry demand curve.

Now suppose two things happen. The different firms come under a single co-ordinated decision maker and all future entry is prohibited. Perhaps the industry is nationalized (but told to keep maximizing profits). Long-run costs, both marginal and average, are unaffected, but now the industry supremo recognizes that higher output bids down prices for everyone. So she draws the marginal revenue curve below the demand curve and concludes that production should be cut back until this marginal revenue crosses the horizontal long-run marginal cost curve. Once monopolized, the industry produces less output at a higher price. It makes permanent supernormal profits thereafter.

Notice the crucial role of blocking competition from entrants. Without this, the attempt to restrict output to raise prices would be thwarted by a flood of output from new entrants. This is one way to think about why OPEC did not succeed for ever in raising oil prices in real terms.

▐▌▌ the absence of a supply curve under monopoly

A competitive firm sets price equal to marginal cost if it supplies at all. If we know its marginal cost curve we know how much it supplies at each price. Aggregating across firms, we also know how much the industry supplies at each price. We can draw the supply curve without knowing anything about the market demand curve. Supply depends *only* on price. We then analyse how supply and demand interact to determine equilibrium price and quantity.

The monopolist sets $MC = MR$. But how far MR is below price depends on how elastic the demand curve is. The monopolist does not have a supply curve independent of what the demand curve is like. What we can say is that the monopolist simultaneously examines demand (hence marginal revenue) and cost (hence marginal cost) when deciding how much to produce and what to charge.

discriminating monopoly

Thus far we have assumed that all consumers must be charged the same price, although this price will depend on the level of output and the position of the demand curve. Unlike a competitive industry, where competition prevents any individual firm charging more than its competitors, a monopolist may be able to charge different prices to different customers.

A discriminating monopoly *can charge different prices to different people.*

This is attractive when it can identify different types of customer whose demand curves are quite distinct. Consider an airline monopolizing flights between London and Rome. It has business customers whose demand curve is very inelastic. They have to fly. Their demand and marginal revenue curves are very steep. The airline also carries tourists whose demand curve is much more elastic. If flights to Rome get too

| Box 3-3 | Telecoms pact signals end of monopolies |

Before 1997 many countries' domestic markets for telecommunications were heavily regulated. Previous editions of our book often used the national phone company as a good example of a monopoly. Some countries, such as Britain and the United States, had been deregulating telecoms for some time, but the 1997 deal, embracing 68 countries, went much further. For example, the entire European Union (www.eu.int) committed itself to complete liberalization of basic telecoms, including satellite networks and mobile phones, by 2003. The World Trade Organization (www.wto.org) estimated that the additional trade generated across national borders could be worth 4 per cent of the world's output in the following decade.

The table below shows how much national monopolies have been eroded by international competition. It shows how the cost of an off-peak 3-minute long-distance call came tumbling down during 1995–99 (cost in pence).

This example reminds us of two things. First, many monopolies are the result of government policy to license only one supplier; such policies can change. Second, firm size must always be considered in relation to the relevant market. When technical breakthroughs in telecom technology made the relevant market much larger – satellites are no respecters of national boundaries – the national phone company was suddenly playing in a much larger game. Sooner or later policy-makers have to recognize such realities.

	France	Germany	Italy	Portugal	Spain	UK
1995	25	35	48	56	48	14
1999	18	11	24	25	38	12

expensive tourists can holiday in Athens instead. Tourists have much flatter demand and marginal revenue curves. Recall why the marginal revenue curve lies below the demand curve. Adding an extra unit of output and sales bids down the price for which existing output can be sold. The more inelastic is the demand curve the more the marginal revenue curve must lie below the demand curve because the higher will be the reduction in revenue from existing output units.

The airline must charge the two groups *different* prices. Since tourist demand is elastic the airline wants to charge tourists a low fare to increase tourist revenue. Since business demand is inelastic the airline wants to charge business travellers a high fare to increase business revenue.

Profit-maximizing output will satisfy two separate conditions. First, business travellers with inelastic demand will pay a fare sufficiently higher than tourists with elastic demand that the marginal revenue from the two separate groups is equated. Then there is no incentive to rearrange the mix by altering the price differential between the two groups. Second, the general level of prices and the total number of passengers will be determined to equate marginal cost to both these marginal revenues. This ensures that the airline operates on the most profitable scale as well as with the most profitable mix.

When a producer charges different customers different prices we say that the producer *price discriminates*. There are many examples of this in the real world. Air fares per mile between London and Frankfurt, almost exclusively an expense account business trip, are among the highest in Europe, but package holidays are much cheaper. Rail operators charge rush-hour commuters a higher fare than midday shoppers whose demand for trips to the city is much more elastic.

Many of the best examples of price discrimination refer to services which must be consumed on the spot rather than to goods which can be resold. Price discrimination in standardized goods is unlikely to work. The group buying at the lower price have an incentive to resell to the group paying the higher price thus undercutting the

---

Figure 3-6 Perfect price discrimination

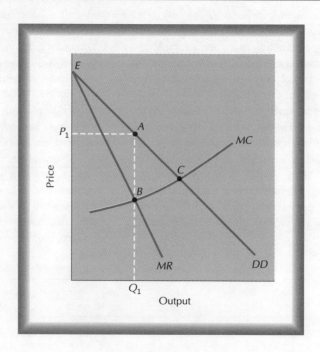

attempt to charge some customers a higher price. Effective price discrimination is feasible only when the submarkets can be isolated from one another to prevent resale.

Figure 3-6 illustrates the case of *perfect price discrimination* where we assume that it is actually possible to charge each and every customer a different price for the same good. Suppose first that the monopolist charges every customer the same price. The profit-maximizing output is Q_1 where MR equals MC and the corresponding price is P_1.

Now suppose the monopolist can perfectly price discriminate, charging a different price for each unit of output sold. The very first can be sold for a price E. Having sold this output to the highest bidder, the customer most desperate for the good, the next unit can be sold to the next highest bidder and so on. As we move down the demand curve DD we can read off the price for which each extra unit can be sold. However, in reducing the price to sell that extra unit, the monopolist no longer reduces revenue from previously sold units. *Hence the demand curve is the marginal revenue curve under perfect price discrimination.* The marginal revenue of the last unit is simply the price for which it can be sold.

Treating DD as the marginal revenue curve we conclude that a perfectly price discriminating monopolist will produce at point C where marginal revenue and marginal cost are equal. Two points follow immediately. First, if price discrimination is possible it is profitable to employ it. In moving from the uniform pricing point A to the price discriminating point C the monopolist adds the area ABC to profits. This represents the excess of additional revenue over additional cost when output is increased. But the monopolist makes a second gain from price discrimination. Even the output Q_1 now brings in more revenue than under uniform pricing. The monopolist also gains the area EP_1A by being able to charge different prices on the first Q_1 units of output rather than the single price P_1. In practice, when firms call in economic consultants one of the main ways these consultants manage to increase the profits of the firm is by devising new ways in which the firm can price discriminate.

Second, whether or not the firm is able to price discriminate affects the output it will choose to produce even if demand and cost conditions remain unaltered. Uniform and discriminatory pricing lead to very different outputs because they affect the marginal revenue obtained from any given total demand curve facing a monopolist.

▬▬ monopoly and technical change

Joseph Schumpeter (1883–1950) argued that it may be wrong to assume the consequence of monopoly is always lower output and higher prices. This ignores the possibility of technical advances, which reduce costs and may allow price reductions and output expansion. A large monopolist with steady profits may find it much easier to fund the research and development (R&D) necessary to make cost-saving breakthroughs. Second, and completely distinct, a monopolist may have a greater *incentive* to undertake R&D.

In a competitive industry a firm with a technical advantage has only a temporary opportunity to earn high profits to recoup its research expenses. Imitation by existing firms and new entrants gradually compete away any supernormal profits. In contrast, by shifting down all its cost curves, a monopoly may be able to enjoy higher supernormal profits for ever. Schumpeter argued that these two forces – greater resources available for R&D and a higher potential return on any successful venture – tend to make monopolies more innovative than competitive industries. Taking a dynamic long-run view, rather than a snapshot static picture, monopolists tend to enjoy lower cost curves which lead them to charge lower prices thereby increasing the quantity demanded.

This argument has some substance. Very small firms typically do little R&D. Many of the largest firms have excellent research departments. Many small firms complain about the problem of trying to raise bank loans for risky research projects. Nevertheless, the Schumpeter argument may overstate the case. Most Western economies operate a *patent* system. Inventors of new processes acquire a temporary legal monopoly for a fixed period. By temporarily excluding entry and imitation the patent laws increase the incentive to conduct R&D without establishing a monopoly in the long run. Over the patent life the inventor can charge a higher price and make handsome profits. Eventually the patent expires and competition from other firms leads to higher output and lower prices. The real price of copiers and microcomputers fell significantly when the original patents of Xerox and IBM expired.

▰▰ recap

- A pure monopoly is the only seller or potential seller in an industry.

- To maximize profits, it chooses output to make *MC = MR* but does not have a supply curve uniquely relating price to output; the relation of price to marginal revenue depends on the demand curve.

- A monopolist aims to cut back output to force up the price. The gap between price and marginal cost is a measure of monopoly power.

- A discriminating monopoly charges higher prices to customers whose demand is more inelastic.

- Monopolies may have more ability and incentive to innovate. In the long run, this is one force for cost reduction.

▰▰ key terms

Monopolist	78
Monopoly power	79
Discriminating monopoly	81

▰▰ review questions

1 The table shows the demand curve facing a monopolist who produces at a constant marginal cost of £5.

Price (£)	9	8	7	6	5	4	3	2	1	0
Quantity	0	1	2	3	4	5	6	7	8	9

Calculate the monopolist's marginal revenue curve. What is the equilibrium output? What is the equilibrium price? What would be the equilibrium price and output for a competitive industry? Explain in words why the monopolist produces a lower output and charges a higher price.

2 Now suppose that, in addition to the constant marginal cost of £5, the monopolist has a fixed cost of £2. What difference does this make to the monopolist's output, price, and profits? Why do we get this answer?

3 Why do golf clubs have different fees for men and women? Is this smart price discrimination or just discrimination?

4 Could a regulation ordering the break up of a monopoly into smaller companies ever lead to *higher* prices?

3-3 imperfect competition

Perfect competition and pure monopoly are useful benchmarks of extreme kinds of market structure. Most markets lie between these two extremes. In nearly half the 800 major product categories in UK manufacturing, 70 per cent of the market is shared by the five largest firms. What determines the structure of a particular market? Why are there 10 000 florists but only a handful of chemical producers? How does the structure of an industry affect the behaviour of its constituent firms? A perfectly competitive firm faces a horizontal demand curve at the going market price. It is a price-taker. Any other type of firm faces a downward sloping demand curve for its product and is called an *imperfectly competitive* firm.

> *An* imperfectly competitive firm *must recognize that its demand curve slopes down.*

For a pure monopoly the demand curve for the firm is the industry demand curve itself. We now distinguish two intermediate cases of an imperfectly competitive market structure.

LEARNING OUTCOMES

When you have finished this section, you should understand

- imperfect competition, oligopoly, and monopolistic competition

- how differences in cost and demand lead to different market structures

- the tangency equilibrium in monopolistic competition

- the tension between collusion and competition within a cartel

- games, and the concepts of commitment and credibility

- why there is little market power in a contestable market

- innocent entry barriers and strategic entry barriers

> *An* oligopoly *is an industry with only a few producers, each recognizing that its own price depends not merely on its own output but also on the actions of its important competitors in the industry. An industry with* monopolistic competition *has many sellers producing products that are close substitutes for one another. Each firm has only a limited ability to affect its output price.*

As with most definitions, the lines between these types of market structure are a little blurred. A major reason is the ambiguity about the relevant definition of the market. Was British Gas a monopoly in gas or an oligopolist in energy? Similarly, when a country trades in a competitive world market, even the sole domestic producer may have little influence on market price. We can never fully remove these ambiguities, but Table 3-4 shows some things to bear in mind as we proceed through this section.

▉▉▉ why market structures differ

We have already drawn attention to the influence of government legislation on market structure. Some industries are legal monopolies, the sole licensed producers. Patent laws may confer temporary monopoly on producers of a new process. Ownership of a raw material may confer monopoly status on a single firm. We now develop a general theory of how the economic factors of demand and cost interact to determine the likely structure of each industry.

The car industry is not an oligopoly one day but perfectly competitive the next. It is long-run influences that induce different market structures. Similarly, although a particular firm may have a temporary advantage in technical know-how or workforce skill, in the long run one firm can hire another's workers and learn its technical secrets. In the long run all firms or potential entrants to an industry essentially have access to the same cost curves.

Chapter 2 discussed minimum efficient scale *MES*, the lowest output at which a firm's long-run average cost curve bottoms out. Table 3-5 relates this to the position of the industry demand curve in order to deduce how different markets will have different structures. When *MES* is tiny relative to the size of the market, there will be room for lots of little firms, each trivial relative to the whole, a good approximation to perfect competition. Conversely, when *MES* occurs at an output nearly as large as the entire market, there is probably room for only one firm. A smaller firm trying to squeeze into the remaining space would be at too great a cost disadvantage because it gets inadequate scale economies.

> *A* natural monopoly *enjoys sufficient scale economies to have no fear of entry by others.*

When *MES* occurs at say a quarter of the market size, the industry will be an oligopoly, with each firm taking a keen interest in the behaviour of its small number of rivals. Monopolistic competition lies midway between oligopoly and perfect competition. But it is the fact that monopolistic competitors all supply slightly different products, such as the location in which you shop, that makes them special.

evidence on market structure

The larger the minimum efficient scale relative to the market size, the fewer will be the number of plants – and probably the number of firms – in the industry. What is the number of plants (*NP*) operating at minimum efficient scale that the current market size could allow? How do we measure how many firms there are in an industry?

Table 3-4   Market structure

	Number of firms	Ability to affect price	Entry barriers	Example
Perfect competition	Many	Nil	None	Fruit stall
Imperfect competition:				
Monopolistic competition	Many	Small	None	Corner shop
Oligopoly	Few	Medium	Some	Cars
Monopoly	One	Large	Huge	Post Office

Table 3-5   Demand, costs, and market structure

Minimum efficient scale relative to market size		
Tiny	Intermediate	Large
Perfect competition	Oligopoly	Natural monopoly

Economists use the *N*-firm concentration ratio to measure the number of important firms in the industry.

> *The* *N*-firm concentration ratio *is the market share of the largest* N *firms in the industry.*

Thus the 3-firm concentration ratio tells us the percentage of the total market supplied by the largest three firms in the industry. If only three firms matter, they will supply almost the whole market. If the industry is perfectly competitive, the largest three firms will account for only a tiny share of the market. Table 3-6 looks at the evidence for the UK, France, and Germany. *CR* is the 3-firm concentration ratio, the market share of the top three firms. *NP* is the number of plants at minimum efficient scale which the market size would allow. If our theory of market structure is correct, industries with large economies of scale relative to the market size – a very low value of *NP* – should exhibit a large *CR*. Such industries should have only a few important firms. Our theory of market structure is compatible with the facts. Industries with room for only very few plants operating at minimum efficient scale, exhibit high degrees of concentration. The largest three firms control almost the whole market.

◼◼◼ monopolistic competition

The theory of monopolistic competition envisages a large number of quite small firms so that each firm can neglect the possibility that its own decisions provoke any adjustment in other firms' behaviour. We also assume free entry and exit from the industry in the long run. In these respects the framework resembles our earlier discussion of *perfect* competition. What distinguishes monopolistic competition is that each firm faces a *downward*-sloping demand curve in its own little niche of the industry.

Its demand curve is not horizontal because different firms' products are only limited substitutes. We have given one example, the location of corner grocers. A lower price attracts some customers from another shop, but each shop will always have some local customers for whom the convenience of a nearby shop is more important than a few pence on the price of a jar of coffee. Monopolistically competitive industries exhibit *product differentiation*. For corner grocers this differentiation is based on location, but in other cases it is based on brand loyalty. The special features of a particular restaurant or hairdresser may allow that firm to charge a slightly different price from other producers in the industry without losing all its customers. Monopolistic competition requires not merely product differentiation, but also limited opportunities for economies of scale so that there are a great many producers who

Table 3-6 Concentration and scale economies in three European countries

Industry	UK		France		Germany	
	CR	NP	CR	NP	CR	NP
Refrigerators	65	1	100	2	72	3
Cigarettes	94	3	100	2	94	3
Petroleum refining	79	8	60	7	47	9
Brewing	47	11	63	5	17	16
Fabrics	28	57	23	57	16	52
Shoes	17	165	13	128	20	197

can largely neglect their interdependence with any particular rival. Many examples of monopolistic competition are service industries where economies of scale are small.

Each firm produces where its marginal cost and marginal revenue are equal. If firms make profits, new firms enter the industry. That is the competitive part of monopolistic competition. As a result of entry, the downward-sloping demand curve of each individual firm shifts to the left. Its market share falls. It reacts to this shift in marginal revenue by cutting output so that marginal cost can fall in line with marginal revenue. Since the firm's demand curve has shifted left but its cost curves are unchanged, it makes lower profits. Entry stops when enough firms have entered to bid profits down to zero for the marginal firm.

In this long-run equilibrium each individual firm's demand curve has shifted enough to the left to just be tangent to its *LAC* curve at the output the firm is producing. That is how we know it makes zero profits. Price equals average cost. Whereas for a perfectly competitive firm, its horizontal demand curve was tangent to *LAC* at the minimum point on the average cost curve, the tangency for a monopolistic competitor lies to the left of this, with both demand and *LAC* sloping down. That is the monopolistic part of monopolistic competition.

Notice two things about the firm's long-run equilibrium. First, the firm is *not* producing at minimum average cost. It has excess capacity. It could reduce average costs by further expansion. However, its marginal revenue would be so low this would not be profitable. Second, the firm retains some monopoly power because of the special feature of its particular brand or location. Price exceeds marginal cost. This helps explain why firms are usually eager for new customers prepared to buy additional output at the *existing* price. It explains why we are a race of eager sellers and coy buyers. It is purchasing agents who get Christmas presents from sales reps, not the other way round.

Box 3-4 | Packaging holidays

In the UK the market for package summer holidays is now worth £7bn a year as people jet off in search of sand and sun. Whereas in 1986 the top 5 chains of travel agents had a combined market share of 25%, by 1998 this had soared to 87%. Evidence of huge economies of scale? Not necessarily.

The industry has been integrating vertically, as travel agents (retail outlets) combine with tour operators (producers of airline and hotel services). Vertical integration can cut costs by allowing better coordination between different stages of the production chain, but it can also enhance market power. The two largest tour operators (Thomson (www.thomson-holidays.com) and Air-

tours (www.airtours.com)) now own the two largest travel agents (Lunn Poly and Going Places). These two firms have a market share of 49%.

The market leaders have been accused of unfair practices. In 1996 Lunn Poly refused to display brochures of First Choice for four months until a new agreement on commissions for travel agents was reached. Small operators claimed to have to pay up to 19% commission to Lunn Poly, while Thomson paid only 10%. Thomson and Airtours argued that their size allowed them to keep prices lower, and that smaller competitors couldn't compete.

Sources: Financial Times, 8 November 1996; *Observer,* 19 September 1999.

▬▬ oligopoly and interdependence

Under perfect competition or monopolistic competition, there are so many firms in the industry that no single firm need worry about the effect of its own actions on rival firms. However, the essence of an oligopolistic industry is the need for each firm to consider how its own actions affect the decisions of its relatively few competitors. What makes oligopoly so fascinating is that the supply decision of each firm depends on its guess about how its rivals will react. First, however, we introduce the basic tension between competition and collusion in all oligopolistic situations.

> Collusion *is an explicit or implicit agreement between existing firms to avoid competition with one another.*

Initially, for simplicity, we neglect the possibility of entry and focus only on the behaviour of existing firms.

the profits from collusion

The existing firms will maximize their *joint* profits if they behave as if they were a multi-plant monopolist. A monopolist or sole decision-maker would organize the output from the industry to maximize total profits. Hence, if the few producers in an industry collude to behave as if they were a monopolist, their *total* profit will be maximized. There is then a backstage deal to divide up these profits between individual firms. By acting jointly, the firms take account of the fact that collectively their marginal revenue is less than the price of their output. Having cut back industry output to the point at which $MC = MR < P$, each firm then faces a marginal profit $(P - MC)$ if only it can expand a little more. Provided its partners continue to restrict output, every individual firm now wants to break the agreement and expand!

Hence oligopolists are torn between the desire to collude, thus maximizing joint profits, and the desire to compete, in the hope of increasing market share and profits at the expense of rivals. Yet if all firms compete, joint profits will be low and no firm is likely to do very well.

cartels

Collusion or co-operation between firms is easiest when formal agreements are legally permitted. Such arrangements are called *cartels*. In the late nineteenth century cartels were common, and they agreed market shares and prices in many industries. Such practices are now outlawed in Europe, the United States, and many other countries. However, secret deals in smoke-filled rooms are not unknown even today. The most famous cartel is OPEC, the Organization of Petroleum Exporting Countries. Active since 1973, its members meet regularly to set price and output levels. Initially, OPEC was very successful in organizing quantity reductions to force up the price of oil. Real OPEC revenues rose 500 per cent between 1973 and 1980. Yet almost from the start, many economists predicted that OPEC, like most cartels, would quickly collapse. Usually, the incentive to cheat is too strong to resist, and once somebody breaks ranks others tend to follow.

In practice, one reason OPEC was successful for so long was the willingness of Saudi Arabia, the largest oil producer, to restrict its output further when smaller members insisted on expansion. By 1986 Saudi Arabia was no longer prepared to play by these rules, and refused to prop up the price any longer. The oil price collapsed from just under $30 to $9 a barrel. Since then, apart from a brief period during the Gulf War, oil prices have fluctuated between $10 and $30 a barrel, but allowing for inflation, real oil prices are much lower than they used to be. OPEC has never recovered the cohesion it had during 1973–85.

the oligopoly kinked demand curve

In the absence of collusion, each firm's demand curve depends on how competitors react. Firms must guess how their rivals will behave.

Suppose that each firm believes that its own price cut will be matched by all other firms in the industry but that an increase in its own price will induce no price response from competitors. Figure 3-7 shows the demand curve DD that each firm would then face. The current price is P_0 and the firm is producing Q_0. Since competitors do not follow suit, a price increase will lead to a large loss of market share to other firms. The firm's demand curve is elastic above A at prices above the current price P_0. Conversely, a price cut is matched by other firms and market shares are unchanged. Sales increase only because the industry as a whole moves down the market demand curve as prices fall. The demand curve DD is much less elastic for price reductions from the initial price P_0.

Marginal revenue MR is discontinuous at Q_0. Below Q_0 the elastic part of the demand curve is relevant, but at the output Q_0 the firm hits the inelastic portion of its kinked demand curve and marginal revenue suddenly falls. Q_0 is the profit-maximizing output for the firm, given its belief about how competitors will respond. The model has one important implication. Suppose the MC curve of a single firm shifts up or down by a small amount. Since the MR curve has a discontinuous vertical segment at the output Q_0, it will remain optimal to produce Q_0 and charge the price P_0. The kinked demand curve model may explain the empirical finding that firms do not always adjust prices when costs change.

It does not explain what determines the initial price P_0. One interpretation is that it is the collusive monopoly price. Each firm believes that an attempt to undercut

---

Figure 3-7 The kinked demand curve

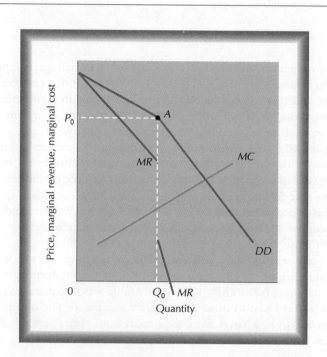

its rivals will provoke them to co-operate among themselves and retaliate in full. However, its rivals will be happy for it to charge a higher price and see it lose market share.

One advantage of interpreting P_0 as the collusive monopoly price is that it contrasts the effect of a cost change for a single firm and a cost change for all firms. The latter will shift the marginal cost curve up for the industry as a whole and increase the collusive monopoly price. Each firm's kinked demand curve will shift upwards since the monopoly price P_0 has increased. Thus we can reconcile the stickiness of a single firm's prices with respect to changes in its own costs alone, and the speed with which the entire industry marks up prices when all firms' costs are increased by higher taxes (as in the cigarette industry) or inflationary wage settlements in the whole industry.

■■■■ game theory and interdependent decisions

A good poker player sometimes bluffs. Sometimes you can clean up with a bad hand, provided your opponents misread it for a good hand. Similarly, by having bluffed in the past and been caught, you may persuade them to keep betting even when you have a terrific hand. Like poker players, oligopolists have to try to second-guess their rivals' moves to determine their own best action. To study how interdependent decisions are made, we use *game theory*.

> A game *is a situation in which intelligent decisions are necessarily interdependent.*

The *players* in the game try to maximize their own *payoffs*. In an oligopoly, the firms are the players and their payoffs are their profits in the long run. Each player must choose a strategy.

> A strategy *is a game plan describing how the player will act or move in every conceivable situation.*

Being a pickpocket is a strategy. Lifting a particular wallet is a move.

As usual, we are interested in equilibrium. In most games, each player's best strategy depends on the strategies chosen by other players. It is silly to be a pickpocket in an area where the police have TV cameras. Equilibrium occurs when each player chooses the best strategy, *given* the strategies being followed by other players. This description of equilibrium, invented by John Nash, is called Nash equilibrium. Sometimes, but not usually, a player's best strategy is independent of those chosen by others. If so, it is called a *dominant strategy*. We begin with an example in which each player has a dominant strategy.

collude or cheat?

Figure 3-8 shows a game[1] which we can imagine is between the only two members of a cartel like OPEC. Each firm can select a high-output or low-output strategy. In each box the coloured number shows firm A's profits and the black number, firm B's profits for that output combination.

---

[1] The game is usually called the Prisoners' Dilemma, because it was first used to analyse the choices facing two people arrested and in different cells, each of whom could plead guilty or not guilty to the only crime that had been committed. Each prisoner would plead innocent if only he or she knew the other would plead guilty.

When both have high output, industry output is high, the price is low, and each firm makes a small profit of 1. When each has low output, the outcome is more like collusive monopoly. Prices are high and each firm does better, making a profit of 2. Each firm does best (a profit of 3) when it alone has high output; for then, the other firm's low output helps hold down industry output and keep up the price. In this situation we assume the low-output firm makes a profit of 0.

Now we can see how the game will unfold. Consider firm A's decision. If firm B has a high-output strategy, firm A does better also to have high output. In the two left-hand boxes, firm A gets a profit of 1 by choosing high but a profit of 0 by choosing low. Now suppose firm B chooses a low-output strategy. From the two right-hand boxes. Firm A still does better by choosing high, since this yields it a profit of 3 whereas low yields it a profit of only 2. Hence firm A has a dominant strategy. Whichever strategy B adopts, A does better to choose a high-output strategy. Firm B also has a dominant strategy to choose high output. Check for yourself that B does better to go high whichever strategy A selects. Since both firms choose high, the equilibrium is the top left-hand box. Each firm gets a profit of 1.

Yet both firms would do better, getting a profit of 2, if they colluded to form a cartel and both produced low – the bottom right-hand box. But neither can afford to take the risk of going low. Suppose firm A goes low. Firm B, comparing the two boxes in the bottom row, will then go high, preferring a profit of 3 to a profit of 2. And firm A will get screwed, earning a profit of 0 in that event. Firm A can figure all this out in advance, which is why its dominant strategy is to go high.

This is a particularly clear illustration of the tension between collusion and competition. In this example, it appears that the output-restricting cartel will never get formed, since each player can already foresee the overwhelming incentive for the other to cheat on such an arrangement. How then can cartels ever be sustained? One possibility is that there exist binding pre-commitments.

A pre-commitment *is an arrangement, entered into voluntarily, which restricts one's future options.*

If both players could simultaneously sign an enforceable contract to produce low output they could achieve the co-operative outcome in the bottom right-hand box, each earning profits of 2. Clearly, they then do better than in the top left-hand box, which describes the non-co-operative equilibrium of the game. Without any pre-

| Figure 3-8 | The Prisoners' Dilemma game |

		Firm B output	
		High	Low
Firm A output	High	1 1	3 0
	Low	0 3	2 2

commitment, neither player can go low because then the other player will go high. Binding pre-commitments, by removing this temptation, enable both players to go low, and both players gain. This idea of pre-commitment is important, and we shall encounter it many times. Just think of all the human activities that are the subject of legal contracts, a simple kind of pre-commitment simultaneously undertaken by two parties or players.

Although this insight is powerful, its application to oligopoly requires some care. Cartels within a country are usually illegal, and we don't seriously believe that OPEC is held together by a signed agreement which could be upheld in international law! Is there some less formal way in which oligopolists can pre-commit themselves not to cheat on the collusive low-output solution to the game? If the game is played only once, this may be difficult. In the real world, the game is repeated many times: firms choose output levels day after day. Suppose two players try to collude on low output. Furthermore, each announces a *punishment strategy*. Should firm A ever cheat on the low-output agreement, firm B promises that it will subsequently react by raising its output. Firm A makes a similar promise.

Suppose the agreement has been in force for some time and both firms have stuck to their low-output deal. Firm A assumes that firm B will go low as usual. Figure 3-8 shows that firm A will make a *temporary* gain today if it cheats and goes high. Instead of staying in the bottom right-hand box with a profit of 2, it can move to the top right-hand box and make 3. However, from tomorrow onwards, firm B will also go high, and firm A can then do no better than continue to go high too, making a profit of 1 for evermore. But if A refuses to cheat today it can continue to stay in the bottom right-hand box and make 2 forever. In cheating, A is swapping a temporary gain for a permanent reduction in profits, and it may well conclude that this is a poor deal. Thus, punishment strategies can sustain an explicit cartel or implicit collusion even when no formal mechanism of pre-commitment exists.

It is all very well to say that you will adopt a punishment strategy in the event that the other player cheats. But you can expect this to have an effect on the other player's behaviour only if your threat is not an empty one.

> A credible threat *is one which, after the fact, you would then find it optimal to carry out.*

In the preceding example, once firm A has cheated and gone high, it is then in firm B's interest to go high anyway. Hence a threat to go high if A ever cheats is a credible threat.

By 1986 many OPEC members had cheated on the low-output agreement, hoping Saudi Arabia would continue its low output. They hoped Saudi threats of retaliation were empty threats. They were wrong. Saudi Arabia punished the cheating of its

---

Box 3-5 | Rubber cartel collapses

In February 1999 Thailand, the world's largest rubber producer, decided to pull out of the International Natural Rubber Organization, claiming that INRO had failed to prop up rubber prices adequately. Thailand complained that large members of INRO had borne too much of the burden of trying to hold down production to boost prices.

smaller partners by raising output. Oil prices collapsed, and OPEC members agreed to behave a bit better in future, allowing a partial recovery in oil prices again.

▓▓▓ entry and potential competition

So far we have discussed imperfect competition between existing firms. We must also think about the effect of potential competition from new entrants to the industry on the behaviour of existing or incumbent firms. Three cases must be distinguished: where entry is trivially easy, where it is difficult by accident, and where it is difficult by design.

contestable markets

Suppose we observe an industry with few incumbent firms. Before assuming it is an oligopoly, we must think hard about entry and exit.

A contestable market *is characterized by free entry and free exit.*

By free exit, we mean that there are no *sunk* or irrecoverable costs; on leaving the industry, a firm can fully recoup its previous investment expenditure, including money spent on building up knowledge and goodwill. A contestable market allows *hit-and-run* entry. If the incumbent firms, however few, are not behaving as if they were a perfectly competitive industry at long-run equilibrium ($p = MC$ = minimum AC), an entrant can step in, undercut them, and make a temporary profit before quitting again.

The theory of contestable markets is controversial. There are many industries in which sunk costs are hard to recover or where the initial expertise may take an entrant some time to acquire, placing it at a temporary disadvantage against incumbent firms. Nor, as we shall shortly see, is it safe to assume that incumbents will not change their behaviour when threatened by entry. But the theory does vividly illustrate that market structure and incumbent behaviour cannot be deduced simply by counting the number of firms in the industry. We were careful to stress that a monopolist is a sole producer *who can completely discount fear of entry*.

innocent entry barriers

Our discussion of entry barriers distinguishes those that occur anyway and those deliberately erected by incumbent firms.

An innocent entry barrier *is one made by nature.*

Absolute cost advantages, where incumbent firms have lower cost curves than those that entrants will face, may be innocent. If it takes time to learn the business, incumbents will face lower costs, at least in the short run; they may already have located in the most advantageous site. In contrast, if incumbents have undertaken investment or R&D specifically with a view to deterring entrants, this is not an innocent barrier. We take up this issue shortly.

Scale economies are another innocent entry barrier. If minimum efficient scale is large relative to the industry demand curve, an entrant cannot get into the industry without considerably depressing the market price, and it may prove simply impossible to break in at a profit. The greater are such innocent entry barriers, the more appropriate it will be to neglect potential competition from entrants. The oligopoly game then reduces to competition between incumbent firms along the lines we discussed in the previous section. Where innocent entry barriers are low, one of two things may happen. Either incumbent firms accept this situation, in which case competition from potential entrants will prevent incumbent firms from exercising much market power – the outcome will be closer to that of perfect competition – or else incumbent firms will try to design some entry barrier of their own.

▰▰▰ strategic entry deterrence

We defined a strategy as a game plan when decision-making is interdependent. The word 'strategic' is used in everyday language, but it has a precise meaning in economics.

> *A* strategic move *is one that influences the other person's choice, in a manner favourable to one's self, by affecting the other person's expectations of how one's self will behave.*

We have already introduced pre-commitment as a strategy move, and we now extend that idea to entry deterrence.

Suppose you are the only incumbent firm. You tell potential entrants that you will flood the market if they come in, causing a price war and big losses for everyone. Since you have a fat bank balance and they are just getting started, they will go bankrupt. So there is no point trying to enter. This is a great outcome for the incumbent firm, since it then gets monopoly profits. But is its threat credible? If it has no spare capacity, how will it quickly produce extra output to bid down the price a lot.

Seeing this, the potential entrant may call its bluff. Suppose instead the incumbent builds an expensive additional factory which will never be used if there is no entry. Its only point is to be available if another firm enters, at which point, as a largely sunk cost, it will be cheap to actually use it. The potential concludes entry is pointless. Provided the initial cost of the factory (spread suitable over a number of years) is less than the extra profits the incumbent keeps making *as a result of having deterred entry*, this entry deterrence is profitable. It is strategic because it works by influencing the decision of *another* player.

> Strategic entry deterrence *is behaviour by incumbent firms to make entry less likely.*

Box 3-6 | Freezing out new entrants?

Unilever (www.unilever.com) is a major player in many consumer products from toothpaste to soap powder. One of its big winners is Wall's ice cream, which has two thirds of the UK market and generates profits of £100 mn/year; retailers' markups can also be as high as 55%. In addition to established rivals such as Nestlé (www.nestle.com) and Haagen Dazs (www.haagen.dazs.com), Unilever has faced new challenges from frozen chocolate bars. Mars has 18% of the market.

A critical aspect of these 'bar wars' is the freezer cabinets in which small shops store ice cream. As the leading incumbent, Unilever, 'loans' these cabinets free of charge to small retailers. Unilever contended that its high market share reflects its marketing expertise (just one Cornetto); Mars argued that Unilever erected strategic barriers to entry, particularly effective in small shops that have space for only one freezer cabinet, by requiring that only Unilever products were stocked in the cabinet they loaned to retailers.

In January 2000 the UK government finally ordered Unilever to stop freezing out competitors.

Source: Economist, 13 January 1996.

Is spare capacity the only kind of pre-commitment available to incumbents? Pre-commitments must be irreversible, otherwise they are an empty threat; and they must increase the chances that the incumbent will fight. Generally, anything with the character of fixed and sunk costs will be of interest: fixed costs artificially increase scale economies and make the incumbent more keen on high output, and sunk costs cannot be reversed. Advertising to invest in goodwill and brand loyalty is a good example. So is product proliferation. If the incumbent has only one brand, an entrant may hope to break in with a different brand. But if the incumbent has a complete range of brands or models, an incumbent will have to compete across the whole product range. Sometimes deterring entry costs incumbents too much money. Entry will then take place. Monopolistic competition is one example.

■■■ summing up

Few industries in the real world closely resemble the textbook extremes of perfect competition and pure monopoly. Most are imperfectly competitive. Game theory in general, and notions such as pre-commitment, credibility, and deterrence in particular, have allowed economists to analyse many of the practical concerns of big business.

What have we learned? First, market structure and the behaviour of incumbent firms are determined *simultaneously*. Economists used to start with a market structure, determined by the extent of scale economies relative to the industry demand curve, then deduce how the incumbent firms would behave (monopoly, oligopoly, perfect competition), then check out these predictions against performance indicators, such as the extent to which prices exceeded marginal cost. Now we realize that strategic behaviour by incumbent firms can affect entry, and hence market structure, except where entry is almost trivially easy.

Second, and related, we have learned the importance of *potential* competition, which may come from domestic firms considering entry, or from imports from abroad. The number of firms observed in the industry today conveys little information about the extent of the market power they truly exercise.

Finally, we have seen how many business practices of the real world – price wars, advertising, brand proliferation, excess capacity or excessive research and development – can be understood as strategic competition in which, to be effective, threats must be made credible by pre-commitments.

■■■ recap

- Imperfect competition exists when individual firms believe they face downward-sloping demand curves.

- When minimum efficient scale is very large relative to the industry demand curve, this innocent entry barrier may produce a natural monopoly in which entry can be ignored.

- At the opposite extreme, entry and exit may be costless. The market is contestable, and incumbent firms must mimic perfectly competitive behaviour, otherwise they would be undercut by a flood of entrants.

- Monopolistic competitors face free entry and exit to the industry, but are individually small and make similar though not identical products. Each has limited monopoly power in its special brand. In long-run equilibrium, price equals average cost. Each firm's downward-sloping demand curve is tangent to the downward-sloping part of its *LAC* curve.

- Oligopolists face a tension between collusion to maximize joint profits and competition for a larger share of smaller joint profits. Without credible threats of punishment by other collusive partners, each firm faces a temptation to cheat.

- Game theory describes interdependent decision-making. In the Prisoners' Dilemma game, each firm has a dominant strategy but the outcome is disadvantageous to both players. With binding pre-commitments, both could be better off by guaranteeing not to cheat on the collusive solution.

- Innocent entry barriers are made in heaven, and arise from scale economies or absolute cost advantages of incumbent firms. Strategic entry barriers are made in boardrooms and arise from credible pre-commitments to resist entry if challenged. Only in certain circumstances is strategic entry deterrence profitable for incumbents.

▬▬▬ key terms

▬▬ review questions

1 An industry faces the demand curve:

Price	1	2	3	4	5	6	7	8	9	10
Quantity	10	9	8	7	6	5	4	3	2	1

(a) Suppose it is a monopolist whose constant *MC* equals 3: what price and output are chosen? (b) Now suppose there are two firms, each with *MC* = *AC* = 3: what price and output will maximize joint profits if they collude? (c) Why do the two firms have to agree on the output each will produce? (d) Why might each firm be tempted to cheat if it can avoid retaliation by the other?

2 Vehicle repairers have sometimes suggested that mechanics should be licensed so that repairs are done only by qualified people. Some economists argue that customers can always ask whether a mechanic was trained at a reputable institution without needing to see any licence. (a) Evaluate the arguments for and against licensing car mechanics. (b) Are the arguments the same for licensing doctors?

3 Think of five adverts on television. Do you think their function is primarily informative, or the erection of entry barriers to the industry?

3-4 e-markets

LEARNING OUTCOMES

When you have finished this section, you should understand

- the special cost characteristics of an e-product: high fixed costs of production but almost zero marginal cost of distribution

- explicit price discrimination and versioning; and the use of bundling to reduce the need for price discrimination

- how specialization in complementary activities gives rise to a role for strategic alliances

- the role of the standard in a network, and the nature of competition between networks to set national or international standards

Electronic commerce is booming. Revenues from e-commerce are forecast to rise between 1999 and 2002 from £70 billion to £550 billion in the United States, and from £13 billion to £150 billion in Western Europe. Just as the service economy displaced the industrial economy in the 20th century, the information economy will dominate the 21st century. A century ago, fortunes were made in railways, mining, and the oil business. Then people like Richard Branson became rich in the service sector. But the richest person on the planet is currently Bill Gates of Microsoft (www.microsoft.com). When he is overtaken, it is likely to be by someone in the e-business. The information revolution is here. It is big business, and changing people's lives in remarkable ways. Yet the laws of economics continue to provide a reliable framework in which to understand what is going on. This section is about microeconomics in action.

First, we discuss the key attributes of information products. Then we examine how producers of these products behave, and hence how the market will develop. How does competition occur? What forms of pricing and other strategic behaviour emerge?

e-products

Table 3-7 documents the rise of the internet. On world stock markets, General Motors (www.gm.com) has already been overtaken by Microsoft. In a handful of years, Yahoo! (www.yahoo.com) and Amazon (www.amazon.com) have almost caught up. Electronic information products are booming.

 *An e-product **can be digitally encoded then transmitted rapidly, accurately and cheaply.***

Table 3-7   Business use of the internet

	1997	1999	2001	2003
Business to business (£bn)	<5	40	320	1130
Business to consumer (£bn)	<5	10	60	150
Millions of devices	100	210	400	720
Milliions of users	100	190	320	490

Source: Financial Times, 24 March 1999.

Examples include music, films, magazines, news, books, and coverage of sport. Information is expensive to assemble and produce but very cheap to distribute. The fixed cost of creating a usable product is large, the marginal cost of distributing it is tiny. This cost structure implies vast scale economies in production. While expansion of output by industrial monopolists is eventually limited by their existing capacity, the reproduction of information products faces no such capacity constraint. The industrial economy was made up largely of oligopolists – Ford, Vauxhall, Fiat, etc. – but we should expect the information economy to be made up largely of monopolies. Moreover, as demonstrated by the birth and precocious childhood of companies like Amazon, Yahoo!, and Freeserve, even existing monopolists are always under threat from unexpected newcomers.

From our previous discussion, you would expect – correctly – that these monopolies would take one of two forms. The first is a dominant firm with a fringe of smaller competitors. Microsoft, inventor of DOS and then Windows, fits the bill well. Microsoft's income stream is now so large that, like, Boeing in the airliner business, it can devote vast sums to R&D. Both take advantage of huge scale economies to become the lowest-cost producer of the industry's standard product.

Other forms of monopoly have to operate in smaller, niche markets, carefully targeted on particular groups of consumers whose diversity of preferences allows these niches to co-exist. Internet firms distribute many products, from airline tickets to dealings in stocks and shares. Monopolistic competition describes these market structures well. However, since the incumbent's advantage is dependent on the segmentation of the market into small niches, its temporary monopoly is vulnerable to competitors who manage to jump across niches. For example, Amazon has recently realized that there is no reason it should confine its activities to taking internet orders for books alone.

pricing information products

Armed only with this chapter, you set up as a consultant (on the internet, of course) to advise firms on how to price information products. Since marginal cost is very low, you expect to drive marginal revenue down almost to zero. But you also want to make profits. Like the phone company, perhaps you should use a two-part tariff.

A two-part tariff *levies an annual charge to cover fixed costs, and a small price per unit related to marginal costs.*

Box 3-7	Been here, got the e-shirt

The production and distribution of information dates back to the first conversation between our most primitive ancestors. Distribution costs have been falling ever since. The printing press slashed costs – think of those monks previously transcribing by hand – and so did the postal service and the telephone. Mail order catalogues are a century old. Browsing did not begin on the internet, it has merely been taken to another dimension. The information economy is different not merely because the distribution costs are dramatically lower but because the distribution of information is now interactive. Customers can manipulate the information they receive and follow-up questions can be processed instantly and cheaply.

Does anyone implement this on the internet? The two most visited UK websites, AOL and CompuServe (early entrants, both American companies, available to subscribers only) charge an annual membership fee and then provide free services. It will be interesting to see whether competition from newer entrants such as Freeserve (www.freeserve.net) leads AOL and CompuServe to abolish annual charges or whether new entrants are simply offering loss leaders to try to overcome switching costs. Economic theory suggests that in the long run some form of annual fee may be part of the solution. Internet suppliers need to earn revenue just like every other business. Unless they can make this revenue from advertising or from selling customer information to other suppliers, membership fees may become part of how pricing develops.

Another lesson you will remember from Section 3-2 is that a monopolist earns more by price discriminating than by charging a uniform price. In revenue terms, the latter allows it to earn the best available rectangle (price × quantity) under the demand curve, whereas perfect price discrimination – a different price for each customer – would allow the monopolist the entire (much larger) area under the demand curve. Where suppliers simply quote a price without knowing the characteristics of the buyer that will show up, it is very difficult to price discriminate. Sometimes, differences in buyers are very obvious, as with package holidaymakers and business travellers. We return to the airline example shortly. However, in many instances, suppliers of goods and services have simply not been able to engage in much price discrimination.

The information revolution has changed all that, since suppliers will frequently have very detailed data on individual purchasers. This allows them to price discriminate, quoting different prices to different customers based on the actual or likely characteristics of the customer. It is precisely because this yields so much more revenue that suppliers are willing to buy lists of customer information from other suppliers. So far, this chapter is standing you in pretty good stead. Let's look at price discrimination in more detail.

What we have described to date is customer-specific price discrimination. Nice work if you can get it. However, distributors of information products have two other tricks even when they cannot buy or establish information about particular customers.

Box 3-8	EMI quit making CDs

In response to internet-induced changes to the music industry, in November 1999, EMI (www.emigroup.com), the world's third largest music company, announced its intention to stop making and distributing compact discs. Having decided CDs had been made obsolete by the ability to download tracks direct from the internet, EMI decided to concentrate on developing and producing music, rather than the business of distributing it. The following table shows how the economics of music distribution are expected to change, with the artist and record label grabbing revenue formerly going to distributors.

Costs and profits on a $15 CD

$ spent on	Traditional retail CD	Internet CD
Promotion	2.50	2.50
Manufacturing	1.00	1.00
Web promotion		1.00
Shipping		1.00
Distribution	3.50	
Retail store	2.00	
Royalty and label profit	6.00	9.50

Source: Financial Times, 3 March 1999.

versioning

Why do publishers supply both hardback and paperback versions of a book, and at very different prices? It is a form of price discrimination that increases total sales revenue. Note that the 'benefit' of the hardback, that justifies the higher price, is not simply its superior physical quality. It is also the fact that it comes out several months earlier. In the information business, old news is no news.

Versioning *is the deliberate creation of different qualities in order to facilitate price discrimination.*

We'll take a bet that you are reading a paperback version of this textbook. It is a pretty safe bet, since there is no hardback version! Delaying publication makes little sense when a student's course starts at a particular time; nor do students need the book to last for 20 years (even though the principles will continue to be relevant!). So little *additional* benefit can be created for a hardback version; given the additional production costs it is not worth doing it.

On the internet, the cost calculation is a little different. Once the product exists, packaging it in various forms incurs little extra cost. Marginal cost of all versions is close to zero. Even small revenue gains from differentiating the product to achieve price discrimination are worthwhile. Sometimes this involves making one version of the product deliberately worse than it could be in order to enhance the value of the premium version. Think again about airlines, who on scheduled flights have economy class and business class. Do businessmen really need a continuous diet of smoked salmon? Is it really optimal to squeeze economy passengers in quite so tight? Even within Europe, business fares can cost double an economy fare; on transatlantic flights the difference can be between £3000 for a business fare and £500 for standard economy fare. Anything that makes people choose business class rather than economy is very profitable. It may actually be revenue enhancing to deliberately make economy worse than it need have been.[2] Once again, suppliers of information products who have made a fine art out of versioning are merely taking previous ideas to their logical conclusion.

bundling

Versioning creates different qualities of the same product in order to allow price discrimination. It occurs when suppliers do not know the characteristics of any individual, but can make guesses about differences across groups of potential purchaser. A different tactic of suppliers is bundling.

Bundling *is the joint supply of more than one product in order to reduce the need for price discrimination.*

Price discrimination is only necessary when different customers behave differently. Suppose one really wants a news channel and another really wants a sports channel. Table 3-8 shows the valuations Edward and Camilla put on each channel. Their tastes for a particular channel differ a lot. Perhaps their tastes for a bundle of channels are more similar.

---

[2] This trick is over 100 years old. Dupuit, the famous 19th-century French economist who was an early advocate of marginal cost pricing in state-run activities, noted that railway companies deliberately provided no roof for third-class carriages in order to boost the demand for second class, where much more revenue could be earned (quoted in Hal Varian, 'Versioning Information Goods', mimeo, University of California at Berkeley, 1997).

If Sky TV (www.sky.co.uk) knows the exact characteristics of each viewer, it gets £32 000 in revenue by perfect price discrimination. How? By charging Edward £6000 to receive the news channel, and £10 000 for the sports channel; and by charging Camilla £10 000 for the news channel and £6000 for the sports channel. If the prices were any higher, Edward and Camilla would simply refuse to sign up to take the channel.

Now assume Sky executives don't have enough detailed information about users to charge different prices to different people. They have to set a single price per channel. For the news channel, if they charge £10 000 only Camilla will sign up. If they charge £6000 they can get both to sign up. Sky does best by charging £6000 for each channel, making £24 000 total revenue (2 × 2 × £6000). But this is a lot worse than the £32 000 that price discrimination would yield. The problem is that to sell a channel to the second subscriber, Sky has to cut the price a lot for the person who would have happily paid more.

Bundling reduces this diversity of people's tastes. Suppose Sky now offers only the two channels as a package. Edward would pay up to £16 000 to get both, so would Camilla. Sky gets £32 000. Bundling is just as good as perfect price discrimination in this example because Edward and Camilla place the same total value on the total package. By bundling news, sports, and movie channels, Sky TV can get more revenue than by selling channels separately at a uniform price to each user.

Although bundling beats uniform pricing across users, it is usually less effective than perfect price discrimination. Suppose in Table 3-8 that the sports channel is worth £4000 rather than £6000 to Camilla. The most she will pay for a total package is £14 000. Selling a package for £14 000 to each of Edward and Camilla earns Sky £28 000. Note that since Edward still values the total at £16 000, price discrimination across users would earn Sky (£16 000 + £14 000), an extra £2000 in revenue for Sky.

However, Sky's informational requirement about individual customers would then be huge. Bundling is therefore often the best suppliers can do in the circumstances. You get bundled all the time. That's why the Sunday papers have all these sections, and why tour operators offer holidays with a week in Florence plus a week on an Adriatic beach. Perhaps Camilla likes frescoes more than Edward, whose own preference tends more towards swimming.

competition versus collaboration

Bundling suggests that most products have more than one attribute or component. From this it is only a short step to the idea that these different components may be produced by *different* firms. More generally, the production and sales of products that are complements rather than substitutes is becoming increasingly prevalent. Software and hardware is an obvious example. Most Microsoft products are operated in computers driven by Intel chips. Nowadays, Apple (www.apple.com) is unusual in

Table 3-8 Bundling TV channels (user value in £000s)

	News	Sports
Edward	6	10
Camilla	10	6

producing both hardware and software. Apple's early success was gradually over-hauled by the strategic alliance of Microsoft and Intel.[3]

A strategic alliance *is a blend of co-operation and competition in which a group of suppliers provide a range of products that partly complement one another.*

Strategic alliances are occurring in other industries, such as airlines, where BA (www.british-airways.com) is currently in the One World partnership with Canadian Airlines, Quantas, Finnair, Iberia, and American Airlines. These alliances allow the different partners to specialize in segments that largely complement one another – travel within the Americas, travel across the Atlantic and within Europe, and travel within Asia and Australasia.

Alliances seek many of the benefits that occur when vertical integration of different production stages occurs within any firm – cost reduction from closer co-ordination and greater specialization. However, an alliance is not a complete merger. It preserves a degree of competition, even between the partners. This may keep all partners on their toes and help assure customers that future profit margins will not become excessive. Whenever switching costs plays a prominent role, current users will pay considerable attention to such signals about possible future behaviour of suppliers.

| Box 3-9 | The hub with the hubbub |

Gatwick Airport's (www.gatwickairport.co.uk) proud boast is 'the hub without the hubbub'. Like airline traffic, internet traffiic needs high-quality infrastructure to convey business across the Atlantic and distribute it within Europe. Gatwick's advantage as a European airline hub is based partly on location. UK hopes of becoming Europe's internet hub are based on the UK's lead in telecom-munications. Other indicators (in 1998) of the UK's lead in telecoms within Europe – a legacy of early liberalization of the telecoms industry in the UK – are shown below.

	UK	Sweden	Netherlands	France	Germany
Transatlantic 'backbone' capacity (megabits/second)	1514	776	600	245	205

Source: Financial Times, 23 June 1999

	US	Japan	UK	France	Germany
% of firms using e-mail	65	72	63	41	48
% of firms with Web site	41	45	37	14	30
% of population on-line	21	6	10	1	5

Source: http:/www.dti.gov.uk/cii

---

[3] These, and many other, fascinating examples are quoted in Carl Shapiro and Hal Varian, *Information Rules*, Harvard University Press, 1999.

◼◼◼ setting standards

One process in which strategic alliances may be especially useful is in the competition to set standards, norms around which economic behaviour is organized.

A standard *is the technical specification that is common throughout a particular network.*

The UK decision to drive on the left is one such standard, the width of railway tracks another, the type of electric plug socket a third. Each is a very strong example of a network externality. There is little point having an AC power supply if the rest of the country has DC power supply. But how are standards originally determined? Usually, as the outcome of competition, which may be economic, political, or both. Strategic alliances help tip the balance in favour of the standard those partners want by demonstrating that a major number of key players are already on this particular network. Underpopulated networks are not worth joining, and sometimes differences in standards are the easiest way to distinguish one network from another.

Typically, as a result of this initial competition to set the standard, one standard is increasingly adopted by everyone. For some of the early networks, this is a valuable triumph as their own standard becomes adopted more widely. Other networks wither as theirs is rejected. Sony (www.sony.com) ploughed a lot of R&D into the Betamax technology for video cassette recorders, but the world adopted its rival, the VHS system that you now have at home.

Alliances, explicit or implicit, help resolve the standards war in favour of the well organized. Why did UK mobile phone company Vodafone (www.vodafone.com) launch a takeover bid for its US counterpart Air Touch, rather than the other way round? The answer lies in standard setting. Early in the 1990s the Europeans managed to resolve the standard that would apply to mobile telephony, creating sufficient of a single market to allow European firms to grow rapidly and enjoy scale economies. American firms were not late into the game. Rather they had three competing standards and never managed to agree which to adopt. While US firms competed with one another inside fragmented regional markets, the Europeans forged ahead to such an extent that their standard was quickly adopted in other continents.

Once standards have been set, competition switches from rivalry over standards to rivalry within the standard. As we explained earlier, this often leads either to a dominant firm (e.g. Microsoft, Intel) using its scale to achieve cost advantages over rivals in current production and greater R&D to sustain this position in the future; or else to a series of temporary monopolies in niche markets, well described by the monopolistic competition model.

◼◼◼ understanding the e-economy

In this section, we have described what is special about the information economy, and how these characteristics affect the behaviour of both users of information and providers of information. Two lessons stand out. First, while the information revolution is truly changing our lives, few of its activities or market tactics are unprecedented. The cost of distributing information has been falling since the printing press was invented. The history of industries such as newspapers, book publishing, and tele-phones already contains examples of most of the phenomena we described in the chapter. Standards, bundling, versioning, alliances, price discrimination – we've seen them all before. What is new about the information economy is the extent to which they are now routinely practised. Second, the revolution in technology has not required any corresponding revolution in economic theory. The existing laws of economics work just fine. Indeed, they are much the best way to make sense of what is happening.

■■ recap

- Information is expensive to produce but very cheap to copy and distribute.

- Information products, with high fixed costs but low marginal cost, are potential monopolies. Where size matters, we get natural monopolies. Where niche markets are smaller, monopolistic competition may prevail. Many existing markets are contestable by new entrants, so many monopolies are temporary.

- Monopolists want to price discriminate when users differ. Information technology may allow personalized pricing. Otherwise, sellers produce different versions of the product, to make discrimination easier, or bundle different products to reduce the need for discrimination.

- Standards are a key feature of a network. Initially, there is competition between networks to set the standard. Once one standard is dominant, there is competition within the network to supply according to that standard.

■■ review questions

1 Why do most undergraduate courses require students to take particular courses in their first year but give them a wide range of options in their final year? Of which supplier tactic in the section is this an example?

2 Give three of your own examples of versioning.

3 'If price discrimination is good for producers, it must be bad for consumers.' Do you agree? Does it matter which consumer you are?

4 What is the difference between a strategic alliance and a cartel?

5 You are Chief Justice of the newly appointed Global Supreme Court, and you have just argued in favour of allowing Microsoft's dominant position to continue. What arguments did you use?

■■ key terms

input markets and income distribution

4-1 the labour market

In winning a golf tournament, a top professional earns more in a weekend than a professor earns in a year. Students studying economics can expect higher career earnings than those of equally smart students studying philosophy. An unskilled worker in the EU earns more than an unskilled worker in India. Few market economies manage to provide jobs for all their citizens wanting to work. How can we explain these aspects of the real world?

In each case the answer depends on the supply and demand for that particular type of labour. We begin our analysis of the markets for inputs or factors of production – labour, capital, and land. We discuss what determines the equilibrium prices and quantities of factors of production in different industries and in the economy as a whole. We begin with the factor called 'labour'. You should be able to guess the structure of this section: demand, supply, equilibrium, problems of disequilibrium and adjustment. It is only because firms want to produce output that they demand factors of production.

  The demand for factors of production is a derived demand *from the demand for the output that the factors are used to produce.*

Each firm simultaneously decides how much output to supply and how many factors to demand. On the supply side we distinguish between the supply of factors to the whole economy and to an individual firm or industry. It takes a long time to train helicopter pilots. Thus the supply of helicopter pilots is almost fixed in the short run. But this total supply of pilots can choose in which industry to work.

Must all industries pay the same wage rate for pilots if they wish to stop pilots moving to higher paying industries? Not quite. Different jobs have different non-monetary characteristics. Helicopter flights to offshore oil rigs are dangerous because of bad weather, and may involve working irregular shifts that make it hard to plan leisure activities during time off. To attract pilots to this industry, it is necessary to pay a higher than average wage rate to offset these disadvantages of the job.

> *An* equalizing wage differential *is the monetary compensation for differential non-monetary characteristics of the same job in different industries so that workers have no incentive to move between industries.*

In the short run, with an almost fixed supply of pilots to the economy as a whole, any increase in the total demand for pilots raises the equilibrium wage of pilots in all industries. But in the longer run the supply of pilots is not fixed. High wages act as a signal for young workers to abandon plans to train as engine drivers and move into the lucrative helicopter business.

Putting demand and supply together we can determine equilibrium prices and quantities in different factor markets. But are these markets always in equilibrium? Are wages sufficiently flexible to restore labour market equilibrium, or might wage responses be sluggish and the labour market out of equilibrium for some time? We show how this relates to unemployment.

the firm's demand for factors in the long run

We begin by discussing the long run in which all factors of production can be fully adjusted. A firm's cost curves show the minimum cost way to produce each possible output level. This depends on the production function, summarizing the alternative production techniques available, and the prices at which different factors of production can be employed. A rise in the price of a unit of labour relative to the price of a unit of capital will lead the firm to switch to a more capital-intensive technique. The firm substitutes away from the input that has become relatively more expensive.

This principle helps explain differences across countries in the capital–labour ratios in the same industry. In the European Union, farmers face high wages relative to the cost of renting a combine harvester. Mechanized farming economizes on expensive workers. In contrast, India has cheap and abundant labour, but capital is relatively scarce and expensive. Indian farmers use much more labour-intensive techniques. Workers with scythes and shovels perform tasks undertaken by combine harvesters and bulldozers in the EU.

The demand for factors of production depends on the level of output and the relative price of the factors themselves. To determine profit-maximizing output, and the corresponding quantities of factors demanded, we calculate the entire total cost curve for all output levels, and then choose profit-maximizing output by equating marginal cost and marginal revenue. An increase in the wage rate will cause the firm to substitute away from labour and towards capital in producing a given output level. But it will also raise the total cost of producing each and every output level.

When we studied consumer decisions in Chapter 2 we saw that a change in the price of a good has both a substitution effect and an income effect. The substitution effect reflects the change in relative prices of different goods and the income effect reflects changes in real income as a result of the price change. The demand for factors works exactly the same way. A higher relative price of labour leads firms to substitute towards the factor that has become relatively cheaper. But there is also an income or output effect. By shifting the marginal cost of producing output, a change in a factor price leads to a different profit-maximizing output.

In the long run an increase in the wage rate will reduce the quantity of labour demanded. The substitution effect leads to more capital-intensive techniques at each output level and the higher marginal cost of output will reduce the amount of output it is most profitable to supply. Similarly, an increase in the price of capital will reduce the quantity of capital demanded. The substitution effect and the output effect go in the same direction. Hence, the more elastic is the demand curve for the firm's output, the more a given increase in the price of a factor of production, and a given shift in the long-run marginal cost curve for output, will lead to a large reduction in the quantity of output produced. And the larger the output effect, the greater will be the reduction in the quantity of all factors demanded.

▄▄▄ the firm's demand for labour in the short run

In the long run the firm can vary its factor intensity by switching from one production technique to another. But in the short run the firm has some fixed factors of production. We now consider the firm's short-run demand for labour when capital is fixed. The marginal product of labour shows how much each extra worker adds to total output, holding other inputs constant. The marginal product increases as the first workers are added because it is hard for the first and second worker to handle all the machinery. Beyond some point, the *diminishing marginal productivity* of labour sets in. With existing machines fully utilized, there is less and less for each new worker to do. As in our discussion of output, we concentrate on the *marginal principle*. Does the cost of a new worker exceed the benefit from having an extra worker?

The marginal value product of labour *is the extra revenue obtained by selling the output an extra worker produces.*

If the firm is perfectly competitive, the marginal value product of another worker is simply the marginal product in physical goods multiplied by the price for which these extra goods can be sold. From this extra revenue from an additional worker, the firm must subtract the extra wage cost. The firm keeps expanding employment so long as the marginal value product of another worker exceeds the wage cost. Once diminishing returns set in, further employment expansion starts to reduce the marginal product of labour in physical goods and hence its marginal value product. The optimal level of employment is where the marginal value product just equals the wage.

monopoly and monopsony power

This theory is easily amended when the firm has *monopoly power* in its output market (a downward-sloping demand curve for its product) or *monopsony power* in its input markets (an upward-sloping supply curve for its inputs so that the firm must offer a higher factor price the more of a factor it wishes to employ).

A firm with monopsony power *is not a price-taker in its input markets. It faces an upward-sloping factor supply curve, and must offer a higher factor price to attract more factors. Hence the* marginal cost of an additional unit of the factor exceeds the factor price. *In expanding its factor use, the firm bids up the price paid to all units of the factor already employed.*

For a perfectly competitive firm, the *marginal value product of labour* (*MVPL*) schedule depicts its marginal revenue from taking on an extra worker. We usually reserve this term for competitive firms who are price-takers in their output markets. *MVPL* is simply the marginal product of labour in physical goods *MPL* multiplied by the output price. We reserve the term *marginal revenue product of labour* (*MRPL*) for firms facing a downward-sloping demand curve for their output.

> *To calculate the* marginal revenue product of labour *we first find the marginal physical product of labour MPL and then calculate the change in the firm's total revenue when it sells these extra goods.*

Figure 4-1 shows the *MVPL* and *MRPL* schedules for two firms with the same technology. Both schedules slope down because of diminishing marginal productivity – a technical property of production – but the *MRPL* schedules slope down more steeply because the firm faces a downward-sloping demand curve for its output and recognizes that additional output reduces the price and hence the revenue earned on previous units of output.

Similarly, although W_0 is the marginal cost of a unit of labour for a competitive firm that is a price-taker in its input market, a monopsonist must recognize that an expansion of employment will bid up the wage rate. Since all workers must be paid the same wage, the marginal cost of an extra worker is then the *MCL* schedule in Figure 4-1.

Any firm will maximize profits when the marginal revenue from an extra worker equals its marginal cost. Otherwise, the firm has the wrong employment level. Thus, a firm that is a price-taker in both its output and input markets employs L_1 workers in Figure 4-1. A firm that is a price-taker in the labour market but not in the output market chooses L_3 workers. A firm that is a price-taker in its output market but not in the labour market chooses L_2 workers. And a firm that is both a monopolist and a monopsonist chooses L_4 workers. For the rest of this chapter we assume that both output and labour markets are competitive. The analysis is easily amended when it is known that the firm has monopoly power in its output market or monopsony power in the labour market.

Figure 4-1 Monopoly and monopsony power

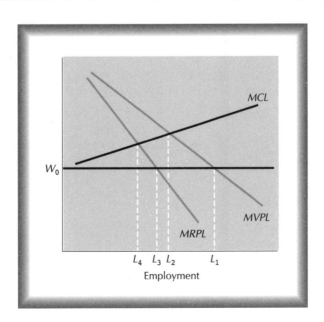

changes in the firm's demand for labour

Consider the effect of a rise in the wage W_0 faced by a competitive firm. Using Figure 4-1, the firm now employs fewer workers than before if W_0 rises. The marginal cost of labour has risen, and intersects the marginal benefits of having a worker (here *MVPL*) at a lower level of employment.

Next, suppose that the competitive firm faces a higher output price. Although the *MPL* remains unaltered in physical goods, this output brings in more money. The *MVPL* schedule shifts up at each level of employment. Hence the horizontal line through the wage W_0 crosses the new *MVPL* schedule at a higher employment level.

Finally, suppose the firm had begun with a higher capital stock. Each worker has more machinery with which to work and will be able to make more output. Although wages and prices remain unchanged, there is an increase in *MPL* in physical goods at each employment level. Hence the *MVPL* schedule shifts upwards. The firm expands employment and output.

For a competitive firm there is a neat way to combine our first two results. Noting that *MVPL* equals the output price P times *MPL*, the extra physical product of another worker, we can write the firm's profit-maximizing condition as wage $W = P \times MPL$. Thus $W/P = MPL$. A profit-maximizing competitive firm will demand labour up to the point at which the marginal physical product of labour equals its *real* wage, its nominal or money wage divided by the firm's output price. If nominal wages and output prices both double, real wages and employment will both be unaffected. But lower real wages move the firm down its *MPL* schedule, taking on more workers until the marginal physical product of labour equals the real wage.

■■■ the industry demand curve for labour

In Figure 4-2 we horizontally add the marginal value product of labour curves for each firm to obtain the $MVPL_0$ schedule for the industry. At the wage W_0 and the price P_0,

Figure 4-2 The industry demand for labour

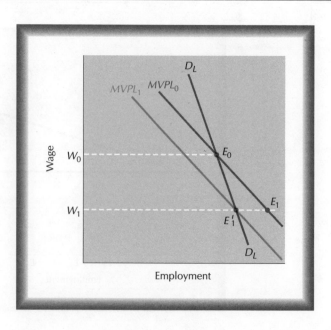

the industry will choose the point E_0. This must be a point on the industry demand curve for labour.

However, $MVPL_0$ is *not* the industry demand curve for labour. It is drawn for a particular output price, P_0. Suppose the wage is cut from W_0 to W_1. At the output price P_0 each firm will wish to move down its $MVPL$ schedule and the industry will wish to expand output and employ labour to the point E_1. In terms of output, the cut in wages has shifted the industry supply curve to the right. At the price P_0 there will now be an excess supply of goods. The increase in supply must bid down the equilibrium price for the industry's product to some lower price P_1. The lower price shifts each firm's $MVPL$ schedule to the left. $MVPL_1$ is thus the new $MVPL$ schedule for the industry at the new price P_1. Hence the industry chooses the point E'_1 at the new wage W_1.

By connecting points such as E_0 and E'_1, we obtain the *industry demand for labour schedule $D_L D_L$* in Figure 4-2. Although each firm constructs its $MVPL$ schedule as if it were a price-taker, the industry demand curve has a steeper slope, since a lower wage will shift the industry output supply curve to the right and reduce the equilibrium price. The more inelastic is output demand, the more a wage cut – through increasing the supply of output – will reduce market price and shift $MVPL$ schedules to the left; and the steeper will be the industry demand curve $D_L D_L$ for labour.

This takes us back to where we began the chapter. The demand for factors of production is a *derived* demand. Firms want factors only because they perceive a demand for their output that it is profitable to supply. It is unsurprising that the elasticity of demand for labour in a particular industry should reflect the elasticity of demand for the product the industry supplies.

the supply of labour

We first discuss individual labour supply.

individual labour supply: hours of work

The effective labour input to the production process is the number of workers multiplied by the hours they work. We approach the analysis of labour supply in two

---

Box 4-1   Boosting UK labour supply

Under New Labour, current UK policies fall under two main headings, *Welfare to Work* and *Making Work Pay*. Both reflect a belief that work allows people to acquire skills and new opportunities: work is a ladder allowing people gradually to climb out of poverty. *Welfare to Work* has two elements, more help in finding a job and more pressure (threat of loss of social security benefits) on those thought to be making little effort to find work. Both raise the incentive to participate in the labour force. *Making Work Pay* deals with incomes of people once they are in the labour force. The Working Family Tax Credit gives money to workers with children, *provided* the parent works a minimum number of hours a week (the limit being set roughly to make it possible for mothers to work while their children are at school).

Both measures attack the poverty trap. To pay for these schemes, the government could have taxed much richer people. Instead, part of the cost is being recouped by faster withdrawal of social security benefits just above the range of the poverty trap. Critics say this is still not a very good answer to the for-whom question.

stages: how many hours people wish to work given that they are in the labour force, and whether or not people wish to be in the labour force at all.

The labour force *is all individuals in work or seeking employment.*

Suppose the individual is in the labour force: how many hours will she wish to work? This will depend on the *real* wage, W/P, the nominal wage divided by the price of goods. If both W and P double, the individual will be able to buy exactly as many goods as before. It is the real wage that measures the amount of goods that can be bought, so it is the real wage that should influence labour supply decisions.

Figure 4-3 shows two possible labour supply curves relating hours of work supplied to the real wage. The curve SS_1 slopes upwards. Higher real wages make people want to work more. But the labour supply curve SS_2 is *backward-bending*. Beyond A, further real wage increases make people want to work fewer hours. The alternative to working another hour is staying at home and having fun. Each of us has only 24 hours a day and we have to decide how to divide these hours between work and leisure. More leisure is nice but by working longer we can get more real income with which to buy consumer goods.

This is a straightforward application of the model of consumer choice in Chapter 2. The choice is no longer between one good and another good, but between goods as a whole and leisure. A higher real wage increases the quantity of goods an extra hour of work will purchase. This makes working more attractive than before and tends to increase the supply of hours worked. But there is a second effect. Suppose you work to get a target real income or a target bundle of goods. You work to get enough to be able to eat, pay the rent, run a car, and have a holiday. With a higher real wage you can have your cake and eat it too. You can work less hours to earn the same target real income and have more time off for fun.

These two effects are precisely the *substitution and income effects* of Chapter 2. An increase in the real wage increases the relative return on working. It leads to a substitution effect or pure relative price effect that makes people want to work more.

Figure 4-3 Individual labour supply

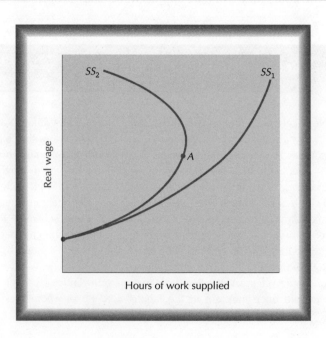

But a higher real wage also tends to raise people's real income. This has a pure income effect. Since leisure is probably a luxury good, the quantity of leisure demanded increases sharply when real incomes increase. This income effect tends to make people work less.

To decide whether or not the substitution effect will dominate the income effect, we must look at actual data on what people do. The empirical evidence for the UK, the United States, and most other Western economies is as follows. For men and women with full-time careers, the substitution effect and the income effect almost exactly cancel out. A change in the real wage has almost no effect on the quantity of hours supplied. The supply curve of hours worked is almost vertical. This conclusion applies to relatively small changes in real wage rates. In most Western countries, the large rise in real wages over the last 100 years has been matched by reductions of ten hours or more in the working week.

Workers care about take-home pay after deductions of income tax. A reduction in income tax rates thus serves to raise after-tax real wages. For the moment we merely note that the empirical evidence on labour supply implies that lower income tax rates should not be expected to lead to a dramatic increase in the supply of hours worked.

individual labour supply: participation rates

If the effect of real wages on the supply of hours is smaller than is often supposed, the more important effect of real wages on labour supply may be the effect on the incentive to enter or participate in the labour force.

The participation rate *is the percentage of a given group of the population of working age who decide to enter the labour force.*

Table 4-1 presents UK data on participation rates for different groups of the population of working age. Most men are in employment or are seeking employment. A smaller but still quite stable percentage of unmarried women are in the labour force. There has been a substantial increase in the number of married women in the labour force, a trend continuing steadily since 1951 when only 25 per cent of married women were in the UK labour force. Similar patterns are observed in other Western countries.

Someone not participating in the labour force is sitting at home. She has lots of leisure but how does she buy consumer goods? She may have inherited wealth, won the lottery, or be supported by her working boyfriend. In many cases, she may be financed by government provision of social security, through unemployment benefit or income support; these may be topped up further by housing benefit and child support. Suppose all this leisure and the goods she buys with her social security cheques give her a utility level U_0.

How much utility could she get by joining the labour force? First, she would lose an hour of leisure for every hour she works. Second, she would lose social security. For every pound earned from work she might lose over 90 pence in withdrawal of

Table 4-1	UK participation rates (%)		
	1971	*1985*	*1996*
Men	92	89	84
Unmarried women	72	74	67
Married women	50	62	72
Source: General Household Survey.			

government support. Since the Treasury coffers are not limitless, governments help the very poor but claw as much money back as they can once people's circumstances improve a little. In addition, going out to work entails several costs – the right clothes, commuting to work, and perhaps paying for child care. It may simply not be worth it.

 The poverty trap *is a situation in which joining the labour force may leave a person worse off than staying at home.*

Suppose the real wage increases. This may now make it possible to break through the poverty trap. Lower real wages make the poverty trap worse. Hence, higher real wages increase the incentive to join the labour force.

What happened to income and substitution effects here? These are tools for comparing two situations in which the individual is able to adjust their behaviour at the margin. The poverty trap is like a high wall that entrants must jump to get into the labour force. Analysis of small changes is not the appropriate procedure. Beginning from a small wage, a small increase in the wage may make no difference. But as wages keep rising, eventually an individual can soar over the wall and finds it worth joining the labour force. For all kinds of reasons, different people face walls of different heights. Hence, as wages in the economy increase, the aggregate labour supply response is continuous. A few more people join with each increase in real wages.

Why does Table 4-1 show such a large increase in labour force participation by married women in the last few decades? First, there has been an important social change in attitudes to married women working. One way to think of this is that the disapproval cost of going out to work has fallen. Second, pressure for equal opportunities for women has tended to raise women's wages, allowing more of them to leap over the wall. Third, the opportunity cost of working has fallen. Labour saving devices within the home allow women to do household chores more quickly; and men now take a (slightly) larger share of these than before.

So we are thinking about things the right way. What do we want to take out of this discussion? First, social influences matter, and can shift labour supply a lot. Second, labour supply to the whole economy will increase with the level of real wages, but not by a lot. It is pretty inelastic. Many people are already in the labour force. Offsetting income and substitution effects mean that further changes in wages have a small effect. The main reason aggregate supply of person hours increases when real

Box 4-2 | Help wanted? or just Help!

The world does not stand still. Technical progress, changing culture and tastes, and easier transport and communications are contributing to the rise and fall of particular industries and skills. The following figure shows forecasts by the US Bureau of Labor Statistics about likely employment trends in the USA.

Source: Economist, 28 September 1996.

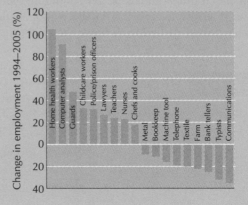

wages rise is that some extra people are able to leap over the wall and join the labour force.

the supply of labour to an industry

Now we discuss the supply of labour to an individual industry. Suppose that the industry is very small relative to the economy as a whole and that it wishes to employ workers with very common skills.

Essentially there are economy-wide markets for plumbers, drivers, and other types of worker. The small individual industry will have to pay the going rate. Jobs in different industries have different non-monetary characteristics, such as risk, comfort, or anti-social hours like night shifts. The idea of the going wage rate must be adjusted industry by industry to allow for the *equilibrium wage differential* which offsets these non-monetary characteristics and makes workers indifferent about the industry in which they work.

Given this adjustment, a small industry will be able to hire as many workers as it wants from the economy-wide labour pool. At this wage rate the industry faces a horizontal labour supply curve. In practice, few industries are this small relative to all the skills they wish to employ. The construction industry is a significant user of plumbers and the freight industry a significant user of lorry drivers. When an industry is a significant user of a particular skill, an expansion of employment in the industry will tend to bid up the wages of that particular skill whose short-run supply is relatively fixed to the economy as a whole. In the short run it will generally be correct to assume that expansion of the industry will bid up the wages of at least some of the workers it employs. The industry's labour supply curve slopes upwards.

In the long run the industry's labour supply curve may be a little flatter. When short-run expansion bids up the wages of computer programmers, more school-leavers will start to train in this skill. In the long run the economy-wide supply will increase and the wages that these workers can earn will fall back again. The individual industry will not have to offer such a high wage in the long run to increase the supply of that type of labour to the industry.

▪▪▪ labour market equilibrium in an industry

Having discussed the industry's labour supply curve, we can combine with its downward-sloping labour demand curve to obtain equilibrium employment and wages in the industry. We can also discuss how this equilibrium can shift. For example, a recession in the output market causes an inward shift in the industry's derived demand for labour. With the upward-sloping labour supply curve unaltered, this leads to a fall in equilibrium wages and employment in the industry.

▪▪▪ transfer earnings and economic rents

Top pianists and top footballers are delighted with the high salaries they can earn, but they would choose the same career even if the pay was less good. Why do they get paid so much? We need to distinguish between transfer earnings and economic rent.

> The transfer earnings *of a factor of production in a particular use are the minimum payments required to induce that factor to work in that job.* Economic rent *(not to be confused with income from renting out property) is the extra payment it receives over and above its transfer earnings.*

In Figure 4-4, *DD* is the labour demand curve for concert pianists and *SS* the supply of pianists to the music industry. Even at a zero wage some dedicated musicians would be concert pianists. Higher wages attract into the industry concert pianists who could have done other things. Because all workers must be paid the same wage rate, equilibrium occurs at E where the wage is W_0 and the number of pianists is L_0. W_0 may be a very large wage. Each firm in the music industry is happy to pay W_0 because their workers are very talented. They have a high marginal product. In the output market (concerts) firms can earn a large revenue. The derived demand curve *DD* for concert pianists is very high.

The supply curve *SS* shows the transfer earnings that the industry may pay to attract pianists into the industry. The first *A* pianists would work for nothing. A wage W_1 would be required to expand the supply of pianists to *B* and W_0 must be paid to increase supply to L_0. If the industry as a whole could make separate wage bargains with each individual pianist, paying each the minimum required to attract them into the industry, the triangle AL_0E is the total transfer earnings the industry would need to pay to attract L_0 pianists.

Figure 4-4	Transfer earnings and economic rent

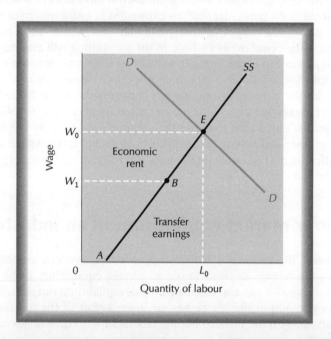

Box 4-3 | Premiership wages

The wage bill in UK Premier League football rose from £50 million in the 1992–93 season to £190 million in the 1997–98 season, while income of the clubs rose from £464 million to £569 million. Spiralling club incomes reflect not only increasing demand as satellite TV retails football to ever wider (and more profitable) audiences, but also greater proficiency in marketing ancillary products like replica shirts. Competition for top talent has seen players get their hands on all of the club's additional revenue.

At the equilibrium position E the last pianist enticed into the industry has transfer earnings W_0 since E lies on the supply curve SS. And it is just worth employing this last pianist, since his marginal value product is also W_0. E lies on the demand curve DD. However, because the industry typically has to pay all workers the same wage, all previous workers must also be paid W_0 even though the labour supply curve SS implies these workers would have worked for less than W_0. These workers whose transfer earnings are less than W_0 are earning *economic rent*. Rent reflects differences in pianists' *supply* decisions not their *productivity* as musicians.

Thus in Figure 4-4 the industry as a whole makes total wage payments equal to the rectangle OW_0EL_0. It pays L_0 workers W_0 each. But these payments can be divided into the total transfer earnings AL_0E and the economic rent $OAEW_0$. Economic rent arises whenever the supply curve of a factor is not horizontal. Economic rent is an unnecessary payment as far as the industry is concerned. By colluding to wage-discriminate, paying each worker his or her transfer earnings alone, the industry could retain all its workers without paying them economic rent. But the entire wage W_0 is a transfer earning as far as a single competitive firm is concerned. If the firm does not match the going rate for the industry, its workers will go to another firm who will employ them, since their marginal value product covers the wage at the equilibrium position E.

In the UK football industry[1] and the US baseball industry, it is currently being asserted that high player salaries are bankrupting the industry. What light does our analysis shed on this issue? First, wages are high because the derived demand is high – crowds at the ground and television rights make it profitable to supply this output – and because the supply of talented players is scarce. The supply curve of good players is steep: even by offering very high wages the industry cannot increase the number of good players by much. Thus there is no simple link between high salaries and the ruin of the game. If supplying the output were not profitable, the derived demand for players would be lower and their wages would be correspondingly reduced.

▪▬ do labour markets clear?

Thus far we have assumed that wage flexibility ensures that labour markets for each industry and for the economy as a whole are in equilibrium. Each market clears at the equilibrium wage and employment level that equates supply and demand. We now examine why it may not be possible to take labour market equilibrium for granted.

minimum wage agreements

The UK minimum wage is £3.70 an hour. If this exceeds the equilibrium wage, firms demand less labour and some workers become unemployed.

> **Workers are** involuntarily unemployed *if they are prepared to work at the going wage rate but cannot find jobs.*

Thus, for low-skill occupations a minimum wage in excess of the free market equilibrium wage will raise the wage for those lucky enough to find jobs but will reduce the total amount of employment relative to the free market equilibrium level of

[1] Football clubs pay transfer fees to another club from whom they wish to take over a player. This idea of transfer fees between clubs should not be confused with the economist's concept of transfer earnings of players, the amount necessary to keep them in the industry.

employment. Minimum wage agreements may explain involuntary unemployment among low-skilled workers.

trade unions

A strong trade union may act in a similar way. If unions in an industry are successful in forcing employers to pay a wage above that which would have prevailed under free competition, the consequence will be a lower level of employment in the industry. By forcing up the wage, the union must accept a loss of employment. The resulting unemployment is collectively voluntary for the union – it chose this action – but may be involuntary for some of the unlucky union members who lose their jobs.

insider–outsider distinctions

Insider–outsider theories emphasize barriers to entering employment in existing firms.

Box 4-4	Minimum wages hurt jobs, don't they?

A minimum wage prices some workers out of a job: by raising wages it slides employment up the demand curve. It must reduce jobs. One of the few certainties in economics. Even politicians understand. Right?

Not so fast. The 'proof' relies on a diagram of a perfectly competitive labour market. People's intuition about economics is often based on perfect competition. What happens when there is a monopsonist, a sole employer in the relevant labour market. A monopsonist recognizes that additional hiring bids up the price of existing workers making the marginal cost of labour exceed the wage. The diagram shows $MRPL$ the marginal revenue product of labour, LS the labour supply curve facing the firm, and MCL the marginal cost of labour to the monopsonist. Equilibrium is where $MRPL$ equals MCL. Employment is N_1 and a wage W_1 is necessary to attract this labour. Crucially, this combination is not on the monopsonist's $MRPL$ curve. The vertical gap between LS and $MRPL$ shows workers are being paid less than their marginal product. Sometimes this is called *exploitation*.

Now suppose the government imposes a minimum wage at W_2. Effectively, the monopsonist will face a *horizontal* labour supply at this wage, at least until N_2 people are hired. Since W_2 is now the

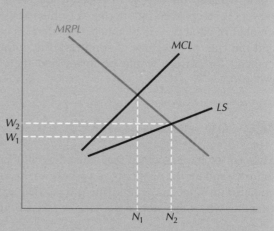

relevant marginal cost of labour, the firm will indeed hire N_2 workers to equate the marginal cost and marginal benefit of hiring. The minimum wage has increased employment, from N_1 to N_2! In effect it has countered the exploitation.

Notice that, beginning at free market equilibrium at a wage W_1, steadily increasing the minimum wage will *increase* employment (sliding the market along the labour supply curve LS) until the minimum wage reaches W_2 at which point employment is maximized. Further increases in the minimum wage now slide the market up the demand curve, steadily *reducing* employment thereafter.

Insiders *have jobs and are represented in wage bargaining.* Outsiders *do not have jobs and are unrepresented in wage bargaining.*

Entry barriers may take several forms: the cost of advertising for workers, interviewing them, and evaluating what sort of job they should be offered; costs of training new workers in activities specific to the firm; and the time taken to build up team-work and for new employees to master their new jobs. These are innocent entry barriers.

But existing workers (insiders) may also succeed in erecting strategic barriers to entry by outsiders, even without the presence of formal trade unions at plant level. For example, they may threaten various forms of industrial disruption if too many outsiders are admitted too quickly, and in many circumstances they would find it easy to obtain mass insider support for such threats if there were any proposal to admit outsiders at a lower wage than that currently being paid to insiders.

When such entry barriers confront outsiders, the insiders will be able to raise their own wage above that for which outsiders would be prepared to work *without* inducing a spate of hiring of outsiders. The outsiders might like to work at the wage currently enjoyed by insiders, but outsiders do not find it attractive to work for the very much lower wage that would be necessary to induce firms to hire them when the economic cost of these various entry barriers is large.

efficiency wage explanations

In the real world, employers face two kinds of problem: they find it hard to tell whether an applicant for a job will be a productive or unproductive worker (a matter of innate ability); and they find it hard to monitor whether workers are trying or shirking even once they are employed. Given the costs of evaluating or screening new workers, and the subsequent costs of monitoring their performance on the job, what is the best policy for a firm? The efficiency wage theory argues that it will be profitable for firms to respond by paying existing workers a wage which on average exceeds the wage for which workers as a whole are prepared to work.

Efficiency wages *are high wages which increase productivity through their incentive effect.*

Paying a wage premium is a device to help retain high-quality workers, even in a world where the firm has some trouble distinguishing between high- and low-quality workers. Moreover, when workers shirk on the job there is a small chance they will get caught. Suppose they get sacked if caught: how big is the penalty for being caught? It is the difference between what the worker currently earns and what the worker will get in unemployment benefit or in some subsequent job. The higher the wage paid by the existing employer, the larger the penalty of being caught shirking.

Minimum wage agreements, trade union power, insider–outsider distinctions, and efficiency wages are all *possible* explanations for insufficient wage flexibility in the short run to maintain the labour market in continuous equilibrium. Whether the labour market is always in equilibrium, and the length of time for which any disequilibrium might persist, are questions to which we return in later chapters.

▰▰ recap

- In the long run, the firm chooses the technique of production to minimize the cost of producing a particular output, and chooses the output at which $MC = MR$.

- A rise in the price of labour will have both a substitution effect and an output effect. Both reduce the demand for labour.

- In the short run, the firm has fixed factors and probably has a fixed production technique. The firm can vary short-run output by varying its variable input, labour. But labour is subject to diminishing returns when other factors are fixed. The marginal physical product of labour falls as more labour is employed.

- A profit-maximizing firm produces the output at which marginal output cost equals marginal output revenue. Equivalently, it hires labour up to the point where the marginal cost of labour equals its marginal revenue product. A perfectly competitive firm equates the real wage to the marginal physical product of labour.

- The *MVPL* schedule for a firm shifts up if the output price increases, the capital stock increases, or if technical progress makes labour more productive.

- Higher industry output reduces the output price in equilibrium. The industry labour demand curve is steeper (less elastic) than that of each firm and is more inelastic the more inelastic is the demand curve for the industry's output.

- For an individual already in the labour force, an increase in the hourly real wage has a substitution effect tending to increase the supply of hours worked, but an income effect tending to reduce the supply of hours worked.

- Individuals with large non-labour income may prefer not to work. Participation rates increase with higher real wage rates, lower fixed costs of working, and changes in tastes in favour of working rather than staying at home. These help explain the trend for increasing labour force participation.

- For a particular industry the supply curve of labour depends on the wage paid relative to wages in other industries using similar skills. Equilibrium wage differentials are the monetary compensation for differences in non-monetary characteristics of jobs in different industries.

- When the labour supply curve to an industry is less than perfectly elastic, the industry must pay higher wages to expand employment. For the marginal worker, the wage is a pure transfer earning required to induce that worker into the industry. For workers prepared to work in the industry at a lower wage, there is an element of economic rent.

- In free market equilibrium, some workers will choose not to work at the equilibrium wage rate. They are voluntarily unemployed. Involuntary unemployment is the difference between desired supply and desired demand at a disequilibrium wage rate. Workers would like to work but cannot find a job.

- There is considerable disagreement about how quickly labour markets can get back to equilibrium if they are initially thrown out of equilibrium. Possible causes of involuntary unemployment are minimum wage agreements, trade unions, insider–outsider distinctions, and efficiency wages.

■■ key terms

■■ review questions

1 In what sense is it true that a firm's decision on how much output to produce is the same thing as its decision on how much labour to demand?

2 (a) Explain why the marginal product of labour eventually declines. (b) Show in a diagram the effect of an increase in the firm's capital stock on its demand curve for labour.

3 Over the last 100 years the real wage has risen but the length of the working week has fallen. (a) Explain this result using income and substitution effects. (b) Explain how an increase in the real wage could cause everyone in employment to work fewer hours but still increase the total amount of work done in the economy.

4 A film producer says that the industry is doomed because film stars are paid an outrageous amount of money. Evaluate the argument being sure to discuss economic rent.

4-2 different kinds of labour

In most European countries men earn more than women and whites earn more than non-whites. Do these stark facts reflect discrimination in the labour market, or simply differences in the productivity of different workers? Workers differ not merely in sex and race but in age, experience, education, training, innate ability, and in whether or not they belong to a trade union. Table 4-2 emphasizes the difference between men and women. Women earn only two-thirds as much per hour as men. These differences partly reflect continuity of employment. Single women do considerably better than married or divorced women and earn almost 90 per cent as much per hour as men. Whether we regard this as discrimination against women who take time off to raise a family is an issue that goes to the heart of our view about how society should be organized.

Table 4-3 considers some of the factors that influence pay differentials for men, the group on which most data are available. It shows separate estimates for workers in trade unions and not in unions. Table 4-3 highlights four sources of pay differentials. People with more education and training earn more money, and these returns to education do not depend much on whether the worker is in a union or not. Notice that it is not just vocational degrees, such as engineering, that enhance earning power. All graduates, including, for example, history and philosophy graduates, seem to earn more than their less educated counterparts.

Personal characteristics also matter. Ethnic minorities earn lower pay even *after allowing for differences in education and work experience*. This is *prima facie* evidence of discrimination. And it may understate the true disadvantage of such minorities if they also enjoy lower educational achievement and work experience because of discrimination elsewhere, for example in schools.

Work experience generally adds to earnings, though at a diminishing rate, especially in manual work, where older workers may not be able to perform all the tasks of which their strong, young colleagues are capable. But experience still matters, even in manual work. Job characteristics also have important effects on pay. Shift work and overtime typically involve additional payments (equalizing wage differentials). Manual workers, perhaps with fewer skills, earn less than non-manuals. And firms in the busy (and expensive) South East region, including London, also have to pay workers more.

Table 4-2 Hourly earnings in the UK, 1998

	Men	Women
Manual	£7.1	£5.2
Non-manual	£12.9	£8.9

Source: Department of Employment, *New Earnings Survey*.

■■■ human capital

Human capital *is the stock of expertise accumulated by a worker. It is valued for its income-earning potential in the future.*

Human capital is the result of past investment and its purpose is to generate future incomes. To invest in another year of school education or a further qualification people may have to make a direct payment, as with fees for private schools, but they also forgo the opportunity to earn immediate income by working. The anticipated benefit of this initial expenditure is either a higher future monetary income or a future job yielding greater job satisfaction. The human capital approach assumes that wage differentials reflect differences in the productivity of different workers. Skilled workers have a higher marginal value product and earn more. In long-run equilibrium, the extra benefit of acquiring skills must just cover the extra cost of acquiring them.

investing in human capital: cost–benefit analysis

Consider the decision of a school-leaver whether to continue in education or take a job immediately. Does investment in further education make sense? There are two costs and two benefits. The immediate costs are for books and fees to continue in education, and the income that could have been earned (the opportunity cost) by taking a job immediately rather than remaining unpaid while in further education, *minus* any income received from the government as an educational grant.

The first benefit occurs in the future and is the stream of *extra* wages that workers with higher education can earn. The second occurs immediately but in a non-monetary

Table 4-3   Pay differentials for UK men

% extra pay for	Union	Non-union
Education and training		
GCSE	+5	+13
A-levels	+16	+21
University degree	+32	+47
Postgraduate degree	+50	+50
Other higher education	+18	+21
Apprenticeship	+11	+9
Personal		
Ethnic minority	−1	−5
Profit share	+2	+11
Years experience		
5	+13	+10
10	+23	+20
15	+30	+28
30	+35	+32
Job character		
South East	+15	+16
London	+23	+15
Manual	−17	−21
Shift work	+12	+8
% overtime	+52	+47

Source: A. Booth, 'Seniority, Earnings and Unions', *Economica*, 1996.

form. It is the fun or consumption value of going to college or university. Most students have a good time. They meet new people, try new sports, discover new rock bands, and do whatever students do.

Like any investment decision, the decision whether or not to continue in higher education rests on comparing current costs and benefits (usually a net cost) with the stream of future costs and benefits (usually a stream of net benefits). It makes sense to go on to further education if the benefits outweigh the costs. But the benefits accrue in the future. Most people would prefer £100 today than a promise of £100 in five years' time. To compare like with like, it is necessary to *discount* or reduce the value of future benefits (or future costs) to place them on a par with benefits or costs incurred today. In the next section we discuss in detail how this should be done. For the moment we can skip the technical details. The general idea will suffice. If the present value, however calculated, of the benefits outweighs the present value of the costs incurred, the educational investment in improving human capital by further education makes sense. If the present value of the benefits is less than the present value of the costs, higher education is a bad investment. It is better to start work immediately.

Table 4-4 shows some estimates of the annual rate of return, spread over one's future lifetime, on two decisions: staying at school from 16 to 18 to sit A-level exams, and going to university at 18. Education beyond 16 yields more than sufficient benefits to pay for the costs: the return is generally positive. Two features deserve further comment.

First, the socio-economic background of the family matters a lot. Children whose fathers work in unskilled or manual get nothing out of A-levels if they then go out to work at 18. Presumably, many of them end up in similar jobs to their fathers. Children from more privileged backgrounds leaving school at 18 get better jobs provided they acquire A-level qualifications. This is compatible with the second feature of Table 4-4, the huge payoff enjoyed from university by children of unskilled or manual fathers. For such children, university is the stepping stone to much better career prospects.

on-the-job training

Firm-specific skills help increase a worker's productivity only if he or she works for that particular firm. Firm-specific human capital could be something as simple as knowing how the filing system works or something as complicated as mastering the

---

Table 4-4 Expected return on education (% per annum over rest of life)

	Father's occupation	
	Professional or manager	Manual or unskilled
Men		
A-level only	6	−1
University	7	25
Women		
A-level only	10	13
University	6	8

Source: R. Bennett, H. Glennerster, and D. Nevison, 'Investing in Skill: To Stay On or Not to Stay On', *Oxford Review of Economic Policy*, 1992.

most efficient way to combine the various production processes of a particular factory. In either case, the skill is virtually worthless to any other firm. *General* skills are those that can be transferred to work for another firm. Examples are learning how to use Windows 2000 or understanding how the stock market works.

The firm can afford to pay for on-the-job training in firm-specific skills. Workers' productivity will be much higher with that firm than with any other firm. The firm is unlikely to lose the worker. The more general or transferable the skill, the more the firm will want the worker to pay the cost of training. No firm will want to invest heavily in training its workers only to see them move to other firms.

Thus, firms offering general or transferable training try to make the workers pay for this. How? By offering an apprentice or training scheme. The worker is working for less than his immediate marginal product. Workers are prepared to invest in human capital because the firm is committed to an age–earnings profile that will allow the worker to recoup the initial investment with interest at a later date. Hence earnings rise much more steeply with age for people with more education.

signalling

Why can a history graduate go on to earn big money in banking? Does education and training on the job raise worker productivity? An alternative explanation is the theory of *signalling*. It could be rational to invest in costly education *even if education adds nothing directly to a worker's marginal product*. The theory assumes that people are born with different innate ability. Some people are good at most things, other people are less smart and on average less productive. But smart people do not all have blue eyes. The problem for firms is to tell which applicants will turn out to be the smart ones with high productivity. Looking at their eyes is not enough.

> Signalling *is the decision to undertake an action in order to reveal inside information.*

In going on in education, the smart people are sending a signal to employers that they are the high-productivity workers of the future. Higher education is *screening out* the smart high-productivity workers. Firms can pay university graduates more because they can be assured that they are the high-ability workers.

> Screening *is the process of learning inside information by observing differences in behaviour.*

To be effective, the screening process must separate the high-ability workers from the others. Why don't lower-ability workers go to university and fool firms into offering

---

Box 4-5 | Good economists in short supply

In June 1999 the Bank of England warned that it was having difficulty recruiting staff with good postgraduate degrees in economics. British students account for only 10 per cent of PhD students in economics in leading UK universities. Why so low? Partly because a good undergraduate economics degree is now worth so much in the City. Professor Andrew Oswald of Warwick University has estimated that economics undergraduates earn about £35 000 a year in their mid-twenties, rising to over £100 000 a year by retirement. The Bank of England can't match these salaries. Nor incidentally can universities. Some of us have to write textbooks to make a decent living!

them high wages? Lower-ability workers could not be confident of passing. The lower-ability people may decide not to go to university: they may not expect to pass, or may feel that to scrape through they will have to work enormously hard.

It seems quite probable that education (even at the highest levels) contributes something to productivity. But there may also be an element of screening in all except purely vocational courses. Some women plan to have a full-time career, either remaining childless or returning to work almost immediately after any children are born. It would make sense for firms to invest in such people but there is a huge problem: how is a firm to tell which young women are planning to stay and which are planning to work only a few years and then have a family? Asking is no good because there is an incentive for young women not to tell the truth.[2]

Can firms and workers co-operate to devise a screening procedure that will persuade young women to reveal their true career plans? Suppose firms offer young workers the choice between a relatively flat age–earnings profile and a much steeper profile that begins at a lower wage but pays a higher wage later in a worker's career. By making the wages in later years sufficiently high, firms could ensure that the two profiles were equally valued by someone planning a lifetime career. The early sacrifice of lower wages would be recouped with interest later. But someone planning to quit the labour force, say at the age of 30, would never opt for the steeper profile: she wouldn't expect to work long enough at the higher wage to recoup the early sacrifice.

By observing whether new recruits accept the steeper age–earnings profile, it might be possible for firms to persuade recruits to reveal their career plans. If women, or any other group with a high risk of quitting at a young age, accept the steeper profile, the firm can embark on training with some confidence that its investment would not be wasted. There is, of course, an issue of credibility. Young workers would need to be assured that they really were exchanging low wages in the early years for suitably higher wages later in their career. And, initially, even career women might be reluctant to accept the steeper profile until they could see a generation of women who, having accepted such a profile and induced the firm to place its training bets, had succeeded in being promoted through the company to earn the suitably higher earnings in the later years of their career.

▨ discrimination

We suspect that there are still a few firms who try to pay female workers less than male workers who are identical in every respect, including the risk of quitting. We might call this overt discrimination.

Discrimination *is the different treatment of people whose relevant characteristics are identical.*

In other cases, traditional age–earnings profiles may give firms a purely economic reason to be cautious about investment in the education and training of women. We have indicated how this more subtle form of discrimination might be changed. But society may discriminate against women in even more subtle ways. For example, our analysis suggests that paternity leave for fathers, the provision of crèches for working

[2] This is a version of the problem of *moral hazard* that we discuss in detail in Section 5-1. However, single women are less likely to interrupt their career than married women. Since firms can discover a woman's marital status, single women on average earn much more than married women. Firms are more likely to invest in training for single women.

parents, or a greater acceptance of part-time working by both sexes, would reduce the incentive for hard-nosed firms to conclude that it is more profitable to train and promote men than women. Whether or not society wishes to organize its work and home life along such principles remains a controversial issue. Pay differentials between men and women depend on much wider factors than the labour market in isolation.

access to education

Thus far we have discussed sex discrimination by firms assuming that they receive male and female applicants of equal calibre. However, it may be that firms treat workers of equal calibre equally but pay men more on average because male workers have more educational qualifications than female workers. If so we must seek the root cause of pay differences by sex not in the labour market, but in education itself.

Table 4-5 shows full-time and part-time UK students in three types of education: FE colleges, university undergraduates, and postgraduates. In 1971 male students greatly outnumbered female students in all forms of further and higher education. By 1998 the gender gap had largely disappeared. Women had overtaken men in FE colleges and in university undergraduate places, and had caught up substantially in postgraduate education.

Why did fewer women previously continue in higher education? There are three possible explanations. First, there may have been genuine discrimination in education. In schools teaching boys and girls, teachers may try harder with boys or encourage more of them to think about further education. Second, women may have had different tastes. The old stereotype of school, marriage, motherhood, and domesticity may still survive in some cases, but this is hard to square with the large number of female students in FE college and undergraduate education.

Finally, we can think about the return to this initial investment in higher education. Equal opportunity legislation and social pressure have increased wages for women, both by reducing sex discrimination for a given job and by increasing the chances of female promotion. Women may now feel that there has been an increase in the future benefits through higher salary opportunities. If so, we should expect more and more women to decide to invest in education. Note, however, the crucial role of expectations or perceptions. Until it becomes evident that women really are being

Table 4-5 UK students 1971–98 (thousands)

	Male		Female	
	71	98	71	98
Further education				
Full time	116	414	95	445
Part time	891	638	630	938
Undergraduate				
Full time	241	491	173	528
Part time	127	168	19	224
Postgraduate				
Full time	33	75	10	63
Part time	15	112	3	102

Source: ONS, Social Trends.

promoted and enjoying the benefits of higher education, the perceived return on higher education may continue to be lower for women than for men, and fewer women than men will invest in postgraduate education.

racial discrimination

Exactly the same general principles may be used to analyse racial discrimination and differences in the earnings of whites and non-whites. West Indians, Indians and Pakistanis are the most important racial minority groups in the UK. Many studies have confirmed the suggestion in Table 4-3 that on average non-whites earn less than whites.

The age–earnings profiles for non-white males are much flatter than the corresponding profiles for white males. White men are much more likely to achieve steady promotion and rising earnings. From our discussion of age–earnings profiles in the previous section, this is likely to imply that whites do more difficult jobs where training and experience are important. Part of the problem for non-white men is not so much the amount of education but the type of education they receive. The payoff to education is very low for non-whites who attend a typical state-run inner-city school.

Two interpretations are possible. Either the quality of education in inner-city schools with predominantly non-white children is poor, or attendance at such schools tends to act as a signal to firms that these children are likely to come from disadvantaged backgrounds. Firms may believe that these potential workers will have lower productivity and be more expensive to train.

Both interpretations imply that firms will be less inclined to employ such workers in jobs that are difficult and require extensive on-the-job training. White workers or non-whites from other educational backgrounds are much more likely to be given the skilled and demanding jobs with which the steeply rising age–earnings profiles are associated. A higher proportion of non-whites will be restricted to unskilled and low-paying jobs.

Table 4-6 completes our examination of racial discrimination. It shows inactivity rates across ethnic groups. Muslim women from Pakistan and Bangladesh have much lower rates of labour force participation. However, this seems to reflect a different attitude to the willingness to supply labour as much as any evidence of discrimination in the demand for their labour. Most minority groups also have unemployment rates well above those for white men or women.

As in our discussion of sex discrimination, it is hard to draw a line between discrimination in the labour market and elsewhere in society. The responsibility of managers is to maximize profits for their shareholders. So long as managers perceive

Table 4-6   Ethnic groups, UK, 1995

	Participation rate (%)		Unemployment rate (%)	
	Men	Women	Men	Women
Whites	86	72	9	7
Blacks	79	65	24	22
Indian	82	63	14	11
Pakistani/Bangladeshi	68	23	29	29

Source: ONS, Labour Market Trends.

that different groups of workers have already acquired different characteristics, or will tend to behave differently during their working lifetimes, managers will wish to treat different groups differently. Unless society as a whole removes the differences in characteristics, opportunities and behaviour of different groups of workers, the eradication of blatant racism or sexism will go only part of the way to eliminating pay differentials between groups of workers.

■■■ trade unions

Trade unions are worker organizations designed to affect pay and working conditions. Do unions protect workers from exploitation by powerful employers or do they use their power to secure unjustified pay increases and oppose technical changes and productivity improvements which might threaten the employment of their members? Before examining these questions we give a brief outline of the importance of unions in the British economy.

By 1980 just over half the civilian labour force in the UK belonged to a trade union. Figure 4-5 shows changes since 1910. After the steady increase in union membership until 1920 there was a massive decline and then recovery in the degree of unionization of the labour force during the inter-war years. Thereafter, there was a long period during which unionization was fairly constant until the late 1960s. The 1970s saw a sharp rise in union membership, which peaked in 1979, since when it has been falling sharply as the industrial economy gives way to the service economy.

what unions do

The traditional view of unions is that they offset the power that a firm enjoys in negotiating wages and working conditions. A single firm has many workers. If each

| **Figure 4-5** | Union membership (% of civilian labour force) |

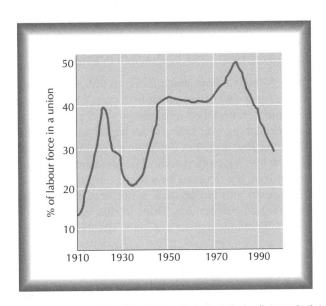

Sources: Bain and Elsheik, *Union Growth and the Business Cycle*, Basil Blackwell, 1976; ONS, *Labour Market Trends*.

worker must make a separate deal with the firm, the firm can make a take-it-or-leave-it offer. A worker with firm-specific human capital, which will be pretty useless in any other firm, may face a large drop in productivity and wages if she rejects the firm's offer. The firm is in a strong bargaining position if it can make separate agreements with each of its workers. In contrast, by presenting a united front, the workers may be able to impose large costs on the firm if they *all* quit. The firm can replace one worker but not its whole labour force. The existence of unions evens up the bargaining process.

Once a union is established, it aims not merely to protect its members but to improve their pay and conditions. To be successful the union must be able to restrict the firm's labour supply. If the firm can hire non-union labour, unions will find it hard to maintain the wage above the level at which the firm can hire non-union workers. This is one reason why unions are keen on closed-shop agreements with individual firms.[3]

 A closed shop *is an agreement that all a firm's workers will be members of a trade union.*

What determines how far the union will trade off lower employment for higher wages in the industry? And what determines how much power unions have to control the supply of labour to particular industries?

The more the union cares about its senior members, the more it is likely to maximize the wage independently of what happens to employment. Senior workers have the most firm-specific human capital and are the least likely to be sacked if total employment in the industry must fall. Conversely, the more the union is democratic and the more it cares about its potential members as well as those actually in employment, the less likely it is to restrict employment to ensure higher wages for those who remain employed in the industry.

When does restricting labour supply by a given amount lead to the largest rise in wages? When the demand for labour is most inelastic. For example, in the last 20 years workers in the electricity supply industry have secured large wage increases. Power stations are very capital-intensive, so the wage bill is a relatively small component of total costs in the industry. Moreover, the consumer demand for electricity is relatively price-inelastic in the short run. For both these reasons, the industry was prepared to meet high wage claims which did not add much to total costs and could in any case be passed on to the consumer.

unionization and wage differentials

Table 4-7 shows how much more an individual union member typically earns than a non-union worker. Union members earn 7.5 per cent more than people not belonging to a union in unskilled jobs, but only 1.5 per cent extra in skilled jobs. Union power has been falling over time. So has the union wage differential. The slope of the labour demand curve is the key determinant of trade union power to raise wages without too great a loss of employment. The demand for labour is a derived demand which depends on the demand for a firm's output.

Consider an industry that is not very competitive, with few domestic firms and little foreign competition. Firms in this industry are making substantial supernormal profits. We would expect unions to get their hands on some of these through higher

---

[3] Unions frequently argue that, in the absence of a closed shop, non-union workers will benefit from improvements in pay and conditions achieved through the efforts of the union. Non-union members are getting a 'free ride' without paying their union subscriptions.

wages which eat into healthy profit margins. At the other extreme, in a perfectly competitive industry, if a union in a single firm raises wages it will simply drive that firm out of business. Only if the union can organize across *the whole industry*, which can then pass these increases on in part to consumers, does the union stand a chance of raising wages.

Studying a large number of industries, Mark Stewart of Warwick University has shown that this is exactly what happens in practice![4] In competitive industries facing significant foreign competition, unions get no wage differential at all. Thus, globalization is undermining the power of national trade unions. In industries sheltered from foreign competition but with a large number of domestic firms, union differentials exist only when the whole industry is unionized. But unions get substantial markups in industries with few domestic firms and little foreign competition.

union wages as compensating differentials

Union wage differentials arise not only from the successful restriction of labour supply. Union work has certain characteristics – a structured work setting, inflexibility of hours, employer-set overtime, and a faster work pace – a whole set of conditions that might be regarded as unpleasant. Perhaps higher wages in such industries are merely *compensating wage differentials* for these non-monetary aspects of the job?

There are two competing views. The first is that, after unions take over and raise wages, firms respond by taking advantage of unions to raise productivity. Work patterns are standardized and the union assists in implementing these new practices. Firms finance higher wages by making workers operate in less pleasant but more productive ways.

The alternative view is that the change in work practices is not an employer *response* to a successful union restriction of labour supply to raise wages, but rather the rationale for the union's existence. Unions emerge in industries where large productivity gains would result from the introduction of unpleasant working conditions. The union exists not to restrict labour supply in total, but to negotiate productivity gains, ensuring that workers receive proper compensating differentials for the unpopular changes in working practices that employers find it profitable to introduce. On this view, the unions do not make separate deals for pay and working conditions; rather, their role is to secure pay increases for changes in working conditions.

| Table 4-7 | Union wage differentials |

% extra for union in	1984	1990
Unskilled	10.5	7.5
Semi skilled	10.5	6.5
Skilled	3.5	1.5

Source: M. Stewart, 'Union wage differentials in an era of declining unionisation', *Oxford Bulletin of Economics and Statistics*, 1995.

[4] See M. Stewart, 'Union Wage Differentials, Product Market Influences and the Division of Rents', *Economic Journal*, 1990.

◼◼ recap

- Different workers get different pay. This reflects personal characteristics such as education, job experience, sex, race, and union status.

- Skills or human capital are the most important source of wage differentials. Human capital formation includes both formal schooling and on-the-job training. Workers with more education and training earn higher lifetime incomes.

- Skilled labour is relatively scarce because it is costly to acquire human capital. The investment decision for human capital involves comparing the present costs with the present value of extra income or other benefits in the future.

- Education is also a screening or signalling device, which indicates to employers the workers of innate ability.

- Under a third of the UK labour force now belongs to a trade union. Unions restrict the labour supply to firms or industries, thereby raising wages but lowering employment. Unions move firms up their demand curve for labour.

- Unions achieve a higher wage differential for their members the more inelastic the demand for labour and the more they are willing or able to restrict the supply of labour. However, some union wage differentials should be viewed as compensation unions have secured in return for changes in work practices that raise productivity but reduce the pleasantness of the job.

◼◼ key terms

◼◼ review questions

1 University-educated workers now earn a larger wage differential than in the 1960s. (a) What effect would this have on the incentive to go to university? Why? (b) Suppose it was shown that going to university added nothing to life-time income potential. Would anyone still go to university? Why?

2 A worker can earn £20 000 a year for the next 40 years. Alternatively, the worker can take three years off to go on a training course whose fees are £7000 per year. If the government provides an interest-free loan for this training, what future income differential per year would make this a profitable investment in human capital?

3 Suppose economists form a union and establish a certificate that is essential for practising economics. How would this help to raise the relative wage of economists? How would the union restrict entry to the economics profession?

4 Apprentices are typically paid low wages. Using the concept of human capital, explain this observation.

4-3 other input markets

Industry needs to increase its capital stock – its machinery, equipment, factory, and office buildings. The car industry has to invest to compete with heavily mechanized foreign producers, the steel industry has to modernize its capital equipment. We examine other factors of production with which labour must co-operate in the productive process. Some issues can be dealt with rather briefly. We have already studied how a firm chooses its production technique in the long run, when all factors can be freely varied, and we are already familiar with the concept of a factor's marginal product. These ideas carry over from the analysis of labour markets to the examination of markets for other factors of production.

Apart from the irreversible decision to acquire education and skills, many aspects of labour market behaviour can be conveniently analysed within a relatively short-run time horizon. Since it takes much longer to adjust other factor inputs, decisions about their use must necessarily take a longer view.

LEARNING OUTCOMES

When you have finished this section, you should understand

- the markets for inputs of capital and land

- distinguish flows over time and stocks measured at a point in time

- simultaneous analysis of the market for renting capital services and the market for buying new capital assets

- the concept of present values

- the difference between nominal and real interest rates

- how land is allocated between competing uses

Having completed our analysis of factor markets, we shall be able to discuss what determines the *income distribution* in an economy. The price of a factor multiplied by the total quantity of the factor employed gives us the earnings or income of that factor. We need to know the prices and quantities of all productive factors if we are to understand how the economy's total income is distributed.

> Physical capital *is the stock of produced goods that contribute to the production of other goods and services.*

The stock of physical capital includes the assembly line machinery used to make cars, railway lines that produce transport services, school buildings that produce education services, dwellings that produce housing services.

> Land *is the factor of production that nature supplies.*

Clearly, this distinction between land and capital can become blurred. By applying fertilizer to improve the soil balance, farmers can 'produce' better land. Because land and capital are sometimes hard to disentangle we discuss these two factors of production in the same chapter. Capital and land are both assets. They do not completely depreciate during the time period during which we examine production decisions by firms.

▪▪▪ physical capital

Table 4-8 shows the level and composition of physical capital in the UK in 1996. (Data on capital take a long time to collect!) 'Dwellings' are primarily owned by private individuals, but some is state owned. Productive fixed capital is plant, machinery and buildings. Inventories are stocks of manufactured goods awaiting sale, partially finished goods (work in progress), and raw materials held for future production. Inventories are capital because they are produced goods which contribute to future production.

The capital input to the production process is about three times the value of annual national output. Investment in physical capital is increasing the capital input to the UK's national production, not only in absolute terms but also relative to the number of workers employed. The economy is becoming more *capital-intensive*. Each worker has more capital with which to work. Because capital depreciates, it takes some investment in new capital goods merely to stand still.

Gross investment *is the production of new capital goods and the improvement of existing capital goods.* Net investment *is gross investment minus the depreciation of the existing capital stock.*

If net investment is positive, gross investment more than compensates for depreciation and the effective capital stock is increasing. However, very small levels of gross investment may fail to keep pace with depreciation and the capital stock will then be falling over time.

▬▬ rentals, interest rates, and asset prices

Table 4-9 emphasizes two crucial distinctions: between *stocks* and *flows*, and between *rental payments* and *asset prices*. The labour market trades a commodity called 'hours of labour services'. Strictly speaking, the hourly wage is the *rental payment* that firms pay to hire an hour of labour. There is no asset price for the durable physical asset called a 'worker' because modern societies do not allow slavery. Since capital can be bought and sold – there are markets for new and used capital – we shall have to be more careful.

Table 4-8	UK capital stock, 1996

	£bn	%
Dwellings	1192	34.0
Productive fixed capital	2144	61.2
Inventories	168	4.8
Total capital stock	3504	100.0

Source: ONS, *UK National Accounts 1998.*

Table 4-9	Stock and flow concepts

	Capital	Labour
Flow input to hourly production	Capital services	Labour services
Payment for flow	Rental rate (£/machine hour)	Wage rate (£/labour hour)
Asset price	£/machine	£/slave, if purchase allowed

A stock *is the quantity of an asset at point in time, such as 100 machines on 1 January 2000. A* flow *is the stream of services that an asset provides during a given interval. The cost of using capital services is the* rental rate *for capital. The* price of an asset *is the sum for which the stock can be purchased outright. By owning a capital asset the purchaser acquires title to the future stream of capital services that the stock will provide.*

Buying a car for £9000 entitles a household to a stream of future transport services. Buying a factory for £100 000 entitles the owner to a stream of future rental payments on the capital services that the factory provides. What will a purchaser be prepared to pay for a capital asset? The answer depends on the value of the rental payments that will be paid in the future for the capital services that the asset stock provides. We have to pay attention to the role of *time* and *interest payments*.

interest rates and present values

Suppose a lender makes a loan to a borrower. At the outset the borrower agrees to repay the initial sum (the principal) *with interest* at some future date. If the loan is £100 for one year at 10 per cent interest per annum, the borrower must repay £110 at the end of the year. The extra £10 (10 per cent of £100) is the interest cost of borrowing £100 for a year. *Interest rates* are usually quoted as a percentage per annum.

Suppose we lent £1 and re-lent the interest as it accrued. After one year we should have £1 plus an interest payment of £0.10. Re-lending the whole £1.10, we should have £1.21 by the end of the second year. The concept of *compound interest* reminds us that the absolute amount by which our money grows increases every year.

At 10 per cent interest per annum, £1 in year 0 is worth £1.10 in year 1 and £1.21 in year 2. Now let us ask the question the other way round. If we offered you £1.21 in two years' time, what sum today would be just as valuable? The answer is £1. If you had £1 today you could always lend it out to get exactly £1.21 in two years' time. Table 4-10 extends this general idea. If £1.21 in year 2 is worth £1 today, then £1 in year 2 must be worth £1/1.21 = £0.83 today. £0.83 today could be lent out at 10 per cent interest to accumulate to £1 in year 2. Similarly, £1 in year 1 is worth only £1/1.10 = £0.91 today.

The present value *of £1 at some future date is the sum that, if lent out today, would accumulate to £1 by that future date.*

The law of compound interest implies that lending £1 today accumulates to ever larger sums the further into the future we maintain the loan and re-lend the interest.

Table 4-10 Interest and present value (PV)

	Year		
	0	1	2
At 10% interest rate:			
value of £1 lent today in:	£1	£1.10	£1.21
PV of £1 earned in:	£1	£0.91	£0.83
At 5% interest rate:			
value of £1 lent today in:	£1	£1.05	£1.10
PV of £ earned in:	£1	£0.95	£0.91

Conversely, the present value of £1 earned at some future date becomes smaller the further into the future the date at which the £1 is earned.

The present value of a future payment also depends on the interest rate. The third row of Table 4-10 shows that a loan of £1 will accumulate less rapidly over time if the interest rate is lower. At 5 per cent interest a loan of £1 cumulates to only £1.10 after two years, compared with £1.21 after two years when the interest rate was 10 per cent in row 1. Hence the fourth row of Table 4-10 shows that the present value of £1 in year 1 or year 2 is larger when the interest rate is only 5 per cent than in the corresponding entry in row 2 where the interest rate is 10 per cent.

Using interest rates to calculate present values of future payments tells us the right way to add together payments at different points in time. For each payment at each date we calculate its present value. Then we add together the present values of the different payments. Now we see how the price of a capital asset should be related to the stream of future payments that will be earned from the capital services it provides. We calculate the present value of the rental payment earned by the asset in each year of its working life and add these present values together. This tells us what the asset is worth today. A useful way to understand the role of interest rates in present-value calculations is to realize that the interest rate represents the *opportunity cost* of the money used to buy the asset.

real and nominal interest rates: inflation and present values

 The nominal interest rate *tells us how many actual pounds will be earned in interest by lending £1 for one year. The* real interest rate *measures the return on a loan as the increase in goods that can be purchased rather than as the increase in the nominal or the money value of the loan fund.*

Box 4-6 | The future's orange, but the present was in the red

How would you like to start a company, make a loss of £229 million pounds in your first year of trading, and watch your share price rise on the stock market? Not a bad beginning.

The Financial Times (12 February 1997) reported that Orange, the mobile phone operator launched in the mid 1990s, 'claimed to have over-taken Vodaphone, the industry leader, in terms of quality, revenues per subscriber and customer churn' (the rate at which existing customers leave the network for bad debt or fraud). Because, like biotechnology, telecommunications seems to many a growth area, stock market analysts often forecast profits in the future even when a young company is making massive losses in its early years. 'Analysts forecast a pre-tax loss of about £150 million for 1997 and a small profit in the

following year' the *Financial Times* reported. Orange's share value is simply the present value of the stream of future profits that shareholders expect to receive. The share price is the present value divided by the total number of shares. Orange's shares rose 5 pence to £2.19 following the 1997 announcement of the £229 million loss, which was lower than the loss shareholders had been expecting! Since Orange's total share value was then £2.6 billion shareholders were obviously doing the present value calculations using expectations of some pretty big profits in the not too distant future.

Nor were they disappointed. By October 1999 Orange was worth £20 billion after a takeover by German competitor Mannesmann.

Suppose the nominal interest rate is 10 per cent and inflation is 6 per cent. By saving for a year, the number of goods we can purchase rises 4 per cent. That is the real interest rate

$$\text{Real interest rate} = \text{nominal interest rate} - \text{inflation rate}$$

To confirm this formula, let us try a second example. Nominal interest rates are 17 per cent and the inflation rate is 20 per cent. Real interest rates are *negative*. It is *costing* you to be a lender. The nominal interest you receive will not compensate for rises in the prices of goods you ultimately wish to purchase.

Table 4-11 shows data on nominal interest rates, inflation, and real interest rates over three decades. The table confirms the pattern found in many countries in many decades. Real interest rates are usually small and positive. Large changes in nominal interest rates occur specifically to offset large changes in inflation rates, preserving real interest rates in their normal range.

How does this distinction between nominal and real interest rates affect the calculation of present values? It is necessary to be consistent. To calculate the present value of a future payment expressed in nominal terms, we should use the discount factor based on the current nominal interest rate. However, if the future payment is expressed in real terms, we should use a discount factor based on the real interest rate.

▪▪▪▪ the demand for capital services

The analysis of the demand for capital services by an industry closely parallels the analysis of labour demand in Section 4-1. The rental rate for capital takes the place of the hourly wage rate. Each represents the cost of employing or using factor services. We emphasize the *use* of *services* of capital. The example to bear in mind is a firm renting a vehicle or leasing office space.

The marginal value product of capital *is the increase in the value of the firm's output when one more unit of capital services is used.*

Given the amounts of labour (and any other factor, such as land) that the firm employs, the marginal value product of capital *MVPK* declines as the amount of capital per worker increases. Although the firm's output price is fixed since it is competitive, the marginal physical product of capital is subject to diminishing returns.

Suppose the firm can rent units of capital at the rental rate R_0. We can think of this as the monthly payment for leasing an office. The firm will rent capital up to the point at which its marginal cost - the rental rate - equals its marginal value product. For a given price and quantity of other factors of production, *MVPK* is the firm's demand

Table 4-11	Nominal and real interest rates and inflation in the UK, 1966–99 (% per annum)							
	66	*71*	*76*	*81*	*85*	*91*	*95*	*99*
Nominal interest rate	6.9	8.9	14.4	13.8	10.6	10.8	6.4	6.0
Inflation rate	3.9	9.4	16.5	11.9	6.1	5.9	2.7	2.2
Real interest rate	3.0	−0.5	−2.1	1.9	4.5	4.9	3.7	3.8

Source: IMF, *International Financial Statistics.*

curve for capital services. For any rental rate we can read off the profit-maximizing level of capital services from the *MVPK* curve. This demand for capital services can be shifted outwards by: (1) an increase in its output price, which makes the marginal *physical* product of capital more valuable, (2) an increase in the level of other factors (chiefly labour), which makes capital more productive, and (3) a technical advance, which increases the physical productivity of capital for any given quantity of other factor inputs.

the industry demand curve for capital services

We need to add horizontally the *MVPK* curves of all firms facing the same rental for capital, but then recognize that higher industry output will bid down output prices and shift *MVPK* curves to the left. Thus the industry demand curve for capital services is steeper than the horizontal sum of each firm's *MVPK* curves. The more inelastic is the demand curve for the industry's output the more inelastic will be the industry's derived demand curve for capital services. Try drawing a diagram like figure 4-2, replacing wages and employment by rental rates and capital use.

■■■ the supply of capital services

Capital services are produced by capital assets. Owning or renting a machine allows a firm to use the input machine-hours. The economist's approach to capital is first to analyse the market for capital services used in production, then to consider what this implies for the market for machines themselves. In so doing, we usually assume that the flow of capital services is directly determined by the stock of capital assets such as machines.

the short-run supply of capital services

In the short run the total supply of capital assets (machines, buildings, and vehicles), and thus the services they provide, is fixed to the economy as a whole. It takes time to change the capital stock. New factories cannot be built overnight. For the whole economy, it makes sense to think of the supply curve of capital services as vertical at a quantity determined by the existing stock of capital assets.

Some types of capital are fixed even for the individual industry. The steel industry cannot change overnight its number of blast furnaces. However, some industries may be able to increase their supply of some types of capital, even in the short run. By offering a higher rental rate for delivery vans, the supermarket industry can attract a larger share of the total quantity of delivery vans that the economy currently possesses. For such types of capital services the industry faces an upward-sloping supply curve. By offering a higher rental rate the industry can increase the supply of delivery van services to that industry.

the supply of capital services in the long run

In the long run the total quantity of capital in the economy can be varied. New machines and factories can be built. Conversely, with no new investment in capital goods the existing capital stock will depreciate and be effectively reduced. Similarly, individual industries can adjust their stocks of capital.

The required rental on capital *is the rental rate that just covers the opportunity cost of owning the capital.*

Suppose you buy a machine to rent out as a business. The machine costs £10 000. If the annual interest rate is 10 per cent, you face an annual opportunity cost of £1000 just for the money tied up. You also know the machine depreciates in value every year, say by £500. The required rental would then be £1500 a year. In the long run, a given quantity of capital services is supplied to the economy only if it earns the required rental. If it earns more, people will build new capital goods. If it earns less, owners of capital will let their assets depreciate and not build new ones.

The long-run supply curve for the industry   Again, our discussion parallels the discussion of labour supply. The preceding analysis determines the supply of capital services to the whole economy. In the long run a very tiny industry can obtain as much of this capital as it wishes, provided it pays the going rental rate. A larger industry may have to pay an increasing rental rate per unit of capital services the larger the fraction of the economy-wide supply it wishes to attract. Thus an industry whose use of capital is significant relative to the whole economy will face an upward-sloping supply curve for capital services.

adjustment in the short and long run

Suppose competition from imports reduces the demand for domestically produced textiles. A lower output price shifts the derived demand curve for capital services to the left. Overnight, the supply of capital services is vertical, determined by previous investment in capital assets. The downward shift in the demand curve leads to a sharp drop in equilibrium rentals on textile machinery. But now machine owners are not getting the required rental. They stop building new machines, and depreciation gradually reduces the effective stock of existing machines. This makes capital services more scarce and bids up the rental. When enough machines have left the industry, one way or another, the rental climbs back to the required rental and long-run equilibrium has been reached. What do producers of new machines do in long-run equilibrium when the stock of machines is constant? They produce just enough new machines to cover depreciation of existing machines.

◼◼◼ land and rents

The distinguishing feature of land is that it is essentially in fixed supply to the whole economy even in the long run. This is not literally true. For example, the Dutch have been able to reclaim from the sea some areas of low-lying land. Similarly, fertilizers may enhance the effective input of land for farming. Nevertheless, it makes sense to think about a factor whose total long-run supply is fixed as a guide to the most important single feature on the market for land.

Figure 4-6 shows the derived demand curve for land DD exactly analogous to the derived demand for capital services. With a fixed supply the equilibrium rental per acre is R_0. An increase in the derived demand, for example because wheat prices have risen, leads only to an increase in the rental to R_1. The quantity of land services is fixed by assumption.

Consider a tenant farmer who rents land. Wheat prices have risen but so have rents. Not only may the farmer be no better off, but the connection between the two rises may not even be recognized. The farmer may complain that high rents are making it hard to earn a decent living. As in our discussion of footballers' wages, it is the high derived demand combined with the inelastic factor supply that cause the high payments for factor services.

Because land is traditionally viewed as *the* asset in fixed supply, economists have taken over the word 'rent', the payment for land services, to the concept of *economic rent*, the excess of actual payments over transfer earnings, which we introduced in Section 4-1.

Land can be used for crops, for grazing, for housing or offices, and even for building roads. How do land prices and land rentals guide the allocation of the fixed total supply between the different possible uses? Suppose there are two industries, housing and farming. Rentals must be equal in the two industries in the long run. Moreover, the rental must equate the fixed supply of land with the total quantity demanded.

Now suppose the government subsidizes housing. The demand for housing land shifts up. Landowners have an incentive to transfer land services from farming to housing, from which they now receive a higher rental. The new equilibrium again equalizes rentals earned in the two sectors while ensuring that the total quantity demanded equals the total quantity supplied. The housing subsidy increases general land rentals and leads farmers to economize on land until its marginal value product rises as much as rentals have.

Figure 4-6   The market for land services

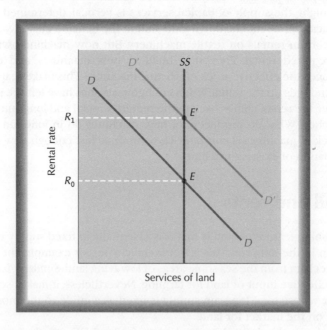

Table 4-12   Real fixed capital per worker, 1996 (£000 per worker, 1996 prices)

Energy and water	873
Agriculture, forestry, fishing	84
Manufacturing	107
Distribution, hotels, catering	39
Construction	14

Source: ONS, *UK National Accounts.*

What about land prices? The land price is the present value of this rental stream discounted at the going interest rate. When rentals rise or interest rates fall land prices increase.

▪▪▪ the facts

The economy is becoming more capital-intensive in its production techniques, a general phenomenon in industrial economies. How does the analysis of this section help us make sense of the facts? Table 4-12 shows UK data on capital intensity in different sectors in 1996. It shows the amount of fixed capital (productive capital minus inventories) per production worker in each sector. A modern power station or sewage plant can be run by a few technical supervisors who keep an eye on the computer screens. Although a large capital-intensive plant is expensive, it can produce a large output at low average cost. It would be much more expensive to produce the same output in a labour-intensive way. Thus it makes sense to choose very capital-intensive production techniques in the gas, electricity, and water industries.

Conversely, construction is very labour-intensive and capital per employee very low. Building a factory involves a number of different tasks that are not easily automated. Service industries such as restaurants, theatres, and hairdressing are also labour-intensive. Human contact and personal services cannot be reproduced by machines.

Why has capital intensity increased in every decade? First, the wage–rental ratio increased, leading industries to substitute capital for labour. In the long run the supply of labour is less elastic than the supply of capital, so real wages rise more than the real rental on capital. This change in relative factor rentals causes further substitution towards capital-intensive techniques. Second, the steady stream of new inventions led to technical advances in production methods. To take advantage of these improvements, firms have to install new capital that *embodies* the latest techniques. There is no point knowing that a breakthrough has been made in robot assembly-line technology unless the robot assembly is actually installed. Labour-saving inventions thus provide an incentive to introduce more capital-intensive methods.

▪▪▪ recap

- Physical capital comprises real assets yielding useful services to producing firms. The main categories are plant and machinery, buildings, and inventories.

- Present value calculations convert future receipts or payments into current values. Because lenders can earn – and borrowers must pay – interest over time, a pound tomorrow is worth less than a pound today. How much less depends on the interest rate. The higher the interest rate, the lower the present value of any future payment.

- Since lending or borrowing cumulates at compound interest, for any given annual interest rate the present value of a given sum is smaller the further into the future that sum is earned or paid.

- The real, or inflation-adjusted, interest rate measures the extra goods a lender can buy by lending for a year and delaying purchases of goods. The real rate of interest is the nominal interest rate minus the inflation rate over the same period.

- The demand for capital services is a derived demand. The firm's demand curve for capital services is its marginal value product of capital curve. Higher levels of the other factors of production and higher output prices shift the derived demand curve up. The industry demand curve is less elastic than the horizontal sum of each firm's curve because it also allows for the effect of an industry expansion in bidding down the output price.

- In the short run the supply of capital services is fixed. In the long run it can be adjusted by producing new capital goods or allowing the existing capital stock to depreciate.

- The required rental is the rental that allows a supplier of capital services to break even on the decision to purchase the capital asset. The required rental is higher the higher is the interest rate, the depreciation rate, or the purchase price of the capital good.

- The asset price is the price at which a capital good is bought and sold outright rather than rented. In long-run equilibrium it is both the price at which suppliers of capital goods are willing to produce and the price at which buyers are willing to purchase. The latter is merely the present value of anticipated future rentals earned from the capital services that the good provides in the future.

- Land is the special capital good whose supply is fixed even in the long run. However, land and capital can move between industries in the long run until rentals on land or on capital are equalized in different industries.

■■ key terms

■■ review questions

1 A bank offers you £1.10 next year for every £0.90 you give it today. What is the implicit interest rate?

2 Discuss the main determinants of the firm's demand curve and the industry's demand curve for capital services. How do these determinants affect the way a tax on the industry's output will shift the industry demand for capital services?

3 The interest rate falls from 10 to 5 per cent. Discuss in detail how this affects the rental on capital services and the level of the capital stock in an industry in the short and long run.

4 Suppose a plot of land is suitable only for agriculture. Can it be true that the farming industry will experience financial distress if there is an increase in the price of land? How would your answer be affected if the land could also be used for housing?

4-4 income distribution

The income of a factor is simply its rental rate multiplied by the quantity of the factor that is employed. In this final section we pull together our discussion of factor markets to examine the distribution of income in the UK.

the functional distribution of income

LEARNING OUTCOMES

When you have finished this section, you should understand

■ the functional distribution of income

■ the personal distribution of income

■ their relation to factor markets

The functional income distribution *shows the division of national income between the different factors of production.*

Table 4-13 shows the total earnings of the different factors of production in the UK in 1998 and compares their shares of national income with the shares they received during 1981–89. There has been relatively little change in the shares of the different factors of production over the last two decades. As the real incomes increased, the real incomes of the different factors of production broadly kept pace.

The aggregate labour supply curve to the economy is relatively inelastic. With an almost vertical labour supply curve, the total number of employed workers was little higher in 1998 than in 1981. The UK capital stock grew considerably faster than the UK labour force. With more capital to work with, labour's marginal product schedule shifted outwards and upwards. When confronted with an almost vertical labour supply curve, the consequence of this steady increase in the demand for labour was to increase the equilibrium real wage. And the combination of real wage growth and a slight increase in the labour force has increased real income from employment since 1981, though the share of income from employment in national income fell a little over this period.

The share of income from profits and rents grew slightly during 1981–98. The quantity of capital employed has been steadily rising, but at roughly the same rate as national output. Since the ratio of capital to output has been fairly constant, a relatively constant share of profits in national income suggests that the rate of return on capital has also been fairly constant over a long period. If the quantity of capital has increased without a permanent fall in its rate of return, the economy cannot simply have moved down a given marginal product of capital schedule; otherwise, the rental on

Table 4-13	UK functional income distribution, 1981–98 (% of national income)

Source (factor of production)	1981–89 average	1998
Employment	64.3	63.4
Self-employment	6.4	5.9
Profits and property rents	29.3	30.7

Source: ONS, *UK National Accounts.*

capital and its rate of return would have been reduced. Rather, the marginal product schedule must have shifted outwards. This was chiefly caused by technical progress.

We know that the supply of land is very inelastic and that the demand for land is a derived demand. As national income increases the derived demand curve for land will shift upwards. Thus it is not surprising that property rents have risen at least in line with national income.

■■■ the personal income distribution

The personal income distribution *shows how national income is divided between different individuals, regardless of the factor services from which these individuals earn their income.*

The personal income distribution is relevant to issues such as equality and poverty. Table 4-14 does not show people whose income is so low that the Inland Revenue do not need to record what their income actually is. Even confining our attention to people with sufficiently high pre-tax incomes that they may be liable for income tax, we can see that pre-tax income is quite unequally distributed in the UK. Looking at the bottom of Table 4-14, 9 per cent of all taxpayers earn 29 per cent of national income. Why should some people earn so much while others earn so little?

Unskilled workers have little training and low productivity. Workers with high levels of training and education earn much more. Some jobs, such as coal mining,

Table 4-14 UK personal income distribution, 1998

| Income range (£000) | Percentage of | |
	Taxpayers	National income
Under 8	24.6	8.6
8–12	23.0	13.7
12–15	13.6	10.9
15–20	15.6	16.2
20–30	14.6	21.3
30+	8.6	29.3

Based on 25 million taxpayers.

Source: ONS, *Social Trends*.

Table 4-15 UK wealth distribution

% of population	% of total wealth
Richest 1%	19
5%	38
10%	51
25%	73
50%	93

Source: ONS, *Social Trends, 1998.*

pay high compensating differentials to offset unpleasant working conditions. Very pleasant, but unskilled, jobs pay much less since many people are prepared to do them. Talented superstars in scarce supply but strong demand may earn very high economic rents.

However, Table 4-14 refers not just to income from the supply of labour services. A major reason why the distribution of personal income is so unequal is that the ownership of wealth, which provides income from profits and rents, is even more unequal. Table 4-15 shows details for the UK for 1994. The most wealthy 1 per cent of the population owns 19 per cent of the nation's marketable wealth and the most wealthy 25 per cent of the population own 73 per cent of the nation's marketable wealth. The stream of profit and rent income to which such wealth gives rise lays a large part in determining the personal distribution of pre-tax *income*.

Surely such an unequal distribution is unfair, and the government should intervene? This normative issue takes us beyond the positive economies studied in Chapters 2–4. Normative issues are what we discuss next.

■■■ recap

- The functional distribution of income between different inputs reflects equilibrium prices and quantities in input markets. Factor shares of national income are quite stable over time.

- The personal distribution of income shows how income is distributed across individuals, through whatever factor supply they earn this income.

- High incomes reflect ownership of attributes or assets in scarce supply and high demand. Markets do not produce equal equality across individuals.

- The bequest of wealth across generations perpetuates advantage and disadvantage. Across individuals, wealth is even more unequally distributed than income.

■■■ key terms

Functional income distribution	143
Personal income distribution	144

■■■ review questions

1 Name three taxes that help equalise the after-tax personal income distribution. Do any taxes have the opposite effect? Did you remember inferior goods?

2 If land is fixed in quantity and quality, can land rentals keep pace with other factor incomes in a growing economy?

3 'Brazil has an unequal personal income distribution. Suggest at least three reasons.

5 welfare economics

5-1 equity, efficiency, and market failure

LEARNING OUTCOMES

When you have finished this section, you should understand

■ horizontal equity and vertical equity

■ the concept of pareto efficiency

■ how the Invisible Hand might make free competitive markets efficient

■ why distortions lead to pure waste that reduce efficiency

■ why externalities lead to inefficiency, and how property rights can solve the problem

■ the market failures that give rise to pollution and congestion

■ other inefficiencies as further examples of missing markets, and explain why such markets fail to exist

In Chapter 1 we pointed out that markets are not the only way society can resolve what, how, and for whom to produce. Communist economies, for example, rely much more heavily on central direction or command. Are markets a good way to allocate scarce resources? What does 'good' mean? Is it fair that some people earn much more than others in a market economy? These are not positive issues about how the economy works but normative issues about how well it works. They are normative because the assessment will depend on the value judgements adopted by the assessor.

> Welfare economics *is the branch of economics dealing with normative issues. Its purpose is not to describe how the economy works but to assess how well it works.*

Left and right wing parties fundamentally disagree about how well a market economy works. The right believes the market fosters choice, incentives, and efficiency. The left stresses the market's failings and the need to supplement it with regulations to protect people from its consequences. How do we cut through the political rhetoric to see what lies behind the disagreement? Two themes recur throughout our discussion. The first is *allocative efficiency*. Is the economy getting the most out of its scarce resources or are they being squandered? The second is *equity*. How fair is the *distribution* of goods and services between different members of society?

equity and efficiency

Economists use two different concepts of equity or fairness.

> Horizontal equity *is the identical treatment of identical people.* Vertical equity *is the different treatment of different people in order to reduce the consequences of these innate differences.*

Horizontal equity would rule out racial or sexual discrimination between people whose economic characteristics and performance were literally identical. Vertical equity is the Robin Hood principle of taking from the rich to give to the poor. Whether or not either concept of equity is desirable is a pure value judgement.

An economy's *resource allocation* is a complete description of who does what and who gets what. Feasible allocations depend on available quantities of inputs and on technology, which affects the productivity of these inputs. The utility derived from any allocation depends on consumer tastes. We want to discuss efficiency and equity properties of various allocations. Equity will always involve value judgements, but it would be nice to keep such judgements as far as possible out of efficiency evaluations. Nearly a century ago, Vilfredo Pareto suggested a definition that he hoped would do this.

> *For a given set of tastes, inputs, and technology, an allocation is* Pareto-efficient *if it is impossible to make one person better off without making at least one other person worse off.*

Suppose there are only two people, Stan and Rudi, and that it is feasible to make up to 10 units of a single good. Any allocation making and distributing less than 10 goods is wasting resources. It is Pareto-inefficient. A free lunch is available. Society could make more goods and give them to either Stan or Rudi (or indeed to both).

Now suppose Stan and Rudi each get 5. To give Stan more, we have to give Rudi less. So giving 5 to each is Pareto-efficient. Notice, however, that *any* distribution using all 10 goods is Pareto-efficient. 10 for Stan and 0 for Rudi is efficient, so too 9 for Stan and 1 for Rudi. Where these various allocations differ is on the equity criterion: 5 for each is more equitable than 10 for Rudi and 0 for Stan. Confronted with an initial allocation of 7 for Rudi and 3 for Stan, suppose it was possible to even things up a bit but only at the cost of losing some goods. Suppose 4 each was possible. This is inefficient but many people would think it more equitable. But is it worth sacrificing 2 goods for Stan to gain 1 for Rudi? Reasonable people will disagree on the answer.

perfect competition and Pareto efficiency

Will a free market economy find a Pareto-efficient allocation 'as if by an Invisible Hand' as Adam Smith first claimed. The remarkable answer is that, under certain conditions, a perfectly competitive economy would indeed be Pareto-efficient. Here is why.

Each consumer voluntarily buys goods until the marginal cost to himself (the price of the good) equals the marginal utility or marginal benefit to himself. The demand curve shows how much consumers buy. Hence at each quantity in Figure 5-1 we can think of the height of the demand curve *DD* as showing the marginal benefit to consumers of getting that quantity of films and devoting the rest of their resources to other goods. Perfectly competitive producers equate price to marginal cost. Hence, at each quantity in Figure 5-1 the height of the supply curve *SS* shows the marginal cost of making that quantity of the good. Economic cost is opportunity cost. So this marginal cost is what consumers could have had instead.

Suppose the economy produces Q_1 films. The marginal benefit to consumers is P_1 well above the marginal cost to producers which is also the marginal benefit of what the resources are producing elsewhere. Society wants more films than Q_1. Where supply and demand intersect, the marginal benefit to society P^* of using resources to make films is identical to the marginal benefit P^* of switching the same resources to make goods elsewhere (giving up this marginal benefit is precisely what the marginal opportunity cost tells us). So no free lunch is available by reallocating resources. The allocation is efficient. Yet no government controller had to make this decision. Each consumer simply pursued her self-interest, buying as much as made sense, and each producer did likewise, making and selling as much as maximized profits. Who made sure that producers and consumers were co-ordinated? Prices did. It was because producers and consumers faced the *same* price that their separate decisions all squared up efficiently.

What about the Invisible Hand? First, we have said nothing about equity. The resulting allocation may well be very unequal as the talented are rewarded more highly than the disadvantaged. The argument is confined to efficiency. Economists feel more comfortable discussing efficiency, where things can be proved by analysis, rather than equity, where every citizen is ultimately entitled to her own opinion. It would be very nice to be able to use the market to achieve efficiency and then confine government activity to redistribution to accomplish the desired degree of equity. However, this is not as easy as it sounds.

Understanding why the Invisible Hand may achieve an efficient allocation also allows us to see how different links in the chain may break down. First, marginal utility to the self-interested cigarette smoker may not be the same as society's marginal valuation of that cigarette. Second, consumers and producers may face *different* prices, for example because goods are taxed; there is then no reason for the market to equate the relevant marginal behaviour of buyers and seller. Third, producers may have monopoly power, so that prices no longer equal their marginal costs and hence

---

Figure 5-1   Competitive equilibrium and Pareto-efficiency

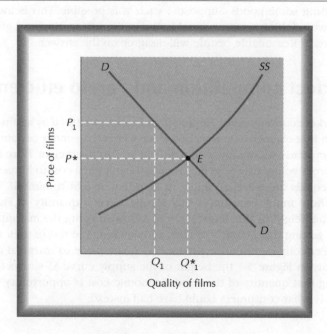

the goods society could have had instead. We examine these and other distortions next.

Second, the act of using taxes and other measures to redistribute in pursuit of equity may itself introduce new distortions, by widening the gap between the price consumers pay and the price producers receive. It is precisely these ambiguities – about the efficiency of the market and about the efficiency cost of redistribution – that make it hard for society to resolve the appropriate degree of reliance on the Invisible Hand unassisted by government intervention.

▰▰▰ distortions and the second best

A distortion *exists whenever society's marginal cost of producing a good does not equal society's marginal benefit from consuming that good.*

taxation as a distortion

Suppose the government wishes to subsidize the poor. To pay for these subsidies the government must tax the rich by taxing the incomes of rich people or the goods that rich people buy. A tax causes a discrepancy between the price the purchaser pays and the price the seller receives. Suppose there is an income tax. Firms equate the marginal value of labour to the gross wage rate, but suppliers of labour equate the after-tax wage rate to the marginal value of the leisure that they sacrifice to work another hour. The income tax ensures that the marginal value product of labour, society's benefit from another hour of work, now exceeds the marginal value of the leisure being sacrificed in order to work. Again this is inefficient.

We can now pose the choice between efficiency and equity in a stark form. If the economy is perfectly competitive, and if the government is happy the distribution of income is equitable, the government need raise no taxes. Perfectly competitive free market equilibrium then allocates resources efficiently. However, if as a pure value judgement the government considers that this distribution of income-earning potential is inequitable, the very act of raising taxes introduces a *distortion*. The resulting equilibrium in the economy is allocatively inefficient.

What should the government do? The answer depends a good deal on the value judgements of the government in power. The more it dislikes the income distribution thrown up by the free market, a distribution reflecting differences in innate ability, human capital, and financial wealth, the more the government is likely to judge that the inefficiency costs of distortionary taxes are a price worth paying to secure a more equitable distribution of income and utility. Conversely, the more the government feels able to tolerate the income distribution thrown up in a free market economy, the more it can resist distortionary taxation and allow competitive free markets to allocate resources as efficiently as possible.

Thus one explanation for the differing attitudes to the market economy is a difference in value judgements about equity. Caricaturing the argument so far, the right supports a free enterprise economy because it considers the most important objective is to maximize the size of the national cake by allocating resources as efficiently as possible. The left supports considerable state intervention because it considers that it is more important to divide the cake more fairly, even if this means having more allocative inefficiency and a smaller cake to share out.

But this is only part of the disagreement. The pursuit of equity through redistribution taxation is not the only distortion that can lead to allocative inefficiency. We consider distortions in the next section. Before leaving our tax example, there is one final point to make.

the second best

When there are no distortions the efficient allocation is first best. *When some distortions cannot be removed, the most efficient of the remaining allocations is called* second best.

If only one distortion remains, eliminating it will achieve the first best or fully efficient allocation. However, and crucially, when more than one distortion exists, removing only one distortion may actually make things worse! Removing all the remaining distortions together would be unambiguously beneficial for efficiency since we could get to the first best. All partial removals of distortions need to be examined on a case by case basis. Sometimes they help, sometimes they don't.

Imagine you were in a large room with two tigers. The tigers are distortions that threaten the efficiency of your lifetime. You are very scared. However, the tigers are pretty preoccupied with each other. Now one of the two tigers dies. The other tiger has nothing to think about except you. Are you better or worse off by the removal of one of the two distortions?

The point is that distortions sometimes offset each other. We always want rid of them all if this is an option. But partial 'improvement' may actually make things worse. Or it may not. Generally, partial removal of weeds from a garden makes it look better. What you need to remember is it all depends on the particular example. The theory of the second best is a really important insight. It says that well meaning intervention can make things worse if the situation has not been analysed and understood properly. It is the systemic effect not the localized effect that counts. One corner may now be without a tiger, but we need to look at the whole room to get the right answer.

■■■ market failure

We use the term *market failure* to cover all the circumstances in which equilibrium in free unregulated markets will fail to achieve an efficient allocation. Market failure describes the circumstances in which distortions prevent the Invisible Hand from allocating resources efficiently.

We now list the possible sources of distortions that lead to market failure.

1 ***Imperfect competition*** It is perfect competition that leads firms to set marginal cost equal to price and thus to marginal consumer benefit. Under imperfect competition, producers set marginal cost equal to marginal revenue, which is less than the price. Therefore, marginal benefit will exceed marginal cost in imperfectly competitive industries. Such industries will tend to produce too little. Expanding output would add more to consumer benefit than it would to production costs or the opportunity cost of the resources used.

2 ***Social priorities such as equity*** Redistributive taxation in the pursuit of equity induces allocative distortions by driving a wedge between the price the consumer pays and the price the producer receives.

3 ***Externalities*** Externalities are things like pollution, noise, and congestion. What they have in common is that one person's actions have direct costs or benefits for other people which that individual does not take into account. The problem arises because there is neither a market nor a market price for things like noise. Hence we cannot expect markets and prices to ensure that the marginal benefits of making a noise are equated to the marginal cost of that noise to other people.

4   *Other missing markets: future goods, risk, and information*   These are further examples of commodities for which markets are absent or limited. We cannot expect markets to allocate resources efficiently if the markets do not exist.

▰▰ externalities

An externality *arises whenever an individual's production or consumption decision directly affects the production or consumption of others other than through market prices.*

Suppose a chemical firm discharges waste into a lake, polluting the water and directly imposing an additional production cost on anglers (fewer and smaller fish) or a consumption cost on swimmers (less pleasant swimming). If there is no 'market' for pollution, the firm can pollute the lake without cost. Its self-interest will lead it to pollute until the marginal benefit of polluting (a cheaper production process for chemicals) equals its own marginal cost of polluting, which is zero. It takes no account of the marginal cost its pollution imposes on anglers and swimmers.

Box 5-1	Rent-seeking

In America, lobbyists catch the early morning plane to Washington DC. In Europe, they find their way to Brussels. Over expense-account lunches, the business of persuasion is conducted. What does all this have to do with the efficiency of the economy?

Suppose a lecturer walks into a class and deposits on the table an open suitcase in which you can all see £10 000 in used banknotes. She gives a brilliant class for an hour, but nobody is listening. All the students are working out if there is any way they can make off with the loot. Nor are they likely to be co-operating. Ian Ironfists is chiefly worried about how to stop his main rival Sam Slugger. Indeed, Ironfists and Slugger can be observed in the lecture parting with their own hard-earned cash to assemble rival teams of students to fight the inevitable lunchtime battle for the suitcase. Micro-economic theory absorbed during the hour's lecture? Zero.

Sources of inefficiency? First, the lecturer's time was *wasted*. Second, at the beginning of the class, society has one suitcase with £10 000, plus the loose change in people's pockets that became used to pay for lunchtime mercenaries. At the end of the lunchtime fight, society will still have one suitcase, £10 000, and some loose change. Total increase in

goods and services as a result of the morning's effort? Nothing. It was a zero-sum game that had no net value added for society. The prospect of *economic rent* or pure surplus – a suitcase worth £10 000 – has led the students to spend their valuable resources (cash in their pocket, time that could have been spent learning more economics) trying to compete for and capture the jackpot.

While government intervention in the economy to offset market failures can, in principle, improve efficiency, intervention can also create opportunities for rent-seeking. Suppose the government regulates the award of franchises to operate railway lines or TV stations. Rival bidders may use up huge amounts of real resources trying to outdo one another. Privately, being in the winning team is so important that it is worth spending a lot to increase your team's chances of winning. But socially it may be close to a zero-sum game. One supplier of railway services or TV programming may be scarcely any better than the other. Where society decides that some form of intervention is necessary to combat market failure, it should still give considerable thought to how to design intervention to minimize government failure. Substantial rent-seeking is one channel through which such government failure may occur.

Conversely, by painting your house you make the whole street look nicer and give consumption benefits to your neighbours. But you paint only up to the point on which your own marginal benefit equals the marginal cost of the paint you buy and the time you spend. Your marginal costs are also society's marginal costs, but society's marginal benefits exceed your own: there is too little housepainting.

In both cases there is a divergence between the individual's comparison of marginal costs and benefits and society's comparison of marginal costs and benefits. Free markets cannot induce people to take account of these indirect effects on other people if there is no market in these indirect effects. At small levels of chemical output, pollution is negligible. The river can dilute the small amounts of pollutant discharged by the chemical producer. But as the discharge rises the costs of pollution rise sharply. Food processers must worry about the purity of their water intake and build expensive purification plants. Still higher levels of pollution start to corrode pipes and contaminate agricultural land.

Figure 5-2 shows the marginal private cost *MPC* of producing chemicals. For simplicity, we assume that *MPC* is constant. It also shows the marginal *social cost MSC* of chemical production. The divergence between marginal private cost and marginal social cost reflects the marginal cost imposed on other producers by an extra unit of the *production externality* of pollution that the chemical producer disregards. The demand curve *DD* shows how much consumers are willing to pay for the output of the chemical producer. If that producer acts as a price-taker, equilibrium is at *E* and the chemical producer's output is *Q* at which the marginal private cost equals the price received by the firm for its output.

However, at this output *Q* the marginal social cost *MSC* exceeds the marginal social benefit of chemicals as given by the corresponding point on the demand curve *DD*. The market for chemicals takes no account of the production externality inflicted on other firms. Since at the output *Q* the marginal social benefit of the last output unit is

| Figure 5-2 | The social cost of a production externality |

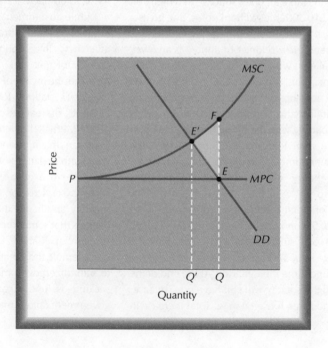

less than the marginal social cost inclusive of the production externality, the output Q is not socially efficient. By reducing the output of chemicals society would save more in social cost than it would lose in social benefit. It would allow society to make some people better off without making anyone worse off.

In fact the socially efficient output is Q', at which the marginal social benefit of the last output unit equals is marginal social cost. E' is the efficient point. How much does society lose by producing at the free market equilibrium E rather than at the socially efficient point E'? The vertical distance between the marginal social cost MSC and the marginal social benefit as given by DD shows the marginal social loss of producing the last output unit. Hence, by expanding from Q' to Q, society loses a total amount equal to the triangle $E'EF$ in Figure 5-2. This measures the social cost of the market failure caused by the production externality of pollution.[1]

Production externalities lead to a divergence between marginal private production costs and marginal social production costs. Similarly, a consumption externality leads to a divergence between marginal private benefits and marginal social benefits. Suppose you plant roses in your front garden. There are no production externalities. The marginal private cost and the marginal social cost of making your garden look nicer are the same, the cost of the plants plus the opportunity cost of your time. Comparing your own costs and benefits, you will decide how nice to make your garden. But you do not take account of the consumption value these improvements have for your neighbours. Since these are benefits too, the marginal social benefit MSB is greater than your marginal private benefit. Hence, from society's viewpoint, you do too little gardening.

property rights and externalities

Suppose your neighbour's tree grows into your garden, obscuring your light and giving you a harmful consumption externality. If the law says that you must be compensated for any damage suffered, your neighbour will either have to pay up or cut back the tree. Your neighbour really likes the tree and wants to know how much it would take to compensate you to leave the tree at its current size. Figure 5-3 shows the marginal benefit MB that your neighbour gets from the last inch of tree size and the marginal cost MC to you of that last inch of tree size. At the tree's current size S_1 the total cost to you is the area $OABS_1$. You simply take the marginal cost OA of the first inch, then add the marginal cost of the second inch, and so on till you get to the existing size S_1. The area $OABS_1$ is what you require in compensation if the tree size is S_1.

Your neighbour is about to pay up this amount. But he has a daughter studying economics. She points out that at the size S_1 the marginal benefit of the last inch is less than the marginal cost to you, which is also the amount you must be compensated for that last inch on the tree. It is not worth your neighbour having a tree this big. Nor, she points out, is it worth cutting the tree down altogether. A tiny tree has little effect on your light and makes the garden next door look nicer.

[1] Conversely, some production externalities have beneficial effects on other producers. A farmer who spends money on pest control on his or her property may reduce the cost of pest control on neighbouring farms. When production externalities are beneficial the marginal social cost will lie *below* the marginal private cost. Suppose we re-label the MSC curve as MPC in Figure 5-2 and re-label the MPC curve as MSC. Free market equilibrium will then occur at E' but E will now be the socially efficient allocation.

At the efficient allocation or tree size S^* the marginal benefit to your neighbour equals the marginal cost to you. Above S^* the neighbour cuts back the tree since the marginal cost (and compensation) exceeds the marginal benefit. Below S^* he or she increases the tree size and pays the marginal compensation that is less than the marginal benefit. At the efficient size S^* your total cost is the area $OAES^*$ and this is the compensation you will be paid. Notice that since a larger tree benefits one party but hurts the other party, *the efficient tree size and efficient quantity of the externality will not be zero.* Rather, it occurs where the marginal benefit equals the marginal cost.

Property rights *are the power of residual control of an asset, including the right to be compensated for externalities.*

First, they affect who compensates whom. They have a distributional implication. Suppose there was no law requiring compensation. It would be worth you paying to have the tree cut back as far as S^* but no further. Beyond that size, you pay more in compensation for the loss of marginal benefit than you save yourself in reduced cost of the externality. So you would pay your neighbour a *total* of EDS_1S^* to compensate for the loss of benefit in cutting the tree back from S_1 to S^*.

Property rights thus have a distributional implication – who compensates whom – but also act to achieve the socially efficient allocation. They implicitly set up the 'missing market' for the externality. The market ensures that the price equals the marginal benefit and the marginal cost, and hence equates the two. Property rights are a way to 'internalize' the externality. If people must pay for it they will take its effects into account in making private decisions and there will no longer be market failure. Why then do externalities like congestion and pollution remain a problem?

There are two obvious reasons why it may be hard to set up this market. The first is the cost of organizing the market. If a factory chimney dumps smoke on a thousand gardens nearby it may be very expensive to collect £1 from each household to bribe the factory to cut back to the socially efficient amount. Second, there is the *free-rider* problem.

Figure 5-3   Property rights

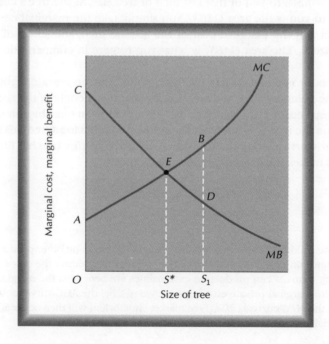

A free-rider, *recognizing that he cannot be excluded from consuming a good, has no incentive to offer to purchase it.*

Suppose someone knocks on your door and says: 'I am collecting bribes from people who mind the factory smoke falling on their gardens. The money I collect will be paid to bribe the factory to cut back. Do you wish to contribute? I am going round 5000 houses in the neighbourhood.' Whether you mind or not, you say: 'I don't mind and won't contribute.' Provided everybody else pays, the factory will cut back and you cannot be prevented from getting the benefits. The smoke will not fall exclusively on your garden merely because you alone did not pay up. Regardless of what other people contribute, there is no incentive for you to contribute: you are a *free-rider*. But everyone else will reason similarly; hence no one will pay, even though you would all have been better off paying and getting the smoke cut back.

▪▪▪ environmental issues

When, for either reason, there is no implicit market for pollutants, there will be over-production of pollutants. Because private producers fail to take account of the costs they impose on others, in equilibrium social marginal cost will exceed social marginal benefit.

If the private sector cannot organize charges for the marginal externalities pollution creates, perhaps the government can? By charging (through taxes) for the divergence between marginal private and social cost, the government could then induce private producers to take account of the costs inflicted on others. This argument for government intervention through taxes is examined in the next chapter. Pollution taxes, especially for water pollution, have been used in France, Italy, Germany, and the Netherlands. But most policy takes a different approach, the imposition of pollution standards that regulate the maximum amount of allowed pollution.

pollution

Since the Clean Air Act of 1956, UK governments have designated clean air zones in which certain types of pollution, notably the smoke caused by burning coal, are illegal. The number of designated clean air zones has increased steadily. Smoke pollution in the UK fell from 2 million tonnes in 1958 to 0.4 million tonnes in 1995. Since 1972 the UK government has steadily reduced the quantity of lead permitted in petrol. Lead emission from vehicles fell by over 80 per cent during 1975-96, even though consumption of petrol rose dramatically.

Since 1951 governments in the UK have imposed increasingly stringent controls on discharges into inland waters. Although we tend to think of *industrial* effluent, sewage is a more important source of pollution. Since 1970 regional water authorities in England and Wales spent (at 1997 prices) an annual average of £3 billion on water purification and sewage treatment. This expenditure was only moderately successful in reducing water pollution. By the late 1980s an even more important problem had been recognized: water pollution from nitrates used as fertilizers on agricultural land. The European Union has laid down tough standards for water purity which will take many years to achieve.

evaluating pollution policy in the UK

Direct regulation of pollution has met with mixed success over the last 30 years. In some cases, for example, the smoke pollution which used to be acute in winter when smoke and fog mixed to produce dense 'smog', tougher standards have led to dramatic improvements in environmental quality. Many rivers are also cleaner, and fish have reappeared.

In other cases, governments have tried to regulate but often been ineffective; it is hard to enforce regulations such as those that prevent ships discharging oil at sea. In yet other cases there has been little attempt to intervene. For example, coal-fired power stations continue to emit large quantities of sulphur dioxide, which the high chimneys are only partially successful in dispersing. And ecologists continue to oppose government policies that allow new coal mines in previously green country-side, or permit the disposal of nuclear waste at sea.

Has the government been tough enough on polluters? Recall that the efficient quantity of pollution is not zero. The fact that pollution still exists is not sufficient to establish that policy has not been tough enough. Where pollution control has been attempted it has usually been crude and simple. Calculations of the social marginal costs and benefits of cutting back pollution tend to be conspicuous by their absence. In part this reflects the difficulty in measuring costs and benefits. Even if doctors were

---

Box 5-2   Acid rain: a bitter controversy

Gases such as sulphur dioxide and oxides of nitrogen are discharged into the atmosphere, dissolved in water vapour, and fall as acid rain. Acid rain poisons fish, destroys forests, and corrodes buildings. The following table shows data for European emissions of sulphur.

It reveals the appalling pollution in Eastern Europe and the ex-USSR, mainly from power stations fuelled by low-grade coal. In Western Europe, the UK is a big exporter of acid rain: prevailing winds blow it east, and Scandinavia is a big loser. It needs a concerted European policy, perhaps even with transfer payments between governments, to deal with externalities across national borders.

Europe is trying to agree a 20 per cent cut in sulphur dioxide emissions and a freeze on emissions of oxides of nitrogen (mainly from car exhausts). But when different countries face a different marginal cost of pollution abatement, and inflict different amounts of marginal damage (polluting unpopulated areas is less costly than polluting densely populated areas), equal cutbacks for all is not the efficient solution. For a given over-all reduction, the efficient solution equates the marginal net benefit (damage reduction minus abatement cost) across different polluters. The following table shows estimates by Professor David Newbery of Cambridge University of the efficient way to achieve a 30 per cent reduction in sulphur dioxide emissions in Europe.

| Sulphur emissions | Million tonnes a year | |
	Produced	Received
E. Europe	6.6	3.7
UK	1.3	0.7
France, Italy, W. Germany	2.3	2.1
Ex-USSR in Europe	2.6	3.5
Scandinavia	0.1	0.5
Other Europe	2.6	3.1

Note: 2 million tonnes received cannot be traced to any particular emitting country.

Efficient cuts in sulphur dioxide emissions (%) (selected countries)

Belgium	69	Austria	16
Holland	65	Spain	10
France	40	Hungary	8
UK	31	Poland	3
Italy	27	Norway	3
Denmark	18	Ex-USSR	3

D. Newbery, 'Acid Rain', *Economic Policy*, October 1990.

unanimous about the effects of lead emission on health, how should society value a marginal increase in the health of current and future generations?

This is not merely a question of efficiency, which we might answer by considering the resources tied up in looking after the sick or the extra output that healthier workers could produce. It is also a question of equity, both within the current generation – poor inner-city children may be most vulnerable to arrested development caused by inhaling lead-polluted air – and across generations.

prices versus quantities

If free markets tend to overpollute, society can reduce pollution either by regulating the quantity of pollution (as it does) or by using the price system to discourage such activities by taxing them. Would it be more sensible to intervene through the tax system than to regulate quantities directly? If each firm were charged the same price or tax for a marginal unit of pollution, every firm would equate the marginal cost of reducing pollution to the price of pollution. Any allocation in which different firms have different marginal costs of reducing pollution is socially inefficient.

However, there are two important qualifications to this argument. First, it would be necessary to monitor the quantity of pollution of each firm in order to assess its tax liability. Second, in order to assess the tax rate or charge for pollution it would still be necessary to calculate the overall costs and benefits of marginal changes in the amount of pollution. If the government has to make a decision on the socially efficient level of pollution anyway, it may be simpler to regulate the quantity directly.

Finally, there is the issue of the uncertainty. Suppose pollution beyond a certain critical level has disastrous consequences, for example irreversibly damaging the ozone layer. By regulating the quantity directly it is at least possible to ensure that the disaster is avoided. Indirect control through taxes or charges runs the risk that the government might do its sums wrong and set the tax too low. Thus, regulating the total quantity of pollution may avoid the worst outcomes. However, by ignoring differences in the marginal cost of reducing pollution across different polluters, it does not reduce pollution in the manner that is cost-minimizing to society. There is no simple answer in an uncertain world.

lessons from the United States

The United States has gone furthest in trying to use property rights and the price mechanism to cut back pollution in a manner that is economically efficient. The US Clean Air Acts (1955, 1970, 1977) have established an environmental policy that includes an *emissions trading programme* and *bubble policy*.

The Acts lay down a minimum standard for air quality, and impose pollution emission controls to particular polluters. Any polluter emitting less than their specified amount obtains an *emission reduction credit (ERC)*, which can be sold to another polluter which wants to go over its allocated pollution limit. Thus, the total quantity of pollution is regulated, but firms that can cheaply reduce pollution have an incentive to do so, and sell off the *ERC* to firms for which pollution reduction is more expensive. In this way we get closer to the efficient solution in which the marginal cost of pollution reduction is equalized across firms.

When a firm has many factories, the bubble policy applies pollution controls to the firm as a whole rather than individual factories. The firm can cut back most in the plants in which pollution reduction is cheapest. Thus, the US policy manages to combine 'control over quantities' for aggregate pollution, where the risks and uncertainties are greatest, with 'control through the price system' for allocating efficiently the way these overall targets are achieved.

▪▪ other missing markets: risk and insurance

When externalities exist, free market equilibrium is inefficient because the externality itself does not have a market or a price. People take no account of the costs and benefits their actions inflict on others. Without a market for externalities the price system cannot bring marginal costs and marginal benefits of these externalities into line. In this section we discuss another 'missing market'.

There is a limited set of *contingent* or insurance markets for dealing with risk. In Chapter 2 we argued that people typically dislike risk. Risk is costly to individuals because it reduces their utility. But does society undertake the efficient amount of risky activities? A complete set of insurance markets allows risk to be transferred from those who dislike risk to those who will bear risk at a price. The equilibrium price or insurance premium would equate the marginal cost and marginal benefit of risk-bearing. The price system would equate social marginal costs and benefits of risky activities. However, problems of adverse selection and moral hazard inhibit the

---

Box 5-3   A lot of hot air?

Chlorofluorocarbons (CFCs) are gases used in things like aerosols. They may destroy the ozone layer that protects the earth from the sun's rays. Without this sunscreen, more people will get skin cancer. But organizing international cutbacks in atmospheric pollution is difficult: each country is tempted to act as a free-rider, enjoying the benefits of other countries' reductions but making no contribution of its own.

The greenhouse effect arises from emissions of CFCs, methane, nitrous oxide and, especially, carbon dioxide. Plants convert carbon dioxide into oxygen. Chopping down forests to clear land for cattle, as the world demand for hamburgers increases, may be good business in the short run, but has a significant effect on the long-run cumulation of greenhouses gases.

The consequence is global warming. People in London and Stockholm get better suntans; people in Africa face drought and famine; and, as icecaps melt, the sea-level rises, flooding low-lying areas. As with acid rain and CFCs, organizing collective international cutbacks has proved difficult because of the free-rider problem.

In 1997 the Kyoto Protocol finally agreed national targets for lower emissions of greenhouse gases. Becoming binding in 2008–12, the agreement will cut emissions by 5 per cent relative to the 1990 level, but by much more relative to the

growth that a do-nothing policy would have allowed. The table below shows 1990 levels, actual behaviour in the 1990s, and the target for 2012. The targets shown in the table are partly the outcome of political compromise. However, in practice different countries face different marginal costs of abatement (cutbacks). It would therefore be more efficient to issue pollution licences and allow these to be traded. Producers facing large marginal costs of cutbacks could buy licences from producers quite happy to do an above-average share of abatement because they face low marginal costs of abatement. By choosing the number of licences, the overall target can be met. By allowing trading in licences, the cutbacks can be allocated to those who can bear them most cheaply.

	1990 emissions (million tonnes)	Change 1990–95 (%)	2012 target (relative to 1990) (%)
Japan	1190	+8	−6
USA	5713	+5	−7
Germany	1204	−12	−21
UK	715	−9	−12
Italy	532	+2	−6
France	498	0	0
Spain	301	+2	+15

organization of private insurance markets. If some risky activities are uninsurable at any price, the price system cannot guide society to equate social marginal costs and benefits.

moral hazard

Insurance companies employ actuaries to calculate the average or statistical chances for aggregate behaviour. They work out how many houses per million will have a fire next year. Since fires in different houses are independent risks, we expect insurance firms to be able to pool the risk over a large number of clients and charge low premiums for fire insurance.

You are sitting in a restaurant and remember you left your car unlocked. Do you abandon your nice meal and rush outside to lock it? You are less likely to if you know the car is fully insured against theft. With full health insurance you are less likely to bother about precautionary check-ups. If the act of insuring increases the likelihood of the occurrence of the thing you wish to insure against, we call this the problem of *moral hazard*.

> Moral hazard *is the exploiting of inside information to take advantage of the other party to the contract.*

Actuarial calculations for the whole population, many of whom are uninsured and will take greater care, are no longer a reliable guide to the risks the insurance company faces and the premiums it should charge. Moral hazard makes it harder to get insurance and more expensive when you do get it. Frequently insurance companies will insure your property only up to a certain percentage of its replacement cost. They will take a large part of the risk, but you will still be worse off if the nasty thing happens. The company is providing you with an incentive to take care and hold down the chances of the nasty thing happening. On average, they pay out less frequently and can charge you lower premia.

adverse selection

Suppose some people smoke cigarettes but others do not. People who smoke are more likely to die young. Individuals know whether they themselves smoke, but suppose the insurance company cannot tell the difference and must charge all clients the same premium rate for life assurance.

Suppose the premium is based on mortality rates for the nation as a whole. People who do not smoke know they have an above-average life expectancy and will find the premium too expensive. Smokers know their life expectancy is lower than the national average and realize that the premium is a bargain. Even though the insurance company cannot tell the difference between the two groups, it can work out that if it charges the premium based on the national average it will attract only smokers and will pay out more than it expected.

> Adverse selection *occurs when individuals use their inside information to accept or reject a contract, so that those who accept are not an average sample of the population.*

One solution is to assume that all clients are smokers and charge the correspondingly high premium to all clients. Non-smokers find it impossible to get insurance at what they believe is a reasonable price. They might be able to volunteer a medical examination in an attempt to prove they are low-risk clients who should be charged a lower price. Medical examinations are in fact compulsory for many insurance contracts now.

To check that you understand the difference between moral hazard and adverse selection, say which is which in the following examples. (1) A person with a fatal disease signs up for life insurance. (2) Reassured by the fact that he took out life assurance to protect his dependants, a person who has unexpectedly become depressed decides to commit suicide. (The first was adverse selection, the second moral hazard.)

One final example before we move on. Borrowers themselves know whether they are high risk or low risk, but suppose it is expensive for lenders to discover which. To cover low risks, the bank can safely lend at 5 per cent interest. To cover high risks, it should lend at 15 per cent. All it knows is that the population has equal numbers of high and low risk borrowers. Since the bank manager can't tell people apart, she decides to charge 10 per cent to everyone. Low risk people don't bother to show up for a loan. The bank's terms are unfair for them. High risk people appear in droves to take advantage of the bargain. The bank charges 10 per cent to people it should be charging 15 per cent. It would go bankrupt. Fortunately, the bank manager's son is doing an economics course and knows a better way. The bank defends against the worst, charging everyone 15 per cent. The bad risk people show up and pay the right price, but low risk people can't borrow at a price they think is fair. The market for loans to them fails to exist. The distortion causes a missing market.

Moral hazard and adverse selection arise because acquiring information is costly, and different people begin with different information. Some of this can be exploited to one's own advantage. Foreseeing this, many markets fail to develop properly in the first place. Without comprehensive markets, the Invisible Hand gets into trouble. And because of the second best, doing quite well in many spheres is no guarantee that the overall outcome is close to the first best.

▉▉▉ quality, health, and safety

Information is incomplete because gathering information is costly. A worker unaware that exposure to benzene might cause cancer will be willing to work for a lower wage than if this information were widely available. The firm's production cost will understate the true social cost and the good will be overproduced. In most countries, governments have accepted an increasing role in regulating health, safety, and quality standards because they have recognized the danger of market failure. The purpose of legislation is twofold: to encourage the provision of information that will allow individuals more accurately to judge costs and benefits, and to set and enforce standards designed to reduce the risks of injury or death.

Politicians often claim that human life is beyond economic calculation and must be given absolute priority at any cost. For example, the UK government repeated this assurance after the Paddington rail disaster in October 1999. An economist will raise two points in reply. First, it is quite impossible to implement such an objective. It is simply too expensive in resources to attempt to eliminate *all* risks of premature death, and in fact we do not do so. Second, in making occupational and recreational choices, for example being a racing driver or going climbing, people do take risks. Society must ask how much more risk-averse it should be than the people it is trying to protect.

Thus, beyond a certain point the marginal social cost of further risk reduction will exceed the marginal social benefit. It will take an enormous effort to make the world just a little safer, and the resources might have been used elsewhere to greater effect. Zero risk does not make economic sense. Economists have long been calling for safety regulations to be subject to cost–benefit analysis. We need to know the costs of making the world a little safer, and we need to encourage society to decide how much it values the benefits.

However, society decides to value the benefit of saving human life, an efficient allocation would adopt health and safety regulations up to the point at which the marginal social cost of saving life by each and every means was equal to the marginal social benefit of saving life. By shying away from the 'unpleasant' task of spelling out the costs and benefits, society is likely to produce a very inefficient allocation in which the marginal costs and marginal benefits are very different in different activities.

Suppose we assume that each regulation is enforced up to the point at which the marginal cost and marginal benefit of saving life are equal *for that activity*. If we can measure the marginal cost directly, we can infer the implicit marginal benefit from saving life through that activity. Economists frequently complain that such calculations reveal very different implicit marginal benefits across activities, which is unsurprising when those responsible for safety standards in building, motoring, medicine, and other areas make no attempt to reach a common view of the marginal social benefit from saving life. For example, estimates for the implicit marginal social benefit from saving life in the UK range from £20 million in the case of building regulations introduced after the Ronan Point disaster to £50 for a rarely used test in pregnant women that might prevent some still-births. Such wide disparities in the social marginal cost of life-saving suggest that society might make big efficiency gains by adopting an integrated approach to cost–benefit analysis of health and safety regulations.

■■■■ recap

- Welfare economics deals with normative issues or value judgements. Its purpose is not to describe *how* the economy works but to assess *how well* it works.

- Horizontal equity is the equal treatment of equals, and vertical equity the unequal treatment of unequals.

- A resource allocation is a description of what, how, and for whom goods are produced. To separate as far as possible the concepts of equity and efficiency, economists use Pareto efficiency. An allocation is Pareto-efficient if no reallocation of resources would make some people better off without making some people worse off.

- For a given level of resources and a given technology, the economy has an infinite number of Pareto-efficient allocations which differ in the distribution of welfare across people.

- Under strict conditions, competitive equilibrium is Pareto-efficient. Different initial distributions of human and physical capital across people generate different competitive equilibria corresponding to each possible Pareto-efficient allocation. When price-taking producers and consumers face the same prices, marginal costs and marginal benefits are equated to prices and hence to each other.

- In practice, governments face a conflict between equity and efficiency. Redistributive taxation drives a wedge between prices paid by consumers (to which marginal benefits are equated) and prices received by producers (to which marginal costs are equated).

- Distortions occur whenever free market equilibrium does not equate marginal social cost and marginal social benefit. Distortions lead to inefficiency or market failure. Apart from taxes, important distortions are imperfect competition (failure to set price equal to marginal cost), externalities (divergence between private and social costs or benefits), and other missing markets in connection with risky goods or other informational problems.

- When a distortion cannot be removed from one market it is not generally efficient to ensure that all other markets are distortion-free.

■ Externalities lead to divergence between private and social costs or benefits because there is no implicit market for the externality itself. When only a few people are involved, a system of property rights may establish the missing market. The efficient solution is rarely a zero quantity of the externality. Transactions costs and the free-rider problem may prevent implicit markets being established. Equilibrium will then be inefficient.

■ When externalities lead to market failure the government could set up the missing market by pricing the externality through taxes or subsidies.

■ In practice, governments often regulate externalities such as pollution or congestion by imposing standards that affect quantities directly rather than by using the tax system to affect production and consumption indirectly.

■ Moral hazard, adverse selection, and other informational problems prevent the development of a complete set of markets. Without these markets the price system cannot equate social marginal cost and benefit for future goods or risky activities.

■■ key terms

■■ review questions

1 An economy has 10 units of goods to share out between two people. (x, y) denotes that the first person gets a quantity x and the second person a quantity y. For each of the following allocations say whether they are (i) efficient and (ii) equitable: (a) (10,0) (b) (7,2) (c) (5,5) (d) (3,6) (e) (0,10). What does 'equitable' mean? If you were making the choice, would you prefer allocation (d) to allocation (e)?

2 In deciding whether or not to drive your car during the rush hour, you think about the cost of petrol and the time of the journey. Do you slow other people down by driving in the rush hour? Is this an externality? Does this mean that too many or too few people drive cars in the rush hour? Would it make sense for city authorities to restrict commuter parking in cities during the day?

3 Explain how an economist might defend laws making it compulsory to wear seat belts in cars.

4 (a) Why might society wish to ban drugs that neither help nor harm the diseases they are claimed to cure? (b) Regulatory bodies are blamed for bad things that happen in spite of the regulations (e.g. a plane crash) but not blamed so much for good things that are prevented (e.g. the quick availability of a safe and useful drug) by stringent tests and regulations. Will regulatory bodies over-regulate the activities under their scrutiny?

5-2 taxes and government spending

How much should the government raise in taxation? Are there good taxes and bad taxes? If taxes are needed to pay for government spending, why do we need government spending in the first place? Table 5-1 shows government spending over four decades. It is important to distinguish government spending on goods and services – schools, defence, the police, and so on – from government spending on *transfer payments*, such as social security, state pensions, and debt interest. Whereas spending on goods and services directly uses up factors of production that could otherwise be employed in the private sector, transfer payments do not directly pre-empt society's scarce resources. Rather, they transfer purchasing power from consumers paying taxes to consumers in receipt of transfer payments or subsidies.

Between 1956 and 1976 there was an increase in the share of national resources directly pre-empted by the government through spending on goods and services. Successive governments have reversed this trend. The second row of Table 5-1 shows government spending on transfer payments. The last row shows the turnaround in total spending since 1976. One reason for trying to reduce government spending is to make room for tax cuts. Table 5-2 shows the *marginal rate of income tax*.

LEARNING OUTCOMES

When you have finished this section, you should understand

- why pure public goods cannot be provided by a market

- average and marginal tax rates; direct and indirect taxes

- tax incidence and tax distortions

- how taxes can compensate for externalities

- supply-side economics

- the Laffer curve

- limits to economic sovereignty

The marginal rate of income tax *is the percentage taken by the government of the last pound that an individual earns. In contrast, the* average tax rate *is the percentage of total income that the government takes in income tax.*

A *progressive* tax structure is one in which the average tax rate rises with an individual's income level. The government takes proportionately more from the rich than from the poor. A *regressive* tax structure is one in which the average tax rate falls as income level rises, taking proportionately less from the rich. The UK was merely part of a worldwide move to cut tax rates, especially for the very rich. Were the tax cuts designed to make the rich richer? Or was their purpose to revive hard work and enterprise? If so, will they work? These questions go to the heart of the current debate.

| Table 5-1 | UK government spending (% of GDP) | | |

Spending on	1956	1976	1999
Goods and services	20.7	25.9	20.8
Transfer payments	13.2	21.0	17.9
Total spending	33.9	46.9	38.7

Sources: ONS, *UK National Accounts*; HM Treasury, *Budget 1999.*

■■■ taxation and government spending

UK government spending, and the taxation that finances it, are now 39 per cent of national output. Table 5-3 shows the composition of government spending and revenue in 1998. Almost half of total government spending, went on transfer payments such as unemployment benefit and debt interest. The other half went on goods and services, especially health, defence, and education. Most government spending is financed through taxation. The most important taxes are income tax and expenditure taxes such as value added tax (VAT). Since state provision of retirement pensions is included on the expenditure side under transfer payments, the pension contributions under the National Insurance Scheme must be included on the revenue side.

Table 5-2 UK income tax rates, 1978–2000

Taxable income (000s of 1999 £)	Marginal tax rate (%) 78–79	86–87	99–00
1 500	34	29	10
5 000	34	29	20
10 000	34	29	20
20 000	45	29	20
30 000	50	40	40
40 000	70	50	40
70 000	83	60	40

Note: Taxable income after deducting allowances. In 1999–2000 a single person's allowance was £4335.

Sources: HMSO, *Financial Statement & Budget Report*; ONS, *Budget 1999*.

Table 5-3 Expenditure and revenue of UK central and local government 1998

Expenditure	£ billion	Revenue	£ billion
Health	46.3	Income tax	86.5
Education	38.1	Corporation tax	30.8
Defence	24.2	Expenditure taxes	103.6
Other current spending	45.0	Social security contributions	54.1
Capital investment	14.3	Taxes on capital	2.0
All goods and services	167.9	Council tax, rates, fees	27.9
Social security	106.1	Other revenue	26.9
Debt interest	30.0	TOTAL REVENUE	331.8
Other transfer payments	25.6	NET SURPLUS	2.2
All transfer payments	161.7		
TOTAL EXPENDITURE	329.6		

Source: ONS, *UK National Accounts*.

■■■ the government in the market economy

How do we justify government spending in a market economy?

> *A* private good, *if consumed by one person, cannot be consumed by another person. A* public good, *even if consumed by one person, can still be consumed by other people.*

Ice cream is a private good. If you eat an ice cream it prevents anyone else from eating the same ice cream. Most goods are private goods. Clean air and defence are examples of public goods. If the air is pollution-free, your consumption of it does not interfere with our consumption of it. If the Navy is patrolling coastal waters, your consumption of national defence does not affect our quantity of national defence. In fact, for a *pure public good* we must all necessarily consume whatever quantity is supplied in the aggregate. We may get different amounts of utility if our tastes differ, but we all consume the same quantity.

The key aspects of public goods are (1) that it is technically possible for one person to consume without reducing the amount available for someone else, and (2) the impossibility of excluding anyone from consumption except at a prohibitive cost. A football match could be watched by a lot of people, especially if it is televised, without reducing the quantity consumed by any individual; but *exclusion* is possible – the ground holds only so many, and the club can refuse to allow the game to be televised. The interesting issues arise when, as with national defence, exclusion of certain individuals from consumption is impossible.

Free-riders   In Section 5-1 we introduced the *free-rider problem* when discussing why bribes and compensation for externalities might not occur. Public goods are especially vulnerable to the free-rider problem if they are supplied by the private sector. Since you get the same quantity of national defence as everyone else, *whether or not you pay for it*, you never purchase national defence in a private market. Everybody else would adopt similar reasoning, and no defence would be demanded even if we all wanted defence. Private markets will not produce the socially efficient quantity. There is a case for government intervention.

The marginal social benefit   Suppose the public good is the purity of the public water supply. Figure 5-4 supposes there are two people. The first person's demand curve for water purity is D_1D_1. Each point on the demand curve shows what the individual would pay for the last unit of purer water. It shows the marginal benefit to the individual. D_2D_2 shows the marginal benefit of purer water to the second individual.

Curve DD gives the marginal social benefit of purer water. Thus at the output Q the social marginal benefit is $P = P_1 + P_2$. We sum vertically at *a given quantity* because everyone consumes the same quantity of a public good. Figure 5-4 also shows the marginal cost of producing the public good. If there are no production externalities the marginal private cost and marginal social cost of production coincide. The socially efficient output of the public good is at Q^*, where the marginal social benefit equals the marginal social cost.

What would happen if the good were privately produced and marketed? Person 1 might pay P_1 to have a quantity Q produced by a competitive supplier pricing at marginal cost. At the output Q the price P_1 just equals the marginal private benefit which person 1 derives from the last unit of the public good. Would person 2 pay to have the output of the public good increased beyond Q? No. Because it is a public good, person 2 cannot be excluded from consuming the output Q which person 1 has commissioned. But, at the output Q, person 2's marginal private benefit is only P_2, which is less than the current price P_1. Person 2 would not pay the higher price necessary to induce a competitive supplier to expand production beyond Q. Person 2 is a free-rider enjoying person 1's purchase Q. And the total quantity privately produced and consumed in a competitive market lies below the socially efficient quantity Q^*.

Revelation of preferences   By constructing the marginal social benefit curve DD, the government can decide how much of the public good it is socially efficient to produce. But how does the government find out the individual demand curves that must be vertically added to get DD? People will understate how much they value the good in order to reduce their own payments, just as in a private market. Conversely, if payments are divorced from the question of how much people would like, people will overstate their private valuations. We are all for safer streets if we do not have to contribute to the cost. In practice, democracies try to resolve this problem through elections of governments. By asking the question, 'How much would you like, given that everyone will be charged for the cost of providing public goods?' society can come closer to providing the efficient quantities of public goods.

Government production   The economist's definition of public goods relies solely on the fact that everyone consumes the same quantity. The free-rider problem implies that private markets will not produce the socially efficient level. It does not imply that the government must produce the goods itself. Public goods are not necessarily produced by the government.

merit goods and bads

> Merit goods *(bads) are goods that society thinks everyone ought to have (ought not to have) regardless of whether they are wanted by each individual.*

Figure 5-4	A pure public good

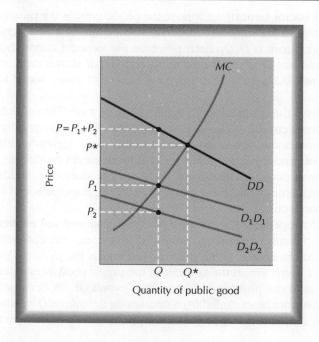

Examples of merit goods are education and health. Merit bads are products such as cigarettes. Since society places a different value on these goods from the value placed on them by the individual, individual choice within a free market leads to a different allocation from the one that society wishes to see.

There are two distinct reasons for merit goods. The first is a version of the externality argument examined in the previous chapter. If more education raises the productivity not merely of an individual worker but of all other workers with whom this worker co-operates, there is a production externality that the individual does not take into account in choosing how much education to purchase. If individuals demand too little education, society should encourage the provision of education. Free schooling to ensure a minimum level of education, communication, and social inter-action might be one way to achieve this.

Conversely, if people take account of the costs to themselves but not the burden on state hospitals in deciding whether or not to smoke and damage their health, society may regard smoking as a merit bad to be discouraged. We shall shortly see how the tax system, in this case a tax on cigarettes, may offset externalities that individuals fail to take into account.

The second aspect of merit goods is where society believes that individuals no longer act in their own best interests. Addiction to drugs, tobacco, or gambling are examples. Economists rarely subscribe to the value judgement of paternalism. The function of government intervention is less to tell people what they ought to like than to allow them better to achieve what they already like. However, the government will sometimes have more information or be in a better position to take a decision. Much as some people hate going to school, they will frequently be glad afterwards that they were made to do so.

■■■ the principles of taxation

Direct taxes *are taxes on income,* indirect taxes *are taxes on spending, and* wealth taxes *are taxes on the value of assets.*

Direct taxes   are taxes on the income of companies or individuals: corporation tax, income tax, and National Insurance contributions (which are income related).

Indirect taxes   Indirect taxes are taxes levied on expenditure on goods and services. The most important tax is value added tax (VAT), which is effectively a retail sales tax. Whereas a sales tax is collected only at the point of final sale to the consumer, VAT is collected at different stages of the production process. However, this is simply passed on to final consumers. But a higher consumer price will reduce the quantity demanded. In turn this will move producers back down their marginal cost curves and alter the net-of-tax price producers require. Later in this section we show how these induced effects determine how the burden of the tax is ultimately divided between producers and consumers. Revenue from VAT is supplemented by other indirect taxes including special duties on tobacco and alcohol, licence fees for motor cars and televisions, and customs duties on imports.

Wealth taxes   In the UK there are two taxes on wealth *per se* rather than on the income derived from wealth. The first is the tax on property values, the main source of revenue for local government. The second is capital transfer tax, which applies to transfers of wealth between individuals, whether as gifts during life or as inheritances after death. How does the UK tax structure compare with that in other countries? Table 5-4 shows the most notable feature of the UK tax system appears to be its low reliance on social security contributions, and high reliance on indirect taxes on spending.

Tax revenue is necessary to pay for government expenditure. We now assess the UK tax system against our two welfare criteria, equity and efficiency.

how to tax fairly

We gave two notions of equity: *horizontal equity*, or the equal treatment of equals, and *vertical equity*, the redistribution from the 'haves' to the 'have-nots'.

> *In taking proportionately more from the rich than from the less well off, income tax reflects the principle of* ability to pay.

The principle of ability to pay thus reflects a concern about vertical equity. A second principle is sometimes applied in discussing the extent to which unequal people should be treated unequally.

> *The* benefits principle *argues that people who receive more than their share of public spending should pay more than their share of tax revenues.*

Car users should pay more towards public roads than people without a car should pay. However, the benefits principle often conflicts directly with the principle of ability to pay. If people who are most vulnerable to unemployment must pay the highest contributions to the government unemployment insurance scheme, it is difficult to redistribute income, wealth, or welfare. If the main objective is vertical equity, the ability to pay principle must usually take precedence.

Although UK income tax is progressive, it is the entire structure of taxes, transfers, and public spending that we must examine before we can judge how much the government is effectively redistributing from the rich to the poor. Two factors make the entire structure more progressive than an examination of income tax alone would suggest. First, transfer payments actually give money to the poor. The old get pensions, the unemployed get unemployment benefit, and, as a final safety net, anyone whose income falls below a certain minimum is entitled to income support. Second, the state provides public goods that can be consumed by the poor, even if they have not paid any taxes. Since the rich tend to sit in their own gardens, public parks help redistribute enjoyment to the poor.

As against these progressive elements of the tax, transfer, and spending structure, there are some *regressive* elements that take proportionately more from the poor. Beer and tobacco taxes are huge earners for the government. Yet the poor spend a much higher proportion of their income on these goods than do the rich. Such taxes reduce the effectiveness of the tax, transfer and spending structure in redistributing from the rich to the poor.

Table 5-4	Sources of tax revenue (% of total taxes)					
Taxes	USA	UK	Germany	France	Sweden	Japan
Direct	45	38	30	22	42	34
Indirect	29	43	30	34	32	28
Social security contributions	25	18	40	43	26	36
Capital	1	1	0	1	0	2

Source: ONS, *Economic Trends*, March 1999.

tax incidence

The incidence *of a tax measures the final tax burden on different people once we allow for all effects of the tax.*

The ultimate effect of a tax can be very different from its apparent effect. Thus to see how taxes (or subsidies) alter people's spending power and welfare, we need to examine tax incidence in more detail.

Figure 5-5 shows the market for labour. *DD* is the demand curve and *SS* the supply curve. In the absence of an income tax (a tax on wages), the labour market will be in equilibrium at *E*. Now suppose the government imposes an income tax. If we measure the gross wage on the vertical axis, the demand curve *DD* is unaltered since it is the comparison of the gross wage with the marginal value product of labour that determines the quantity of labour demanded by firms. Workers' preferences or attitudes are also unchanged, but it is the wage net of tax that workers compare with the marginal value of their leisure in deciding how much labour to supply. Thus, although *SS* continues to show the labour supply curve in terms of the after-tax wage, we must draw in the higher schedule *SS′* to show the supply of labour in terms of the gross or pre-tax wage. The vertical distance between *SS′* and *SS* measures the amount of tax being paid on earnings from the last hour's work.

DD and *SS′* show the behaviour of firms and workers at any gross wage. The new equilibrium is at *E′*. The gross wage is *W′* at which firms demand *L′*. The vertical distance between *A′* and *E′* measures the tax being paid on earnings from the last hour of work. Thus the after-tax wage is *W″* at which workers are happy to supply a quantity of hours *L′*. Relative to the original equilibrium, the tax on wages has raised the pre-tax wage to *W′*, but lowered the after-tax wage to *W″*. It has raised the wage that firms pay but lowered the take-home wage for workers.

| **Figure 5-5** | A tax on wages |

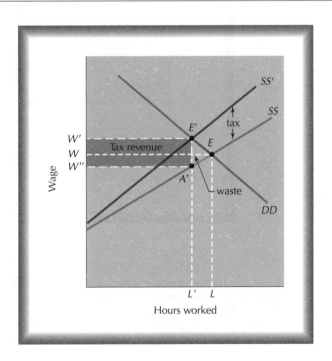

The tax wedge *is the gap between the price paid by the buyer and the price received by the seller.*

The incidence of the tax has fallen on *both* firms and workers even though, for administrative convenience, the tax may be collected directly from workers. The incidence or burden of a tax cannot be established by looking at who actually hands over the money to the government. Taxes usually alter equilibrium prices and quantities and these induced effects must also be taken into account. However, we can draw one very general conclusion. The more inelastic the supply curve and the more elastic the demand curve, the more the final incidence will fall on the seller rather than the purchaser.

Figure 5-6 depicts the extreme case in which the supply curve is completely inelastic. In the absence of a tax, equilibrium is at *E* and the wage is *W*. Since the vertical supply curve *SS* implies that a fixed quantity of hours *L* will be supplied whatever the after-tax wage, the imposition of a tax on wages leads to a new equilibrium at *A′*. Only if the pre-tax wage is unchanged will firms demand the quantity *L* that is supplied. Hence the entire incidence falls on the workers. To check you have grasped the idea of incidence, draw for yourself a market with an elastic supply curve and an inelastic demand curve. Show that the incidence of a tax will now fall mainly on the purchaser.[2]

taxation, efficiency, and waste

We have been considering the equity implications of a tax. But we must also think about the efficiency implications of a tax. We can use Figure 5-5 again. Before the tax is imposed, labour market equilibrium is at *E*. The wage *W* measures both the marginal

Figure 5-6	Taxing a factor in inelastic supply

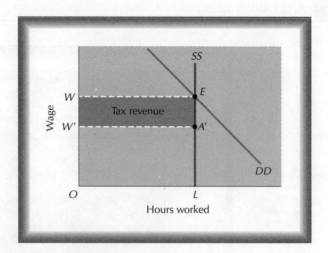

[2] By now you may be wondering whether we always show the effect of a tax as a shift in the supply curve. We do, provided we wish to measure the pre-tax price of the good or service on the vertical axis. If we want to measure the after-tax price on the vertical axis, the effect of the tax will be to shift not the supply curve but the demand curve. We get exactly the same conclusions as before.

social benefit of the last hour of work and its marginal social cost. The demand curve *DD* tells us the marginal value product of labour, the extra benefit society could have from extra goods produced. The supply curve *SS* tells us the marginal value of the leisure being sacrificed in order to work another hour, the marginal social cost of extra work. At *E* marginal social cost and benefit are equal, which is socially efficient.

When the tax is imposed, the new equilibrium is at *E'*. The tax *A'E'* increases the wage to firms to *W'* but reduces the after-tax wage for workers to *W''*. But there is an additional tax burden or deadweight loss that is pure waste. It is the triangle *A'E'E*. By reducing the quantity of hours from *L* to *L'*, the tax causes society to stop using hours on which the marginal social benefit, the height of the demand curve *DD*, exceeds the marginal social cost, the height of the supply curve *SS*. By driving a wedge between the wage firms pay and the wage workers receive, the tax induces a distortion destroying the efficiency of free market equilibrium.

must taxes be distortionary?

Government needs tax revenue to pay for public goods and to make transfer payments. Must taxes create distortions and lead to inefficiency? Figure 5-6 shows what happens when a tax is levied but the supply is completely inelastic. There is no change in the equilibrium quantity. Since the quantity is unchanged, there is no distortionary triangle or deadweight burden. The equilibrium quantity remains the socially efficient quantity.

We can make this into a general principle. When either the supply or the demand curve for a good or service is very inelastic, the imposition of a tax will lead only to a small change in quantity. Hence the deadweight burden triangle must be small. Given that the government must raise some tax revenue, the smallest amount of total waste will be achieved when the goods that are most inelastic in supply or demand are taxed most heavily. This principle finds practical expression in the UK tax system. The most heavily taxed commodities are alcohol and tobacco. Alcohol and tobacco have an inelastic demand.

So far, we have discussed the taxes that would do least harm to the allocative efficiency of the economy. Sometimes the government can levy taxes which actually improve efficiency and reduce waste. The most important example is when externalities exist. Cigarette smokers pollute the air for other people but take no account of this in deciding how much to smoke. They give rise to a harmful consumption externality. Figure 5-7 shows the supply curve *SS* of cigarette producers. Since there are no production externalities, *SS* is also the marginal social cost curve. *DD* is the private demand curve showing the marginal benefit of cigarettes to smokers. Because there is a harmful consumption externality, the marginal social benefit *DD'* of cigarette consumption is lower than *DD*.

In the absence of a tax, free market equilibrium is at *E*, but there is over-consumption of cigarettes. The socially efficient quantity is *Q** since marginal social cost and marginal social benefit are equated at *E**. Suppose the government levies a tax, equal to the vertical distance *E*F*, on each packet of cigarettes. With the tax-inclusive price on the vertical axis, the demand curve *DD* is unaffected, but the supply curve shifts up to *SS'*. Each point on *SS'* then allows producers to receive the corresponding net-of-tax price on *SS*. After the tax is introduced, equilibrium is at the point *F*. The socially efficient quantity *Q** is produced and consumed. Consumers pay the price *P'* and producers receive the price *P''* after tax has been paid at the rate *E*F* per unit.

Only the tax rate *E*F* per unit guides the free market to the efficient allocation. This is exactly the amount of the externality on the last unit when the efficient quantity *Q** is produced. By levying a tax at precisely this rate, consumers are induced to behave as if they took account of the externality, though in fact they take account only of the tax-inclusive price. Whenever externalities induce distortions, the government can improve efficiency by levying taxes. The fact that alcohol and tobacco have harmful externalities provides a reason for taxing them heavily.

■■■ taxation and supply-side economics

Suppose the government adopts a less ambitious spending programme and is therefore able to reduce income tax rates. What will be the consequences?

First, by spending less on goods and services, the government will free some resources for use by the private sector. If it were true that the private sector uses resources more productively than the public sector, the transfer of resources might directly produce more output. The total supply of goods and services would rise. Whether or not the private sector does use resources more productively than the government remains a contentious issue.

What about the effects of lower tax rates? Income taxes introduce a distortion that leads to a level of work that is socially inefficient. With lower taxes and a smaller distortion there would be a lower dead-weight burden. Since the distortion leads to a level of work that is lower than the socially efficient amount, cutting income taxes would also increase the amount of work done in the economy. How large could this effect be? It all depends on the elasticity of labour supply. The more inelastic the labour supply, the lower is the distortion introduced by any particular income tax rate.

In Chapter 4 we argued that the supply curve of labour input (hours times people) is quite inelastic. Cutting income tax *will* increase the supply of labour input, chiefly by attracting new workers into the labour force. But the total effect on labour supply might not be as large as some proponents of tax cuts believe. In contrast, the tax cut enthusiasts believe that income tax is a major distortion and labour supply is very

---

Figure 5-7 Taxes to offset externalities

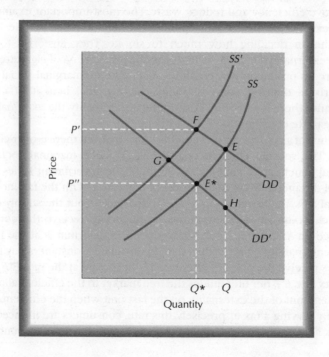

elastic. The socially efficient quantity of labour input would then be much larger than the equilibrium level under current tax rates. One illustration of this view is the famous Laffer curve, named after one of President Reagan's most influential advisers.

> *The* Laffer curve *shows how much tax revenue is raised at each possible tax rate.*

Suppose that all government tax revenue was raised through income tax. Figure 5-8 shows that with a zero tax rate the government would raise zero revenue. At the opposite extreme, with a 100 per cent income tax rate, there would be no point working and again tax revenue would be zero. Beginning from a zero rate, a small increase in the tax rate will yield some tax revenue. Initially revenue rises with the tax rate, but beyond the tax rate t^* higher taxes have major disincentive effects on work effort and revenue falls.

Professor Laffer's idea was that many 'big government–big tax' countries are now at tax rates above t^*. If so, tax cuts would be the miracle cure. The government would actually raise *more* revenue by cutting taxes. By reducing the tax distortion and increasing the amount of work *a lot*, lower taxes would be more than compensated by the extra work and incomes to which the tax rates were applied. It is not the shape of the Laffer curve that is in dispute. Rather, what many professional economists have disputed is that these economies do *in fact* have tax rates above t^*. Most economists' reading of the empirical evidence is that our economies lie to the left of t^*. Cutting income tax rates may eliminate some of the deadweight burden of distortionary taxation, but governments should probably expect their tax revenue to decline if such policies are put into effect.

◼◼◼ local government

Thus far we have been chiefly interested in the principles of central government. In this section we examine the economics of local government. Local government expenditure may cover a variety of things, from sweeping the streets to providing local schooling. In turn this must be financed through taxes. Some of these taxes will

---

Figure 5-8 The Laffer curve

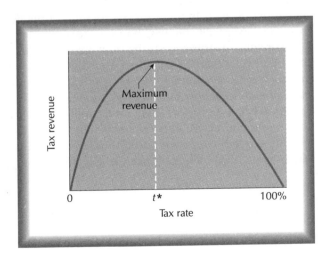

be local, but some will come from central government revenue raised through the national tax system. Finally, local government is responsible for some types of regulation, for example land use or *zoning* laws.

economic principles

Why don't we make central government responsible for everything? First, diversity matters. People are different and don't want to be treated the same. Civic pride is necessarily local. Second, people feel that central government is remote from their particular needs. Even if central government paid attention to local considerations, it would find it hard to do so efficiently.

We turn now to two important models of local government. The first is the Tiebout model.[3] This model emphasizes diversity. Some people want a lot of local expenditure on public services and are prepared to pay high local taxes; others want to pay lower local taxes even though this means lower public services. If all local governments are the same, everyone is unhappy with the compromise. The Tiebout model is sometimes called the *invisible foot*: people move to the area providing the package of spending and taxes they want. The invisible foot brings about an efficient allocation of resources through competition between local governments.

In practice, the invisible foot is sometimes a very imperfect incentive structure. First, it may be hard to move between local authorities. For example, being born in a neighbourhood may entitle you to a higher place in the queue for housing provided by that local authority. Second, if much of local authority revenue comes from central government, the levels of spending and taxes may be insensitive to the wishes of local residents.

Earlier in the chapter, we stressed the distinction between efficiency and equity. Even if the invisible foot led to efficiency, it might also lead to inequity. The rich are likely to cluster together in suburbs. Then they pass zoning laws specifying a minimum size for a house and its garden. This makes it impossible for the poor to move to that neighbourhood. By forming an exclusive club, the rich ensure that their taxes do not go to supporting the poor. And the poor get stuck with one another in inner-city areas whose governments face the biggest social needs but the smallest local tax base.

The Tiebout model assumes that residents mainly consume the public services provided by their own local authority. But when each unit of local government is responsible for a small geographical area, this may be a bad assumption. If an inner-city supplies free art galleries, financed out of taxes on inner-city inhabitants, the rich still come in from the suburbs to make use of these facilities. Conversely, inner-city inhabitants spend their Sundays enjoying countryside facilities supported by taxes raised out of town. In these cases, provision of public services in one area confers a beneficial externality on neighbouring areas.

Economic theory suggests the right answer to this problem. Unless the externality can be priced (charging suburban users but not city dwellers for entry to subsidized galleries and opera houses), the most efficient solution is to widen the geographical area of each local government until it includes most of the people who will use the public services it provides. Thus, for example, it may make sense to have an integrated commuter rail service and inner-city subway, and to subsidize it to prevent people driving through congested streets; but only a local government embracing both the suburbs and the inner city is likely to get close to the efficient policy.

[3] Charles Tiebout, 'A Pure Theory of Local Expenditures', *Journal of Political Economy*, 1956.

These two theories of local government pull in opposite directions, and the right answer lies somewhere in between. The assumptions of the Tiebout model favour a lot of small local government jurisdictions to maximize choice and competition between areas. The model emphasizing externalities across areas suggests larger jurisdictions to 'internalize' externalities than would otherwise occur.

■■■ economic sovereignty

Thus far, we have discussed a single country in isolation. In a democratic country insulated from the rest of the world, the government is sovereign: while it retains democratic support and observes existing laws, it has the final say in policy design. Where it dislikes existing laws it may also be able to initiate legislation to amend previous laws. Sometimes central government chooses to delegate powers to local government. We now ask how interactions with the rest of the world affect the sovereignty of national governments.

> Economic sovereignty *is the power of national governments to make decisions independently of those made by other governments.*

Even in an economy closed to the outside world, governments cannot do anything they like. Within market economies they have to work within the forces of supply and demand. It is more efficient to have high tax rates on things for which the demand or supply is inelastic: high tax rates on things with elastic supply and demand induce large distortions since equilibrium quantity is very sensitive to the price. We now apply this insight to economies open to interactions with the rest of the world.

International capital is now highly mobile across countries. Suppose the UK government tries to levy a large tax on capital in Britain. Lots of capital will quickly move elsewhere to escape the high taxes. The *tax base*, in this example the quantity of capital available for taxing in Britain, quickly shrinks. So the high tax *rates* may raise little tax *revenue*. In contrast, since people are much less mobile than capital across national boundaries, the tax base for taxation of workers' incomes in Britain is much less sensitive to tax rates than the tax base for capital taxes.

Even people are more mobile across national boundaries than they were a few decades ago. Communication is easier, transport costs are lower, satellites pay no attention to national frontiers on a map. Migration affects not just taxation but government spending. Suppose a country wishes to implement a generous welfare state. As a closed economy, all it has to worry about is how much of its tax base disappears from work into leisure. If welfare is too generous, people may not work enough. As an open economy, it also has to worry whether more generous welfare provision will lead to more migration into the country as foreigners take advantage, legally or illegally, of the generous welfare provision.

Thus closer economic integration with other countries – through trade in goods and movement of factors of production – effectively undermines the sovereignty of nation states. If the rate of income tax was 80 per cent in Liverpool but 20 per cent in Manchester, one would expect some pretty dramatic movement of capital and of people from Liverpool to Manchester. The tax base in Liverpool would evaporate (even die-hard Everton supporters could commute from Manchester for Everton's home games). The local government of Liverpool has limited local sovereignty because it is effectively in competition with Manchester.

As modern technology undermines even barriers between countries, the same process is at work. The economic sovereignty of nation states, their freedom to do what they want, is steadily being constrained by the pressure of competition from foreign countries. More than one in ten beer cans now sold in England was bought by

British households in France, hopping across the English Channel to take advantage of lower rates of alcohol taxation in France. UK Chancellors, caught between the pressure to raise revenue and the need to reduce alcohol taxes to prevent the UK booze business being undercut, have recently opted for a compromise and made little changes to alcohol taxes. They have already lost the sovereignty to set tax rates at the high levels that they would have liked.

National sovereignty is undermined not merely by competition between countries for tax bases but by two other considerations. The first is other sorts of cross-country spillovers such as acid rain, greenhouse gases, or the threat of pollution from a nuclear accident. Banning nuclear power generation in southern England may have limited value if northern France is studded with nuclear power stations.

The second is the scope for redistribution. Economics is about equity as well as efficiency. In an important sense, the right jurisdiction for government is the area within which citizens feel sufficient identity with one another that the rich are prepared to pay for the poor, and the fortunate are prepared to assist the unlucky, without resentment becoming entrenched. Many of the nation states of Europe have long histories and retain strong national identities. But these are not always set in stone. The Irish question has troubled Britain for centuries. More recently, countries such as Belgium and Italy have faced strong internal pressures for division. In the opposite direction, some Europeans now feel as much a citizen of Europe as of their own particular nation state.

It is clearly not the case that nation states are obsolete. But they are beginning to come under pressure. And further developments in technology are likely to increase the transnational scope both of economic interactions and of cultural identity. The proliferation of e-commerce and the use of the internet for entertainment will only accelerate this process.

■ recap

- In industrialized economies, government revenues come mainly from direct taxes on personal incomes and company profits, indirect taxes on purchases of goods and services, and contributions to state-run social security schemes. Government spending comprises spending on goods and services and transfer payments.

- Government intervention in a market economy should be assessed against the criteria of distributional equity and allocative efficiency. A progressive tax and transfer system takes most from the rich and give most to the poor. The UK tax and transfer system is mildly progressive.

- Externalities are cases of market failure where intervention may improve efficiency. By taxing or subsidizing goods that involve externalities, the government can induce the private sector to behave as if it takes account of the externality.

- A pure public good is a good for which one person's consumption does not reduce the quantity available for consumption by others. A free market will undersupply a public good because of the free-rider problem.

- Except for taxes designed to offset externalities, taxes are generally distortionary. By driving a wedge between the selling price and the purchase price, they prevent the price system achieving the equality of marginal costs and marginal benefits. The amount of the deadweight burden is higher the higher is the marginal tax rate and the size of the wedge, and the more elastic are supply and demand.

- The incidence of tax describes who ultimately pays the tax. The more inelastic is demand relative to supply, the more a tax will fall on purchasers as opposed to sellers.

■ Rising tax rates initially increase tax revenue but eventually lead to such large falls in the equilibrium quantity of the taxed commodity or activity that revenue starts to fall again.

■ The economic sovereignty of nation states is being affected by increasing integration of countries within the world economy. As national tax bases become more mobile they become more elastic and harder to tax by a single country. Pollution spillovers also inflict transnational externalities. In both cases, co-operation between countries is needed for a more efficient solution. However, national policies also reflect national identities.

key terms

review questions

1 Which of the following are public goods? (a) the fire brigade; (b) clean streets; (c) refuse collection; (d) cable television; (e) social toleration; (f) the postal service. Explain and discuss alternative ways of providing these goods or services.

2 Classify the following taxes as progressive or regressive. (a) 10 per cent tax on all luxury goods; (b) taxes in proportion to the value of owner-occupied houses; (c) taxes on beer; (d) taxes on champagne.

3 There is a flat-rate 30 per cent income tax on all income over £2000. Calculate the average tax rate (tax paid divided by income) at income levels of £5000, £10 000, and £50 000. Is the tax progressive? Is it more or less progressive if the exemption is raised from £2000 to £5000?

4 (a) Suppose labour supply is completely inelastic. Show why there is no deadweight burden if wages are taxed. Who bears the incidence of the tax? (b) Now suppose labour supply is quite elastic. Show the area that is the deadweight burden of the tax. How much of the tax is ultimately borne by firms and how much by workers? (c) For any given supply elasticity show that firms bear more of the tax the more inelastic is the demand for labour.

6 | governing the market

6-1 industrial policy and competition policy

LEARNING OUTCOMES

When you have finished this section, you should understand

- how industrial policy seeks to offset market failures

- reasons for locational externalities

- consumer surplus and producer surplus

- the social cost of monopoly power

- UK competition policy in theory and practice

- the regulation of potential mergers, both in theory and in practice

What do Durex, Valium, and Cornflakes have in common with household gas supplies and mobile phones? The answer is that the London Rubber Company, Hoffman LaRoche, Kelloggs, British Gas, Cellnet, and Vodafone have all been the subject of investigations by the Competition Commission, which exists to monitor the behaviour of large firms and check the possible abuse of monopoly power.[1] In this chapter we examine government intervention to enhance market efficiency.

Competition policy *aims to enhance economic efficiency by promoting or safeguarding competition between firms.*

The instruments of competition policy include rules about conduct of firms and rules about the structure of industries. The former aims to prevent abuse of a monopoly position. The latter seeks to prevent monopolies arising, for example by breaking up existing monopolies or by stopping mergers that create new monopolies.

Some industries were traditionally viewed as natural monopolies: scale economies were so large that breaking them up made no sense and competition from other firms provided no competitive discipline. In many countries, especially in Europe, these had become nationalized industries, run by the state to provide continuous supervision in

---

[1] Prior to 1999, the Competition Commission was known as the Monopolies and Mergers Commission.

the social interest. Since 1980 the UK has pioneered the privatization of many of the state-owned firms, and other countries have followed. Since scale economies do not vanish with privatization, continuing regulation has been necessary in many instances. We describe this regulatory revolution in the next section. First, we deal with cases in which scale economies are less acute and competition policy therefore offers a more promising avenue for intervention.

Before so doing, we discuss other motives for intervention to increase the efficiency of industrial production.

Industrial policy *aims to offset externalities that affect production decisions by firms.*

We discuss four such channels for market failure: invention and knowledge creation, in which it is difficult to prevent hard-earned progress being pirated by others; spillovers into other countries, which provide opportunities for policy competition between governments; capital market failures, which explain why new businesses are so hard to start; and locational externalities that explain why car stylists cluster in Turin and why Chinese restaurants cluster in London's Soho district.

■■■ industrial policy

inventions and the patent system

It is hard to trade information: the buyer needs to see it, and having seen the information then has no incentive to pay for it! Suppose a company develops a product in secret, and then markets it. If other firms quickly imitate the new invention, competition will rapidly compete away the profits on this new product. Since everyone can foresee that this will occur, few resources will be devoted to searching for inventions, even though they are socially valuable.

Inventions are a public good. The problem arises because the inventor cannot privately appropriate the benefits since imitators cannot be excluded. The solution to this market failure is a patent system.

A patent *is a temporary legal monopoly awarded to an inventor who registers the invention.*

The temporary monopoly provides, before the fact, the assurance that if the search for a new discovery is successful the inventor will be able to cash up after the fact. Why is the legal monopoly only temporary? Otherwise, successful inventors would have an entrenched entry barrier which would prevent competition for all time. The trick in designing a successful patent system is to provide a big enough incentive for invention, but not such a large and long-lived cushion that the benefits of competition are suppressed for ever.

research and development (R&D)

Research *is the process of invention.* Development *makes research commercially viable.*

Why should governments, even those committed to allowing market forces to work, spend several billion pounds of taxpayers' money promoting R&D? This seems to indicate widespread agreement that there are market failures in R&D which the patent system alone is insufficient to offset. Economics provides several insights into what may go wrong with market forces in R&D. First, large projects can be very risky for an individual company. Boeing, the largest plane manufacturer in the world, has described each new project as 'betting the company': failure on one new project could threaten the very existence of the company. Private individuals may be risk-averse, and this applies even to executives of large corporations. Consequently, private firms may undertake less R&D than is socially desirable.

If private decision-makers require a high expected return before being willing to assume such risks, why should society demand any less? Essentially for two reasons. First, the government can *pool* the risks across a large number of projects in its portfolio. Second, even if projects go wrong, the government can spread the burden very thinly across the population: 1 per cent on everybody's income tax rate for a year should cover even the biggest disaster. Thus, the population as a whole should require only a small risk premium, much smaller than that required by executives in an individual company who may face personal disaster if the project turns sour.

It should also be noted that no patent system can be watertight. Indeed, as we remarked above, to make it so would effectively be to suppress all future competition indefinitely. In these circumstances, a further argument for public support of R&D may be because private firms realize they will not be able to appropriate for themselves all the benefits of their efforts. Some imitation will occur, but it will be insufficiently clear-cut to guarantee that a law suit will not be protracted and expensive. Moreover, other inventors may be stimulated by what they see to make a breakthrough in an entirely different area. New breakthroughs build on past discoveries. These provide additional motives for R&D support as part of an effective industrial policy.

strategic international competition

In Chapter 3 we discussed how individual firms might try to erect strategic entry barriers to preserve and enhance their market power. Such considerations also apply in international competition between large firms. For a concrete example, consider again the commercial airliner industry. Effectively, there are two large firms left in

---

Box 6-1 Turning research into business success

Harvard Business School guru Professor Michael Porter is famous for his work on what gives countries a competitive edge. He gives the UK pretty low marks, calculating that it is only the thirteenth most effective of the industrial nations at deriving commercial benefit from science and technology. 'In the UK, people say we want more entrepreneurs but we don't want them to become rich.' Porter advocates a reduction in capital gains tax faced by successful entrepreneurs, and better tax breaks for research and development expenditure. The table below shows the ratio of patents (a measure of commercial application of ideas) to citations (the number of academic references to scientists' work, an indicator of scientific research output). The UK scores poorly.

International patents per 1000 scholarly citations, 1975–95

Japan	267	Italy	108
Germany	266	Canada	97
Switzerland	266	Finland	89
Austria	150	UK	87
France	135	Denmark	57
Sweden	130	Australia	46
Netherlands	120	Spain	25

Source: Financial Times, 11 December 1998.

the world market. Boeing (www.boeing.com) is much the largest and has an entire product range, from the relatively small twin-engined 737 to the 747, the Jumbo. Another American firm, McDonnell-Douglas (www.boeing.com), had a smaller product range, and in 1996 decided to merge with Boeing. The other major player is the European consortium Airbus Industrie (www.airbus.com), in which British Aerospace (BAe) (www.bae.co.uk) has a stake.

Airbus Industrie asked the governments of its member producers (Germany, France, the UK, and Spain) for *launch aid*, a grant or loan on favourable terms to help with R&D on new aircraft. Will Airbus succeed even without government support? If the answer is yes, public subsidies are simply a transfer payment to Airbus shareholders, for which there is no strong rationale. Second, will other European governments support Airbus even if the UK does not? If so, the UK government may be able to act as a free-rider. However, governments that systematically try to do this will eventually get a bad reputation.

Suppose the UK government has decided that it cannot free-ride on other governments: either it pays its share of launch aid or the whole project collapses. What are the benefits of providing launch aid? If Airbus pulls out, Boeing-McDonnell-Douglas will be the sole producer without fear of competition. In that event, Boeing will surely cash up, raising the price of aircraft. British airlines and ultimately British consumers will pay high prices, and Boeing can earn monopoly profits. It may well be worth preventing this.

If the UK could have been sure that McDonnell-Douglas would have stayed independent, and provided effective competition to Boeing, it *might* have been worth allowing Airbus to fold: European consumers would still have got the benefit of cheaper planes. But this strategy would have been risky. Launch aid may be seen as a pre-commitment by European governments not to allow Airbus to be bullied out of the industry. Boeing may conclude that there is no point attempting a price war to try to force Airbus out. If European governments can display the credible threat to back Airbus if necessary, Boeing shareholders are only going to lose by an unsuccessful price war. Hence, the pre-commitment may *prevent* a price war which might otherwise occur.

sunrise and sunset industries

Sunrise *industries are the emerging new industries of the future.* Sunset *industries are those in long-term decline.*

Sunrise industries include information technology and genetics. Sunset industries in Western economies include the old heavy industries such as steel and shipbuilding which are now suffering from massive excess capacity as these industries have been undercut by more efficient producers in the Pacific basin. Why not leave such changes to market forces? What are the market failures that might justify government intervention through industrial policy? We begin with the sunrise industries.

First, there may be imperfections in the market for lending to new companies and new industries. Banks and other lenders may be too risk-averse, or too unfamiliar with the new business, to lend the money needed through the early loss-making years. Second, the market may be slow to provide the relevant training and skills: Catch 22 (until the industry exists, people won't perceive the need for developing such skills; but without the skills, the industry cannot exist).

These arguments suggest that it may be possible to provide a rationale for an industrial policy to subsidize sunrise industries. But certain questions must be answered satisfactorily. First, why are markets so short-sighted and uninformed? If existing lenders or trainers get it wrong, why don't new firms come in and do a better job? If the answer is entry barriers, this confirms the close relation between industrial policy and competition policy. Second, even if markets get it wrong, can the government do better? The strategy of trying to outguess the market by 'picking winners' is now highly discredited.

Sunset industries present different problems. For example, the government may or may not attach importance to local unemployment when industries with a heavy geographical concentration are allowed to go under all at once. It *may* be desirable to spend what could otherwise be dole money on temporarily subsidizing lame ducks to ease the transition. Sometimes, however, a sharp shock is required to signal the extent of the adjustment eventually required and the government's commitment to seeing that adjustment is actually made.

Strategic considerations may be important here too. Suppose for example there are two remaining producers in an industry which has now contracted to the point when it can profitably support only one firm. Each firm would like to be the one to survive. They are playing an exit game of chicken. One of two things may happen, neither of which is socially desirable. First, the industry survives with two firms for much longer than is socially efficient. Second, the firm with the smaller financial backing may be the first to crack, even if it can produce at slightly lower cost than its richer rival. In such circumstances, an industrial policy that seeks faster and more efficient rationalization of the sunset industry may be advantageous.

■ economic geography

Why do fashion designers cluster in Milan and most Formula 1 racing teams have their production headquarters in the Thames Valley?

Economic geography *means that a firm's location affects its production costs. A beneficial* locational externality *occurs when a firm's production costs are reduced by locating near similar firms.*

Why might a firm's costs of production depend on its geographical proximity to other firms? Explanations fall under three headings: the interaction of scale economies and risk, transport and transactions costs, and technological spillovers.

Suppose a worker invests in very specific skills, such as designing racing cars, and there is only one employer in the local labour market. The worker is very dependent on the particular employer: having skills this specific is risky. With a cluster of similar employers, risks of workers fall. They no longer require such a large 'risk premium' or 'compensating differential' in their wage. Labour is therefore cheaper for firms. Where did scale economies come into the argument? Without them, each locality could have a tiny smattering of every firm. It is the presence of (some) scale economies that forces firms into all or nothing choices between different locations.

A second reason for clustering of producers is transport costs. Shops may cluster because of transport costs for consumers – one trip gets you to a street with lots of shops stocking what you want – but larger producers cluster because of features of production. Closeness to raw materials is an obvious example. Discovering a coal seam or iron ore leads to a profusion of heavy industrial businesses in the locality.

Most significant of all is probably the spillover in technology itself. In addition to Formula 1 car producers, famous examples include Silicon Valley in California and Route 128 around Boston, clusters of computer-based producers who find it advantageous to be in proximity. Although they are in competition with one another, they also feed off each other's ideas just as the most competitive of university professors still attend each other's seminars. Although articles get published two years later in journals, at which point ideas become accessible worldwide, discussions with the professor next door about some state of the art idea may yield a huge competitive edge over professors (research producers) elsewhere. The same holds good in businesses from software design to satellite technology.

This concept of a locational externality allows us to make clearer a concept that politicians have discussed for years but which previously economists have had considerable trouble providing with a coherent interpretation.

> *The* industrial base *of a country or region is a measure of the stock of existing producers available to provide such locational externalities.*

The emphasis on 'industrial' carries the presumption that the externalities are more significant for producers than for consumers, because of the specificity of investments required and minimum size that scale economies impose. Although ring-road super-stores cluster together to offer adjacent carpet stores, DIY shops, and garden centres, competition between *different* local clusters is intense. The degree of market failure is small.

In contrast, where the minimum efficient scale of specific investments is large, countries or regions may find there are two equilibria – one in which nobody enters and one in which many firms enter, each enjoying benefits from the presence of the other. Yet achieving the second outcome efficiently requires co-ordination of the

---

Box 6-2   State Aids in the EU

Every time an EU government gives yet another 'final subsidy' to its ailing national airline, there is a howl of protest from other airlines trying to compete. The European Union has been trying, with modest success, to crack down on the practice of State Aids. Examples include outright subsidies to ailing firms, but also other forms of discriminatory treatment such as special tax breaks. Getting rid of State Aids is not easy.

EU competition policy, by viewing transfers to individual firms as distortions, takes the view that State Aids are bad for efficiency within the Single Market. This has been the traditional view of economists. However, economics is like a sausage machine: you get out what you put in. Within models with few market failures, State Aids add an unnecessary market failure and diminish efficiency. However, within the last decade, two new areas of economic analysis have shown how a useful role for State Aids might exist. The first is the new industrial economics, for example strategic international competition between firms, as between Boeing and Airbus, where knowledge that Airbus has State Aids may affect the behaviour

of Boeing in ways favourable to Europe. The second is the new economic geography, where locational externalities may provide incentives for governments to bid for inward investment (e.g. of Japanese car producers) which then augments the industrial base of its host nation. From the viewpoint of the EU as a whole, it is desirable that such inflows go to the place where their contribution will be largest. An implicit auction, in which member states each bid to attract investment (by offering tax advantages, investment grants, etc.) may then be an efficient mechanism for revealing where the locational externalities are greatest.

State aid to manufacturing, 1994–96 (% of net output)

6	Greece, Italy
4	Germany
3	Belgium, Denmark, Spain
2	Luxembourg, Portugal, France, Ireland, Finland
0	UK

entry decision of different producers to internalize the externality facing each firm: it neglects the benefits that its own entry creates for other firms.

Before this is taken as a blank cheque to pursue industrial subsidies, it should be recalled that in the 1970s and 1980s industrial policy had some spectacular failures in many countries. Any time a large private firm experienced difficulties, this was prima facie evidence that intervention was required to 'preserve skills', 'maintain an international presence' in the industry, or 'take account of the needs of suppliers'. The new economic geography is not an alibi for backing losers or for freezing the industrial structure in a changing world.

▪▪▪ the social cost of monopoly power

When firms have monopoly power, price and social marginal benefit of the last output unit exceed the private and social marginal cost of producing that last output unit. From society's viewpoint the industry is producing too little. Expanding output would add more to social benefit than to social cost.

In Section 6-2 we take up the case of natural or pure monopoly. We begin with a more general discussion of all forms of imperfect competition and monopoly power. Intermediate forms of imperfect competition require some economies of scale to limit the number of firms an industry can support. Nevertheless, to introduce the idea of the social cost of monopoly power it is convenient to ignore economies of scale altogether. We thus ask the following question: what would happen if a competitive industry were taken over by a single firm which then operated as a multi-plant monopolist? Figure 6-1 shows how this question may be answered. Under perfect

Figure 6-1 The social cost of monopoly

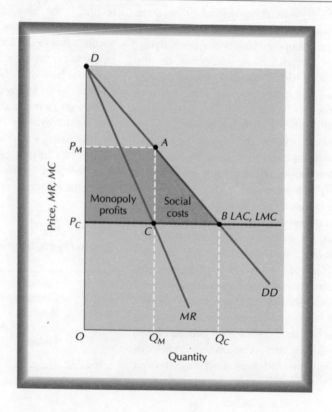

competition *LMC* is both the industry's long-run marginal cost curve and its supply curve. With constant returns to scale, *LMC* is also the long-run average cost curve of the industry. Given the demand curve *DD*, competitive equilibrium is at *B*. The competitive industry produces an output Q_C at a price P_C.

Now the industry is taken over by a monopolist, who produces an output Q_M at a price P_M thus equating marginal cost and marginal revenue. The area $P_M P_C AC$ shows the monopolist's profits from selling Q_M at a price in excess of marginal and average cost. The triangle *ACB* shows the deadweight burden or social cost of monopoly power. Why? Because at Q_M the social marginal benefit of another unit of output is P_M but the social marginal cost is only P_C. Society would like to expand output up to the competitive point *B* at which social marginal benefit and social marginal cost are equal. The triangle *ACB* measures the social profit or excess of benefits over costs from such an output expansion. Conversely, by reducing output to Q_M the monopolist imposes a social cost equal to the area *ACB*.

Since the demand curve measures the marginal benefit to consumers of each unit of output and the marginal cost curve measures the extra resources used to make each unit of output, the area between *DD* and *LMC* up to that output always measures the total surplus to be divided between producers and consumers.

> **Producer surplus** *is the excess of revenue over total costs. Total costs are shown by the area under the LMC curve up to this output.*

> **Consumer surplus** *is the triangle showing the excess of consumer benefits over spending. It is the area under the demand curve at this output minus the spending rectangle.*

In Figure 6-1, at the output Q_M producer surplus is the rectangle labelled profits and consumer surplus is the triangle DAP_M above this. But this output is inefficient because it does not maximize the sum of consumer and producer surplus. That is maximized at output Q_C at which the area between the demand curve and the *LMC* curve is maximized.

> *The* social cost of monopoly *is the failure to maximize social surplus. When output is below the socially efficient level, the* deadweight burden *triangle shows the social surplus that has been sacrificed.*

In fact, the welfare cost of monopoly may be greater than the deadweight burden triangle itself. Since monopoly may yield high profits to the firm, firms will expend large quantities of resources in trying to acquire and secure monopoly positions. They may advertise too much, not to provide information about the product, but to raise the fixed cost of being in the industry, thereby making it harder for new firms to enter.

Box 6-3   Price discriminating monopoly

The social cost of monopoly arises only because the monopolist cannot price discriminate. Perfect price discrimination would make the demand curve and marginal revenue curve coincide – selling new units would no longer bid down the price on existing sales. Then the monopolist would produce the socially efficient output. Price discrimination is possible only in special circumstances. Consumers must not be able to set up a second-hand market. Price discrimination in goods is hard.

Similarly, firms may devote large quantities of resources trying to influence the government in order to obtain favourable judgements which enhance or preserve their monopoly power. They may also deliberately maintain extra production capacity so that potential entrants can see that any attempt at entry will be matched by a sharp increase in production by existing firms, forcing price reductions which in the short run will be unprofitable for all but which may bankrupt the entrant first. From the economy's viewpoint, resources devoted to lobbying the government or maintaining over-capacity may also be largely wasted.

Modern economic analysis emphasizes yet another consideration, the role of information. Those running a monopoly are likely to have inside information about the firm's true cost opportunities. They know more than either the shareholders or any potential regulator. Perhaps the monopolist could really have lower costs than it has, but the managers can't be bothered putting in the effort. Economists sometimes call this 'managerial slack' or 'X-inefficiency'. The failure of competition effectively gives the firm an 'information monopoly' on its own cost possibilities. Outsiders can't find out.

When a competitive firm gets lazy it loses market share and may even go out of business. When a monopoly gets lazy it simply makes a little less profit than it might. From the social viewpoint, its cost curves are unnecessarily high. In Figure 6-2 *LMC* is the marginal cost of a firm striving for cost efficiency. The monopolist takes advantage of its information monopoly to enjoy an easy life and has higher costs *LMC'*. Suppose the monopolist could be broken up into identical firms (in the example there are constant returns to scale). Competition between firms would not merely make each set price equal to marginal cost, it would reveal managerial slack and force firms to attain the lower cost curve *LMC*. The monopolist would produce output Q_M at a price P_M. The competitive industry produces Q_C at a price P_C. Thus the economy moves from E' to E. Notice that the social gain is hugely larger than the triangle $E'FG$.

At the monopoly output Q_M, consumer surplus, the excess of their benefits over what they paid, was $P_M JE'$. HFE P_M was the declared profit of the monopolist, $KFHP_C$

Figure 6-2   An information monopoly

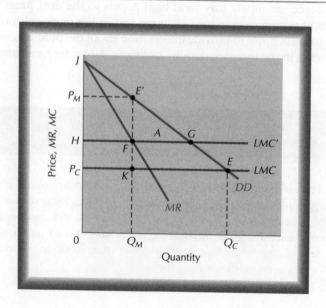

the hidden profit that the monopolist took as the easy life, and OQ_MKP_C the costs that even an efficient firm would have had to incur. In contrast, when equilibrium moves from E' to E, the *additional* social profits are the whole triangle $E'KE$.

So far we have assumed monopolists are lazy 'fat cats'. If it takes resources (effort, investment, etc.) to lower costs, the gain from abolishing monopoly will be smaller than in Figure 6-2 but still larger than the triangle $E'FG$. For these reasons, the precise extent of the social cost of monopoly remains a subject of continuing controversy. Nevertheless, few governments believe that the social cost of monopoly is sufficiently small that it can safely be ignored. We shortly examine the policies which have been adopted to restrict the degree of monopoly power exercised by large firms.

Our discussion relates only to the efficiency losses arising from imperfect competition. Society might also have views on two other aspects on monopoly performance: the amount of *political* power that large companies are in a position to exert, and the *distributional* issue of fairness in relation to the large supernormal profits that a monopolist can earn.

the distribution of monopoly profits

Suppose the government imposes a profits tax: what effect would this have on the monopolist's output decision? The way to maximize after-tax profits is to maximize pre-tax profits. Provided the government does not take all the extra pre-tax profit in taxes, increasing pre-tax profits must always increase post-tax profits. Hence the monopolist will produce exactly the same output as in the absence of a profits tax and, facing the same demand curve, will charge the same price as before.

One last issue. A monopolist may have sunk costs in the past, for example in R&D or in building factory capacity. Viewed from today, these have already been incurred and the position of today's cost curve is independent of whether or not the government taxes monopoly profits. However, had the firm known that profits would be subject to a windfall tax, perhaps the monopolist would never have incurred large R&D costs in the first place. Thus, an occasional surprise windfall tax may be able to remove monopoly profits without any adverse incentive effects on efficiency. However, the expectation that there would be regular resort to such a device would undermine incentives to invest. Costs would become higher than they need have been.

must liberalization help?

By now you may be assuming that more competition is always better. But in Chapter 5 we introduced the theory of the second best. Beginning from a distorted position, elimination of *all* market failures would always increase efficiency. But partial elimination or reduction can occasionally make things worse: sometimes two distortions somewhat offset each other. Removing just one makes the other one worse. More competition is not always better

Suppose there are large economies of scale and a falling average cost curve. A monopolist is bad for the reasons outlined already, but it does at least produce on a large scale and allow society to benefit from scale economies. Suppose the government insists on more competition, say entry of a second producer. Dividing the market, both firms fail to reap many scale economies. More competition may reduce profit margins and drive price closer to marginal cost; it may also reduce information monopolies (we can see what the other firm is charging), forcing more expenditure on cost reduction to shift cost curves down. But if scale economies are big enough, both producers will still have larger costs than the original monopolist. Society may be worse off because it has to spend more resources on production.

The second example is called cream skimming

Cream skimming *is entry only in the profitable parts of the business, thereby undermining scale economies elsewhere.*

Suppose a postal monopoly is required to have a uniform service provision: it has to deliver throughout the UK at a uniform price. A private entrant would want to take on profitable parcel delivery in cities but not unprofitable parcel delivery to remote rural areas. If it is allowed to cream skim the profitable bits alone, it reduces the scale economies of the large producer in other areas and might even jeopardize the entire operation.

▮▮▮ competition policy

Figure 6-3 provides a convenient guide to the remainder of this chapter. It divides possible outcomes into four regions. In the top left box, competition is possible and desirable, what we might call the normal case. In the top right box, some kind of competition would be possible but it is not desirable. In this box, scale economies are important and entry by other firms would lead to cream skimming or to small-scale high-cost activities by all firms. In the bottom right, the situation is one of natural monopoly. Huge scale economies preclude any possiblility of open competition. In the bottom left box, the incumbent has sufficient power to deter entry if things are left to the market. But scale economies are not that significant. Society would gain more from greater competition, if only it could be secured, than it would lose from giving up economies of large scale by allowing entry.

Figure 6-3 divides up our analysis into competition policy, the topic in the remainder of this section, and regulation, the topic of the next section. Competition policy is about the two boxes in the left-hand column. It concerns situations in which promotion of competition is likely to be beneficial. This can be achieved by setting rules for conduct or by taking steps to ensure a market structure in which competition can then take place.

Figure 6-3 | Assessing competition

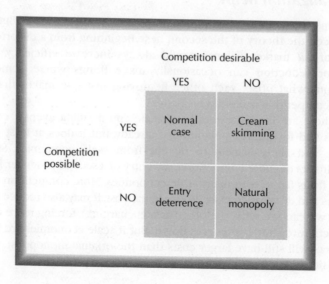

In the United States, much of competition policy has been based on achieving a structure favourable to competition. UK competition policy has been more pragmatic, assessed on a case by case basis, without any prior presumption that the existence of monopoly power is against the public interest.

competition law in the UK

Legislation has been steadily extended since the Monopoly and Restrictive Practices Act of 1946. Restrictive practices have been separately examined since the establishment of the Restrictive Practices Court in 1956. Monopoly policy was comprehensively reassessed in the 1973 Fair Trading Act and amended in the Competition Acts of 1980 and 1998. The 1973 Act introduced a Director-General of Fair Trading to supervise many aspects of competition and consumer law including the regulation of quality and standards. The Director-General is responsible for monitoring company behaviour and, subject to a ministerial veto, can refer individual cases to the Competition Commission for a thorough investigation. A company can be referred if it supplies more than 25 per cent of the total market. The Commission can also be given cases where two or more distinct firms by implicit collusion operate to restrict competition.

The Competition Commission *is charged to investigate whether or not a monopoly, or potential monopoly, acts against the public interest.*

There is no presumption that monopoly is necessarily bad, and the Commission is charged to investigate whether or not the monopoly acts against the public interest, a brief that may be widely interpreted though in recent years there has been increasing emphasis on the 'maintenance and promotion of effective competition'.

The Restrictive Practices Court examines agreements between firms supplying goods and services in the UK, for example agreements on collusive pricing behaviour. All agreements must be notified to the Director-General of Fair Trading, who will refer them to the Court unless they are voluntarily abandoned or judged of trivial significance. The Court will find against these agreements unless they satisfy one of eight 'gateways' or justifications, for example that their removal would cause serious and persistent unemployment in the area. Thus for restrictive practices the burden of proof lies on the companies to show that they are acting in the public interest: in contrast, the legislation on monopolies is more open-minded, requiring the Commission to make the case that companies are acting against the public interest.

The UK is subject to the monopoly legislation of the European Union as well. Article 85 of the Treaty of Rome is rather similar to the UK legislation on restrictive practices. Agreements have to be notified and they are likely to be outlawed. Article 86 bans the abuse of a 'dominant position' as a monopolist. The 1998 Competition Act sought to bring UK policy more in line with European Law. In particular, the previous terms of reference of the Competition Commission were supplemented by two new Prohibitions. Essentially, there is a ban on agreements that prevent, restrict, or distort competition in the UK (though exemptions can still be granted if this is judged in the public interest), and a ban on conduct that amounts to abuse of a dominant position within the UK.

UK competition policy in practice

The Competition Commission (www.competition-commission.gov.uk) has wide powers to make recommendations, and the Secretary of State to act on these recommendations, yet only a few companies have been penalized as a result of investigations. More frequently, the Commission has relied on informal assurances that criticized behaviour will be discontinued.

The Commission has investigated a wide range of cases, from beer to breakfast cereals and from contraceptives to cross-Channel ferries. Because the Commission is charged to investigate each case with an open mind, its judgements have tended to stress different aspects of behaviour in different cases. Certainly a high market share has not been sufficient to attract an unfavourable judgement. On the other hand, cost reduction has not been sufficient to avoid censure by the Commission. Hoffman LaRoche was praised as 'a highly competent organization with a product range of high quality', but its enormous profits, sometimes as high as 60 or 70 per cent on capital employed, were held to be unjustified and the Commission recommended that the price of both Librium and Valium be halved.

Unilever subsidiary Birds Eye Wall's (BEW) was accused of freezing out the competition by distributing wrapped ice cream primarily through dedicated distribution outlets on terms that did not allow these outlets to handle products that competed with BEW. The case was eventually referred to the Competition Commission.

In 1998 the Commission ruled that there was no evidence that BEW had refused to supply other wholesalers, but that BEW had supplied some regional wholesalers on less favourable terms than those granted to its own distributors. The Commission concluded that BEW had restricted and distorted competition, found no offsetting benefits to the public interest, and recommended that BEW be required to supply wholesalers on the same terms as its dedicated distributors.

The Commission also has the power to investigate regulated industries such as utilities that we discuss more fully in Section 6-2. In 1999 it reported on claims that charges by Cellnet, Vodafone, and BT for calls from fixed phones to mobile phones were too high. It concluded that emerging competition in telecommunications was not yet sufficient to discipline these powerful suppliers, and that at the end of 1998 charges made by Vodafone and Cellnet were 22 per cent above the public interest benchmark – calculated for a hypothetical supplier, with the scale economies corresponding to a 25 per cent market share, and a 16.5 per cent return on capital – and that BT charges for calling into a mobile phone were 50 per cent above a public interest benchmark. The Commission recommended that the licences of Cellnet, Vodafone, and BT be modified to impose price ceilings on these particular charges.

restrictive practices

Since restrictive practices legislation was first introduced, over 5000 agreements have been registered, the vast majority of which were abandoned even before they were taken to the Court. Most explicit price-fixing has gone. These facts look impressive but overstate the success of policy against restrictive practices. First, they may simply have forced collusive agreements underground. Second, the various 'gateways' have permitted some agreements to be ratified, and the wisdom of some of these ratifications has been challenged. Finally, it is possible that tighter control of restrictive practices agreements between firms is one of the factors that provide an incentive for mergers, a subject we take up shortly. By formally merging, companies could continue their old practices within the merged company and take their chance if they got investigated by the Commission.

assessing UK competition policy

Legislation on restrictive practices has eliminated many cases of blatant anti-competitive behaviour. The Director-General of Fair Trading now has powers to promote the provision of better consumer information (e.g. the Trade Descriptions Act) and to monitor general company behaviour. And the Competition Commission has identified some practices that many regard as undesirable. Would a more radical and comprehensive anti-monopoly policy have been better for society?

Large scale may be necessary to achieve minimum efficient plant size, and the cost of breaking up large companies may be considerable. Large scale may also promote better management, co-ordination, and research. Co-ordination via cartels or single ownership may facilitate better planning when products are close complements in production.

When tariffs on imports are low and transport costs are moderate, domestic producers may face severe international competition. Without knowing the size of the relevant market in which firms are competing, large size cannot immediately be equated with uncompetitive behaviour.

Nor is it obvious that the government should always oppose large profits. Profits are the carrot that encourages firms to take risks in a market economy. Many firms take risks that do not come off. But if potential risk-takers are assured that success will immediately invite investigation by the Competition Commission and an order to cut prices and eliminate excess profits, there will be less risk-taking in the economy. Society has to decide how much risk-taking it wishes to encourage and to allow a proper return to risk-taking as an economic cost against accounting profits.

These doubts about the merit of a blind pursuit of perfect competition lie behind the UK policy and the judgements of the Competition Commission. Thus policy has considered each case on its merits. Monopoly policy should not be independent of other aspects of government policy. Large firms make more sense when the UK is competing within a large European market. We might wish to be tougher on large firms if the government is pursuing a policy of protection with high import tariffs.

■■■ mergers

Two existing firms can join together in two different ways.

> *One firm may make a* takeover bid *for the other by offering to buy out the shareholders of the second firm.*

Managers of the 'victim' firm will usually resist since they are likely to lose their jobs, but the shareholders will accept if the offer is sufficiently attractive.

> *A* merger *is the voluntary union of two companies where they think they will do better by amalgamating.*

We must ask whether mergers are in the public interest, since mergers help to create monopoly power.

> *By a* horizontal merger *we mean the union of two firms at the same production stage in the same industry. By a* vertical merger *we mean the union of two firms at different production stages in the same industry. In* conglomerate mergers, *the production activities of the two firms are essentially unrelated.*

A horizontal merger may allow exploitation of economies of scale. One large car factory may be better than two small ones. (Notice that this requires that each of the original companies were producing below minimum efficient scale.) In vertical mergers it is often claimed that there are important gains to co-ordination and planning. It may be easier to make long-term decisions about the best size and type of steel mill if a simultaneous decision is taken on the level of car production to which steel output forms an important input. Since conglomerate mergers involve companies with completely independent products, these mergers have only small opportunities for a direct reduction in production costs.

Two other factors are frequently mentioned as potential benefits of mergers. First, if one company has an inspired management team it may be more productive to allow this team to run both businesses. Managers of course are very fond of this explanation for mergers. Economists have tended to be more sceptical. Second, by pooling their financial resources, the merging companies may enjoy better credit-worthiness and access to cheaper borrowing. If companies achieve any of these benefits, they will increase productivity and lower the cost of making any specified output level. These private gains are also social gains, since society can use less resources to achieve the same output. If these were the only considerations, social and private calculations would coincide.

However, there are two reasons for private and social assessments to diverge. First, the merger of two large firms will give them the monopoly power that derives from a large market share. The merged company is likely to restrict output and increase prices, a deadweight burden for society as a whole.

Second, the merged company may be able to use its *financial* power as distinct from its power derived from current market share. This danger is especially apparent in conglomerate mergers. A car producer and a food manufacturer cannot merge to gain economies of scale in production; but they can use their joint financial resources to start a price war in one of these industries. By forcing out some existing competitors, or merely holding this increased threat over potential entrants, they may be able to increase their market share in the long run, deter entry, and charge high prices for evermore. In framing merger policy, the government must therefore decide whether the potential social gains from reduced costs and more efficient production are outweighed by the social costs of monopoly power that might arise.

mergers in practice

Table 6-1 shows annual averages of takeovers and mergers involving only UK firms. It shows dramatic merger booms in the late 1980s and again after 1995. What was going on? First, the two merger booms coincided with high values of the stock market, when the cost of financing mergers was low. Since one way in which a firm finances a takeover is by giving some of its shares to shareholders in the other company, a booming stock market raises both the bidding power of takeover raiders and the value of the companies for which they are bidding. It was the value of the mergers, even more than the number of them, which was the key aspect of the merger booms.

Table 6-1 UK takeovers and mergers 1972–98 (annual averages)

	Number	Value (1998 £bn)
1972–78	640	1.4
1979–85	490	4.2
1986–89	1300	43.1
1990–94	590	9.5
1995–98	580	31.2

Sources: British Business 1989; Business Trends 1997; ONS, First Release 1999.

Conversely, 1990–94 was a period of recession, high real interest rates and expensive borrowing. The benefit of mergers was reduced and the cost increased.

Second, mergers are often associated with opportunities to rationalize industrial structure. Two major developments in European markets have been the run up to the creation of the Single European Market in 1992, and the corresponding reorganization that took place before the euro was launched in 1999. A larger market increases opportunities for scale economies (a greater private incentive to create large firms) and enhances competition (reducing the need for society to worry about mergers creating monopoly power).

Third, the combination of new technology and deregulation has been changing market structure both in the UK and in its main trading partners. Segmentation of national markets has been breaking down in telecoms, financial services, and many other industries. Cross-border mergers have allowed leading players to respond to larger markets.

The increase in effective market size in the last 15 years has also influenced the type of mergers taking place. Conglomerate mergers had grown steadily in the 1960s and 1970s, becoming a third of all mergers by the early 1980s. However, financial deregulation has made it easier to raise finance and reduced the importance of

---

Box 6-4 Sky's the limit for Man United

In late 1998, British Sky Broadcasting launched a huge bid to take over UK football giants Manchester United. The bid was referred to the Competition Commission, which turned it down. The Commission emphasized Premier League matches. TV rights, for the whole Premier League, are sold collectively by the Premier League to various TV companies. Much the largest fees are paid by BSkyB. Its very high market share of premium football viewing gives it market power.

The Commission argued that if collective selling of Premier League rights continued, BSkyB would gain an unfair advantage over other TV bidders through the influence and information it would acquire as a result of merger with Man United. Aware of this, potential bidders would be reluctant to bid, further enhancing BSkyB's dominant position. If, instead, the collective sale of Premier League rights was replaced by deals between individual clubs and broadcasters, merger of the top club and top broadcaster would again have adverse effects on competition.

The Commission also considered that the merger would have adverse effects on football itself. It would reinforce the existing gap between rich and poor clubs, even within the Premier League. And it would give BSkyB too much influence over regulation of football by the Premier League. Moreover, if the merger then provoked a small number of other clubs and broadcasters into similar mergers, the rich–poor gap would widen still further.

The Commission's judgement was based on its assertion that 'the relevant football market in which Manchester United operates is no wider than the matches of Premier League clubs' (http://www. mmc.gov.uk/bskyb.htm). But was this correct? In 1999 Man United were European champions and won the world cup championship in Tokyo, but they did it on the cheap, partly because so many of their young stars had grown up in the Man United youth programme. BSkyB's money would have allowed Man United to match salaries in Series A in Italy. The Premier League has never been able to (afford to) attract the top Brazilian stars.

This example shows again the difficulty in defining the relevant market in which to assess competition policy. Should it be the UK, Europe, or the global market? Once it extends beyond a single country, which competition authority should have jurisdiction? Easy questions with difficult answers.

the financial muscle that provided one of the motives for conglomerate mergers. Disappointing performance of these hybrid companies has increasingly led to demerger and a renewed focus on the original core business. In contrast, the erosion of segmented national markets has led to a boom in horizontal mergers.

merger policy

The proliferation of large companies through merger would not have been possible had the government been operating a tough anti-merger policy. Individual cases have been scrutinized to see if they were against the public interest. Indeed, it is only since 1965 that mergers have been subject to public scrutiny at all. There are now two grounds for referring a prospective merger to an investigation by the Competition Commission: (1) that the merger will promote a new monopoly as defined by the 25 per cent market share used in deciding references for existing monopoly positions, or (2) that the merger involves the transfer of at least £70 million worth of company assets.[2]

Since the legislation was introduced in 1965, only about 4 per cent of all merger proposals have been referred to the Competition Commission. Thus for much of the period government policy has been to consent to, or actively encourage, mergers. In believing that the benefits would outweigh the costs, British merger policy reflected two underlying assumptions. The first was that the cost savings from economies of scale and more intensive use of scarce management talent could be quite large. The second was that the UK was effectively part of an increasingly competitive world market so that the monopoly power of the merged firms, and the corresponding social cost of the deadweight burden, would be small. Large as they were, the merged firms would still be small in relation to European or world markets, and would face relatively elastic demand curves which gave little scope for raising price above marginal cost.

Nevertheless, it would be wrong to suppose that all mergers were approved. Nearly half of the mergers actually referred to the Competition Commission were found to be against the public interest, and the effects of the legislation went beyond the cases actually referred. Investigation was a lengthy process taking many months, a delay during which company share prices could move considerably and upset the original negotiations about the terms on which the relative shares of the companies should be valued. In practice, even the threat that a merger might be referred was often sufficient to induce the companies to abandon the merger.

[2] The asset valuation was £5 million during 1965-80, £15 million during 1980-84, and £30 million during 1984-94.

▣▣ recap

- The social cost or deadweight burden of monopoly power arises because marginal cost is set equal to marginal revenue, which is less than price and marginal consumer benefit.

- The easy life may lead monopolists to make inadequate efforts to reduce costs, adding to the social cost of monopoly.

- Industrial policy seeks to offset market failures in production; offsetting monopoly power is the object of competition policy. The two are frequently related.

- Patents provide a temporary legal monopoly for successful inventors, and hence an incentive to look for inventions.

- Many governments believe that the social return on R&D exceeds its private return. Some benefits of R&D spill over to other firms, creating an externality.

- Economic geography is based on locational externalities arising in training, transport, and knowledge creation. The industrial base is the existing locational stock available.

- In the UK any firm with more than 25 per cent of the market can be referred to the Competition Commission, which must then consider whether or not the monopoly is against the public interest. The Commission takes account of a wide range of factors in making a judgement.

- Anti-competition agreements between firms, such as collusive price-fixing, must be notified and are generally outlawed.

- Mergers may be horizontal, vertical, or conglomerate. Conglomerate mergers have the smallest scope for economies of scale. The recent merger boom has largely been in horizontal mergers to take advantage of larger markets caused by globalization, European integration, and deregulation.

- In principle, mergers can be referred to the Competition Commission if they will create a firm with a 25 per cent market share or if they involve assets of over £70 million. In practice, few mergers satisfying these criteria are actually referred.

▣▣ key terms

▣▣ review questions

1 With constant AC and MC equal to £5, a competitive industry produces 1 million output units. Taken over by a monopolist, output falls to 800 000 units and the price rises to £8. AC and MC are unchanged. How would you calculate the social cost of monopoly? What is it?

2 Quite apart from aid to sunrise industries, UK policy provides substantial tax breaks for those investing in small firms. Do you think the issues discussed in this chapter can be used to justify such a policy?

3 Most footballs in the world are made in a small village in Pakistan. Why do football producers cluster together? Why not in Switzerland?

6-2 privatization and regulation

'In every great monarchy in Europe the sale of the Crown lands would deliver a much greater revenue than any which these lands ever afforded to the Crown. When the Crown lands had become private property, they would, in the course of a few years, become well improved and well cultivated.'

Adam Smith, *The Wealth of Nations* (1776)

This section deals with the boundary between the public sector and the private sector. As suggested by Adam Smith, the controversy is over 200 years old. Section 6-1 discussed the role of policy in cases where promoting competition was feasible and likely to enhance efficiency. Now, we discuss industries in which scale economies are considerable. Competition may not be feasible or may require sacrificing scale economies to an extent that makes competition undesirable. Before 1980 such industries were thought to require so much regulation that they might as well be state owned.

Nationalization *is the acquisition of private companies by the public sector.*

After 1980 the UK pioneered a programme of privatization that has now been emulated in countries as diverse as France, Japan, Mexico and Hungary. Some countries, like the Czech Republic which began the 1990s with 97 per cent of its economy in state hands, were so keen to privatize quickly that they gave away state enterprises to private shareholders for only a nominal price!

 Privatization *is the return of state enterprises to private ownership and control.*

It was the intention in the UK that subsequent regulation of privatized companies would be as light and unintrusive as possible. For this reason, the changes were sometimes called deregulation. In industries without big scale economies this was indeed possible. In the industries on which we mainly focus in this chapter – utilities such as electricity, gas, water, telecommunications – more extensive regulation, with regard to structure not just conduct, is required whenever international competition is not vigorous.

natural monopoly

A natural monopoly faces huge opportunities for scale economies. In private hands, it sets marginal cost equal to marginal revenue, which is well below price and social marginal benefit. Hence a natural monopoly produces too little output from society's point of view. What can the government do? If it breaks up the firm into a lot of small firms, it will lose scale economies and waste resources. If instead it orders the monopoly to raise output to the socially efficient level, the firm will lose money. Private firms cannot be forced to lose money forever. They shut down instead.

A natural monopoly's *average costs keep falling as its output rises. It can undercut smaller competitors. Since* LMC *lies below* LAC *at all outputs for which* LAC *is still falling, a natural monopoly loses money if forced to price at marginal cost.*

One solution is to compromise. The monopolist is forced to produce more than the output that maximizes private profit, but not so much more that profits become negative. A better solution may be a two-part tariff.

A two-part tariff *means that users pay a fixed sum to access the system and then a price per unit that reflects marginal cost of production.*

Provided the fixed charge does not deter anyone from joining the system, the efficient output can then be achieved. Consumers use the system until marginal cost equals marginal benefit, and producers can break even because they separately recover fixed costs (the source of scale economies) through the fixed charge. Thus, for example, phone companies charge a quarterly line rental (the fixed charge) and a price per call.

The two-part tariff is not always a feasible solution. If the fixed charge has to be *very* high it may induce people to abandon consumption of the commodity altogether. Moreover, whereas it may be easy to collect fixed charges from consumers with telephone or gas installations, it is harder to enforce a fixed charge for the right to travel by rail and a fare per journey reflecting marginal cost. The costs of enforcing such a system might be enormous.

The third solution to the natural monopoly problem is to order the monopolist to produce at the socially efficient output but to provide a government subsidy to cover the losses that this will inevitably imply. However, the government will wish to be closely concerned with the operation of the company to ensure that this does not provide a blanket guarantee to underwrite whatever losses the company makes through its own stupidity or inefficiency. Thus, where the subsidy solution is adopted there is a pressure for the government to become involved in the entire running of the industry so that all operations can be carefully monitored.

If such industries are nationalized so they can produce closer to the socially efficient output, it is inevitable that they will make losses and require a subsidy.

The fact that nationalized industries make losses is not sufficient to prove that they are not *minimizing costs or producing the wrong output from society's viewpoint.*

Three problems recur in attempts to adopt *any* of the above solutions to the problem of natural monopoly. First, once information is costly for monitors to acquire it is hard to ensure that the industry does minimize costs. Unnecessarily high costs can be passed on under average cost pricing (solution 1), can result in a higher fixed charge to ensure break-even under a two-part tariff (solution 2), or can require a larger subsidy (solution 3).

The second problem is regulatory capture.

Regulatory capture *implies that the regulator gradually comes to identify with the interests of the firm it regulates, eventually becoming its champion, not its watchdog.*

Clearly, the regulated devote considerable time, effort, and money to lobbying and otherwise trying to influence the regulator. A sense of public duty is the only reason for the regulator to resist. It can become an unequal contest. More subtly, the regulated firm has all the inside information about its own activities, information which it is the whole purpose of the regulator to try to acquire. Of necessity, regulators build up contacts with the regulated. At the end of long conversations, the regulator can feel quite sympathetic to the problems as perceived by the regulated.

Third, regulators may have difficulty making credible commitments about their future behaviour. For example, the regulator may seek to encourage the monopolist to

---

Box 6-5 | Airline deregulation

Lessons from the United States Internal US flights were deregulated in 1978. Entry barriers were removed, and by 1984 the number of airlines had risen from 36 to 120, fares were down 30 per cent, and passenger use was up 50 per cent. Fuller planes meant lower costs. More frequent service meant greater passenger convenience. Free marketeers rejoiced as their predictions came true.

The story changed after 1984. Cutthroat competition led to bankruptcies and mergers. By 1989 only 27 airlines survived. The top 12 controlled 97 per cent of the market. Fares rose. By 1997 airline profits reached $5 bn. Powerful incumbent airlines erected strategic entry barriers to consolidate their market share. They moved to a single airport (the hub) out of which long-haul flights operated. A system of feeder services (the spokes) first flew passengers to the hub. The hub-and-spoke system made it hard for small airlines to challenge the major airlines. Second, the majors also owned the reservation system used by travel agents to locate empty seats. By programming the computer to show their own flights first, they put new entrants at a disadvantage. Finally, they offered air miles that could be cashed in only with the same airline.

Regulation in Europe European scheduled air travel was extensively regulated until 1997. Flights between European capitals were often restricted to one airline from each of the two countries, such as Iberia and Alitalia on the Madrid–Rome route. Competition was sometimes nominal; the two airlines divided their joint revenue equally. Fares were strictly controlled. Scheduled air travel was specifically exempt from EC Competition Law.

The consequence? High fares. Moreover, when firms have extensive product market power, trade unions will grab a big slice of these excess profits:

lack of competition will show up as much in inflated costs as in high profits. The table shows how beautifully this theory fits the facts. Apart from the UK, where domestic deregulation had begun in the 1980s, all continental airlines paid much more than their US counterparts, despite average living standards being much higher in the USA than in, say, Spain or Portugal.

In the 1990s, European airlines were increasingly subject to normal competition law. 'EU completes air travel deregulation programme' reported *The Times* (2 April 1997) but then pointed out that, because of congestion at major airports, new entrants would have to operate out of secondary airports. While incumbents retain access to prime 'landing and takeoff slots' at favoured airports, life will remain difficult for new entrants. In March 1999, the High Court in London ruled that slots at Heathrow could be traded freely for cash. The European Commission thinks small airlines will be unable to afford to buy these slots.

Labour costs per worker, 1987 (USA = 100)

	Cockpit staff	Cabin crew
8 US airlines	100	100
British Airways	120	68
Sabena (Belgian)	307	139
UTA (French)	298	161
Lufthansa (German)	325	143
Alitalia (Italian)	232	211
TAO (Portuguese)	167	93
SAS (Scandinavian)	258	146
Iberia (Spanish)	200	132

Sources: F. McGowan and P. Seabright, 'Deregulating European Airlines', *Economic Policy*, 1990; *The Times*, 2 April 1997; *Financial Times*, 10 February 1998.

invest by promising 'light' regulation in the future. But once the investment is made and a cost sunk, the regulator then faces temptations to change the ground rules, toughening requirements. Foreseeing all this, the monopolist never invests in the first place. The equilibrium is one of underinvestment because the regulator faces commitment problems.

During 1945–80, many European governments concluded that the least bad solution to these three problems was nationalization.

nationalized industries

By nationalized industries we mean not the state provision of public goods, such as defence, nor of services supplied without charge, such as state education, but of private goods for sale in the market-place. Even by 2000 some UK firms remained under state control (e.g. the Post Office and Nuclear Electric).

Although natural monopoly was the commonest reason for nationalization, three other motives sometimes played a role. The first was externalities. One reason the London Underground has yet to be privatized is that the failure of politicians to price roads properly allows huge pollution and congestion externalities to go unchecked. Subsidizing public transport may then be the second-best policy. A second reason was value judgements about equity or fairness. A private profit-maximizing railway would close many rural lines. Society may think this would severely reduce the welfare of citizens in remote areas and undermine national unity. If so, its choices are to legislate that private suppliers must subsidize rural railways if they wish to be in the train business, or to nationalize the whole thing. Third, it may be important to co-ordinate different parts of a network. As a nationalized industry, British Rail could think about the entire system. The fragmentation of the industry after privatization has led to externalities. For example, when Railtrack (www.railtrack.co.uk) invests in better infrastructure, the main gain may accrue to train operators not Railtrack itself.

We now discuss in more detail how society might wish investment and pricing decisions to be made within the public sector.

investment decisions

An investment project is profitable if the present value of the stream of future operating profits exceeds the initial cost of the new capital. Since firms do the most profitable projects first, investment proceeds until the marginal project is reached. At this point the present value of future profits just equals the cost of the capital. The same statement can be made using flows instead of stocks. Investment proceeds as long as the rate of return exceeds the interest rate that represents the opportunity cost of the funds tied up.

The same principles carry over into social investment decisions provided we use social not private measures of costs, benefits and the discount rate.

The initial cost of capital good   In the absence of other distortions, this is simply the private cost of the capital project. However, if externalities exist they should be taken into account. Local unemployment might reduce the social opportunity cost of construction workers below the market wage. Without the project the people would have made nothing else. Even the Treasury understands that where projects reduce unemployment they also reduce payments for unemployment benefit. A second possible externality arises from economic geography. Where *building* capital goods fosters production externalities (e.g. skill development), the right place to take this into account is in adjusting the 'social price' of the capital good.

Valuing the stream of future costs and benefits   Society will wish to use social not private values of costs and benefits. Externalities are one source of divergence between private and social. Consumer surplus is another. A private firm thinks the annual benefit is the steam of profits. For society the benefit is the entire area under the demand curve up to this ouput. Social profit coincides with monopoly profits only when the monopolist can price discriminate. With uniform pricing, the profit rectangle ($OP \times OQ$) is always smaller than the total consumer benefit. Notice, for later, that even when we measure *total* social benefit by the area under the demand curve, the *marginal benefit* is still given by the height of the demand curve at the output actually produced.

Choosing the discount rate   If public sector projects use a different discount rate from private sector projects, this will lead to a distortion between public and private investment.

> *The* discount rate *is the interest rate used in calculating present values of future streams of benefits or costs.*

However, there are two reasons why the (second-best) compromise still involves public-sector discount rates below private ones. First, the public sector handles risk better. Even a huge loss on a major project would imply only a tiny change in income tax rates. The risk is spread more thinly: the public sector has more 'shareholders'.

Second, public investment displaces not just private investment but private consumption. Governments finance public-sector investment out of taxation that reduces take-home pay and high-street spending. Households can shift resources between current and future consumption by saving today to accumulate wealth for tomorrow. The after-tax interest rate shows the terms on which one can be swapped for the other. For efficiency, public sector investment should offer the same rate of return.

First best would thus be the same return on public investment, private investment and private saving. Distortions from tax rates and differences in ability to handle risk make this unattainable. The most efficient compromise (the second best) involves a public sector discount rate below the private rate but above the post-tax interest rate.

pricing decisions

But for distortions elsewhere in the economy, nationalized industries should set prices at marginal cost. Private marginal cost should be adjusted for any production or consumption externalities that arise, thus ensuring that society equally values the marginal cost and marginal benefit from the last unit of output. Social marginal cost also takes account of any distributional value judgements the government wishes to impose. Prices should reflect short-run social marginal costs. In the short run, existing capacity is fixed and does not enter marginal cost. Long-run marginal cost *LMC* also include the appropriate opportunity cost of the capital itself (on an annual basis, this is depreciation and interest on money tied up).

Thus, when demand and marginal benefit are low, *SMC* lies below *LMC* because the cost of capital is not included in *SMC*. However, *SMC* becomes vertical once a plant's full capacity is reached. Hence if demand is large, pricing at *SMC* leads to prices well in excess of *LMC*. This is precisely the signal that further investment to increase capacity is socially profitable. Once capacity has also been chosen optimally in the long run, *SMC* and *LMC* will coincide.

Peak load pricing   In Chapter 3 we argued that a private monopolist would make higher profits if it were possible to price discriminate, charging different prices to customers whose demand curves were effectively distinct. The problem with price discrimination in *goods* is that low-price customers resell to higher-price customers, thus tending to equalize the prices customers actually pay. Resale is not a problem when the commodity is a service (train journeys, electricity supply), which must be consumed as it is purchased.

A producer of electricity faces a high demand for electricity at breakfast time and dinner time, moderate demand throughout the rest of the day, and very little demand at night. To cater for demand at peak times it has to build extra power stations, which are idle when demand is lower. Thus in the long run, taking account of the capacity cost of building the extra power stations, the marginal cost of supplying peak users is very high. Users at different times impose very different marginal costs on society. It makes sense to charge peak users higher prices to reflect the higher marginal costs they impose.

> Peak load pricing *is a system of price discrimination whereby peak time users pay higher prices to reflect the higher marginal cost of supplying them.*

Peak load pricing has two attractive consequences. Not only are peak users paying for the high marginal costs they impose, but also those users who would not mind consuming at a different time (e.g. households with night storage heaters, who can use electricity at a time when marginal costs are low) are induced by cheaper prices to switch to consuming at off-peak times. By spreading total daily consumption more evenly, society reduces peak demand and has to devote less resources to building power stations whose number is determined by peak usage.

Efficient pricing policy makes prices vary with short-run marginal cost. Off-peak users do not exhaust full capacity and pay the marginal operating cost c exclusive of capacity charges for the marginal plant. Peak users with the demand curve pay a higher price on the vertical part of the *SMC* curve through which their demand curve passes.

Given this efficient pricing structure, what is the efficient quantity of investment? Investment should increase capacity up to the point at which the once-and-for-all cost of a new plant equals the present value of operating profits when the efficient pricing structure is in operation. Equivalently, on a flow basis, the average daily price should cover long-run marginal cost inclusive of capacity costs.

To sum up, prices should be set at short-run marginal cost, the actual opportunity cost of the resources to society. When there is a daily or seasonal pattern in demand, peak load pricing reflects the different short-run marginal costs of supplying different customers at different times of day or times of year. The amount of total demand met on the vertical part of short-run marginal cost curves will then depend on the level of total capacity. At low capacity, prices will frequently be high since they are set on the vertical part of the short-run marginal cost curves. In the long run, investment and the efficient level of capacity should be determined to ensure that, when pricing at short-run marginal cost, average daily or yearly prices equal long-run marginal cost.

Telephone pricing in the UK   Peak load pricing and two-part tariffs try to get the relevant price as close to marginal cost as possible. This makes sense whether the aim is maximization of profit or social profit. Next time you see the quarterly telephone bill, take a look at it in closer detail. You will find you have been charged a quarterly rental independent of the number of calls made, and then in addition a charge per minute that you make a call: a two-part tariff. Since the telephone regulator OFTEL cares about efficiency, the rental should roughly cover the capacity charge, while the price per unit should cover short-run marginal cost *SMC*. This in turn should follow the principle of peak load pricing.

Households and businesses wake up in the morning and want to get started on a new day's communication by phone. By evening, there are fewer people left to call, and by the middle of the night most of us are asleep. Those who wish to make daytime calls should pay the high price required to choke off demand at full capacity. Conversely, when the weekend network is deserted because business is asleep, *SMC* and price should be much lower. Table 6-2 shows that actual prices of British Telecom closely follow both principles: two-part tariff and peak load pricing.

nationalized industries' performance

By 1967 the large UK public sector was being run according to sophisticated principles of pricing and investment as set out above. Civil servants who helped run these industries were masters of the intricacies of the social discount rate, peak load pricing, two-part tariffs and consumer surplus. So what went wrong?

Three things. First, the analysis assumed perfect (i.e. costless) information. In practice, firms always had inside information and the government became worried that there were insufficient ways of preventing unnecessary cost escalation. Cost curves were higher than they should be. Second, there were several types of commitment problem. The government found it difficult to resist pressure for wage increases in the public sector. Managers of nationalized industries couldn't argue that the 'shareholders' couldn't afford it. The shareholder was the Treasury and it could always find more money. Hence managers in nationalized industries found it hard to resist wage claims. They also found it hard to fire people. Strikes against dismissals made politicians nervous. Sometimes the minister would pick up the phone and find a way to do a deal.

Commitment problems also applied to investment. Investment by the nationalized industries is part of government spending and contributes to the budget deficit. Of course it also contributes to future government earnings but politicians under short-term pressure had a habit of cancelling long-term investment plans by nationalized industries. So nationalized industries had inefficient levels of investment. However much the privatized utilities are now blamed for poor infrastructure in railway signalling or water supply, half a century of underinvestment while they had been nationalized obviously contributed to the problem.

There were other types of 'government failure'. Politicians wanted plants located in their constituencies, wanted wage freezes during periods of overheating, wanted additional spending during recessions, all of which distorted decision making within nationalized industries. They had been nationalized to solve a market failure: now they were at least as vulnerable to government failure.

Third, people began to realize that a goldfish might look big in a small jar but small in a large lake. Increasing integration of different national economies began to introduce competition through imports or entry by foreign companies. As the size of

| Table 6-2 | BT price of a local call, 2000 |

	Day	Evening	Weekend
Pence/minute	4	1	1

Note: Quarterly fixed rental £23.63.

Source: British Telecommunications.

the relevant market increased, the potential market power of firms of a given size diminished. Industries previously viewed as natural monopolies might be subject to more competition in the future, reducing the case for state control.

■■■ public versus private

Efficiency does not fall like rain from the sky. It needs sustained effort and leadership by management. How do incentives differ in the public and private sectors?

incentives for private managers

In theory, private managers' performance is monitored by actual and potential share-holders. If managers do badly, the company's directors may be voted out of office at the annual general meeting of shareholders. Moreover, if bad management is perceived by the stock market, share prices will be lower than they might have been and a takeover raider may see an opportunity to buy up the company, install a better management, improve profits, and hence make capital gains when share prices subsequently rise. Together, these threats are supposed to discipline managers and keep them on their toes.

In practice, these threats are weak and not very credible. Individual shareholders face a free-rider problem: provided other shareholders monitor the management, everything will be fine. So everyone tends not to bother. Second, takeover raids typically bid up the share price significantly; the incumbent management has considerable leeway before it is likely to get into trouble and be out of a job. Finally, incumbent managers have a lot of insider information about the true state of the firm, information not available to existing shareholders or potential raiders.

Because shareholders know all this, they try to give managers a direct incentive to care about profits and cost reduction. Senior executives get large profit-related bonuses. These are a carrot, for those who like carrots; but shareholders have no accompanying stick, which effective two-handed discipline would require.

In these circumstances, we cannot guarantee that private management will be efficient unless it is subject to effective competition and challenge, either from other competitors in the market-place or from a tough and watchful regulatory body. When the private firm is very large, and therefore subject to little domestic competition, and also produces in a sector sheltered from imports and foreign competition, it is quite likely to be a relatively sleepy monopolist unless it has regu-lators to whom it must account. And these regulators must be capable of resisting regulatory capture.

incentives for public managers

If private managers sometimes face a weak market mechanism for discipline and control, public sector managers face no market mechanism at all. Everything depends on the effectiveness of the government as a watchdog. In principle, the government might do this at least as effectively as private markets. It too can offer performance-related bonuses, and it does not face the free-rider problem which confronts individual shareholders. On the other hand, its civil servants probably have less training in business evaluation than do private sector analysts, and, of greatest importance, there is the overwhelming political temptation for the government to hijack the nationalized industries and make them an instrument of whatever is the pressing problem of the day.

the importance of ownership

It follows from the arguments above that the transfer of *ownership* from public to private sector may not in itself be the most important issue. Neither public nor private owners are good at monitoring managements. If ownership transfer to the private sector has any direct benefit, it is the one we cited above: it makes it less easy for governments to use industries to meet the requirements of other political dictates. On the other hand, it should not be imagined that private industries are immune from such considerations. If you doubt this, talk to any private oil company involved in the North Sea. Such companies have at times faced a petroleum revenue tax rate of over 90 per cent, way above anything they were led to expect when they first went into the North Sea.

Thus, most economists agree that the key issue is not ownership itself but rather the severity of the market competition, or its substitute regulatory policy, which the industry faces. Sheltered monopolies will be sleepy and slack no matter who owns them. Conversely, the major benefits of privatization are likely to stem not from literally returning ownership to the private sector, but rather from associated measures which make it clear to managers that they are expected to compete effectively and efficiently. The litmus test of this assertion is the fact that so many UK nationalized industries managed to improve their performance in the run-up to privatization, *while they were still in public ownership*. However, over the longer run, privatization may represent a useful commitment by government not to interfere too closely in the day-to-day running of the industry.

selling the family silver?

Some people worry that selling off state assets mortgages the country's future. Others think privatization makes the state better off. Is there any simple way through the confusion in the public debate? You already know enough to work out the answer for yourself. The market price of an asset is simply the present value of the income stream to which it entitles the owner. Suppose a fair price is £100. If we sell you the asset, we get £100 in cash but you get an asset worth £100. Neither of us is better or worse off than before. Of course, if we underprice the asset we are selling, perhaps because we want large queues of buyers so we can claim how popular it is, we make a loss on the sale and you make a profit. That is one way the government could be worse off by privatization.[3]

How could the government be better off by privatization? Essentially for the reason first advanced by Adam Smith in the quotation at the start of this chapter. If nationalized industries previously had bad performances, they would have been worth little had they been sold at that stage. If management policy is changed *prior* to privatization, the present value of future profits rises at this point, and it is this that is the source of improvement to the public finances, not the subsequent change of ownership.

Finally, notice that the question of mortgaging the future hinges crucially on what is done with the privatization revenue. If it is invested in physical capital for the public sector or used to retire outstanding government debt, it is not at all imprudent. Only if it is 'blown', for example on a tax-cut-financed consumer boom, can the government be said to be piling up financial trouble for future governments.

---

[3] Most UK privatizations do seem to have been underpriced. The government believed there was an externality in encouraging wider share ownership, and was prepared to subsidize this activity.

▪▪▪ privatization in practice

Table 6-3 shows average annual real revenues from privatization under the Conservative Government during 1980-97 from sales of nationalized industries such as British Telecom, British Gas, British Airways, British Steel, the water companies and most of electric power. At 1997 prices, almost £67 billion in revenue was raised during 1980-97. People quickly figured out that buying shares at the offer price was a good deal; hence the queues of eager buyers featured on the TV news. However, the attempt to encourage wider share ownership was substantially frustrated. Having made their capital gains, individuals soon sold their shares to the big pension funds and insurance companies that were eager to have a portfolio close to the market average. Earlier, we stressed the importance of the extent of competition that the newly privatized companies would face. We distinguish two cases.

enough competition, little market failure

Examples in this group include Jaguar, Cable & Wireless, British Aerospace, and British Airways. Some firms were not that large, but many were huge. We place them in this group because they were subject to acute international competition. In general, firms in this group have been quite successful after privatization.

market power and regulation

Having privatized most of the smaller companies first, by 1984 the government turned to sales of the giant corporations that were close to natural monopolies. Whereas water and electricity were broken up into different private companies between which there might be a degree of competition, British Telecom (BT) and British Gas were privatized intact. The privatizing of giant firms not subject to severe international competition is unlikely to be attractive unless accompanied by regulation.

will national markets survive?

Nationalization was not an unmitigated success, and we are gradually learning in Europe that the alternative policy response – leave natural monopolists in the private sector but regulate their activities – is also full of difficulties. In the United States, where regulation was always preferred to public ownership, the same conclusion was reached long ago: regulatory capture and informational problems create serious difficulties for public policy.

Perhaps a bit of lateral thinking is needed. Instead of imperfectly intervening to control a monopolist within a small market, why not try to expand the market? A large market may support competition between many firms where each of them has to be large to take advantage of economies of scale. This is a key aspect of the programme to 'complete the internal market' within Europe. How easily the market can be

Table 6-3 UK privatization revenues 1980–97 (annual averages, 1997 £bn)

80–83	84–86	87–90	91–93	94–97
0.2	1.5	4.5	7.8	5.0

Source: HM Treasury.

widened affects the regulatory strategy that should be adopted for a particular industry. For example, gas and telecommunications should not be treated similarly. For some time to come, British Gas (www.britishgas.co.uk) will inevitably have a powerful market position within the UK, although it will of course face competition from other energy sources. In contrast, exciting changes are taking place in telecommunications, which are likely to promote much greater competition.

Box 6-6 | The private finance initiative

In 1992 the government introduced the Private Finance Initiative (PFI). The government claimed it was an innovative way of drawing on private-sector expertise to finance and manage public projects. Critics claimed it was largely a scam for lowering the apparent size of the budget deficit.

The PFI transforms government departments and agencies from owners and operators of assets to ongoing purchasers of services from the private sector. Private firms become long-term service providers not just upfront asset builders. Rather than paying for the capital cost of road building, the government becomes a continuing purchaser of miles of maintained highway.

During 1992–98 £11 billion such deals were signed, of which 27 per cent was accounted for by the Channel Tunnel Rail Link alone; another 33 per cent by other transport schemes such as roads, bridges, and rail and tram developments; and 12 per cent by hospitals and other health-sector projects. In 1996 the scheme was extended to local authorities under the name Public Private Partnership Programme.

The Treasury insists the principal aim is to draw on private-sector management expertise and risk control. The government was fed up with cost overruns on public projects. Under the PFI, the private sector is responsible for risks within its control. The government is only responsible for overruns arising from wider risks outside the contractors' control. Of course, the dividing line is ambiguous. London and Continental Railway, responsible for the largest PFI project, the Channel Tunnel Rail Link, has kept asking for more money than the level specified in its original bid.

What about the budgetary implications? First, any benefit of private-sector efficiency has to be set against the fact that the government can borrow more cheaply than the private sector. The private sector bears the initial construction costs, which it finances by borrowing. Yet the lower credit rating of privately financed projects (compared with a government rating of AAA, Greenwich Hospital's bonds are rated BBB, and Docklands Light Railway bonds rated A), can mean anything up to an extra one percentage point on the interest rate that must be paid. Private-sector efficiency has to offset more than this if the government is to benefit by the arrangement.

Second, the PFI allows the government to escape the initial capital cost of building a road or a prison in exchange for incurring two future costs: the ongoing cost of 'renting' the road or prison service from the asset provider, and the possible liability for cost increases outside the control of the private supplier. Making proper allowance for the latter in today's budget estimates is no easy matter.

Many future flows are not properly accounted for in the government accounts. This is not how the stock market behaves. Think of all these internet companies currently valued at billions of pounds merely because they will earn revenues at some future date.

As PFI projects gradually build up the flow of fees to be paid to private-service providers of what were previously public projects, this will automatically tend to raise the flow of government spending in the future.

For further details, see www.treasury-projects-taskforce.gov.uk

regulatory reform

What lessons should have been learned from the experience of nationalizing natural monopolies? First, regulators need to be independent of government to make credible the promise not to interfere all the time. This has been accomplished by establishing the independent regulators whose acronyms punctuate the media: OFTEL, OFWAT, OFGEM, and so on. Each regulatory agency has objectives clearly laid down by Parliament but is responsible for their implementation through regulatory policy.

Second, attention must be paid to information asymmetries and possible cost escalation by natural monopolists. In essence, two systems of regulation of *conduct* are possible: a price ceiling or a ceiling on the rate of return (sometimes called 'cost-plus'). Regulatory design faces a tradeoff when the firm has an information monopoly on its true costs. A price ceiling gives the monopolist all the benefit of cost reduction that is unobservable by the regulator; a cap on the rate of return would force prices down with costs.

If that was the only problem, a price cap offers much better incentives. But if the monopolist faces other risks, rate of return regulation enables unforeseen developments to be passed on to consumers, whereas a price cap makes the monopolist bear all of the risk. Efficient risk-sharing might employ at least some elements of rate-of-return regulation.

Despite the case for some compromise between these two methods, UK regulation has plumped entirely for the price-cap method, putting the full force of regulation behind the pressure for cost reduction. This was pioneered with the privatization of BT in 1984 which has been subject to an '$RPI - X$' price ceiling. What this means is that its *nominal* prices can rise by the same percentage as the retail price index, minus X per cent. X is therefore the annual rate of reduction in *real* prices. Since the telecommunication industry is enjoying rapid technical progress, it should be able to reduce costs year after year. The regulator sets X. During 1984–89, X was 3 per cent. It was then raised to 4.5 per cent and then 6.25 per cent. During its first ten years as a private company, BT's real prices fell by 43 per cent.

Subsequent regulators have used a similar approach. In regulating the water companies, OFWAT (www.open.gov.uk/ofwat) adopted '$RPI + K$' to reflect the fact that the real price of water needs to increase if water companies are to improve

Box 6-7	The biggest privatizer of all?

The UK pioneered privatization under Margaret Thatcher and John Major. By 1997 the UK did not have that much left to sell. Continental Europe has been catching up fast, and countries such as Italy and France may eventually raise even more from privatization than the UK did. So far, the UK has resisted privatizing the Post Office, but the Dutch post office has already been sold, and Germany's giant 'Bundespost', Europe's biggest letter carrier, is scheduled for sale in 2000.

Privatization receipts 1993–98 (£bn)

Italy	56	UK	22
France	36	Sweden	12
Spain	28	Holland	11
Germany	23	Portugal	10

Source: Observer, 7 March 1999.

quality (and indeed quantity!) by undertaking the substantial investment that was for so long neglected when water was a nationalized industry. The level of *K* averaged around 5.5 per cent during 1990–95 although it varied slightly across the different regional water companies according to OFWAT's assessment of the need for investment.

In 1999, after an investigation by the Competition Commission was critical of charges for mobile phones, Vodafone and Cellnet were set a price ceiling of RPI − 9 during each of 1999 and 2000. Regulating conduct is not the only option available to regulators. It would also be possible to think about breaking up the company to change the structure of the industry. In the 1980s, the US phone company AT&T (www.att.com) was broken up into 'baby Bells', each serving a region of the US but sharing the same network for interregional calls.

Many industries are vertically integrated, combining an upstream facility, the basic transmission network, with downstream activities such as local distribution. The basic network is a natural monopoly – we only want one national grid for electricity – but downstream activities may offer more opportunities for competition. Obviously, access to the network has to be available at reasonable prices, and the regulator needs to monitor this. A key issue is whether the firm that runs the network should also be allowed to compete with other downstream distributors. The answer depends on whether either vertical externalities or opportunities for strategic behaviours give the network monopolist undue power in the downstream market.

In privatizing BT, the government decided to allow BT to compete in downstream activities. Subsequent experience has shown that Mercury offered only limited competition; BT may now be facing tougher competition from cable TV companies that are now allowed simultaneously to offer phone calls down the same cable. Indeed, after more than a decade of regulatory experience, UK practice has moved steadily towards greater regulation of structure, which began with the electricity privatization in which the grid and the distribution companies were kept clearly distinct. Similarly, the privatization of British Rail led to the creation of Railtrack to supply the infrastructure network, and the award of regional operating franchises to companies such as Virgin Trains and Connex.

recap

- Nationalization is the acquisition of private companies by the public sector. Privatization is the sale of public-sector firms to the private sector.

- A natural monopoly faces a falling average cost curve. Marginal cost lies below average cost. Pricing at marginal cost implies losses.

- A two-part tariff may allow the monopolist to set the appropriate marginal charge and recover losses via the fixed charge.

- Ideally, state-run firms should price at marginal social cost and invest until price just covers long-run marginal social cost, including the annual interest cost of the initial capital expenditure.

- Regulatory capture occurs when the regulator becomes the champion of the industry that it is supposed to regulate.

- Privatization was a response to the view that some state companies were not natural monopolies, and that even natural monopolies were better handled by arms' length regulation that committed the government not to intervene perpetually.

- Transfer of ownership makes credible the fact that the firm does not have limitless government backing (though governments do bail out even private companies from time to time!).

- Selling assets at a fair price leaves government wealth unaltered.

- Many privatized firms now face intense competition, often from abroad. However, natural monopolies have required a new framework of regulation. This has favoured price-capping, administered by independent regulatory agencies and subject to periodic review.

- Increasingly, the UK has been driven to regulate not merely conduct but structure. Some parts of a natural monopoly have been hived off and become suitable for competition.

- The Private Finance Initiative uses private finance to build projects and private management to run them. The government then pays a service charge to use the asset.

key terms

review questions

1 Why do sports clubs have both an initial membership fee and an annual subscription for people who are already members?

2 An MP has suggested that since British Telecom is regulated by OFTEL it would make sense to establish OFAIR to regulate British Airways. Would it?

3 'Cheap season tickets keep commuters off congested rush-hour roads.' 'Commuters should pay extra since most trains lie idle the rest of the day.' Adjudicate between these views. Does the answer depend on how cars and parking are being priced?

4 'The Channel Tunnel, built with private money, was then unable to keep up the interest payments on its debts. It should never have been built.' Discuss.

5 Did you remember the distinction between private and social valuation of costs and benefits in answering question 4? Identify five sources of difference between private and social?

6 Why is the Private Finance Initiative a compromise between fixed-price and cost-plus contracts?

7 | aggregate demand and national income

7-1 macroeconomic accounts

LEARNING OUTCOMES

When you have finished this section, you should understand

■ how to construct national income accounts

■ the circular flow between households and firms

■ the equality of leakages from, and injections to, the circular flow

■ the role of the government and the foreign sector

■ important omissions from the usual measures of national income

Macroeconomics *is the study of the economy as a whole.*

Macroeconomics is concerned not with the details of individual products or industries but with the economy as a whole. Microeconomics places the emphasis on a detailed understanding of particular markets. To achieve this amount of detail or magnification, many of the interactions with other markets are suppressed. Microeconomics is a bit like looking at a horse race through a pair of binoculars. It is great for details, but sometimes we get a clearer picture of the whole race by using the naked eye. In contrast, macroeconomics is concerned with the interaction of different parts of the economy, it relies on a different simplification to keep the analysis manageable. Macroeconomics simplifies the building blocks in order to focus on how they fit together and influence one another. Our notion of the individual details is more blurred but we can give our full attention to the whole picture. We are more likely to notice the horse sneaking up on the rails.

Almost every day the media refer to the problems of inflation, unemployment, and slow growth. These issues are widely discussed; they help determine the outcome of elections, and make some people interested in learning more about macroeconomics. What the government can and should do is the subject of lively debate both within economics and in the country at large.

■■■ **the facts**

We begin with some key facts on recent inflation, economic growth, and unemployment. Table 7-1 shows average rates of annual inflation and output growth over the last two decades. Although the UK has experienced higher inflation than Switzerland, Japan, or the United States, its inflation rate has still been much lower than that of many other countries. Figure 7-1 shows the annual inflation rate in the UK over a much longer period.

| **Figure 7-1** | The inflation rate in the UK |

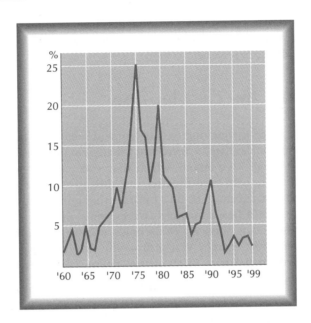

Source: ONS, *Economic Trends.*

| **Table 7-1** | Inflation and real output growth, 1980–97 (% per annum) |

Country	Inflation	Growth
Argentina	234	0.9
Brazil	362	2.9
Israel	65	4.7
Korea	6	8.5
Italy	8	1.9
UK	5	2.6
Sweden	5	1.7
France	4	1.5
USA	3	2.8
Japan	1	2.9
Switzerland	3	0.8

Source: World Bank, *World Development Report.*

Table 7-1 also shows the average annual rate of growth of real output in selected countries. Korea and Israel have grown significantly faster than the European countries such as the UK, Switzerland, and France. Switzerland, with the lowest inflation rate, has almost the *lowest* growth rate of real output. Brazil, with an inflation rate 100 times as large, grew three times as quickly.

Since 1980 Europe has faced high unemployment. Table 7-2 shows that unemployment rates increased much more in Europe than in Japan or the United States. The 1970s was a period of poor macroeconomic performance throughout the world. In almost every country there was a decline in the growth of both real GNP and real GNP per person, a rise in unemployment rates, and an increase in inflation.

In the 1980s and 1990s many people became disenchanted with the old economic policies. As Western economies started to slow down and both inflation and unemployment rose, people began to feel that the old policies were no longer working. Since 1981 governments have steadily brought inflation under control. However, unemployment has remained stubbornly high and growth has not recovered to the pace seen before 1973.

■■■ the circular flow

We begin by ignoring the government sector and transactions with other countries. Households own the factors of production or inputs to the production process. They own their own labour, which they can rent out to firms in exchange for wages. They also own firms themselves. Although other factors of production such as capital and land appear to be held by firms, they are ultimately owned by households. Households earn factor incomes (wages, rents, profits), which are payments by firms for these factor services. Households use their incomes to buy goods and services from firms, thereby giving firms the money to pay for the factor services used in production. Figure 7-2 shows this *circular flow* between households and firms.

> *The* circular flow *shows how real resources and financial payments are exchanged between firms and households.*

The inner loop shows the transfers of real resources between the two sectors and the outer loop shows the corresponding flows of money in a market economy.

Figure 7-2 suggests that there are three ways of measuring the amount of economic activity in an economy: (*a*) the value of goods and services produced, (*b*) the level of factor earnings, which represent the value of factor services supplied, or (*c*) the value

Table 7-2	Unemployment (% of labour force)		
	1980	1989	1998
USA	7.2	5.3	4.5
Japan	2.0	2.2	4.1
France	5.8	9.3	11.7
Italy	5.6	10.0	11.9
UK	6.2	7.3	6.3
Belgium	9.3	7.5	9.5
Holland	6.0	6.9	4.0
Sweden	2.0	1.5	8.3

Source: OECD, *Economic Outlook*.

of spending on goods and services. Since all payments are the counterparts of real resources, and since for the moment we assume that all payments must be spent on purchasing real resources, we must get the same estimate of total economic activity whether we measure the value of production, the level of factor incomes, or spending on goods and services.

Factor incomes must equal household spending since we assume that all income is spent. The value of production must equal total spending on goods and services since we assume that all goods are sold. The value of output must equal the value of household incomes: since profits are sales minus the direct payments to hire land, labour, and capital, and since these profits ultimately accrue to the households which own the business, household incomes must equal the value of production. Once we have learned to measure the level of economic activity through this system of *national income accounting*, we can begin the analysis of the basic macroeconomic issues such as inflation, unemployment, and economic growth.

Figure 7-2 leaves out important features of the real world: saving and investment, government spending and taxes, transactions between firms and with the rest of the world. We need a comprehensive system of national accounting which addresses these complications.

national income accounting

Gross domestic product *(GDP) measures the output produced by factors of production located in the domestic economy regardless of who owns these factors.*

First, we extend our simple circular flow to recognize that transactions do not take place exclusively between a single firm and a single household. Firms hire labour services from households but buy raw materials and machinery from other firms. To avoid double counting, we use the concept of value added.

| **Figure 7-2** | The circular flow between firms and households |

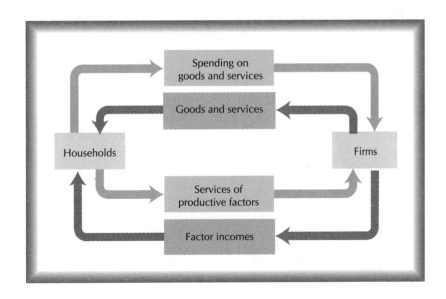

Value added *is the increase in the value of goods as a result of the production process.*

Value added is calculated by deducting from the value of the firm's output the cost of the input goods used up in producing that output. Closely related is the distinction between final goods and intermediate goods.

Final goods *are goods purchased by the ultimate user, either consumer goods purchased by households or capital goods such as machinery purchased by firms.* Intermediate goods *are partly finished goods which form inputs to another firm's production process and are used up in that process.*

Thus, ice cream is a final good but steel is an intermediate good which some other firm uses as an input to its production process. In classifying capital goods as final goods, we suppose they are not used up in subsequent production. In the language of Chapter 2, they do not depreciate or wear out. Shortly, we shall see how depreciation may be handled.

Table 7-3 should keep you straight. Steelco is a firm that supplies steel to a robot maker Robotco and a car firm Carco. Robotco turns steel into robots, capital goods used in the car industry. Carco makes cars using robots and steel. If we count up the total sales in the economy, it comes to £11 000. But this involves double counting: intermediate goods (steel) are counted both when sold originally by Steelco and again when the goods the steel helps make (robots and cars) are sold on to final users (households or firms that no longer use them up in further production).

Value added is just net output after subtracting off produced materials that are used up during the process. Labour is used up in the process but was not produced further back in the chain by another supplier. We only have to net out goods that we will count somewhere else. GDP is £7000 whichever of the last three columns we use to evaluate it. Final spending makes sure we do not count intermediate goods separately. Value added nets out properly. And only net output can be passed on to households as factor incomes.

investment and saving

What happens if value added is £7000 but households decide only to spend £5000?

Saving *is the part of income not spent on goods and services.* Investment *is the purchase of new capital goods by firms from other firms.*

| Table 7-3 | Calculating GDP |

Good	Seller	Buyer	Gross sale	Value added	Final spending	Factor incomes
Steel	Steelco	Robotco	£1 000	£1 000	–	£1 000
Steel	Steelco	Carco	£3 000	£3 000	–	£3 000
Robot	Robotco	Carco	£2 000	£1 000	£2 000	£1 000
Cars	Carco	Consumers	£5 000	£2 000	£5 000	£2 000
Gross sales			£11 000			
GDP				£7 000	£7 000	£7 000

If households earn £7000 but only spend £5000, who is contributing the other £2000 in the final spending measure of GDP? It must be firms spending £2000 on new capital goods made by other firms. This £2000 is also additional value added and therefore the source of the extra £2000 in factor incomes, over and above the £5000 households themselves spent buying goods from firms.

The circular flow automatically recycles money between firms and households. Saving is a leakage *from the circular flow, money for households not returned to firms. Investment is an* injection *to the circular flow, money for firms that did not originate with households. As a matter of definition, leakages must equal injections.*

We can make the same point another way. Let us use Y to denote GDP, C to denote consumer spending, I to denote purchases of investment goods by firms, and S to denote saving by households. First, as a matter of definition, Y equals $(C + S)$. Saving is the part of income not consumed. Second, as a matter of definition, Y equals $(C + I)$. GDP equals spending on final goods by households and firms. Together this tells us that, as a matter of definition, S equals I. Not only by accident, not only in equilibrium, but always. By definition.

What happens if firms cannot sell all the output that they produce? Surely this leads to a difference between the output and expenditure measures of GDP? Final goods are goods not used up in the production process during the period. Suppose that Carco's sales were not £5000 but only £4000. It is left with £1000 worth of cars which must be stockpiled.

Inventories or stocks *are goods currently held by a firm for future production or sale.*

Because they have not been used up in production and sale during the current period, stocks are classified as capital goods. Adding to stocks is investment in working capital. When stocks are run down, we treat this as negative investment or disinvestment. Now we can keep the national accounts straight. When Carco sells only £4000 of the £5000 worth of cars produced in the period, we treat the inventory investment of £1000 by the car producer as final expenditure. As in Table 7-3, the output and expenditure measures of GDP are each £7000. But spending on final goods now comprises: car producer (£2000 on machines, £1000 on stocks), household-consumer (£4000 on cars).

Many people find this confusing. The trick is to distinguish between classification by commodity and classification by economic use. When a steel producer makes *and sells* steel we show this as production of an intermediate good. Since it has been passed on to someone else, our expenditure measure will pick it up further up the chain of production and sales. But when a firm adds to its stocks we must count that as final expenditure because it will not show up anywhere else in this period's accounts.

▰▰▰ the government

Governments raise revenue both through direct taxes T_d levied on incomes (wages, rents, interest, and profits) and through indirect taxes or expenditures taxes T_e (VAT, petrol duties, cigarette taxes). Taxes meet two kinds of expenditure. Government spending on goods and services G comprises purchases by the government of physical goods and services.

But governments also spend money financing *transfer payments* or benefits, B. These include pensions, unemployment benefit, and subsidies to private firms (investment grants) and to state-owned firms (covering losses). Transfer payments are payments that do not require the provision of any goods or services in return. Transfer payments add to neither national income nor national output. They are not included in GDP. There is no corresponding value added or net output produced. In contrast, spending G on goods and services produces net output, gives rise to factor earnings in the firms supplying this output, and hence to additional spending power of the households receiving this income. Hence government spending G on goods and services should be included in GDP.

National income accounts provide a logically coherent set of definitions and measures of national output. However, taxes drive a wedge between the price the purchaser pays and the price the seller receives. Thus we can choose to value national output either at market prices inclusive of indirect taxes on goods and services, or at the prices received by producers after indirect taxes have been paid.

GDP at market prices *measures domestic output inclusive of indirect taxes on goods and services.* GDP at basic prices *measures domestic output exclusive of indirect taxes on goods and services. Thus GDP at market prices exceeds GDP at basic prices by the amount of revenue raised in indirect taxes (net of any subsidies on goods and services).*

Measuring consumption C, investment I, and government spending G on goods and services, at market prices inclusive of indirect taxes, the value added or net output of the economy is given by $(C + I + G)$. Hence

$$\text{GDP at market prices} \equiv C + I + G$$

Subtracting indirect taxes (net of subsidies) T_e

$$Y \equiv \text{GDP at basic prices} \equiv C + I + G - T_e$$

We now use Y to denote GDP at basic prices. The right-hand side is the final expenditure measure of GDP and the net output measure of GDP, each at basic prices. The output, expenditure, and income measures of GDP at basic prices are all equal. Figure 7-3 shows that direct taxes and transfer benefits do affect the circular flow of payments. Household incomes at basic prices Y are supplemented by benefits B less direct taxes T_d. This gives us personal disposable income.

Personal disposable income *is household income after direct taxes and transfer payments. It shows how much households have available for spending and saving.*

Personal disposable income equals $(Y + B - T_d)$. Saving is the amount of disposable income not spent on consumption.

$$S \equiv (Y + B - T_d) - C$$

Proceeding round the top loop of Figure 7-3, consumption C at market prices is now supplemented by injections of investment spending I and government spending G. From $(C + I + G)$ or GDP at market prices, we subtract indirect taxes T_e to get back to Y or GDP at basic prices. Together, our definitions of GDP and saving imply

$$C + S - B + T_d \equiv Y \equiv C + I + G - T_e$$

Since these expressions are identically equal,

$$S + T_d + T_e \equiv I + G + B \text{ and } S - I \equiv G + B - T_d - T_e$$

The first identity tells us the total leakages or withdrawals from the circular flow of payments – money that leaks out through household savings and taxes to the government – exactly equals the injections to the circular flow – investment spending by firms and government spending on goods and services and on transfer benefits that put money back into the system. Total leakages must equal total injections; otherwise we would have made a bookkeeping error and the sums would not add up.

The second identity makes a similar point. Taking firms and households together, net withdrawals from the circular flow $S - I$ (the financial surplus of the private sector) must be exactly offset by net injections $G + B - T_d - T_e$ from the government sector (the financial deficit of the government). The private sector can run a surplus only if the government runs a deficit, and vice versa.

■■■■ the foreign sector

We now consider an *open economy*, which trades with other countries.

Exports (X) *are goods that are domestically produced but sold abroad.* Imports (Z) *are goods that are produced abroad but purchased for use in the domestic economy.*

Hence net final expenditure on domestic goods (GDP) becomes

$$Y \equiv C + I + G + X - Z - T_e \equiv C + I + G + NX - T_e$$

where NX denotes net exports $(X - Z)$.

What about leakages from and injections to the circular flow? Imports represent a leakage, but exports are an injection. Augmenting (1) and (2)

$$S + (T_d + T_e - B) + Z \equiv I + G + X \quad \text{and} \quad S - I \equiv (G + B - T_e - T_d) + NX$$

Figure 7-3 The government and the circular flow

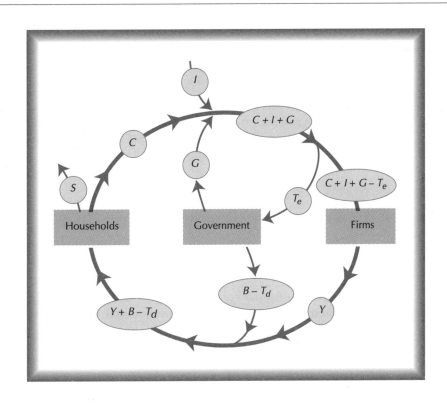

Total leakages must still equal total injections. Imports are an extra source of leakages and exports an extra source of injections of money to the circular flow.

Moreover, a private sector surplus $S - I$ is a net leakage from the circular flow. It must be matched by a net injection of the same amount. This injection can come either from a government deficit $(G + B - T_e - T_d)$ or from net exports NX, the excess of export earnings over import spending. The surplus of the private sector must be matched by the budget deficit of the government plus the trade deficit of foreigners.

from GDP to GNP or GNI

To complete the national accounts we must deal with two final problems. Thus far we have assumed that all factors of production are domestically owned: all net domestic output accrues to domestic households as factor incomes. But this need not be the case. When Nissan owns a car factory in the UK, some of the profits will be sent back to Japan to be spent or saved by Japanese households. Similarly, when immigrant workers send some of their wages back home to support relatives, or foreign owners of UK property or shares in UK companies send home some of their income from property rents or company dividends, there is a discrepancy between the factor incomes earned in the UK and the factor incomes accruing to UK households.

Conversely, UK households earn income from factor services that they supply in foreign countries. Since most income flows between countries are not labour income but income from interest, dividends, profits, and rents, they are shown in the national accounts as the flow of *property income* between countries. The net flow of property income into the UK is the excess of inflows of property income from factor services supplied abroad over the outflows of property income from factor services by foreigners in the UK.

When there is a net flow of property income between the UK and the rest of the world, the output and expenditure measure of GDP will no longer equal the total factor incomes earned by UK citizens. We use the terms *gross national product* (GNP) or *gross national income* (GNI) to measure GDP adjusted for net property income from abroad.

GNP (or GNI) *measures total income earned by domestic citizens regardless of the country in which their factor services were supplied. GNP (or GNI) equals GDP plus net property income from abroad.*

Thus, if the UK has an inflow of £2 billion of property income from abroad but an outflow of £1 billion of property income accruing to foreigners, UK GNP, measuring income earned by UK citizens, will exceed UK GDP, measuring the value of goods produced in the UK, by £1 billion.

from GNP to national income

The final complication is depreciation.

Depreciation *or capital consumption measures the rate at which the value of the existing capital stock declines per period as a result of wear and tear or of obsolescence.*

Depreciation is a flow concept telling us how much our effective capital stock is being used up in each time period, an economic cost because it measures resources used in the production process. We now recognize that machinery wears out. In consequence, the *net* output of the economy is reduced. Accordingly, we subtract depreciation from GNP to arrive at net national product (NNP) or national income.

National income *is the economy's net national product. It is calculated by subtracting depreciation from GNP at basic prices.*

We have now developed a complete set of national accounts. You are probably wondering how you are going to remember all these new concepts. Figure 7-4 may help to keep you straight.

■■■ what GNP measures

Since depreciation is rather difficult to measure, and consequently may be treated differently in different countries or during different time periods, in practice most economists make comparisons using GNP, which avoids the need to argue about depreciation.

nominal and real GNP

Nominal GNP *measures GNP at the prices prevailing when income was earned.*

Since it is physical quantities of output that yield people utility or happiness, it can be very misleading to judge the economy's performance by looking at nominal GNP.

Real GNP, *or GNP at constant prices, adjusts for inflation by measuring GNP in different years at the prices prevailing at some particular calendar date known as the base year.*

The most common measure of inflation in the UK is the annual percentage increase in retail prices. However, consumption expenditure is only one component of GNP.

Figure 7-4 | National income accounting: a summary

Composition of spending on GNP	Definition of GDP	Definition of NNP	Definition of national income	Factor earnings
Net property income from abroad	Net property income from abroad	Depreciation		
G			Indirect taxes	
	GDP at market prices	NNP at market prices	National income (NI) = NNP at basic prices	Rental income
I				Profits
NX				Income from self-employment
C				Wages and salaries

GNP at market prices (also GNI at market prices)

GNP also includes investment, government spending, and net exports. To convert nominal GNP to real GNP we need to use an index that reflects what is happening to the price of all goods. This index is called the GNP deflator.

The GNP deflator *is the ratio of nominal GNP to real GNP expressed as an index.*

GNP in the UK rose from £25 billion in 1960 to over £855 billion in 1998. Yet without knowing what happened to the price of goods in general it is impossible to judge what happened to the quantity of output over this period. On average, prices in 1998 were 13 times those in 1960. In consequence, the change in real GNP was much less dramatic than the change in nominal GNP over the same period. Hence we see the vital importance of distinguishing between nominal and real GNP.

per capita real GNP

Real GNP tells us about the whole economy. We may be interested in a different question: what was happening to the standard of living of a representative person?

Per capita real GNP *is real GNP divided by the total population. It is real GNP per head.*

Even per capita real GNP is only a crude indicator. The more the income distribution is changing over time, the less reliable is the change in per capita real GNP as an indicator of what is happening to any particular person.

a comprehensive measure of GNP

Coverage of the GNP accounts should be as comprehensive as possible. In practice, we encounter two problems. First, some outputs, such as noise, pollution, and congestion, are nuisances. We should make an adjustment for these 'bads' by subtracting

---

| Box 7-1 | GNP is underestimated, but don't tell the government! |

The famous gangster Al Capone was never charged with murder or gun running, but he was eventually convicted of income tax evasion. Taxes are evaded not only by smugglers and drug dealers but also by gardeners, plumbers, street vendors, and many others offering goods and services 'for cash'. Since government estimates of GNP are derived from tax statistics, the 'hidden' or 'underground' economy is not reported in GNP.

Economists have devised various ways to come up with some rough estimates of the size of the hidden economy. One way is to keep track what people spend. Maria Lacko used the stable relationship between household consumption of electricity and its two main determinants – income and weather temperature – to estimate incomes by

studying available data on electricity consumption and temperature. The hidden economy is large both in the former communist economies, where the new private sector is not yet part of official statistics, and in several Mediterranean countries that have a long history of having trouble getting their citizens to pay their taxes.

Estimated size of the hidden economy (% of GNP)

Poland	34	Denmark	16	Netherlands	8
Hungary	31	Finland	11	Australia	7
Spain	21	Germany	11	France	6
Greece	20	USA	10	Japan	3
Italy	16	UK	10		

Source: M. Lacko, *Hungarian Hidden Economy in International Comparisons*, Institute of Economics, Budapest, 1996.

from the traditional GNP measure an allowance for all the nuisance goods created during the production process. This is a perfectly sensible suggestion but it is almost impossible to implement. These nuisance goods are not traded through markets, so it is hard to quantify the level of their output or the costs they impose on society.

Many valuable goods and services are excluded from GNP because they are not marketed and therefore hard to measure accurately. These activities include household chores, do-it-yourself activities, and unreported jobs.

Deducting the value of nuisance outputs and adding the value of unreported and non-marketed incomes would make GNP a more accurate measure of economy's production of goods and services. But there is another important adjustment that must be made if we are to use GNP as the basis for calculations of national economic welfare. People get enjoyment not merely from goods and services, but also from leisure time.

Suppose people in Leisuria value leisure more highly than people in Industria. Other things equal, people in Industria will work more hours and produce more goods and services. Industria will have a higher measured GNP. It would be silly to say this proves that people in Leisuria have a lower level of enjoyment. By choosing to work less hard they are revealing that the extra leisure is worth at least as much as the extra goods that could have been produced by working longer hours.

Because it is difficult and expensive to collect regular measurements on non-marketed and unreported goods and bads and to make regular assessments of the implicit value of leisure, real GNP inevitably remains the most commonly used measure of economic activity. Although far from ideal, it is the best measure we have that is available on a regular basis.

Box 7-2 The quality of life

Familiar statistical measures, such as GDP, omit many of the things we really care about. However, governments could decide to spend more money collecting statistics. In 1998, UK Deputy Prime Minister John Prescott announced plans to produce a 'happiness index' measuring the quality of life. The index includes 13 'headline indicators': economic growth, social investment, health, education and training, employment, housing quality, climate change, air pollution, transport, water quality, land use, waste disposal, and wildlife. Many of these indicate aspects of 'environmental capital'. Keeping track of depreciation of, and investment in, environmental capital may be one way to promote sensible use of natural resources.

▣▬ recap

- Macroeconomics is the study of the economy as a whole. Inflation, unemployment, and growth are three key macroeconomic issues.

- Households supply the services of factors of production to firms that use them to produce goods and services. Firms pay factor incomes to households, who in turn use this money to purchase the goods and services produced by firms. This process is called the circular flow of payments.

- Gross domestic product (GDP) is the value of output of the factors of production located in the domestic economy. It can be measured in three equivalent ways: value added in production, factor incomes including profits accruing to entrepreneurs, or final expenditure.

- Leakages from the circular flow are payments by firms to households not automatically returned to firms as spending by households on the output of firms. Savings, taxes, and imports are leakages. Injections are sources of revenue to firms that do not arise from household spending. Investment by firms, spending on goods and services by the government, and exports are all injections. As a matter of definition, total leakages must equal total injections.

- GDP at market prices values domestic output at prices inclusive of indirect taxes. GDP at basic prices measures domestic output at prices exclusive of indirect taxes. Gross national product (GNP), also called gross national income (GNI), adjusts GDP for net property income from abroad.

- National income is net national product (NNP) at basic prices. NNP is GNP minus the depreciation of the capital stock during the period.

- Nominal GNP measures income at current prices. Real GNP measures income at constant prices. The index of prices used to make this adjustment is the GNP deflator.

- Per capita real GNP divides real GNP by the population.

- Real GNP and per capita real GNP are still very crude measures of national and individual welfare. GNP takes no account of non-market activities, bads such as pollution, valuable activities such as work in the home, and production unreported by tax evaders. Nor does GNP measure the value of leisure.

▣▬ key terms

▪▪▪ review questions

1 This question deals with the value added accounting. The table shows final sales and purchases of intermediate goods by firms connected with car production:
What is the contribution of the car industry to GNP?

	Final sales	Intermediate goods purchases
Car producer	1000	270
Windscreen producer	199	12
Tyre producer	83	30
Car radio producer	30	5
Steel producer	47	0

2 GNP at market prices is £300 billion. Depreciation is £30 billion and indirect taxes are £20 billion. There are no subsidies. (a) What is the value of national income? (b) Explain why and how depreciation leads to a discrepancy between GNP and national income. (c) Explain why indirect taxes enter the calculation.

3 (a) Suppose the crime rate falls and the police force can be halved. Former police officers get jobs in private industry at the same wage as police officers. Explain why there is no change in GNP. (b) Is society better or worse off? (c) What does this suggest about including police expenditure as part of GNP?

4 Explain whether the following activities should appear in a comprehensive measure of GNP: (a) time spent by students in lectures; (b) the income of muggers; (c) the time spent by boxing match spectators; (d) the wage paid to traffic wardens who issue parking tickets; (e) dropping litter.

7-2 short-run equilibrium output

LEARNING OUTCOMES

When you have finished this section, you should understand

- actual output and potential output

- short-run equilibrium output

- determinants of desired consumption and desired investment

- the effects of a shift in aggregate demand

- the multiplier

- the paradox of thrift

Since 1960 real GNP in the UK has grown on average at 2.3 per cent per annum. But there have been marked cycles around this rising trend in real GNP. Real GNP actually fell during 1973–75, 1979–81, and 1989–92. In between, it grew 10 per cent during 1975–79, 26 per cent during 1981–89, and 24 per cent during 1992–98. One aim of macroeconomics is to explain why real GNP fluctuates as it does. In this chapter we analyse the forces determining real GNP.

To construct a simple model, we ignore the discrepancies between national income, real GNP, and real GDP. Henceforth, we use national income, total output, and GNP interchangeably. We begin by distinguishing *actual* output from *potential* output.

Potential output *is the output the economy would produce if all factors of production were fully employed.*

Potential output tends to grow smoothly over time as the economy's stock of factors of production increases. Population growth adds to the labour force. Investment in education, training, and new machinery gradually increases the stock of human and physical capital. Technical advances allow any given stock of factors to produce more output. Together, these explain why the UK has grown on average at 2.3 per cent per annum since 1960.

Potential output is not the maximum output the economy could conceivably produce – if compelled to work 18 hours a day, doubtless we could all produce more. Rather, it is the output that could be sustained if every market in the economy were in long-run equilibrium. Thus, potential output includes an allowance for 'normal unemployment'. Some people don't want to work at the equilibrium wage rate, and, in a constantly changing economy, others are temporarily in between jobs. Potential output in the UK, and in many other countries of Western Europe, probably corresponds to an unemployment rate of between 5 and 10 per cent.

Suppose actual output falls below potential output. Workers become unemployed and firms have idle machines or spare capacity. A key issue in macroeconomics is how quickly market forces will return output to its potential or full employment level. Macroeconomics emphasizes how disturbances in one part of the economy induce changes in other parts of the economy which may feed back on the first part, exacerbating the original disturbance.

We cannot examine this important issue by *assuming* that the economy is always at its full employment potential output, for that would be to assume that the problem could never arise. Instead, we must construct a model in which departures from potential output are a logical possibility, examine the market forces that would then be set in motion, and form a judgement about the success or otherwise of market forces in restoring output to its full employment potential.

Thus we begin by studying a model with two crucial properties. First, all prices and wages are fixed at a given level. Second, at these prices and wage levels, there are workers without a job who would like to work and firms with spare capacity they would find profitable to use. Thus the economy has spare resources. Under these circumstances, we do not need to analyse the supply side of the economy in detail. Any increase in output and employment will happily be supplied by firms and workers until full employment is reached.

Since, below potential output, firms happily supply as much output as is demanded, the actual quantity of total output is *demand-determined*. It depends only on the level of *aggregate demand*, the total amount that people want to spend on goods and services in the economy as a whole. This is the essence of the model of income and output determination in this chapter.

Initially, we focus on the demand-determined model of output and employment first developed by John Maynard Keynes in *The General Theory of Employment, Interest, and Money*, published in 1936. Keynes used the model to explain the high levels of unemployment and low levels of output that persisted in most industrial countries throughout the 1930s in the Great Depression.

After the publication of the *General Theory* in 1936, most young economists became Keynesians, advocating government intervention to keep output close to potential. In the 1950s and 1960s, this approach was challenged by *monetarists*, whose intellectual leader was Milton Friedman. They argued, correctly, that even if Keynesian analysis helped us think about depressions it was a poor tool for understanding inflation, which monetarists attribute to a growth in the money in circulation. We develop an approach that builds on the best insights of both Keynesians and monetarists.

■■■ aggregate demand

In the absence of the government and the foreign sector, there are two sources of demand for goods: consumption demand by households, and investment demand for new machines and buildings by firms. Using AD to denote aggregate demand, C to denote consumption demand, and I to denote investment demand, $AD = C + I$. Consumption demand and investment demand are determined by different economic groups and depend on different things.

consumption demand

Households buy goods and services ranging from cars and food to cricket bats, theatre performances, and electricity. In practice, these consumption purchases account for about 90 per cent of personal disposable income.

> Personal disposable income *is the income households receive from firms, plus transfer payments received from the government, minus direct taxes paid to the government. It is the income that households have available for spending or saving.*

Given its disposable income, each household must decide how to divide this income between spending and saving. A decision about one is necessarily a decision about the other. One family may be saving to buy a bigger house; another may be spending more than its income, or 'dissaving', by taking the round-the-world trip it has always wanted.

Many factors affect the consumption and savings decisions of each household and thus the aggregate level of planned consumption and planned savings. We examine these in Chapter 8. But to get started, a single simplification will take us a long way. We assume that, in the aggregate, households' consumption demand is larger the larger is aggregate personal disposable income. Figure 7-5 shows the relationship between desired aggregate consumption and total income that we assume in the rest of this chapter. To be specific we assume $C = 8 + 0.7Y$.

The consumption function *shows the level of aggregate consumption desired at each level of personal disposable income.*

Our simplified model has no government, no transfer payments, and no taxes. Hence personal disposable income equals national income. Figure 7-5 shows desired consumption C at each level of *national* income. The consumption function is a straight line. *Autonomous* consumption demand is unrelated to the level of income. Households wish to consume 8 even when income is zero.[1] The slope of the consumption function is the marginal propensity to consume.

The marginal propensity to consume *is the fraction of each extra pound of disposable income that households wish to consume.*

In Figure 7-5 the marginal propensity to consume (*MPC*) is 0.7. If income rises by £1, desired consumption rises by 70p.

investment spending

Income is the key determinant of household consumption plans as described by the consumption function. What about the factors determining the investment decision by firms?

Figure 7-5 Aggregate demand

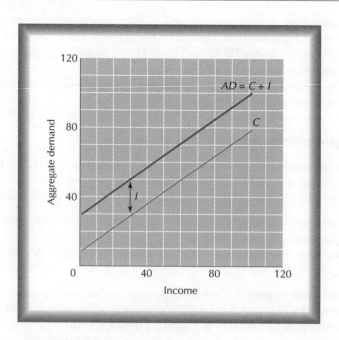

---

[1] This minimum consumption is needed for survival. How do households finance this spending when their incomes are zero? In the short run they dissave and run down their existing assets. But they cannot do so for ever. The consumption function may be different in the short run from in the long run, an idea we discuss in Chapter 8.

Investment demand *consists of firms' desired or planned additions to physical capital (factories and machines) and to their inventories.*

Inventories are goods held for future production or sale.

Firms' demand for investment depends chiefly on firms' current guesses about how fast the demand for their output will increase. There is no close connection between the current *level* of output and current guesses about how demand and output will *change*. Sometimes output is high and rising, sometimes it is high and falling. Since there is no close connection between the current level of income and firms' guesses about how the demand for their output is going to change, we begin our analysis of aggregate demand by making the simple assumption that investment demand is autonomous. We assume that desired investment I is constant, independent of current output and income. In Chapter 8 we discuss investment demand in more detail. In our simplified model, aggregate demand is simply households' consumption demand C plus firms' investment demand I.

Aggregate demand *is the amount that firms and households plan to spend on goods and services at each level of income.*

the aggregate demand schedule

Figure 7-5 shows the *aggregate demand schedule*. In this example, the given amount I that firms wish to spend on investment is 22. Given the consumption function $C = 8 + 0.7Y$, the aggregate demand schedule AD is a vertical distance 22 higher than the consumption function at each income level. Since each extra unit of income adds 0.7 to consumption demand and nothing to investment demand, aggregate demand increases by 0.7. The AD schedule is parallel to the consumption function and the slope of both is given by the marginal propensity to consume. We now show how aggregate demand determines the level of output and income.

▰▰▰ equilibrium output

Whenever aggregate demand falls below its full employment level, firms can't sell as much as they would like. We say there is *involuntary* excess capacity. Workers can't

---

| **Box 7-3** | Movements along the aggregate demand schedule and shifts in the schedule |

The aggregate demand schedule is a straight line whose height depends on the total amount of autonomous spending: autonomous consumption demand plus investment demand. The slope is the MPC. For a given level of autonomous demand, changes in income lead to *movements along* a given AD schedule.

The level of autonomous demand is influenced by many things which we examine in Chapter 8. It is not fixed for all time. But it *is* independent of income. The purpose of the AD schedule is to separate out the change in demand directly induced by changes in income. All other sources of changes in aggregate demand must be shown as *shifts* in the AD schedule. For example, if firms get more optimistic about future demand and decide to invest more, autonomous demand increases and the new AD schedule is parallel to, but higher than, the old AD schedule.

work as much as they would like. There is *involuntary* unemployment. We now require a definition of short-run equilibrium. We cannot use the definition that we used in microeconomics, namely the output at which both suppliers and demanders were happy with the quantity being purchased and sold. We now wish to contemplate a situation in which firms and workers would be delighted to produce more goods and supply more labour. Suppliers are frustrated. But we can at least require that demanders are happy.

> *When prices and wages are fixed, the output market is in* short-run equilibrium *when aggregate demand or planned aggregate spending just equals the output that is actually produced.*

Thus, spending plans are not being frustrated by a shortage of goods. Nor are firms producing more output than they can sell. In short-run equilibrium the output produced exactly equals the output demanded by households as consumption and by firms as investment. Figure 7-6 shows income on the horizontal axis and planned spending on the vertical axis. It also includes the 45° line, which reflects any point on the horizontal axis on to the same point on the vertical axis. Beginning, for example, at an income of 40 on the horizontal axis, we go vertically up to *B* on the 45° line, then horizontally along to the same value of 40 on the spending axis.

We draw in the *AD* schedule from Figure 7-5. This crosses the 45° line at *E*. Since *E* is the *only* point on the *AD* schedule that is also on the 45° line, it is the only point at which income and desired spending are equal. Equilibrium output is 100. Firms are producing 100. That output is equal to income. At an income of 100 we can read from the *AD* schedule that the demand for goods is also 100.

Suppose output and income are only 40. Since the consumption function is $C = 8 + 0.7Y$, consumption demand is 36. But investment demand is always 22; aggregate demand is 58; but output is only 40. There is excess demand, and spending plans cannot be realized at this output level. Conversely, at all outputs above the equilibrium level of 100, aggregate demand will be less than income and output.

Figure 7-6 The 45° diagram and equilibrium output

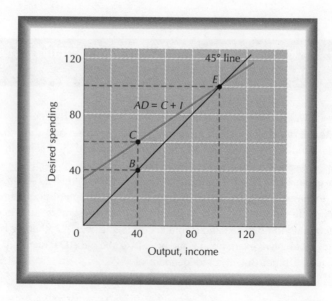

adjustment towards equilibrium

Suppose the economy begins with an output of 30, below the equilibrium output. Table 7-4 shows that aggregate demand of 51 exceeds production of 30. If firms have inventories they can sell more than they have produced by running down stocks for a while. Note that this destocking is *unplanned*; planned changes of stocks are already included in the total investment demand *I*. If firms cannot meet aggregate demand by unplanned destocking, they have to turn away customers. Either response – unplanned destocking or turning away customers – is a signal to firms that they should increase their output levels. At *any* output level below 100, aggregate demand exceeds output firms get signals to start raising their output.

Conversely, if output is initially above its equilibrium level, output exceeds aggregate demand. Firms cannot sell all they have produced, make *unplanned* additions to inventories, and respond by making plans to cut output.

Table 7-4	Aggregate demand and output adjustment

Y	I	C = 8 + 0.7Y	AD = C + I	Y − AD	Unplanned stocks	Output
30	22	29	51	−21	Falling	Rising
80	22	64	86	−6	Falling	Rising
100	22	78	100	0	Zero	Constant
120	22	92	114	+6	Rising	Falling

Box 7-4	Spending like there's no tomorrow

Nowadays Nigel Lawson advertises diets. He used to be Chancellor of the Exchequer. At the height of the Lawson boom in the late 1980s, heady optimism and easy access to credit made UK consumers spend a lot. Personal saving collapsed as people bought champagne, sports cars, and houses. The boom years didn't last long. As inflation got out of control, the government had to take action to slow the economy down. House prices fell. People found their mortgages were larger than the value of their houses. To pay off this 'negative equity', householders had to raise saving sharply in the early 1990s. By 1999 personal saving was collapsing again. . . .

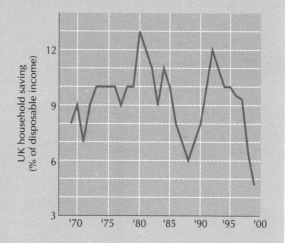

Although in this chapter we assume a constant marginal propensity to save, Chapter 8 discusses more sophisticated theories of consumption and saving.

equilibrium output and employment

In this example the equilibrium level of income and output is 100. Firms sell all the goods they produce and households and firms buy all the goods they want. But there is nothing that guarantees that 100 is the level of full employment or potential output. The whole point of our analysis is that the economy can end up with an output level below potential without any forces being present to move output towards the potential level. Firms have no incentive to hire unemployed workers since there is no prospect of increasing the level of output beyond its existing level of 100. At the given level of prices and wages, the lack of aggregate demand blocks an expansion of output to the full-employment level.

another approach: planned saving equals planned investment

Equilibrium income equals planned investment plus planned consumption. Thus, planned investment equals equilibrium income minus planned consumption: $I = Y - C$. However, planned saving S is the part of income Y not devoted to planned consumption C. Thus $S = Y - C$. Equilibrium occurs where planned investment equals planned savings: $I = S$. Equilibrium income makes households plan to save as much as firms are planning to invest. Figure 7-7 shows how this works out. Using the data in Figure 7-6, since the consumption function is $C = 8 + 0.7Y$, the saving function must be $S = Y - C = -8 + 0.3Y$.

The saving function *shows desired saving at each income level.*

Since planned investment I is 22 whatever the level of income, the equilibrium level of income that makes planned savings equal to planned investment is $Y = 100$, exactly as in Figure 7-6.

If income exceeds its equilibrium level of 100, households want to save more than firms want to invest. But savings is the part of income not consumed. Thus, households are not planning enough consumption, together with firms' investment plans, to purchase the total amount of output being produced. Unplanned inventories pile up

---

Figure 7-7 At equilibrium output planned investment equals planned saving

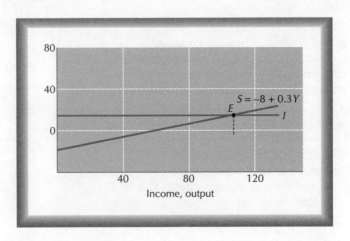

and firms reduce output. Conversely, when output is below its equilibrium level, planned investment exceeds planned saving. Together, planned consumption and planned investment exceed actual output. Firms make unplanned inventory reductions and increase output. Either way, output tends to adjust towards its equilibrium level of 100.

the distinction between planned and actual

Equilibrium output and income will satisfy one of two equivalent conditions. Aggregate demand must equal income and output. In other words, planned consumption plus planned investment must equal actual income, output, and spending. Equivalently, planned investment must equal planned saving. In the last chapter we showed that *actual* investment is *always* equal to *actual* saving, purely as a consequence of our national income accounting definitions. When the economy is not in equilibrium, unplanned investment or disinvestment in stocks or unplanned saving (frustrated consumers) always ensures that actual investment, planned plus unplanned, equals actual saving, planned plus unplanned.

▄▄▄ a fall in aggregate demand

Suppose firms became pessimistic about the future demand for their output. In consequence they reduce their current investment demand. Specifically, suppose planned investment falls from 22 to 13. In Figure 7-7 the horizontal line showing investment demand will fall by 9. Hence equilibrium output will fall. But how much? Since the slope of the saving function is 0.3, we move left 10 for every 3 we go down. Thus a vertical fall of 9 in investment demand induces a horizontal reduction of 30 in output. Equilibrium output falls from 100 to 70. Only when output falls this much is planned saving again in line with planned investment.

Until adjustment is complete, planned saving exceeds the new lower level of planned investment. But actual saving and investment are always equal. Unplanned inventory investment makes up the difference during adjustment. When investment demand falls, firms cannot initially sell their previous output and unplanned stock-building occurs. This is a signal to cut output and begin adjustment. When the new equilibrium is reached, adjustment is complete and planned investment is again equal to planned saving.

Indeed, on the way to this point, firms may temporarily reduce output below the new equilibrium. Why? In order to get rid of the excess stocks they have accumulated during adjustment. Later we argue this is one cause of the cycles in output that we call the business cycle.

▄▄▄ the multiplier

In the preceding example, investment demand fell by 9 but equilibrium output fell by 30.

> *The* multiplier *is the ratio of the change in equilibrium output to the change in autonomous demand that caused the output change.*

The multiplier exceeds 1 because planned saving is not very responsive to income. It takes a large change in income to alter planned saving by the amount that planned investment has changed.

The marginal propensity to save MPS *is the part of each unit of extra income not spent on extra consumption. Thus* MPS = *(1* − MPS*).*

Generalizing Figure 7-7 to any saving function, each unit fall in investment demand requires a fall in output of (1/*MPS*) to reduce planned saving by the same amount. Hence

$$\text{Multiplier} = 1/MPS = 1/[1 − MPC]$$

The larger the marginal propensity to consume, the hence the lower the marginal propensity to save, the larger is the multiplier.

▪▪ the paradox of thrift

What happens to *actual* saving when households *desire* to save less? Planned investment is unaltered. Hence in equilibrium planned saving cannot have changed!

The paradox of thrift *says that a change in desired saving has no effect on the equilibrium level of saving since planned investment is unaltered.*

How can we reconcile a desire to save less at each income level with an uncharted quantity of saving? The answer is that equilibrium income must increase. Take a look again at Figure 7-7. A lower desire to save will induce a downward shift in the saving function. Hence it intersects the line for planned investment at a larger level of output. A desire to save less is a desire to consume more. Aggregate demand increases, boosting output.

In this chapter, we are concentrating on short-run effects. A greater desire to save would reduce aggregate demand and reduce output. Why then do politicians keep urging us to save more? They may have in mind the effect in the longer run. In the short run, we discuss saving and investment independently and assume there are no forces to get aggregate demand to its full employment level. In the long run, wages, prices, and other variables have time to adjust. Not only may these market forces restore long-run equilibrium, they may introduce links between saving and investment. With long-run output at full capacity, politicians may be hoping that a desire to save more may induce other changes that induce an increase in planned investment.

▪▪ recap

▪ Aggregate demand is planned spending on goods (and services). The *AD* schedule shows aggregate demand at each income level.

▪ Autonomous consumption is desired consumption at zero income. The marginal propensity to consume (*MPC*) is the fraction by which consumption rises when income rises by a pound. The marginal propensity to save (*MPS*) is the fraction of an extra pound of income that is saved, *MPC* + *MPS* = 1.

▪ For given prices and wages, the goods market is in equilibrium when output equals planned spending or aggregate demand. Equivalently, at the equilibrium level of income, planned saving equals planned investment.

▪ The equilibrium level of output is demand-determined because we assume that prices and wages are fixed at a level that implies an excess supply of goods and labour.

- A rise in planned investment increases equilibrium output by a larger amount.

- The multiplier is the ratio of the change in output to the change in autonomous demand which caused output to change. In the simple model of this section, the multiplier is $1/(1 - MPC)$ or $1/MPS$. The multiplier exceeds 1 because MPC and MPS are positive fractions.

- The paradox of thrift shows that a reduced desire to save leads to an increase in output but no change in the equilibrium level of planned savings, which must still equal planned investment.

■■ key terms

■■ review questions

1 Suppose the consumption function is $C = 0.7Y$ and planned investment is 45. (a) Draw a diagram showing the aggregate demand schedule. (b) If actual output is 100, what unplanned actions will occur? (c) What is equilibrium output?

2 Planned investment is 150. People decide to save a higher proportion of their income: the consumption function changes from $C = 0.7Y$ to $C = 0.5Y$. (a) What happens to equilibrium income? (b) What happens to the equilibrium proportion of income saved? Explain. (c) Using a saving-investment diagram, show the change in equilibrium output.

3 Which part of actual investment is not included in aggregate demand? Why not?

4 (a) Find equilibrium income when investment demand is 400 and the consumption function is $C = 0.8Y$. (b) Would output be higher or lower if the consumption function were $C = 100 + 0.7Y$?

7-3 fiscal policy and foreign trade

LEARNING OUTCOMES

When you have finished this section, you should understand

- how government spending and taxes affect aggregate demand and equilibrium output

- the balanced budget multiplier

- automatic stabilizers

- the structural budget and the inflation-adjusted budget

- the limits to active fiscal policy

- how foreign trade affects equilibrium output

Fiscal policy is the government's decisions about spending and taxes.

We extend our model of income determination to include the effects of fiscal policy, then take up three issues.

Stabilization policy consists of government actions to try to keep output close to potential output.

We analyse both the possibilities and the difficulties of using fiscal policy for stabilization. The second issue is the significance of the government's budget deficit.

The budget deficit is the excess of government outlays over government receipts.

During 1960–99 the only periods when the UK goverment was not in deficit were 1969–70, 1988–90 and 1999. We examine the size of the deficit and ask how much we should worry about it. The government finances its deficit mainly by borrowing from the public. As a result of this borrowing, the government builds up its debts to the public.[2] By 1999 the UK national debt was £350 billion, or about £5900 per person. The third fiscal policy issue we examine is the effects of the national debt.

The national debt is the stock of outstanding government debt.

Most of this chapter is about the government and aggregate demand. We know from section 7-1 that GDP is $C + I + G + X - Z$. To complete our model of income determination we must add not merely the government but also the effect of foreign trade. Exports X and imports Z are each nearly 30 per cent of UK GDP. The UK is a very open economy, and the effects of foreign trade are too important to be ignored even in a simple model.[3] We conclude this chapter by discussing income determination when foreign trade is included.

■■■ the government and aggregate demand

Since it is cumbersome to keep distinguishing between GDP at market prices and GDP at basic prices, we assume all taxes are direct taxes. In the absence of indirect taxes, measurements at market prices and at basic prices coincide. Until the final section of this chapter, we continue to ignore foreign trade.

---

[2] Government is responsible not merely for its own deficits but also for losses made by nationalized industries. The public sector net cash requirement (PSNCR) is the government deficit plus net losses of nationalized industries.

[3] In contrast, net property income is 1 per cent of GNP. We continue to treat GNP and GDP as equivalent.

In this simplified model, aggregate demand AD equals consumption demand C, plus investment demand I plus government demand G for goods and services.

In the short run government spending G need not vary with the level of output and income. We assume G is fixed by the government. This level reflects how many hospitals the government wishes to build, how large it wants defence spending to be, and so on.

Note that we can think of $(I + G)$ as planned injections. Although actual injections always equal actual leakages, only at equilibrium output do planned injections equal planned leakages. Planned leakages depend on output but planned injections do not. To extend Figure 7-7, we need to work out how the presence of the government affects planned leakages.

The government levies taxes and pays out transfer benefits. *Net taxes* are taxes minus transfers. If the net tax rate t is constant, then net taxes $NT = tY$, and household disposable income YD is $Y(1 - t)$. Thus if households save 30 pence of each extra pound of disposable income, the new saving function becomes $S = -8 + 0.3 (1 - t)Y$. Planned leakages, the value of planned $S + NT$, are therefore $-8 + [t + 0.3(1 - t)]Y$ which is also $-8 + [0.3 + 0.7t]Y$. Hence higher net tax rates t make planned leakages more sensitive to national output.

Figure 7-8 extends Figure 7-7 by adding government spending demand G to planned injections, and by amending planned leakages to include the effect of taxes as well as saving. The line for planned leakages is therefore steeper than in Figure 7-7. Equilibrium output occurs where the two lines cross.

the effect of changes in fiscal policy

Suppose there is an increase in aggregate demand because planned government spending increases. Looking at Figure 7-8 it is easy to see that an upward shift in the horizontal line for planned injections must lead to a higher equilibrium output. Output has to increase to raise planned leakages in line with the higher planned injections. Hence higher government spending boosts equilibrium output.

| **Figure 7-8** | Equilibrium output |

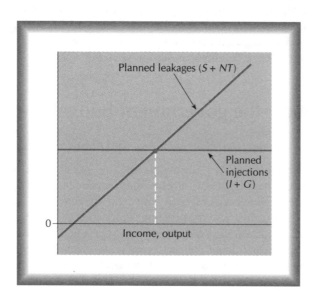

An increase in planned investment, another planned injection, would have the same effect on equilibrium output. What about the size of the effect in Figure 7-8 compared with Figure 7-7? Since planned leakages are *more* sensitive to output in Figure 7-8 – since there is a leakage to taxes as well as to saving – the upward-sloping line is steeper. Hence the output effect of any given increase in planned injections is smaller. Output no longer has to rise so much in order to accomplish the required change in planned leakages. The multiplier is smaller.

What about the effect of a change in the net tax rate? Thinking again in terms of Figure 7-8, a higher net tax rate makes the planned leakages line steeper. Hence it intersects the given planned injections line at a lower equilibrium output. With higher leakages for any output level, it takes a lower output to make planned leakages equal to planned injections.

the balanced budget multiplier

Suppose we now combine a tax increase and an increase in government spending. To keep things simple, suppose initial equilibrium output is 1000, the net tax rate is 0.2 and the initial level of government spending is 200. Hence initially $G = NT = 200$.

Consider an increase of 100 in government spending matched by a rise in the net tax rate to 0.3. Given that initial equilibrium output is 1000, this implies $G = NT = 300$, so there should be no effect on output. Injections and leakages each increased by 100.

Not so fast! The higher tax rate also reduces disposable income YD by 100. For a given propensity to save out of disposable income, this means that planned saving falls, and hence planned leakages fail to increase by as much as planned injections. Hence equilibrium output has to rise to increase planned leakages in line with the higher level of planned injections!

The balanced budget multiplier *states that an increase in government spending plus an equal increase in taxes leads to higher equilibrium output.*

We could have reached the same conclusion by thinking about aggregate demand and consumption instead of thinking about planned injections and planned leakages. An additional 100 in government spending adds a full 100 to aggregate demand ($C + I + G$). Additional taxes of 100 reduce disposable incomes by 100. However, the marginal propensity to consume out of disposable income is less than 1. Hence consumption demand falls by less than 100 when disposable income falls by 100. On balance aggregate demand ($C + I + G$) increased since the rise in G outweighs the fall in C. Hence equilibrium output increases.

▪▪ the government budget

A budget *describes spending and financing plans.*

The government budget describes its plans for government spending and net tax rates. The budget is in surplus when revenue exceeds expenditure, and in deficit when spending exceeds revenue. Thus, the budget deficit is $G - tY$.

Since government spending G on goods and services is assumed to be independent of output, whereas net tax revenue varies with Y, for given levels of G and t we should expect the budget deficit to vary with output. Other things equal, high output means high tax revenue and a budget surplus; low output means low tax revenue and a budget deficit.

investment, saving, and the budget

Could an increase in government spending so increase equilibrium output that tax revenue rises more than government spending? Actually, we can show this is impossible. Again we use the equality of planned leakages and injections. Thus in equilibrium $[S + NT] = G + I$.

Equivalently, $[S - I] = [G - NT]$. Investment is fixed, but higher government spending boosts output and hence saving. Thus the $[S - I]$ increases. Although the output increase boosts net tax revenue, the budget deficit must nevertheless increase.

The same reasoning helps us think through the effect of a rise in the net tax rate. We know this reduces equilibrium output. Hence, on the left-hand side, saving falls both because output is lower and because disposable incomes are reduced by the tax increase. With investment unaffected, the left-hand side moves in the negative direction. So must the right-hand side. Net tax revenue must increase, even though equilibrium output is lower.

deficits and the fiscal stance

Is the size of the budget deficit a good measure of the government's *fiscal stance*? Can we tell from the size of the deficit whether fiscal policy is *expansionary* and aiming to increase national income, or *contractionary* and trying to reduce national income?

In itself, the deficit is *not* a good measure of the government's fiscal stance. The deficit can change for reasons that have nothing to do with fiscal policy. Even though government spending and tax rates remain unaltered, if investment demand drops output will fall. In turn this will reduce the government's net tax revenue and increase the budget deficit. The government will take in less revenue from taxes and have to pay out more transfer payments such as unemployment benefit.

In particular, for given levels of government spending and tax rates, we expect the budget to show larger deficits in recessions, when income is low, than in booms, when income is high. Suppose aggregate demand suddenly falls. The budget will go into deficit. Someone looking at the deficit might conclude that fiscal policy was expansionary and that there was no case for further tax cuts or further increases in government spending on goods and services. But that might be wrong. The deficit may exist because of the recession.

the structural budget

We can indicate the fiscal stance by calculating the *structural* or *cyclically-adjusted budget*.

> The structural budget *shows what the budget would have been if output had been at full-employment output.*

The structural budget uses existing rates of tax and social security, but adjusts the net revenue they yield by hypothetically adjusting output to its fuul employment level.

inflation-adjusted deficits

A second reason why the actual government deficit may be a poor measure of fiscal stance concerns the distinction between real and nominal interest rates. Official measures of the deficit treat the whole of the nominal interest paid by the government on the national debt as an item of government expenditure. It would make more sense to count only the *real* interest rate times the outstanding government debt as an item of expenditure which contributes to the deficit.

 The inflation-adjusted budget *uses real not nominal interest rates to calculate government spending on debt interest.*

Suppose inflation is 10 per cent, nominal interest rates are 12 per cent, and real interest rates are 2 per cent. From the government's viewpoint, the interest burden is only really 2 per cent on each £1 of debt outstanding. Putting the matter differently, although nominal interest rates are 12 per cent, even at constant tax rates inflation will inflate future nominal tax revenue at 10 per cent a year, providing most of the revenue required to meet the high nominal interest rates. Similarly, from the private sector's viewpoint, although bondholders are getting a nominal income of 12 per cent from the government, this represents a real return of only 2 per cent, and it is the latter that will determine the real value of the fiscal stimulus the government is providing via transfer payments in the form of debt interest to the private sector.

▉▉ automatic stabilizers and active fiscal policy

Shifts in aggregate demand or planned injections have less effect on equilibrium output when the multiplier is low. When planned leakages are very responsive to output, shifts in planned injections have a small effect on equilibrium output.

 Automatic stabilizers *are mechanisms in the economy that reduce the response of GNP to shocks.*

Box 7-5 | Better measures of fiscal stance

During the mid 1970s, nominal interest rates were 15 per cent, but annual inflation averaged 16 per cent: real interest rates were negative. Begg (1987) shows that counting real not nominal interest in the budget deficit reduced it from 5.5 per cent to only 1 per cent during 1975–77. Quite a difference! Now inflation is much better under control, so the inflation correction is less important.

One should still remember the other correction – for the effect of the business cycle on tax revenues. Remember that the UK experienced the Lawson boom in the late 1980s, then the Major slump in the early 1990s, before enjoying steady growth after 1993. Thus the structural budget deficit

should be larger than the actual deficit in the late 1980s (when boom conditions temporarily boosted government revenues), smaller than the actual deficit in the early 1990s (the recession cut tax revenue and boosted unemployment benefit). After several years of steady recovery, the discrepancy between the two should have been much smaller by the late 1990s. The table below confirms these predictions.

Recent estimates by the UK Treasury suggest that, after two years, a 1 per cent increase in output (relative to potential output) leads to an improvement in the budget deficit or surplus by 0.75 per cent of GDP.

Average annual deficit (central and local government)	1988–90	1991–94	1995–97	1998–2000
Actual deficit (% of GDP)	0.2	5.8	4.6	−0.1
Structural deficit (% of GDP)	2.5	4.6	3.8	−0.3

Sources: OECD, *Economic Outlook*; D. Begg, 'UK Fiscal Policy since 1970', in R. Dornbusch and R. Layard (eds), *The Performance of the UK Economy*, Oxford University Press, 1987; HM Treasury, *Budget 99*.

Income tax, VAT, and unemployment benefit are important automatic stabilizers. Whenever income and output fall, government payments of unemployment benefits rise and government receipts of income tax and VAT fall. These factors help to ensure that the net tax rate is sufficiently high to reduce the size of the multiplier by a considerable amount.

Automatic stabilizers have one great advantage. They work automatically. Nobody has to decide whether there has been a shock to which the government should now respond. By reducing the responsiveness of the economy to shocks, automatic stabilizers help ensure that output does not fall to catastrophic levels. In an open economy, imports are another automatic stabilizer.

| Box 7-6 | The limits on active fiscal policy |

Why can't shocks to aggregate demand immediately be offset by fiscal policy?

1 Time lags It takes time to recognize that aggregate demand has changed. It may take six months to collect reliable statistics. Even then, it takes time to change fiscal policy. Long-term spending plans on hospital construction or on defence cannot be changed overnight. And once the policy change has been implemented it takes time to work through all the steps of the multiplier process before the full effect of the new fiscal policy is felt.

2 Uncertainty The government faces two major sources of uncertainty in deciding how much fiscal policy should be changed. First, it does not know for certain the values of key magnitudes such as the multiplier. It only has estimates obtained from past data. Second, since fiscal policy takes time to work, the government has to forecast the level that aggregate demand will have reached by the time fiscal policy has had its full effects. Mistakes made in forecasting non-government sources of autonomous demand, such as investment, may lead to incorrect decisions about the fiscal changes currently required.

3 Induced effects on autonomous demand Our simple model treats investment demand and the autonomous component of consumption demand as given. But this is only a simplification. Changes in fiscal policy may lead to offsetting changes in other components of autonomous demand. If the government estimated these induced effects incorrectly, fiscal changes will not have the expected effects. We discuss this issue in Chapter 8.

Why doesn't the government expand fiscal policy when unemployment is persistently high?

1 The budget deficit When output is low and unemployment is high, the budget deficit is likely to be large. Fiscal expansion will make the deficit even larger. The government may refuse to undertake a fiscal expansion either because of worries about the size of the deficit itself, or because of worries that a large deficit will lead to inflation.

2 Maybe we're at full employment! Our simple model assumes that there are resources involuntarily unemployed that would like to work. Output is demand-determined. Fiscal expansion raises demand and output. Suppose, however, that we are in full long-run equilibrium at potential output. Now there are no spare resources to be mopped up by expansion of aggregate demand. If the government believes that high unemployment and low output are not the result of a fall in aggregate demand, but rather the result of a decline in the willingness to work or to supply output, it may conclude that fiscal expansion is pointless. Later chapters discuss the supply side of the economy and explore this argument in greater detail.

active or discretionary fiscal policy

Although automatic stabilizers are always at work, governments also use *active* or *discretionary* fiscal policies which alter spending levels or tax rates in order to stabilize the level of aggregate demand close to full-employment output. When other components of aggregate demand are abnormally low, the government stimulates demand by cutting taxes, increasing spending, or both. Conversely, when other components of aggregate demand are abnormally high, the government raises taxes or reduces spending.

▓▓▓ the national debt and the deficit

The government's total outstanding debts are called the *national debt*.

The UK government ran large actual deficits in the 1970s. Hence the nominal value of its debt increased sharply from £33 billion in 1971 to £113 billion in 1981. Yet in many of these years the nominal deficit was actually a real surplus once the appropriate inflation-accounting is employed. The *real* debt was falling, not rising. Moreover, when the economy is growing in *real* terms, real tax revenue will be rising, and the public sector can service a growing real debt without having to increase *tax rates*.

These two arguments – inflation adjustment of the deficit and the growth of real incomes and the real tax revenue from given tax rates – suggest that in many countries debt may not be out of control. Although nominal deficits have dramatically raised the nominal debt, the ratio of nominal debt to nominal GDP may well have *fallen*. In fact, the debt/GDP ratio in 1999 was two-thirds of its level 30 years earlier (Table 7-5). Public fears of a UK debt explosion were misplaced.

There are two theoretical reasons why concerns about the national debt may be overstated. First, the vast majority of UK debt is owed to UK citizens who hold government bonds. It is a debt we owe ourselves as a nation. Second, some of the money which the public sector has borrowed in the past has been used to finance physical investment or investment in human capital, which will raise *future* tax revenue and help pay off the debt. Prudent businesses sometimes borrow to finance profitable investment, and there is no reason why a prudent public sector should not do likewise.

Box 7-7	'You've never had it so prudent'

This is what Prime Minister Tony Blair told the Labour Party Conference in 1999. His Chancellor, Gordon Brown, not only gave the Bank of England independent control of interest rates (to stop politicians being tempted to boost the economy too much), but also introduced a Code for Fiscal Stability (for the same reason).

The **Code for Fiscal Stability** commits the government to a medium-run objective of financing all current government spending out of current revenues.

Borrowing-financed deficits are allowed only to finance public-sector investment (which should eventually pay for itself by raising future output and hence future tax revenues). A medium-run perspective is needed because the actual deficit fluctuates over the business cycle even if tax rates remain constant. Chancellor Brown's 'golden rule' means that government debt accumulation in the long run (because of borrowing to finance investment) should be accompanied by higher output and tax revenue without requiring any change in tax rates.

Why, then, should a sensible economist worry about the scale of the public debt at all? Two reasons. First, *if* the debt becomes large relative to GNP, high tax rates may be required to meet the debt interest burden. High tax rates may have disincentive or distortionary effects.

Second, if the government is unwilling to raise tax rates beyond a certain point (because of the adverse effects mentioned above) or is unable to raise tax rates beyond a certain point (because businesses and rich individuals would then emigrate), a sufficiently large debt may lead to large deficits which the government can finance only by borrowing or printing money. Since borrowing merely compounds the problem, eventually the temptation to print money on a massive scale may become irresistible. That is how hyperinflations start. By the late 1990s, UK government debt, as a percentage of GDP, was lower than in 1970. In many European countries, it has risen steadily for two decades. Government debt is over 100 per cent of GDP in countries like Belgium and Italy. Such high debt levels are especially worrying when real interest rates are high.

This completes our introduction to fiscal policy, aggregate demand, and the economy. We conclude the chapter by extending our model of aggregate demand and income determination to include foreign trade.

◼◼◼ foreign trade and income determination

In this section we take account of the economy's exports X, goods domestically produced to be sold to the rest of the world, and its imports Z, goods produced by the rest of the world but purchased by domestic residents. Table 7-6 shows UK exports, imports, and net exports $X - Z$. Net exports are very small relative to GDP.

The trade balance *is the value of net exports. When exports exceed imports the economy has a* trade surplus. *When imports exceed exports, the economy has a* trade deficit.

Table 7-5	UK national debt, 1969–99 (net public sector debt as % of GDP)

1973	1979	1985	1991	1999
60	48	46	28	41

Source: OECD, *Economic Outlook*; HM Treasury, *Budget 99*.

Table 7-6	UK foreign trade, 1950–98 (percentage of GDP)

	Exports	Imports	Net exports
1950	23	23	0
1960	20	21	−1
1970	22	21	1
1980	27	25	2
1998	26	27	−1

Source: ONS, *Economic Trends*.

When a household spends more than its income, it dissaves, or is in deficit, and must run down its assets (in bank accounts or holdings of industrial shares) to meet this deficit. Similarly, when a country runs a trade deficit with the rest of the world, the country as a whole must sell off some assets to foreigners to pay for this deficit.

Table 7-6 shows that the UK is a very open economy. Exports and imports are each over a quarter of GDP. In the United States, exports and imports are about 12 per cent of GDP. Foreign trade is much more important for most European countries than for a very large country like the United States. Net exports $X - Z$ add to our measures of GDP. Hence, the equilibrium condition for the goods market must now be expanded to[4] $Y = C + I + G + X - Z$.

What determines the desired levels of exports and imports? The demand for our exports depends chiefly on what is happening in foreign economies. For a small country like the UK, the level of foreign income and foreign demand for our exports is largely unrelated to the level of income in our domestic economy. Hence we treat the demand for our exports as autonomous. At any particular instant it is at a given level but this level will change when demand conditions alter in the rest of the world.

Imports from the rest of the world may be raw materials for domestic production or items consumed directly by households, such as a Japanese television or a bottle of French wine. Demand for imports is likely to rise when domestic income and output rise.

The marginal propensity to import (MPZ) *is the fraction of each additional pound of national income that domestic residents wish to spend on extra imports.*

At each income level, the difference between export demand and import demand is the demand for net exports. At low levels of income, net exports will be positive. There will be a trade *surplus* with the rest of the world. At high levels of income, there will be a trade *deficit* and net exports will be negative. By raising import demand while leaving export demand unchanged, an increase in a country's income will reduce the trade surplus or increase the trade deficit.

net exports and equilibrium income

Figure 7-9 shows how equilibrium output is determined. The horizontal line $I + G + X$ shows planned injections. The upward-sloping line $S + NT + Z$ shows planned leakages. Equilibrium output Y^* adjusts planned leakages until they are the same level as planned injections.

the multiplier in an open economy

By adding a third leakage through imports Z, an open economy has planned leakages $(S + NT + Z)$ that are even more responsive to output than in our previous discussion. The line for planned leakages $(S + NT + Z)$ in Figure 7-9 should therefore be steeper than for planned leakages $(S + NT)$ in Figure 7-8 which in turn should be steeper than for planned leakages S in Figure 7-7.

The flatter the planned leakages line, the larger the effect on equilibrium output of any given upward shift in planned injections. Hence the output multiplier may be large in a closed economy with no government, but is much smaller in an open economy with a government sector.

---

[4] This condition also implies $Y + Z = C + I + G + X$. Domestic output Y plus output Z from abroad equals final demand or final expenditure $C + I + G + X$.

Nevertheless, increases in planned injections, whether from higher investment, higher government spending, or higher exports, raise equilibrium output a bit. Conversely, a higher savings rate, a higher tax rate, or a higher marginal propensity to import all have the effect of making the planned leakages line steeper and reducing equilibrium output.

import spending and employment

A common view is that imports steal jobs from the domestic economy. Final expenditure demand $C + I + G + X$ is met partly through goods produced abroad rather than through goods produced at home. Thus, by reducing imports, we can create extra output and employment at home. This view is correct, but also dangerous. It is correct because higher consumer spending on domestic rather than foreign goods *will* increase aggregate demand for domestic goods.

The view that import restrictions are always good for domestic output and employment is dangerous because it ignores the possibility of retaliation by other countries. By reducing our imports, we cut the exports of others. If they retaliate by doing the same thing, the demand for our exports will fall. In the end, nobody gains employment but world trade disappears.

Figure 7-9 Equilibrium output

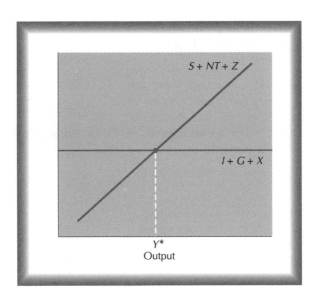

▰▰ recap

- The government enters the circular flow by purchasing goods and services, and by levying taxes (net of transfer benefits) which lower the marginal propensity to consume out of national income.

- An increase in government purchases increases planned injection and equilibrium output. A higher tax rate increases planned leakages and reduces equilibrium output.

- An equal initial increase in government spending and taxes raises output. This is the balanced equilibrium budget multiplier.

- Higher government spending increases the budget deficit. An increase in the tax rate reduces the budget deficit.

- The budget deficit is not a good indicator of the fiscal stance. The structural budget calculates whether the budget would be in surplus or deficit if income were at its full-employment level. It is also important to inflation-adjust the deficit.

- Automatic stabilizers reduce fluctuations in GNP by reducing the multiplier. Leakages act as automatic stabilizers.

- In addition, the government may also use active or discretionary fiscal policy to try to stabilize output. In practice, we should not expect active fiscal policy to be capable of perfect stabilization of output.

- The national debt grows as a result of budget deficits.

- In an open economy, exports are a source of demand for domestic goods but imports are a leakage since they represent a demand for goods produced abroad.

- Exports are determined mainly by conditions abroad and can be treated as autonomous spending unrelated to domestic income. The marginal propensity to import MPZ tells us how much of each extra pound of national income goes on additional demand for imports.

- Taxes and imports reduce the value of the multiplier.

- An increase in exports increases domestic output and income. An increase in the marginal propensity to import reduces domestic output and income.

- The trade surplus is the excess of exports over imports. The trade surplus is larger the smaller is the level of income. An increase in exports increases the trade surplus.

▰▰ key terms

review questions

1 Suppose equilibrium output in a closed economy is 1000, consumption is 800 and investment is 80. (a) What is the level of government spending on goods and services? (b) Suppose investment rises by 50 and the marginal propensity to save out of national income is 0.2. What is the new equilibrium level of C, I, G, and Y? (c) Suppose instead that G had risen by 50. What would be the new equilibrium of C, I, G, and Y? (d) Suppose full-employment output is 1200. By how much would G now have to be raised to get the economy to full-employment output?

2 In equilibrium, desired savings equal desired investment. True or false? Explain.

3 Why does the government bother to raise taxes when it could borrow to cover its spending?

4 Suppose $MPZ = 0.4$, $t = 0.2$, and $MPS = 0.2$. investment demand rises by 100. (a) What happens to the equilibrium level of income and the equilibrium level of net exports? (b) Suppose exports, rather than investment, increase by 100. How does the trade balance change?

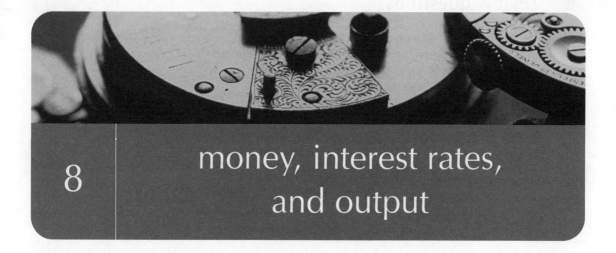

money, interest rates, and output

8-1 money and banking

I n songs and popular language, 'money' stands for many things. It is a symbol of success, a source of crime, and it makes the world go around.

> Money *is any generally accepted means of payment for delivery of goods or settlement of debt. It is the* medium of exchange.

Dog's teeth in the Admiralty Islands, sea shells in parts of Africa, gold during the nineteenth century: all are examples of money. What matters is not the physical commodity used but the social convention that it will be accepted without question as a means of payment.

 **money and its functions**

Although the crucial feature of money is its acceptance as the means of payment or medium of exchange, money has three other functions. It serves as a unit of account, as a store of value, and as a standard of deferred payment. Money, the medium of exchange, is used in one-half of almost all exchange. Workers exchange labour services for money. People buy or sell goods in exchange for money. We accept money not to consume it directly but because it can subsequently be used to buy things we do wish to consume. To see that society benefits from a medium of exchange, imagine a barter economy.

 A barter economy *has no medium of exchange. Goods are simply swapped for other goods.*

In a barter economy, the seller and the buyer *each* must want something the other has to offer. To see a film, you must hand over in exchange a good or service that the cinema manager wants. There has to be a *double coincidence of wants*.

Trading is very expensive in a barter economy. People spend a lot of time and effort finding others with whom they can make mutually satisfactory swaps. Since time and effort are scarce resources, a barter economy is wasteful. The use of money – any commodity *generally* accepted in payment for goods, services, and debts – makes trading more efficient. By economizing on time and effort spent in trading, society can use these resources to produce extra goods or leisure, making everyone better off.

other functions of money

The unit of account *is the unit in which prices are quoted and accounts are kept.*

In Britain prices are quoted in pounds sterling; in the United States in dollars. It is usually convenient to use the units in which the medium of exchange is measured as the unit of account as well. However, there are exceptions. During rapid inflation people often find it more convenient to use dollars as the unit of account. Prices are quoted in dollars but payment is made in local currency, the medium of exchange.

Money is a store of value *because it can be used to make purchases in the future.*

To be accepted in exchange, money *has* to be a store of value. Nobody would accept money as payment for goods supplied today if the money was going to be worthless when they tried to buy goods with it tomorrow. But money is neither the only nor necessarily the best store of value. Houses, paintings, and interest-bearing bank accounts all serve as stores of value. Since money pays no interest and its real purchasing power is eroded by inflation, there are almost certainly better ways to store value.

Box 8-1	Travellers' tales

The following contrast between a monetary and barter economy is reproduced from the World Bank, *World Development Report*, 1989.

Life without money

'Some years since, Mademoiselle Zelie, a singer, gave a concert in the Society Islands in exchange for a third part of the receipts. When counted, her share was found to consist of 3 pigs, 23 turkeys, 44 chickens, 5000 cocoa nuts, besides considerable quantities of bananas, lemons and oranges . . . as Mademoiselle could not consume any considerable portion of the receipts herself it became necessary in the meantime to feed the pigs and poultry with the fruit.' W. S. Jevons (1898)

Marco Polo discovers paper money

'In this city of Kanbula [Beijing] is the mint of the Great Khan, who may truly be said to possess the secret of the alchemists, as he has the art of producing money . . . He causes the bark to be stripped from mulberry trees . . . made into paper . . . cut into pieces of money of different sizes. The act of counterfeiting is punished as a capital offence. This paper currency is circulated in every part of the Great Khan's domain. All his subjects receive it without hesitation because, wherever their business may call them, they can dispose of it again in the purchase of merchandise they may require.' *The Travels of Marco Polo*, Book II

Finally, money serves as a *standard of deferred payment* or a unit of account over time. When you borrow, the amount to be repaid next year is measured in pounds sterling. Although convenient, this is not an essential function of money. UK citizens can get bank loans specifying in dollars the amount that must be repaid next year. Thus the key feature of money is its use as a medium of exchange.

different kinds of money

In prisoner-of-war camps, cigarettes served as money. In the nineteenth century money was mainly gold and silver coins. These are examples of *commodity money*, ordinary goods with industrial uses (gold) and consumption uses (cigarettes) which also serve as a medium of exchange. To use a commodity money, society must either cut back on other uses of that commodity or devote scarce resources to additional production of the commodity. But there are less expensive ways for society to produce money.

> A token money *is a means of payment whose value or purchasing power as money greatly exceeds its cost of production or value in uses other than as money.*

A £10 note is worth far more as money than as a 7.5 × 14 cm piece of high-quality paper. By collectively agreeing to use token money, society economizes on the scarce resources required to produce money. Since the manufacturing cost is tiny, why doesn't everyone make £10 notes? The essential condition for the survival of token money is restriction of the right to supply it. Private production is illegal.[1] Society enforces the use of token money by making it *legal tender*. The law says it must be accepted as a means of payment. In modern economies, token money is supplemented by IOU money.

> An IOU money *is a medium of exchange based on the debt of a private firm or individual.*

A bank deposit is IOU money because it is a debt of the bank. You can write a cheque and the bank is obliged to pay whenever the cheque is presented. Bank deposits are a medium of exchange because they are generally accepted as payment.

■■■ modern banking

When you deposit your coat in the theatre cloakroom, you don't expect the theatre to rent your coat out during the performance. In effect, banks lend out some of the coats in their cloakroom. A theatre would have to get your particular coat back on time, which might be tricky. A bank finds it easier because one piece of money looks just like another.

> Bank reserves *are the money available in the bank to meet possible withdrawals by depositors. The* reserve ratio *is the ratio of reserves to deposits.*

Unlike other financial institutions, such as pension funds, the key aspect of banks is that some of their liabilities are used as the medium of exchange: cheques allow their deposits to be used as money.

---

[1] The existence of forgers shows that society is economizing on scarce resources by producing money whose value as a medium of exchange exceeds its direct production cost.

The money supply *is the value of the stock of the medium of exchange in circulation.*

At any time, some people are writing cheques on a Barclays account to pay for goods purchased from a shop that banks with Lloyds; and others are writing cheques on Lloyds' accounts to finance purchases from shops banking with Barclays. The *clearing system* is the process of interbank settlement of the net flows required between banks as a result.

Table 8-1 shows the balance sheet of UK commercial banks in 1999. The banks' assets were mainly loans to firms and households, and purchases of financial securities such as bills and bonds issued by governments and firms. It is the fact that many securities are very liquid – easily sellable at a predictable price – that means banks can lend short term and still get it back if depositors then withdraw their money. In contrast, many loans to firms and households are quite illiquid. The bank cannot easily get its money back in a hurry. Note that modern banks get by with very few cash reserves in the vault. In Table 8-1 these are so small they are not even recorded separately.

Liabilities of commercial banks include sight and time deposits. Sight deposits mean the depositor can withdraw money 'on sight' without any notice; chequing accounts are sight deposits. Time deposits, which pay higher interest rates, require the depositor to give a period of notice before withdrawing money. Banks then have more time to organize the sale of some of their high-interest assets in order to have the cash available to meet these withdrawals. Certificates of deposit (CDs) are large 'wholesale' time deposits, a one-off deal with a particular client for a specified period, usually paying quite generous interest rates. The other liabilities of banks are various 'money market instruments', short-term and highly liquid borrowing by banks.

the business of banking

A bank is a business and its owners or managers aim to maximize profits. A bank makes profits by lending and borrowing. To get money in, the bank offers favourable terms to potential depositors. British banks increasingly offer interest on sight deposits and usually offer free chequing facilities to people whose sight deposits or current accounts do not fall below a certain level. They do not charge directly for the expenses of clearing and processing cheques. And they offer better interest rates on time deposits.

Table 8-1 Balance sheet of UK commercial banks, March 1999

Assets	£bn	Liabilities	£bn
In foreign currency		In foreign currency	
Securities	242	Deposits and money market instruments	1050
Loans	883	Other liabilities	93
Other assets	24		
In sterling		In sterling	
Securities	71	Deposits and money market instruments	832
Loans	861	Other liabilities	146
Other assets	40		
	2121		2121

Next, the banks have to find profitable ways to lend what has been borrowed. Table 8-1 shows how the banks lend out their money. In sterling, most is lent as advances of overdrafts to households and firms, usually at high interest rates. Some is used to buy securities such as long-term government bonds. Some is more prudently invested in liquid assets. Although these do not pay such a high rate of interest, the bank can get its money back quickly if people start withdrawing a lot of money from their sight deposits. And some money is held as cash, the most liquid asset of all.

The bank uses its specialist expertise to acquire a diversified portfolio of investments though depositors merely observe that they get an interest rate on their time deposits or free chequing facilities. Without the existence of the intermediary, depositors would have neither the time nor the expertise to decide which of these loans or investments to make. UK banks hold reserves that are only 2 per cent of the sight deposits that could be withdrawn at any time. This shows the importance of the other liquid assets in which banks have invested. At very short notice, banks could cash in liquid assets easily and for a predictable amount. The skill in running a bank entails being able to judge how much must be held in liquid assets including cash, and how much can be lent out in less liquid forms that earn higher interest rates.

banks as creators of money

To keep the arithmetic simple, suppose banks use a reserve ratio of 10 per cent. Initially, people pay £1000 into the banking system. Banks have assets of £1000 cash and liabilities of £1000 deposits, which is money they owe to depositors. If banks were like cloakrooms, that would be the end of the story. However, banks realize that they do not need all deposits to be fully covered by cash reserves.

Suppose banks create £9000 of overdrafts. Think of this process as the simultaneous loan of £9000, which appears on the asset side of the balance sheet, and the granting to customers of £9000 of deposits, against which they can now write cheques, which therefore appear as £9000 of deposits on the liability side of the balance sheet. Now the banks have £10 000 of total deposits – the original £1000 corresponding to money paid in, plus the new £9000 as the counterpart to the overdraft – and £10 000 of total assets, comprising £9000 in loans and £1000 cash in the vaults. The reserve ratio is now 10 per cent.

It does not even matter whether the 10 per cent ratio is imposed by law or whether it is merely the profit maximizing estimate of smart behaviour by banks that balance risk and reward. The risk is the possibility of being caught short of cash, the reward is the interest rate spread.

The interest rate spread *is the amount by which interest rates on loans exceed interest rates on deposits.*

How did banks create money in this example? Originally, there was £1000 of cash in circulation. That was the money supply. When paid into bank vaults, it went out of general circulation as the medium of exchange. But the public acquired £1000 of bank deposits against which cheques could be written. After the overdrafts were created, the public had £10 000 of deposits against which cheques could be written. The money supply had increased from £1000 to £10 000. Banks created money.

■■ the monetary base and the money multiplier

To complete our analysis of how the money supply is determined we need to examine what determines the amount of cash that will be deposited with the banking system. Through the *central bank*, the Bank of England in the UK, the government controls the issue of token money in a modern economy.

> *The* monetary base *or stock of* high-powered money *is the quantity of notes and coin in private circulation plus the quantity held by the banking system.*

How much of the monetary base will be held by commercial banks as cash reserves? In the simplified example of the previous section, we assumed that the general public deposited all its cash with the banks. But this is only a simplification. Even people with deposit accounts and cheque-books carry some money around in their pockets. We do not write out a cheque for a bus fare.

But there are other reasons why people hold cash. Many people do not trust banks. They keep their savings under the bed. Remarkably enough, only three-quarters of British households have chequing accounts. Other people hold cash because they wish to make illegal or unreported transactions in the 'black economy'. How is the money supply related to the monetary base, the amount of notes and coin issued by the central bank? The answer to this question is the money multiplier.

> *The* money multiplier *is the ratio of the money supply to the monetary base.*

The value of the money multiplier depends on two key ratios, the banks' desired ratio of cash reserves to total deposits, and the private sector's desired ratio of cash in circulation to total bank deposits.

Banks' desired ratio of cash reserves to total deposits determines how much they will multiply up any given cash reserves into deposit money. The *lower* the desired cash reserves ratio, the larger the quantity of deposits the banks will create against given cash reserves and the *larger* will be the money supply. Similarly, the *lower* the private sector's desired ratio of cash in circulation to private sector bank accounts, the *larger* will be the money supply for any given quantity of high-powered money issued by the central bank. Since a higher fraction of the monetary base is deposited in the banking system, the banks are able to create more bank deposits.

We give an exact formula for the money multiplier in Box 8-2. Suppose that banks wish to hold cash reserves equal to 1 per cent of their total deposits and that the

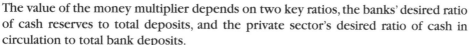

Box 8-2 | The money multiplier

Suppose banks wish to hold cash reserves R equal to some fraction c_b of deposits D, and that the private sector holds cash in circulation C equal to a fraction c_p of deposits D. Thus

$$R = c_b D \quad \text{and} \quad C = c_p D.$$

The monetary base, or stock of high-powered money, H, is either in circulation or in bank vaults. Hence

$$H = C + R = (c_p + c_b)D.$$

Finally, the money supply is circulating currency C plus deposits D. Hence

$$M = C + D = (c_p + 1)D.$$

These last two equations give us the money multiplier, the ratio of M to H

$$M/H = (c_p + 1)/(c_p + c_b) > 1.$$

Using the data of Table 8-2,

$$c_p = 22.8/750.5 = 0.03, \quad c_b = 6/750.5 = 0.008,$$

and the money multiplier is

$$M/H = (1.03)/(0.038) = 27,$$

which is simply the ratio of M4 to M0.

private sector wishes to hold cash in circulation equal to 3 per cent of the value of private sector sight deposits. The formula given implies that the money multiplier would be 27. Each £100 increase in the monetary base leads to a rise of £2700 in the money supply.

The higher the interest rate banks can earn by lending relative to the interest rate (if any) that banks must pay depositors, the more banks will wish to lend and the more they will take chances with a low ratio of cash reserves to outstanding sight deposits. Conversely, the more unpredictable are withdrawals from sight deposits and the fewer lending opportunities the banks have in very liquid loans, the higher cash reserves they will have to maintain for any level of deposit lending.

What about the public's desired ratio of cash in circulation to deposits? In part this depends on institutional factors, for example whether firms pay wages by cheque or cash. In part it depends on tax rates and the incentive to hold cash to make untraceable payments in the process of tax evasion. Credit cards reduce the amount of cash used. Credit cards are a temporary means of payment, a *money-substitute* rather than money itself. When you sign a credit card slip, the slip itself cannot be used to make further purchases. Within a short period you have to settle your account by using cash or a cheque, the ultimate means of payment. Nevertheless, since credit cards allow people with chequing accounts to carry less cash in their pocket, their increasing use will probably reduce the desired ratio of cash to sight deposits with banks.

■■■ measures of money

Money is the medium of exchange, and the money supply is cash in circulation (outside banks) plus bank deposits. It sounds simple, but it isn't. Two issues arise: which bank deposits, and why only bank deposits?

We can think of a spectrum of liquidity. Cash, by definition, is completely liquid. Sight deposits (chequing accounts) are almost as liquid, though all of us can remember a situation in which we met problems trying to pay by cheque. Time deposits (savings accounts) used to be much less liquid, but nowadays many people have provisions for automatic transfer between savings and chequing accounts when the latter runs low. Savings deposits are almost as good as chequing accounts.

UK statistics now also distinguish between *retail* and *wholesale* deposits. Retail deposits are those made in high street branches at the advertised rate of interest. Wholesale deposits are big one-off deals where the (corporate) depositor negotiates an interest rate with the bank. But these too can be quite liquid.

Until the 1980s, everyone was pretty clear what a bank was, and hence whose deposits counted towards the money supply. Financial deregulation has blurred this distinction, both in the UK and the USA, and is starting to do so in continental Europe. Until about 1980, UK banks did not lend for house purchase and cheques on building society deposits could not be used at the supermarket checkout. Now 'banks' compete vigorously for house mortgages, and building society cheques are widely accepted as a means of payment. The case for excluding building society deposits from measures of the money supply has gradually collapsed.

Figure 8-1 shows different monetary aggregates and their relation to one another. M0 is the wide monetary base: cash in circulation outside the banks, cash inside banks, and the banks' own accounts with the Bank of England. M0 is the narrowest measure of money. Wider measures begin from cash in circulation. Adding all sight deposits, we get the M1 measure, which used to be considered a good measure of narrow money. Augmenting that by UK private sector time deposits and CDs gives M3 which used to be called sterling M3. That used to be considered the best definition of broad money.

Since there is a spectrum of liquidity, there may be no good place to draw a line and say that everything narrower than this is money, everything wider than this is not. We used to keep track of M0, M1, and M3. All of these measures ignore balances in foreign currency and refer purely to cash and bank deposits in sterling. This approach has been made obsolete by the increasing use of building society deposits as means of payment, and by the conversion of many building societies to commercial banks.

To reflect the new reality, monetary statistics now combine banks and building societies, as shown in Figure 8-1. Now the government routinely publishes statistics only on M0 and M4. Advances in technology, and financial deregulation (which led to greater competition and many more financial products on offer), have made it increasingly easy for customers to substitute between 'broad' and 'narrow' money. Once we leave the monetary base, the first sensible place to stop is M4. Table 8-2 gives actual data for 1999.

| Figure 8-1 | UK monetary aggregates (sterling) |

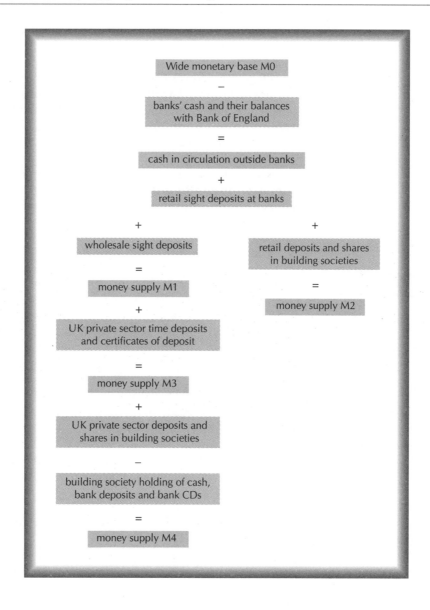

▆▆ competition between banks

Financial deregulation, allowing the new entry of more and more banks, has made modern banking a very competitive business. Banks compete with one another both in the interest rates they offer to attract deposits and in the interest rates they charge borrowers for loans.

The interest rate spread covers the cost of providing banking services. When spreads exceed this amount, they generate profits for banks. Profits act as a signal for new banks to enter, which tends to compete away spreads. With more banks, interest rates on bank loans fall. Increased competition for deposits also raises interest rates paid to depositors. Both effects reduce the spread.

Equilibrium in the banking industry occurs at the point at which it is not worth attracting any more deposits in order to make more loans. The marginal cost of funds, the deposit interest rate, plus the marginal cost of doing banking business, plus any equilibrium profit margin, just equals the marginal revenue that can be earned on making new bank loans (inclusive of any appropriate allowance for possible default). In a perfectly competitive industry, any supernormal profits are competed away eventually by free entry.

Although regulated less than before, banking regulation has not completely disappeared. Moreover, there are substantial scale economies in banking, and competition is therefore imperfect. For both reasons, equilibrium profit margins in banking are usually positive. Nevertheless, once we know the exact market structure, we have a good idea of how interest rates on deposits and loans are likely to be related. And, other things equal, further deregulation of banks is likely to reduce interest rate spreads further.

Competition between banks and the influence of regulation therefore affect how much cash it is *optimal* for profit-maximizing banks to suck into the banking system. These two forces also affect the size of cash reserves it is optimal for banks to hold. The key ratios c_p and c_b in Box 8-3 that determine the size of the money multiplier are not fixed constants but the outcome of the competitive behaviour of banks themselves.

Table 8-2	Narrow and broad money in the UK, June 1999, sterling (£ billion)

	wide monetary base M0	28.8
−	banks' cash and balances at the Bank	−6.0
=	cash in circulation	22.8
+	banks' retail deposits	404.5
+	building society's deposits and shares	104.7
+	wholesale deposits	266.3
	money supply M4	798.3

Source: ONS, *Financial Statistics*.

Box 8-3 | A beginner's guide to the financial markets

Financial asset A piece of paper entitling the owner to a specified stream of interest payments for a specified period. Firms and governments raise money by selling financial assets. Buyers work out how much to bid for these assets by calculating the present value of the promised stream of payments. Assets are frequently retraded between individuals before the date at which the original issuer is committed to repurchase the piece of paper for a specified price.

Cash Notes and coin, paying zero interest. The most liquid asset.

Bills Financial assets with less than one year until the known date at which they will be repurchased by the original borrower. Suppose the government sells three-month Treasury bills. In April the government sells a piece of paper simultaneously promising to repurchase it for £100 in July. Bills do not pay interest, but if people bid £97 in April they will effectively make 3 per cent by holding the bill till July, quite a decent annual return. As July gets nearer the price at which the bill is retraded will climb towards £100. Buying it from someone else in June for £99 and reselling to the government in July for £100 still yields 1 per cent in a month, or over 12 per cent a year at compound interest. Because Treasury bills can easily be bought and sold, and because their price can only fluctuate over a small range (say, between £97.5 and £98 in May when they expire in July), they are highly liquid. People can get their money back quickly and have a good idea how much they would get if they had to sell.

Bonds Longer-term financial assets. If you look under government bonds in the *Financial Times* (www.FT.co.uk) you will find a bond listed as Treasury 5% 2004. In the year 2004 the government guarantees to repurchase this bond for £100 (the usual repurchase price). Until then the person owning the paper will get interest payments of £5 a year. Bonds are less liquid than bills, not because

they are hard to sell, but because the price for which they could be sold, and the amount of cash this would generate, is more uncertain. We now explain why by looking at the most extreme kind of bond.

Perpetuities Bonds that are never repurchased by the original issuer, who pays interest for ever. Usually called Consols (consolidated stock) in the UK. Consols 2.5% pay £2.5 a year for ever. Most consols were issued when interest rates were very low. People originally would have bid around £100 for this consol. Suppose interest rates on other assets rise to 10 per cent. Consols are traded between people at around £25 each so that new purchasers of these old bonds get about 10 per cent. Notice two things. The person *holding* a bond makes a capital loss when other interest rates rise and the price of the bonds falls. Second, since the price of Consols was once £100 and is now only £25, there is much more volatility in Consol prices than in the price of Treasury bills. The longer the remaining life of the bond, the more its current price can move around. Hence although bonds can easily be bought and sold, they are not very liquid. If you buy one today, you do not have a very good idea exactly how much you would get if you had to sell out in six months' time.

Gilt-edged securities Government bonds in the UK. Gilt-edged because there is no danger of the government refusing to meet the interest payments.

Corporate shares (equities) Entitlements to receive corporate dividends, the part of firms' profits paid out to shareholders rather than retained to finance new investment in machinery and buildings. In good years, dividends will be high, but in bad years dividends may be zero. Hence a risky asset which is not very liquid. Firms could even go bust, making the shares completely worthless.

▪▪▪ recap

- Money has four functions: a medium of exchange or means of payment, a store of value, a unit of account, and a standard of deferred payment. It is its use as a medium of exchange that distinguishes money from other assets.

- In a barter economy, trading is costly because there must be a double coincidence of wants. Using a medium of exchange reduces the costs of matching buyers and sellers and allows society to devote scarce resources to other things. A token money has a higher value as a medium of exchange than in any other use.

- Token money is accepted either because people believe it can subsequently be used to make payments or because the government declares it legal tender. The government controls the supply of token money.

- Modern banks attract deposits by acting as financial intermediaries. A national system of clearing cheques, a convenient form of payment, attracts funds into sight deposits. Interest-bearing time deposits attract further funds. In turn, banks lend out money as short-term liquid loans, as longer-term less liquid advances, or by purchasing securities.

- Sophisticated financial markets for short-term liquid lending allow modern banks to operate with very low cash reserves relative to deposits. The money supply is currency in circulation plus deposits.

- The monetary base M0 is currency in circulation plus banks' cash reserves. The money multiplier is the ratio of the money supply to the monetary base, and exceeds unity. The money multiplier is larger (a) the smaller is the desired cash ratio of the banks and (b) the smaller is the private sector's desired ratio of cash in circulation to deposits.

- Financial deregulation has allowed building societies into the banking business. M4 is a broad measure of money and includes deposits at both banks and building societies.

▪▪▪ key terms

▪▪▪ review questions

1 (a) A person trades in a car when buying another. Is the used car a medium of exchange? Is this a barter transaction? (b) Could you tell by watching someone buying mints (white discs) with coins (silver discs) which one is money?

2 Initially gold coins were used as money but people could melt them down and use the gold for industrial purposes. (a) What must have been the relative value of gold in these two uses? (b) Explain the circumstances in which gold could (i) become a token money, and (ii) disappear from monetary circulation completely.

3 In what sense do commercial banks create money?

4 (a) Would it make sense to include travellers' cheques in measures of the money supply? (b) season tickets for the train? (c) credit cards?

5 Sight deposits = 30, time deposits = 60, banks' cash reserves = 2, currency in circulation = 12, building society deposits = 20. Calculate M0 and M4.

8-2 central banking and the monetary system

A central bank *acts as banker to the commercial banks and is responsible for setting interest rates.*

Originally private institutions in business for profit, central banks came under public control as their activities as bankers to their respective governments grew, and as governments have placed increasing emphasis on manipulating interest rates. Founded in 1694, the Bank of England (www.bankofengland.co.uk) was not nationalized until 1947. The Bank is responsible for issuing banknotes, and also acts as banker to the government and to the commercial banks. Deposits with the Bank are liabilities of the Bank. Its assets are government securities and outstanding loans to commercial banks. Unlike commercial banks, the central bank cannot go bankrupt. It can always print more money.

LEARNING OUTCOMES

When you have finished this section, you should understand

- the key roles of the central bank

- how the central bank can affect the money supply

- the determinants of money demand

- how money market equilibrium is achieved

- comparative static experiments that alter money market equilibrium

- why a nominal anchor is needed, and how the central bank uses the interest rate instrument to pursue intermediate targets

the Bank and the money supply

The money supply is partly a liability of the Bank (currency in private circulation) and partly a liability of banks (bank deposits). We now describe the ways in which the Bank *might* seek to affect the money supply: reserve requirements, the discount rate, and open market operations.

reserve requirements

A required reserve ratio *is a minimum ratio of cash reserves to deposits that the central bank requires commercial banks to hold.*

If a reserve requirement is in force, banks can hold more than the required cash reserves but they cannot hold less. If their cash falls below the required amount, they must immediately borrow cash, usually from the central bank, to restore their required reserve ratio.

When the central bank imposes a reserve requirement in excess of the reserve ratio that prudent banks would anyway have maintained, the effect is to reduce the creation of bank deposits, reduce the value of the money multiplier, and reduce the money supply for any given monetary base. Similarly, when a particular reserve requirement is already in force, any increase in the reserve requirement will reduce the money supply. Thus a reserve requirement acts like a tax on banks by forcing them to hold a higher fraction of their total assets as bank reserves and a lower fraction as loans earning high interest rates.

the discount rate

The second instrument of monetary control available to the central bank is the discount rate.

> *The* discount rate *is the interest rate that the Bank charges when the commercial banks want to borrow money.*

When the discount rate was an important part of monetary control in the UK it used to be known as Bank Rate, or Minimum Lending Rate (MLR). Suppose banks think the *minimum* safe ratio of cash to deposits is 10 per cent. It does not matter whether this figure is a commercial judgement or a required ratio imposed by the Bank. On any particular day, banks are likely to have a bit of cash in hand.

By setting the discount rate at a penalty level in excess of the general level of interest rates, the Bank can induce commercial banks voluntarily to hold additional cash reserves to reduce the danger of having to go to the Bank for more cash. Since bank deposits now become a lower multiple of banks' cash reserves, the money multiplier is reduced and the money supply is lower for any given level of the monetary base.

open market operations

> *An* open market operation *occurs when the central bank alters the monetary base by buying or selling financial securities in the open market.*

Whereas the previous two methods of monetary control operate by altering the value of the money multiplier, open market operations alter the monetary base. Since the money supply is the monetary base multiplied by the money multiplier, they alter the money supply. Suppose the Issue Department of the Bank prints £1 million of new banknotes and uses them to purchase government securities on the open market. There are now £1 million fewer securities in the hands of the banks or the private sector, but the monetary base has increased by £1 million. Some will be held in private circulation but most of it will be deposited with the banking system, which can now expand deposit lending against its higher cash reserves.

◼◼ lender of last resort

Modern fractional reserve banking allows society to produce the medium of exchange with relatively small inputs of scarce resources: land, labour, and capital. However, there is a price to be paid for this efficient production of the medium of exchange. Any system of fractional reserve banking is vulnerable to financial panics. Since banks have insufficient reserves to meet a simultaneous withdrawal of all their deposits, any hint of large withdrawals is likely to become a self-fulfilling prophecy as people scramble to get their money out before the banks go bust. The threat of financial panics can be avoided, or at least greatly diminished, if it is known that the Bank of England stands ready to act as a lender of last resort.

> *The* lender of last resort *stands ready to lend to banks and other financial institutions when financial panic threatens the financial system.*

The Bank's role as lender of last resort does not merely preserve a sophisticated and interconnected system of modern finance in which the failure of one bank would bring many others crashing down. It also reduces one major uncertainty in the day-to-day process of monetary control. If depositors were subject to fluctuating moods of optimism and pessimism about the solvency of banks, there would be wild swings in the private sector's desired ratio of cash in circulation to bank deposits and corresponding fluctuations in the value of the money multiplier.

the demand for money

In 1965 the amount of money (M4) in the UK was £17 billion. By 1999 it was £783 billion. Why were UK residents prepared to hold 46 times as much money in 1999 as in 1965? We single out three variables that determine money demand: interest rates, the average price of goods, and real income.

the motives for holding money

Money is a stock. It is the quantity of circulating currency and deposits *held* at any given time. Holding money is not the same as *spending* money when we go to the cinema. We hold money now to spend it later.

Money is the medium of exchange, for which it must also serve as a store of value. In these two functions of money we must seek the reasons why people wish to hold it. People can hold their wealth in various forms – money, bills, bonds, equities, and

Box 8-4	The repo market

In American movies, people falling into arrears on their loans have their cars repossessed by the repo man. In the mid 1990s, London finally established a repo market. Other European financial centres, such as Frankfurt and Milan, had operated repo markets for years. Surely the ultracautious Bundesbank was not a major player in dubious car loans?

A gilt repo is a *sale and repurchase agreement*. A bank sells you a gilt with a simultaneous agreement to buy back the gilt at a specified price on a particular future date. You pay cash to the bank today and get a predictable amount of cash (plus interest) back at a known future date. You have effectively made a deposit in the bank and your short-term loan is secured or 'backed' by the gilt which is temporarily registered in your ownership. Thus repos use the outstanding stock of *long-term* assets (here gilts) as backing for a new set of secured *short-term* loans.

Reverse repos are the other way round. Now you get a short-term loan from the bank by initially selling gilts to the bank, accompanied by an agreement for you to repurchase the gilts at a specified date in the near future at a price agreed now. Just as repos are secured temporary fixed-term deposits,

reverse repos are effectively secured temporary fixed term loans by the bank.

Repos and reverse repos are clearly very like other short-term loan lending and borrowing. They can even be used as the basis for open market operations by the central bank. In the UK, the Bank of England used to conduct open market operations by buying and selling Treasury Bills; the Bundesbank and Banca d'Italia made much more extensive use of repo and reverse repo transactions. But they achieved much the same purpose. Now the Bank of England also uses the repo market for open market operations designed to alter the monetary base.

The repo market allowed gilts to be used as collateral for more liquid short-term lending and borrowing. It increased the extent of financial intermediation. As the cost of lending and borrowing fell, more people made deposits to banks and borrowed from banks. The Bank of England estimated that this increased the money supply M4 by as much as £6 billion at the start of 1996 when the gilt repo market began in the UK.

Source: Bank of England, *Inflation Report*, May 1996.

property. For simplicity we assume that there are only two assets: money, the medium of exchange that pays no interest, and bonds, which we use to stand for all other interest-bearing assets that are not directly a means of payment. How should people divide their wealth at any instant between money and bonds?

> *The* opportunity cost of holding money *is the interest given up by holding money rather than bonds.*

People will hold money only if there is a benefit to offset this cost. We now consider what that benefit might be.

The transactions motive

Without money, making transactions by direct barter would be costly in time and effort. Holding money economizes on the time and effort involved in undertaking transactions. If all transactions were perfectly synchronized, we would earn revenue from sales of goods and factor services at the same instant we made purchases of the goods and services we wish to consume. Except at that instant, we need hold no money at all.

> *The* transactions motive *for holding money reflects the fact that payments and receipts are not perfectly synchronized.*

We need to hold money between receiving payments and making subsequent purchases. How much money we need to hold depends on the value of the transactions we wish to make and the degree of synchronization of our payments and receipts.

Money is a nominal variable not a real variable. We do not know how much £100 will buy until we know the price of goods. If all prices double, both our receipts and our payments will double in nominal terms. To make the same transactions as before we will need to hold twice as much money.

> *The* demand for money *is a demand for* real *money balances.*

Hence when the price level doubles, other things equal we expect the demand for nominal money balances to double, leaving the demand for real money balances

---

Box 8-5 Financial regulation or lifeboat operations?

Systemic risk provides a powerful rationale for government intervention in financial markets: externalities matter. Allowing one institution to go under may bring down many others.

Any intervention carries its own risk, often one of moral hazard. Insuring depositors against loss removes their incentive to monitor the institutions' management, and gives managers perverse incentives to go for broke. They cash up if things go well, but the government pays if things go badly.

In the UK, regulation of banks is now the responsibility of the Financial Services Agency. Capital adequacy requirements ensure that shareholder capital has to be sufficient to stand a pretty large loss, thereby reducing the chance of bankruptcy and a financial panic.

There may still be a case to supplement this with last-resort lending by the central bank. In the UK, with its seafaring tradition, this is called a 'lifeboat operation'. The Bank either lends directly to the troubled institution or simply floods the market with money which, as we shall shortly see, causes a reduction in interest rates. This boosts business confidence to an extent sufficient to remove the source of the crisis. When the panic dies down, the Bank can undo this temporary injection of liquidity so there are no long-run effects on the money supply.

unaltered. People want money because of its purchasing power in terms of the goods it will buy. People hold real money balances because they want to make transactions. Real national income is a good proxy for the total real value of the transactions people undertake. Thus we assume that the transactions motive for holding real money balances will increase when real national income increases.

The second factor affecting the transactions motive for holding money is the synchronization of payments and receipts. Suppose that, instead of shopping throughout the week, households do all their shopping on the day they get a salary cheque from their employers. Over the week, national income and total transactions are unaltered, but people now *hold* less money over the week.[2]

A nation's habits for making payments change only slowly. In our simplified model we assume that the degree of synchronization remains constant over time. Thus we focus on real national income as *the* measure of the transactions motive for holding *real* money balances.

The precautionary motive   Uncertainty about the precise timing of receipts and payments gives rise to a precautionary motive for holding money. Suppose you buy a lot of interest-earning bonds and try to get by with only a small amount of money. You are walking down the street and spot a great bargain in a shop window. But you do not have enough money to take advantage immediately of this opportunity. By the time you arrange to cash in some bonds, the sale may be over.

> *In an uncertain world, there is a* precautionary motive *to hold money. In advance, we decide to hold money to meet contingencies the exact nature of which we cannot yet foresee.*

If the degree of uncertainty remains roughly constant over time, it is the volume of transactions that will determine the benefits from holding real money balances for precautionary reasons. Thus, other things equal, the higher is real national income the stronger will be the precautionary motive for holding money.

Together, the transactions and precautionary motives provide the main reasons for holding the medium of exchange. They are the motives most relevant to the benefits from holding a narrow measure of money. The wider measure, M4, includes interest-earning deposits. The wider the definition of money, the less important will be the transactions and precautionary motives that relate to money as a medium of exchange, and the more we must take account of money as a store of value in its own right.

The asset motive   Suppose we forget all about the need to transact. We think of a wealthy individual or a firm deciding in which assets to hold wealth. At some distant date there may be a prospect of finally spending some of that wealth, but in the short run the objective is to earn a good rate of return. Some assets, such as industrial shares, on average pay a high rate of return but are also quite risky. When share prices fall, shareholders can make a capital loss which swamps any dividend payment to which they are entitled. As well as holding some risky assets, people will keep some of their wealth in safe assets.

> *The* asset motive *for holding money arises because people dislike risk. People are prepared to sacrifice a high average rate of return to obtain a portfolio with a lower but more predictable rate of return.*

---

[2] By allowing us to pay all at once when the statement arrives monthly, credit cards have this effect.

The asset motive for holding money is important when we consider broad measures of money such as M4.

the demand for money: prices, real income, and interest rates

The transactions, precautionary, and asset motives suggest that there are benefits to holding money. But there is also a cost, the interest forgone by not holding interest-earning assets instead. People hold money up to the point at which the marginal benefit of holding another pound just equals its marginal cost. Figure 8-2 illustrates how much money people will choose to hold.

On the horizontal axis we plot quantities of real money balances, nominal money in current pounds divided by the average price level of goods and services. The horizontal line *MC* shows the marginal cost of holding money, the interest forgone by not holding bonds. The height of *MC* depends on the level of interest rates. The *MB* schedule shows the marginal benefit of holding money. We draw the *MB* schedule for a given level of real national income measuring the level of transactions undertaken. For a given level of real income, the marginal benefit of the last pound of money holdings declines as we hold more real money.

Given the level of our real income, desired money holdings occur at point *E*. For any level of real money below the level *L*, the marginal benefit of another pound exceeds its marginal cost in interest forgone. We should hold more money. Above *L*, the marginal cost exceeds the marginal benefit and it is not worth holding as much money as this. The optimal level of money holding is *L*. If all prices of goods and services double but interest rates and real income remain unaltered, neither the *MC* schedule nor the *MB* schedule shift. The desired point remains *E* and the desired level of *real* money remains *L*. Since prices have doubled, individuals will hold twice as much nominal money to preserve the level of their real money balances at *L*.

If interest rates on bonds increase, the opportunity cost of holding money rises. Figure 8-2 shows this as an upward shift from *MC* to *MC'*. The desired point is now *E'* and the desired quantity of real money holdings has fallen from *L* to *L'*. Higher interest rates reduce the quantity of real money balances demanded.[3]

Finally, we consider the effect of an increase in real income. At each level of real money holdings, the marginal benefit of the last pound is higher than before. With more transactions to undertake and a greater need for precautionary balances, a given quantity of real money does not make life as easy as it did when transactions and real income were lower. The benefit of a bit more money is now greater. Hence we show the *MB* schedule shifting up to *MB'* when real income increases. Thus an increase in real income increases the quantity of real money balances demanded.

Thus far we have focused on the demand for M0. Wider definitions of money must also recognize the asset motive for holding money. To explain the demand for M4 we interpret *MC* as the *extra* return that could be obtained on average by putting the last pound into risky assets rather than time deposits, which are safe but yield a lower return. An increase in the average *interest differential* between risky assets and time deposits shifts the opportunity cost schedule from *MC* to *MC'* and reduces the quantity of time deposits demanded. An increase in wealth shifts the marginal benefits schedule from *MB* to *MB'* and increases the quantity of time deposits demanded.

---

[3] If π is the inflation rate and r the nominal interest rate on bonds, the real return on bonds is $r - \pi$. But in purely financial terms the real return on money is $-\pi$. That is the rate at which the purchasing power of money is being eroded by inflation. Hence the differential real return between bonds and money is $(r - \pi) - (-\pi) = r$. The *nominal* interest rate is the opportunity cost relevant to real money demand.

explaining the rise in money holdings from 1965 to 1999

We now return to the question with which we began this section. Why did nominal money holdings increase from £17 billion in 1965 to £783 billion in 1999? Our discussion has identified three factors: prices, real income, and nominal interest rates.

Although nominal money holdings grew 46-fold, the average price level also grew between 1965 and 1999. Once we divide nominal money by the price index to obtain real money, real money balances quadrupled over the period. Yet real GDP more than doubled. Higher real income and real output increase the quantity of real money demanded. Nominal interest rates hardly changed. Why then has real money demand increased much more than real GDP?

The intense increase in competition forced banks to pay ever more generous interest rates on *deposits*, thereby *reducing* the cost of holding broad money, most of which is now interest-bearing deposits. The opportunity cost of holding an interest-bearing deposit is the small spread between the deposit rate and the interest rate you might have earned on Treasury bills. This cost of holding money is now much smaller than it used to be.

■■■ equilibrium in financial markets

We have explained the forces determining the supply of money and the demand for money. We now combine supply and demand to show how equilibrium is determined. The real money supply L is the nominal money supply M divided by the price level P. We now issue a warning that should never be forgotten.

The central bank controls the nominal money supply. *When the price of goods is fixed, the central bank also controls the* real money supply. *But if we allow the price level to change, changes in nominal money will tend to lead to changes in the price level. It is then much harder for the central bank to control the real money supply.*

| Figure 8-2 | Desired money holdings |

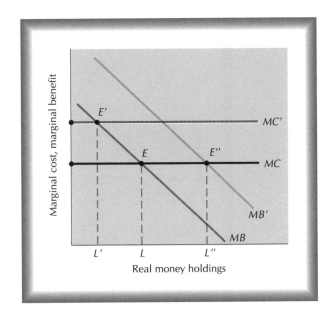

For the moment we ignore this difficulty. With given prices, the central bank can determine both the nominal and the real money supply.

money market equilibrium

The money market *is in* equilibrium *when the quantity of real balances demanded equals the quantity supplied.*

Figure 8-3 shows the demand curve *LL* for real money balances for a given level of real income. The higher the interest rate and the opportunity cost of holding money, the lower the quantity of real money balances demanded. With a given price level, the central bank controls the quantity of nominal money and real money. The supply curve is vertical at this quantity of real money L_0. Equilibrium is at the point *E*. At the interest rate r_0 the quantity of real money that people wish to hold just equals the outstanding stock L_0.

Suppose the interest rate is r_1, lower than the equilibrium level r_0. There is an excess demand for money given by the distance *AB*. Only when interest rates rise to r_0 is excess demand eliminated.

changes in equilibrium

A shift in either the supply curve or the demand curve for money will alter equilibrium in the money market.

A fall in the money supply   Suppose the central bank reduces the money supply. Given our assumption that the price level is given, this contraction in nominal money will also reduce the real money supply. It takes a higher interest rate to reduce the demand for real balances in line with the lower quantity supplied. Hence a reduction in the real money supply leads to an increase in the equilibrium interest rate. Conversely, an increase in the real money supply reduces the equilibrium interest rate.

Figure 8-3   Money market equilibrium

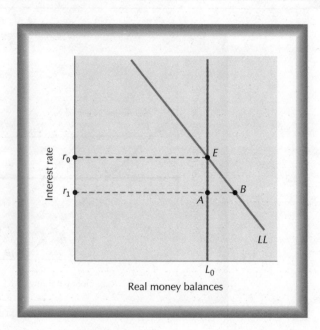

An increase in real income   An increase in real income increases the marginal benefit of holding money at each interest rate, and increases the quantity of real balances demanded. Since people wish to hold more real balances at each interest rate, the equilibrium interest rate must rise to keep the quantity of real balances demanded equal to the unchanged real supply. Conversely, a reduction in real income will reduce the equilibrium interest rate.

An increase in banking competition   A once-and-for-all increase in banking competition, reflected by a permanent increase in interest rates paid on bank deposits, will increase the demand for bank deposits at any level of market interest rates r. The money demand curve shifts up. For a given money supply, this bids up equilibrium market interest rates.

▰▰ monetary control

We begin by examining the practical problems entailed when the Bank tries to implement the textbook theory of monetary control, namely the use of open market operations to determine the monetary base and the use of reserve requirements and the discount rate to influence the size of the money multiplier.

monetary base control

Suppose first that the Bank imposes a cash reserve requirement on the banks. This acts as a tax on banks, preventing them from undertaking business that they would otherwise have found profitable. Modern banks, with access to sophisticated telecommunications, will try to find ways round these controls. They may well conduct lending business with domestic firms through markets in Frankfurt or New York.

To avoid this problem, the Bank can dispense with a *required* cash ratio and rely on open market operations and changes in the monetary base to work through a money multiplier whose size is determined by the cash ratio that banks wish to hold for purely commercial purposes. This is one reason why UK formal reserve requirements were scrapped in the early 1980s.

Nevertheless, the Bank argues that there is one key problem in trying to work through the monetary base: the Bank's role as lender of last resort. When the banks

Box 8-6	The big issue

Like the UK, Japan had a huge property price boom in the late 1980s and then an even more severe collapse in the early 1990s. Japanese banks took a big hit as the value of their loans and other assets fell drastically. Fears about the health of the banking system then led to a loss of consumer confidence and a collapse of private spending.

The Bank of Japan (www.boj.or.jp/en) eased monetary policy to try to help banks and get people spending again. Interest rates fell steadily as the Bank printed money. On 3 March 1999 it issued 1800 billion yen (about £9 billion), driving short-term interest rates to 0.02 per cent! With interest rates down to zero, further open-market operations between money and short-term securities were pretty pointless. The Bank of Japan then started discussing whether it should buy government bonds as a device for pumping yet more money into the economy.

wish to increase lending and deposits they can *always* get extra cash from the Bank.

Moreover, by offering generous interest rates, banks can also get more of the cash previously held by the public outside the banks. How can banks afford to pay such generous rates on time deposits? Because the demand for bank loans is not very sensitive to interest rates.

control through interest rates

Figure 8-4 shows again the market for money. We draw the money demand schedule *LL* for a given level of real income. If the central bank were able to control the money supply, then, for a given level of goods prices, it could fix the real money supply, say at L_0. The equilibrium interest rate would be r_0.

Alternatively, the central bank can fix the interest rate at r_0 and provide whatever money is required to clear the market at this interest rate. The central bank announces that it is ready to deal in interest-bearing assets in unlimited quantities at r_0. In equilibrium, the central bank will end up supplying exactly the quantity of money demanded at the interest rate r_0. The money supply will be L_0.

The central bank can fix the money supply and accept the equilibrium interest needed to make demand equal supply, or can fix the interest rate and supply whatever money is then demanded.

Faced with all the problems in trying to control the money supply directly, the Bank has preferred to set interest rates and then provide the money the market demanded. This is one reason why, in practice, the Bank has frequently been prepared to act as lender of last resort without charging a penalty rate.

Figure 8-4 Interest rates and monetary control

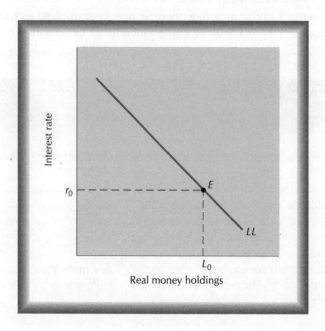

▰▰ targets and instruments of monetary policy

When the position of the money demand schedule is uncertain, fixing the money supply makes the interest rate uncertain, whereas fixing the interest rate makes the money supply uncertain. If the *effects* of monetary policy on the rest of the economy operate primarily through the interest rate, this is an important reason to view monetary policy as the choice of interest rates rather than the choice of money directly. In any case, the latter is almost impossible. Table 8-2 showed that 97 per cent of M4 is bank deposits, and only 3 per cent is cash directly issued by the central bank. In practice, therefore the central bank always conducts monetary policy by choosing interest rates. Interest rates are the instrument of monetary policy.

> *The* monetary instrument *is the variable over which the central bank exercises day to day control.*

Two other concepts lie behind our subsequent discussion of monetary policy. One is the *ultimate objective* of monetary policy in macroeconomics. Objectives could include price stability, output stabilization, manipulation of the exchange rate, and reducing swings in house prices.

Second, in pursuing its ultimate objective, what information does a central bank use at its frequent meetings to decide about interest rates? It probably tries to get up-to-date forecasts of as many variables as possible. Sometimes, however, it concentrates on one or two key indicators, such as the recent behaviour of prices, the exchange rate, or the money supply.

> *An* intermediate target *is the key indicator used as an input to frequent decisions about where to set interest rates.*

Although every central banker knows that interest rates are the instrument about which policy decisions are made, interest rates may be chosen to try to keep the intermediate target on track. New data on the money supply (largely bank deposits) comes out faster than new data on the price level. In the heyday of monetarism, central banks responded to new information by changing interest rates to try to meet medium-run targets for money growth. In terms of Figure 8-4 it was as if they were fixing the money supply not interest rates.

Throughout the world, over the last decade there have been two key changes in the design of monetary policy. First, central banks have been told that their ultimate objectives should concentrate more on inflation control and less on other things. Second, money has become less important as an intermediate target. The financial revolution has reduced its reliability as a leading indicator of what is happening to inflation. Increasingly, central banks are using *inflation forecasts* as the intermediate target to which interest rate policy responds.

■■ recap

- The Bank of England is the UK central bank acting as banker to the banks and to the government. Because it can print money it can never go bust. It acts as lender of last resort to the banks.

- The Bank is responsible for implementing the government's monetary policy. It controls the monetary base through open market operations, purchases and sales of government securities. In addition, the Bank can affect the size of the money multiplier by imposing reserve requirements on the banks, or setting the discount rate for last resort loans at a penalty level which encourages banks to hold excess reserves.

- The demand for money is a demand for real balances. The quantity of real balances demanded falls as the interest rate rises. Increases in real income increase the quantity of real balances demanded at each interest rate.

- Interest rates adjust to ensure that the money market is in equilibrium.

- An increase in the real money supply reduces the equilibrium interest rate. An increase in real income increases the equilibrium interest rate.

- The Bank finds it difficult to control the money supply exactly. Imposing artificial regulations drives banking business into unregulated channels. Monetary base control is difficult since the Bank is committed to act as a lender of last resort and supply cash when needed. In practice, the Bank has preferred to control the money supply by operating directly on interest rates and allowing the demand for money to determine the quantity of money that must then be supplied. Interest rates are the instrument of monetary policy.

- Because interest rates take time to affect the economy, intermediate targets are used as leading indicators relevant to the interest rate decision.

■■ key terms

■■ review questions

1 Suppose the Bank required commercial banks to hold 100 per cent cash reserves against deposits. What happens to the value of the money multiplier?

2 What effect do you expect the widespread adoption of credit cards to have on the precautionary demand for money by households? Explain.

3 Suppose banks raise interest rates on time deposits whenever interest rates on bank loans and other assets rise. (a) Will a rise in the general level of interest rates have a large or a small effect on the demand for time deposits? (b) If the government is worried about the effect of high interest rates on electors who have large loans to finance house purchases, does this imply that it will be easy or difficult for the government to reduce M4 by a large amount?

4 What are the desirable properties of a good leading indicator?

8-3 interest rates and output

In this section we extend our simple model of income determination. We explain why lower interest rates boost aggregate demand and national income. We examine how the money market and the output market interact to determine simultaneously the equilibrium level of income *and* interest rates. We then examine how the government can affect equilibrium income by monetary and fiscal policy in this extended model. Finally, we discuss how the government can use a mix of monetary and fiscal policy to manage or control the level and composition of aggregate demand.

LEARNING OUTCOMES

When you have finished this section, you should understand

- how interest rates affect aggregate demand

- the effects of a monetary and a fiscal expansion

- *IS* and *LM* curves

- how output and interest rates react to shocks in either the goods market or the money market

- that different mixes of monetary and fiscal policy can achieve the same output but at different interest rates

▰▰ interest rates and aggregate demand

We look first at consumption demand.

interest rates, consumption, and saving

In Chapter 2 we argued that changes in (real) interest rates have both income and substitution effects. The substitution effect makes people want to save more and consume less today because the relative reward for saving has risen. The income effect also makes people save more if initially they were borrowers. Higher interest rates make borrowers poorer and they have to consume less. However, higher interest rates make lenders richer, so for them the income effect goes the other way. Putting all this together, economic theory offers the possibility that higher interest rates increase planned saving and reduce consumption demand, but it is not exactly clear cut.

Income and substitution effects apply only when people can freely choose between consumption and saving both before and after the change in interest rates. Yet in practice many people have trouble borrowing as much as they would like, even at the going interest rate. Lenders fear of moral hazard (a borrower vanishing with the money) and adverse selection (borrowers have inside information about whether they are a bad risk or not) mean that lenders often require collateral.

> *Borrowers offer* collateral *to lenders when they hand over legal title to assets that the creditor can then seize if the borrower defaults on the loan.*

Building societies and banks often keep the deeds to a property until a loan is paid off.

Lower interest rates tend to boost the price of assets by increasing the present value of the income that they generate. Hence lower interest rates increase the value of collateral. This may allow people to borrow more than before. If they were unhappy before about not being able to borrow, they will now take advantage of better creditworthiness to borrow and spend. This applies to businesses but also to households.

The credit channel of monetary policy *is the effect of lower interest rates in boosting aggregate demand by increasing the value of collateral.*

other influences on consumption demand

Chapter 7 examined how planned consumption and saving depended on disposable income. Interest rates were conveniently ignored as one of the other things equal. Are there other influences a more complete theory of consumption demand should restore?

The ability to lend and borrow allows consumers to shift resources through time. In principle it is their long-run resources that should influence spending decisions. Consumption today should depend not just on current disposable income and interest rates but also on today's expectations of future income. Other things equal, higher expected future income should increase planned spending today. Most students expect to have future incomes that greatly exceed their limited incomes while at school or university. That is why they run up debts. They are borrowing against future incomes to spend a bit more today. Diminishing marginal utility means that low consumption hurts a lot. Better to have fewer yachts later and a few more beers today.

We shall continue to treat expectations of future incomes as one of the 'other things equal' in thinking about consumption demand. However, these expectations can change radically. In the Lawson boom years of the late 1980s, people were expecting a rosy future. By the early 1990s they were much more pessimistic. The consumption function shifted up and then down again. The saving function did the converse.

Some economists have argued that an implication of this more sophisticated view is that fiscal policy may be weaker than suggested in the previous chapter. A tax cut boosts disposable income today, but also adds to the budget deficit and government debt. Consumers begin to foresee that taxes may need to rise in future to pay off the debt. Hence consumers reduce estimates of their future disposable income. This argument was first noticed nearly 200 years ago by David Ricardo.

Ricardian equivalence *asserts that tax cuts have no effect on aggregate demand if people foresee that they will induce equivalent tax increases in the future.*

Ricardo himself thought that, in its extreme form, the argument was unlikely to be true empirically. Today most economists agree with that assessment. Nevertheless, it contains a useful insight. Present policies may have future consequences. To understand behaviour, we think about the total effect of the policy not just its immediate and obvious impact.

investment demand

In Chapter 7 we treated investment demand as autonomous, or independent of the current level of income and output. In this section we begin to analyse the forces that determine the level of investment demand. Here we focus on the role of interest rates. Other determinants of investment demand are considered later.

Total investment spending comprises investment in fixed capital and investment in working capital. Fixed capital includes factories, houses, plant, and machinery. Working capital consists of stocks or inventories. Although the total volume of stockbuilding or destocking is quite small, this component of total investment is volatile and contributes significantly to changes in the total level of investment.

How are we to organize our thoughts about investment? Our model of planned injections in a closed economy distinguishes investment I, and government spending G on goods and services. Public investment is part of G, and we continue to treat government demand as part of the government's general fiscal policy. Thus we assume that G is fixed at a level determined by the government. In this section it is the determination of private investment demand I on which we focus.

investment in fixed capital

Firms add to their plant and equipment because they foresee profitable opportunities to expand their output, or because they can reduce costs by moving to more capital-intensive production methods. British Telecom needs new equipment because it is developing new products for data transmission. Nissan needs new assembly lines because it is substituting robots for workers in car production.

In each case, the firm has to weigh the benefits from new plant or equipment – the increase in profits – against the cost of investment. But the benefit occurs only in the future, whereas the costs are incurred immediately as the plant is built or the machine purchased. The firm must compare the value of extra future profits with the current cost of the investment. The firm has to ask whether the investment will return enough extra profits to pay back *with interest* the loan used to finance the original investment. The higher the interest rate, the larger must be the return on a new investment before it will match the opportunity cost of the funds tied up in it.

At any instant there is a host of investment projects that the firm *could* undertake. Suppose the firm ranks these projects, from the most profitable to the least profitable. At a high interest rate, only a few projects will earn enough to cover the opportunity cost of the funds employed. As the interest rate falls, more and more projects earn a return at least as great as the opportunity cost of the funds used to undertake the investment. Hence the firm will undertake more investment. Figure 8-5 plots the investment demand schedule *II* describing this relationship between interest rates and investment demand.

> *The* investment demand schedule *shows how much investment firms wish to make at each interest rate.*

If the interest rate rises from r_0 to r_1, fewer investment projects will cover the opportunity cost of the funds tied up, and desired investment will fall from I_0 to I_1.

What determines the height of the schedule *II*? Two things: the cost of the new machines, and the stream of profits to which new machines give rise. For a given stream of expected future profits, an increase in the purchase price of new capital goods will reduce the rate of return earned on the money tied up in investment. Hence fewer projects will match the opportunity cost of any particular interest rate. Since the level of desired investment will be lower at each interest rate, an increase in the cost of new capital goods will shift the investment demand schedule *II* downwards.

Similarly, if the firm becomes less optimistic about future demand for its output, it will reduce its estimates of the stream of profits that will be earned on each of the possible investment projects. For a given cost of new capital goods, the return on each project will fall. At each interest rate there will now be fewer projects matching the opportunity cost of the funds. Since desired investment will fall at each interest rate, a lower level of expected future demand and profits will shift the investment demand schedule downwards.

The investment demand schedule *II* can be used to analyse both business investment in plant and machinery and residential investment in housing. Can we say anything about the slope of the schedule? The longer the economic life of the capital good, the larger the fraction of its total returns that will be earned in the relatively distant future and the more the original cost of the goods will have accumulated at compound interest before the money can be repaid. Hence a small change in interest rates has a more important effect, the longer the economic life of the capital good. The investment demand schedule will be flatter for long-lived houses and factories than for very short-term machinery. A rise in interest rates is more likely to choke off long-term than short-term projects.

inventory investment

There are two reasons why firms *plan* to hold inventories or stocks of raw materials, partly finished goods, and finished goods awaiting sale. First, the firm may be speculating, or betting on price increases. When oil prices were rising sharply, many firms bought large stocks of oil, believing it would be cheaper to buy it now rather than later. Similarly, firms may hold finished goods off the market hoping to get a better price for them in the near future.

Second, firms may plan to hold stocks for the same reasons households plan to hold money. Corresponding to the transactions motive for holding money is the fact that many production processes take time. A ship cannot be built in a month, or even a year in many cases. Some stocks are simply the throughput of inputs on their way to becoming outputs. But there is also a motive corresponding to the precautionary motive for holding money. Suppose demand for the firm's output suddenly increases. Since plant capacity cannot be changed overnight, the firm may have to pay large overtime payments if it is to meet the upsurge in its order book; so it may be cheaper to carry some stocks in reserve with which to meet any sudden upswing in demand. Similarly, in a temporary downturn, it may be cheaper to continue production and pile up stocks of unsold goods than to incur expensive redundancy payments in order to reduce the workforce and cut back production.

Figure 8-5   The investment demand schedule

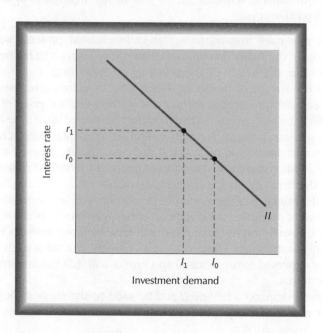

These are the benefits of holding inventories. What about the costs? By holding on to goods that could have been sold, or purchasing goods whose purchase could have been delayed, the firm is tying up money that could have been used elsewhere to earn interest. Hence the cost of holding inventories is the interest paid on the money that could have been earned by selling them or that was laid out to purchase them.

Thus we can also regard the investment demand schedule *II* in Figure 8-5 as being relevant to planned investment in increasing inventories. For any given assessment of the benefits of holding inventories, an increase in the interest rate increases the marginal cost of holding inventories. Hence an increase in interest rates makes firms reduce desired investment in inventories.

In this section we have established two points. First, an increase in interest rates will affect all types of investment decisions. From now on we suppose there is an aggregate investment demand schedule relating planned investment to the level of the interest rate. Second, an increase in the cost of capital goods or a reduction in expected future profit opportunities will lead to a downward shift in the investment demand schedule. A decrease in the cost of capital goods or greater optimism about future profits will shift the schedule upwards. Since ideas about future profits can sometimes be revised quite drastically, it is possible that the investment demand schedule could shift around quite a lot.

▌▌▌ money, interest rates, and equilibrium output

In Chapter 7 we showed how an increase in aggregate demand – equivalently, a fall in planned leakages – would increase equilibrium output. Can monetary policy do this? Suppose people are worried that short-run equilibrium output is well below the full-employment level of output. We could relax the intermediate target for monetary policy. Until we learn how to analyse prices that can vary, it does not yet make sense to discuss relaxing the Bank of England's inflation target. For the moment we assume that the intermediate target is a fixed nominal money supply.

Increasing the nominal money supply target induces the Bank to cut interest rates. Lower interest rates increase the demand for money in line with the higher supply. You now know that lower interest rates also increase the demand for goods. If that was the end of the story, we could still use the model of Chapter 7. Monetary policy would simply be one of the 'other things equal' behind a particular schedule of aggregate demand and schedule of planned leakages. Changing monetary policy would shift these schedules as before.

What is new is that the induced change in output *then affects money demand itself*. Section 8-2 discussed the role of income or output as a proxy for the transactions to which the benefit of holding money is related. Hence, when monetary policy cuts interest rates to boost aggregate demand, the induced rise in output causes a partial rise in interest rates again. Since the new target monetary supply remains constant, money demand must remain at this new level. As output increases, it takes a rise in interest rates to prevent money demand from rising. Higher interest rates increase the cost of holding money and offset the increase in the benefit of holding money.

Could the induced increase in interest rates be large enough to reverse their initial fall? It can't. It is only the fact that output has risen that is putting upward pressure on interest rates after their initial cut. If interest rates were as high as originally, output would not have risen. But then there would be no induced pressure on interest rates. To sum up, relaxing monetary policy leads to a fall in interest rates and increase in equilibrium output. However, these effects are partly damped by the feedback from output to interest rates necessary to keep the money market in equilibrium.

■■■ fiscal policy and crowding out

The same kind of process operates when the initial cause of higher aggregate demand is a fiscal expansion. Suppose there is an exogenous increase in government spending. In Chapter 7 we calculated the multiplier effect in raising equilibrium output. Now the effect is smaller. Higher output increases money demand and interest rates must rise to keep money demand in line with an unchanged target for money supply. Higher interest rates reduce private spending on investment and perhaps consumption too. Higher government spending has partly crowded out private spending.

Crowding out *is the reduction in private demand caused by higher government spending that bids up interest rates when the intermediate target for monetary policy is unaltered.*

As in discussing monetary policy, the induced effects never reverse the direction of the initial effect. If interest rates rose enough to make private demand fall by more than government demand for goods had increased, total output would be lower. But then there would be nothing to bid up interest rates in the first place.

Our discussion of the effects of monetary and fiscal policy on output and interest rates has emphasized the connection of the goods market and the money market. Interest rates affect both markets, and so does income. We need to think about both markets at once.

■■■ the *IS–LM* model

It would be nice to be able to draw both money market and output market in the same diagram. The *IS–LM* model plots interest rates and income in the same diagram since these are the two variables linking the two markets.

| Figure 8-6 | Simultaneous equilibrium for money and output |

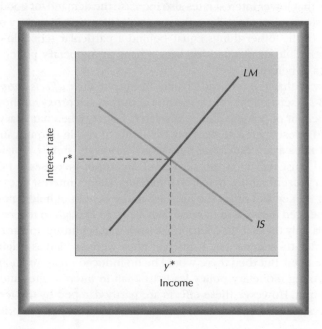

The IS *curve, which relates only to the output market, shows combinations of income and interest rates that make actual output equal aggregate demand (equivalently, equate planned leakages and injections). The* LM *curve, which relates only to the money market, shows combinations of income and interest rates that keep money demand equal to the fixed money supply target.*

With only firms and household we get equilibrium output when planned investment I equals planned saving S. Hence the shorthand IS. Similarly, think of money demand as a demand for liquidity L which must equal the money supply M. Hence LM.

Figure 8-6 shows simultaneous equilibrium in the markets for money and output. The IS curve slopes down: other things equal, lower interest rates boost planned investment and hence equilibrium output. Apart from interest rates, anything that affects equilibrium output must be shown as shifting the IS curve. Higher government spending, lower tax rates, greater export demand, more optimism about future profits or consumer incomes; any of these would shift IS upwards. Adverse changes would shift IS downwards.

The LM curve slopes up to show that, for a given money supply target, money demand cannot change if the money market is to clear. Higher output would increase money demand; it must be accompanied by higher interest rates to reduce money demand again. What would shift the LM curve? An increase in the money supply target would require higher money demand. At any given interest rate, only higher output can increase money demand. The LM curve must shift to the right. A lower money supply target would shift it to the left.

Equilibrium occurs where the IS and LM curves intersect. The equilibrium interest rate is r^* and equilibrium income is Y^*. Figure 8-6 allows us immediately to show the effects of monetary and fiscal policy that we discussed previously. A monetary policy expansion shifts the LM curve to the right, causing both an increase in income and a cut in interest rates. The eventual fall in interest rates is less than the vertical distance by which the LM curve shifts down. The induced rise in output does some of the job of raising money demand in line with higher money supply, so interest rates don't have to do the job unassisted.

A rise in government spending shifts the IS curve upwards in Figure 8-6. This causes an increase in both income and interest rates. Because interest rates rise to maintain money market equilibrium (keep the economy on the LM curve), the eventual increase in income is less than the horizontal shift right in the IS curve. Crowding out damps the increase in equilibrium output and reduces the multiplier. Implicitly, Chapter 7 held interest rates constant and computed the distance by which the IS curve shifted to the right when aggregate demand increased.

It would of course be possible for the Bank of England to react to a fiscal expansion by changing its intermediate monetary target in order to keep interest rates at their original level. The effect in Figure 8-7 would be to make the LM curve horizontal at the interest rate that the Bank had decided to maintain. Then equilibrium output would increase by the full amount of the rightward shift in the IS curve, and we would rediscover the multiplier formula from Chapter 7.

This is shown in Figure 8-7. When the fiscal expansion causes IS_0 to shift to IS_1, a simultaneous monetary expansion allows a new equilibrium at E_2. Income increases to Y_2 and no crowding out occurs.

▮▮▮ demand management and the policy mix

Although fiscal decisions will determine the government's budget deficit, it is not essential to finance the deficit by printing money. The government can also sell bonds and borrow from the private sector. Hence, if it chooses, the government can pursue independent monetary and fiscal policies.

Demand management *is the use of monetary and fiscal policy to stabilize the level of income around a high average level.*

Nevertheless, monetary and fiscal policy are not interchangeable. They affect aggregate demand through different routes and have different implications for the *composition* of aggregate demand.

Figure 8-7 can be used to analyse the mix of monetary and fiscal policy. Suppose the government aims to stabilize income at the level Y_1. The figure shows two different ways in which this can be done. One option is to have an expansionary or *easy* fiscal policy with high government spending, low tax rates, or both. This leads to a high *IS* schedule, which we show as IS_1. To keep income in check with such an expansionary fiscal policy, it is necessary to have a *tight* monetary policy. With a low money supply the *LM* schedule lies far to the left, which we show as LM_0.

Equilibrium at E_1 meets the objective of attaining an income level Y_1. Since government spending is a large component of aggregate demand, it requires a high equilibrium interest rate to keep investment and consumption demand in check so that total income is no larger than Y_1. Thus the mix of easy fiscal policy and tight monetary policy means that government spending G will be a relatively large share of national income and private spending $(C + I)$ a relatively small share.

Alternatively, the government can adopt a tight fiscal policy (a lower *IS* schedule, IS_0) and an easy monetary policy (a schedule LM_1, further to the right). The target income Y_1 is still attained but at the lower interest rate corresponding to the new equilibrium E_3. With easy monetary policy and tight fiscal policy, the share of private expenditure $(C + I)$ will be higher and the share of government expenditure lower than at E_1. With lower interest rates, there is less crowding out of private expenditure.

Figure 8-7 Fiscal expansion shifts the *IS* schedule

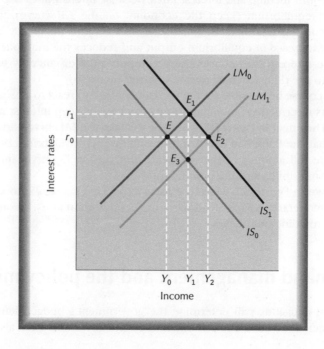

taking stock

We have now completed the first stage of macroeconomics. You have learned how to analyse the demand side of the economy. This is all we need provided we assume there is spare capacity and that prices and wages are fixed. To relax these assumptions we now need to introduce supply. Even when you have mastered the analysis of supply and demand, and adjustment of prices, the demand analysis of the previous two chapters will remain an important part of the story, especially in the short run.

recap

- An increase in interest rates may reduce consumption demand, and certainly reduce investment demand.

- The investment demand schedule shows this negative relationship between the interest rate and the demand for investment. Higher expected future profits or a lower cost of new capital goods will shift the investment demand schedule upwards.

- An increase in the money supply reduces interest rates and increases equilibrium output.

- A fiscal expansion increases output, money demand, and interest rates, thus crowding out or partially displacing private consumption and investment demand.

- The *IS* schedule shows the combinations of interest rates and income compatible with goods market equilibrium. As interest rates increase, equilibrium income falls. Other stimuli to aggregate demand shift the *IS* schedule upwards showing higher equilibrium income at each interest rate.

- The *LM* schedule shows combinations of interest rates and income compatible with money market equilibrium. With a given money supply target, higher income must be accompanied by higher interest rates to keep money demand unchanged. An increase in the supply of money shifts the *LM* schedule to the right. Equilibrium in both markets occurs at the point at which the *IS* and *LM* schedules intersect.

- A given income level can be attained by easy monetary policy and tight fiscal policy or by the converse. In the latter case the equilibrium interest rate is higher and private spending lower.

key terms

review questions

1 Suppose people not previously allowed bank overdrafts get credit cards on which they can borrow up to £500 each. What happens to the consumption function and the saving function? Why?

2 'Higher money supply increases consumption and investment, and hence income. Higher income increases interest rates. Hence higher money supply increases interest rates.' Evaluate this proposition using diagrams to check your answer.

3 Fiscal policy takes the form of government subsidies to firms undertaking investment. Monetary policy involves an open market sale of government bonds. Explain what this policy mix does to the level of GNP and to its composition as between consumption, investment, and government expenditure on goods and services.

4 Suppose firms expect a huge boom in a couple of years. What happens today to investment, income, and interest rates?

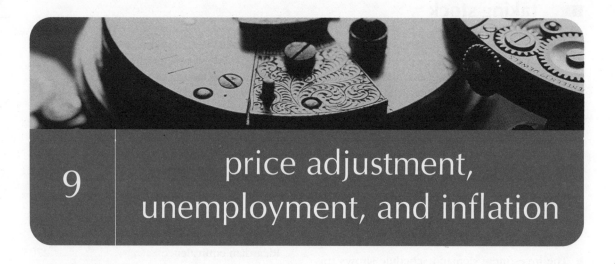

| 9 | price adjustment, unemployment, and inflation |

9-1 prices and aggregate supply

LEARNING OUTCOMES

When you have finished this section, you should understand

- how the price level affects aggregate demand

- the classical model of output and price determination

- effects of monetary and fiscal policy in this model

- why wage adjustment is sluggish in the short run

- how temporary output gaps may emerge

- effects of supply shocks

By assuming prices are fixed and that the economy has spare resources, simple Keynesian models can ignore the supply decision. It appears that boosting aggregate demand will always lead to higher output. But as full capacity approaches, prices will start to rise. Nor can the economy produce indefinitely above its normal full capacity level. This section introduces aggregate supply and examines how prices adjust to the balance of supply and demand. In a short enough period, there is no time for prices to change, and much of our previous analysis remains relevant. In a long enough period, prices can fully adjust. This section allows you to understand the transition from short run to long run.

▆▆▆ the classical model of aggregate supply

To get started, we first look at the opposite extreme to price rigidity, namely complete price flexibility.

 The classical model *analyses the economy when wages and prices are fully flexible.*

We can think about the classical model either as an assertion of instant flexibility, something that only a few economists believe, or as a description of what happens in the long run after full adjustment is complete, something much more reasonable.

Suppose the price level P, the nominal wage W, and the nominal money supply M all double. Nothing real has changed. Real money M/P and real wages W/P are unaltered. In real terms, the economy should be unaltered. The classical model says that real variables are affected other by real variables. Changing a nominal variable has no real effects once all adjustment is complete. Nominal variables only affect other nominal variables.

In the classical model, *output supply is always at Y^* the level of potential output, and is independent of the price level. Potential output is determined by real variables.*

◼◼◼ aggregate demand and the equilibrium price level

How does the price level affect aggregate demand and bring it into line with this level of aggregate supply. The key insight is to understand that one of the 'other things equal' in our analysis is the intermediate target for the *nominal* money supply. Yet it is the *real* money supply which is relevant to money market equilibrium, since the demand for money is a desire for real purchasing power.

Suppose the price level falls. For given nominal money, there is now more real money. Other things equal, interest rates have to fall to keep the money market in equilibrium. Lower interest rates also boost aggregate demand and output. Conversely, a rise in the price level reduces the real money supply, raises interest rates, and reduces output.

Technically, the effects work by shifting the *LM* curve.[1] This curve shows combinations of interest rates and output that maintain real money demand in line with real money supply, treating as given the level of nominal money. The *LM* curve doesn't care whether the real money supply changed because nominal money was reduced or because prices were higher. Either way, real money demand must fall and the curve shift to the left. At each output we need higher interest rates than before.

Figure 9-1 shows the level of potential output Y^*. Changes in any of the relevant 'other things equal' (such as labour supply or productivity) can alter Y^*. Holding these constant, Y^* is fixed. To show this, we draw the vertical aggregate supply curve *AS*. We also plot *IS* and *LM* curves showing combinations of interest rates and income consistent with short-run equilibrium in output and money markets. We begin with *IS* and *LM* and hence equilibrium at *A*.

fiscal expansion

A fiscal expansion boosts aggregate demand and shifts the *IS* curve to *IS'*. In Chapter 8 we held the *LM* curve constant and deduced that short-run equilibrium would move to *B* with higher output and higher interest rates. However, output is now above potential output. This must create excess demand and bid up prices. The classical model says that when prices have fully adjusted the economy is at *C*. In the classical model, output is always at Y^*. Higher prices have shifted the *LM* curve upwards by

[1] This is the most reliable effect, on which we focus. Increasing the value of real money may also shift the *IS* curve outwards, directly boosting aggregate demand, through the credit channel effect. More real money means firms and households have better collateral and may be able to borrow more at any particular interest rate. This borrowing boosts demand for goods.

reducing the real money stock. It now takes higher interest rates at each output to make money demand lower, in line with a lower real money supply. Since aggregate output is unchanged, the fiscal expansion has been completely offset by lower private demand on consumption and investment. These fall because interest rates have risen. The new equilibrium level of prices is what has brought all these changes about.

> *In the* classical model, *there is complete crowding out. Higher government spending leads to an equivalent reduction in private spending, since total output cannot change.*

To check you have understood, ask yourself what happens when government spending falls. Don't read on. Draw a diagram now. Did you notice you can use Figure 9-1 in reverse! Beginning at *C*, the *IS* curve shifts from *IS'* to *IS*, inducing a fall in prices and a rightward shift from *LM'* to *LM*, and a new equilibrium at *A*. The cut in government spending crowds in an equal amount of private spending through lower interest rates.

monetary expansion

Next suppose the nominal money supply is increased by 20 per cent. In the previous chapter this shifted the *LM* curve to the right and caused lower interest rates and higher output. Not in the classical model. The initial expansion causes a boom that bids up prices, and undoes the increase in real money that got the whole process going. Once prices have risen enough to completely restore real money and the position of the *LM* curve to where they began, the new equilibrium is established. Higher nominal money has fed into an equivalent percentage increase in prices (and other nominal variables like wages), leaving all real variables unaltered. This is the context in which monetarism is completely correct.

Figure 9-1 Prices, supply and output

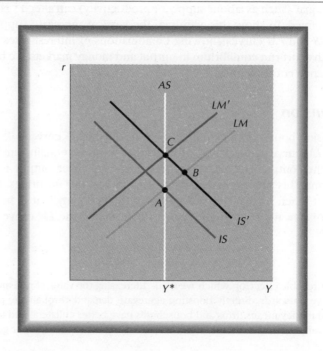

Monetarists *argue that changes in nominal money only affect prices and other nominal variables.*

Notice the importance of the implicit 'other things equal' assumption. Even within the classical model, money is not the only cause of changes in prices. Figure 9-1 showed how fiscal expansion would change prices, in order to change real money and crowd out private spending, to keep output at Y^*.

■■■ supply shocks

A change in aggregate supply itself also changes prices. If potential output falls, something must reduce aggregate demand. If neither monetary nor fiscal policy change, the price level will do the job. Using Figure 9-1 again, imagine Y^* moves to the left. Since original output now exceeds potential output, this bids up prices, reduces the real money stock, bids up interest rates, and shifts the *LM* curve left until it intersects the *IS* curve at the new lower level of potential output.

A permanent adverse supply *shock leads to a rise in the price level unless the government takes other action to reduce aggregate demand.*

For example, the same reduction in real money could instead have been achieved by cutting the nominal money supply and leaving prices unaltered. Either way, the supply shock requires a compensating shift in the *LM* curve and a *change* in *M/P*. During such episodes we should not expect changes in the behaviour of nominal money and the price level to be closely correlated. Once we accept that potential output can change, we should expect the government to be interested in policies that enhance potential output.

Supply-side policies *aim to increase potential output.*

These work not through aggregate demand but by changing microeconomic incentives affecting aggregate supply. Examples include policies to stimulate labour supply (see Section 3-1) or boost productivity. We discuss such policies further in Section 9-2.

This completes our discussion of the classical model. The key to understanding it is that any departures from potential output induce price changes that shift the *LM* curve by the amount required to restore potential output. Even when price adjustment is sluggish, induced shifts in the *LM* curve remain the key, as we now show.

Box 9-1	Anchors away!

Now we understand why the economy needs a nominal anchor. After complete adjustment, market forces really determine real variables like *M/P* and *W/P*. Once we fix say *M*, the real value *M/P* then determines *P* and the real value *W/P* determines *W*. We could instead have fixed *P* or *W*, but we have to fix one. Otherwise all nominal variables could be anything. If the required value of *M/P* was 2, this could be achieved by *any* combination in which there was twice as much nominal money as the price level. In this section we use a monetary target as the nominal anchor. Later we discuss the use of an inflation target (which is really like choosing *P*, given where *P* was last year).

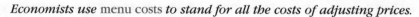 price and output adjustment in the short run

If the classical model always applied, output would always be at potential output, aggregate demand would be largely irrelevant, and Chapter 8 would have been a waste of your time. In practice, prices and wages are unlikely to be instantly flexible. Output can therefore deviate from potential output in the short run.

reasons for sluggish price adjustment

Some firms are in long-run relationships with their customers. Instead of continuously varying prices in line with market conditions, it may be better for both parties to adjust prices more gradually. There may also be direct costs of adjusting prices.

Economists use menu costs *to stand for all the costs of adjusting prices.*

Price catalogues have to be reissued, managerial time has to be used up deciding by how much to change prices, customers and sales reps have to be informed.

Although these arguments justify some price stickiness based on product market considerations, the strongest reason to believe prices are sticky comes from labour market behaviour. Wage costs are often a very large part of total costs. Even if firms were to adjust prices quickly when marginal costs change, costs themselves may be sluggish to reflect changes in market conditions.

Long-run relationships matter even more in the labour market, where team-building, trust, and acquisition of firm-specific skills all take time to develop. It makes more sense for workers' pay to reflect longer-term considerations. This argument is reinforced if firms have better access to borrowing than do their workers. By smoothing out wages over the business cycle, firms provide a valuable service to workers who might otherwise face temporary periods of low income. Workers unable to borrow against better times would then have to cut back consumption a lot. Diminishing marginal utility means that this would be very costly to workers.

Nor could a firm and its workforce be in continuous negotiations about how wages should next be changed. Spending too much time negotiating means less time spent on production. When negotiations have fixed costs, it is optimal to undertake them less frequently. In practice, therefore, most wage agreements last at least a year.

These are nearly always agreements about the level of nominal wages. Although the deal will make provision for agreed rates of overtime payments, the entire schedule of payments will not be renegotiated for at least a year. During that time, any change in prices of goods will have the effect of changing *real* wages.

consequences of sluggish wage adjustment

Suppose consumers become optimistic about the future, consumption demand increases, and the IS curve shifts to the right in Figure 9-2. In the short run, firms inherit nominal wage agreements and there is no need to raise prices much in order to be happy to supply extra output. A bit of overtime will do for a while. Although the long-run supply curve is always vertical at Y^*, in the short run firms are prepared to supply extra output if they get somewhat higher prices. This moderate rise in prices shifts the LM curve to LM_1 in Figure 9-2 since the real money stock falls.

Compared with Chapter 8, where prices were assumed fixed, short-term changes in prices thus damp the expansion a little by bidding up interest rates more quickly. But prices have not risen to the long-run level. Short-run equilibrium output remains above Y^*. The economy is enjoying a boom.

What happens next? The next time wages are renegotiated, workers take advantage of the boom to press for higher real wages. In addition, they have to ensure nominal wages catch up the price increase that took place during the last agreement. For both reasons, nominal wages increase, though probably not all the way to their long-run equilibrium level.

Firms pass on higher wage costs in higher prices, the real money supply falls again, and the new LM curve is LM_2. Output is falling back towards its long-run equilibrium, but the boom has not been completely extinguished. Subsequent rounds of wage negotiation raise wages further, leading to further price rises and further shifts in the LM curve. At LM_3 the new long-run equilibrium has been reached, and we are back in the classical model. To check you understand, draw your own diagram for the effects of a cut in the money supply target.

Your diagram should show an initial shift left in the LM curve, then its subsequent rightward shift in several steps until it returns to its initial position. Monetary contraction causes a slump which gradually puts downward pressure on wages and prices until both have fallen enough to restore the real money supply to its original position. At that point, long-run equilibrium is restored.

▰▰ summing up

How long it takes to complete this transition from short run to long run is one of the most controversial questions in macroeconomics. Some economists think it is very rapid, so that the insights of the classical model quickly become relevant. Other economists think the Keynesian model of the previous chapter remains relevant for a very long time. The mainstream view is probably somewhere in the middle. Within a year, price adjustment has begun. But it takes somewhere between two and five years to complete.

Table 9-1 summarizes the mainstream view. In the short run, overtime and short-time working take most of the strain in adjusting the supply of output. In the medium

---

Figure 9-2 | Short-run dynamics

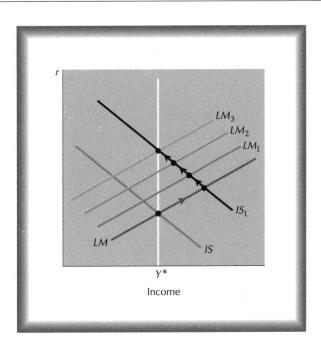

run, not only has adjustment of wages and prices begun, but firms are also hiring or firing in order to adjust hours back towards normal. In the long run, all adjustment is complete.

 The output gap *is the percentage deviation of actual output from potential output.*

Box 9-2 shows output gap estimates by the Organization for Economic Cooperation and Development (OECD). Output gaps cannot arise in the classical model.

a temporarily adverse supply shock

Earlier, we noted that a permanent reduction in potential output will cause a price increase unless the government takes other action to reduce aggregate demand. What

Table 9-1	Labour market adjustment		
	Short run (3 months)	Medium run (1–2 years)	Long run (3–5 years)
Wages	Largely given	Beginning to adjust	Fully adjusted
Hours of work	Demand determined	Mix of hours and	Normal work week
Employment	Largely given	employment adjusting	Full employment

Box 9-2	OECD estimates of output gaps 1980–2000

The figure shows the UK slump of the early 1980s, as the Thatcher government fought to conquer inflation caused by previously high demand plus the second oil shock to the supply side; the boom of the mid 1980s; which in turn prompted another recession as government tightened policy to control inflation; and the steady recovery since 1993.

Germany also experienced a recession in the early 1980s as the Bundesbank raised interest rates to fight inflation from the second oil shock. At the end of the 1980s, German Unification led to a massive boost to demand as the government ran a large budget deficit in order to finance restructuring in East Germany. Again, the Bundesbank responded to overheating by raising interest rates, causing a subsequent contraction of demand. We also show data for Finland, which initially benefited from an opening of trade to the east, but then suffered a dramatic collapse in its export markets in the early 1990s as the former Soviet Union imploded.

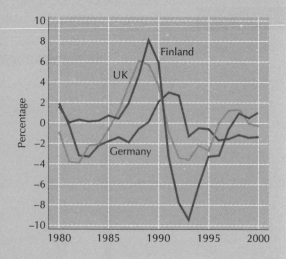

about a temporary supply shock? The division between temporary and permanent is less straightforward than you may imagine. An earthquake obviously changes something real: it destroys physical capital and reduces potential output. Similarly, if workers become scarce and unions succeed in getting higher real wages to reflect this, the effect is permanent. Potential output falls and prices increase.

What about a union that presses for a wage increase unjustified by any change in scarcity of productivity? Now it all depends on how the government reacts. One option is to hang tough. Initially, firms pass on higher wages into higher prices. This reduces the real money supply, makes the *LM* curve shift left, raises interest rates, and causes a recession. As unemployment develops, workers realize they are pricing themselves out of jobs. They gradually cut wages, prices fall back again, and the economy claws its way back to full employment. In the long run, the wage increase is defeated, but it takes a recession in the short run to bring this about.

Alternatively, the government may be terrified of recession. Instead, it can accommodate the wage increase. The easiest method is a monetary expansion.

Monetary policy accommodates a nominal shock *when it changes the intermediate monetary target to prevent the shock having real effects.*

When prices and wages increase, the government increases the money supply to prevent the real money stock being eroded. This avoids the recession but at the cost of accepting the permanent increase in prices. Repeated accommodation therefore leads to inflation.

▰▰ recap

- Prices affect aggregate demand by changing the real value of a fixed nominal money supply.

- The classical model assumes prices and wages have adjusted fully. Output is always at potential output.

- The equilibrium price level adjusts the real money supply to the level that makes aggregate demand equal to potential output. Changes in fiscal and monetary policy change prices but not output.

- Monetarism identifies changes in money as the main cause of changes in prices.

- Supply-side policies seek to enhance potential output.

- In practice prices change slowly because wage adjustment is sluggish.

- Until prices change fully, shifts in aggregate demand can affect real output. The output gap is the deviation of output from potential output.

- Permanent supply shocks change the price level unless other policies adjust aggregate demand. Nominal shocks do not change potential output. The long-run effect of nominal shocks on prices depends on whether or not policy accommodates them.

▰▰ key terms

▪▪▪ review questions

1 The New Deal leads large numbers of additional people to join the labour force. Discuss the effects on output and prices, in the short run and in the long run.

2 Suppose the government wants to maintain stable prices during this transition. How could policies be adjusted to achieve the government's aim?

3 What would be the effect of a permanent increase in VAT? Discuss both supply and demand effects.

4 When is monetarism incorrect?

9-2 unemployment

In the early 1930s, more than one-quarter of the UK labour force was unemployed. High unemployment means that the economy is throwing away output by failing to put its people to work. It also means misery, social unrest, and hopelessness for the unemployed. Over the following 40 years, macroeconomic policy was geared to avoiding a rerun of the 1930s. Figure 9-3 shows that it succeeded.

In the 1970s, views about unemployment began to change. People began to reject the Keynesian pessimism about the ability of the economy to respond to shocks by quickly restoring full employment. The classical model began to be more widely accepted as a description of the way the economy works even in the fairly short run.

By the 1970s, governments in many countries began to perceive an even greater danger to economic and social stability, the danger of high and rising inflation. Thus by the 1980s many governments had embarked on tight monetary and fiscal policies to try to keep inflation under control. The combination of restrictive demand policies and adverse supply shocks led to a dramatic increase in unemployment in most countries in the 1980s

---

| **Figure 9-3** | UK Unemployment (%) |

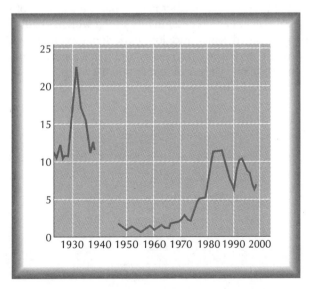

Sources: B. R. Mitchell, *Abstract of British Historical Statistics* and B. R. Mitchell and H. G. Jones, *Second Abstract of British Historical Statistics*, Cambridge University Press; ONS, *Economic Trends*.

(see Table 9-2). In the 1990s, unemployment has receded a bit in the UK and the United States but in Continental Europe remains a major problem. Will high unemployment continue?

Not everyone wants a job. Those who do are called the labour force.

The labour force *comprises all those people holding a job or registered as being willing and available for work.*

The postwar growth of the labour force has been caused less by an increase in the population of working age than by an increase in participation rates by married women.

The unemployment rate *is the percentage of the labour force without a job but registered as being willing and available for work.*

stocks and flows

Unemployment is a stock concept measured at a point in time. Like a pool of water, its level rises when inflows (the newly unemployed) exceed outflows (people getting new jobs or quitting the labour force altogether). Figure 9-4 illustrates this. Beginning with people working, there are three ways to become unemployed. Some people are sacked or made redundant (job-losers); some are temporarily laid off but expect eventually to be rehired by the same company; and some people voluntarily quit their existing jobs. But the inflow to unemployment can also come from people not previously in the labour force: school-leavers (new entrants), and people who once had a job, then ceased even to register as unemployed, and are now coming back into the labour force in search of a job (re-entrants).

People leave the unemployment pool in the opposite directions. Some get jobs. Others give up looking for jobs and leave the labour force completely. Although some of this latter group may simply have reached the retirement age at which they can draw a pension, many of them are discouraged workers.

Discouraged workers *are pessimistic about finding a job and leave the labour force.*

Table 9-3 shows that the pool of unemployment is not stagnant. Even with 1.8 million unemployed, this number is less than the number of people entering and leaving the pool *every* year. A recession hits young workers badly. Unlike established workers with accumulated skills and job experience, young workers have to be trained from scratch, and firms frequently cut back on training when times are tough. Youth unemployment exceeds the national average.

| Table 9-2 | Unemployment (%) |

	1972	1982	1999
UK	4.0	11.3	6.7
Ireland	8.0	13.5	6.4
Italy	6.3	8.4	12.3
Sweden	2.7	3.2	5.6
France	2.8	8.1	12.4
EU	3.2	9.4	11.2
USA	5.5	9.5	4.2

Source: OECD, Economic Outlook.

■■■ types of unemployment

Economists used to classify unemployment as frictional, structural, demand-deficient, or classical.

Frictional unemployment *is the irreducible minimum level of unemployment in a dynamic society.*

It includes people whose physical or mental handicaps make them almost unemployable, but it also includes the people spending short spells in unemployment as they hop between jobs in an economy where both the labour force and the jobs on offer are continually changing. In the longer run, the pattern of demand and production is always changing. In recent decades industries such as textiles and heavy engineering have been declining.

Structural unemployment *arises from the mismatch of skills and job opportunities when the pattern of demand and production changes.*

A skilled welder made redundant at 50 may have to retrain in a new skill more in demand in today's economy. But firms may be reluctant to take on and train older workers. Such workers become the victims of structural unemployment.

| **Figure 9-4** | Labour market flows |

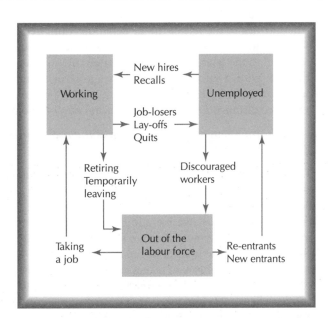

| **Table 9-3** | Flows into and out of unemployment (millions of people) |

	1998
Inflow to unemployment	3.2
Outflow from unemployment	3.3
Stock of unemployed	1.8

Source: ONS, *Labour Market Trends*.

Demand-deficient unemployment *occurs when output is below full capacity.*

Until wages and prices have adjusted to their new long-run equilibrium level, a fall in aggregate demand will lead to lower output and employment. Some workers will want to work at the going real wage rate but will be unable to find jobs. Since the classical model assumes that flexible wages and prices maintain the economy at full employment, classical economists had some difficulty explaining the high unemployment levels of the 1930s. Their diagnosis of the problem was partly that union power was maintaining the wage rate above its equilibrium level and preventing the required adjustment from occurring.

Classical unemployment *arises when the wage is deliberately maintained above its equilibrium level.*

It can be caused either by the exercise of trade union power or by minimum wage legislation. The modern analysis of unemployment takes the same types of unemployment but classifies them differently. Modern analysis stresses the difference between *voluntary* and *involuntary* unemployment.

the natural rate of unemployment

Figure 9-5 shows the market for labour. The labour demand schedule LD slopes downwards, showing that firms will take on more workers at a lower real wage. The schedule LF shows how many people want to be in the labour force at each real wage. An increase in the real wage increases the number of people wishing to work. The schedule AJ shows how many people accept job offers at each real wage. The schedule lies to the left of the LF schedule, both because some people are inevitably between jobs at any instant, and because a particular real wage may tempt some people into the labour force even though they will accept a job offer only if they find an offer with a rather higher real wage than average. Labour market equilibrium occurs at the point E. The employment level N^* is the equilibrium or full-employment level. The distance EF is called the natural rate of unemployment.

The natural rate of unemployment *is the rate of unemployment when the labour market is in equilibrium.*

This unemployment is entirely *voluntary*. At the equilibrium real wage w^*, N_1 people want to be in the labour force but only N^* want to accept job offers; the remainder don't want to work at the equilibrium real wage. Which of our earlier types of unemployment must we include in the natural rate of unemployment? Certainly all frictional unemployment. But we should also include structural unemployment. The issue is not why the worker became redundant (the decline of the steel industry), but why the worker refuses to take a lower wage as a dishwasher in order to get a job.

What about classical unemployment, for example where unions maintain wages above their equilibrium level? This is shown in Figure 9-5 as a wage rate w_2 above w^*. Total unemployment is now AC, which exceeds EF. At the wage w_2, BC workers are voluntarily unemployed, but an additional AB workers are involuntarily unemployed, since A shows hiring by firms and B shows desired labour supply at this wage rate.

A worker is involuntarily unemployed *if he or she would accept a job offer at the going wage rate.*

However, through their unions, workers collectively decide to opt for the wage rate w_2 in excess of the equilibrium wage, thereby reducing the level of employment. Hence for workers as a whole we must regard the extra unemployment as voluntary.

Keynesian or demand-deficient unemployment is entirely involuntary and arises when wages have not yet adjusteda to restore labour market equilibrium. Suppose in Figure 9-5 that the original labour demand schedule is high enough to intersect *AJ* at *B*. Equilibrium unemployment is *BC*. Now labour demand falls to *LD* as in Figure 9-5. Before wages adjust, *BC* remains voluntary unemployment but *AB* is involuntary unemployment, pure spare capacity. Boosting labour demand again could move the economy from *A* back to *B*. However, in the absence of an increase in demand, involuntary unemployment will slowly bid wages down, moving the economy from *A* down to *E*. If this takes a long time, policies to boost demand may be preferable.

Thus we can divide total unemployment into the equilibrium or natural rate – the equilibrium level determined by normal labour market turnover, structural mismatch, union power, and incentives in the labour market – and Keynesian unemployment, sometimes called demand-deficient or cyclical unemployment – the disequilibrium level of involuntary unemployment caused by the combination of low aggregate demand and sluggish wage adjustment.

In the short run, Keynesian unemployment is the part of total unemployment that the government could help mop up by using fiscal and monetary policy to boost aggregate *demand*, rather than waiting for wage and price reductions to increase the real money supply and lower interest rates. In contrast, the natural rate of unemployment tells us the part of unemployment that will not be eliminated merely by restoring aggregate demand to its full-employment level. The natural rate is the 'full-employment' level of unemployment. To reduce the natural rate, *supply-side* policies operating on labour market incentives will be needed.

| **Figure 9-5** | The natural rate of unemployment |

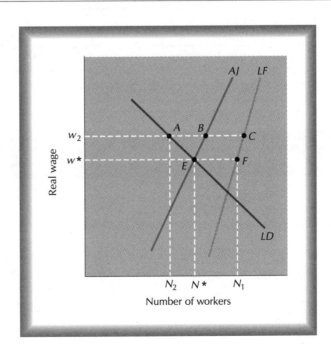

■■■ why is unemployment so high?

How much did unemployment rise because of a higher natural rate of unemployment, and how much because of deficient demand? Table 9-4 shows the average unemployment rate during seven periods, from 1956–59 through to 1991–95. The top row shows the steady rise in the average unemployment rate in successive periods.

The second row shows that there was a steady rise in the natural or equilibrium rate of unemployment, which quadrupled between the 1950s and the 1980s. Indeed, until the start of the 1980s, almost *all* the increase in unemployment reflected a deterioration of supply-side factors and the consequent rise in the natural rate of unemployment. Since the early 1980s, the natural rate of unemployment has remained obstinately high. Increasing skill mismatch contributed to a higher natural rate of unemployment. The labour market is not very good at processing workers as they step out of one job and hope to step into another.

More generous unemployment benefit may entice more people into the labour force, shifting *LF* to the right in Figure 9-5. More significantly, it shifts *AJ* to the left. People spend longer in unemployment searching for the right job. For both reasons, equilibrium unemployment increases. Higher benefits caused some of the increase in equilibrium unemployment, though less than is sometimes supposed. Rises in trade union power, especially in the 1970s, had a marked effect on equilibrium unemployment, as did the tax wedge between the cost of labour to the firm and the take-home pay of the worker.

Up to 1980, actual unemployment was very close to its equilibrium rate – hardly surprising, since this was the objective of the demand management policies in force. However, while the rise in unemployment up to 1980 was due to supply-side factors, since 1980 the story is rather different. The determined attempt of governments

Table 9-4 UK unemployment 1956–95

Unemployment rate (%)	56–59	60–68	69–73	74–80	81–87	88–90	91–95
Actual rate	2.2	2.6	3.4	5.2	11.1	7.3	9.3
Estimated natural rate	2.2	2.5	3.6	7.3	8.7	8.7	8.9

Sources: R. Layard, S. Nickell, and R. Jackman, *Unemployment*, Oxford University Press, 1991; S. Nickell, 'Inflation and the UK Labour Market' in T. Jenkinson, *Readings in Macroeconomics*, Oxford University Press, 1996.

Box 9-3 The lump-of-labour fallacy

Would a shorter work week allow the same total work to be shared between more workers, leaving fewer unemployed? The demand for labour (hours × people) depends both on the cost of hiring workers and on how productive they are.

A normal shift probably includes an hour of dead time (coffee breaks, tidying up, chatting), a fixed cost that yields scale economies to longer shifts. Shorter work weeks thus have higher average costs, and reduce hiring. They also give workers less income to spend on goods. Few economists think a shorter working week is the cure for unemployment.

to improve the supply side did halt the decline, which may have been quite an achievement.

Table 9-4 also shows that, when actual unemployment rose to 10 per cent and above, much of the unemployment was Keynesian, or due to deficient demand. During 1981–87, of the actual unemployment rate of 11.1 per cent, only 8.7 per cent was equilibrium unemployment: the rest was due to insufficient demand. Given the depth of the recession during 1990–92, when unemployment rates again reached double digits, the UK again experienced significant Keynesian unemployment. By the late 1990s, this spare capacity had been removed by an expansion of demand.

■■■ supply-side economics

Keynesians believe that the economy can deviate from full employment for quite a long time, certainly for a period of several years. Monetarists believe that the classical full-employment model is relevant much more quickly. But everyone agrees that in the long run the performance of the economy can be changed only by affecting the level of full employment and the corresponding level of potential output.

income tax cuts

One of the key themes of supply-side economists is the benefits that stem from reducing the marginal rate of income tax.

> *The* marginal rate of income tax *is the fraction of each extra pound of income that the government takes in income tax.*

We discussed tax rates and work incentives in detail in Section 3-1. We pointed out that a cut in marginal tax rates, and a consequent increase in the take-home pay derived from the last hour's work, tend to make people substitute work for leisure. But against this *substitution effect* must be set an *income effect*. People have to do less work

---

Box 9-4	Did the tax carrot work?

The evidence from the past

A lower *marginal* tax rate makes people *substitute* work for leisure. But tax cuts also make workers better off. This *income effect* makes them want to consume more leisure, and hence work less.

The UK evidence shows that tax cuts have a negligible effect on the labour supply decision of men and single women. But for married women, higher take-home pay does encourage labour force participation.

The Thatcher programme

During the 1980s the Thatcher government embarked on a major programme of tax cuts and

tax reforms. The basic rate of income tax fell from 33 to 25 per cent and for top income-earners from 83 to 40 per cent. Many politicians anticipated a considerable increase in the labour supply, yet most economists were pessimistic because of the evidence from the past.

The Thatcher programme is assessed by C. V. Brown, 'The 1988 Tax Cuts, Work Incentives and Revenue', *Fiscal Studies*, 1988. The cut in the basic rate of income tax had no detectable effect at all. The massive cut in the marginal tax rate of top earners had a small effect in stimulating extra hours of work by the rich. The evidence from the past stood up well to this major change of tax policy.

to obtain any given target living standard. Thus, theoretical economics cannot prove that income tax cuts increase the desired labour supply, and in fact most empirical studies confirm that, at best, tax cuts lead to only a small increase in the supply of labour.

Figure 9-6 examines a cut in marginal tax rates. The labour demand schedule LD shows that firms demand more workers at a lower real wage. We draw a steep schedule LF showing that higher after-tax real wage rates, at best, lead to only a small increase in the number of people wishing to be in the labour force. The schedule AJ shows how many people wish to accept job offers at each real wage. It is drawn for a given (real) level of unemployment benefit. Hence the horizontal distance between the AJ and LF schedules – voluntary unemployment at each real wage – decreases as the real wage rises relative to the given level of unemployment benefit.

Suppose there is a marginal income tax rate equal to the vertical distance AB. Equilibrium employment will then be N_1. Why? At the employment level N_1 firms are happy to hire this quantity of labour at the gross wage w_1. Subtracting the income tax rate AB, N_1 workers want to take job offers at the after-tax wage w_3. Thus N_1 is the equilibrium level of employment. The horizontal distance BC shows the natural rate of unemployment, the number of workers in the labour force not wishing to work at the going rate of take-home pay.

Suppose income taxes were abolished. The gross wage and the take-home pay now coincide, and the new labour market equilibrium is at E. Note that two things have happened. First, equilibrium employment has risen. Second, the natural rate of unemployment has fallen from BC to EF. A rise in take-home pay relative to unemployment benefit reduces voluntary unemployment. Similar effects would be obtained if, instead of cutting income tax, the level of unemployment benefit were cut. For a given labour force schedule LF, fewer people would now wish to be unemployed at any real wage. Hence the schedule AJ, showing acceptances of job offers, would shift to the right.

| Figure 9-6 | A cut in marginal income tax rates |

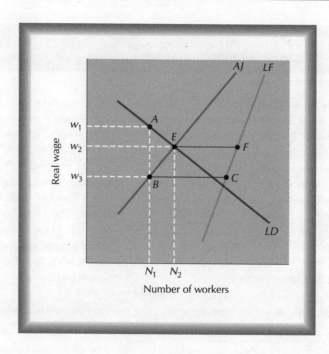

other policies aimed at labour supply

By restricting job acceptances, unions force firms up the labour demand schedule. The equilibrium real wage is higher but equilibrium employment lower. Since a higher real wage reduces employment but (slightly) increases the number of people wishing to be in the labour force, in raising real wages unions increase the natural rate of unemployment. Collectively, labour opts for higher wages and more unemployment.

Conversely, the natural rate of unemployment will be reduced if the power of organized labour is weakened. Unions will be less successful in restricting labour supply and forcing up wages. Government intervention in the labour market to weaken the monopoly power of trade unions should be classified as a supply-side policy aimed at reducing the natural rate of unemployment and increasing equilibrium employment and potential output.

Policies aimed at reducing frictional and structural unemployment should also be included in supply-side economics. Their objective is to shift the *AJ* schedule to the right relative to the labour force schedule *LF*. Such policies include grants that allow

---

Box 9-5   'The graphs the EU Commission dare not publish'

Brussels riven by job market row – A controversial report linking unemployment to rigidities in the labour market has split the Commission' reported the *Financial Times*. The first graph shows, for 14 EU members, the correlation between the degree of labour market regulation and the percentage of the labour force with jobs. The second graph shows, for some OECD countries, the correlation between the employment rate and the cost of firing a worker. The figures show a high degree of regulation and high costs of dismissal are each associated with a lower employment rate. If correlation proved causality, this would clinch the case for deregulation.

Suppose you had to make the case for labour market regulation. If the labour market worked perfectly there would be no need for intervention. Regulations may have been designed to *offset* existing market failures thereby enhancing efficiency. The countries with the largest distortions have the lowest employment rates, but also the largest government intervention to ameliorate the consequences of these distortions. Of course, to be persuasive, you'd have to identify exactly what these distortions were (market power of large employers, externalities in training, etc.) and explain why the particular forms of regulation made things better not worse. You might or might not be able to show this

Source: Financial Times, 8 November 1996.

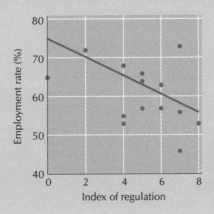

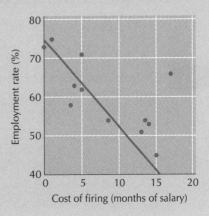

redundant workers to retrain in relevant skills, government measures introduced to help school-leavers develop skills and job experience for the first time, and special measures to encourage the long-term unemployed back into the labour force. By making the labour force more suited to employers' needs, such policies aim to allow firms to make wage offers that unemployed workers will find acceptable. Hence such measures reduce voluntary unemployment. Section 3-1 contains more details of recent policies to boost labour supply.

policies aimed at the demand for labour

Because the *AJ* and *LF* schedules get closer together at higher real wages, anything that increases labour demand will have a small beneficial effect on equilibrium unemployment. Giving workers more capital with which to work will increase their productivity and raise the benefit of workers to firms; so will better technology. Labour demand will also increase if, in real terms, firms receive a higher price for their output. In later chapters we discuss when exchange rate changes may have this effect.

■■■ eliminating Keynesian unemployment

Suppose the government boosts aggregate demand: what effect will this have if the economy begins with involuntary unemployment and hence spare capacity?

On average, boosting aggregate demand by 1 per cent will not increase employment by 1 per cent or reduce unemployment by 1 percentage point. Table 9-5 shows two periods of demand growth and two periods of rapid demand decline. In practice, booms lead initially to a sharp increase in shift lengths and hours worked; slumps lead to the abolition of overtime, the introduction of short time, and a marked decline in hours worked.

Hence in the short run changes in demand and output lead to smaller changes in the level of employment. When output grew 17 per cent between the second quarter of 1992 and the second quarter of 1998 employment increased by only 7 per cent. Moreover, changes in employment do not lead to corresponding changes in unemployment. The last two rows of the table show that rapid expansion or contraction of employment leads to smaller changes in unemployment.

One reason for this result is the 'discouraged worker effect'. When unemployment is high and rising, some people who would really like to work get so pessimistic that they give up looking for a job. Since they are no longer registered as looking for work, they are not recorded in the labour force or considered to be among the unemployed. Conversely, in a boom many people who had previously given up looking for work

Table 9-5 Output, employment, and unemployment

Cumulative change in	79ii–81ii	86ii–88ii	90ii–91ii	92iv–98ii
Real GDP (%)	−7.8	+9.1	−3.4	+16.8
Employment (%)	−6.3	+2.5	−2.9	+6.8
Employed (million)	−1.7	+0.5	−0.7	+1.5
Unemployed (million)	+1.4	−0.9	+0.6	−1.2

Source: ONS, *Economic Trends*.

come back into the labour force since there is now a good chance of finding a suitable job. Hence in booms and slumps recorded employment data change by more than recorded unemployment data.

■■■ costs of unemployment

the private cost of unemployment

It is important to distinguish between voluntary and involuntary unemployment. When individuals are voluntarily unemployed, they reveal that they do better by being unemployed than by accepting the job offers that they face at the going wage rate. Under these circumstances the private cost of unemployment (the wage forgone by not working) is less than the private benefits for being unemployed. What are these benefits?

First, the individual is entitled to transfer payments from the government. Second, there is the value of leisure. By refusing a job, some people are revealing that the extra leisure is worth more to them than the extra disposable income if they took a job. Third, some people expect to get a better job after a temporary spell of unemployment. These future benefits must be set against the current cost of lower disposable income.

When people are involuntarily unemployed, the picture changes. Involuntary unemployment means that people would like to work at the going wage but cannot find a job because there is excess labour supply at the existing wage rate. These people are worse off as a result of being unemployed. The distinction between voluntary and involuntary unemployment may affect our value judgement about how much attention should be paid to the unemployment problem. When unemployment is involuntary, people are suffering more and the case for helping them is stronger.

the social cost of unemployment

Again we distinguish between voluntary and involuntary unemployment. When unemployment is voluntary, individuals prefer to be unemployed. Does this mean that unemployment is also good for society as a whole?

There is one obvious discrepancy between individual benefit and social benefit. For an individual, unemployment benefit is one of the benefits of being unemployed. But this transfer payment gives no corresponding benefit to society as a whole. To this extent, the value judgement that we ought to support the unemployed inevitably entails a cost in allocative inefficiency. It encourages too many people to be voluntarily unemployed.

However, this does not mean that society should go to the opposite extreme and eliminate voluntary unemployment completely. First, society is perfectly entitled to adopt the value judgement that it will maintain a reasonable living standard for the unemployed, whatever the cost in resource misallocation. Second, even in terms of allocative efficiency, the efficient level of voluntary unemployment is certainly above zero.

In a changing economy, it is important to match up the right people to the right jobs. Getting this match right allows society as a whole to produce more output. Freezing the existing pattern of employment in a changing economy will eventually lead to a mismatch of people and jobs. The flow through the pool of unemployment is one of the mechanisms through which society reallocates people to more suitable jobs and increases total output in the long run. If unemployment benefits make this transition smoother, society may gain.

Involuntary or Keynesian unemployment has an even higher social cost. Since the economy is producing below capacity, it is literally throwing away output that could have been made by putting these people to work. Moreover, since Keynesian unemployment is involuntary, it may entail more human and psychological suffering than voluntary unemployment. Although hard to quantify, it is also part of the social cost of unemployment.

Box 9-6   Hysteresis and high unemployment in Europe

Supply and demand curves are supposed to be independent of one another. The labour supply curve or job acceptances schedule *JA* shows the number of people willing to work at each real wage whatever the position of the labour demand curve *LD,* and vice versa. But this assumption may be wrong.

The initial equilibrium is at *E*. Something then makes the labour demand curve shift left to *LD'*. Suppose this in turn *causes* a permanent reduction in labour supply: *JA* shifts to *JA'*. When labour demand reverts to its original level *LD*, the new equilibrium is at *F*, not *E*. The short-run history of the economy has affected its long-run equilibrium.

> Hysteresis *makes long-run equilibrium depend on the path followed in the short run.*

Hysteresis is a possible explanation of high and persistent unemployment in Europe. We now examine some channels through which it might work.

The insider–outsider distinction Outsiders are the unemployed without jobs. Only insiders with jobs participate in wage bargaining. At *E* there are lots of insiders in work and they ensure that real wages are low enough to preserve their own jobs. When a recession occurs, *LD* shifts to *LD'*. Some insiders get fired and become outsiders. Eventually, market forces will restore labour demand to *LD* again. But now there are fewer insiders than originally. They exploit their scarcity by pressing for higher wages for themselves, rather than encouraging their firms to rehire. The economy gets trapped in the high-wage, low-employment equilibrium at *F* instead of the low-wage, high-employment equilibrium at *E*. Thereafter, only long-run supply-side measures aimed at breaking

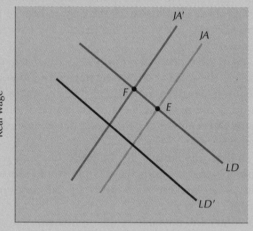

down insider power (e.g. less job protection) can gradually shift *JA'* to the right again.

Discouraged workers Again, the economy begins at *E*. It has a skilled and energetic labour force. A temporary recession leads to unemployment and a culture in which people stop looking for jobs. When demand picks up, labour supply has been permanently reduced and equilibrium reverts to *F*, not *E*. Only long-term supply-side measures to restore the work culture will succeed.

Policy implications of hysteresis First, once the problem has emerged, it is dangerous to try to break out of it simply by expanding aggregate demand. Supply-side policies, needed to restore aggregate supply, take a long time to work.

Second, precisely because the problem is so hard to cure once it occurs, it is even more important not to let demand fall in the first place. The payoff to demand management is higher than in an economy with a *unique* long-run equilibrium, where all that is at stake is how quickly the economy gets back to its original point.

▰▰ recap

- People are either employed, unemployed, or out of the labour force. The level of unemployment rises when inflows to the pool of the unemployed exceed outflows. Inflows and outflows are large relative to the level of unemployment.

- Unemployment can be classified as frictional, structural, classical, and demand-deficient. In modern terminology, the first three types are voluntary unemployment and the last is involuntary, or Keynesian, unemployment. The natural rate of unemployment is the equilibrium level of voluntary unemployment.

- In the long run, sustained rises in unemployment must reflect increases in the natural rate of unemployment. During temporary recessions, Keynesian unemployment is also important.

- Supply-side economics aims to increase equilibrium employment and potential output, and to reduce the natural rate of unemployment, by operating on incentives at a microeconomic level.

- Hysteresis means that short-run changes can move the economy to a different long-run equilibrium. It may explain why European recessions have raised the natural rate of unemployment substantially.

- Society would not benefit by driving the natural rate of unemployment to zero. Some social gains in higher productivity are derived from the improved matching of people and jobs that temporary spells of unemployment allow.

- Keynesian unemployment is involuntary and represents wasted output. Society may also care about the human misery inflicted by involuntary unemployment.

▰▰ key terms

▰▰ review questions

1 What is the discouraged-worker effect? Suggest two reasons why it occurs.

2 'The microchip has caused a permanent increase in the level of unemployment.' Carefully examine this assertion.

3 How would high unemployment be explained by (a) a Keynesian, (b) a classical economist?

4 Explain how tax cuts reduce unemployment. Does it matter whether the economy began at the natural rate of unemployment?

9-3 inflation

O ne of the first acts of the Labour government in 1997 was to make the Bank of England independent, with a mandate to achieve low inflation.

Inflation *is a rise in the average price of goods over time.* Pure inflation *is the special case in which all prices of goods and factors of production are rising at the same rate.*

Persistent inflation over many years is quite a recent phenomenon. In the UK the *price level* was no higher in 1950 than it had been in 1920. Figure 9-7 shows that the UK price level fell quite sharply during some of the interwar years when inflation was negative. Yet after 1945 there was not a single year in which the price level fell. Since 1950 the price level has increased by a factor of 20, more than its increase over the previous three centuries. This broad picture applies in most of the advanced economies.

| Figure 9-7 | The annual UK inflation rate 1920–99 |

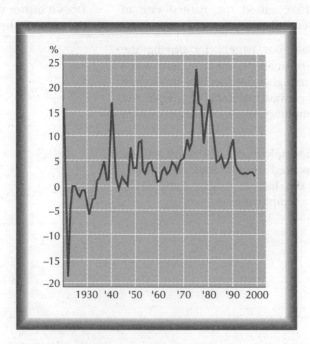

Sources: B. R. Mitchell, *European Historical Statistics 1750–1970*, Macmillan, 1975, and OCED, *Economic Outlook*.

▬▬▬ money and inflation

Since interest rates can change quickly, we assume that the money market is always in equilibrium. Hence the supply of real money M/P always equals the demand for real money L. Since money demand depends on income and interest rates, we can remind ourselves of this by writing it as $L(Y, r)$. Thus $M/P = L(Y, r)$. When L stays constant, the quantity theory of money will hold.

> *The* quantity theory of money *says that changes in nominal money* M *lead to equivalent changes in prices* P, *but have no effect on real output.*

In Section 9-2 we showed that this is true in the classical model.

However, the quantity theory needs interpreting with care. First, money is not the only cause of changes in prices. Fiscal policy or permanent supply shocks can also have this effect. Second, causation may not always run from money to prices. It could go the other way, as when monetary policy accommodates an increase in nominal wages. Third, real money demand L may not be constant over the period. Hence the real money supply will have to change, making M and P behave differently. In the short run, price sluggishness raises the possibility of booms and slumps during which output and interest rates change. Since these affect money demand, again the correlation between money and prices will break down.

While there need be no short-run correlation between money and prices, the same is not true in the long run. Then, we may as well use the classical model and treat output as fixed at Y^*. Milton Friedman has said inflation is always a monetary phenomenon. At least in the long run this is correct. Whether or not money growth is the original cause of inflation, unless the nominal money supply keeps growing inflation will burn itself out, like a fire without oxygen. Fixing nominal money means that steadily increasing prices steadily reduce real money. Interest rates increase steadily, and the ever-increasing slump must eventually smother inflation.

Whether inflation is causing money growth or vice versa, there must be a good correlation between the two in the long run. Figure 9-8 confirms this using annual averages over a 25-year period. One reason this is true is that real variables usually change slowly. Show us two variable growing at over 50 per cent a year and we'll take a bet they are both nominal variables.

▬▬▬ inflation and interest rates

Table 9-6 shows nominal interest rates and inflation for selected countries in 1998. High inflation is usually accompanied by high nominal interest rates in order to keep real interest rates at sensible levels. Irving Fisher first noticed this relationship.

Table 9-6   Inflation and interest rates 1998 (% per annum)

	Inflation	Interest rate
Turkey	85	75
Ecuador	36	50
Jamaica	14	25
Nigeria	10	14
South Africa	7	17
Switzerland	0	1

Source: IMF, *International Financial Statistics*.

The Fisher hypothesis *says that higher inflation should be accompanied by higher nominal interest rates.*

The Fisher hypothesis means that the quantity theory of money is correct for changes in the level of nominal money but not for changes in its growth rate. When we double the level of money and prices, there is no ongoing inflation after adjustment is completed. Thereafter all variables can return to their original real level, as the quantity theory predicts. Suppose, however, we move from zero money growth to annual money growth of 10 per cent. Eventually, inflation is 10 per cent a year (otherwise real money would be changing for ever), but what about interest rates?

If the real interest rate is about 2 per cent, then nominal interest rates change from 2 per cent to 12 per cent when inflation rises permanently to 10 per cent. But changes in nominal interest rates *change* the quantity of real money demanded. The quantity theory fails to predict this change. However, once the new equilibrium is reached, in which all nominal variables grow at 10 per cent thereafter, the quantity theory works from then onwards.

hyperinflation

Hyperinflation *means high inflation, often defined as above 50 per cent per month.*

Ukraine's annual inflation reached 10 000 per cent in 1993. The most famous hyperinflation is Germany during 1922–23. Germany lost the First World War. The German government had a big deficit, which it financed largely by printing money. The sixteenfold increase in the nominal money supply in 1922 was tiny compared with the increase in 1923. The government had to buy faster printing presses. In the later

| Figure 9-8 | Money growth and inflation 1970–95 |

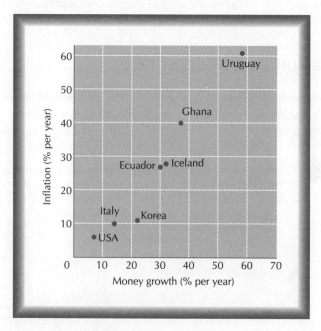

Source: IMF, *International Financial Statistics*.

stages of the hyperinflation they took in old notes, stamped on some more zeros, and reissued them as larger-denomination notes in the morning.

Prices increased by a factor of 75 in 1922 but by considerably more in 1923. By October 1923 it took 192 million reichmarks to buy a drink that had cost 1 reichmark in January 1922. People carried money around in wheelbarrows when they went shopping. According to the old joke, thieves used to steal the barrows but leave the almost worthless money behind.

The flight from money   When the inflation rate is π and the nominal interest rate r, the real return on non-interest-bearing money is simply $-\pi$, which shows how quickly the real value of money is being eroded by inflation. The extra real return on holding interest-bearing assets rather than money is $(r - \pi) - (-\pi) = r$. Even though people care about real rates of return, the *nominal* interest rate measures the cost of holding money. Nominal interest rates rise with inflation. During the German hyper-inflation the cost of holding money became enormous.

> The flight from money *is the collapse in the demand for real money during hyperinflation.*

People were paid twice a day so they could shop in their lunch hour before the real value of their cash depreciated too much. Any money not immediately spent was quickly deposited in a bank where it could earn interest. People spent a lot of time at the bank.

What lessons can we draw? First, *rising* inflation and *rising* interest rates can significantly reduce the demand for *real* money balances. Hyperinflations are a rare example in which a real quantity (real money balances) can change quickly and by a large magnitude. Second, and as a direct result, money and prices can get quite out of line when inflation and nominal interest rates are rising. Prices rose by six times as much as nominal money between January 1922 and July 1923, reducing the real money supply by 82 per cent, in line with the fall in real money demand.

Box 9-7	The quantity theory of money

The quantity theory of money is sometimes written as:

$$MV = PY.$$

The velocity of circulation V is the ratio of nominal income PY (prices P times real income Y) to nominal money M. When prices adjust to maintain real income at its full employment level, assumed constant, a change in M leads to an equivalent change in P, *provided velocity V stays constant.* What is velocity? It is the speed at which the stock of money is passed round the economy as people transact. How do we assess whether velocity is likely to remain constant, as the simple quantity theory requires?

The quantity theory equation can be rearranged as:

$$M/P = Y/V.$$

The left-hand side is the real money supply. We can think of the right-hand side as real money demand. It rises if real income rises and falls if velocity rises. But we have argued that real money demand is determined by real income and nominal interest rates, which measure the opportunity cost of holding money. Hence, even in the classical model, velocity is constant only if interest rates are constant.

■■ deficits and money growth

In the short run, a budget deficit can be financed by issuing bonds rather than printing money. Hence there is no reason to expect a close short-run correlation between budget deficits and increases in the money supply. Nor need there be any longer run correlation, provided the government remains solvent and able to borrow in financial markets.

However, when government debt gets large relative to the government's ability to raise taxes to pay debt interest, people may get scared and stop lending more to the government. A weak government in fiscal trouble may then have little option but to print money. Then the correlation between deficits and money creation gets stronger.

Money growth helps the budget in two different ways. First, as real income grows, the demand for real money rises. Hence the real money supply M/P can increase. The government can increase nominal money without increasing the price level.

Seigniorage *is the value of real resources acquired by the government by printing money without causing inflation.*

However, when money supply growth exceeds growth of real money demand, this causes inflation. This may also be a source of revenue for the government.

At constant real income, the pure inflation tax *is the real resources the government obtains from printing nominal money.*

It is important to understand that printing *nominal* money does not necessarily provide more *real* resources to cover a budget deficit. Think of the outstanding stock of real money as the tax base, the thing to be taxed, and think of inflation as the tax rate, the rate at which the real value of government monetary liabilities are being eroded.

Real tax revenue from inflation is the tax rate times the tax base, in other words the inflation rate times the level of real money stock. But this stock must be demanded. Higher inflation rates reduce the base for the inflation tax by reducing money demand. Beyond some inflation rate, the demand for real money falls so much that the government actually gets *less* revenue from further increases in inflation.

This explains what is going on in a hyperinflation. The government's finances are in a mess and it now owes a lot. In real terms, the budget deficit is larger than the maximum real revenue that even the inflation tax can raise. As the government prints more and more money, things actually get worse.

■■ inflation and unemployment

We begin by discussing one of the most famous and infamous relationships in postwar macroeconomics. It is known as the Phillips curve.

the Phillips curve

In 1958, Professor A. W. Phillips of the London School of Economics demonstrated a strong statistical relationship between annual inflation and annual unemployment in the UK. Similar relationships were found to hold in other countries, and this relationship quickly became known as the Phillips curve. It is shown in Figure 9-9.

The Phillips curve *shows that a higher inflation rate is accompanied by a lower unemployment rate. It suggests we can* trade off *more inflation for less unemployment, or vice versa.*

The Phillips curve seemed the answer to the problem of choosing macroeconomic policy. It showed the menu of choices available. Governments simply had to decide how much extra inflation to tolerate in exchange for lower unemployment. They picked a point on the Phillips curve and set fiscal and monetary policies to achieve the corresponding level of aggregate demand and hence unemployment.

The Phillips curve in Figure 9-9 shows the trade-off that people believed they faced in the 1960s. In those days UK unemployment was scarcely ever over **2** per cent of the labour force. But people sincerely believed that if they did the unthinkable, and cut back aggregate demand until unemployment rose to 2.5 per cent, the inflation rate would fall to zero.

Today, of course, we know that there have been years since 1970 when *both* inflation and unemployment were over 10 per cent. Something happened to the Phillips curve. The simple Phillips curve ceased to fit the facts.

Let's try to work out why. Suppose we begin in long-run equilibrium with no inflation and unemployment at its natural rate U^*. Beginning from this position, there is a once-off increase in the level of nominal money, which then remains constant thereafter. With sluggish wage and price adjustment, initially real money increases, interest rates fall, output increases, and unemployment falls. The boom then starts to bid up prices. The economy has moved from E to A in Figure 9-9.

Higher prices now start to reduce the real money stock, bid up interest rates and slowly bring the economy back to long-run equilibrium. As the boom unwinds, inflation falls and unemployment rises again. The economy slides along the Phillips curve from A back to E. Conversely, something that causes an initial fall in aggregate demand induces a slump, taking the economy from E to B, with higher unemployment and falling prices. Thereafter, falling prices lead to rises in the real money supply and boost the economy back to full employment. It moves up the Phillips curve from B back to A.

We draw two conclusions. First, it was wrong to interpret the Phillips curve as a *permanent* trade-off between inflation and unemployment. Rather, it shows the temporary trade-off while the economy is adjusting to a shock to *aggregate demand.*

Figure 9-9	The Phillips curve

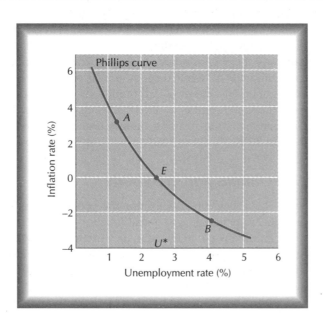

An increase in aggregate demand requires a *temporary* period of inflation to reduce real money balances and get aggregate demand back to its full-employment level.

Second, the speed with which the economy moves back along the Phillips curve depends on the degree of flexibility of money wages, and hence of prices. Extreme monetarists believe that this flexibility is almost instantaneous. In contrast, the model of more sluggish wage adjustment that we developed in Section 9-1 means that the economy takes much longer to adjust fully to any shock to aggregate demand. Movements along the Phillips curve back to long-run equilibrium take much longer.

This examination of short-run adjustment is a useful beginning to our analysis. But it is only a beginning. First, we have assumed that the long-run equilibrium involves a constant nominal money supply and zero inflation. Second, we have assumed that all shocks are to aggregate demand rather than to aggregate supply. And, finally, we have assumed that the natural rate of unemployment remains constant over time. Once we recognize these three complications we shall be able to understand the complete picture.

the vertical long-run Phillips curve

Suppose nominal money grows steadily in the long run. Is there any reason why output, employment, and unemployment should differ from the levels that these variables would attain if there were no inflation? People care about real variables not nominal variables. In long-run equilibrium, nominal money and nominal wages can grow at the *same* rate as prices. Neither the real money supply nor real wages are being eroded by inflation. And if nominal interest rates rise in line with inflation to maintain the real interest rate, neither lenders nor borrowers are doing better or worse as a result of inflation.

In thinking about the Phillips curve, Milton Friedman suggested that we recognize that the long-run equilibrium values of most real variables will be unaffected by the inflation rate. In Figure 9-10 we show this as a vertical long-run Phillips curve. The real economy can adjust to any long-run rate of nominal money growth and inflation. Beginning from E, with nominal money and prices growing at the rate π_1, suppose something reduces aggregate demand. The economy moves from E to A in Figure 9-10. The recession puts downward pressure on inflation. Prices now grow more slowly than nominal money, and the real money supply expands.

This stimulus gradually moves the economy along the short-run Phillips curve PC_1, from A back to E. Conversely, any increase in aggregate demand would initially slide the economy up PC_1, but then induce additional inflation that would erode real money and move the economy back to E again. The short-run Phillips curve still describes the short-run trade-off while the economy is adjusting to a demand shock. But the height of the short-run curve is determined by the level of expected inflation, which in long-run equilibrium is π_1. Friedman's insight was that, during the 1970s and 1980s, governments were printing money faster than ever before. Inflation expectations increased. The short-run Phillips curve shifted up to a high level.

expectations and credibility

Since E is a long-run equilibrium, the economy could stay there for ever. Suppose a new government wants to defeat inflation. It says it is cutting money growth from π_1 to π_2. If only people believed it, they might adjust wage claims immediately, allowing the economy to move straight from E to F. A sufficiently credible government could simply talk expectations down. Later we will see that this is what central bank independence is all about.

Suppose, however, people don't believe the new government, expecting it to be just as inflationary as its predecessor. Workers get large rises in nominal wages, and financial markets set high nominal interest rates, just to defend against the high inflation they think is coming. To their surprise, the government does what it says and cuts money growth. Initially, this causes a slump since real money falls. The economy moves from E to A in Figure 9-10. There is a slump and unemployment rises. But the government is expecting better news next year. Now that the private sector sees money growth has fallen, the short-run Phillips curve will shift down to PC_2 to reflect lower inflation expectations, making life easier for the government in future.

This may happen. However, weak governments sometimes abandon tough medicine half way through. The unpopularity of unemployment at A may lead the government to revert to high money growth in the following year to try to restore equilibrium at E with lower unemployment. If so, the short-run Phillips curve may not fall. Realizing that disinflation will then be protracted, the government may even give up disinflation completely.

This example shows the crucial role of expectations, and explains why governments go to such lengths to try to convince the public of their good intentions.

changes in the natural rate of unemployment

In the long-run, the Phillips curve is vertical at the natural rate of unemployment U^*, the level of voluntary unemployment when the labour market is in equilibrium. In the previous section we discussed the forces that could change the natural rate of unemployment. We also argued that the natural rate had steadily increased since the mid-1960s. Structural unemployment had increased, and organized workers had secured real wage increases in excess of their productivity increases. An increase in the natural rate of unemployment *shifts* the vertical long-run Phillips curve to the right. It continues to pass through the natural rate of unemployment, which has increased.

Figure 9-10 Expectations and credibility

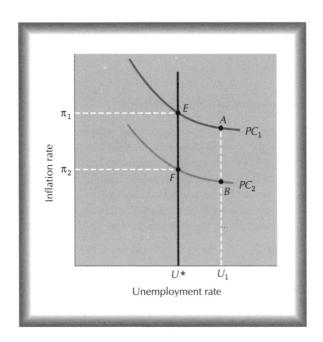

inflation and unemployment since 1960

The original Phillips curve seemed to offer a permanent trade-off between inflation and unemployment. Moreover, it suggested that both inflation *and* unemployment could be extraordinarily low. In the 1960s and the early 1970s, many governments were committed to maintaining full employment even in the short run. Any shock that tended to increase inflation – whether a wage claim by a trade union or a rise in the cost of a raw material – was accommodated by an increase in the money supply to prevent a reduction of the real money supply in the short run. Since governments were often raising the rate of money growth but rarely reducing it, money growth and inflation gradually increased. That explains why inflation rose above its level of the 1960s. Since the mid-1970s, government policy has changed in many countries. The emphasis is now on keeping inflation down. That is why inflation has fallen since the early 1980s.

What about unemployment? We now understand that the Phillips curve is vertical in the long run at the natural rate of unemployment. An increase in the natural rate of unemployment in many countries is an important component of the rise in actual unemployment in those countries. But it is not the whole story. We understand now that the short-run Phillips curve shows the *temporary* trade-off between inflation and unemployment while the economy is adjusting to an aggregate demand shock and gradually working its way back to potential output and the natural rate of unemployment. The height of the short-run Phillips curve depends on current expectations about future inflation and money growth.

At the beginning of the 1980s, inflation was high because it had been high in the recent past. Anti-inflation policies were only just beginning to bite. When tight money was first introduced, the real money supply was cut since inflation did not fall immediately. Aggregate demand fell and the economy moved to the right along the short-run Phillips curve. In addition to a high natural rate of unemployment, many countries were experiencing a short-run Keynesian slump. Involuntary unemployment was also high.

In the 1990s, many European economies were trying to reduce inflation to very low levels to show they were fit candidates for monetary union. Even countries such as the UK that were undecided about whether to join still pressed ahead with tight policies to get inflation down. These policies helped keep European unemployment at high levels. But once inflation had been defeated, continuing tight policies was unnecessary. British unemployment has fallen a lot since 1993, both because it is no longer in recession and because supply side-prices have reduced U^* a little..

an aggregate supply shock

What is the effect of an aggregate supply shock such as the doubling of oil prices? Overnight, inflation increases as firms pass on increased costs in higher prices. Suppose there has not yet been time for employment to change. What happens next depends on what the government does, and on what people expect the government to do. Suppose the government does *not* accommodate the shock. Money growth remains unchanged. With higher inflation, the real money supply is reduced, interest rates rise, and aggregate demand falls. There is a Keynesian slump and stagflation.

 Stagflation *is a period of both high inflation and high unemployment. It is often caused by an adverse supply shock.*

Gradually, involuntary unemployment bids down wages or moderates wage increases. The inflation rate falls below the fixed rate of money growth, and the real money supply starts to expand again. Eventually the economy gets back to the natural rate of unemployment. Since money growth has remained unchanged, in the long run the inflation rate has not been altered by the adverse supply shock.

Suppose instead that the government *had* accommodated the aggregate supply shock. When inflation first increased, the government simply raised permanently the rate of money growth to match this higher inflation rate. There would be no reduction in the real money supply, even in the short run. Aggregate demand would not be reduced in the short run and there would be no increase in unemployment. But the economy would be left with permanently higher rates of money growth and inflation.

▰▰▰ the costs of inflation

People dislike inflation. And governments think it worth while to adopt tight fiscal and monetary policies aimed at reducing inflation, even though in the short run these policies may mean higher unemployment and lower output. Why exactly is inflation such a bad thing?

inflation illusion?

Some of the arguments most commonly used to show why inflation is a bad thing are in fact quite spurious, and suggest that people may suffer from inflation illusion.

> *People have* inflation illusion *when they confuse nominal and real changes. People's welfare depends on real variables, not nominal variables.*

It is incorrect to say that inflation is bad because it makes goods more expensive. If *all* nominal variables are increasing at the same rate, people have larger nominal incomes and can buy the same physical quantity of goods as before. If people think about their nominal expenditure without recognizing that their nominal incomes are also increasing, they have inflation illusion. It is real incomes that tell us how many goods people can afford to buy.

A second kind of illusion is more subtle. Suppose there is a sharp increase in the real or relative price of oil. In countries that import large quantities of oil, people will now be worse off. The country as a whole has to divert goods from domestic consumption to exports in order to earn the extra foreign currency with which to purchase the more expensive oil imports. Hence domestic consumption per person has to fall. However, it can fall in one of two ways.

The first way is if workers do not ask for 'cost-of-living' wage increases to cover the higher cost of oil-related products. Real wages fall since the old level of nominal wages now buys fewer goods. There is no increase in either domestic prices or domestic wages. The domestic economy has adjusted to the adverse supply shock without inflation. And people are inevitably worse off.

Suppose instead that people try to maintain their old standard of living. Workers put in for cost-of-living increases to restore their real wages, and firms protect their profit margins by increasing prices in line with higher wage and fuel costs. There is a lot of domestic inflation, which the government accommodates by printing extra money. Eventually the economy settles down in its new long-run equilibrium position. People must still be worse off. The rise in the real oil price has not disappeared by magic. It still takes more domestic exports, made possible by lower domestic consumption, to pay for the more expensive oil imports. Hence in the new long-run equilibrium workers will find that their real wages have been reduced and firms may find that their profit margins have been squeezed.

What people notice is that there has been a period of rising wages and rising prices, but that somehow wages did not manage to keep up with price rises. Real wages fell.

But people draw the wrong conclusion. It was not the inflation that made them worse off, but the rise in oil prices.

So far, we have examined some spurious arguments about why inflation is a bad thing. The subsequent discussion has two central themes. First, was the inflation fully expected in advance? Or are people still adjusting to inflation which took them by surprise? Second, do our institutions, including government regulations and the tax system, enable people to adjust fully to inflation once they have come to expect it? The costs of inflation depend on the answer to these two questions.

complete adaptation and full anticipation

Imagine an economy in which inflation is 10 per cent a year for ever. Everybody knows it, anticipates its continuation, and can take it into account when making wage bargains or lending money. All prices, money wages, and the nominal money supply grow at 10 per cent a year. Inflation is eroding neither real incomes nor the real money supply. The economy is at full employment. Government policy is also fully adjusted. Nominal taxes are being changed every year to keep real tax revenue constant. Nominal government spending is increasing at 10 per cent a year so that real government spending is constant.[2]

Nominal interest rates have risen to the constant level necessary to maintain the equilibrium real interest rate when inflation is 10 per cent a year. Share prices are rising with inflation to maintain the real value of company shares on the stock exchange. The tax treatment of interest earnings and capital gains has been adjusted to take account of inflation. In real terms, taxation of interest earnings and capital gains remains unaffected by inflation.[3] Pensions and other transfer payments are being raised every year, in line with expected inflation.

This economy does not suffer from inflation illusion. Individuals and the government fully expect a 10 per cent inflation and have adjusted as fully as they can to minimize its effect on real variables. This was the insight that lay behind the long-run vertical Phillips curve in the previous section. But even in this ideal world, is complete adjustment possible?

Shoe-leather costs   Earlier in this section, we explained that nominal interest rates usually rise with inflation to preserve the real rate of interest. But the nominal interest rate is the opportunity cost of holding money. Hence when inflation is higher, people hold less money balances. We examined the flight from money during hyperinflation as an extreme example of this relation between inflation and the demand for real balances.

Society uses money to economize on the time and effort involved in undertaking transactions. When high nominal interest rates induce people to economize on holding real money balances, society must use a greater quantity of resources in undertaking transactions and therefore has less resources available for production and consumption of goods and services. We call this the *shoe-leather cost* of higher inflation.

---

[2] For simplicity we assume there is no productivity growth, no changes in supply or demand conditions, and hence a given level of full employment and potential output. Pure inflation could also happen, of course, in an economy with underlying real growth of output and employment.

[3] During times of inflation, many people worry about a country's international competitiveness. We discuss this in the next chapter. We shall see that it is also possible to adjust the exchange rate over time so that a country's real competitiveness remains unaffected by inflation.

Shoe-leather costs *stand for all the extra time and effort people put into transacting when they try to get by with lower real balances.*

Menu costs   When prices are rising, price labels have to be changed. For example, menus have to be reprinted to show the higher price of meals.

The menu costs *of inflation refer to the physical resources required to reprint price tags when prices are rising (or falling).*

The faster the rate of price change, the more frequently menus have to be reprinted if real prices are to remain constant.

Among the menu costs of inflation we should probably include the effort of doing mental arithmetic. When the inflation rate is zero it is easy to walk into a shop and see that a pound of steak costs the same as it did three months ago. But when inflation is 25 per cent a year, it takes a bit more effort to see what has happened to the real price of steak. Although people without inflation illusion try to think in real terms, the mental arithmetic required involves real time and effort.

Even when inflation is perfectly anticipated and the economy has fully adjusted to inflation, it is impossible to avoid shoe-leather costs and menu costs. Although these costs become very significant when the inflation rate reaches hyperinflation levels, they suggest that the social cost of living with 20 per cent inflation for ever might not be too large. However, this applies to the case in which society is best able to adjust to inflation. As we now see, the costs of inflation will be larger in other situations.

fully anticipated inflation

In this section we assume that the inflation is fully anticipated but that institutional factors prevent people from implementing some of the changes that would be required if nominal variables are to adjust in line with expected inflation. Because nominal variables are prevented from fully adjusting, inflation then affects more real variables than the shoe-leather and menu effects identified above.

Taxes   Tax rates may not be fully inflation-adjusted. The first problem is fiscal drag.

Fiscal drag *is the increase in real tax revenue when inflation raises nominal incomes and pushes people into higher tax brackets in a progressive income tax system.*

Here is a simple example. Suppose income below £2000 is untaxed but people pay income tax at 30 pence in the pound on all income over £2000. Initially, a person with an income of £3000 pays tax at 30 per cent on the income over £2000. Thus income tax paid is £300. Suppose that after ten years of inflation all wages and prices have doubled but the tax brackets and tax rates remain as before. The person's income is now £6000. Nominal tax paid is 30 per cent on the £4000 by which nominal income exceeds £2000. Hence nominal tax paid is £1200. Thus, although wages and prices have only doubled, nominal taxes paid have increased fourfold. Fiscal drag has increased the real tax burden. The government is benefiting from the inflation at the expense of private individuals.

To make the tax system inflation-neutral, nominal tax brackets must be increased in line with inflation. In the above example, if the real tax exemption limit had been pre-served by raising the nominal limit from £2000 to £4000 when other nominal variables doubled, everything would be inflation-adjusted. When governments adjusted the nominal tax bands upwards to offset inflation this used to be portrayed as a cut in income tax or increased government generosity. This is pure inflation illusion. The adjustments are required merely to maintain the real burden of income tax unchanged. In countries such as the UK and the United States, this logic has now been accepted. Tax bands are now automatically increased in line with inflation unless a deliberate government policy to the contrary is adopted.[4]

Taxing capital   Income tax levied on interest income is also affected by inflation. Suppose there is no inflation and the nominal and real interest rates are both 4 per cent. With a 30 per cent tax rate, the after-tax real return on lending is 2.8 per cent a year. Now suppose inflation is 10 per cent a year and nominal interest rates rise to 14 per cent to maintain the pre-tax real interest rate of 4 per cent. But in the current tax system in most countries, lenders must pay income tax at 30 per cent on nominal income. Hence the after-tax nominal interest rate is 9.8 per cent (0.7×14). Subtracting the 10 per cent inflation rate, the after-tax *real* interest rate is actually *negative*. This compares with the 2.8 per cent after-tax real interest rate when inflation was zero.

What goes wrong? When inflation is 10 per cent, nominal interest rates are 14 per cent. But 10 per cent of this is not real income, merely a payment for keeping up with inflation. Only 4 per cent is the real interest rate providing real income. But income tax applies to the whole 14 per cent. Hence higher inflation reduces the real return on lending because the tax system is not properly inflation-adjusted.

Higher inflation rates must have real effects in such a system. If, as we have assumed, the pre-tax nominal interest rate rises fully in line with inflation to preserve the pre-tax interest rate to borrowers, then higher inflation makes lenders lose out. Conversely, higher inflation *could* lead to even higher nominal interest rates to preserve the real after-tax interest rate to lenders. But then the real pre-tax interest rate to borrowers would rise with inflation. Either way, the government is benefiting by higher real tax revenue. Individual borrowers or lenders are losing out.

Capital gains taxation provides another example. Suppose people have to pay the government 30 per cent of any capital gains they make when buying and selling shares. When inflation is zero only real gains are taxed. But when inflation is 10 per cent, nominal share prices must rise merely to preserve their real value. People have to pay capital gains tax even though they are not making real capital gains.

Taxing profits   Inflation may also increase the real burden of taxation on company profits. Here is a simple example. Suppose a company holds some stocks of finished goods awaiting sale. In an inflationary world, the nominal value of these stocks will increase over time. If these capital gains are treated as taxable company profits, firms will have to pay more taxes even though the real value of their stocks remains unchanged. Such inconsistencies in the tax system would disappear if firms and the government moved over to inflation accounting.

Inflation accounting *is the adoption of definitions of costs, revenue, profit and loss that are fully inflation-adjusted.*

Thus institutional imperfections help explain why inflation can have real effects even when individuals have fully anticipated that inflation. Until institutions are fully adjusted to inflation, these effects can be significant. In many instances it is the government that stands to gain most by inflation.

---

[4] How about indirect taxes? Percentage taxes on value, such as VAT, automatically increase nominal tax revenue in proportion to inflationary rises in the price level. However, *specific* duties, such as £5 a bottle on whisky, need to be raised as the price level rises. In the UK there is no *automatic* formula for raising such duties. Each year the government makes a decision about how much to raise them.

unexpected inflation

Previously, we assumed that inflation was fully anticipated. Now we discuss problems that arise when inflation takes people by surprise.

Redistribution   When prices rise unexpectedly, the losers are people who own nominal assets and the gainers are people with nominal liabilities. The terms of the original nominal contract to buy or sell, lend or borrow, may have been written to take full account of expected inflation, but they cannot have incorporated inflation that subsequently takes people by surprise.

In one sense, since to every borrower there corresponds a lender, one person's gain is another person's loss. In the aggregate the two cancel out. But unexpected inflation results in a redistribution of income and wealth, in this case from lenders to borrowers. This has two consequences. First, it may lead to economic dislocation. For example, some people may have to declare bankruptcy, which in turn may affect other people. Second, we have to adopt a value judgement about whether we like the redistribution that is taking place.

One of the most important redistributions is between the government and the private sector. Unexpected inflation reduces the real value of all outstanding nominal government debt. Not only is the real money supply reduced, but the real price at which the government has to buy back its bonds is reduced. Equivalently, the government has a higher nominal tax revenue with which to buy back bonds at the already agreed nominal price.[5]

Does this redistribution matter? This is a tricky question. If the government is better off it may be able to cut taxes and undo the effect of such a redistribution. But typically, the people who lent to the government and lost out through unexpected inflation tend not to be the same people who will benefit from any tax cuts the government then can offer.

The old and the young   In practice, many of the people who lend by buying nominal assets are the old. Having paid off their mortgages and built up savings during their working life, they may well have put their wealth into nominal bonds to provide income during retirement. These people lose out when there is unexpected inflation and the real value of the bonds falls. They also lose out if they keep their wealth in non-interest-bearing money, either in a current account or under the bed.

The nominal debtors are the young, and especially those just entering middle age, who have a large mortgage to move into a large house to see them through the process of bringing up a family. Having borrowed a fixed sum to buy a house, they gain when unexpected inflation increases house prices and nominal incomes without any matching increase in the nominal sum they owe the bank or building society. Unexpected inflation redistributes from the old to the young.

uncertainty about inflation

Uncertainty about future inflation increases the complexity of making long-term plans since a much wider range of possible (nominal) outcomes must be investigated. As with shoe-leather costs, this increases the real resources that society must expend in making plans, undertaking transactions, and doing business. Second, people dislike risk. The extra benefits of the champagne years are poor compensation for the years

---

[5] Why do we emphasize unexpected inflation? Because expected inflation was already built into the terms on which bonds were originally issued.

of starvation. People would rather average out these extremes and live comfortably all the time. The psychic costs of worrying about how to cope with the bad years may also be important.

When people must enter into nominal contracts, an increase in uncertainty about the inflation rate increases the uncertainty about the eventual real value of the nominal bargains that people are currently making. This is a genuine cost of inflation. There is some empirical evidence that inflation rates change by more when inflation is already high. Hence higher average inflation rates may be accompanied by more uncertainty about inflation. If so, this imposes a real cost. It may be a very important cost.

◼◼◼ pre-committing to low inflation

This approach takes a long-run view. It is concerned not with the temporary costs of first getting inflation down, but with how to *keep* inflation down. Box 9-8 provides evidence that central bank independence is a useful pre-commitment to tight monetary policy and low inflation. Indeed, institutional pre-commitment was a favourite theme of the 1990s as the following examples show.

The Maastricht Treaty   Signed in 1991, the treaty set out conditions both for entering EMU and after admission to EMU. The first requirement was to avoid loose fiscal policy: a ceiling of 3 per cent on budget deficits relative to GDP (though this may yet be interpreted in relation to the structural budget to allow some modest and temporary overshoot during recessions). High-debt countries were also supposed to initiate actions to bring their debt/GDP levels below 60 per cent. Moreover, EMU entrants first had to succeed in disinflating to low levels, measured both directly by changes in price indexes and indirectly by nominal interest rates (the Fisher effect again!).

Not only did EU governments have to sign up for tight policy in the 1990s and beyond, EMU hopefuls had to undertake institutional reform, making their national central banks formally independent. And the Maastricht Treaty confirmed that the new European Central Bank was constitutionally independent and mandated to pursue price stability.

Outside Europe   The US central bank – the Federal Reserve – is already pretty independent, and many other central banks, from Canada to New Zealand have also seen their independence enhanced. Within the United States, a succession of Congressional resolutions have also forced the United States to end large budget deficits and move much closer to budget balance.

UK policy 1992–97   Despite losing the peg to the Deutschmark when the UK left the Exchange Rate Mechanism in 1992, subsequent inflation has been remarkably low. UK monetary policy worked as follows. First, the Chancellor announced his inflation target for the coming years. Second, each month Treasury and Bank officials tried to agree on a recommendation about the stance of monetary policy that would achieve this medium-run objective while looking after the short-term needs of the real economy. At the monthly meeting of Chancellor and Governor, the arguments would be considered *then the Chancellor alone would decide*.

Since previous Chancellors always 'took the Bank's views into account', what was new about this procedure? Two things. First, since the minutes of the Governor–Chancellor meeting were published a few weeks later, any objections by the Bank were highly publicized. Second, the Bank was given responsibility to produce a quarterly *Inflation Report*, openly published and *completely free from any Treasury control*. The Report quickly became very influential, because of its clear analysis, and the envy of other central banks. Despite the UK's success in maintaining low inflation since 1992, there were some who thought high European unemployment, an absence of adverse supply shocks, and the need to keep open the possibility of joining EMU had made this a period in which high inflation was in any case unlikely.

UK policy since 1997   On taking office in May 1997, the new Chancellor, Gordon Brown, quickly announced that the Bank of England would acquire 'operational independence' in deciding the level at which interest rates should be set. The Bank would endeavour to achieve an inflation target laid down by the Chancellor. Thus, the Bank would not itself choose this target. For example, in an emergency (e.g. a doubling of oil prices) the government could announce a temporarily higher target rather than

---

Box 9-8	Central bank independence

Central bankers are cautious people unlikely to favour rapid money growth and inflation. So why do these occur? Either because the government cares so much about unemployment that it never tackles inflation, or because it is politically weak and ends up with a budget deficit which it finances, at least to some extent, by printing money. Essentially, inflation arises when governments overrule cautious bankers. Proposals for central bank independence mean *independence from the government*.

Suppose this could be achieved, and monetary policy on average was tighter. Hence, in the long run, where it is the level of full capacity output that counts, independent central banks should lead to lower inflation without any reduction in real output. That, after all, is what the vertical long-run Phillips curve is all about. Central bank independence is a pre-commitment by government to keep money tight and inflation low.

The two figures below show that both predictions of the theory work out in practice – countries with more independent central banks have lower average inflation, yet there is no evidence that real output growth is lower in the long run.

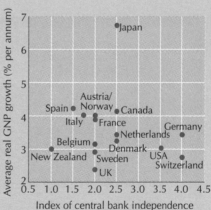

Source: A. Alesina and L. Summers, 'Central bank independence and macroeconomic performance: some comparative evidence', *Journal of Money, Credit, and Banking*, May 1993.

force the Bank to initiate a drastic recession simply to bid prices down again very quickly. Nevertheless, any such change in the target would be politically difficult except in truly exceptional circumstances. Operational independence would thus act as a pre-commitment to policies favouring low inflation.

■■■ the Monetary Policy Committee (MPC)

Since 1997 UK monetary policy has been set by the Bank of England's Monetary Policy Committee (www. bankofengland.co.uk)], which meets monthly to set interest rates to try to hit the inflation target laid down by the Chancellor. Currently the target is 2.5 per cent annual inflation, plus or minus 1 per cent. If the MPC misses its target range, the Governor is obliged to write to the Chancellor explaining why.

An inflation target *is an intermediate target for setting interest rates. It serves as a nominal anchor.*

In this section, we discuss three questions. Why was the MPC given an inflation target rather than a target for the path of nominal money. How does it work? And how easy has it been for the MPC to decide where to set interest rates?

inflation targets

Without a nominal anchor, there is nothing to tie down the price level or any other nominal variable. Market forces determine real variables such as money M divided by prices P. Setting interest rates can influence M/P but not separately determine M and P. An intermediate target – an announced path for one of the nominal variables – is also required. For example, for a given path for M, once we know interest rates and output we know money demand M/P and can therefore work out the price level P.

Figure 9-11 UK interest rates, 1974–99

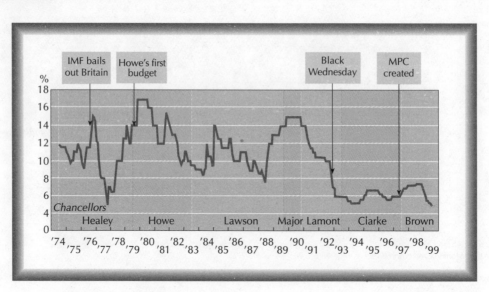

Source: Financial Times, 11 June 1999.

An inflation target is instead a path for prices themselves. It is an alternative to a nominal money target. Two reasons have made inflation targets increasingly popular. First, since we care about inflation, it seems natural to target inflation itself. Second, changes in banking behaviour caused by changes in competition and regulation have led to quite large and unpredictable changes in the demand for money. When banks offer better interest rates on deposits, they cut the cost of holding money. If the central bank has difficulty forecasting the demand for real money balances, it may be unsure what target for nominal money growth will achieve the path of inflation rate it really desires.

Because this seems obvious, why were money growth targets ever popular? Partly because data on money supply comes out much faster than data on the price level. However, given the headache of trying to forecast money demand, central banks would now rather predict what the price level data is going to be.

back to the future

Not only do lags in data mean that the MPC has to forecast where the economy is today, it also has to recognize that interest rate medicine does not work immediately. In fact, it can take up to two years for a change in interest rates to have its full effect on private behaviour. Hence the MPC has to *forecast* the path of prices at least two years into the future merely to know where to set interest rates *today*! On occasion, the MPC may raise interest rates even though current inflation is under control. This means that, in the absence of any change in interest rates, the MPC is forecasting that inflation will be too high. It then has to act quickly to keep inflation on track.

so far so good

Most people give the MPC high marks for their performance so far. It was prepared to change interest rates even when this was unpopular, and inflation remained close to 2.5 per cent as a result. Since inflation expectations were therefore low, nominal interest rates were low relative to the bad old days when inflation was high. Figure 9-11 shows the history of UK interest rates since 1974. Although the Bank's operational independence in setting interest rates was granted in 1997, the decisive break actually occurred in 1992 when sterling left the Exchange Rate Mechanism and changed nominal anchors from a pegged exchange rate to an inflation target. The MPC has been building on the earlier success during 1992–97.

▰▰ recap

- The quantity theory of money asserts that changes in prices are caused chiefly by equivalent changes in the nominal money supply. In practice, prices cannot immediately adjust to changes in nominal money, so interest rates or income alter to change money demand. In the long run, changes in interest rates can break any simple relation between nominal money and prices.

- A 1 per cent increase in inflation leads roughly to a 1 per cent increase in nominal interest rates so real interest rates are roughly unchanged. Higher inflation reduces the demand for real money. The flight from money during hyperinflation is a spectacular example.

- In the short run, there need be no close relation between the size of the budget deficit and the growth of the nominal money supply.

- The original Phillips curve showed a trade-off between inflation and unemployment. We now recognize that the short-run Phillips curve is a temporary trade-off showing how unemployment and inflation adjust to shocks to aggregate demand.

- In the long run the Phillips curve is vertical. The height of the short-run Phillips curve depends on underlying money growth and expected inflation. To shift the Phillips curve downwards people must believe inflation will be lower in the future.

- Some of the claimed costs of inflation are illusory. The true costs of inflation depend on whether it was anticipated and on the extent to which the economy's institutions allow complete inflation-adjustment.

- Uncertainty about future inflation rates imposes costs on people who dislike risk. Uncertainty may be greater when inflation is already high.

- Operational independence of central banks is designed to remove the temptation faced by politicians to boost the economy too much.

- Inflation targets are an alternative nominal anchor to targets for nominal money.

■■■ key terms

■■■ review questions

1 (a) How do you explain the following data? (b) Is inflation always a monetary phenomenon?

1996	Money growth	Inflation
	%	%
France	4	2
Japan	11	1
Germany	10	1
Holland	13	2
USA	−5	3
Italy	4	3

Source: The Economist.

2 Looking at data on inflation and unemployment over ten years, could you tell the difference between supply shocks and demand shocks?

3 Name five groups which lose out during inflation. Does it matter whether this inflation was anticipated?

4 How much of the popular dislike of inflation do you think is due to illusion?

10 open economy macroeconomics

10-1 exchange rates and the balance of payments

Exports and imports are each about 10 per cent of the size of GNP in the United States, 20 per cent in Japan, and 30 per cent in the UK, France, and Germany. Even in the United States, the exchange rate, international competitiveness, and the trade deficit are major issues. International considerations will be even more important in more open economies such as the UK, Germany, and Holland.

 Open economy macroeconomics *is the study of economies in which international transactions play a significant role.*

In this chapter we show how international transactions affect the domestic economy. The effects of monetary and fiscal policy are very different in an open economy from the effects we discussed in a closed economy. The international environment is not merely an afterthought which can be discussed separately from macroeconomics: in open economies it is intrinsic to the way these economies work.

LEARNING OUTCOMES

When you have finished this section, you should understand

- the forex market

- balance of payments accounting

- the concepts of internal and external balance

- the effects of monetary and fiscal policy under fixed exchange rates

- the effects of devaluation in the short run, medium run, and long run

- what determines floating exchange rates

▰▰▰ the foreign exchange market

The foreign exchange (forex) market *is the international market in which one national currency can be exchanged for another. The price at which the two currencies exchange is the* exchange rate.

For UK residents, an exchange rate of $1.6/£ measures the international value of sterling; the number of units of foreign currency (dollars) that exchange for one unit of the domestic currency (pounds).

As in any market, the equilibrium price depends on supply and demand. If there are only two countries, the UK and the United States, who is bringing a supply of dollars to the forex market wishing to exchange them into pounds? This demand for pounds comes from two sources. First, American consumers pay in dollars but British exporters want to be paid in pounds. Second, American residents wishing to buy British assets (shares in ICI or UK Treasury bills) must convert their dollars into pounds before these assets can be purchased. Conversely, a supply of pounds arises from UK imports of goods produced in the United States, and from UK residents wishing to purchase assets in the United States.

Figure 10-1 shows the resulting supply of pounds SS and demand for pounds DD. At the equilibrium exchange rate of e_1 the quantity of pounds supplied and demanded is equal. What would change this equilibrium rate? If, at each sterling price, the demand by Americans for British goods or assets increases, the demand schedule for pounds, DD, will shift to the right, increasing the equilibrium dollar–sterling exchange rate.

When the dollar–sterling exchange rate increases we say the pound has *appreciated*, because the international value of sterling has risen. Conversely, when the dollar–pound exchange rate falls we say that the pound has *depreciated*. Its international value is lower.

alternative exchange rate regimes

An exchange rate regime *is a description of the conditions under which national governments allow exchange rates to be determined.*

Figure 10-1 The forex market

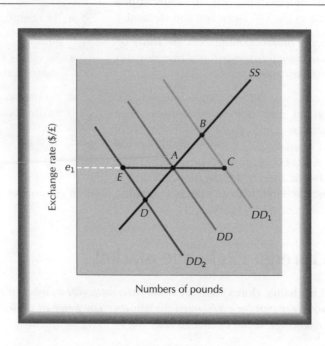

In a fixed exchange rate *regime, national governments agree to maintain the convertibility of their currency at a fixed exchange rate.*

A currency is convertible *if the government acting through the central bank, agrees to buy or sell as much of the currency as people wish to trade at the fixed exchange rate.*

The fixed exchange rate e_1 would be the free market equilibrium rate if the supply schedule were SS and the demand schedule DD. The market would clear on its own.

Suppose now that the demand for pounds shifts from DD to DD_1. Americans get hooked on whisky and need more pounds to pay for extra imports of UK whisky. In a free market, the equilibrium point would now be B and the pound would appreciate against the dollar. At the fixed exchange rate e_1 there is an excess demand for pounds equal to AC. Since the currency is convertible, this excess demand is satisfied by people asking the Bank of England for AC pounds which the Bank is committed to supply on demand. The Bank prints AC additional pounds and sells them in exchange for $(e_1 \times AC)$ dollars, which are added to the UK foreign exchange reserves.

The foreign exchange reserves *are the stock of foreign currency held by the domestic central bank.*

Now suppose the demand schedule for pounds shifts to the left to DD_2. Few foreigners want British goods or assets, and the demand for pounds is correspondingly low. The free market equilibrium exchange rate would lie below e_1 in the absence of any intervention by the central bank. However, the central bank is committed to defending the fixed exchange rate e_1. At this rate, there is an excess supply of pounds EA. The central bank must demand EA pounds, which it pays for by selling $(EA \times e_1)$ dollars from the foreign exchange reserves. When the central bank is forced to buy or sell pounds to support the fixed exchange rate, we say that the central bank *intervenes* in the forex market.

If the demand for pounds on average is DD_2, the Bank will be running down the UK foreign exchange reserves to support the pound at e_1. Under these circumstances, we say that the pound is overvalued. As reserves start to run out, the government may try to borrow foreign exchange reserves from the International Monetary Fund [IMF (www.imf.org)], an international body which exists primarily to lend to countries in short-term difficulties. But at best this is only a temporary solution. Unless the demand for pounds increases in the long run, it will be necessary to *devalue* the pound.

In a fixed exchange rate regime, a devaluation (revaluation) *is a reduction (increase) in the exchange rate that governments commit themselves to maintain.*

Thus, in November 1967 the UK government, after consultations with other governments, devalued the pound from \$2.80/£ to \$2.40/£.

In a floating exchange rate *regime, the exchange rate is allowed to attain its free market equilibrium level* without *any government invervention using the foreign exchange reserves.*

Thus, in Figure 10-1 the demand schedule shifts from DD_2 to DD to DD_1 would be allowed to move the equilibrium point from D to A to B.

Of course, it is not necessary to adopt the extreme regimes of pure floating on the one hand and perfectly fixed exchange rates on the other hand. *Dirty floating* describes a regime in which intervention is used to offset large and rapid shifts in supply or demand schedules in the short run, but where the exchange rate is gradually allowed to find its equilibrium level in the longer run. There are many kinds of exchange rate regime. If we understand the two polar cases – fixed exchange rates and freely floating exchange rates – we can see how the intermediate cases would work. Before studying macroeconomics under each of these regimes, we explain balance of payments accounting.

■■■ the balance of payments

The balance of payments *is a record of all transactions between residents of one country and the rest of the world.*

Taking the UK as the domestic country and the United States as the 'rest of the world', all international transactions that give rise to an inflow of pounds to the UK are entered as credits in the UK balance of payments accounts. Outflows of pounds are shown as debits, and are entered with a minus sign. Similarly, inflows of dollars to the United States are credits in the US balance of payments accounts but outflows are debits. Table 10-1 shows the actual UK balance of payments accounts in 1998.

The current account *of the balance of payments records international flows of goods, services, and transfer payments.*

Visible trade refers to exports and imports of goods (cars, food, steel). *Invisible trade* refers to exports and imports of services (banking, shipping, tourism). Together, these make up the trade balance or net exports of goods and services.

However, the trade balance is not identical to the current account on the balance of payments. We must also take account of transfer payments between countries (foreign aid, budget contribution to the EU) and of the net flow of property income (interest, profits, dividends) which arises when residents of one country own income-earning assets in another country. The flow of net property income leads to a discrepancy between GDP and GNP.

Now we turn to transactions on the capital account of the balance of payments.

The capital account *of the balance of payments records international transactions in financial assets.*

Table 10-1 shows a net outflow of £9 billion in 1988. The outflow of money from the UK to buy physical and financial assets abroad exceeded the inflow of money to the UK as foreigners bought assets in the UK. The balancing item is a statistical adjustment, which would be zero if all previous items had been correctly measured. It reflects a failure to record all transactions in the official statistics. Adding together the current

Table 10-1	UK balance of payments, 1998 (£bn)

Visible exports	169
Visible imports	−190
Invisibles: credits	182
Invisibles: debits	−160
(1) CURRENT ACCOUNT	1
(2) CAPITAL ACCOUNT	−9
(3) Balancing item	8
(4) UK BALANCE OF PAYMENTS (1 + 2 + 3)	0
(5) Official financing	0

Source: IMF, *International Financial Statistics.*

account (1), the capital account (2), and the adjustment (3) we obtain the UK *balance of payments* in 1998. It so happens it just balanced in 1998.

The balance of payments shows the net inflow of money to the country when individuals, firms, and the government make the transactions they wish to undertake under existing market conditions. It is in surplus (deficit) when there is a net inflow of money (outflow of money).

The final entry in Table 10-1 is *official financing*. This is always of equal magnitude and opposite sign to the balance of payments in the line above, so that the sum of all the entries is *always* zero. Official financing measures the international transactions that the government must take to *accommodate* all the other transactions shown in the balance of payments accounts. What is this official financing?

floating exchange rates

Suppose first that the exchange rate is freely floating and there is no government intervention in the forex market. The government neither adds to nor runs down the foreign exchange reserves. The exchange rate adjusts to equate the supply of pounds and the demand for pounds.

The supply of pounds arises from imports to the UK or purchases of foreign assets by UK residents. It measures the outflows from the UK, the negative items on the balance of payments accounts of the UK. Conversely, the demand for pounds arises from UK exports and purchases of UK assets by foreigners, and measures the inflows to the UK, the positive items on the UK balance of payments accounts. With a freely floating exchange rate, the quantities of pounds supplied and demanded are equal. Hence inflows equal outflows and the balance of payments is exactly zero. There is no government intervention in the forex market and no official financing.

Since the balance of payments is the sum of the current account and the capital account, under floating exchange rates a current account surplus must be exactly matched by a capital account deficit, or vice versa. What is true for the country as a whole is also true for an individual. Think of your own balance of payments account with all other individuals. If your income exceeds your spending, you run a current account surplus in your transactions with other people. This surplus adds to your assets. You add to your cash balances or your bank account, or buy shares or property. The increase in your asset holdings matches the excess of your income over your spending.

Similarly, for the country as a whole a current account surplus, or net inflow from abroad, must be matched by an increase in the country's holding of foreign assets. Since the government is not adding to the foreign exchange reserves, this must show up in the capital account as a capital account deficit exactly matching the current account surplus. The capital account deficit shows the outflow of money as domestic residents add to their holding of foreign assets. The balance of payments, the sum of the current and capital accounts of the balance of payments, must be zero when there is a freely floating exchange rate.

fixed exchange rates

With a fixed exchange rate, the balance of payments need not be zero. When there is a deficit, total outflows exceed total inflows on the combined current and capital accounts. How is the deficit financed? Since there is a deficit, the supply of pounds to the forex market, corresponding to the wish to import or acquire foreign assets, exceeds the demand for pounds, corresponding to the wish to export or the desire of foreigners to acquire domestic assets. Hence the balance of payments deficit is exactly the same as the excess supply of pounds in the forex market.

To maintain the fixed exchange rate, the central bank has to offset this excess supply of pounds by demanding an equivalent quantity of pounds. The central bank runs down the foreign exchange reserves, selling dollars to buy pounds. In the balance of payments accounts this shows up as 'official financing'. When there is a balance of payments deficit (surplus), reserves must be sold (bought).

■■■ components of the balance of payments

We begin with the concept of the real exchange rate.

the real exchange rate and competitiveness

Once again, we must distinguish nominal and real variables. International competitiveness is measured by the real exchange rate.

> The real exchange rate *measures the relative price of goods from different countries when measured in a common currency.*

Suppose we measure the real exchange rate by comparing dollar prices of goods produced in the two countries. We can define the UK's real exchange rate as

$$\text{Real exchange rate} = \frac{\text{£ price of UK goods}}{\text{\$ price of US goods}} \times (\$/£). \tag{1}$$

An increase in the real exchange rate, by increasing the price of UK goods relative to US goods when measured in the same currency, makes the UK less competitive relative to the United States. Conversely, a fall in the UK's real exchange rate makes the UK more competitive in international markets.

Equation (1) says the real exchange rate can depreciate for three different reasons: a depreciation of the nominal exchange rate; a rise in the price of foreign goods; or a reduction in the price of domestic goods. The arithmetic doesn't care which. Thus, if the UK has 10 per cent annual inflation and the US has no inflation, the UK's real exchange rate depreciates, and it becomes more competitive, if and only if its nominal exchange rate depreciates by more than 10 per cent a year.

Given the actual behaviour of prices at home and abroad, it is useful to keep track of the hypothetical path the nominal exchange rate would have had to follow to keep competitiveness constant.

> The purchasing power parity *(PPP) exchange rate path is the path of the nominal exchange rate that would keep the real exchange rate constant over a given period.*

the current account

Exports   In Chapter 7 we made the simple assumption that export demand for domestic goods and services was given. We now recognize that the demand for UK exports will be influenced chiefly by two things. First, the higher the level of income in the rest of the world, the higher will be the demand for UK exports. Second, the lower the UK's real exchange rate and the higher the level of UK competitiveness in world markets, the higher will be the demand for UK exports.

Imports   For imports we simply tell the same story in reverse. Import demand will be larger the higher is the level of domestic income, the relationship we recognized in Chapter 7 through the marginal propensity to import. But import demand will also be larger the higher is the real exchange rate and the cheaper are foreign goods relative to domestic goods when both are measured in the domestic currency.

Other items on the current account Other items include foreign aid and spending on military bases abroad, matters of government policy. Also on the current account we include the net flow of interest, dividend, and profit income between countries, which arises because residents of one country hold assets in another. The size of this net flow of income depends on the pattern of international asset-holding and on the level of interest rates, profits, and dividends at home and abroad.

capital account items

These arise through international purchases and sales of assets, and have become increasingly important since 1945 for two reasons. First, computers and telecommunications have made it almost as easy for a British resident to transact in the financial markets of New York, Frankfurt, Zurich, Tokyo, and Hong Kong as it is in London. Second, the elaborate system of controls, restricting international transactions on the capital account, have gradually been dismantled.

The world's financial markets now have two crucial features. First, capital account restrictions have been almost entirely abolished. Funds can be freely moved from one country to another in search of the highest rate of return. Second, there are billions and billions of pounds that are internationally footloose and capable of being switched between countries and currencies when assets in one currency seem to offer a higher rate of return than assets elsewhere. If the owners of these funds are prepared to transfer them entirely to the currency in which assets seem to offer the highest rate of return, and if there are no obstacles to such transfers, we say that international financial capital is 'perfectly mobile' between countries.

> Perfect capital mobility *means that an enormous quantity of funds will be transferred from one currency to another whenever the expected rate of return on assets in one country is higher than in another.*

The movement of these funds from one country to another could lead to capital account flows that would swamp the typical flows of imports and exports we observe on the current account.

> Speculation *is the purchase of an asset for subsequent resale, in the belief that the total return – interest or dividend plus the capital gain – will exceed the total return that can be obtained in other assets.*

In international asset markets, capital gains arising from changes in exchange rates form an important part of the expected rate of return on an asset. You have £100 to invest for a year. Suppose UK interest rates are 10 per cent a year but interest rates in the United States are zero. Keeping your funds in pounds, you will have £110 at the end of the year. But what if you convert them into dollars at the beginning of the year, lend in dollars for a year, and then convert the money back into pounds at the end?

Suppose initially the exchange rate is $2/£. Your £100 will buy $200. At a zero interest rate you will still have $200 at the end of the year. But suppose that sterling has depreciated by 10 per cent during the year. At the end of the year the exchange rate is $1.80/£. Your $200 will convert back to £110 at the end of the year. Although you get no interest by investing in dollars for a year, you make a capital gain of 10 per cent on holding dollars, whose value relative to pounds increases by 10 per cent during the year.

In this example you end up with £110 whether you lend in dollars or pounds during the year. If the pound had depreciated by more than 10 per cent (the excess of the UK interest rate over the US interest rate), the capital gain on holding dollars would have outweighed the loss of interest, and the total return on lending in dollars rather than pounds would have been larger. Conversely, if the pound had depreciated against the dollar by less than the interest rate differential, you would have earned a higher total return by keeping your money in pounds. Equation (2) summarizes this important result.

$$\text{Return on foreign lending} = \text{foreign interest rate} + \text{domestic currency depreciation} \tag{2}$$

In a world of almost perfect international capital mobility, there will be an enormous capital outflow whenever the total return on foreign lending exceeds the total return on domestic lending, the domestic interest rate. There will be a huge capital inflow when the return on domestic lending exceeds the return on lending abroad. And net flows on the capital account of the balance of payments will be small only when the total return on foreign lending is broadly in line with the return on lending in the domestic currency.

Perfect capital mobility implies that investors equate expected total returns on assets in different currencies. Interest differentials must be offset by expected exchange rate changes. This is called the interest parity condition.

▰▰ internal and external balance

We now discuss the relation between the state of the economy – boom or recession – and the external balance or current account on the balance of payments. Figure

---

Figure 10-2 Internal and external balance

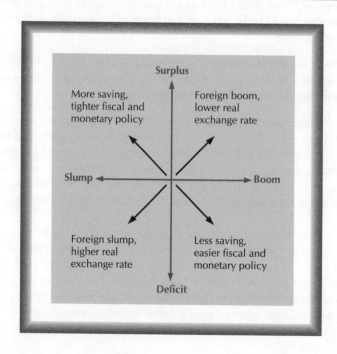

10-2 shows the different combinations of boom and recessions and current account surpluses and deficits.

$$Y = C + I + G + (X - Z). \tag{3}$$

Domestic output Y equals aggregate demand, which arises from spending on consumption; investment; goods and services purchased by the government; and net exports, that is the excess of exports X over imports Z.

> *A country is in* internal balance *when aggregate demand is at the full-employment level. A country is in* external balance *when the current account of the balance of payments just balances.*

In the absence of government intervention in the forex market, the capital account of the balance of payments must also be in balance at this point. In Figure 10-2 the point of internal *and* external balance is the intersection of the two axes, where there is neither a boom nor a slump, and neither a current account surplus nor a deficit.

The combination of internal and external balance is the long-run equilibrium of the economy. Output is at full capacity. With external balance, not only is the current account in balance, but there is no long-term pressure to change the stock of foreign exchange reserves, nor any permanent flows on the capital account.

Figure 10-2 shows the shocks that in the short run can move the economy away from internal and external balance. One of the main lessons of Figure 10-2 is that most shocks in an open economy will simultaneously move the economy away from *both* internal and external balance.

Without any policy change, will the economy be able to adjust to any shock and get back to the point of both internal and external balance? And can macroeconomic policy be used to make this transition easier? Since the economy behaves very differently under fixed and floating exchange rate regimes, we have to analyse the two regimes separately.

■■■ monetary and fiscal policy under fixed exchange rates

The trade balance depends on income levels at home and abroad, and on competitiveness. In the long run, internal balance at home and abroad fixes domestic and foreign incomes at full capacity levels. Hence there is a level of competitiveness compatible with external balance. If a country's real exchange rate is too low, it will have a trade surplus; if it is too high, it will have a trade deficit.[1]

Notice three further points. First, in the long run, if external balance implies $X - Z$ is zero, internal balance then implies that domestic demand $(C + I + G)$, must equal potential output. Second, real exchange rates must be constant in long-run equilibrium. Under a regime fixing nominal exchange rates, domestic and foreign inflation rates must eventually be equal. Otherwise, competitiveness and the trade balance would keep changing for ever. Third, under fixed exchange rates, expected exchange rate changes should normally be zero. Hence the interest parity condition means that interest rates must match foreign interest rates if a massive capital flow is to be avoided.

---

[1] For most countries, the trade balance and the current account are similar. There are exceptions. Japan, with a large stock of foreign assets, has important interest income from them. Many poor countries have big foreign debts, on which they need to pay interest.

the balance of payments and the money supply

We now highlight a key mechanism through which external balance is restored when the economy is not in long-run equilibrium. Suppose the economy is running a balance of payments deficit. Two things are happening. First, on average, private individuals are withdrawing money from circulation. They need this money to acquire the foreign exchange with which to purchase foreign goods and assets. The domestic money supply is being reduced by exactly the amount of the balance of payments deficit.

Second, the government is intervening in the forex market. The balance of payments deficit is exactly matched by official financing, as we saw earlier in the chapter. The government is selling foreign exchange reserves, thereby supplying foreign currency to the market. In exchange, the central bank is obtaining pounds sterling which effectively have been withdrawn from circulation.

Thus, under fixed exchange rates, the money supply is not determined exclusively by the original decision of the government about how much money to print. When the economy has a balance of payments deficit, the monetary outflow will be reducing the domestic money supply below the value it would otherwise have attained. Conversely, with a surplus on the balance of payments, the domestic money in circulation will be augmented by the inflow of money from abroad. Suppose the government does not wish the domestic money supply to be reduced when there is a balance of payments deficit. The government can undo the effect by offsetting action at home.

Sterilization *is an open market operation between domestic money and domestic bonds the sole purpose of which is to neutralize the tendency of balance of payments surpluses and deficits to change the domestic money supply.*

adjustment under given policies

Consider a domestic shock that reduces aggregate demand. In a closed economy, a slump would bid down prices, boosting real money and thus cutting interest rates, to restore full employment. How does adjustment differ in an open economy with a fixed exchange rate facing almost perfect international capital mobility?

Initially, there is still a slump. Imports fall and the trade balance increases. But current account effects are swamped by what happens on the capital account. Lower income reduces money demand. However, any tendency for interest rates to fall immediately prompts a massive and immediate capital outflow that reduces the money supply until it has fallen in line with money demand. Interest rates are immediately restored to foreign levels. This follows directly from equation (2) and the interest parity condition.

The adjustment mechanism is thus completely different from a closed economy, in which slumps slowly cure themselves by bidding down prices and boosting the real money supply. Instead, the slump bids down prices and, at a fixed nominal exchange rate, slowly boosts competitiveness. This increases aggregate demand and restores internal balance.

A final point. When the economy gets back to internal balance, it will now have a trade surplus and no longer be in external balance. Current account surpluses mean additional income. GNP exceeds GDP. Even if the latter is fixed eventually by potential output, the former can grow, and provides a source of additional demand. As consumption increases again, domestic demand recovers, the economy now over-heats, and the induced reduction in competitiveness eventually restores external balance. Now GNP and GDP are the same, the internal balance can also be restored.

A shock from abroad Suppose the shock initially affects net exports not domestic demand. Now the boom or slump that the trade shock causes will induce changes in prices and competitiveness that gradually reverse the effect on net exports. Adjustment is now much simpler.

monetary policy under fixed exchange rates

When price adjustment is sluggish, an increase in the nominal money supply increases the real money supply in the short run, and tends to reduce domestic interest rates. With perfect capital mobility, this leads to a capital account outflow until the domestic money supply has been reduced to its original level and interest rates have returned to world levels. Hence domestic monetary policy is powerless in a fixed exchange rate regime when capital mobility is perfect.

Perfect capital mobility means that the government cannot fix independent targets for both the money supply *and* the exchange rate. Under fixed exchange rates, the government has to accept the domestic money supply that makes domestic and foreign interest rates equal.

This is equivalent to the assertion that sterilization will not work. When attempts to increase the domestic money supply are frustrated by a capital account deficit and a monetary outflow, the government can try to pump yet more money into the economy. With interest rates again below world levels, owners of international funds withdraw yet more money.

fiscal policy under fixed exchange rates

In contrast, in an open economy fiscal policy is *more* powerful in the short run than in a closed economy.

In a closed economy, fiscal policy leads to two kinds of crowding out. In the short run, a fiscal expansion increases output but bids up interest rates, moderating the output increase. And in the long run, higher demand bids up prices and reduces the real money stock, raising interest rates until consumption and investment demand fall to restore aggregate demand to its full-employment level. In an open economy, capital account flows peg interest rates at world levels and prevent induced changes in interest rates.

Hence, in the short run a fiscal expansion has a larger effect in an open economy with a fixed exchange rate.

▬▬ devaluation

We now assess the consequences of a devaluation. We distinguish its effects in the short run, the medium run, and the long run. Initially, we assume that the domestic country begins from internal and external balance. This allows us to highlight the effect of the devaluation itself. Then we consider whether devaluation may be the appropriate policy response to a shock that has already moved the economy from its long-run equilibrium position.

the short-run effect

When prices and wages adjust slowly, the immediate effect of a devaluation is to improve international competitiveness. Resources will be drawn into domestic industries such as car production, which can now compete more effectively with imported cars, and will be drawn into export industries, which can now compete more effectively in foreign markets. However, there are two points to note.

First, although devaluation tends to increase the quantity of net exports $(X - Z)$, the initial response may be quite slow. Overnight, there may be a lot of contracts outstanding that were struck at the old exchange rate. Similarly, it may take time to build up production capacity in the domestic industries making goods for export or to substitute for goods formerly imported. Second, devaluation may not improve the trade balance in the short run. The trade balance refers to value not volume. Because quantity responses are initially low, cutting international prices of UK goods may initially move the current account into deficit. In the longer run, quantities are more responsive and net trade revenues increase.[2]

the medium-run effect

For convenience, we re-write equation (3)

$$Y = (C + I + G) + (X - Z). \tag{4}$$

The supply of domestic goods Y equals aggregate demand, which comprises domestic absorption $(C + I + G)$ plus net export demand $(X - Z)$. A devaluation increases net export demand $(X - Z)$. What happens next depends crucially on aggregate supply.

If the economy begins with Keynesian unemployment, the economy has the spare resources to produce extra goods and can meet this increase in aggregate demand. Output will increase and unemployment will fall. But if the economy begins at full employment, the economy as a whole cannot produce more goods. The higher aggregate demand will quickly bid up prices and wages. The economy's international competitiveness is reduced, and net exports start to fall again. When domestic prices and wages have risen by the same percentage as that by which the exchange rate was initially devalued, the real exchange rate and competitiveness have returned to their original levels.

If for some reason the government intended the devaluation to improve the current account balance permanently, the devaluation should be accompanied by fiscal policy to reduce domestic absorption. Since there is now no upward pressure on domestic prices, the higher international competitiveness and lower exchange rate can be sustained in the medium run.

the long-run effect

It is real variables, not nominal variables, that matter. Can altering the nominal exchange rate permanently change the value of real variables?

Suppose a devaluation has been accompanied by tighter fiscal policy in order to allow the economy to meet the higher demand for net exports without any direct upward pressure on prices. Although this takes care of demand-side effects on prices, we must also think about supply-side effects. Domestic firms that import raw materials will want to pass on these cost increases in higher prices. Workers who buy imported consumer goods, from food to TV sets, will conclude that the cost of living has increased, and they will demand nominal wage increases to maintain the value of

---

[2] Thus we have established that a devaluation may lead first to a deterioration of the current account of the balance of payments but then to an improvement in the current account. Economists sometimes describe this response as the *J-curve*. As time elapses after the devaluation, the current account falls down to the bottom of the J but then improves and rises above its initial position.

their real wages. These price and wage increases lead other firms and other workers to react in similar fashion.

Thus, in the absence of any real change in the economy, the eventual effect of a devaluation will be an increase in all other nominal wages and prices in line with the higher import prices, leaving all real variables unchanged. Eventually, a devaluation will have no effect. Most of the leading computer models of the UK economy, models based on past data, conclude that the effects of a sterling devaluation are almost completely offset by a rise in domestic prices and wages by the end of five years.

Table 10-2 shows the effect of the sterling devaluation by 15 per cent in 1967. The first row shows that it took two years before the current account moved from deficit into surplus. As we explained, a devaluation will not improve the value of the current account until quantities of imports and exports have time to respond. In the third row we show an indicator of fiscal policy. In 1967, UK unemployment was low and the economy was close to full employment. The economy had few spare resources with which to produce extra goods for export or import substitution. In 1969, fiscal policy was tightened substantially, reducing domestic absorption and allowing an improvement in net exports. The government (including the nationalized industries) actually ran a surplus in 1969.

The final row of the table shows the real exchange rate, the relative price of UK goods to foreign goods when measured in a common currency. It shows two things. First, instead of using the 15 per cent devaluation to reduce export prices in foreign currencies, UK exporters responded in part by raising prices and profit margins. Only about half the competitive advantage was passed on to foreign purchasers as lower foreign prices for UK goods. Second, even by 1970 we can see competitiveness being eroded. Domestic wages had started to rise as workers asked for cost of living wage increases to meet higher import prices. By 1970 the real exchange rate had begun to rise again.

Devaluation and adjustment   A devaluation is likely to lead to a temporary but not a permanent increase in competitiveness relative to the position that would have been attained without the devaluation. But devaluation may be the simplest way to change competitiveness quickly. It may be a useful policy when the alternative adjustment mechanism is a domestic slump and a protracted period of gradual wage and price reduction until competitiveness is increased.

Table 10-2   The 1967 sterling devaluation

	1967	1968	1969	1970
Current account (£b)	−0.3	−0.2	0.5	0.8
Balance of payments (£b)	−0.7	−1.4	0.7	1.4
Budget deficit (% of GDP)	5.3	3.4	−1.2	0
$/£	2.8	2.4	2.4	2.4
Real exchange rate (1975 = 100)	109	102	102	103

Source: ONS, Economic Trends.

■■ floating exchange rates

We now turn to freely floating exchange rates in the absence of any government intervention in the forex market. In this section we explain how the level of the exchange rate is determined.

the long-run path

We argued that only one real exchange rate is compatible with internal and external balance in the long run. In this sense, the current account plays a large role in exchange rate determination. A country finding oil, and better able to export than before, could survive with a permanently higher real exchange rate.

Knowing the real exchange rate in the long run, how do we work out the corresponding path for the nominal exchange rate? We also need to know how domestic and foreign prices behave. A small country has no effect on how the rest of the world behaves. We simply form the best guess about the likely path of foreign prices. What about domestic prices?

Floating exchange rates restore domestic monetary sovereignty since the government no longer needs to intervene in the forex market. Knowing the path of the domestic target for monetary policy (whether a path for nominal money, or an explicit inflation target) we can deduce the likely path of domestic prices in the long run. Knowing the required real exchange rate, and the paths of domestic and foreign prices, we can deduce the path the nominal exchange rate will eventually follow when all adjustment is complete.

Essentially, in the long run this is the purchasing power parity path for the nominal exchange rate. If domestic inflation exceeds foreign inflation for ever, the nominal exchange rate must depreciate for ever to maintain the real exchange rate and competitiveness at the appropriate long-run level.

In the long run, the current account is centre stage in determining floating exchange rates. Countries cannot depart from external balance indefinitely. But in the short run, the role of the current account is dwarfed by the threat of capital movements. Forex traders need to balance their books day by day. Hence in the short run, the capital account can drive the exchange rate a long way away from the path that would balance the current account.

speculation

Holders of funds in sterling will compare the interest rate obtained by lending on sterling assets with the expected total return that can be obtained by temporarily lending abroad instead. It is the *total* return that counts. The total return from lending in a foreign currency (dollars) is the interest rate on dollar assets such as US government bonds plus the capital gain (loss) from a depreciation (appreciation) of the dollar–sterling exchange rate while the money is lent abroad.

Since speculators cannot be certain how exchange rates are going to change over time, it is the *expected* exchange rate changes, and hence the expected capital gains or losses from temporarily lending abroad, that influence decisions today about which currency looks the most attractive.

Suppose UK interest rates are 2 per cent higher than US interest rates. Why don't holders of funds move all their funds into sterling? What would make them indifferent about which country they lent in? Suppose speculators expect the pound to depreciate by 2 per cent a year against the dollar. People investing in pounds will get 2 per cent extra interest but make a 2 per cent capital loss on the exchange rate change relative to the alternative strategy of lending in dollars. The extra interest just compensates for the expected loss and most speculators won't mind where they hold their funds. Since there are no massive flows between currencies, the forex market can be in equilibrium. The dollar–sterling exchange rate falls at 2 per cent a year as everyone expected, and investors get the same return on their money in either currency.

What would happen if UK interest rates suddenly rose and were now 4 per cent higher than interest rates in the United States? Everyone will try to move into pounds. Almost instantaneously, this will bid up the dollar–sterling exchange rate. How high will it rise? Until it has reached such a high level that most people expect the pound then to fall at 4 per cent a year thereafter. Only then will the capital losses expected on funds lent in pounds be sufficient to offset the 4 per cent interest differential, and only then will people stop wanting to get their money into pounds.

Why do speculators believe that a higher value of the pound today makes it more likely that the exchange rate will fall in the future? Because smart speculators figure out that eventually the exchange rate has to return to the only path compatible with external balance in the long run. If the exchange rate does not seem to be moving in that direction, eventually the government is going to have to take some drastic action to restore external balance.

Thus we can sum up the complete theory of exchange rate determination as follows. In the long run, the exchange rate will have to follow the path which offsets differential inflation rates across countries and allows long-run equilibrium at the unique real exchange rate compatible with external balance. But in the short run the nominal exchange rate can depart significantly from this path and competitiveness can change by a large amount.

In the long run, countries with high inflation rates also have higher nominal interest rates. That is the Fisher relation we discussed in Chapter 9. Hence in the long-run equilibrium when the exchange rate is falling along the PPP path, the speculators are quite happy too. The capital losses on the depreciating exchange rate are just offsetting the high nominal interest rates earned by lending in that currency.

But when a country has higher interest rates in the short run than it is expected to have in the long run, the currency will temporarily be attractive to owners of international funds. To stop them all moving their funds into the currency to take advantage of these high interest rates in the short run, the currency will have to appreciate, perhaps significantly, above its purchasing power parity path. Only then are speculators likely to believe that the exchange rate will fall sufficiently in the near future to provide capital losses that offset the high interest rates that are temporarily on offer. In the short run, large movements in the exchange rate may be required to prevent the massive flows on the capital account which would be incompatible with day-to-day equilibrium in the forex market.

■■■ monetary and fiscal policy under floating exchange rates

In a closed economy with sluggish wage and price adjustment, both monetary and fiscal policy have real effects in the short run, although the economy eventually returns to full employment or internal balance. In an open economy with fixed exchange rates, highly mobile international funds make monetary policy almost powerless in the short run but increase the power of fiscal policy. Under floating exchange rates the converse is true: monetary policy is powerful in the short run, but the effectiveness of fiscal policy is reduced.

monetary policy

Suppose that the foreign price level and the foreign money supply are fixed. The rest of the world has no inflation. Its nominal and real interest rates are constant and equal, perhaps at 3 per cent per annum. The domestic economy begins in internal and external balance, also with a constant money supply and constant wages and prices. Since there is no domestic inflation, domestic nominal and real interest rates are also 3 per cent.

In this long-run equilibrium, domestic and foreign interest rates are equal. But with neither domestic nor foreign inflation, speculators recognize that the nominal exchange rate can remain unchanged for ever. It is at the level that secures the level of competitiveness appropriate to external balance in long-run equilibrium. Hence speculators have no wish to transfer funds between currencies. It is a full long-run equilibrium.

Figure 10-3 shows this nominal exchange rate as e_1. Suppose that at time t there is a once-and-for-all reduction in the nominal money supply by 50 per cent. Eventually domestic prices and wages will fall by 50 per cent. Thus in the long run it will require an appreciation of the nominal exchange rate, a doubling from e_1 to e_2, to restore the real exchange rate to its long-run equilibrium level.

However, domestic prices adjust sluggishly. In the short run, a reduction in the nominal money supply will also reduce the real money supply. Thus the immediate effect is to raise domestic interest rates in order to reduce the demand for money and maintain equilibrium in the domestic money market. Now speculators are keen to invest large amounts in pounds. To choke off a massive inflow of funds on the capital account, the sterling exchange rate must rise *above* its new long-run equilibrium position e_1. We say that the exchange rate must overshoot the change eventually required.

When the exchange rate jumps from e_1 to e_3, speculators realize that it will have to fall to get back to its new long-run equilibrium e_2. The anticipated falls in the exchange rate mean anticipated capital losses for those holding sterling rather than dollars, and

| Figure 10-3 | Exchange rate overshooting |

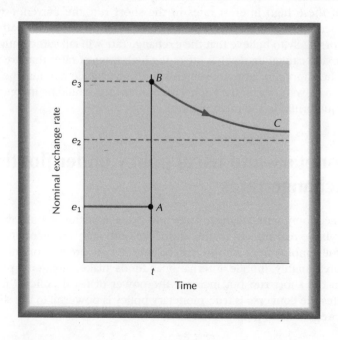

these offset the higher sterling interest rate. The exchange rate converges on its new equilibrium by moving along the path *BC* as time elapses.

The path gets steadily flatter over time. Initially the fall in the nominal money supply caused a large reduction in the real money supply and a big increase in domestic interest rates. But gradually domestic prices and wages start to fall, increasing the real money supply and reducing sterling interest rates. As the interest differential falls, it requires a slower and slower exchange rate depreciation to prevent massive international flows of funds. And, of course, the smart speculators had already figured that out in deciding that an initial jump in the exchange rate to e_3 was exactly what was required to keep them happy with the currency in which their funds were held.

So monetary policy can have a powerful effect in the short run. Changes in the real money supply and domestic interest rates not only influence domestic absorption, as in a closed economy, but also induce large changes in the nominal exchange rate and the level of competitiveness, which are only slowly eroded as domestic wages and prices adjust.

Again we emphasize that the government cannot choose independent targets for both the money supply and the exchange rate. Under a *fixed* exchange rate, there will be a net monetary flow on the balance of payments until, given domestic prices, the domestic real money supply equals the demand for real balances at the domestic level of real income and world interest rates. Domestic interest rates must match foreign interest rates in order to prevent massive capital flows when interest rates are known to be fixed.

In contrast, under a *floating* exchange rate the balance of payments is exactly zero. Combining currency and capital accounts, there are no international monetary flows. Thus the government can determine the domestic money supply at any level it chooses. But the government must then accept the path for the exchange rate that clears the forex market and keep the speculators happy. Equally, even without any official financing, the government can peg the exchange rate simply by announcing that it will match foreign interest rates for ever. As foreign interest rates change, the government simply alters the domestic money supply to maintain domestic money market equilibrium at the required interest rate.

fiscal policy

Whereas the effect of interest rate changes on the exchange rate and competitiveness makes monetary policy a more powerful tool with which to influence aggregate demand under floating exchange rates, the effect of interest rate changes on the exchange rate reduces the short-term effectiveness of fiscal policy.

Suppose the government undertakes a fiscal expansion, say by increasing the level of government spending. This increases aggregate demand and bids up interest rates. The higher interest rate leads to an immediate appreciation of the nominal exchange rate to choke off an inflow of funds. In a closed economy, higher interest rates partially crowd out private expenditure by reducing consumption and investment demand. But in an open economy with floating exchange rates, the induced reduction in the demand for net exports further reduces the power of a fiscal expansion to stimulate aggregate demand in the short run.

the pound since 1980

Figure 10-4 shows the behaviour of the nominal and real sterling exchange rates since 1980. We show the exchange rate against a basket of the currencies most important for the UK's international trade. The UK's real exchange rate had appreciated substantially during 1977–80. First, a tight monetary policy had been introduced to fight inflation. Until domestic prices and wages adjusted, the squeeze in real money meant high interest rates and a sharp appreciation in the nominal exchange rate. Second, the UK found oil. We discuss its effects in the next section.

After 1981, competitiveness gradually improved as the real exchange rate fell. In part, this can be explained by the overshooting story. The period 1979–81 was a time of sharp appreciation, and subsequently this was gradually reversed. The UK boom of the mid-1980s was partly built on falls in the real exchange rate and greater international competitiveness. However, domestic tax cuts and monetary growth eventually caused the economy to overheat. A government still committed to low tax rates responded with very sharp increases in UK interest rates. These led to a sharp exchange rate appreciation to stave off a speculative inflow. The late 1980s were partly a rerun of the late 1970s.

In 1990 the UK joined the Exchange Rate Mechanism and pegged its nominal exchange rate against other EU countries. Inflation had risen to 10 per cent and the government wanted a rapid improvement before the next election. When eventually the squeeze proved tougher than the economy could stand, speculators foresaw an inevitable easing of monetary policy, lower interest rates, and a devaluation of sterling. On Black Wednesday in September 1992 they bailed out of the pound. The UK government abandoned the attempt to hold the exchange rate and suspended membership of the EMS.

Figure 10-4 shows the sharp depreciation of both nominal and real exchange rates in late 1992. Increased competiveness gave the UK an export boom during 1993–95 that helped pull the country out of recession. However, one theme of this chapter has been that nominal devaluation is unlikely to achieve permanent increases in competitiveness. By the end of 1996 the real exchange rate had returned to its level of 1992. The UK's European partners tightened their fiscal policy in efforts to meet the Maastricht criteria for EMU, whereas the UK relied on high interest rates to control inflation. This bid up sterling, very sharply, in real terms. Britain's temporary period of export-led growth quickly petered out.

Figure 10-4 The exchange rates (1990 = 100)

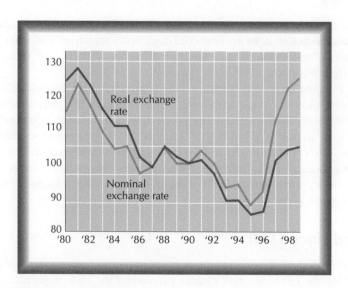

Source: IMF, *International Financial Statistics.*

■■ North Sea oil

By the late 1970s the UK was beginning to exploit the large reserves of oil discovered in the North Sea. The doubling of oil prices in 1979–80 increased the importance of these reserves. What effect did this have on the exchange rate?

Let's think first about long-run equilibrium with internal and external balance. External balance means that imports equal exports. The UK was formerly a large oil-importer. This trade deficit was offset by a surplus on other trade, primarily trade in manufactured goods. Suppose, for simplicity, that the oil discovery made the UK self-sufficient in oil. To preserve external balance, the UK had to give up its trade surplus in manufactured goods. The monetary mechanism that brought this about was a rise in the real exchange rate and a reduction in competitiveness.

For a given domestic money supply and given domestic prices, there was an appreciation of the exchange rate required for external balance in the long run. Recognizing this, speculators realized that, unless the exchange rate rose immediately, there would be foreseen capital gains as it gradually climbed to its higher long-run value. Since this made holding funds in pounds more attractive than before, the exchange rate had to rise immediately to choke off the potential inflow of funds.

Thus, sterling's real exchange rate rose especially sharply in the period 1979–81 because there was simultaneously a move to tighter monetary policy and a sharp increase in the real value of the UK's oil reserves. And in the period 1981–87 there was an improvement in competitiveness, both because of the gradual recovery from over-shooting, and because a world slump had reduced the world demand for oil and the real price of oil.

By the mid-1980s, a considerable part of North Sea oil reserves had been extracted. The importance of oil extraction to the UK economy rapidly diminished.

■■ recap

- The demand for domestic currency arises from exports, and purchases of domestic assets by foreigners; the supply of domestic currency arises from imports and purchases of foreign assets. Floating exchange rates equate supply and demand in the absence of government intervention in the forex market.

- Under fixed exchange rates, the government meets an excess supply of pounds by running down foreign currency reserves in order to demand pounds. Conversely, any excess demand for pounds at the fixed exchange rate is met by increasing the foreign exchange reserves and supplying pounds to the market.

- In the balance of payments accounts, monetary inflows are recorded as credits and monetary outflows are recorded as debits. The current account shows the balance on trade in goods and services plus net income earned from assets owned in other currencies. The capital account shows net purchases and sales of assets. The balance of payments is the sum of the current and capital account balances.

- Under floating exchange rates, a current surplus must be offset by a capital deficit or vice versa. Under fixed exchange rates, a balance of payments surplus or deficit must be matched by an offsetting quantity of official financing.

- The real exchange rate adjusts the nominal exchange rate for prices at home and abroad, and is the relative price of domestic to foreign goods when measured in a common currency. A rise in the real exchange rate reduces the competitiveness of the domestic economy.

- An increase in domestic (foreign) income increases the demand for imports (exports). An increase in the real exchange rate reduces the demand for exports, increases the demand for imports, and reduces the demand for net exports.

- Holders of international funds compare the domestic interest rate with the total return from temporarily lending abroad. This return is the foreign interest rate plus the depreciation of the international value of the domestic currency over the period of the loan. Perfect international capital mobility means that an enormous quantity of funds will shift between currencies when the perceived rate of return differs across currencies.

- Internal balance occurs when aggregate demand is at the full-employment level. External balance occurs when the current is zero. Both are necessary for long-run equilibrium.

- A balance of payments deficit leads to an equivalent reduction of the domestic money supply. A balance of payments surplus increases the domestic money supply by an equal amount.

- Under fixed exchange rates and perfect capital mobility, monetary policy is almost powerless. Domestic interest rates are pegged at world levels.

- Fiscal policy is a powerful tool under fixed exchange rates. Fiscal expansion no longer bids up domestic interest rates in the short run.

- A devaluation is a reduction in the fixed exchange rate. With sluggish price adjustment, its immediate effect is to increase competitiveness and aggregate demand. With spare resources, output increases. But at full employment, net exports can increase only if domestic absorption is reduced by tighter fiscal policy.

- In the long run, devaluation is unlikely to have much effect. But devaluation could speed up the adjustment process when a shock requires an adjustment in competitiveness to restore internal and external balance.

- Under floating exchange rates, the long-run value of the nominal exchange rate will be determined to secure external balance, given prices at home and abroad. But in the short run it is determined by speculative considerations, and must change to prevent massive flows on the capital account.

- Under floating exchange rates, monetary policy is a powerful short-term tool. A reduction in the money supply increases domestic interest rates and leads to a sharp appreciation of the exchange rate, which overshoots its long-run level. The fall in competitiveness, until domestic prices and wages adjust, sharply reduces aggregate demand in the short run.

- Fiscal policy is now a weaker tool in the short run. Fiscal expansion increases interest rates and the exchange rate, crowding out not merely domestic consumption and investment but also net exports.

- A deterioration in the oil-related part of the current account eventually requires an equivalent improvement in other items on the current account to preserve overall external balance. This is achieved through a fall in the real exchange rate.

■■■ key terms

■■■ review questions

1 A country has a current account surplus of £6 billion but a capital account deficit of £4 billion. (a) Is its balance of payments in deficit or surplus? (b) Are the country's foreign exchange reserves rising or falling? (c) Is the central bank buying or selling domestic currency?

2 For over 20 years, Japan has run a persistent trade surplus. How is this compatible with the statement that countries must eventually get back to external balance?

3 Rank the following three situations according to the ability of monetary policy to affect real output and employment in the short run: (a) a closed economy; (b) an open economy with fixed exchange rates; (c) an open economy with floating exchange rates. Explain. Assume the same speed of wage and price adjustment in each case.

4 Newsreaders say that 'the pound had a good day' whenever the sterling exchange rate rises on the forex market. (a) Under what circumstances might an appreciation of the exchange rate be desirable? (b) Undesirable?

10-2 the international monetary system

LEARNING OUTCOMES

When you have finished this section, you should understand

- the gold standard

- the adjustable peg Bretton Woods system

- the rise of capital mobility and the reasons for speculative attacks within adjustable peg systems

- motives for co-ordination of national macroeconomic policies

- the European Monetary System

We begin the section by briefly reviewing the possible exchange rate regimes. Then we discuss the relative merits of the different regimes. We conclude the section by looking at some of the questions raised by the possibility of international economic co-operation and *policy co-ordination*.

■■■ exchange rate regimes

An exchange rate regime *is the policy rule for intervening in the forex market.*

Table 10-3 summarizes the regimes that we shall be discussing: the gold standard, a currency board, the adjustable peg, managed floating, and freely floating exchange rates.

■■■ the gold standard

First, the government of each country fixed the price of gold in terms of its domestic currency.

The par value of gold *is the price of gold in terms of domestic currency.*

Second, the government maintained the *convertibility* of domestic currency into gold. The government bought and sold as much gold as people wished to transact at the par value. Third, the government follows a rule that links domestic money creation to the government's holdings of gold. This is called *100 per cent gold backing* for the money supply. Each pound in circulation was backed by an equivalent value of gold in the vaults of the central bank.

Since people could trade gold between countries, but the price of gold was fixed in each country, the nominal exchange rate was therefore fixed.

The gold standard *was a monetary union based on fixed gold prices, convertible currencies, and complete gold backing for the money supply.*

Table 10-3 Exchange rate regimes

	Exchange rate	
Forex intervention	Fixed	Flexible
None		Free float
Automatic	Gold standard, Currency board	
Some discretion	Adjustable peg	Managed float

balance of payments adjustment under the gold standard

Suppose Americans decide to spend more on imports of goods produced in the UK. Britain now has a trade surplus. The UK will enjoy an export-led Keynesian boom in the short run since aggregate demand for British output has increased. Conversely, the United States faces a recession and a balance of payments deficit. This provides an automatic international adjustment mechanism. Initially the UK payments surplus leads to an increase in the stock of pounds in circulation and the stock of gold at the Bank of England. Gradually, the higher domestic money supply puts further upward pressure on domestic prices by reducing interest rates and increasing aggregate demand for goods.

As prices rise, the UK gradually becomes less competitive since the nominal exchange rate remains fixed. When UK prices have risen, and UK competitiveness fallen, to the extent required to restore balance of payments equilibrium, international flows of money and gold cease. With the domestic money supply unchanging, there is no further pressure on domestic prices. Internal and external balances have been restored. Of course, exactly the opposite effects are happening in the United States.

Thus the gold standard does provide an automatic mechanism for adjusting imbalances in the trade and payments of different countries in the world economy. However, adjustment is far from instantaneous. The speed of adjustment depends on the speed with which domestic prices and wages adjust to the pressures of excess supply or excess demand.

The gold standard in action was not quite the same as the idealized version described here. Since the money supply was not usually 100 per cent backed by gold, the changes in official gold reserves incurred while defending the parity value of the exchange rate did not necessarily lead to identical changes in domestic money supplies.

The gold standard had one big benefit and one large drawback. By tying the domestic money supply closely, if not perfectly, to the stock of gold, it effectively ruled out persistent money creation of a large scale and ruled out persistently high inflation rates. However, since the major mechanism by which full employment could be restored was a fall in domestic prices and wages, which might take many years to adjust fully to a large fall in aggregate demand, the period of the gold standard was a period in which individual economies were vulnerable to long and deep recessions.

the adjustable peg and the dollar standard

In an adjustable peg regime, *exchange rates are normally fixed but countries are occasionally allowed to alter their exchange rate.*

This system, in operation for a quarter of a century after the Second World War, became known as the Bretton Woods system after the small American town where the details of the system were first hammered out.

Because other countries agreed to fix their exchange rates against the dollar (and hence against each other), this system also became known as the dollar standard

Each country announced a par value for its currency against the dollar. Under the dollar standard, currencies were convertible against dollars rather than gold. At the fixed exchange rate, central banks were committed to buy or sell dollars from their stock of foreign exchange reserves or dollar holdings. They were committed to intervene in the foreign exchange market to defend the exchange rate against the dollar.

The crucial difference between the gold standard and the dollar standard was that there was no longer 100 per cent backing for the domestic currency. Britain's domestic money supply did not have to bear any relation to the stock of dollars held by the Bank of England as foreign exchange reserves. Governments in Britain and other countries could print as much money as they wished.

Why does this matter? Because it inhibits the adjustment mechanism built into the gold standard. Countries with a balance of payments deficit lost gold and their domestic money supply fell. Eventually this put downward pressure on the price level and began to increase competitiveness. Under the dollar standard, countries with a balance of payments deficit lost money, but there was nothing to stop the domestic government printing more money to restore the domestic money supply to its original level. Thus governments of deficit countries could delay deflationary pressure from monetary contraction.

Such policies were unlikely to be feasible for ever. As the balance of payments deficit persisted, the government eventually ran out of foreign exchange reserves. Then the country had to devalue its exchange rate, moving to a lower par value against the dollar, to attempt permanently to increase competitiveness and remove the underlying imbalance in international payments. Thus the first problem with an adjustable peg system is that it does not necessarily provide an *automatic* mechanism for resolving imbalances in international payments. Rather, deficit countries tended to stave off the required adjustment until a major crisis had built up, and then undertake a significant exchange rate devaluation. In such circumstances, speculators had a field day. If a country was in balance of payments difficulties there was no danger that its exchange rate would be *raised*. Speculators faced a one-way bet against the central bank that was trying to defend the exchange rate.

The dollar standard had a second drawback. The US government could always finance an American balance of payments deficit by printing more dollars. In the mid-1960s the United States began to run much larger payments deficits, partly because of heavy military spending in Vietnam. In consequence the world's supply of outstanding dollars increased rapidly. By increasing the world's money supply, this process began to increase the inflation rate throughout the trading world.

▆▆ floating exchange rates

We discussed floating exchange rates at length in Section 10-1. Here, we discuss further the evolution of high international capital mobility. World trade had collapsed in the 1930s during the Great Depression. Countries responded by trying to get a larger share of the smaller cake. They raised tariffs and engaged in competitive devaluation against one another. But other countries retaliated. All this did was make the international cake get even smaller.

The postwar architects of the Bretton Woods system were determined to restore exchange rate stability. With free capital mobility, this requires small interest rate differentials across countries. In 1945 this seemed implausible. Hence the architects of Bretton Woods decided to outlaw private capital movements.

Capital controls *prohibit, restrict, or tax the flow of private capital between countries.*

This made it easy to defend fixed exchange rates. The central banks were the biggest players in town. But the rise of global financial markets gradually made relaxation of capital account controls inevitable. Daily trading in forex markets is now dominated by speculators, not just by their actual trades but by the possibility that they might move huge sums around.

This increases the difficulty of defending fixed exchange rates, which no longer works through the volume of forex intervention, now small relative to the size of private funds. Rather governments defend exchange rates by setting interest rates that induce private players to bid the currency to the right place. In terms of Figure 10-1, governments no longer intervene by mopping up excess supply or excess demand, rather they take interest rate action to shift the demand and supply curves themselves.

Whenever this use of interest rates seems too much a surrender of domestic sovereignty, government may fall back on floating exchange rates as an alternative. Floating also tends to avoid the one-way bet that sometimes induces a speculative attack on a fixed exchange rate regime.

▪▪▪ speculative attacks on pegged exchange rates

Most people still remember Black Wednesday when the UK was forced to depreciate and abandon the EMS. More recently, supposedly pegged exchange rates were successfully attacked in Mexico (1994), many Asian countries (1997), and Brazil (1999). When the speculators have more money than the central bank, the foreign exchange reserves can't always hold the line.

Raising interest rates may also be unconvincing if the domestic economy obviously can't stand the pain. Politically, it may be impossible to sustain the tough policy. Speculators understand that if they push hard enough, the government will have to cave in.

> *A* speculative attack *occurs when a country faces a sharp loss of reserves, a sharp depreciation, or both.*

There are several interpretations of such a speculative attack. One is that it is correcting a policy mistake. Where a country has such a large budget deficit that it needs to print money, it is bound to have inflation, and promising to peg the nominal exchange rate makes little sense. However, many of the Asian economies, such as Korea and the Philippines, attacked in 1997, appeared to have no such problem.

A second interpretation is that there are two possible equilibrium exchange rates. Without any attack, the original peg is fine. For example, the exchange rate may be a little overvalued, but the cost of devaluing (raising inflation expectations) may outweigh the cost of having a small amount of uncompetitiveness. However, once attacked, the cost of repelling the attack must be added to the scales. It may tip the balance, making it optimal now to accept defeat, and take the (temporary) advantage of higher competitiveness that the devaluation achieves. Whether the peg survives or not depends entirely on whether speculators decide to attack.

Attacks can, however, be very costly. When domestic banks have borrowed in foreign currency, these debts increase when the exchange rate falls and may bankrupt the banks and cause a widespread loss of confidence. Suppose a country wants to be less vulnerable to attack, what can it do?

repelling boarders

Three types of response have been adopted. First, one can try to reduce capital mobility making it easier to defend these fixed but adjustable exchange rate pegs. This was the solution adopted by those designing the Bretton Woods system after the Second World War. However, from the 1970s onwards, controls were progressively dismantled as a global financial system was created. It also became harder and harder to enforce controls – smart bankers found offshore ways of doing the same business.

One form of control that might stand a chance in the modern world is a tiny tax on financial transactions, first proposed by Nobel prize winner James Tobin. Paying a tiny once-off tax on a 10-year investment would be almost trivial, the same tax on holding a foreign asset for two hours would take away all the profits. Hence a Tobin tax would mainly hit short-term 'hot money'. Capital controls have been used quite successfully in Chile, and were introduced by Malaysia in 1997 after its currency was attacked. Whether the global economy is consistent with widespread controls remains a contentious issue. Small emerging markets can probably use them. The more highly integrated a country is with the world's financial markets, the harder it will be.

If capital controls are not to be the answer, the exchange rate regime has to become more robust. Pegged exchange rates are an uncomfortable halfway house: usually pegged but sometimes adjustable. While they are pegged the central bank is obliged to try to defend them, even when a one-way bet is emerging. But because they are not completely pegged, the speculators can win in the end. If this is the diagnosis, the solution may be to retreat to one of the safer extremes: float or peg completely. Thus, a second solution for repelling boarders and avoiding spectacular exchange rate crashes is simply to float. Let the speculators punch thin air. They can take the currency down, but, if it was for no good reason, the currency will probably come up again. Most Asian exchange rates have now recovered from 1997.

The alternative is to make the peg much more credible, akin to the old gold standard. One popular device is a currency board.

> A currency board *is a constitutional commitment to peg the exchange rate by giving up monetary independence.*

A currency board removes the ability of the central bank to change the monetary base. Balance of payments surpluses (deficits) become the only source of expansion (contraction) of the monetary base. Suppose a country has a deficit because it imports too much. Importers take domestic money to the currency board to get the foreign exchange they need; the board simply keeps the domestic money which is retired from circulation. Countries with currency boards in 1999 include Estonia, Bulgaria, and Argentina.

Like all pre-commitments, it hurts when it has to take the strain. Since the country loses monetary independence, it cannot use interest rates for domestic reasons. If it has any trouble doing the right thing with fiscal policy, it can get into trouble. If its banks face bankruptcy, it is difficult to ease credit conditions to help them. If it is possible a country may have to give up even a currency board, speculators may still attack.

Thus no solution is ideal. If any single solution was perfect, everyone would have been doing it long ago. We now consider some other issues that arise in choosing between fixed and floating exchange rates.

■■■ international policy co-ordination

By policy co-ordination, we mean a concerted attempt by a group of countries to formulate policy collectively. At one extreme, this might eventually imply a supra-national body to which national sovereignty is subordinated. At the other extreme, we might mean agreements to brief other governments about one's own policy, and to exchange information. In between lie a spectrum of arrangements which specify some 'rules of the game' subject to which national governments still have a measure of discretion.

What do governments stand to gain by co-ordinating macroeconomic policy to some extent? Like oligopolists, governments are essentially interdependent, the outcome for each depending on the policies pursued by others. Like oligopolists, they face a tension between the incentive to collude and the incentive to compete. Collusion allows them to 'internalize' the externalities they otherwise impose on one another when each sets policy without regard for its impact on the welfare of others. But there is also an incentive to compete by cheating on collective agreements.

the externality argument for co-ordination

The most obvious externality imposed by non-cooperative behaviour is the externality acting through the exchange rate. Suppose a government wants to get inflation down. An exchange rate appreciation will reduce prices directly by making imports cheaper.

But what works for a country in isolation cannot work for the world as a whole. We cannot all appreciate our exchange rates. A rise in the $/£ rate is necessarily a fall in the £/$ rate. Countries that use exchange rate appreciation to reduce their own inflation effectively export inflation abroad. That is the externality they fail to take into account.

In principle, policy co-ordination can solve this market failure: countries can agree not to use exchange rate policy in this manner. As with other collusive or co-operative agreements, an effective punishment threat is required to prevent individual countries from subsequently cheating on the agreement. If this can be devised, the agreement will be credible, and all countries may benefit.

Box 10-1	Exchange rate regimes and inflation

The table shows evidence assembled by the IMF in a study of 136 countries' inflation behaviour over three decades (1960–90). A hard peg is adjusted only rarely; a soft peg is frequently realigned (usually devaluations!). The table confirms that countries that have pursued more stringent exchange rate regimes have typically had inflation below the world average, and also had more stable inflation rates than the rest of the world.

The IMF rightly concludes that ability to sustain a tough exchange rate policy may be a symptom of sound macroeconomic policy as well as a cause of it.

% deviation from annual average in all 136 countries	Exchange rate regime			
	Hard peg	Soft peg	Intermediate	Float
Average inflation:				
All countries	−1.1	3.3	5.5	7.2
Rich and upper-middle-income	−2.3	−0.6	7.6	8.0
Poor and lower-middle-income	−0.4	5.2	4.0	6.6
Volatility of inflation				
All countries	−1.5	0.2	2.6	1.4
Rich and upper-middle income	−3.1	0.6	1.2	−1.2
Poor and lower-middle-income	2.2	−0.1	4.4	6.8

Source: IMF, World Economic Outlook 1996.

the reputation argument for co-ordination

It is possible that a government would like to keep inflation under control by tight policies but is unable to resist reflating the economy as the next election draws near. Because everyone knows this will happen, inflation expectations remain high and inflation is hard to control even at the start of the government's period of office.

Such a government might be glad if it could make a binding pre-commitment which ruled out the option to reflate as the next election drew near. An independent Bank of England is such a pre-commitment, but policy co-ordination may offer an alternative.

Why do people go to Weightwatchers or Alcoholics Anonymous? Because, alone, they are too weak to stick to their resolutions. Joining a club provides peer discipline. Even in everyday language, it shows commitment. You look silly if you subsequently pull out. Policy co-ordination may act in a similar way. Hence it may allow national governments to make credible the promises that would otherwise be incredible. That is the second argument for policy co-ordination.

We now turn to a closer examination of one of the most studied recent examples of co-ordination, the European Monetary System.

■■■ the European Monetary System

In March 1979 the members of the European Community (*including* the UK) founded the European Monetary System (EMS).

The EMS *was a system of monetary and exchange rate co-operation in Western Europe.*

The important features of the EMS were as follows. First, the European Currency Unit (ECU) was used as a unit of account for transactions between EC governments. The ECU was simply a bundle of the constituent currencies (including sterling). Second, member governments each deposited 20 per cent of their foreign exchange reserves with the European Monetary Co-operation Fund, and received ECUs in exchange. These funds were to be available for short-term central bank intervention in foreign exchange markets. It was only the third but key provision, the Exchange Rate Mechanism (ERM), in which the UK did not initially participate.

Under the ERM, *each country fixed a nominal exchange rate against each other ERM participant, though collectively the group floated against the rest of the world.*

Each country in the ERM could allow its exchange rate to fluctuate within a band of ±2¼ per cent of the parities it has agreed to defend. When the currency hit the edge of a band, *all* central banks in the ERM countries were obliged to intervene to try to defend the parity. The ERM had two other features: realignments were allowed but had to be unanimously agreed by participants of the ERM.

the EMS up to 1992

Table 10-4 shows the realignments of the major ERM currencies during 1979–91. (Recall that the UK did not join until 1990 and left again in 1992.) Two facts stand out. First, realignments largely followed the strategy of restoring purchasing power parity. The relatively high-inflation countries (initially Italy and France) were allowed nominal exchange rate devaluations. Second, whereas there was a realignment almost every six months between 1979 and 1983, after 1983 realignments were much less frequent. Between 1987 and 1991 there was no realignment.

Did the EMS exert financial discipline? Were France and Italy forced to live with tight German policies and low German inflation? Not initially. When they became uncompetitive at fixed nominal exchange rates, they were soon allowed to devalue to improve competitiveness. Typically, realignments did not *fully* restore purchasing power parity, so some discipline was being exerted. After 1983 discipline was much stricter. Thus, the EMS was founded when its members had very different inflation rates, but these were gradually brought into line. The EMS played some role in this. It did not reflect a political will to do this quickly, nor did it instantly force countries to harmonize policies. But over time, it did have an effect.

One final aspect of the EMS experience should be mentioned. It reduced nominal exchange rate volatility in the short run. Nor did its members experience the dramatic swings in real competitiveness to which the floating sterling and dollar were subject over the same period.

why did it work up to 1992?

Only part of the success of the EMS should be attributed to policy convergence. Most countries initially had foreign exchange controls which prevented large capital account flows. This allowed fixed bilateral parities to survive even when interest rates were out of line. Only occasionally was the prospect of a realignment so imminent that exchange controls had trouble stemming the speculative tide. Following the Single European Act of 1986, which sought to create an integrated market within the EU, the major EMS countries committed themselves to remove all foreign exchange controls by June 1990. Greece, Spain, and Portugal were allowed until 1992.

The UK joined the ERM in 1990. In Section 10-3 we discuss the ERM in the 1990s and the economics of EMU.

Table 10-4 EMS realignments, 1979–91 (date and percentage realignment)

Date	DM	FF	DG	IL	BF	DK	LF	IP
Sept. 79	+2.0					−2.9		
Nov. 80						−4.8		
Mar. 81				−6.0				
Oct. 81	+5.5	−3.0	+5.5	−3.0				
Feb. 82					−8.5	−3.0	−8.5	
June 83	+4.3	−5.8	+4.3	−2.8				
Mar. 83	+5.5	−2.5	+3.5	−2.5	+1.5	+2.5	+1.5	−3.5
July 85	+2.0	+2.0	+2.0	−6.0	+2.0	+2.0	+2.0	+2.0
Apr. 86								−8.0
Jan. 87	+3.0		+3.0		+2.0			
Cumulative	+23.7	−9.1	+19.1	−18.7	−3.3	−6.2	−5.3	−9.5

DM (Deutschmark), etc.

▒▒ recap

- Under the gold standard, each country fixed the par value of its currency against gold, maintained the convertibility of its currency into gold at this price, and linked the domestic money supply to gold stocks at the central bank. It was a fixed exchange rate regime.

- In the absence of capital flows, countries with a trade deficit faced a payments deficit, a monetary outflow, and a reduction in gold stocks. By inducing a domestic recession which put downward pressure on wages and prices and increased competitiveness, this provided an automatic adjustment mechanism.

- The postwar Bretton Woods system was an adjustable peg in which fixed exchange rates could occasionally be adjusted. Effectively, it was a dollar standard. But the domestic money supply was no longer linked to the stock of foreign exchange reserves.

- Unlike fixed exchange rates, floating exchange rates can cope with permanent differences in domestic inflation rates. They are also less vulnerable to speculative attack.

- International policy co-ordination allows policy-makers to take account of the externalities they impose on each other and may allow individual governments to commit themselves to policies that would otherwise not be credible.

- The UK was always a member of the European Monetary System but did not join its most important feature, the Exchange Rate Mechanism, until 1990 and left again in 1992. The early survival of the ERM depended on capital account controls.

▒▒ key terms

Exchange rate regime	340
Par value of gold	340
Gold standard	340
Adjustable peg regime	341
Dollar standard	341
Capital controls	342
Speculative attack	343
Currency board	344
EMS	346
ERM	346

▒▒ review questions

1 How did the dollar standard differ from the gold standard? Explain the differences in (a) the automatic adjustment mechanism, (b) financial discipline.

2 What would happen in the long run if floating exchange rates did not return to their PPP path? How can speculators make use of the knowledge that PPP will eventually be restored?

3 What are the advantages and disadvantages of a currency board?

4 When the UK left the ERM in September 1992 the news had different effects on the UK stock market and the UK bond market. Which market rose strongly? What was worrying the other market?

10-3 the economics of EMU

from EMS to EMU

By 1988, capital controls had been abolished as part of the programme to establish a single market within the EU. Some policy-makers realized that it was only a matter of time before speculators attacked the pegged exchange rates of the ERM. One possible solution was to go forward rapidly to completely fixed exchange rates.

A monetary union *has permanently fixed exchange rates within the union, an integrated financial market, and a single central bank setting the single interest rate for the union.*

A monetary union need not have a single currency. English and Scottish currencies circulate side by side in Edinburgh. What matters is that the exchange rate is certain and that a single authority (the Bank of England) sets the interest rate for both.

In 1988, the European heads of state established the Delors Committee to recommend how to get to European monetary union. Interestingly, the Committee was not

Box 10-2	The ERM: a quick history lesson

- The 1923 hyperinflation changed German history. Now Germans hate inflation. The constitution of the Bundesbank (Buba) makes stable prices its key objective.

- With mobile capital, pegging the exchange rate means the same interest rate in both countries. The issue is who sets the single interest rate. Initially, capital controls allowed the ERM to duck this issue.

- By the mid-1980s, the Deutschmark became the nominal anchor of the ERM. The Buba set interest rates for purely German reasons, and other countries then followed suit.

- Germany thus felt safe, and other countries enjoyed rapid falls in inflation expectations now the Buba was seen to be in charge.

- From the start of the ERM the Buba had a private understanding with the German government that the Buba would not defend weaker

currencies if this threatened inflation in Germany.

- In mid-1992, several exchange rates appeared overvalued. Germany proposed a general realignment but this was declined by other countries. The Buba intervened massively to help the lira and sterling, but both were forced out of the ERM by speculators and depreciated substantially. The peseta, escudo and punt were devalued but stayed in the ERM.

- A new attack on the French franc in 1993 led to a face-saving redesign of the ERM to allow the franc to survive. Central parities remained unaltered but bands were widened to 15 per cent either side of the parity.

- In 1996, the lira rejoined the ERM at a rate not much lower than it had left it. Partner countries were angry about the boom the UK and Italy had enjoyed by devaluing in 1992.

asked to discuss whether EMU was a good idea. The Delors Committee recommendations became the basis of the Treaty of Maastricht in 1991.

European Monetary Union was to be attempted in three stages. Stage 1, which began in 1990, saw any remaining capital controls abolished, and the UK encouraged to join the ERM (it did that autumn). Realignments within the ERM were to be frowned on but impossible. In Stage 2, which began in January 1994, a new European Monetary Institute was to begin preparing the ground for EMU, realignments were to be even harder to obtain, and excessive budget deficits were to be discouraged though not outlawed.

Stage 3, in which exchange rates were irreversibly fixed and the single monetary policy would begin, would start in 1997 provided a majority of potential entrants fulfilled the 'Maastricht criteria' (this deadline was not achieved). Otherwise, EMU would begin in January 1999 with whatever number of countries then met the criteria. Monetary policy in EMU would be set by an independent central bank, mandated to achieve price stability as its principal goal.

 The Maastricht criteria *for joining EMU said that a country must already have achieved low inflation and sound fiscal policy.*

The monetary criteria said that to be eligible, a potential entrant had to have low inflation, low nominal interest rates (market confirmation of low inflation expectations), and two prior years in the ERM without any devaluation. This last requirement was to prevent competitive devaluations or 'last realignments' as EMU approached.

The fiscal criteria said budget deficits must not be excessive, interpreted to mean that budget deficits should be less than 3 per cent of GDP; and that the debt/GDP ratio should not be over 60 per cent. Tight fiscal policy would mean there was little pressure on the central bank to bail out fiscal authorities.

Many economists complained that the Maastricht criteria were caution taken to extremes. An independent central bank with a tough constitution was an adequate pre-commitment to low inflation. It was unnecessary to constrain fiscal policy as well. Indeed, since national governments would no longer have a national interest rate or national exchange rate policy to deal with purely national circumstances, leaving them fiscal room for manoeuvre might be a good idea. The Maastricht deal reflected the balance of power in the negotiations. At the time, Germany ran the EMS and trusted itself to do so in its own interests. Why would Germany give up such a good position? Only if EMU was going to be super safe. The Maastricht criteria were the price of getting Germany on board.

sterling and UK membership

What arguments were advanced against UK membership of the ERM and EMU? First, until the late 1980s, North Sea oil made sterling behave differently from other European currencies. As UK oil production wound down, this objection evaporated.

Second, whereas the core countries of Europe are now very integrated with one another, offshore UK is less integrated with the rest of Europe. A common policy may be less suitable. Table 10-5 shows the composition of UK trade and how it has changed since the UK joined the EU in 1973. The trend is clear. The UK is getting more integrated with continental Europe all the time, even if from a lower baseline than some other European countries.

Third, the UK has a greater tradition of macroeconomic sovereignty: it seems to have more to lose. Whereas ERM countries had been in an ERM in which the 'single' interest rate was increasingly set by Germany alone, sterling floated during the entire period except for the two years of its ERM membership in 1990–92.

However, the absence of capital controls and the power of the speculators limit monetary sovereignty whatever the exchange rate regime. The Bank of England has often wished to raise interest rates for domestic reasons, to cool down a housing boom, but been unprepared to do so because higher interest rates would bid up further the value of the floating pound, exacerbating the woes of UK exporters. The Bank has often found itself hoping for interest rate rises in Frankfurt and Washington that would allow it to raise sterling interest rates without causing a further appreciation of sterling.

Finally, Black Wednesday (16 September 1992) makes it hard for UK politicians to appear too in favour of EMU. Then Chancellor John Major had taken the UK into the ERM in 1990 to combat rising inflation at the end of the Lawson boom. Unfortunately, this coincided with German reunification. Big subsidies to East Germany caused German overheating. When Chancellor Kohl refused to raise taxes, the Bundesbank raised interest rates to cool down the German economy. Interest rates high enough to do this job were far too high for Germany's partners in the ERM. This provoked the crisis of 1992–93.

German unification was the biggest country-specific economic shock in postwar Europe. It may not be a good guide to how EMU will fare. Indeed, the mandate of the European Central Bank to take an EU-wide view will prevent it reacting in such extreme fashion to the needs of one country. But UK voters remember the UK flirtation with a single European interest rate as an unhappy experience.

During 1996–98, EU countries scrambled frantically to get their budget deficits below the 3 per cent Maastricht limit to be eligible for EMU. There was fiscal tightening in continental Europe. Since the UK was enjoying the effects of looser policy after 1992 – the whole point of leaving the ERM had been to reduce interest rates and stimulate the economy – the UK business cycle got out of phase with the rest of Europe. This had little to do with any structural difference. It simply reflected the fact that while the UK had its foot on the accelerator its EU partners still had the brakes on tight. By the end of the decade, the UK was having to start worrying about overheating at a time when the rest of the EU was finally coming out of its policy-induced recession and looking forward to a period of steady growth. Eleven countries (all of those that wished to go ahead) were deemed in spring of 1998 to be fit and ready for EMU at the start of 1999.

With looser fiscal policy but as strong a commitment to low inflation, the UK inevitably had higher interest rates than its EU partners. Even if the UK wanted to join EMU, it would require tighter fiscal policy to make EMU interest rates appropriate for the UK. Announcing a 'tax for Europe' would have been political suicide in the UK, even though the Treasury did manage to raise tax revenue quite substantially by a host of less visible measures.

Table 10-5	UK trade patterns (%)		
	EU	*N. America*	*Rest of world*
1972	34	17	49
1998	57	15	28

Source: UN, *International Trade Statistics*.

▄▄▄ the economics of EMU

In 1999, Professor Robert Mundell won the Nobel Prize for Economics, in part for his pioneering work on optimal currency areas.

An optimal currency area *is a group of countries better off with a common currency than keeping separate national currencies.*

Mundell and the economists who came after him identified three attributes that might make countries suitable for a currency area. First, countries that trade a lot with each other may have little ability to affect their equilibrium real exchange rate against their partners in the long run; but they may face temptations to devalue to gain a temporary advantage. A fixed exchange rate rules out such behaviour and allows gains from trade to be enjoyed.

Second, the more similar the economic and industrial structure of potential partners, the more likely it is they face common shocks, which can be dealt with by a common monetary policy. It is country-specific shocks that pose difficulties for a single monetary policy.

Third, the more flexible are the labour markets within the currency area, the more easily any necessary changes in competitiveness and real exchange rates can be accomplished by (different) changes in the price level in different member countries.

Conversely, countries gain most by keeping their monetary sovereignty when they are not that integrated with potential partners, have a different structure, and hence are likely to face different shocks, and cannot rely on domestic wage and price flexibility as a substitute for exchange rate changes.

To these purely economic arguments, we should add an important political argument. Currency areas are more likely to work when countries within the area are prepared to make at least some fiscal transfers to partner countries. In practice, this cultural and political identity may be at least as important as any narrow economic criteria for success.

is Europe an optimal currency area?

Those who have studied the structure of national economies, and the correlation of shocks across countries, generally reach the following conclusions.[3] First, Europe is quite, but not very, integrated. Second, there is a clear inner core of countries – the usual suspects – who are more closely integrated than the rest.

However, the act of joining EMU is likely to change the degree of integration, possibly quite substantially. The Single Market will be underpinned by EMU, enhancing integration of product markets and removing the need for national legislation that is partly responsible for existing segmentation of markets. There is also independent evidence that countries which trade a lot have more correlated business cycles. Moreover, countries which belong to currency unions tend historically to trade much more with each other than can be explained simply by the fact that their exchange rates are fixed.[4] These pieces of evidence imply that it may be possible

[3] See T. Bayoumi and B. Eichengreen, 'Shocking aspects of European monetary unification', in F. Giavazzi and F. Torres (eds.), *Adjustment and Growth in the European Monetary Union*, Cambridge University Press, Cambridge, 1994; and T. Bayoumi and B. Eichengreen, 'Operationalizing the theory of optimum currency areas', Discussion Paper 1484, Centre for Economic Policy Research, London, 1996.

[4] A. Rose, 'One money, one market', *Economic Policy*, 2000.

successfully to start a currency union before all the microeconomic pre-conditions are fully in place. The act of starting may speed up the process.

the Stability Pact

The Stability Pact, ratified by the Treaty of Amsterdam in 1997, confirmed that the Maastricht fiscal criteria would not merely be entry conditions for EMU but would continue to apply after countries joined the monetary union. Some EMU members have debt/GDP ratios of close to 100 per cent. Reducing these towards 60 per cent may take decades. The real focus has been on the 3 per cent ceiling for budget deficits.

In principle, countries exceeding the limit may have to pay fines unless their economy is in evident recession (automatic stabilizers mean tax revenues fall in a slump). To avoid this, and to retain the ability to use fiscal expansion as a last resort in a slump, countries may aim for something more like budget balance in normal times. Note that if budgets are roughly in balance over the business cycle, but output grows for ever, debt/GDP ratios should exhibit trend decline, whatever their cyclical behaviour. This may eventually lead to the tough conditions of the Stability Pact being eased.

the European Central Bank

The single monetary policy is now set in Frankfurt by the European Central Bank *(ECB). National central banks have not been abolished, but the board of the ECB sets the interest rate on the euro.*

The ECB mandate says its first duty is to ensure price stability, but it can take other aims into account provided price stability is not in doubt. In 1999, the ECB cut interest rates when Germany and Italy were stagnating and there was little sign of inflation.

Whereas the Bank of England is very transparent, revealing its inflation forecast and publishing minutes of meetings of its Monetary Policy Committee, the ECB has had a more difficult job. On the one hand, it wished to appear transparent. On the other hand, it needed to emphasize continuity with the Bundesbank, whose tradition had been not to publish the minutes and to give monetary growth forecasts pride of place as a leading indicator of inflation. Moreover, it may be easier for ECB board members to take a truly European interest, even if against the direct interest of the country from which they come, if voting records are not revealed.

One issue yet to be fully resolved is how the ECB will interact with the 11 national fiscal authorities. Since no procedure exists for co-ordinating fiscal policy, fiscal authorities may sometimes face temptations to free-ride on others: when Euroland is overheating, let other countries take the unpopular measures to tighten fiscal policy. Proponents of the Stability Pact point out that it helps redress this balance, keeping fiscal free-riding in check.

fiscal federalism?

One reason for the survival of the monetary union that we call the United States is its federal fiscal structure. When a particular state has a slump, it pays less income tax revenue to Washington, and gets more social security money from Washington, without any decisions having to be taken. This is automatic stabilizers at work, courtesy of federal tax rates and federal rates of social security payments. Conversely, a booming state pays more tax revenue to Washington, and gets less social security money back.

A federal fiscal system has a central government setting taxes and expenditure rules that apply in its constituent states or countries.

When state income increased $1, the state paid an extra 30 cents in income tax and got an extra 10 cents in social security. Originally, economists thought that this meant each state was effectively insured up to about 40 cents in the dollar. Euroland has no federal fiscal structure on anything like this scale. The pessimists concluded that EMU would come under pressure from country-specific shocks.

The idea was correct but the sums were wrong. The original US calculations would have been correct if they described a world in which state incomes were completely uncorrelated. In practice, of course, the correlation is quite high. Hence, when one state slumps and gets help from Washington, many other states are slumping and also getting help. But this increases US government debt and means *every* state has to pay higher future taxes.

But an individual state could have done that on its own, without membership of the federal 'mutual insurance' club. It could have borrowed in the slump to boost its own fiscal spending, and paid it back later when times were better. Making allowance for this, US states are probably insured more like 10 cents in the dollar than 40 cents. However, the Stability Pact might *prevent* individual EMU countries behaving in this way, by restricting their ability to borrow in bad times.

macroeconomic policy in an EMU member

Figure 10-5 shows what life is like for an EMU member. Interest rates are set by the ECB in Frankfurt. From an individual country's viewpoint, it is as if the *LM* curve is horizontal at r_0. Suppose the initial level of the *IS* curve allows equilibrium at *A*. Aggregate demand equals potential output.

Now the country faces a shock that shifts the *IS* curve down to IS_1. With full monetary sovereignty, the country might have reduced its own interest rate to restore full employment output at *C*. This might still happen in EMU if the country is very correlated with other EMU countries. Then the ECB will react to what is happening throughout Euroland and cut interest rates for everybody.

Figure 10-5 A member of Euroland

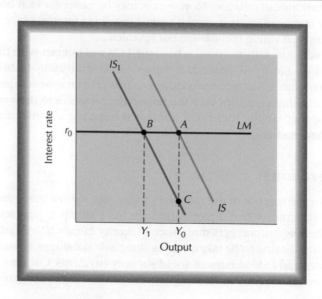

At the opposite extreme, if no other countries face the IS curve shock and the country is too small to influence Euroland data to which the ECB reacts, then interest rates will remain at r_0. The country now faces two choices. Provided it does not infringe the Stability Pact, it can use fiscal policy to shift IS_1 to the right, or it can wait for its labour market to do the same thing.

How does this work? At B the country is facing a slump. This gradually bids down wages and prices. At the fixed nominal exchange rate against its partners, this makes the country more competitive. Higher exports and lower imports shift the IS_1 curve to the right. If wage and price flexibility is high enough, there may be no need for fiscal policy. However, given that many European labour markets are quite sluggish, sensible use of fiscal policy may speed up the process.

▓▓ recap

- A monetary union means permanently fixed exchange controls, free capital movements, and a common monetary policy.

- In abolishing capital controls by 1992, the EMS was already committed to almost complete harmonization of monetary policy. The UK became a full EMS member in 1990, but withdrew in 1992.

- The Delors Report recommended progress to EMU in three stages. Stage 1 began on 1 July 1990 and envisaged exchange rate stability gradually increasing. In 1994 in Stage 2, the new institutions began rehearsing their eventual role, though as yet without formal power. In 1999, Stage 3 established the European Central Bank to run monetary policy. Exchange rates between EMU members were fixed for ever.

- The Maastricht criteria say that EMU entrants, including future ones, must have shown low inflation, low interest rates, and stable nominal exchange rates before entry; and must have budget deficits and government debt under control.

- EMU members must continue to obey the Stability Pact, which fines countries for excessive budget deficits, except when they are in recession.

- In EMU, countries can change their competitiveness through the slow process of domestic wage and price adjustment. In the absence of any federal fiscal system, individual member states are likely to want to retain control of fiscal policy as a last resort for dealing with crises.

▓▓ key terms

Monetary union	349
Maastricht criteria	350
Optimal currency area	352
European Central Bank	353
Federal fiscal system	354

▓▓ review questions

1 Suppose two countries fix their exchange rate for ever, but they have foreign exchange controls preventing private sector capital account flows between them. Is this a monetary union? If not, why not?

2 Why might a country join a monetary union that was not an optimal currency area?

3 Set out the arguments used for and against UK membership of EMU. Which do you find the most persuasive?

11 | growth and cycles

11-1 economic growth

LEARNING OUTCOMES

When you have finished this section, you should understand

- determinants of economic growth

- how economics became called the dismal science

- the neoclassical model of economic growth

- the growth performance of advanced and less advanced countries

- whether growth rates can be altered by economic policy

- the costs of growth

In 1999 real GDP in the UK was 10 times its level of 1870. Real income per person quintupled over that period. On average, we are richer than our grandparents but less rich than our grandchildren will be. Table 11-1 shows that these long-term trends were even more pronounced in other countries. Over the same period 1870–1999, in Japan real income per person grew 27-fold.

Economists have always been fascinated by the theory of economic growth. In 1798 Thomas Malthus's *First Essay on Population* predicted that output growth would be far outstripped by population growth until starvation and death brought the latter into line with the former, the origin of the notion of economics as 'the dismal science'. Some countries still seem stuck in a Malthusian trap, but others have clearly broken through into sustained growth and prosperity. We examine how they did it. As Table 11-1 shows, adding even 0.5 per cent to the annual growth rate makes an enormous difference after a few decades.

▬▬ economic growth

The growth rate of a variable is its percentage increase per annum.

 Economic growth *is the rate of change of real income or real output.*

Yet GDP (and GNP) are very incomplete measures of *economic* output; it is difficult to account for the introduction of new products; and there is no direct relationship between GDP and happiness.

GDP as a measure of economic output

GDP measures the net output or value added of an economy by measuring goods and services purchased with money. It omits output which is not bought and sold and therefore is unmeasured. The two most important omissions are leisure and externalities such as pollution and congestion.

In most industrial countries, the length of an average work week has fallen by at least ten hours a week since 1900. In choosing to work fewer hours per week, people reveal that the extra leisure is worth at least as much as the extra goods that could have been produced by working harder. But when people decide to swap washing machines for extra leisure, recorded GDP is reduced; hence, GDP understates the true economic output of the economy. Conversely, the output of pollution reduces the net economic welfare that the economy is producing and ideally should be subtracted from GDP. For example, sulphur dioxide emissions from coal-fired power stations lead to 'acid rain', destroying vast acres of German and Scandinavian forests. With comprehensive national income accounting, this output of acid rain would have been deducted from GDP.

new products

In 1870 people did not have televisions, cars or computers. Although statisticians do their best to compare the value of real GDP in different years, the introduction of new products creates a genuine difficulty in trying to make comparisons over time.

GDP as a measure of happiness

Even with an accurate and comprehensive measure of GDP, two problems remain. First, should we be interested in total GDP or in GDP per capita? Total GDP indicates the size of an economy, which may tell us something about its clout in the world. However, if we care about the happiness of a typical individual in an economy, it makes more sense to look at GDP per capita.

Table 11-1 Per capita real GDP, 1870–1999

	Per capita real GDP	
	Ratio of 1999 to 1870	Annual growth (%)
Japan	27	2.7
USA	10	1.8
Australia	4	1.2
Sweden	14	2.2
France	10	1.9
UK	5	1.3

Source: Angus Maddison, 'Phases of Capitalist Development', in R. C. O. Matthews (ed.), *Economic Growth and Resources*, vol. 2, Macmillan, 1979; updated from IMF, *International Financial Statistics*.

Even so, real GDP per person is a very imperfect indicator of the happiness of the typical individual within a country. When income is shared equally between its citizens, a country's per capita real GDP does tell us what each and every person is getting. But countries such as Brazil have very unequal income distributions. A few people earn a lot and a lot of people earn only a little. It is possible for such countries to have fairly high per capita real income while many of their citizens are really quite badly off.

Finally, we note that, even when GDP is adjusted to measure leisure, pollution, and so on, higher per capita GDP does not necessarily lead to greater happiness. Material goods are not everything. But they do help.

a recent phenomenon?

A very small increase in the annual growth rate has substantial results when its impact is cumulated over a long period. Had we been growing for thousands of years, we'd be even richer now than we are. In fact, it is only in the last two and a half centuries that per capita levels of real income have been persistently increasing.

In the long run, changes in output caused by fluctuations around potential output are swamped by the effect of persistent growth on potential output itself. In the long run, it is in changes in the level of potential output that we must seek the explanation of economic growth.

Potential output grows either because the quantity of inputs grows, or because a given quantity of inputs produces greater output. Measuring inputs is hard but not impossible. We have to keep track of the use of labour, of capital, of land (the environment), and perhaps of energy. How much output any given bundle of inputs produces depends on the productivity of these inputs.

Our grandparents had the same 24 hour day as us, and may even have been fitter, since they got more exercise. Why did they produce less output? We must have accumulated advantages in the meantime. These advantages can be physical, in which case we call them capital, or can be ideas, in which case we call them knowledge accumulated through technical progress. We begin by discussing the evolution of this knowledge in more detail.

■■■■ technical knowledge

At any given time, a society has a stock of technical knowledge *about ways in which goods can be produced.*

Some of this knowledge is written down in books and blueprints, but much is reflected in working practices learned by hard experience.

Technical advances come through invention, *the discovery of new knowledge, and* innovation, *the incorporation of new knowledge into actual production techniques.*

inventions

Major inventions can lead to spectacular increases in technical knowledge. The wheel, the steam engine, and the modern computer are obvious examples. Industrialized societies began only when productivity improvements in agriculture allowed some of the workforce to be freed to produce industrial goods. Before then, almost everyone had to work the land merely to get enough food for survival.

Embodiment of knowledge in capital   To introduce new ideas to actual production, innovation frequently requires investment in new machines. Without investment, bullocks cannot be transformed into tractors even if the knowhow for building tractors is available. Major new inventions may thus lead to waves of investment and innovation as these ideas are put into practice. Just as the mid-nineteenth century was the age of the train, we are now in the age of the microchip.

Learning by doing   Human capital can matter as much as physical capital. Workers get better at doing a particular job as they have more practice. The most famous example is known as the Horndal effect, after a Swedish steelworks built during 1835–36, and kept in the same condition for the next 15 years. Without changes in the machinery or the size of the labour force, output per worker-hour nevertheless rose by 2 per cent a year. Eventually, however, as skills become mastered, further productivity increases become harder and harder to attain.

▄▄▄ growth and accumulation

We organize our discussion around a simple production function

$$Y = A \times f(K, L). \tag{1}$$

Variable inputs capital K and labour L combine to produce a given output $f(K, L)$. The function f tells us how much we get out when we use specified quantities of the inputs K and L. This relationship never changes. We capture technical progress separately through A, which measures the extent of technical knowledge at any date. As technical progress takes place, we get more output from given inputs. A increases in value. In this simple framework, we assume that land is fixed. It is one of the other-things-equal assumptions, and need not feature explicitly in the analysis.

Malthus, land, and population

One of the earliest doomsters was the Reverend Thomas Malthus, writing in 1798. Living in a largely agricultural society, Malthus worried about the fixed supply of land. As a growing population tried to work a fixed supply of land, the marginal product of labour would diminish and agricultural output would fail to increase in line with population. The per capita food supply would fall until starvation started to reduce population to the level that could be fed from the given supply of agricultural land. This dire prediction earned for economics the name 'the dismal science'.

In terms of equation (1), when people are starving they have to consume all their income. Without savings, society cannot invest in capital, so K is zero. The production function then has diminishing returns to labour: adding more workers to fixed land drives down productivity.

Some of the poorer developing countries today face this *Malthusian trap*. Agricultural productivity is so low that almost everyone must work on the land if enough food is to be produced. As population grows and agricultural output fails to keep pace, famine sets in and people die. If better fertilizers or irrigation manage to improve agricultural output, population quickly expands as nutrition improves, and people are driven back to starvation levels again.

Yet Malthus's prediction did not prove correct for all countries. Today's rich countries managed to break out of the Malthusian trap. How was this achieved? First, they managed to improve agricultural productivity (without an immediate population increase) so that some workers could be transferred to industrial production. The capital goods thus produced included better ploughs, machinery to pump water and drain fields, and transport to distribute food more effectively. As capital was applied in agriculture, output per worker increased further, allowing yet more workers to be released to industry while maintaining sufficient food production to feed the growing population. Second, the rapid technical progress in agricultural production led to large and persistent productivity increases, reinforcing the effect of moving to more capital-intensive agricultural production. In terms of equation (1), increases in A and in K allowed output to grow faster than labour, causing a *rise* in living standards.

Thus we conclude that even the existence of a factor whose supply is largely fixed need not make sustained growth impossible. If capital can be accumulated, more and more capital can be substituted for fixed land, allowing output to grow at least as rapidly as population, and it is possible that continuing technical progress will allow continuing output growth even when one factor is not increasing. Moreover, the price mechanism provides the correct incentives for these processes to occur. With a given supply of land, increasing agricultural production will increase the price of land and the rental that must be paid for land. This provides both an incentive to switch to production methods that are less land-intensive (heavy fertilizer usage, battery chickens), and an incentive to concentrate on technical progress which will allow the economy either to get by with less land or, effectively, to increase the supply of land. A similar argument applies to any natural resource in finite supply.

capital accumulation

In the late 1950s, Bob Solow of MIT assembled the nuts and bolts of the neoclassical growth theory that has formed the basis of empirical work ever since.[1] It is a theory of growth because it asks why potential output grows in the long run. It is *neoclassical* because it does not ask how actual output gets to potential output. Over a long enough period, the only question of interest is what is happening to potential output itself. So neoclassical growth theory simply assumes that actual and potential output are equal.

Over this horizon, output, labour, and capital are growing. What about equilibrium in the long run? Usually, equilibrium means that things are not changing. Hence we apply equilibrium not to levels but to growth rates and ratios.

> Along the steady-state path, *output, capital and labour are all growing at the same rate. Hence output per worker and capital per worker are constant.*

The steady state is the long-run equilibrium in growth theory.

We assume that labour grows at a constant rate n. To keep things simple, we also assume that some constant fraction s of income is saved; the rest is consumed. Aggregate capital formation (public and private) is the part of output not consumed (by both public and private sectors). Investment first widens and then perhaps deepens capital.

> In a growing economy, capital-widening *extends the existing capital per worker to new extra workers.* Capital-deepening *raises capital per worker for all workers.*

Keeping capital per person constant requires more investment per person (1) the faster is population growth n (extra workers for whom capital must be provided) and

---

[1] Solow won a Nobel Prize for his work on long-run growth. He is also famous for his one-liners. Since, in short-run analysis, he is an unrepentant Keynesian, many of his famous remarks are aimed at those who believe that prices clear markets quickly: 'Will the olive, unassisted, always settle exactly half way up the martini?'

(2) the more capital per person k that has to be provided. In Figure 11-1 we plot the link nk along which capital per person is constant.

Adding more and more capital per worker k increases output per worker y, but with diminishing returns: hence the curve y in Figure 11-1. Since a constant amount of output is saved, sy shows the saving per person. Since saving and investment are equal, it also shows investment per person. In the steady state, capital per person is constant. Hence investment per person sy must equal nk, the investment per person needed to keep k constant by making capital grow as fast as labour. k^* is the steady-state capital per person, and y^* the steady-state output per person. Capital and output grow at the same rate n as labour along this steady-state path.

Figure 11-1 also shows what happens away from the steady state. If capital per worker is low, the economy begins to the left of the steady state. Per capita saving and investment sy exceeds nk, the per capital investment required to keep capital in line with growing labour. So capital per person rises. Conversely, to the right of the steady state, sy lies below nk and capital per person falls. Figure 11-1 says that, from whatever level of capital the economy begins, it gradually converges on the (unique) steady state.

a higher saving rate

Suppose people permanently increase the fraction of income saved, from s to s'. We get more saving, more investment, and hence a faster rate of output growth. Oh no we don't! Figure 11-2 explains why not. There is no change in the production function, which relates output to inputs. At the original savings rate s, the steady state is at E as before. At the higher savings rate, $s'y$ shows savings and investment per person. At F it equals nk, the per capita investment needed to stop k rising or falling. Thus F is the new steady state.

F has more capital per worker than does E. Productivity and output per worker are higher. That is the permanent effect of a higher saving rate. It is an effect on levels, not

---

Figure 11-1   Neoclassical growth

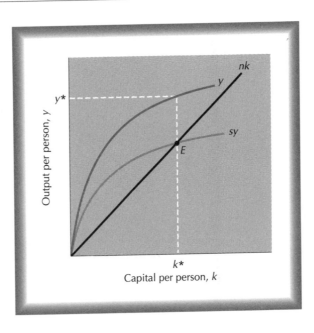

on growth rates. In *any* steady state, L, K, and Y all grow at the same rate, and that rate is determined 'outside the model': it is the rate of growth of labour and population. We return to this issue shortly.

To make the transition from E to F, there must be a temporary period in which capital grows faster than labour; only then can capital per worker rise as required. A higher savings rate, if successfully translated into higher investment to keep the economy at full employment, will lead to faster output growth for a while but not for ever. Once capital per worker rises sufficiently, higher rates of saving and investment go entirely in capital widening, which is now more demanding than before. Further capital deepening, the basis of productivity growth, cannot continue without bound.

growth through technical progress

We have made a lot of progress, but we still have some problems. First, the theory does not fit *all* the facts. So far, the theory says that output, labour, and capital all grow at rate n. Although it is true that capital and output do grow at the same rate, in practice both grow more rapidly than labour. That is why we are better off than our great grand-parents.

The answer may lie in technical progress, which we ignored in trying to explain output growth entirely through growth in factor supplies (population growth and the accumulation of capital). It turns out that *labour-augmenting technical progress* would do the trick. Population growth might eventually double the number of workers. Imagine instead that the number of workers is constant but that new knowledge allows the same workers to do the work of twice as many as before, as if the population had grown.

Labour-augmenting technical progress *increases the effective labour supply.*

Suppose this progress occurs at rate t. Effective labour input grows at rate $(t + n)$ because of technical progress and population growth. Now go back to Figure 11-1, and

---

Figure 11-2 A higher savings rate

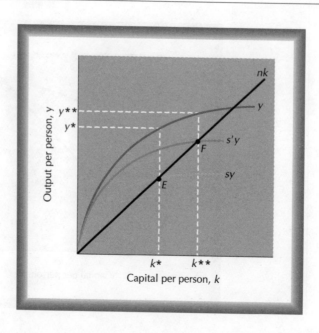

simply put $(t + n)k$ instead of nk. To make this valid, we have to measure capital and output not per worker but per worker-equivalent. Worker-equivalents are created by population growth or technical progress. Otherwise the diagram is identical.

E remains the steady state. Output per worker-equivalent and capital per worker-equivalent are constant. Since worker-equivalents grow at rate $t + n$, so must capital and output. Since actual workers increase at rate n, output and capital per actual worker each increase at rate t. Now our growth theory fits all the facts.

It remains uncomfortable that the two key growth rates, n and t, remain determined outside the model. For that reason, for the next 30 years the main use of this growth theory was in growth accounting: showing how to decompose actual output behaviour into the parts explained by changes in various inputs and the part residually explained by technical progress. We next examine the results of accounting for growth.

◼◼◼ growth in the OECD

The Organization for Economic Cooperation and Development [OECD (www.oecd.org)] is a club of the world's richest countries, ranging from industrial giants like the United States and Japan to smaller economies like New Zealand, Ireland, and Turkey. Table 11-2 shows the growth of OECD countries since 1950. The table shows the sharp productivity slowdown after 1973 in all OECD countries. Several explanations have been put forward. Some economists have emphasized the role of increasing pollution control and other regulations which, though socially desirable, had the consequence of raising production costs and reducing *measured* output and hence *measured* productivity.

1973 was also the year of the first OPEC oil price shock, when real oil prices quadrupled. This had two effects. First, it diverted R&D towards very long-term efforts to find alternative energy-saving technologies. These efforts may take decades to pay off and show up in improvements in actual productivity. Second, the higher energy prices made much of the capital stock economically obsolete overnight. Energy-guzzling factories were simply too expensive to operate and had to be closed down. The world effectively lost a considerable part of its capital stock, and this inevitably reduced output per head. Of course, for a time firms tried to struggle on with their existing factories. In practice, scrapping took a long time, though it was given renewed impetus by the second sharp rise in oil prices in 1980–81. That is why its effects were drawn out over such a long period.

Having discussed differences in growth across sub-periods, we now discuss differences across countries. The one sheds light on the other. The fact that all the OECD countries move together across sub-periods shows that many aspects of growth

| Table 11-2 | Average annual growth in real output per person employed (%) |

	OECD	Japan	Germany	Italy	France	Sweden	UK	USA
1950–73	3.6	8.0	5.6	5.8	4.5	3.4	3.6	2.2
1973–79	1.4	2.9	3.1	2.9	3.0	1.5	1.6	0
1979–90	1.5	3.0	1.6	1.9	2.6	1.7	2.1	0.7
1990–99	1.3	0.9	3.4	1.3	1.4	1.9	1.5	1.3

Sources: S. Dowrick and D. Nguyen, 'OECD Comparative Economic Growth 1950–85', *American Economic Review*, 1989; OECD, *Economic Outlook*.

may not be within a country's own control. Technical progress is diffused across countries quite quickly, wherever it originated. Countries are increasingly dependent on the same global economy.

the convergence hypothesis

Figure 11-1 has a unique steady state at E, and, whatever the level of capital per worker with which an economy begins, the figure implies that it will eventually converge to E. Poor countries with a low inheritance of capital grow extra rapidly until they reach the steady-state growth rate of output and capital; rich countries with a very high inheritance of capital grow at below-average rates until capital per worker falls back to its steady-state level k^*.

When capital per worker is low, it doesn't take much investment to equip new workers with capital (capital-widening), so the rest of investment can go on raising capital per worker (capital-deepening). When capital per worker is already high, it takes a lot of saving and investment just to maintain capital-widening, let alone to deepen capital. This is one reason for the convergence hypothesis.

The convergence hypothesis *asserts that poor countries grow more quickly than average, but rich countries grow more slowly than average.*

This explanation for convergence relies purely on the effect of capital accumulation. A second explanation for convergence or 'catch-up' operates through a different channel. Technical progress no longer falls out of the sky at a fixed rate. Suppose

---

Box 11-1 | Standards of living and the convergence hypothesis

The table below shows World Bank estimates of per capita income in 1997 and of its annual real growth during 1980–97. Three points stand out. First, the east Asian economies – China, Korea, Hong Kong, Thailand, Singapore – grew very quickly. Even India is now growing steadily. Second, convergence cannot be a powerful force in the world or the very poorest countries would be growing very rapidly. In reality, poor countries stay poor. Third, within the rich OECD countries, convergence is much more reliable. The richest OECD countries tend to grow less quickly than the poorer OECD countries. These conclusions apply not just in the particular data shown below – they are widely replicated in all empirical studies.

Per capita GNP (000s of 1997 US $) and annual % growth 1980–97

	1997 level ($000)	1980–1997 growth (%)		1997 level ($000)	1980–1997 growth (%)
Poor & middle income			OECD		
Mozambique	0.1	−1.2	Portugal	10.5	2.9
Bangladesh	0.3	2.3	Spain	14.5	2.0
Nigeria	0.3	−1.2	Ireland	18.3	4.2
China	0.8	11.0	Italy	20.1	1.4
Indonesia	1.1	5.5	UK	20.7	2.0
Philippines	1.2	1.1	France	26.5	2.0
Turkey	3.1	1.7	USA	28.7	1.7
Korea	10.5	7.8	Switzerland	44.3	1.6

Source: World Bank, *World Development Report*.

instead we have to invest real resources (universities, research labs, R&D) in trying to make technical improvements. It is rich countries that have the human and physical capital to undertake these activities, and it is in rich countries that technical progress is made. However, once discovered, new ideas are soon disseminated to other countries.

Since poorer countries do not have to use their own resources to make technical break-throughs, they can devote their scarce investment resources to other uses such as building machines. By slipstreaming the richer countries, they can temporarily grow faster.

■■■ endogenous growth

Solow's theory makes economic growth depend on population growth and technical progress. Both proceed at given rates. The subsequent literature on catch-up makes technical progress respond to economic and political factors. But it would be nice to have an even stronger link with economic behaviour and the consequent rate of economic growth. We want to make growth *endogenous*, or determined within our theory.

> Endogenous growth *occurs in models in which the steady-state growth rate can be affected by economic behaviour and economic policy.*

Saving, investment, and capital accumulation lie at the heart of growth. In Solow's theory, applying more and more capital to a given path for population runs into the diminishing marginal product of capital. It cannot be the source of permanent growth in productivity.

We know there must be diminishing returns to capital alone at the level of individual firms; otherwise one firm would get more and more capital, become more productive at a constant or increasing rate, and gradually take over the entire world! Because we know that this holds at the level of the firm, economists had always assumed that it held also at the level of the economy.

However, there may be significant externalities to capital. Higher capital in one firm increases productivity in *other* firms. When British Telecom invests in better equipment, other firms immediately can do things that were impossible before. The insight also applies to human capital. Training by one firm has beneficial externalities for others. Thus the production function of each individual firm exhibits diminishing returns to its own capital input, but also depends on the capital of other firms. No firm, acting in isolation, would wish to raise its capital without limit. But when all firms expand together the economy as a whole may face constant returns to aggregate capital.

Consider the following simple example of the aggregate economy. Because there are no diminishing returns in the aggregate, per capital output y is proportional to capital per person k. To isolate the role of accumulation, suppose there is no technical progress. Thus $y = Ak$ where A is constant. Given a constant saving rate s and population growth at rate n, consider whether there exists a steady state in which capital per person grows at rate g. If so, investment for capital-deepening is gk and investment for capital-widening, to keep up with population growth, is nk. Hence in per capita terms

$$\text{Gross investment} = (g + n)k = sy = sAk = \text{saving}$$

from which the steady-state growth rate g is

$$g = (sA - n). \tag{2}$$

Why does this confirm the possibility of *endogenous* growth? Because it depends on parameters that could be influenced by private behaviour or public policy. In the Solow model, without technical progress, steady-state growth is always n, whatever the savings rate s or the level of productivity A. Equation (2) says that any policy that succeeded in raising the saving rate s would *permanently* increase the growth rate g. Similarly, any policy that achieved a once and for all increase in the *level* of A, for example greater workplace efficiency, would permanently increase the growth rate of k. And since $y = Ak$, this would translate into permanently faster output growth. Not only is it possible for government policy to affect growth within this framework, there is also some presumption that government intervention may increase efficiency. Firms neglect the fact that, in raising their own capital, they also increase the productivity of *other* firms' capital. Government subsidies to investment might offset this externality.

There are many potential channels of endogenous growth. For example, instead of assuming technical progress occurs exogenously, we can model the industry that undertakes R&D with the objective of producing technical progress. Constant returns in this industry will generate endogenous growth. In fact, constant returns to aggregate production of any *accumulatible* factor (knowledge, capital, etc.) will suffice.

Note, too, that endogenous growth models explain why growth rates in different countries might permanently be different. This might explain why convergence does not take place and why some countries remain poor indefinitely.

While endogenous growth theory has been an exciting development, it also has its critics. Most of these criticisms boil down to one key point. Whatever the relevant accumulatible factor, why should there be *exactly* constant returns in the aggregate? With diminishing returns, we are back in the Solow model where long-run growth is exogenous. With increasing returns, the economy would settle not on steady growth but on ever more rapid expansion of output and capital. We know historically that this is not occurring. So for endogenous growth only constant returns to accumulation will do. Some people think this seems just too good to be true.

▮▮▮ the costs of growth

Some people believe that the benefits of economic growth are outweighed by the costs. Pollution, congestion, and a hectic life-style are too high a price to pay for a rising output of cars, washing machines, and video games.

Since GNP is a very imperfect measure of the net economic value of the goods and services produced by the economy, there is no presumption that our objective should be to maximize the growth of measured GNP. We discussed issues such as pollution in Chapter 5. In the absence of any government intervention, a free market economy is likely to produce too much pollution. However, complete elimination of pollution is also wasteful. Society should undertake activities accompanied by pollution up to the point at which the marginal benefit of the goods produced equals the marginal pollution cost imposed on society. Pollution taxes or regulation of environmental standards can be used to move the economy towards an efficient allocation of resources in which marginal social costs and benefits are equalized.

The full implementation of such a policy would probably reduce the growth of measured GNP below the rate that is achieved when there is no restriction on activities such as pollution and congestion. And this is the most sensible way in which to approach the problem. It tackles the issue directly. In contrast, the 'zero-growth' solution tackles the problem only indirectly.

The zero-growth proposal *argues that, because increases in measured GNP are accompanied by additional costs of pollution, congestion, and so on, the best solution is to aim for zero growth of measured GNP.*

The problem with the zero-growth approach is that it does not distinguish between measured outputs that are accompanied by activities with social costs and measured outputs that give rise to no pollution or congestion. It does not provide the correct incentives. When society believes that there is too much pollution, congestion, environmental damage, or stress, the best solution is to provide incentives that directly reduce these phenomena. Simply restricting overall growth in measured output is a terribly crude alternative which is distinctly second best.

Of course, some of these difficulties might be removed if economists and statisticians could devise a more comprehensive measure of GNP which included all the 'quality of life' activities (clean air, environmental beauty, etc.) that yield genuine consumption benefits but at present are not captured in measured GNP. Inevitably voters and commentators tend to judge government performance according to how well the economy is doing on some international league table of published and measurable statistics. A more comprehensive measure of GNP might remove some of the conflicts that governments feel between fostering growth of output as currently measured and encouraging measures to improve the quality of life.

recap

- Economic growth is the percentage annual increase in real GNP or per capita real GNP in the long run. It is a very imperfect measure of the rate of increase of economic well-being.

- Aggregate output can be increased either by increasing the inputs of land, labour, capital and raw materials, or by increasing the output obtained from given input quantities. Technical advances are an important source of productivity gains.

- The simplest theory of growth has a steady state in which capital, output, and labour all grow at the same rate. Whatever its initial level of capital, the economy tends to converge on this steady-state path. This theory can explain output growth but not productivity growth.

- Labour-augmenting technical progress allows permanent growth of labour productivity, and enables even the simplest growth theory to fit many of the facts.

- There is a tendency of economies to converge, both because capital-deepening is easier when capital per worker is low and because of catch-up in technology. Implementing technical change may depend on how well society is organized to buy off (or defeat) the losers.

- Theories of endogenous growth are built on constant returns to accumulation.

key terms

review questions

1 'Britain produces too many scientists but too few engineers.' What kind of evidence might help you decide if this is true? Will a free market lead people to choose the career that most benefits society?

2 Name two economic bads. Suggest feasible ways in which they might be measured. Should they be included in GNP? *Could* they be?

3 'If the convergence hypothesis is correct, the poor African countries should have grown long ago!' Is this correct? Do any of the newer approaches to economic growth help explain why some countries remain so poor?

4 'It is because we know Malthus got it wrong that we take a more relaxed view about the fact that some minerals are in finite supply.' Is there a connection? Explain.

11-2 the business cycle

After a deep recession during 1990–92, the UK left the Exchange Rate Machanism in 1992, reduced interest rates, and allowed the pound to depreciate substantially. The new Chancellor, Kenneth Clarke, presided over a steady recovery. Prime Minister Major delayed the General Election until May 1997, the last possible date, in the hope that an increasing 'feel-good factor' would win the election for the Conservatives.

This episode illustrates many of the issues that we examine in this chapter. First, is there a business cycle? We know output fluctuates a lot in the short run, but a cycle does not mean merely temporary departures from trend: it also requires a degree of regularity. Can we see it in the data? If we can, how do we explain it? If we can explain it, why did economic recovery after 1992 not boost the feel-good factor and government popularity as it had done in the past.

We also explore the international dimension. Can a single country display cycles that are out of phase with those in its trading partners?

LEARNING OUTCOMES

When you have finished this section, you should understand

- trend growth and economic cycles around this path

- theories of why business cycles occur

- whether potential output itself can cycle

- whether national business cycles are becoming more correlated

- recent UK business cycles

▄▄▄ trend and cycle: statistics or economics?

In practice, aggregate output and productivity do not grow smoothly. In some years they grow very rapidly but in other years they actually fall.

> The trend path of output *is the smooth path it follows in the long run once the short-term fluctuations are averaged out.*

> The business cycle *is the short-term fluctuation of total output around its trend path.*

Figure 11-3 presents a stylized description of the business cycle. The black curve shows the steady growth in trend output over time. But actual output follows the coloured curve. Point *A* represents a *slump*, the bottom of a business cycle. At *B* the economy has entered the *recovery* phase of the cycle. As recovery proceeds, output climbs above its trend path, reaching point *C*, which we call a *boom*. Then the economy enters a *recession* in which output is growing less quickly than trend output, and is possibly even falling. Point *E* shows a *slump*, after which recovery begins and the cycle starts again. Output grows most quickly during a recovery and grows least quickly (and possibly actually falls) during a recession.

Figure 11-4 shows the annual percentage growth of real GDP and of real output per employed worker in the UK during 1970–99. Output and productivity were growing most rapidly in 1964, 1968, 1973, and 1986–88 and growing least rapidly in 1966, 1974–75, 1980–81, and 1990–92. The figure makes three basic points. First, the growth of output and productivity is far from smooth in the short run. Second, although the economy is not subject to perfectly regular cycles, there does seem to be evidence of a pattern of slump, recovery, boom, and recession. Finally, in the short run there is a close relation between changes in output and changes in output per person. These are the facts that we seek to explain.

Any series of points may be decomposed statistically into an average trend and fluctuations around that trend. We begin by assuming that potential output grows smoothly. Later we shall consider whether potential output itself can fluctuate significantly in the short run. For the moment, we assume that deviations of actual output from trend reflect departures of aggregate demand and actual output from their full-employment level. What causes business cycles?

Figure 11-3 The business cycle

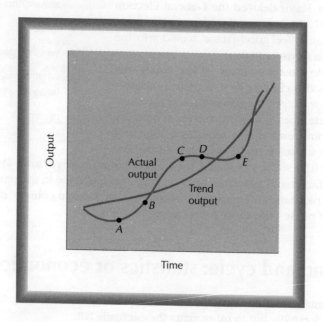

Figure 11-4 UK cycles in output and productivity

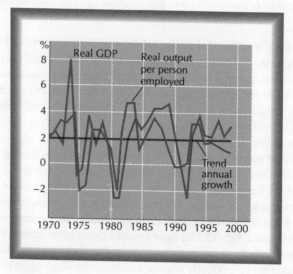

Source: ONS, *Economic Trends*.

It is possible to argue that the factors on which aggregate demand depends just happen to fluctuate in the short run and that the observed fluctuations in output merely reflect this. However, we should not wish to call this an *explanation* of the business cycle: it does not tell us why these influences on aggregate demand happen to fluctuate in quite a regular way.

One version of this approach does at least claim to be a theory. It is known as the *political business cycle.* Suppose voters have short memories and are heavily influenced by how the economy is doing immediately prior to the election. Suppose, too, that the government understands how to use monetary and fiscal policy to manipulate aggregate demand in the short run. To maximize its chances of re-election, the government adopts a tight monetary and fiscal policy just after it has been elected, manipulates the economy into a slump, and then adopts expansionary monetary and fiscal policy just before the election is due. Since the economy has spare resources during the slump, it is possible to make output grow considerably faster than its trend growth rate during the period immediately before the election. The voters think that the government has got things under control and votes them in for another term of office.

The political business cycle *arises from cycles in policy between general elections.*

This theory provides a reason for fluctuations and also suggests why business cycles tend to last about five years – that is the period between elections in countries such as the UK. And it probably does contain a grain of truth. On the other hand, it supposes that voters are pretty naive. In 1997 the Major government lost the election even though output was growing strongly. Voters thought Labour could do even better.

■■■ theories of the business cycle

If government policy is not the source of the business cycle, in which components of aggregate demand can the cycle originate? International trade helps explain how cycles get transmitted from one country to another, but we really require a theory of domestic business cycle to initiate the process.

The very notion of a cycle suggests sluggish adjustment. If the economy responded immediately to any shock we should expect to see sharp rises and falls in economic activity but not sustained periods of recession or recovery. Since a theory of a domestic cycle must be based on consumption or investment spending, it seems plausible that investment spending is the most likely candidate. Whereas households can in principle adjust their consumption spending relatively quickly, changes in investment spending are likely to take more time. Firms are unlikely to rush into major and irreversible investment projects and new factories cannot be built overnight. Hence we concentrate on investment as the most likely source of the business cycle.

the multiplier–accelerator model of the business cycle

The multiplier–accelerator model distinguishes the consequences and the causes of a change in investment spending. The consequence is straightforward. In the simplest Keynesian model, an increase in investment leads to a larger increase in income and output in the short run. Higher investment not only adds directly to aggregate demand, but by increasing incomes adds indirectly to consumption demand. In Chapter 7 we referred to this process as the multiplier.

What about the cause of a change in investment spending? Firms invest when their existing capital stock is smaller than the capital stock they would like to hold. When firms are holding the optimal capital stock, the marginal cost of another unit of capital just equals its marginal benefit, the present value of future operating profits to which it is expected to give rise over its lifetime. This present value can be increased either by a fall in the interest rate at which the stream of expected future profits is discounted or by an increase in the future profits expected.

In previous chapters we have focused on the role of changing interest rates in changes in investment demand. However, real interest rates don't change very much. The simplest way to calculate the present value of a new capital good is to assess the likely stream of *real* operating profits (by valuing future profits at *constant prices*) and then discount them at the *real* interest rate. Hence in practice changes in interest rates may *not* be the most important source of changes in investment spending. Almost certainly, changes in expectations about future profits are more important. If real interest rates and real wages change only slowly, the most important source of short-term changes in beliefs about future profits is likely to be beliefs about future levels of sales and real output. Other things equal, higher expected future output is likely to raise expected future operating profits and increase the benefit from a marginal addition to the current capital stock.

The accelerator model of investment *assumes that firms guess future output and profits by extrapolating past output growth. Constant output growth leads to a constant level of investment and a constant rate of growth of the desired capital stock. It takes* accelerating *output growth to* increase *the desired level of investment.*

Of course, the accelerator is only a useful simplification. A complete model of investment would allow both for the effect of changing output (and other forces) in changing expected future profits and the desired capital stock, and the role of changes in interest rates in altering the present value of these expected future profits, and hence the incentive to invest today. Nevertheless, many empirical studies confirm that the accelerator is a useful simplification.

Precisely how firms respond to changes in output will depend on two things: first, the extent to which firms believe that current output growth will be sustained in the future; second, the cost of quickly adjusting investment plans, capital installation, and the production techniques thus embodied. The more costly it is to adjust *quickly*, the more firms are likely to spread investment over a longer period.

We now show how a simple version of the multiplier–accelerator model can lead to a business cycle. In Table 11-3 we make two specific assumptions, although the argument holds much more generally. First, we assume that the value of the multiplier is 2. Each unit of extra investment increases income and output by 2 units. Second, we assume that current investment responds to the growth in output *last* period. If last period's income grew by 2 units, we assume that firms will increase current investment by 1 unit. The economy begins in equilibrium with output Y_t equal to 100. Since output is constant, last period's output change was zero. Investment I_t is 10, which we can think of as the amount of investment required to offset depreciation and maintain the capital stock intact.

Suppose in period 2 that some component of aggregate demand increases by 20 units. Output increases from 100 to 120. Since we have assumed that a growth of 2 units in the previous period's output leads to a unit increase in current investment, the table shows that in period 3 there is a 10-unit increase in investment in response to the 20-unit output increase during the previous period. Since the assumed value of the multiplier is 2, the 10-unit *increase* in investment in period 3 leads to a further increase of 20 units in output, which increases from 120 to 140.

In period 4 investment remains at 20 since the output growth in the previous period was 20. Thus output in period 4 remains at 140. But in period 5 investment reverts to its original level of 10, since there was no output growth in the previous period. This fall of 10 units in investment leads to a multiplied fall of 20 units in output in period 5. In turn this induces a further fall of 10 units of investment in period 6 and a further fall of 20 units in output. But since the rate of output change is not accelerating, investment in period 7 remains at its level of period 6. Hence output is stabilized at the level of 100 in period 7. With no output change in the previous period, investment in period 8 returns to 10 units again and the multiplier implies that output increases to 120. In period 9 the 20 unit increase in output in the previous period increases investment from 10 to 20 units and the cycle begins all over again.

The multiplier-accelerator model *explains business cycles by the dynamic interaction of consumption and investment demand.*

The insight of the multiplier-accelerator model is that it takes an *accelerating* output growth to keep increasing investment. But this does not happen in Table 11-3. Once output growth settles down to a constant level of 20, investment settles down to a constant rate of 20 per period. Then in the following period, the level of investment must *fall*, since output growth has been reduced. The economy moves into a period of recession, but once the rate of output fall stops accelerating, investment starts to pick up again.

This simple model should not be regarded as the definitive model of the business cycle. If output keeps cycling, surely firms will stop extrapolating past output growth to form assessments of future profits? Firms, like economists, will begin to recognize that there is a business cycle. The less firms' investment decisions respond to the most recent change in past output, the less pronounced will be the cycle. Even so, this simple model drives home a simple result which can be derived in more realistic models. When the economy reacts sluggishly, its behaviour is likely to resemble that of a large oil tanker at sea: it takes a long time to get it moving and a long time to slow it down again. Unless the brakes are applied well before the desired level of the capital stock is reached, it is quite likely that the economy will overshoot its desired position. It will have to turn round and come back again.

Ceilings and floors The multiplier-accelerator model can generate cycles even without any physical limits on the extent of fluctuations. Cycles are even more likely

Table 11-3 The multiplier–accelerator model of the business cycle

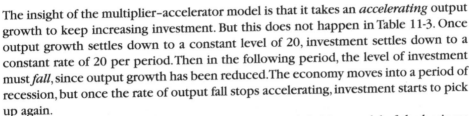

Period t	Change in last period's output $(Y_{t-1} - Y_{t-2})$	Investment I_t	Output Y_t
$t = 1$	0	10	100
$t = 2$	0	10	120
$t = 3$	20	20	140
$t = 4$	20	20	140
$t = 5$	0	10	120
$t = 6$	−20	0	100
$t = 7$	−20	0	100
$t = 8$	0	10	120
$t = 9$	20	20	140

when we recognize the limits imposed by supply and demand. Aggregate supply provides a *ceiling* in practice. Although it is possible temporarily to meet high aggregate demand by working overtime and running down stocks of finished goods, output cannot expand indefinitely. In itself this tends to slow down growth as the economy reaches a boom. Having overstretched itself, the economy is likely to bounce back off the ceiling and begin a downturn. Conversely, there is a *floor*, or a limit to the extent to which aggregate demand is likely to fall. Gross investment (including replacement investment) cannot actually become negative unless, for the economy as a whole, machines are being unbolted and sold to foreigners. Thus although falling investment may be an important component of a downswing, investment cannot fall indefinitely, whatever our model of investment behaviour.

fluctuations in stockbuilding

Thus far we have emphasized investment in fixed capital. Now we consider inventory investment in working capital. Firms hold stocks of goods even though these have a cost, namely the interest payments on the funds tied up in producing the goods for which no revenue from sales has yet been received. What is the corresponding benefit of holding stocks? If output could be instantly and costlessly varied it would always be possible to meet sales and demand by varying current production. Holding stocks makes sense because it is expensive to adjust production *quickly*. Output expansion may involve heavy overtime payments and costs of recruiting new workers. Cutting output may involve expensive redundancy payments. Holding stocks allows firms to meet short-term fluctuations in demand without incurring the expense of short-run fluctuations in output.

Consider how firms respond to a fall in aggregate demand. Wages will not respond fully and immediately to allow firms to cut prices and boost aggregate demand to eliminate the short-term fluctuation in the quantity of output demanded. Nor, since output adjustment on a large scale is expensive, do firms immediately react by reducing output substantially and laying off large numbers of workers. In the short run, firms undertake the adjustments that can be made most cheaply. They reduce hours of overtime and possibly even move on to short-time working. If demand has fallen substantially, this still leaves firms producing a larger output than they can sell. Firms build up stocks of unsold finished output.

If aggregate demand remains low, firms gradually reduce their workforce, partly through natural wastage and partly because it becomes cheaper to sack some workers than to meet the interest payments on ever larger volumes of stocks. And as wages gradually fall in response to higher unemployment, prices can be reduced, the real money supply increases, interest rates fall, and aggregate demand picks up again. However, firms are still holding all the extra stocks which they built up when the recession began. Only by increasing output *more slowly* than the increase in aggregate demand can firms eventually sell off these stocks and get back to their long-run equilibrium position.

Hence a fall in aggregate demand will be accompanied by a gradual process of output reduction. And once aggregate demand starts to pick up again, output will increase more slowly until stocks have been sold off and output can return to its full-employment level. Thus changes in stocks help explain why output adjustment is so sluggish; they explain why the economy is likely to spend several years during the phase of recovery or recession.

Now we can make sense of the behaviour of productivity shown in Figure 11-4. Output per worker tends to rise during the boom and fall during the slump. Output adjusts more quickly than employment. This is what we would expect, given the adjustment story we have developed. A fall in demand is met initially by cutting hours and increasing stocks. With a shorter work week, output per worker falls. Only as the recession intensifies do firms undertake the costlier process of sacking workers and restoring hours to their normal level. Conversely, a boom is the time when output and overtime are high and productivity per worker peaks.

real business cycles

Our account of the business cycle is completely compatible with the earlier analysis of the sluggishness of wage adjustment in the short run. The view that output fluctuates around the trend level of potential output fits nicely with our account of adjustment in Chapter 8, which might be succinctly described as Keynesian in the short run but classical or monetarist in the long run.

Not all economists share our assessment of how the economy works. In particular, there is an influential school known as the New Classical economists whose intellectual leader is Professor Robert Lucas of the University of Chicago. One of the key assumptions of the New Classical school, is that all markets clear almost instantaneously. Effectively, output is almost always at its full-employment level.[2]

> Real business cycle theories *explain cycles as fluctuations in potential output itself.*

Proponents of the theory argue that macroeconomics is intrinsically about dynamics over time, and that simplifications such as the consumption function, or even *IS–LM* analysis, are too simple to be useful.

Rather, we need firmly to base theories of firms and households in a microeconomic analysis of choice between the present and the future. For example, this approach would view each household as making a plan to supply labour and demand goods both now and in the future in such a way that lifetime spending was financed out of lifetime income plus any initial assets. Such plans would then be aggregated to get total consumption spending and total labour supply. An equivalently complex story would apply to firms and investment.

One implication of this approach is that it is no longer helpful to distinguish between supply and demand. If labour supply and consumption demand are part of the same household decision, things that induce the household to change its demand also induce it to change its supply.

For this reason, real business cycle theorists simply discuss what happens to actual output, which reflects both supply and demand and, by assumption, equates the two at potential output. In this view, the economy is then bombarded with shocks (e.g. breakthroughs in technology, changes in government policy) which alter these complicated plans and give rise to equilibrium behaviour that looks like a business cycle.

Why is this approach called the *real* business cycle approach? In the classical model changes in nominal money only affect other nominal variables, such as prices and wages, but do not affect real variables. Since real business cycle theorists believe in the classical model, they take it for granted that the source of business cycles must be in real shocks. In contrast, a Keynesian would argue that sluggish adjustment of nominal wages and prices give ample time for nominal shocks (e.g. money) to have significant real effects as well. We now give an example of real business cycle analysis in action.

---

[2] For an accessible introduction to these issues, see the lively exchange between Charles Plosser and Greg Mankiw in the *Journal of Economic Perspectives*, Summer 1989.

intertemporal substitution: a key to persistence

Real business cycle theories need to combine rapid market adjustment to equilibrium with the smooth or sluggish behaviour of aggregate output over the business cycle. Intertemporal substitution means making trade-offs over time, postponing or bringing forward actions in the sophisticated long-run plans of households and firms. This behaviour can cause effects to persist and look like part of a business cycle.

Suppose the Nintendo genie visits while we are all asleep. When we wake up, our productivity has doubled. But the game lasts only a year. We know that by next year our productivity will have returned to normal. We will face a temporary productivity shock, a blip in our technology. What should we do?

We are definitely wealthier after the genie's visit. We are pleased it happened. We could simply behave as before, working just as hard and investing just as much. In that case, our extra productivity would make extra output this year, but it is output that we would blow entirely on consumption this year. We would get little extra utility out of the hundredth bottle of champagne, and we would be making no provision for the future. There must be a better way.

We could put in a temporary spurt of extra work while we are superproductive, but in itself that would only exacerbate the problem: even more champagne today, still nothing extra for tomorrow. In fact, because leisure is a luxury and because we are better off than before, we may feel like taking it easy and doing less work.

We need a way of transferring some of our windfall benefit into future consumption. The solution is investment. A sharp rise in the share of output going to investment will provide more capital for the future, thereby allowing higher future consumption even after our productivity bonus has evaporated. Once we get to the future, being then richer than we would have been without the genie, we may in consequence work less hard than we would have done, since leisure is a luxury.

The point of this example is to show that even a temporary shock can have effects that persist well into the future. Persistence occurs both through investment (in human as well as physical capital) and through intertemporal labour substitution – deciding when in one's life to put the effort in.

Real business cycle theories still need to be worked out fully. To date, they seem vulnerable to two possible criticisms. First, they are usually theories of persistence rather than of cycles. Shocks have long drawn out effects, but rarely are these cyclical effects. Thus, to 'explain' business cycles, so far real business cycle theorists have had to assume a cyclical pattern to the shocks themselves. The theory is therefore incomplete. Second, and related, since the most widely researched example involves shocks to technology, a cyclical pattern of shocks implies that in some years technical knowledge actually diminishes: we forget how to do things. Not just once, but regularly every few years. This may be a bit hard to swallow.

policy implications

Even if research on real business cycles has much still to accomplish, it does have one vital message for macroeconomic policy. If the theory is right, it destroys the case for trying to stabilize output over the business cycle. Fluctuations in output are fluctuations in an equilibrium output that efficiently reconciles people's desires. For example, in the parable of the Nintendo genie, the induced effects on investment, labour supply, output, and consumption implement people's preferred way to take advantage of the beneficial opportunity. Trying to prevent these ripples is misguided policy.

While this caveat is important, it undermines the case for stabilization policy only if we buy totally the assumptions of complete and instant market-clearing and the absence of any externalities. For most economists these assumptions are too extreme to reflect the real world, and so valid reasons for stabilization policy remain. Even so, real business cycles contain an insight that every economist should acknowledge: there is no reason why potential output should grow as smoothly as trend output. The latter is a statistical artefact whose construction, averaging, forces it to be smooth.

■■■ an international business cycle?

National politicians want all the credit when output is high but produce a cast-iron alibi when the economy turns sour. They say domestic difficulties were caused by the world recession. How good is their alibi? Figure 11-5 shows business cycles in the four largest countries of the EU. It confirms that countries of the EU move quite closely with one another.

Although national circumstances play some role, these patterns warn us how inter-dependent the leading countries have become in the modern world. Economies are becoming more open. In product markets, protectionist policies are being removed, through global institutions like the World Trade Organization and through regional integration as in the creation of a Single European Market.

Improvements in transport and telecommunications also favour greater integration of product markets; and when R&D costs are large, producers need a global market if they are to recover their overheads. Product market integration provides an inter-national transmission mechanism through exports and imports. This is not the only channel through which one country affects another. Increasingly, we have a global financial market. Closer financial integration increases the likelihood that different countries pursue similar monetary policies.

Thus, the business cycle is transmitted from one country to another not just through private sector decisions about imports and exports (and their induced effects on labour supply, investment, and consumption), but also, sometimes, through induced changes in the economic policy of other governments.

| **Figure 11-5** | EU business cycles (% GDP growth) |

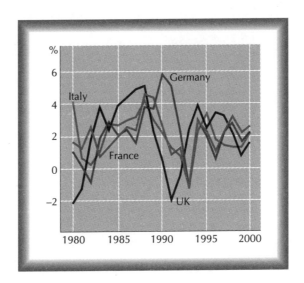

Source: OECD, *Economic Outlook*.

■■ **recovery after 1992**

As we remarked in earlier chapters, the 1980s saw financial reform in most countries. Deregulation of credit, and greater competition in its supply, was particularly marked in the United States and the UK. The recession of the early 1990s was the first world recession since the financial revolution. Did this make any difference?

Imagine you had been a consumer in the boom of 1986–88. Life looked rosy, and for the first time in modern history financial institutions were competing vigorously to lend you money. So, of course, you borrowed. The boom surely wouldn't end just yet, would it? Table 11-4 shows the collapse of the saving rate. There was a consequent rise in UK household debt. When the crash came, you got very badly hurt. Around the world, interest rates were suddenly very high as governments tried to stop economies overheating at the end of the 1980s. The interest cost of your huge debt soared.

Worse still, the collateral you had offered when you borrowed – your house or your portfolio on the stock market – was suddenly much less valuable. Higher interest rates lower asset prices by reducing the present value of the future income that the assets provide. In the UK, Japan, and the United States, the three countries where consumer debt had risen most in the 1980s, asset prices had fallen 25 per cent by 1992.

Table 11-4 shows clearly how consumers responded. Having acquired too much debt in the 1980s, they tried to put things right at the start of the 1990s. They saved a larger fraction of their incomes in order to try to repay some of the debt and bring it back to manageable proportions. However, it can be a slow process. When debt is nearly as large as income, and only a small fraction of income is saved, debt cannot be paid off very quickly. This continuing 'debt overhang' explains why the feel-good factor was slow to return after 1992. It helps explain why consumer spending recovered only slowly and why the Major government lost the 1997 election. Paradoxically, the success of the Major government in defeating inflation after 1992 paved the way for reductions in nominal interest rates and a recovery in the housing market. Table 11-4 shows that by 1999, the saving rate had collapsed again as consumers went on another spending spree.

Table 11-4	UK household saving (% of disposable income)

1982	1988	1992	1996	1999
10	4	12	10	5

Source: ONS, *Economic Trends*.

■■■ recap

- The trend path of output is the long-run path after short-run fluctuations are ironed out. The business cycle describes fluctuations in output around this trend. Cycles last about five years but are not perfectly regular.

- The political business cycle argues that the government manipulates the economy to make things look good just before an election.

- Cycles require either sluggish adjustment or intertemporal substitution. We also have to explain why cycles are fairly regular.

- The multiplier–accelerator model highlights the dependence of investment on expected future profits, and assumes that expectations reflect past output growth. This model delivers a cycle but assumes that firms are pretty stupid.

- Full capacity and the impossibility of negative gross investment provide ceilings and floors that limit the extent to which output can fluctuate.

- Fluctuations in stockbuilding are important in the business cycle.

- Real business cycles assume that output is always at potential and that fluctuations are in potential output itself. A desire for some intertemporal smoothing can generate persisting reactions to changes. Generating cycles is more difficult.

- Some swings in potential output do occur, but many short-run fluctuations probably reflect Keynesian departures from potential output. Aggregate demand and aggregate supply both contribute to the business cycle.

- Increasing integration of world financial and product markets has made most countries heavily dependent on the wider world. Business cycles in the rich countries are closely correlated.

- Recovery from the recession of 1990–92 was slow and weak. One key difference from previous cycles was the large burden of household debt accumulated during financial deregulation in the 1980s. By the late 1990s, consumer confidence had returned.

■■■ key terms

■■■ review questions

1 Look again at Figure 11-4. Can you say which fluctuations in output were caused by changes to aggregate supply and which by changes to aggregate demand? Does the cyclical behaviour of productivity help to answer this question?

2 'If firms could forecast future output and profits accurately, there could not be a business cycle.' Is this true?

3 Would it be more helpful for the world economy if all the largest countries elected governments on the same day? Why, or why not?

4 What is real about a business cycle?

11-3 macroeconomics: a final assessment

This section discusses remaining disagreements between macroeconomists, and why these exist.

areas of disagreement

We begin by asking why economists disagree at all. Surely, by looking carefully at the evidence we can say which views are correct and which must be rejected as inconsistent with the facts?

Positive economics relates to how the world actually works. Normative economics relates to different value judgements about what is desirable. Some disagreements between macroeconomists arise from differing value judgements. However, many important disagreements are disagreements in the positive economics of how the world actually works. Unlike some of the physical sciences, economists can rarely undertake controlled laboratory experiments. In practice, we have to try to unscramble historical data to make judgements about how the economy works.

Even so, empirical research in economics does not always offer clear-cut answers. Suppose, for example, we wish to study how the economy works when exchange rates are floating. Since many relevant data, such as GDP, are available only quarterly, we have only 100 separate pieces of data since freely floating exchange rates were adopted in 1973. For some purposes we simply do not have sufficient data to offer more than tentative conclusions. Economists who don't like these tentative conclusions argue that as yet the case against them remains unproved.

Moreover, we live in a world that is constantly evolving. Even if we had a good estimate of the empirical magnitudes in the demand for money during 1950–80, should we expect these to be relevant in the 1990s, when credit cards have been adopted on a wide scale? The truthful answer may be that as yet it is simply too early to say. Only when credit cards have been in widespread use for a long time shall we be able to measure their impact with more confidence. And, of course, by then we will be worrying about the effect of the internet on the demand for money.

Empirical economists do the best they can. In some cases their research is rather persuasive and their conclusions are widely accepted. Few people dispute that current consumption and the current demand for money are influenced by what is happening to current income. But in other cases empirical research is much less conclusive. Although economists agree about many aspects of positive economics, some disagreements will inevitably remain. We now pick out key disagreements that are not mere quibbles about points of detail. They fundamentally affect one's view of the world and the policy decisions one is likely to support.

market clearing

A market clears and is in equilibrium when the quantity sellers wish to supply equals the quantity purchasers wish to demand. Whether, and if so how quickly, all markets clear remains the most important issue in macroeconomics. At the one extreme we have the classical analysis which assumes that all markets clear. The economy is then at full employment and potential output. In these circumstances a monetary expansion will increase prices but not output, and a fiscal expansion will crowd out private consumption and investment until aggregate demand is restored to its full-employment level. At the other extreme, Keynesian analysis assumes that markets, especially the labour market, do not clear. With imperfect wage flexibility, a reduction in the aggregate demand for goods and the demand for labour leads to lower output and employment. In such a situation, expansionary fiscal and monetary policy can increase real output.

Do markets clear or not? It is interesting how the onus of proof changes over time. Before Keynes's *General Theory*, most economists took it for granted that markets cleared and tried to explain periods of high unemployment within this framework. In the immediate postwar period, most economists took it for granted that markets did not clear continuously and sought to interpret macroeconomics within the Keynesian paradigm.

In the 1970s the pendulum swung back again. It became fashionable to say that the Keynesian assumption of wage stickiness could not be given any plausible microeconomic foundation. Since the 1980s the pendulum has been in motion again. New Keynesian economists began to articulate microeconomic foundations for wage stickiness, and fewer economists believe there is a presumption that markets automatically clear.

is long-run equilibrium unique?

Suppose an economy begins in long-run equilibrium but then experiences a *temporary* shock which drives it to a different position in the short run. What happens when the shock has disappeared? Does the economy, sooner or later, go back to the original equilibrium, or does it settle down in a new, *permanently different*, long-run equilibrium?

The latter case is called *hysteresis*. We introduced it in Chapter 9 when discussing unemployment, but the same argument applies to aggregate supply and potential output. Hysteresis exists when the path an economy follows in the short run affects which long-run equilibrium it eventually reaches.

Whether or not hysteresis is quantitatively an important phenomenon is one of the most controversial issues of the last ten years. The more economists believe that hysteresis matters, the more they argue that the easiest way to prevent its damaging effects is to prevent the economy from entering a recession in the first place. In contrast, economists who believe that hysteresis is not very important can take a more relaxed attitude to temporary recessions since they believe that these have no long-term consequences.

expectations formation

Most economists accept that beliefs about the future are an important determinant of behaviour today. For example, consumer spending will depend both on how much today's households wish to spend out of their expected future incomes *and* on how today's households decide what future incomes to expect. Some important disagreements between economists can be traced to different beliefs about how expectations are formed. For simplicity, we divide the possible approaches to this question into three categories.

Exogenous expectations   Some economists remain almost completely agnostic on the vital question of how expectations are formed. When analysing the behaviour of the economy, they simply treat expectations as exogenous or given. Expectations are one of the inputs to the analysis. The analysis can display the *consequences* of a change in expectations – for example, an increase in expected future profits might increase firms' investment spending at each level of interest rates – but the analysis does not investigate the *cause* of the change in expectations. In particular, it is unrelated to other parts of the analysis. With given expectations, there is no automatic feedback from rising output to expectations of higher profits in the future.

Exogenous expectations *are not explained within the model.*

Extrapolative expectations

One simple way to make expectations endogenous, or determined by what is going on elsewhere in the analysis, is to assume that people forecast future profits by extrapolating the behaviour of profits in the recent past, or extrapolate past inflation in order to form expectations of inflation in the near future.

Extrapolative expectations *assume that the future will be similar to the recent past.*

Proponents of this approach suggest that it offers a simple rule of thumb and corresponds to what many people seem to do in the real world.

Rational expectations

Suppose the rate of money growth is steadily increasing and inflation is steadily accelerating. Extrapolating past inflation rates will persistently under-forecast future inflation. Many economists believe that it is implausible that people will continue to use a forecasting rule that makes the same mistake (under-forecasting of future inflation, say) period after period.

The hypothesis of rational expectations *assumes that, on average, people guess the future correctly.*

They do not use forecasting rules that systematically give too low a forecast or too high a forecast. Any tendency for expectations to be systematically in error will quickly be detected and put right.

This in no way says that everybody gets everything exactly right all the time. We live in a risky world where unforeseeable things are always happening. Expectations will be fulfilled only rarely. Rational expectations says that people make good use of the information that is available today and do not make forecasts that are already knowably incorrect. Only genuinely unforeseeable things cause present forecasts to go wrong. Sometimes people will underpredict and sometimes they will overpredict. But any systematic tendency to do one or other will be noticed and the basis of expectations formation will be amended until guesses are on average correct.

short run and long run

Where it is agreed that certain policies have short-run benefits but long-run costs, or vice versa, different groups of economists may adopt differing value judgements about how these gains and losses should be traded off. In part, the differing policy prescriptions offered by different groups of economists can be seen as reflecting differing judgements about the relative importance of the short run and the long run.

In practice, these judgements are closely connected with the three issues on which we have already focused. The more quickly one believes markets clear, the less scope there will be for demand management in the short run and the greater will be the importance attached to supply-side policy aimed at increasing potential output over the longer run. Conversely, the more one believes in the possibility of high levels of

Keynesian unemployment in the short run, the more likely one is to judge that the short-run benefits of getting back to full employment are more important than any tendency thus induced to reduce the level of potential output in the long run. Similarly, the more one wishes to focus on very short-run analysis, the more plausible it becomes that expectations can somehow be treated as given in the short run; and the more one wishes to discuss what is happening in the long run, the more important it is likely to be to take account of how expectations are changing over time. And the more one believes in hysteresis, the more one must look after the short run in order to look after the long run.

■■■ a summing up

Table 11-5 provides a convenient summary of disagreements in macroeconomics. We group views into four current schools of economic thought: New Classical, Gradualist Monetarist, Moderate Keynesian, and Extreme Keynesian. In column 1 we show the issues on which they have to take a position. These are the speed of market clearing, the nature of expectations formation, and the implicit time horizon. Given these, the table shows inference each school draws about full employment, which may also depend on the assessment of whether hysteresis and multiple equilibria is a serious possibility. Finally, Table 11-5 records how these judgements are reflected in differing recommendations for policy design.

Thus, New Classical economists are optimists on market clearing and therefore emphasize the need for supply-side policies to change the equilibrium position itself. At the other end of the spectrum, extreme Keynesians are sufficiently pessimistic about market adjustment that they emphasize the need for demand management at all times.

Table 11-5   A stylized picture of competing views

	New Classical	Gradualist Monetarist	Moderate Keynesian	Extreme Keynesian
Market clearing	Very fast	Quite fast	Quite slow	Very slow
Expectations	Rational – adjust quickly	Adjust more slowly	Could be fast or slow to adjust	Adjust slowly
Long run/ short run	Not much difference since fast adjustment	Long run more important	Don't neglect short run	Short run very important
Full employment	Always close	Never too far away	Could be far away	Could stay away
Hysteresis	No problem	No problem	Might be big problem	Big problem
Policy conclusion	Demand management useless; supply side needed	Supply side more important; avoid wild swings in demand	Demand management important too	Demand management what counts

■■■ recap

- Although there is much about which all economists agree, there remain some important differences of opinion, both in the positive economics of how the world actually works and in the normative economics of how the government should behave.

- It is desirable that economic theories should be tested against the facts. However, in some cases such tests are unlikely to yield conclusive answers.

- In seeking to understand the major schools of macroeconomic thought, it is helpful to bear in mind their attitude to four key issues: the speed with which the labour market clears, the way in which expectations are formed, the possibility of hysteresis, and the relative importance of the short run compared with the long run.

■■■ key terms

■■■ review questions

1 As compared with a closed economy, how is the speed of adjustment likely to differ (a) in an open economy with a fixed exchange rate? (b) in an open economy with a floating exchange rate?

2 Identify each of the following statements with one of the four schools: (a) Reducing inflation is easy and will not be accompanied by an increase in unemployment. (b) Expansionary monetary and fiscal policy will always increase output unless there is a sudden surge of imports. (c) It is always worth incurring a temporary increase in unemployment to obtain a permanent inflation reduction. (d) The government can always generate a domestic slump and reduce inflation, but the cost in output forgone could be quite high in the short run.

12 | trade and development

12-1 trade theory and trade policy

International trade is a part of daily life. Britons drink French wine, Americans drive Japanese cars, and Russians eat American wheat. The basis of international trade is *exchange* and *specialization*. International differences in the availability of raw materials and other factors of production lead to international differences in production costs and goods prices. Through international exchange, countries supply the world economy with the commodities that they produce relatively cheaply and demand from the world economy the goods made relatively cheaply elsewhere.

These benefits from trade are reinforced if there are economies of scale in production. Instead of each country having a lot of small producers, different countries concentrate on different things and everyone can benefit from the cost reductions that ensue. Because foreign competition may make life difficult for some voters, governments are frequently under pressure to restrict imports. We conclude the section by discussing trade policy and whether it is ever a good idea to restrict imports.

LEARNING OUTCOMES

When you have finished this section, you should understand

- patterns of international trade
- comparative advantage and the gains from trade
- two-way trade in the same product
- the welfare economics of tariffs, quotas, and export subsidies

■■■ trade patterns

Since every international transaction has both a buyer and a seller, one country's imports must be another country's exports. To get an idea of how much trade takes place, we can count the total value of exports by all countries or the total value of imports. To count both imports and exports would be to count every transaction twice.

Table 12-1 shows the value of world exports and, as a benchmark, the value relative to GNP in the world's largest single economy, the United States. In real terms world trade has grown rapidly since 1950, at an average annual rate of 7.5 per cent. International trade has been playing an increasingly important part in national economies. Between 1960 and 1995, UK exports as a fraction of GNP rose from 18 per cent to 27 per cent. Details for selected countries are shown in Table 12-2. By 1998, world exports were nearly 20 per cent of world GNP.

The Great Depression of the 1930s and the Second World War virtually destroyed international trade. It was not until the 1960s that world trade again reached its level of 1928. As trade has grown, the interdependence of national economies has increased. Like many of the countries shown in Table 12-2, Britain is now a very open economy. Smaller countries are of course more open; when New York trades with California it does not count as *international* trade. Events in other countries affect our daily lives much more than they did 20 years ago.

world trade patterns

Fifty per cent of world trade is between different industrial countries, and only 14 per cent does not involve industrial countries at all. World trade and world income are organized around the rich industrial countries.

Services account for most of the GDP of rich countries and are a rapidly growing part of international trade, but from a small baseline. The reason trade in goods – or merchandise trade – remains important is that many countries import goods, add a little value and then re-export them. The value added makes a small contribution to GDP but gross flows of imports and exports of goods are large.

Table 12-3 distinguishes between *primary commodities* (agricultural commodities, minerals, and fuels) and manufactured or processed commodities (chemicals, steel,

Table 12-1 The value of world exports

	1928	1935	1950	1973	1998
World exports					
(billions of 1990 £)	277	117	176	931	5460
(% of US GNP)	57	27	20	40	64

Sources: League of Nations, *Europe's Trade*, Geneva, 1941; IMF, *International Financial Statistics; National Income Accounts of the United States, 1928–49*.

Table 12-2 Exports as % of GDP

	1967	1998
Belgium	36	75
Netherlands	43	55
UK	18	27
France	14	26
Italy	17	26
USA	5	11
Japan	10	11

Source: IMF, *International Financial Statistics*.

cars, etc.). We show the breakdown of exports and imports for selected countries. Although the EU is chiefly an exporter of manufactures, primary commodities account for one-fifth of exports. And although the EU has to import many raw materials, imports of wholly or partly finished manufactures account for three-quarters of EU imports. US trade exhibits the same general pattern.

comparative advantage

We start by showing the benefits of trade when there are international differences in the opportunity cost of goods.

> *The* opportunity cost *of a good is the quantity of other goods sacrificed to make one more unit of that good.*

Suppose a closed economy with given resources can make video recorders or shirts. The more resources are used to make videos, the less resources can be used to make shirts. The opportunity cost of videos is the quantity of shirt output sacrificed by using resources to make videos instead. Opportunity costs tell us about the *relative* costs of producing different goods.

> *The* law of comparative advantage *states that countries specialize in producing and exporting the goods that they produce at a lower relative cost than other countries.*

There are many reasons why relative costs may differ across countries. We begin with a very simple model in which technology is the source of the difference. The United States and the UK produce two goods, video recorders and shirts. Labour is the only factor of production and there are constant returns to scale. Table 12-4 shows it takes 30 hours of American labour to produce one video and 5 hours to produce one shirt. UK labour is less productive. It takes 60 hours of British labour to produce one video and 6 hours to produce one shirt.

costs and prices

For simplicity, we assume that there is perfect competition. Hence the price of each good equals its marginal cost. Since there are constant returns to scale, marginal costs equal average costs. Hence prices equal average costs of production. Because labour is the only input, average costs are given by the value of labour input per unit of output, the unit labour cost. American workers earn $6 an hour and British workers £2 an hour (No minimum wage in this example!). Table 12-4 shows the unit labour

Table 12-3 Trade patterns, mid-1990s

	EU	N. America	Asia
% of exports			
Primary	19	21	16
Manufactures	79	73	83
% of imports			
Primary	25	18	28
Manufactures	73	79	69

Source: GATT, International Trade.

costs of the two goods in each country. In the absence of international trade, each country produces both goods and these unit labour costs are the domestic prices for which the goods are sold.

American unit labour requirements are *absolutely* lower for *both* goods than those in the UK. But American labour is *relatively* more productive in videos than in shirts. It takes twice as many labour hours to produce a video in the UK as it does in the United States but only 6/5 times as many hours to produce a shirt. These relative productivity differences are the basis for international trade.

allowing international trade

Suppose the countries can now trade with each other. We make two key points. First, if each country concentrates on producing the good that it makes relatively cheaply, the two countries together can make more of *both* goods. Trade leads to a pure gain, additional output to be shared between the two countries. Second, the free market will provide the right incentives for this beneficial trade to occur.

The countries trade. Since they use different currencies, a foreign exchange market must be set up and an equilibrium exchange rate established. In long-run equilibrium there is external balance. The values of exports and imports are equal. Suppose we begin at a high value of the pound that makes the UK uncompetitive in both goods. Now consider lower and lower exchange rates. When the exchange rate is low enough, the UK is able to compete by exporting one good. Which one? The one it is relatively better at making. A low enough exchange rate establishes external balance.

> *Regardless of a country's domestic production costs or* absolute advantage *in producing goods more cheaply, there always exists an exchange rate that will allow that country to produce at least one good more cheaply than other countries when all goods are valued in a common currency. At the equilibrium exchange rate, the country must have at least one good it can export to pay for its imports.*

comparative advantage

This pattern of trade and production illustrates the law of comparative advantage. Countries specialize in producing the goods they make *relatively* cheaply. The reason that production and trade patterns depend on *comparative* advantage and *relative* costs is that the level of the equilibrium exchange rate will take care of differences in absolute advantage.

Table 12-4 Production techniques and costs

	USA	UK
Unit labour requirement (hours/output unit)		
Videos	30	60
Shirts	5	6
Wage per hour	$6	£2
Unit labour cost		
Videos	$180	£120
Shirts	$30	£12

The principle of comparative advantage has many applications in everyday life. Suppose two students share a flat. One is faster both at making the dinner and at vacuuming the carpet. But if tasks are allocated according to absolute advantage, the other student is not helping at all. The jobs will get done most quickly if each student does the task at which he or she is relatively faster.

differences in capital–labour ratios

A *relatively* abundant supply or endowment of one factor of production tends to make the cost of renting that factor relatively cheap. Goods that use that factor relatively intensively will therefore be relatively cheap. They will be the goods in which the country has a comparative advantage. Thus the UK, which is relatively generously supplied with capital relative to labour, should export capital-intensive cars to Hong Kong. Hong Kong, which is relatively well endowed with labour, should export labour-intensive textiles to the UK. Differences in relative factor supply are an important explanation for comparative advantage and the pattern of international trade.

Figure 12-1 offers some evidence in favour of this analysis. It emphasizes skills, or human capital, rather than physical capital, although, of course, the two are usually correlated. Countries with scarce land but abundant skills tend to have the high shares of manufactures in their exports; countries with lots of land but few skills typically export raw materials. The figure also shows regional averages. Africa lies at one end, the industrial countries at the other.

We now have two explanations for comparative advantage or international differences in relative production costs. First, there are international differences in technology: differences in relative physical productivity and relative unit labour requirements. Second, even if countries have access to the same technology, the

Figure 12-1	Comparative advantage and export composition (125 countries and regional averages)

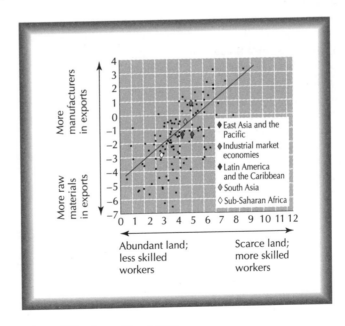

Source: World Bank, *World Development Report, 1995*.

domestic relative price of goods may differ across countries because the relative cost of renting factor inputs differs across countries. Where a factor is in relatively abundant supply, goods that use that factor relatively intensively are likely to be relatively cheaper than in other countries.

■■ intra-industry trade

The theory suggests that different countries have a comparative advantage in different goods and specialize in producing these goods for the world economy. It explains why the UK exports cars to Hong Kong and imports textiles from Hong Kong. It does not explain why the UK exports cars (Rovers, Jaguars, etc.) to Germany while simultaneously importing cars (Mercedes, Audis, etc.) from Germany.

Intra-industry *trade is two-way trade in goods made within the same industry.*

Of course, a Jaguar is not exactly the same commodity as a Mercedes, nor is Danish Carlsberg exactly the same commodity as Fosters lager. We are now discussing industries each making a wide range of different, and highly substitutable, products which enjoy some brand allegiance.

In analysing intra-industry trade, we must take account of three factors. First, consumers like a wide choice of brands. They don't want exactly the same car as everyone else. Second, there are important economies of scale. Instead of each country trying to make small quantities of each brand in each industry, it makes sense for the UK to make Jaguars, Germany to make Mercedes, and Sweden to make Volvos,

Box 12-1	Comparative advantage and the gains from trade

The table summarizes earlier data on unit labour requirements (ULR) in labour hours per unit output, unit labour cost (ULC) in domestic prices, and opportunity cost (OC) in domestic goods forgone. With lower unit labour requirements, the United States has an *absolute advantage* in both goods. One way to calculate *comparative advantage* is to compare ULRs across countries. Relative to the UK, the United States needs relatively less labour to produce videos than to produce shirts. The United States has a comparative advantage in videos, the UK in shirts.

Alternatively, we can compare opportunity costs, OC. By sacrificing 6 shirts, the United States gets 30 labour hours which make an extra video. 6 shirts cost 1 video. The opportunity cost of a video is 6 shirts in the United States and 10 shirts in the UK. But the opportunity cost of a shirt in the UK (1/10 of a video) is less than in the United States (1/6 of a video). Hence, again, the United States has a comparative advantage in videos and the UK in shirts.

The gains from trade

To produce 60 shirts, the UK gives up production of 6 videos. To produce 6 videos, the United States gives up only 36 shirts. Trade and international specialization allow the world economy to have an extra 24 shirts with no loss of videos. Or if the United States produces another 10 videos, giving up 60 shirts, the world economy has an extra 4 videos with no loss of shirts. These are the *gains from trade.*

	ULR	ULC	OC
USA			
Videos	30	$180	6 shirts
Shirts	5	$30	1/6 video
UK			
Videos	60	£120	10 shirts
Shirts	6	£12	1/10 video

and then swap them around through international trade. Third, the tendency to specialize in a particular brand, to which the demand for diversity and the possibility of scale economies gives rise, is limited by transport costs. Intra-industry trade between Germany and Sweden is likely to be larger than intra-industry trade between Germany and Japan.

gainers and losers

Countries trade because they have a comparative advantage based either on a relative advantage in technology or on relative factor abundance, or because different countries specialize in producing different brands when economies of scale exist. In the latter case the gain from trade is the reduction in average costs that economies of scale allow. Since it takes less factor input to make each output unit, the world economy can produce more goods from its given stock of factor inputs. In the former case, where trade is based on cross-country differences in opportunity costs, Box 12-1 shows that trade again allows the world economy to produce more output from any given stock of factor inputs.

These results tell us that the world economy gains when countries first begin international trade: some trade is better than no trade. But they do not tell us that everything that happens in the world economy makes everyone better off. We now give two examples of the conflicts to which international trade gives rise.

refrigeration

At the end of the nineteenth century, the invention of refrigeration enabled Argentina to become a supplier of frozen meat to the world market. Argentina's exports of meat, non-existent in 1900, had risen to 400 000 tons a year by 1913. The United States, with exports of 150 000 tons in 1900, had virtually stopped exporting beef by 1913.

Who gained and who lost? In Argentina the entire economy was transformed. Cattle grazers and meat exporters attracted resources. Owners of cattle and land gained; other land users lost out because, with higher demand, land rents increased. Argentine consumers found their steaks becoming more expensive as meat was shipped abroad. Although Argentina's GNP increased significantly, the benefits of trade were not equally distributed. Some people in Argentina were worse off. In Europe and the United States, cheaper beef made consumers better off. But beef producers lost out because beef prices fell.

Refrigeration opened up the world economy to Argentinian beef producers. As a whole, the world economy gained. In principle, it would have been possible for the gainers to compensate the losers and still have something left over. But, in practice, gainers do not often offer compensation to losers. So some people lost out. In this example the major losers were beef producers elsewhere in the world, and other users of land in Argentina.

the UK car industry

The second example is the UK car industry. Table 12-5 shows that, as recently as 1971, imports of cars were only 15 per cent of the domestic market while exports were 35 per cent of the sales of UK car producers. Since 1971 UK car manufacturers have been losing their share of the domestic market to foreign imports. By 1996 imports were 59 per cent of the UK market. Exports recovered in the 1990s, in part because Nissan and Toyota established major UK plants to produce not just for the UK market but for export within the EU.

UK car buyers and producers of foreign cars benefited from the increase in UK imports of cheaper foreign cars. But Rover, the major UK car producer, had a tough time and there were huge redundancies among its workforce. The UK government faced pressure to restrict UK imports of cars to prevent further job losses in the car industry.

Restricting car imports to the UK would help the UK car industry but raise car prices to UK consumers of cars. Should the government heed the wishes of producers or consumers? More generally, how should we decide whether to restrict imports or have free unrestricted trade in all goods? We now develop the general theory of how to analyse the costs and benefits of tariffs or other types of trade restriction. In so doing, we move from *positive economics*, the analysis of the reasons for, and the pattern of, world trade, to *normative economics*, the study of how the government should choose its trade policy.

the economics of tariffs

An import tariff *requires the importer of a good to pay a specified fraction of the world price to the government.*

If t is the tariff rate, expressed as a decimal fraction (e.g. 0.2), the domestic price of imported goods will be $(1 + t)$ times the world price of the imported good. By raising the domestic price of imports, a tariff helps domestic producers but hurts domestic consumers.

the free trade equilibrium

In Figure 12-2 we study the domestic market for cars. Suppose the UK faces a given world price of cars, say £10 000 per car, shown by the solid horizontal line. Schedules *DD* and *SS* represent the demand for cars by UK consumers and the supply of cars by UK producers. We assume that domestic and foreign cars are perfect substitutes. Consumers will buy whichever is cheaper.

At a price of £10 000, UK consumers wish to purchase Q_d cars. They want to be at the point *G* on the demand curve. Domestic firms wish to produce only Q_s cars at this price. The difference between domestic supply Q_s and domestic demand Q_d comes from imports.

equilibrium with a tariff

Now the government levies a 20 per cent tariff on imported cars. Car importers have to charge £12 000 to cover their costs inclusive of the tariff. The broken horizontal line at this price shows that importers are willing to sell any number of cars in the

Table 12-5	The UK car industry			
		1971	*1990*	*1996*
Ratio of:				
Imports to home sales		0.15	0.51	0.59
Exports to UK car output		0.35	0.33	0.51

Source: ONS, Annual Abstracts of Statistics.

domestic market at a price of £12 000. The tariff raises the domestic tariff-inclusive price above the world price.

What is the effect of the tariff on domestic consumption and production of cars? By raising domestic car prices, the tariff encourages domestic car production. Firms increase production from Q_s to Q_s'. The tariff provides protection for domestic producers by raising the domestic price at which imports becomes competitive. In moving up the supply curve from point C to point E, domestic producers whose marginal costs lie between £10 000 and £12 000 find that they can now survive because the domestic price of imports has been raised by the tariff.

On the demand side, the price increase moves consumers up their demand curve from point G to point F. The quantity of cars demanded falls from Q_d to Q_d'. From the consumers' viewpoint, the tariff is like a tax. Consumers have to pay more for cars.

Figure 12-2 shows the combined effect of the increase in domestic production and the reduction in domestic consumption: namely a fall in imports. Imports fall both because domestic production increases *and* because domestic consumption is reduced. For any given tariff, the extent of the reduction in imports will depend on the slopes of the domestic supply and demand schedules. The more elastic these schedules are, the more a given increase in the domestic tariff-inclusive price will reduce imports. When both schedules are very steep, the tariff-induced rise in the domestic price will have little effect on the quantity of imports.

costs and benefits of a tariff

Figure 12-3 provides a detailed accounting of the costs and benefits of imposing a tariff. We have to be careful to distinguish *net costs to society* from *transfers* between one part of the economy and another. We start by noting that, after the tariff has been imposed, consumers purchase the quantity Q_d'. Since the price to the consumer has risen by £2000, consumers are spending (£2000 $\times$ Q_d') *more* than it would previously have cost them to buy the same quantity Q_d' at the world price. We begin by

---

Figure 12.2 The effect of a tariff

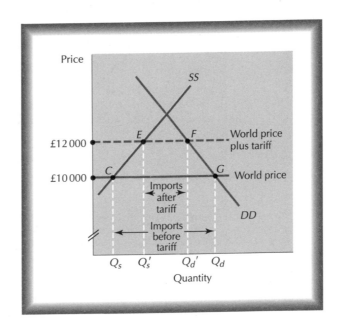

discussing who gets these extra payments, which in total are given by the area *LFHJ* in Figure 12-3.

Some of the extra consumer payments go to the government, whose revenue from the tariff is the rectangle *EIHF*, being the tariff of £2000 per imported car times $(Q_d' - Q_s')$ the number of imported cars. This transfer, *EIHF*, from consumers to the government is *not* a net cost to society. For example, the government may use the tariff revenue to reduce income tax rates.

Increased consumer payments also go in part to firms as extra profits. Firms receive a higher domestic price for their output. The supply curve shows how much firms need to cover the extra cost of producing Q_s' rather than Q_s. Hence the area *ECJL* shows the increase in firms' profits. It measures the extra revenue from higher prices not required to meet increased production costs. Thus *ECJL* represents a transfer from consumers to the pure profits or economic rent earned by firms. It is not a net cost to society as a whole.

What about the shaded area *A*? This is part of the area *LFHJ* showing extra consumer payments, but it is neither revenue for the government nor extra profits for firms. It *is* a net cost to society: the cost of supporting inefficient domestic firms.

The supply curve *SS* shows the marginal cost of making the last car in the home economy. But society *could* import cars from the rest of the world in unlimited quantities at the world price £10 000. This world price is the true marginal cost of cars to the domestic economy. The triangle *A* shows the resources that society is wasting by producing the quantity $(Q_s' - Q_s)$ domestically when it could have been imported at a lower cost. The resources drawn into domestic car production could be used more efficiently elsewhere in the economy.

There is a second net loss to society, the triangle labelled *B*. Suppose the tariff was abolished and free trade restored. The quantity of cars demanded would increase to Q_d. The triangle *B* shows the excess of consumer benefits, as measured by the height

Figure 12-3 The welfare costs of a tariff

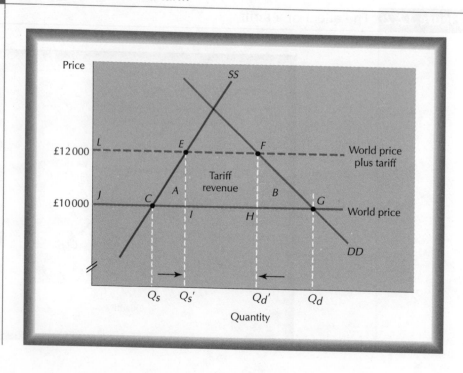

of the demand curve showing how much consumers are prepared to pay for the last unit demanded, over the marginal costs of expanding from Q_d' to Q_a, the world price at which imports could be purchased. Conversely, by imposing the tariff, society incurs a net loss equal to the shaded triangle B. It shows the net benefit society has given up by reducing the quantity of cars purchased by consumers.

To sum up, when we begin from free trade equilibrium and then impose a tariff, the subsequent rise in the domestic price leads both to transfers and to pure waste. Money is transferred from consumers to the government and to producers. As a first approximation, the net cost of these transfers to society as a whole is zero. This approximation is exact only if all consumers are identical and share equally in the ownership of firms and in the benefits of whatever the government does with the tariff revenue.

But in addition to the transfers and potential distributional effects, a tariff involves pure waste. In the post-tariff equilibrium, the domestic price of cars exceeds the world price. Since consumers buy cars until the marginal benefits of the last car equals the price they have to pay, the last car purchased is worth more to consumers than the world price at which the country as a whole could get another car. Consumers are consuming too little. Conversely, domestic producers are producing too many cars. In Figure 12-3 the two triangles A and B show the waste arising from domestic overproduction and domestic underconsumption of cars. They are a *deadweight burden* or pure waste. This is the *case for free trade*.

Does this mean that tariffs should never be imposed?

■■■ good and bad arguments for tariffs

Table 12-6 lists some of these arguments. We group them under several headings. The *first-best* argument is a case where a tariff is *the* best way to achieve a given objective. *Second-best* arguments are cases where the policy would indeed be beneficial but where there is another policy that would be even better if only it could be implemented. Non-arguments are cases in which the claimed benefits are partly or completely fallacious.

the optimal tariff: the first-best argument

In presenting the case for free trade, we were careful to assume that the domestic economy could import as many cars as it wished without bidding up the world price of cars. For a small economy this may be a reasonable assumption. However, when a country's imports form a significant share of the world market for a commodity, a higher level of imports is likely to bid up the world price.

Table 12-6 Arguments for tariffs

Type	Example
First-best	Foreign trade monopoly
Second-best	Way of life, Anti-luxury, Infant industry, Defence, Revenue
Strategic	Games against foreigners
Non-argument	Cheap foreign labour

In this case, the world price of the last unit imported is *lower* than the true cost of the last import to the domestic economy. The domestic economy should recognize that, in demanding another unit of imports, it raises the price it has to pay on the quantity already being imported. But in a free trade world without tariffs, each individual will think only about the price that he or she pays. Although no single individual bids up the price, collectively the individuals of the domestic economy bid up the price of imports.

Under free trade, each individual buys imports up to the point at which the benefit to that individual equals the world price the individual must pay. Since the collective cost of the last import exceeds its world price, the cost of that import to society exceeds its benefit. There are too many imports. Society will gain by restricting imports until the benefit of the last import equals its cost to society as a whole.

> *When a country has monopoly power in international trade, the* optimal tariff *can restore imports to the level at which social marginal cost and social marginal benefit are equal.*

Only when a country does not bid up the world price of its imports is the cost to society of the last unit imported equal to the world price. Then and only then is the optimal tariff zero. There is no longer any reason to discourage imports. That is the case for free trade under those circumstances.

The optimal tariff is a straightforward application of the principles of efficient resource allocation which we discussed in Chapter 5.

second-best arguments for tariffs

We now introduce the principle of targeting.

> *The* principle of targeting *says that the most efficient way to attain a given objective is to use a policy that influences that activity directly. Policies that attain the objective but also influence other activities are* second best *because they distort these other activities.*

The optimal tariff is a first-best application of the principle of targeting precisely because the source of the problem is a divergence between social and private marginal costs in trade itself. That is why a tariff on trade is the most efficient solution. The arguments for tariffs that we now examine are all second-best arguments because the original source of the problem does not directly lie in trade. The principle of targeting assures us that there are ways to solve these problems at a lower net social cost.

Way of life   Suppose society wishes to help inefficient farmers or craft industries. It believes that the old way of life, or sense of community, should be preserved. It levies tariffs to protect such groups from foreign competition.

But there is a cheaper way to attain this objective. A tariff helps domestic producers but also hurts domestic consumers through higher prices. A production subsidy would still keep farmers in business and, by tackling the problem directly, would avoid hurting consumers. In terms of Figure 12-3, triangle *A* shows the net social cost of subsidizing domestic producers so they can produce Q_s' rather than Q_s. But a tariff, the second-best solution, also involves the social cost given by the triangle *B*.

Suppressing luxuries   Some poor countries believe it is wrong to allow their few rich citizens to buy Rolls-Royces or luxury yachts when society needs its resources to stop people starving. A tariff on imports of luxuries will reduce their consumption but, by raising the domestic price, may also provide an incentive for domestic producers to use scarce resources to produce them. A consumption tax tackles the problem directly, and is more efficient.

Defence   Some countries believe that, in case there is a war, it is important to preserve domestic industries that produce food or jet fighters. Again, a production subsidy rather than an import tariff is the most efficient way to meet this objective.

Infant industries   One of the most common arguments for a tariff is that it allows infant industries to get started. Suppose there is *learning by doing*. Only by actually being in business will firms learn how to reduce costs and become as efficient as foreign competitors. A tariff provides protection to new or infant industries until they master the business and can compete on equal terms with more experienced foreign suppliers.

Society should invest in new industries only if they are socially profitable in the long run. The long-run benefits must outweigh the initial losses during the period when the infant industry is producing at a higher cost than the goods could have been obtained through imports. But in the absence of any divergence between private and social costs or benefits, an industry will be socially profitable only if it is privately profitable.

If the industry is such a good idea in the long run, society should begin by asking why private firms can't borrow the money to see them through the early period when they are losing out to more efficient foreign firms. If the problem is that banks or other lenders are not prepared to risk their money, society should ask whether the industry is such a good idea after all. And if the industry does make sense but there is a problem in the market for lending, the principle of targeting says that the government should intervene by lending money to private firms.

Failing this, a production subsidy during the initial years is still better than a tariff, which also penalizes consumers. And the worst outcome of all is the imposition of a *permanent* tariff, which allows the industry to remain sheltered and less efficient than its foreign competitors long after the benefits of learning-by-doing are supposed to have been achieved. We return shortly to the question of why so many tariffs exist that are justified by the infant industry argument.

Revenue   In the eighteenth century, most government revenue came from tariffs. Administratively, it was the simplest tax to collect. Today this remains true in some developing countries. But in modern economies with sophisticated systems of accounting and administration, the administrative costs of raising revenue through tariffs are not lower than the costs of raising revenue through income taxes or taxes on expenditure. The balance of tax collection should be determined chiefly by the considerations examined in Chapter 5: the extent to which taxes induce distortions, inefficiency, and waste, and the extent to which they bring about the distribution of income and wealth desired by the government. The need to raise revenue is not a justification for tariffs themselves.

strategic trade policy

In Chapter 3 we argued that game theory is a useful tool in analysing strategic conflict between oligopolists. In international trade, strategic rivalry may exist directly, between the giant firms or 'national champions' of different countries, or indirectly, between governments acting on their behalf.

In Chapter 6 we argued that strategic international competition might provide one rationale for domestic industrial policy. We used the example of commercial aircraft.

The British government initially subsidized British Aerospace in its participation in Airbus Industrie not only as a pre-commitment to deter Boeing from trying to force Airbus out of the industry, but perhaps also to try to induce the third producer, McDonnell-Douglas, to quit.

Similar considerations arise in trade policy. Levying a tariff on imports, thereby protecting domestic producers, may deter foreigners from attempting a price war to force the domestic producers out of the industry, and may prevent foreign producers from entering the industry.

This sounds like a very general and robust argument for tariffs, but it should be viewed with considerable caution. If it is attractive for one country to impose tariffs for this purpose, it may be equally attractive for foreigners to retaliate with tariffs of their own. We then reach an equilibrium in which little trade takes place, domestic giants have huge monopoly power since they no longer face effective competition from foreigners, and all countries suffer.

All countries may be led to impose tariffs even though all would be better off if they were abolished. This suggests there is a role for international co-operation to agree on, and subsequently enforce, low tariff levels.

Dumping   Although the preceding discussion relates to tariffs, it can also be applied to trade subsidies.

> Dumping *occurs when foreign producers sell at prices below their marginal production cost, either by making losses or with the assistance of government subsidies.*

Domestic producers say this is unfair and demand a tariff to protect them from this foreign competition. If we could be assured the foreigner would supply cheap goods indefinitely, we should say thank you, close down our more expensive industry, and put our resources to work elsewhere. To this extent, dumping is a non-argument for a tariff.

Much more likely, however, the foreign producers, with or without the assistance of their governments, are engaged in predatory pricing intended to drive our producers out of the industry. Once the foreigners achieve monopoly power in world markets, they intend to raise prices and cash up. If so, it may be wise for our government to resist. Even so, for reasons we explained earlier, a production subsidy is the efficient way to insulate our producers from this threat. A tariff has the undesirable side effect of distorting consumer prices.

non-arguments for tariffs

Cheap foreign labour   Home producers frequently argue that tariffs are needed to protect them from cheap foreign labour. However, the whole point of trade is to exploit international differences in the relative prices of different goods. If the domestic economy is relatively well endowed with capital, it benefits from trade precisely because its exports of capital-intensive goods allow it to purchase *more* labour-intensive goods from abroad than would have been obtained by diverting domestic resources to production of labour-intensive goods.

As technology and relative factor endowments change over time, countries' comparative advantage alters. In the nineteenth century Britain exported Lancashire textiles all over the world. But textile production is relatively labour-intensive. Once the countries of Southeast Asia acquired the technology, it was inevitable that their relatively abundant labour endowment would give them a comparative advantage in producing textiles.

New technology frequently gives a country a temporary comparative advantage in particular products. As time elapses, other countries acquire the technology, and relative factor endowments and relative factor costs become a more important determinant of comparative advantage. Inevitably, the domestic producers who have lost their comparative advantage start complaining about competition from imports using cheap foreign labour.

The basic proof of the gains from trade tells us that in the long run the country as a whole will benefit by facing facts, recognizing that its comparative advantage has changed, and transferring production to the industries in which it now has a comparative advantage. And our analysis of comparative advantage promises us that there *must* be some industry in which each country has a comparative advantage. In the long run, trying to use tariffs to prop up industries that have lost their comparative advantage is both futile and expensive.

Of course, in the short run the adjustment may be painful and costly. Workers lose their jobs and must start afresh in industries where they don't have years of experience and acquired skills. But the principle of targeting tells us that, if society wants to smooth this transition, some kind of retraining or relocation subsidy is more efficient than a tariff.

why do we have tariffs?

Aside from the optimal tariff argument, there is almost nothing to be said in favour of tariffs. Economists have been arguing against them for well over a century. Why are tariffs still so popular?

Concentrated benefits, diffuse costs   A tariff on a particular commodity helps a particular industry. It is relatively easy for firms and workers in an industry to organize effective political pressure, for they can all agree that this single issue is central to their livelihood, at least in the short run. But if the tariff is imposed, the cost in higher consumer prices is borne by a much larger and more diverse group of people whom it is much harder to organize politically. Hence the politicians are more likely to heed the vociferous, well-organized group lobbying *for* tariffs, especially if they are geographically concentrated in an area where, by voting together, they could have a significant effect on the outcome of the next election.

▬▬ tariff levels: not so bad?

In the nineteenth century world trade grew rapidly in part because the leading country, the UK, pursued a vigorous policy of free trade. In contrast, US tariffs averaged about 50 per cent, although they had fallen to around 30 per cent by the early 1920s. As the industrial economies went into the Great Depression of the late 1920s and 1930s, there was increasing pressure to protect domestic jobs by keeping out imports. Tariffs in the United States returned to around 50 per cent, and the UK abandoned the policy of free trade that had been pursued for nearly a century. The combination of world recession and increasing tariffs led to a disastrous slump in the volume of world trade, further exacerbated by the Second World War.

WTO

After the war there was a collective determination to see world trade restored. Bodies such as the International Monetary Fund and the World Bank were set up and many countries signed the General Agreement on Tariffs and Trade (GATT), a commitment to reduce tariffs successively and dismantle trade restrictions.

Under successive rounds of GATT, tariffs fell steadily. By 1960, US tariffs were only about one-fifth their level at the outbreak of the Second World War. In the UK, the system of wartime quotas on imports had been dismantled by the mid-1950s, after which tariffs were reduced by nearly half in the ensuing 25 years. Europe as a whole has moved towards an enlarged EU in which tariffs between member countries have been abolished. The GATT Secretariat, now called the World Trade Organization, began the latest round of negotiations – the Seattle round – in 2000, and late in 1999 the USA and China announced an agreement paving the way for Chinese membership of the WTO.

Thus, tariff levels throughout the world are probably as low as they have ever been. And world trade has seen four decades of rapid growth, arising at least in part from the success of GATT in removing trade restrictions. Figure 12-4 shows that lower transport costs have reinforced this trend.

■■■ other trade policies

Tariffs are not the only form of trade policy.

Quotas *are restrictions on the maximum quantity of imports.*

For example, the EU now has a ceiling on imports of steel from Eastern Europe. Although quotas restrict the *quantity* of imports, this does not mean they have no effect on domestic prices of the restricted goods. With a lower supply, the equilibrium price will be higher than under free trade.

Thus quotas are rather like tariffs. The domestic price to the consumer is increased, and it is this higher price that allows inefficient domestic producers to produce a

---

Figure 12-4 Falling transport costs

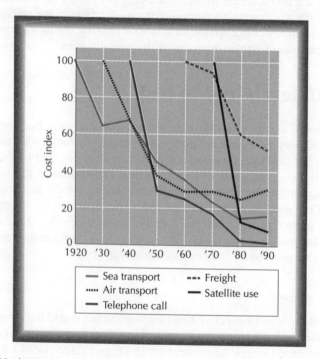

Source: World Bank, *World Development Report, 1955.*

higher output than under free trade. Quotas lead to social waste for exactly the same reasons as tariffs.

Because quotas raise the domestic price of the restricted good, the lucky foreign suppliers who succeed in getting some of their goods sold will make large profits on these sales. In terms of Figure 12-3, the rectangle *EFHI*, which would have accrued to the government as revenue from a tariff, now accrues to foreign suppliers or domestic importers. It represents the difference between domestic and world prices on the goods that are imported, multiplied by the quantity of imports allowed.

If these profits accrue to foreigners they represent a net social cost of quotas over and above the costs of imposing an equivalent tariff. However, the government could always auction off licences to import and so recoup this revenue. Private importers or foreign suppliers would be prepared to bid up to this amount to get their hands on an important licence.

Non-tariff barriers *are administrative regulations that discriminate against foreign goods and in favour of home goods.*

They may take the form of delaying imports at the frontier, ordering civil servants to use goods made at home, or merely a publicity campaign to 'buy British'. Non-tariff barriers may also be more subtle. Contracts can specify standards with which domestic producers are familiar but foreign producers are not. The 1992 programme aimed to end non-tariff barriers inside the EU.

Export subsidies *protect domestic firms by offering government help in competing with foreign firms.*

Figure 12-5 shows the economics of an export subsidy. Suppose the world price of a computer is £5000. Under free trade, domestic consumers would purchase a quantity Q_d at point G on their demand curve, producers would make a quantity Q_s at point E on their supply curve, and a quantity *GE* would be exported.

Figure 12-5 An export subsidy

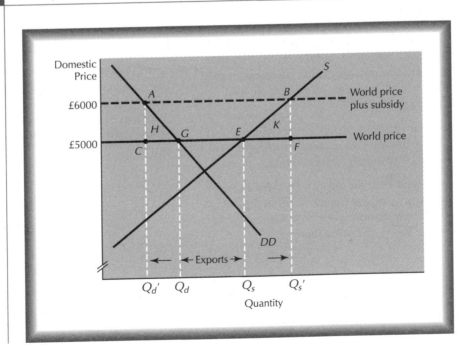

To boost the computer industry, the government now imposes a 20 per cent *export subsidy* applying only to computers that are exported. On such goods, domestic producers now earn a total of £6000. No firm will sell at home for £5000 when it can sell abroad and get £6000. The supply to the domestic market will be curtailed to Q_d' so that consumers are prepared to pay this price. Total domestic production increases to Q_s' and exports are AB.

Although the subsidy increases exports, it does so at the net social cost given by the shaded triangles H and K. Triangle H measures the net social cost of reducing domestic consumption from Q_d to Q_d'. The consumer benefits from the extra consumption would have exceeded the world price or social marginal cost at which the economy would always have obtained computers. Triangle K measures the social cost of increasing output from Q_s to Q_s' even though the marginal domestic cost of using these extra resources exceeds the price being received from the foreigners who buy computers.

Just as with a tariff, an export subsidy is usually a second-best policy. Even if the country did wish to increase its output of computers, it would be cheaper to use a production subsidy, incurring the cost of the triangle K, but avoiding the rise in the domestic price and the cost of the triangle H.

▨▨ recap

■ World trade has grown rapidly over the previous 40 years, and is dominated by the developed industrial countries. Primary commodities make up about 25 per cent of world trade; the rest is trade in manufactures.

■ Countries trade because they can buy goods more cheaply from other countries. Differences in international production costs arise from differences in technology and factor endowments. Economies of scale also lead to international specialization.

■ Countries produce the goods in which they have a comparative advantage, or produce relatively cheaply. By exploiting international differences in opportunity costs, trade leads to a pure gain.

■ Countries tend to produce and export goods that use intensively the factors with which the country is relatively well endowed.

■ Intra-industry trade occurs because of scale economies and consumer demand for diversity. The gain from trade is now a larger market and the lower costs that this enables.

■ If trade is to balance, and the foreign exchange market is to be in equilibrium, each country must have a comparative advantage in at least one good. The level of the equilibrium exchange rate copes with international differences in absolute advantage.

■ Although international trade can benefit the world as a whole, some people will lose out unless the gainers compensate the losers.

■ By raising the domestic price, a tariff reduces consumption but increases domestic production. Hence imports fall.

■ A tariff leads to two deadweight losses that are net social costs: overproduction by domestic firms whose marginal cost exceeds the world price, and underconsumption by consumers whose marginal benefit exceeds the world price.

■ When a country affects the price of its imports, the world price is less than the social marginal cost of importing. This is the case for the optimal tariff. Otherwise, arguments for tariffs are usually second-best solutions. A production subsidy or consumption tax would achieve the objective at lower social cost.

■ Export subsidies raise domestic prices, reducing consumption but increasing output and exports. As with a tariff, they involve waste. Goods are exported for less than society's marginal production cost and for less than the marginal benefit to domestic consumers.

■ Tariffs have fallen substantially since the Second World War, partly in response to the disastrous collapse of world trade under tariff restrictions of the 1930s.

■ Trade protection is usually harmful to society. Yet governments frequently adopt it because it is an easy option politically.

▄▄ key terms

▄▄ review questions

1 'A country with uniformly low productivity can only lose by allowing foreign competition.' Discuss this assertion in detail.

2 'Large countries gain less from world trade than small countries.' True or False? Why?

3 Stereos, wine, transistor radios, steel sheeting: which of these do you think will have high intra-industry trade? Why?

4 To preserve its national heritage, society bans exports of works of art. (a) Is this better than an export tax? (b) Who gains and who loses from the export ban? (c) Will this measure encourage young domestic artists?

12-2 less developed countries

LEARNING OUTCOMES

When you have finished this section, you should understand

- the handicaps with which developing countries begin

- whether reliance on comparative advantage is a secure route to prosperity

- the role of industrialization and the export of manufactures

- the international debt crisis

- the role of structural adjustment in future development

- the importance of aid from rich countries

In Europe or the United States a drought is bad for the garden; in poor countries it kills people.

Less developed countries (LDCs) are those with low levels of per capita output.

In May 1974, the General Assembly of the United Nations passed a resolution calling for a New International Economic Order (NIEO). It called for international co-operation to reduce the widening gap between the developed and the developing countries. The resolution reflected the feeling of many LDCs that the world economy is arranged to benefit the industrial countries and exploit the poorer countries. Since 1974 we have had a quarter of a century of talk about restructuring the world economy – but not much action.

world income distribution

In 1997, 35 per cent of the world's people lived in low-income countries, with an average annual income of about £220 per person. In the rich countries, people enjoyed an average annual income of about £16 000 per person. *Most of the world's people live in poverty beyond the imagination of people in rich Western countries.* And, of course, not everyone in a country gets exactly the average income. Even in some middle-income countries, many people live in great poverty.

Table 12-7 shows data on per capita income, life expectancy at birth, and adult illiteracy. The low-income countries are very badly off on every measure. Nevertheless, the situation of low-income countries has improved since 1965. Table 12-8 shows a marked increase in life expectancy in low-income countries, a clear indication that the quality of life has improved since 1965. Per capita income grew in all groups of countries. Although low-income countries achieved real growth, in absolute terms they fell even further behind the rest of the world.

Table 12-7 World welfare indicators, by country group, late 1990s

	Low income	Middle income	Rich industrial
Per capita GNP (£)	220	1180	16 060
Life expectancy at birth (years)	59	68	78
Adult illiteracy (%)	47	18	<5

Source: World Bank, *Development Report* (various issues).

404

the north and the south

The north–south distinction sees the world divided into the rich north and the poor south. Those in the south claim the right to a larger share of the world's income, and their claims are on the rich countries of the north. The north–south division is essentially the same as the division between the industrialized countries and the LDCs.

People living in the industrial north may be interested in the problems of LDCs not merely out of a concern for fairness and an abhorrence of poverty. An increase in world trade will usually benefit everyone concerned. Even from a purely selfish standpoint, the north has many reasons to be interested in the economic development of the LDCs.

▇▇▇ economic development in low-income countries

Why do so many countries have such low per capita real GNP? To get to this position, they must have grown slowly for a long time. We examine the special problems faced by countries with very low incomes.

Population growth The growth of per capita real income depends on the growth of total real income relative to the growth of population. In rich countries birth control is widespread; in poor countries much less so. In the absence of state pensions and other benefits, having children is one way people can try to provide security against their old age when they are no longer able to work. In recent decades the population of low-income countries has been growing at about 2.5 per cent per annum; in rich countries annual population growth is less than 1 per cent per annum. Merely to maintain per capita living standards, poor countries have to increase total output much faster than rich countries.

A rapidly expanding labour force can allow rapid GNP growth if other factor inputs are expanding at an equal rate. The problem for poor countries is that they cannot expand supplies of land, capital, and natural resources at the same rate as the labour force. Decreasing returns to labour set in.

Resource scarcity Dubai is generously endowed with oil and has a per capita GNP in excess of the United States or Germany. Most of the world's low-income countries have not been blessed with natural resources that can profitably be exploited. And having resource deposits is not enough: it takes scarce capital resources to extract mineral deposits.

Table 12-8 World development, 1965–97

Country income group	Per capita real growth (% p.a.)	Life expectancy at birth	
		1965	1997
Low	2.1	50	59
Middle	1.6	52	68
Rich	2.6	71	78

Source: World Bank, Development Report (various issues).

Capital   The rich countries have built up large stocks of physical capital which make their labour forces productive. Poor countries have few spare domestic resources to devote to physical investment. Most domestic resources are required to provide even minimal consumption. Financial loans and aid allow poor countries to buy in machinery and pay foreign construction firms. However, LDCs frequently complain that financial assistance is inadequate.[1]

Human capital   Without resources to devote to investment in health, education, and industrial training, workers in poor countries are often less productive than workers using the same technology in rich countries. Yet without higher productivity, it is hard to generate enough output (surplus to consumption requirements) to increase investment in people as well as in machinery.

Social investment in infrastructure   Developed countries achieve economies of scale and high productivity through specialization, which is assisted by sophisticated networks of transport and communications. Without expensive investment in power generation, roads, telephone systems, and urban housing, poor countries have to operate in smaller communities which are unable fully to exploit the possibility of scale economies and specialization.

Conflict   In addition to these narrow economic reasons, some people believe that the poorest regions have been those where colonially imposed boundaries made little sense and where colonial rule did not sufficiently prepare the indigenous people for administration. The end of empire then left governments without wide domestic support, and both internal and international conflict followed.

We now discuss the extent to which the world economy can help. However, we do not focus exclusively on the very poorest countries. The group of countries classified as LDCs also includes the newly industrialized countries – countries such as Mexico and Brazil which are well on their way to becoming rich countries. In some cases these middle-income countries have developed in the way the poorest countries hope to develop. But together, the LDCs share many grievances about the way the world economy operates.

▃▃ development through trade in primary products

In Section 12-1 we analysed the gains from trade when countries specialize in the commodities in which they have a comparative advantage. We saw that relative factor abundance is an important determinant of comparative advantage. In many LDCs, the factor with which they are relatively most abundantly supplied is land. This suggests that LDCs can best take advantage of the world economy by exporting goods that use land relatively intensively.

Primary products *are agricultural goods and minerals. Their production relies heavily on the input of land.*

---

[1] At the 1996 Food Summit, Jacques Diouf, Director of the Food and Agriculture Organization said his annual budget was 'less than what nine developed countries spend on dog and cat food in six days, and less than 5 per cent of what inhabitants of just one developed country spend on slimming products every year'. *The Times*, 14 November 1996.

In this section we study LDC exports of primary commodities, both the 'soft' commodities – agricultural products such as coffee, cotton, and sugar – and the 'hard' commodities or minerals, such as copper or aluminium. As late as 1960, exports of primary commodities accounted for 84 per cent of all LDC exports. Nevertheless, many LDCs have become sceptical of the route to development through specialization in production of primary products. Today, less than half of all LDC exports are primary products.

trends in primary commodity prices

Table 12-9 shows that, with the exceptions of petroleum, where supply was effectively curtailed by OPEC, and gold, where the price used to be artificially controlled, the trend in real prices of primary products has been downwards for the last two decades. This can be attributed both to increased supply and to reduced demand. On the demand side, technical advances such as artificial rubber and plastics have reduced the price for which many raw materials can be sold in industrial markets.

On the supply side, the problem has been the success of the LDCs in increasing productivity and output. LDCs invested in better drainage and irrigation, better seeds, and more fertilizers. Asian agriculture was transformed by the 'green revolution'. Mineral producers developed more capital-intensive mining methods. The concerted effort of LDCs to increase output and obtain more export earnings contributed to the fall in the real price of the commodities that they were trying to sell.

price volatility

A second disadvantage of concentrating on the production of primary products is that their real prices tend to be very volatile, because both the supply and the demand are price-inelastic. On the demand side, people need food and industrial raw materials. On the supply side, crops have already been planted and perishable output has to be marketed whatever the price. Because both supply and demand curves are very steep, a small shift in one curve will lead to a large change in the equilibrium price.

export concentration

Fluctuations in the real price of primary products lead to volatile export earnings and fluctuations in GNP in those LDCs that concentrate on producing primary products for the world economy. The real price of, say, cocoa is volatile. Suppose Ghana faces a 50 per cent drop in cocoa prices: its export earnings fall 11 per cent, which is catastrophic. Of course, Ghana does very well when cocoa prices soar. But Ghana's entire economy will be buffeted by changes in the world cocoa market.

Table 12-9 Real price of primary products 1955–99 (1995 = 100)

	55	75	85	95	99
Petroleum	57	180	229	100	125
Gold	43	120	118	100	62
8 other metals	152	200	128	100	71
28 soft products	186	217	129	100	70

Source: IMF, International Financial Statistics.

commodity stabilization schemes

Suppose primary producers got together to organize a stabilization scheme for a particular primary product. By stabilizing the price of the commodity, the scheme would stabilize the export earnings of countries heavily dependent on exports of that commodity. Figure 12-6 shows how the scheme would work. *DD* shows the inelastic demand curve for the commodity. The total supply curve of competitive producers fluctuates between SS_1 and SS_2 depending on the state of the harvest. In a free market, equilibrium will oscillate between points A_1 and A_2 on the demand curve. Since demand is inelastic, these oscillations imply major changes in the commodity price.

> A buffer stock *is an organization aiming to stabilize a commodity market. It buys when the price is low, sells when the price is high.*

Suppose a bumper harvest means the supply curve is SS_1. The buffer stock organization can buy a quantity *AB*, leaving a quantity *OQ* to be purchased by other buyers at a price *P*. If the government runs the buffer stock, the country's exports will be *Q* at the price *P*.

The buffer stock stores the commodity in warehouses. When there is a harvest failure, the producers' supply curve will be SS_2. Rather than allow free market equilibrium at the point A_2, the buffer stock sells off a quantity *CA* from the warehouse. Together with new production *PC*, this implies that again the total quantity exported is *Q* and the price is *P*. Thus the activities of the buffer stock organization not only stabilize the commodity price at *P* but, by stabilizing the quantity of exports at *Q*, stabilize export earnings.

At which price should the buffer stock aim to stabilize the market? If the only aim is the elimination of price volatility, the price should be stabilized at the level that implies neither accumulation nor decumulation of buffer stock holdings in the long run.

Figure 12-6 Commodity price stabilization

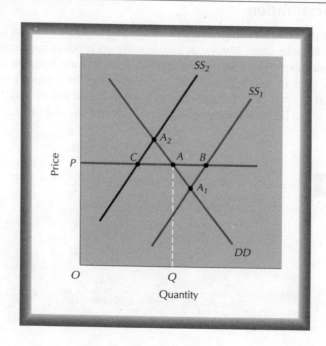

There have been attempts by LDCs to organize commodity price stabilization schemes in coffee, cocoa, and tin. Sometimes these take a simple form. For example, when there has been a bumper coffee crop in Brazil, the world's largest coffee producer, the Brazilian government has purchased coffee from Brazilian farmers and simply burned it. When demand is inelastic, the buffer stock could also try to stockpile goods systematically in order to force up prices on average, and raise revenue for producers. But none of the LDCs has managed to copy OPEC's example with much success. For many primary commodities, governments have to deal not with a few large oil fields but with a large number of small producers who are much harder to organize.

One problem with the strategy of supply restriction to force up the price is that there is an incentive for individual producers to cheat on the collective agreement. When price is forced above marginal cost, each producer has an incentive to produce more than the agreed output. Yet if all producers cheat, the price will come tumbling down or the buffer stock will be forced to acquire enormous warehouse stocks to keep this production off the market.

development through industrialization

Many countries have concluded that the route to development lies not through increased specialization in production of primary products but in the expansion of industries that produce manufactures. We discuss two very different forms that industrial development has taken.

import substitution

When world trade collapsed in the 1930s, many LDCs found their export revenues reduced by more than 50 per cent. Not unnaturally, some LDCs resolved never again to be so dependent on the world economy. After the war, they began a policy of import substitution.

> Import substitution *is a policy of replacing imports by domestic production under the protection of high tariffs or import quotas.*

Import substitution reduces world trade and involves suppressing the principle of comparative advantage. LDCs used tariffs and quotas to direct domestic resources away from the primary products in which they had a comparative advantage, into industrial manufacturing where they had a comparative disadvantage.

International trade theory suggests that this policy is likely to be wasteful. Countries are using more domestic resources to make manufactured products than would have been required to make the exports to finance imports of the same quantity of manufactures.[2] Import substitution was pursued partly because LDCs wanted to reduce their specialization in particular primary commodities, and partly because these countries associated a developed industrial sector with the high productivity levels observed in the rich industrial countries. Import substitution has one great danger and one possible merit.

The danger is that import substitution may prove a dead end. In the short run, the policy is costly because domestic manufactures are being produced using more resources and at a higher cost than the country's social marginal cost of these goods, namely the world price at which they could be imported. And, although domestic

[2] By closing itself off from the world economy, the communist bloc also pursued import substitution on a grand scale. It was not an economic success.

industry may expand quite rapidly behind tariff barriers while imports are being replaced, once import substitution has been completed economic growth may come to an abrupt halt. The country is now specialized in industries in which it has a comparative *disadvantage*, and further expansion can come only from expanding *domestic* demand.

The possible merit is that comparative advantage is a dynamic, not a static, concept. A tariff may help an infant industry even though production subsidies would achieve the same outcome at lower social cost. By developing an industrial sector and learning to use the technology, LDCs may eventually come to have a comparative advantage in some industrial products. Thus import substitution may not be an end in itself. It may be a preliminary phase in which industry gets started, as a prelude to export-led growth.

 Export-led growth *stresses production and income growth through exports rather than the displacement of imports.*

exports of manufactures

The real success stories of the last three decades are the countries that have made this transition and are no longer high-tariff countries but rather are successful exporters

---

Box 12-2 | Fickle capital flows hurt LDCs

During the 1990s, capital mobility increased. Many LDCs attracted foreign capital in large amounts. In 1997 East Asia caught a cold. Country after country faced a speculative attack on its exchange rate peg. Even countries with healthy 'fundamentals' were attacked. Since Asian banks had borrowed in foreign currency, drastic falls in exchange rates led to large increases in the real value of bank liabilities, making the banking system bankrupt and inducing further panic.

The table below shows the dramatic depreciation of real exchange rates. The IMF found itself organizing large rescue packages. Where these helped restore solvency, the depreciated 'super-competitive' exchange rate then allowed recovery in 1998. As confidence returned, exchange rates climbed to more reasonable levels, as the table shows.

Lessons of the crisis? First, allowing massive capital inflows is dangerous: what flows in can also flow out. Increasingly, LDCs are encouraged to float the exchange rate as a way of limiting the capital inflow. Second, retaining some restrictions on capital flows may not be such a bad idea, at least until the domestic banking system is well regulated and more robust. Third, LDCs should not borrow too much in foreign currency, whose domestic value increases when the exchange rate plunges. Fourth, the IMF success came at a price, and not only for the rich countries who paid its bills. Bailing out foreign investors raises expectations of future bail-outs. Some critics said that if the IMF had not bailed out Mexico in 1995, the Asian crisis of 1997 would not have been so bad.

	Indonesia	Korea	Malaysia	Thailand	Philippines
Real exchange rates (1990–96 = 100)					
June 1997	105	95	111	107	115
Dec. 1997	62	66	80	72	89
June 1998	33	76	79	87	92
Dec. 1998	71	85	77	98	91

Source: World Bank, *Global Development Finance 1999*.

of manufactures. Instead of withdrawing from the world economy, they are turning it to their advantage. This has been particularly true in the countries of South East Asia, including China.

Should producers of manufactures in the rich countries worry about competition from Asian producers of manufactures? High-tech industries aside, will the 'tigers' wipe out producers of labour-intensive manufactures in Europe, North America, and even Japan? Although we tend to think of LDCs exporting very labour-intensive low-quality manufactures such as cheap textiles, this stereotype is outdated. It remains true that textiles are the largest single manufactured commodity exported by LDCs, but exports of machinery and consumer durables are growing the most rapidly. LDCs are now major producers of everything from cars to transistors and television sets. How will the industrial countries react?

The principle of comparative advantage suggests that established industrial economies should reallocate factors to industries in which their comparative advantage now lies, industries such as genetics and telecommunications, which use relatively intensively the capital and technical expertise with which the rich countries are relatively well endowed.

However, the adjustment process is costly. Factories have to be closed, outdated plant written off, and workers retrained. The LDCs are justifiably frightened that their strategy of economic development through industrialization and export-led growth through manufactures will be frustrated by protection in their industrial markets. The movement for an NIEO does not want merely an assurance that the rich countries will not impose tariffs and other restrictions on imports from LDCs. It would like the industrial countries to go further: to accelerate imports of manufactures from LDCs by actually imposing tariffs on imports from other industrial countries. At present, the prospects for such discrimination in favour of LDCs seem small.

development through borrowing

A third route to economic development is by external borrowing, and a third complaint of LDCs about the way the world economy works is that borrowing terms are too tough. LDCs have traditionally borrowed in world markets to finance an excess of imports over exports. By importing capital goods, LDCs were able to supplement domestic investment financed by domestic savings.

the international debt crisis

Remember the basic balance of payments arithmetic:

$$\text{Current account deficit} = \text{trade deficit} + \text{debt interest} = \text{increase in net foreign debt}$$

The international debt crisis *arose when many poor countries were no longer able to pay interest on their foreign debts.*

Debt hurts only when the real interest rate is positive: only then does a country have to sacrifice real resources to repay the debt in the future. A crucial reason why a debt crisis emerged after 1980 was the rise in real interest rates. Indeed, for many of the previous decades real interest rates were actually negative, and debtor countries were being subsidized in real terms by creditors. It is arguable that the right measure of a country's ability to pay is not its GNP but its export earnings. Hence in Table 12-10 we look at the ratio of debt service to exports. Debt service is the flow of interest payments on the existing debt. The increase in the ratio of debt service to exports has increased much more sharply than the simple debt/GNP ratio. It explains why debtor countries were hurting so much.

Default and debt rescheduling   Suppose the only way to meet the burden of debt interest (and repayment of the original loan) is to plunge your economy into a deep and long recession. This will slash imports and allow export revenue to go to servicing the debt. Politically, you are in big trouble. Voters won't put up with austerity for long.

Do you have any other options? First, you can call in the IMF and the World Bank. Under their *adjustment programmes* you can probably get a short-term loan to pay your other creditors. But these international agencies will insist that you take tough action to get the long-run position under control. Second, you can go to your creditors – in this case mainly the large private banks of the world's richest economies – and seek a debt rescheduling.

Debt rescheduling *is an agreement with creditors to pay back over a longer payback period with a lower repayment per period.*

If you think your economy will expand in the future this may be a good strategy, and you can grow your way out of trouble without too much short-run pain.

If things are even more desperate, you may consider outright default or refusal to repay what you owe. Obviously, this deals with the immediate burden of the debt, but what are the costs? In the most extreme case, governments of the creditors may think about sending in their armies, though this has almost never happened. But governments of creditors might attempt to exert what leverage they could through international negotiations, trade embargoes, and so on. Economists are more interested in a direct market mechanism which might have the same deterrent effect.

When countries borrow in world financial markets, they do not all face the same interest rate. Like individuals, riskier countries face higher interest rates, which build in a *risk premium* to cover the possibility of default. Hence it is possible that countries that default face prohibitive risk premia when they try to borrow in the future. The knowledge that this will happen may be sufficient to deter them from defaulting in the first place.

What has happened in practice? First, there have been very few outright defaults. Second, and somewhat surprisingly, there is very little evidence that, as a country's debt position becomes more risky, the financial markets substantially raise the interest rate on new borrowing. So the deterrent effect may be small. In practice, much of the problem has been met by debt rescheduling. Creditors have preferred to get some money back over a longer period rather than provoke debtors to announce outright

Table 12-10   Debt service (% of net exports)

	1970	1980	1997
Argentina	22	37	64
Columbia	12	16	29
Brazil	12	63	62
Mexico	24	50	37
Venezuela	3	27	33
Burundi	2	10	29
Kenya	6	21	21

Source: World Bank, *World Development Report*.

default. And, finally, under international pressure from governments, the creditor banks have actually written off much of the debt. This means they acknowledge that it is never going to be repaid even though the debtor has not explicitly announced a complete default. Many famous Western banks announced operating losses as they set off bad debts against their healthy profits from domestic operations.

■■■ development through structural adjustment

Poor countries are poor not because they have massive unused capacity but because their level of potential output is so low. Investment may be necessary to improve human and physical infrastructure, but investment is not sufficient. We only have to recall that the Soviet bloc spent decades restraining consumption in order to create resources for high levels of investment. By the 1970s and 1980s, the rate of return on this investment was close to zero. Their economies stagnated.

Productivity growth need not come from additions to capital: it can also come from using more efficiently the resources already available. Countries that have been exposed to the world economy have grown more rapidly than those which had cut themselves off behind protective tariffs. One theme of advice to LDCs in the 1990s was an emphasis on structural adjustment.

> Structural adjustment *is the pursuit of supply-side policies aimed at increasing potential output by increasing efficiency.*

Examples of such policies are reductions in government subsidies to industry, privatization, lower levels of protection against imports, broader and less distortionary tax rates, less government intervention to ration and allocate credit by quota rather than by price. This pursuit of microeconomic efficiency has usually been underpinned by a recommendation to abolish large budget deficits, financed by money creation and causing endemic inflation.

Structural adjustment policies were already being encouraged in LDCs before the Soviet bloc abandoned central planning after 1989, but the former communist 'transition economies' were encouraged to make structural adjustment the centre-piece of reform. Even in OECD economies, greater stress on supply-side policies after 1980 took a long time to work and appears to have had only modest measurable success. LDCs sometimes claim that unpalatable medicine is being forced down their throats as the price for loans and aid from rich countries. Two rejoinders are possible.

First, what the doctor dispenses is rarely pleasant but it is often useful. Second, we have increasing evidence, for example from transition economies, that those which have embraced structural adjustment with more enthusiasm have also generally achieved greater subsequent economic success. In part this is a chicken-and-egg phenomenon. Countries confident of their future prospects and committed to reform may embrace structural adjustment more easily; countries fearful of the future and in which the debate still rages about which economic system is appropriate are countries more likely to find reasons to go slow on structural adjustment. Neverthe-less, in economics as in medicine, we have little evidence that delaying the treatment is usually good for the patient.

■■■ aid

Many of the complaints of the poor south come down to the view that the rich north should provide them with more aid.

Aid *is an international transfer payment from rich countries to poor countries.*

Such aid can take many forms: subsidized loans, outright gifts of food or machinery, or technical help and the free provision of expert advisers. The basic issue is a moral or value judgement about equality. Within a country the government usually makes transfer payments to the poor, financed by taxes on the rich, thereby implementing a view of society as a whole that the income distribution thrown up by market forces is unfair and inequitable.

The same value judgement lies at the heart of aid or transfer payments between countries. However, it is complicated by two additional factors. First, within a country with a sense of national identity and social cohesion, it may seem right that the government should be concerned with *all* its citizens. But there is no single government of the world that can accept worldwide responsibility for welfare. Governments of individual countries, and the citizens they represent, may feel much less responsibility for the welfare of people of a different nationality in a distant country, of which they have little knowledge or experience. Second, the issue is complicated by history. Many people of the south feel that the prosperity of the north was first established during a colonial period when the resources of the south were exploited. Aid seems at least partial compensation. The northern countries do not share this interpretation of history.

aid and the recipient countries

If aid is to be given, does it matter in what form it is given? Many LDCs believe the single most important contribution the rich countries can make is to provide free access for the LDCs to the markets of the developed countries. 'Trade, not aid' is the slogan. Just as the best service a domestic government can render a 30-year-old redundant steel worker may be to provide retraining to allow a useful working life for another 30 years, LDCs believe that trade rather than handouts is a more effective and more lasting form of assistance and encouragement.

Critics of existing aid programmes also argue that the donor countries should do more to check up on who is actually benefiting from their transfers. It is argued that too much aid finds its way into the hands of the ruling elite in the recipient countries rather than the poorest people for whom it was intended.

Of course, some people in rich countries like to exaggerate the extent of government corruption in poorer countries. More practically, recipient governments dislike donors telling them what to do, and it is usually necessary to channel aid through recipient governments.

aid and migration

The quickest way to equalize world income distribution would be to permit free migration between countries. Residents of poor countries could go elsewhere in search of higher incomes. And in emigrating, they would increase the capital and land per worker for those who stayed behind.

Nor is this idea entirely fanciful. The massive movements of population from Europe to the Americas and the colonies in the nineteenth and early twentieth centuries represented an income-equalizing movement of this sort. Since the Second World War the major migrations have been temporary, although the steady flow of Mexicans (illegally) across the US border is one major exception. More common has been the EU's use of temporary migrant labour from Turkey, the Balkans, and North Africa, which countries have all benefited from payments sent home to their families by workers temporarily abroad. Similarly, Egypt, India, and Pakistan receive significant transfer payments from workers temporarily abroad. And in 1989–90 we saw substantial westward migration from Eastern Europe as the barriers came tumbling down.

None the less, there is no free and unrestricted immigration to the rich countries today. Indeed, even migrant workers are frequently outlawed. One difference between conditions today and conditions during the massive migrations of the nineteenth century is that there are now extensive systems of welfare and public health in rich countries. Quite apart from any racial or religious arguments, opponents of immigration say that existing residents would end up subsidizing unskilled immigrants who would spend most of their lives receiving public handouts.

The United States grew extremely quickly during the period of large-scale immigration. With economies of scale, it is not clear that existing residents inevitably lose out by admitting immigrants. Although fascinating, the question is largely academic. At present there is little prospect of the rich countries allowing immigration on a significant scale, least of all from the poorest countries of the world economy.

◼◼◼ recap

- The call for a New International Economic Order (NIEO) was an attempt by LDCs to get a larger share of the world's income and wealth. It reflected the extreme inequality between the rich north and the poor south. Half the world's population had an annual income of scarcely more than £220 per person in 1996.

- The south complains that (a) markets for their primary products are controlled by the north; (b) northern protectionism is hampering their prospects for industrial development; (c) borrowing is too expensive; (d) austere and unpopular domestic policies are being forced upon them; and (e) simple justice dictates that the north should take practical steps to close the north–south gap.

- In the world's poorest countries, population growth is faster than the rate at which supplies of other factors can be increased. Hence labour productivity is low and, after provision for consumption, there are few spare resources to increase human and physical capital. It is hard to break out of this vicious circle.

- The downward trend in real prices, price volatility, and danger of extreme concentration in a single commodity have made LDCs reluctant to pursue development by exploiting a comparative advantage in primary products. Buffer stocks and cartel supply restrictions have proved difficult to organize, with the conspicuous exception of OPEC.

- LDCs are increasing their export of labour-intensive manufactures. Although the LDCs are beginning from a small base, their market share could quickly become much more significant.

- Industrial countries are tempted to protect their declining manufacturing industries. Yet they would probably do better by encouraging adjustment towards the industries in which their comparative advantage now lies.

- Structural adjustment policies aim to improve incentives and the efficiency with which existing resources are used.

- LDCs ran large deficits, financed by external borrowing. Larger debts and high interest rates led to threats of default and an international debt crisis.

- Increasing financial market integration in the 1990s led to large capital inflows to LDCs. When investors got scared, many LDCs faced drastic crises.

- Trade may help the LDCs more effectively than aid. Migration would help equalize world incomes but there is little prospect of rich countries allowing significant immigration.

FOUNDATIONS OF ECONOMICS

◼◼◼ key terms

◼◼◼ review questions

1 Discuss two forces tending to reduce the real price of agricultural produce in the long run.

2 Why have LDCs been particularly successful in exporting textiles, clothing, and leather footwear?

3 (a) Describe how a buffer stock scheme works. (b) What could go wrong? (c) Why don't private speculators smooth out prices of primary products in any case? (d) Does your answer to (c) help you answer (b)?

4 How could rich countries best help the poor countries?

5 Why might a floating exchange rate insulate an LDC from capital flows more effectively than a pegged exchange rate?

index